Jean Monnet

ALSO BY FRANÇOIS DUCHÊNE

The Case of the Helmeted Airman: W. H. Auden's Poetry
With Geoffrey Shepard: *Managing Industrial Change in Europe*
With Edward Szczepanik and Wilfrid Legg: *New Limits on European
Agriculture: Politics and the Common Agricultural Policy*

Jean Monnet

THE FIRST STATESMAN OF INTERDEPENDENCE

François Duchêne

W. W. NORTON & COMPANY
NEW YORK • LONDON

The text of this book is composed in Garamond #3,
with the display set in Koch Antiqua.
Composition and manufacturing by the Maple-Vail Book Manufacturing Group.
Book design by Chris Welch.

Library of Congress Cataloging-in-Publication Data

Duchêne, François.
Jean Monnet : the first statesman of interdependence /
François Duchêne.
p.   cm.
Includes bibliographical references (p.   ) and index.
1. Monnet, Jean, 1888–1979.   2. Statesmen—Europe—Biography.
3. European federation.   I. Monnet, Jean, 1888–1979.   II. Title.
D413.M56D73   1994
940.5′092—dc20
[B]   93-34404

ISBN 0-393-03497-6

W. W. Norton & Company, Inc., 500 Fifth Avenue, New York, N.Y. 10110
W. W. Norton & Company Ltd., 10 Coptic Street, London WC1A 1PU

2   3   4   5   6   7   8   9   0

WITH MUCH LOVE
TO

ANNE

WHO HAS MADE THIS POSSIBLE

Under your inspiration, Europe has moved closer to unity in less than twenty years than it had done before in a thousand. . . . You are transforming Europe by the power of a constructive idea.

—*President John F. Kennedy*

The French happened to have Jean Monnet . . . and he was a revolutionary.

—*Dag Hammarskjöld*

For me, a great man is a man in public life who deliberately causes something important to happen, the probability of which seemed low before he took up the task.

—*Isaiah Berlin*

Politics is the art of the possible. . . . [Monnet] . . . enlarged the possible.

—*Michel Rasquin, Luxembourg Minister of Economic Affairs*

He wasn't the only one . . . but we knew he was the yeast in the dough.

—*Michel Gaudet, Legal Counsel to the High Authority*

The greatest risk of all would be to do nothing and change nothing.

—*Jean Monnet*

We are uniting people, not forming a coalition of states.

—*Jean Monnet*

Contents

Photographs follow page 190

Foreword

On Friday, March 20, 1979, I attended the funeral of Jean Monnet, who had died in his ninety-first year. The fifteenth-century country church was filled with heads of state and chiefs of government of the six nations then members of the European Community, including French President Giscard D'Estaing and German Chancellor Helmut Schmidt. So far as I now remember, I was the only non-official American present except for Monnet's old friend John H. McCloy. During the Catholic service the music consisted of songs and instrumental pieces from each member state of the European Community. Then, unexpectedly, sandwiched among the European classics, came a loud and lively rendition of "The Battle Hymn of the Republic".

After the service McCloy and I greeted Jean's widow, Silvia Monnet. In spite of her understandable grief, she was gleeful on one point. "Did you hear 'The Battle Hymn of the Republic'? You know that that was one of Jean's favourites." But, she said with a mischievous smile, "those European leaders here were all totally confused; there wasn't one of them who even knew what that music was all about. Wasn't that wonderful?"

In a sense that incident reflected the essence of Jean Monnet. He was, of course, a Frenchman; more than that, he was a European and, in a larger sense, a man sensitive to the culture and opinion of all parts of the globe.

François Duchêne has now produced a biography of the quality that Jean so richly deserves. His story is superbly written, thoroughly documented and wisely analysed. It tells us a great deal about one of the most extraordinary personalities of modern times—a little man from Cognac who, by the power of an indomitable will and the lever of a deeply felt idea, transformed Europe from a coterie of competing states mired in ancient rivalries to a Europe in which goods and people could move freely and European solutions be provided for European problems.

Coal and steel had special significance in the early 1950s, since those commodities had furnished the basic raw materials for fighting two world wars. Monnet, who passionately abhorred war as cruel, wasteful and irrational, presciently foresaw that, when the Second World War ended, the pooling of coal and steel (the traditonal sinews of war) not only might soften national rivalries but—even more important—might help tie West Germany tightly to the West.

Many of us have by now so long focussed on the Cold War and the menace of the Soviet Union that we find it hard to realise that the dark spectre overhanging Europe in the early postwar years was the threat of a resurgent Germany. In that atmosphere, Monnet clearly predicted that the French government would be moved by conditioned reflex to try, as its predecessors had unsuccessfully sought, to block Germany's aggressive instincts by massive force and by inhibiting its economic recovery. At the same time, Americans, seeking to rehabilitate Germany as the engine of European economic recovery, were already assisting that truncated new state to rebuild.

Monnet sought a fresh solution that would reconcile those conflicting pressures. Under the Schuman Plan which he proposed, Germany would be permitted, even encouraged, to rebuild, but within the framework of a united Europe rather than a totally independent nation state. Of course, a united Europe would not be easy to achieve. Monnet had seen the failure of many well-intentioned efforts to achieve cooperation among governments, and those examples had convinced him that unless the national governments were to transfer substantive power to some supranational institution, the result would be mere organised impotence. That had been the case with other international institutions formed.

But Monnet knew also that he could never persuade governments to give up sovereignty over a wide spectrum of their affairs. Still, he thought, they might well be willing to yield portions of their sovereignty in a discrete economic sector. His thinking was roughly equivalent to the blitzkrieg tank warfare tactics General de Gaulle had futilely advocated in Paris during the late 1930s: concentrate all available power at a specific point in a narrow sector, then break through. After that, they can spread out behind the lines. So Monnet believed that, once the breakthrough had been accomplished in the sector of coal and steel, the scope and jurisdiction of the new institutions could then be expanded.

There was a well-conceived method in this apparent madness. All of us working with Monnet well understood how irrational it was to carve a limited economic sector out of the jurisdiction of national governments and subject that sector to the sovereign control of supranational institutions. Yet, with his usual perspicacity, Monnet recognised that the very irrationality of

this scheme might provide the pressure to achieve exactly what he wanted—
the triggering of a chain reaction. The awkwardness and complexity
resulting from the singling out of coal and steel would drive member governments to accept the idea of pooling other production as well.

I knew Monnet well during the last three decades of his life and, along
with a handful of others, worked closely with him whenever he summoned
me. He expected great output from all who worked with him, but I never
spent a long night seeking to meet one of his requests without feeling that
my effort was for a spacious purpose.

Among the most striking of the several aspects unique about the Monnet
phenomenon is that he accomplished a profound redrawing of the economic
map of Europe without ever holding elective office. He succeeded because,
among other things, he notably lacked any personal ambition. Because he
never challenged a political figure as a rival, he could easily gain the friendly
attention of that politician whenever he needed it.

Nor was Monnet in the slightest degree impressed by rank or title. He
had an instinct for the real *loci* of power, and he quickly ascertained from his
friends who in any position of authority might be worth educating. Then,
having identified his target for persuasion, he sought the acquaintance of the
individual of lesser rank in his target's chain of command who actually prepared the initial drafts of documents that provided his boss with advice and
new initiatives. He sometimes spent day after day with that lowly but tactically placed minion.

Monnet was known to his friends as an incorrigible optimist, yet his
optimism did not stem from a Panglossian conviction that all was for the
best in the best of posssible worlds, but rather from a faith in the logic of
events and the essential rationality of people—a daunting faith in the ineluc-
table direction of deeply moving forces. Thus, as I constantly discovered, he
was never put off course by disappointments; instead, he would say with a
Gallic shrug: "What has happened has happened, but it does not affect anything fundamental. We have had a useful setback; now we must build on it
as an asset rather than an obstacle".

An example of this, as Duchêne also reports, occurred when I was present
at Monnet's thatched roof cottage at Houjarray near Paris in June 1950 for a
Sunday of work. During the afternoon, three or four cabinet ministers from
other delegations also arrived. Then a telepone call gave us the shocking and
quite unanticipated news that the North Korean army had invaded South
Korea.

After a mere moment of reflection, Monnet took me aside to say: "You
Americans will never permit the Communists to succeed with such aggression; you cannot afford to let them begin the erosion of lines drawn during
the postwar years. Yet unfortunately, an American intervention in Korea
could clearly jeopardise the Schuman Plan. It would almost certainly increase

American insistence on a larger German role in the defence of the West and that could create panic in Europe. We both know what the rearming of Germany could mean".

Monnet feared, in other words, that the prospect of a rearmed Germany could lead the French to hesitate before entering the Coal and Steel Community with the Germans. Yet he reacted as usual when confronted by a new obstacle. We should, Monnet decided, push promptly forward with a scheme to organise European defence roughly along the lines of the Schuman Plan. So he enlisted the support of political leaders such as Prime Minister René Pleven, who had earlier assisted Monnet in the League of Nations Polish loan negotiations.

Monnet's tactic was to persuade the French government to take a public position rejecting German rearmament on a national basis but advocating the formation of a European army that would include units from Germany within a European Defence Community.

On October 24, 1950, Pleven presented such a plan to the French Assembly, which approved it. Then began what the perceptive commentator Raymond Aron described as "the greatest ideological and political debate France had known since the Dreyfus affair". In the end, as we now know, the European Defence Community foundered on the rock of resurgent French nationalism, but meanwhile, the European concept was kept alive.

Unlike most of his countrymen, Monnet believed that Europe could be effectively rebuilt on the foundation of a Franco-German rapprochement rather than the old idea of an entente between France and Great Britain. He also believed that its effectiveness would be greatly enhanced if Britain were to join at the outset in building such a political edifice. He knew the British well and greatly respected their skills in politics and in shaping institutions. Yet, though he spent a great deal of effort trying to persuade his British friends to "be present at the creation", he was neither dismayed nor surprised when they held off. The British, he told me, had an infallible instinct for the *fait accompli:* "If we go forward and show concrete results, they will join at the right time".

Of course, history largely proved him right. When the British began to feel the economic hardship of exclusion from the Community and to fear that such exclusion might jeopardise their cherished "special relationship" with the United States, they took steps to join. Although Britain's first efforts were frustrated by de Gaulle's myopic nationalism, she finally took her place in Brussels.

Though Monnet had no illusions about the possibility of changing human nature, he was convinced that by altering the conditions under which people lived they would necessarily adapt to the new reality. "Europe", he said, "will not be conjured up at a stroke, nor by an overall design. It will be attained by concrete achievements generating an active community of interest".

With his astute sense of timing, Monnet was firmly convinced that novel ideas should be advanced at moments when the contradictions of the *status quo* forced political leaders to question their own assumptions. Thus, as he himself wrote in his *Memoirs:* "I've always believed that Europe will be established through crises and not the sum of the outcome of those crises".

His working methods were extraordinary. Although he produced highly persuasive documents, I never saw him write anything himself. For a long time, I was one of his overworked amanuenses, and I can speak with authority only about how we worked together with me serving as his intellectual punching bag. We would talk together without restriction until he abruptly stopped with the comment: "That's enough for now. Try a draft that distills what we have said to one another and let me have it in the next two hours". Even a simple letter he was writing would go through multiple drafts. On one occasion I remember, we put a document through twenty-three drafts, only to decide at the end that the second draft stated exactly what he wanted to say.

Monnet thought most effectively when he not only talked but walked. Whenever I stayed overnight at his house in Houjarray, we would breakfast together, then Jean would hand me a gnarled walking stick, throw open the door and say: "Start talking". I would describe to him recent developments in America or whatever else I thought might interest him. Then, as we climbed up over the sunlit hills, he would suddenly grab my arm and point out a bucolic scene, saying: "Isn't that beautiful! Can you imagine a more lovely view than this? This is a great country, and we must see that its qualities are put to good use". Then once more he would turn, abruptly seize my arm and say: "Start talking again".

In the course of our walks, he would identify by name and then describe his neighbours. He made clear his admiration for the French peasants among whom he proudly numbered himself. He admired their earthy sense, their frugality, their obstinacy and their ability to negotiate a hard bargain. I used to tease him from time to time by saying: "Jean, stop acting like a peasant". That comment always made him proud, and he would often respond with a puckish grin, "Why should I? I *am* a peasant". As I worked with him longer, I recognised that he derived much of his skill as a negotiator from his peasant's sense of feeling close to the land.

To see Monnet as a whole and understand the full basis for his place in history, I commend you to read and ponder François Duchêne's masterful biography, which, better than almost any other similar chronicle I have ever read, conveys a picture of the subject in all his complexities and genius.

Sooner or later, once history has worked its magic in providing a longer perspective, his full and unique contribution to the unity not only of Europe but of the West will be fully recognised. Then historians can give his massive achievements their proper and well-deserved rank.

GEORGE W. BALL

Acknowledgements

T his book would not have been written without the exceptional efforts of a number of old friends. Leonard Tennyson and Robert Schaetzel originally conceived the idea, and Robert Schaetzel, with his usual energy and enthusiasm, raised from the MacKnight Foundation the first funds which triggered all those that followed. He paved the way for sustained help from the Secretariat of the European Commission in Brussels, thanks to Emile Noël. The European Cultural Foundation in Amsterdam, whose executive director is Raymond Georis, provided the third basic contribution that launched the work. Periods of research at the Harry S. Truman Library in Independence, Missouri (on John Gillingham's recommendation), and the Seeley Mudd Library at Princeton (the depositary of the Dulles papers) were much helped by fellowships from the two organisations. A sizable part of the costs of editing and delivering two thousand pages of interviews was defrayed by the European Historical Archives in Florence. Without these supports, it would have been impossible to follow the track to the far-flung places of a mobile career.

Leonard Tennyson has shown endless kindness in putting me up—and up with me—in Washington for months of research. What might have been testing times have, on the contrary, strengthened an old friendship. Two friends have also helped more than any author has a right to expect. Jacques Van Helmont, who worked close to Monnet for a quarter century and has a rare ability to recall with precision the context and detail of events in which he took part, has responded in patient detail to some version of every chapter and has provided many insights, which will be evident from the text. Some of these comments are archive material in themselves. Max Kohnstamm, who carried out much of Monnet's diplomacy for two decades, especially in Germany and the Low Countries, has given me free run of his diary of the period and of his abundant archives, especially of the United States–Euratom agreement he negotiated from the European side. Long interviews with him based on the diaries have taken me repeatedly to the Kohnstamms' house in the Ardennes, where the warmth of Kathleen Kohnstamm's hospitality and the beauty of her garden make work a rare pleasure.

Other friends have also been exceedingly helpful. Edmond Wellenstein has commented on two chapters from his wealth of experience of the events under review. Anthony Hartley, from his reading of German sources and in many conversations, has given me an understanding I would not otherwise have had of the historical background of German policy. So has John Gillingham, who sent me an advance copy of his book on the European Coal and Steel Community, which draws heavily on German records. Daniel and Jeanne Singer kindly and invaluably lent my wife and me their flat in Paris for two successive Augusts. Ulrica Dunlop has been exceedingly kind in providing information from Sweden. It has been stimulating to absorb the views of historians, some of whom I disagree with and who nevertheless have compelled me to review my assumptions.

One's experience with archives varies greatly. On the whole, it is easier, quicker and cheaper to work in North America than in most European centres, but there are wide variations, especially in Europe, where archives can range from the costly to the costive. There are exceptionally helpful teams at the Harry S. Truman Library in Independence, Missouri, and at the European Historical Archives in Florence. I am very grateful to Anne Morton, the head of research and reference at the Hudson Bay Company archives in the Provincial Archives of Manitoba, Winnipeg, for pointing me to more material by correspondence than I might myself have located on the spot. I am greatly indebted to Miriam Camps, William Diebold, John Leddy, Lord Perth, Robert Schaetzel and John Tuthill for liberal access to their papers or to particular items of special interest.

Grateful thanks are also due to seven people for providing texts that were all the more informative for being unpublished either at the time or now. They are, in alphabetical order: the distinguished diplomatic historian Jean-Baptiste Duroselle, who has allowed me to quote from a long, unpublished chapter, "Le rôle de Jean Monnet à Londres", about Monnet's activities during the First World War, which he prepared for Monnet's *Memoirs* and which contains rare items; Anjo Harryvan, for his and A. E. Kersten's study of Dutch diplomacy in the period before the Messina conference, later published as "The Netherlands, Benelux and the relance européenne 1954–55", in E. Serra (ed.), *IP Rilancio dell'Europa e i Trattati di Roma;* a friend of fifty years, Richard Mayne, for allowing me the use of his manuscript book of 1973, *The Father of Europe: The Life and Times of Jean Monnet,* which is particularly valuable because it exploits archives of the Action Committee for the United States of Europe which have not yet been classified or freely released by the Fondation Jean Monnet pour L'Europe in Lausanne; Ruggero Ranieri, for his thesis "L'Espansione alla prova del Negoziato—l'Industria italiana e la Comunità del Carbone e dell'Acciaio 1945–1955"; Charles Rutten, who has retired from his career as the Dutch permanent representative to the institutions of the European Community, for his insider's memorandum on his earlier chief Jan Beyen's role in launching the European Common Market, "Het Nederlandse Aandeel in de Totstandkoming van de Gemeenschappelijke Markt inzonderheid in de periode maart–juni 1955"; and Pascaline Winand for her thesis *Presidents' Advisers and the Uniting of Europe,* since published in a revised version as *Eisenhower, Kennedy and the United States of Europe.*

A number of librarians have taken much time and trouble responding to requests, notably Chantal Bonazzi at the Section Contemporaine of the Archives Nationales and François Gasnault and Mme. Dijoux at the Ministère des Finances in Paris, Françoise Nicod at the Fondation Jean Monnet in Lausanne, Pierre Pascal at the Mairie of Cognac and Françoise-Marie Peemans at the archives of the Belgian Ministry of External Affairs in Brussels. Their help has been much appreciated.

Thanks are due also to the Fondation Jean Monnet, directed by Henri Rieben, for supplying free of charge useful publications exploiting its archives, and to the same Fondation, to Mrs. Aline Ramsay and to the Photographic Department of the European Commission in Brussels and the Bundespressestelle in Bonn for providing photographs, wherever possible, on the same terms.

Finally, I would like to thank the sixty-eight participants in, and observers of, Monnet's activities, many of them relatives and friends of his, who have given me interviews and often the most generous hospitality as well. A few spoke without being recorded, but sixty interviews have been taped, representing well over two thousand pages of evidence. They cover every phase of Monnet's career from the early 1930s onward. Interviews on their own do not suffice, because people tend to remember general impressions, purposes and results better than critical paths, details and dates, but they are invaluable correctives to the archives. They reveal assumptions at the time and in the thick of the mêlée about the background, about participants' motives and about the perceived ranking of different factors, which rarely get written down. Where the informants have agreed (in over fifty cases), interviews will be deposited in the historical archives of the European Community in Florence. And, here again, from a personal point of view, many of the interviews have been an opportunity to renew cordial relations of long standing and to make new ones, which has been one of the pleasures of preparing this volume.

Introduction
WHY JEAN MONNET?

Although Marshall McLuhan's electronic global village looms ever nearer, the international arena is almost entirely without the laws and institutions which give legitimacy to states at home. The devouring wars of the early half of the century showed the ruin that can come of such a vacuum. How does one produce appropriate forms of decision-making for a context which affects everyone more and more but lacks any contractual base?

Traditional predatory militarism by great powers was suppressed in 1945, but in other respects the problem has continued to grow. For instance, as physical distances shrink, the number of countries steadily multiplies. In 1878, three empires covered eastern Europe. In 1992, twenty-four governments covered the same ground, possibly with more to come. The United Nations started life after the war with 55 member states; it ended 1993 with 170.

This is in part a result of growing democracy. Ironically, however, the more democratic a system is and the more representative of domestic interests, the more it emphasises roots rather than horizons. There is no deep or widespread constituency for international ties, which nevertheless exist. The risk in these conditions is that the costs of an interdependent world will exceed the benefits.

Since the end of the Cold War, the United Nations has offered one approach to an international order. Behind the United Nations lies the relative hegemony of the West. This is better than nothing. But a collection of states cannot act coherently. And no oligarchy can in the long run be legitimate in a world of would-be self-determination. There is a need for other approaches.

In many ways, the boldest experiment of this kind since the watershed of 1945 has been provided by the European Union, formerly called the European Community.[1] This has involved a radical kind of contract in which states delegate at least some powers of decision to common bodies.

Of course, this solution has been devised to meet the peculiar needs of a continent that is only just recovering from the loss of its old political preeminence. But the very difficulties that have been encountered, the solutions to overcome them and the problems posed inside and outside the Union—in short, the process itself—have wider lessons and effects.

For centuries, Europe has been a region of many states and wars. Now, it has suddenly formed a partial union, embracing several once-great powers, which could spread to the whole continent. This virtually amounts to a change in political civilisation, despite the fact that the European integration movement has never claimed, like the Bolsheviks, to transform social values from within. Reformers of other persuasions used, for that reason, to regard it as below the salt. Yet Leninism has collapsed and the Union has so far withstood crises and remains. By creating a civil framework where none had existed, it has bred half a continent to a new life and become a magnet to the rest.

Unity, as a response to loss of mastery over the environment, might seem mere common sense. But common sense has not been much in evidence in the past in inducing former great powers to rise above old rivalries. The city-states of ancient Greece and Renaissance Italy have become models of failure in the genre. Achieving the obvious required too much creative power.

In fact, European Union is that rarest of all phenomena in history, a studied change of regime. It is the reverse of conquest and quite distinct both from incremental adjustment, which is the political norm, and from revolution, which is the social equivalent of an earthquake.

In 1950, six states sat down to form the European Community—Belgium, France, West Germany, Italy, Luxembourg and the Netherlands. Britain, Denmark and Ireland joined in 1973, Greece in 1981 and Portugal and Spain in 1986. German reunification in 1990 brought in East Germany as well. The Union, with 340 million people, is now, after China and India, the third most populous political grouping in the world.

It has changed the European ground rules. They used to be dictated by an aggressive competition between states repeatedly breaking out in wars. Now, for the first time, they follow the norms of civil society. Joint govern-

---

1. European Union began as a series of separate European Communities (for coal and steel, 1952; nuclear energy, 1958; the common market, 1958) with some bodies (the Assembly and Court of Justice) in common. In 1967, all the institutions (including the Commissions and Councils of Ministers) became common. The Treaty of Maastricht, signed on December 11, 1991, and aiming at monetary integration and greater political cooperation, has made the institutions into pillars of a single European Union.

ing bodies flatten frontiers as barriers to the rule of law. Relations between states reflect domestic standards instead of threatening them. All this exerts a great power of attraction. Virtually every European society aspires to join the Union. A new dynamic has been born.

IT WOULD BE naïve to imagine that any one leader, or even group of leaders, could claim the credit for changes as large as these. Yet one man more than others has personified European unity. This was Omer Marie Gabriel Jean Monnet, understandably known as Jean Monnet. He was born in Cognac on Friday, November 9, 1888, in the era of horse-drawn carriages. He died in his ninety-first year, in the country not far to the west of Paris, on Friday, March 16, 1979, ten years after the first man landed on the moon.

In 1963, President John F. Kennedy said that by a "constructive idea", Monnet had done more to unite Europe in twenty years than all the conquerors in a thousand. In 1976, the council of the heads of government of the European Community's nine states (as they then were) proclaimed him the one and only "Honorary Citizen of Europe". There is still no other.

"Europe", the achievement for which Monnet is most known, is not in fact his only claim to fame. For sixty years, he was one of the most fertile sources of administrative and political schemes in this century. Yet he has been, and is, almost unknown to the public. People look wary in conversations as it dawns on them that he was not Claude Monet, the painter. He was a figure even adherents found it hard to classify. As Baron Robert Rothschild, a Belgian diplomat, has said, he was "neither a civil servant nor a politician. He was in a category of his own".

Jean Monnet was never voted in by a constituency; he was never part of an elected government: he never held the reins of power, as commonly understood in a democracy. His few platform appearances were models of histrionic incompetence. His voice failed to carry. His delivery stumbled. He had no instinct for projecting an aura in public.

A civil servant could operate well enough within such limits. To succeed as a statesman, however, almost defies belief. Monnet has often been dismissed as a technocrat. He suffers, in fact, from not fitting into any known political cubby-hole. The French commander-in-chief in 1914, General Joseph Joffre, when asked who had won the first battle of the Marne—the "miracle" of the Marne—gave the famous answer that he could not say, but that he knew who would have lost it. Those entrusted with power enjoy the benefit of the doubt for what is pursued in their name. They carry the responsibility. Not to hold formal authority deprives one of this consecration. The burden of proof turns against the unofficial actor or adviser. His influence has to be demonstrated, a notably difficult thing to do, and if established, shared with those who accepted the advice.

At the same time, to the extent that a man like Monnet is not easily perceived outside the circle of those who knew him at first hand, he becomes a grey eminence, a man of mystery, cloaked in occult power, a patch of darkness where conspiracy theories breed. He can be credited with an influence and magic he did not possess. He is, in the eye of the beholder, both smaller than his real self, because what he did cannot be solidly grasped, and larger, because the area in which he operated casts a shadow any part of which may, rightly or wrongly, be ascribed to him.

A study of a man who may have shaped history must try to sift body from shadow. The task is greater when the subject's claims melt into his creations, as those of Monnet do. To disentangle these elements and cast as much light as possible on the man at work is the aim of this book. The ten chapters of the first part of the study, under the general title of "Actions", examine his career chronologically. The three chapters of the second part, under the heading of "Legacy", discuss his methods, policies and achievements.

HOW WAS IT that Monnet was widely thought by detractors as well as admirers to be almost inexplicably effective? His secret, if he had one, came of a combination of creative and critical faculties. He appealed to the romantic in people through the idealism of his goals and to the expert in them through the realism of his means.

Robert Marjolin, himself a man of consequence in the history of European unity, has referred to Monnet's "exceptional ability to conceive original ideas, ideas at any rate to which he was able to give an air of originality, combined with an extraordinary talent for putting them into practice". He added that he had never encountered anyone with "anything like Monnet's persuasive power" in a small group or a tête-à-tête.

Jelle Zijlstra, who was for many years Minister of Economics, then Finance Minister and finally Prime Minister of the Netherlands and knew Monnet well throughout that time, has stressed a third factor. "I never have met a man before or since who had Monnet's single-mindedness. He had at any specific period one thing he wanted to achieve. Exceptionally, two—but never three. And then, with all his powers of persuasion, of personal magnetism, he forced a solution. It's the difference between intellectual power and will-power. . . . He was a very clever man, okay; he had brains. But this power!"

Such force of personality may seem more overwhelming than persuasive. Sir Michael Palliser, a former head of the British Foreign Office, has noted that Monnet was "a very good listener . . . but, I think, not a very patient man. Underneath that calm manner, there was a good deal of impatience". Theodore White has written that in the 1940s Monnet was "known for his abrupt manners, tart tongue, sharp mind". But "he did love ideas. . . . When he talked of how and where you plant ideas, he talked not like an intellectual, but like a good gardener inserting slip cuttings into old stock".

And at least one of those who worked close to him in later days, the translator of his *Memoirs*, Richard Mayne, has remembered the experience as a mixture of domestic detail and high politics.

Monnet was highly egocentric in that whatever engaged him was the only important thing in the world. But he was always committed to the job in hand and was by the standards of politics utterly selfless. Bernard Clappier, a future governor of the Bank of France, and John J. McCloy, America's postwar proconsul in Germany, both thought Monnet a hard taskmaster, yet noted that his subordinates "adored him". He gave them the heady feeling they were at the centre of affairs and making history. One has explained that he allowed people a great deal of scope; another that unlike many, he never resented a subordinate's success. He opened up horizons, whether for his staff or, by his policies, for his fellow Europeans.

For all his impact on it, Monnet was not a man of the establishment. He was far closer to his native Cognac than to the pomp of power. He spoke often to basic values in ways uncommon with public men:

- "There is nothing more dangerous than victory"
- "Crises are opportunities"
- "What you say is too clear to be true"
- "Why should there be a border beyond which I treat men differently from those on my side?"

Hidden beneath his energy and will, there was a large capacity for feeling. There is an entry in his diary when he was invited to a hunt. It is typical that he went because he had no preconceptions. He was horrified at what he saw. "It is an abominable sight, these mangy riders, followed by a caravan of cars, pursuing a magnificent stag until it drops so they can kill it and hand it to the dogs. . . . I was unable to watch this sickening spectacle and returned home on foot".

Yet Monnet was also honed to action as to a game of chess. His attitude to any given move was similar to Paul Valéry's definition of originality in a poem, that it should be so specific to its moment and purpose that it could never have been the same before or be repeated in the future. This, not Henry Ford's lack of respect for the past, was the core of Monnet's antihistoricism. He suspected history of being a crutch for those who hoped relying on it would be easier than thinking for themselves.

Monnet was the same with high and low. He never tried to seem brilliant, nor (except in rare peremptory squalls) would he raise his rather low voice. He also had a charming smile. Nothing was forced. Yet sooner or later, he would determine the course of the conversation. He was not cultured, but his attitude to living, his reserve, spoke of an old civilisation. He regarded himself as a man of action, was rather puritan in some ways—Anne Morrow

Lindbergh, the wife of Charles Lindbergh, noted in 1926 that he "is embarrassed (a little) when you thank him for something"—and disliked rhetorical effects. Yet his schemes tended to the large scale; he let himself go at least once to admit there had to be a utopian strain in all political achievement; and his highest word of commendation for a statesman was to call him, as he called Roosevelt and Willy Brandt, "generous". He was given at once to world perspectives and minute attention to detail and made sure he never lost the connecting thread.

Paul Reuter, the international lawyer to whom Monnet first talked of what became the Schuman Plan, has left a graphic sketch. "He was small and stocky . . . and sometimes had a sly smile. I have seen him wrapping people round his little finger, seducing them. He could do that. But basically he was a passionate man, ardent and imaginative, a completely disinterested man. I won't say he was proud or modest, they are not always that different, but he was not vain or imbued with self. . . . He was generous in human relations, not small-minded . . . Contact with him was direct, simple, informal, but he was imperious too . . . he could squeeze you like a lemon. . . . He picked the flowers of politics and left the rest to the navvies".

In short, Monnet was a rich and complex personality. He had an ability to seem to live in service of an ideal yet bring people up short by earthy judgements; to be calculating yet to show up routine professional calculations as wanting; all these feeding off controlled but burning energy. In short, the creator is as interesting as the creations, and one of the intriguing quests is for the links between the two.

PART I

Actions

ONE

A Talent at Large

1888—1938

Jean Monnet was born on Friday, November 9, 1888, in Cognac, a town
situated on the mild Charente River, some forty miles inland, halfway
down the green Atlantic coast of France. The Renaissance king, François I,
was born in the castle five hundred years ago. After the Reformation, Cognac
became a Calvinist bastion. A century later the quality of its brandy was
discovered almost by accident. Today, it is a cream and grey place typical of
the French provinces. Towards the river it is greyer than most because a dark
fungus thrives on brandy fumes and furs up the warehouse walls. Most of
these treasure hoards have quasi-classical facades and in the case of the best
spirits the technical term for them is a "paradise", but to the casual eye they
come perilously close to "dark satanic mills" without the chimneys. Yet they
stand in one of the most rural regions of what was in Monnet's youth a
deeply rural country. Foreigners, struck by Monnet's rooted, practical personality, spoke of him jokingly as a "French peasant". This was not just a
foreigners' picturesque stereotype. Frenchmen who knew him well nursed
the same impression. Hervé Alphand, one of the important postwar officials,
noted in his war-time diary: "Monnet attracts me with his quasi-peasant
approach, his acute intelligence, his wariness, his drive". Hubert Beuve-
Méry, the founder of France's world-class postwar daily paper, *Le Monde,*
referred to "his obstinacy, like a peasant determined to sell his cow", and a
younger man, René Foch, reversed the image, observing "his circumspect
manner of inspecting a problem from every angle . . . like a peasant buying
a cow". The former president Valéry Giscard d'Estaing has spoken of his
having "the air of a refined peasant".

After the Second World War, Monnet wanted to round off the land on
which his house stood. Like the previous owner of his house, he put in a bid
for the plot that stood in the way. The neighbour refused, as he had done

before. "As long as I own this land, I can say *merde* to anyone". So Monnet went and bought another, better plot in the village and offered it to the neighbour in exchange. This time, the neighbour could not refuse. Peasant had met peasant. Monnet also took his superstitions seriously, if that is a peasant characteristic, and seemed to be a walking barometer, to judge by the number of times he tapped his chest and complained of the "heaviness of the weather". Salt would be thrown over the left shoulder and wood respectfully touched.

One often finds a whiff of the soil in Frenchmen before 1914, a Clemenceau, a Claudel, a Cézanne, and many others, none of them peasants. They even looked somewhat similar. Monnet carried traces of that world to his dying day. He was short, dark, slim in youth, a bit of a dandy, and in later life sturdy. In those later years, he ate and drank sparely and was not fat, but everything about him was faintly circular. He had a round face with trim moustache, a small barrel body and—was it an illusion or did he have a hint of bandy legs? His movements were unhurried. He spoke only when he knew what he wanted to say. In later years, his voice was veiled and gravelly and he cleared his throat a lot. "Things have never come easily to me".

Monnet did have peasant antecedents. His paternal grandfather had owned a vineyard. He had lived to 102, and Monnet often told a story of his falling into the river, fishing, when over 90. His maternal grandfather, a cellarman at Hennessy, became one of the skilled foremen who are the guardians of quality in the wine and brandy trades. Monnet was only two generations away from peasant growers and workers and closely in touch with both.

However, this was only the more remote part of the background. Though Monnet's father, Jean-Gabriel Monnet, wore wooden clogs as a boy and started as a salesman, he had, by 1897, become chairman of a cooperative of small-holders set up in 1838 to compete with the big names in brandy, the Martells, Hennessys and the like (several of them Irish and eighteenth century in origin). Though it came to be known as J. G. Monnet & Co., it had earlier called itself (in the English version) the United Vineyard Proprietors' Company of Cognac. The elder Monnet had risen to be a minor member of the merchant aristocracy of Cognac. He was described by John Davenport, in a *Fortune* profile Monnet liked, as "a witty temperamental Prince Charming whose one great aim in life was to see Monnet brandy cover the earth". The "big house" (with two Corinthian columns in the hall) in which the younger Monnet grew up was conceived for commercial entertaining and the dignity of the firm, not just domestic ease. Reflecting such a childhood, Monnet's expensively simple habits were simultaneously those of the well-off and steeped in the values of a small community where gratuitous show was a mark of dubious character.

In truth, Monnet was more squire than peasant. His long-lasting domestic helps, usually a married couple, cook and chauffeur, seem always to have regarded him with respect verging on devotion. He valued character and the individual, and tied neither to rank. As his early assistant, René Pleven, later a prime minister of France on two occasions, has put it, he "was a republican from the provinces, . . . attached to his corner of the world . . . and to the principles on which the democratic Third Republic was based".[1] His yardstick was the upright individual, of any class, deserving the respect of a local community which knew him from childhood.

However, if Cognac was in one way a narrow provincial community, it was also international, the miniature world capital of brandy. Monnet believed it was the only town in France with a street named after Richard Cobden, the English high priest of free trade. "The people of Cognac", wrote Monnet, "were not nationalist at a time when France was". France, in those pre-1914 years, was (intermittently) haunted by the dream of reversing the defeat by Prussia in 1870–71. But she had only 60 per cent of the population of the new Germany, and the gap was widening. To make it up, there was a tremendous emphasis on morale as the make-weight against matériel. It fed the vitalism imbibed by the young Charles de Gaulle from writers influential at the time, like Maurice Barrès and Charles Péguy. There was none of this in Monnet's Cognac, with its matter-of-fact outlook on overseas markets. For his part, "the power of Great Britain was universally respected and very impressive to a young Frenchman who was ready to regard that country and its Empire as the natural place for him to work. Between Cognac and London, there were direct links that by-passed Paris. . . . At Cognac, one was on equal terms with the British: in Paris, one was somewhat under their influence".

A Cognac childhood fathered the man in other ways. Cognac salesmen travelled the world to hawk their wares. Markets could be swayed by a host of influences. Salesmen were questioned back home on political and economic conditions wherever they went. The Monnets kept open table for their envoys and foreign customers who came from Britain, Germany, Scandinavia and America. Judgement on distant markets depended on personal ties and one's assessment of the messenger. Throughout life, Monnet was liable, on report of a supposed fact, to ask: "Who told you that?" "Saturday was the day when we were visited by the men from the country, the distillers who supplied us with raw spirit. . . . There was more than a business relationship between them and my father, there was friendship and mutual trust". For Monnet, informal talk at mealtimes was one of the keys to work; and

---

1. The French Third Republic lasted from the end of the Franco-Prussian War in 1871 to the fall of France in 1940. The postwar Fourth Republic, in many ways its continuation, was much shorter-lived, from 1946 to 1958. In the latter year, General de Gaulle brought in the Fifth Republic, which operates today.

work itself the passport to friendship. Although in some respects his intelligence was very abstract, his approach to action latched almost physically on to the psychology of people and situations he faced. He kneaded the human dough. It was an outlook very foreign to the university-educated mind.

In old age, Monnet remembered his father as "a very intelligent, rather quiet man. People were attracted to him . . . they had affection for him". Nevertheless, the young Jean seems to have been much closer to his mother, who was "very kind . . . and very strict". Née Maria Demelle, she was thirteen years younger than her husband and only nineteen when her first child Jean was born. He was desperately unhappy when he was sent to boarding school and had to be brought home. Even in day school, he was so restless that he was given a dispensation to get up and move around the class during lessons. Much later, the reference books understandably referred to Monnet as an "economist". In fact, little attracted to books, he left school at sixteen, after his first *baccalauréat,* to learn the English basic to a cognac merchant. He was apprenticed for two years to a family connection in the City, the financial district of London. It was the first of his lifelong links with the English-speaking world. In those days, such ties were relatively rare. With time, Monnet's English and American cultures (he had touches of both) became second nature. He spoke a fluent and idiomatic though not always correct English. Yet even apart from his accent, he could never have been taken for any but a Frenchman. Though he could profess a well-nigh "American" optimism and dress in old Savile Row clothes, he still reminded the journalist Anthony Sampson of Hercule Poirot. (True, Poirot was Belgian, but the caricature was pre-1914 French.) His Frenchness did not prevent him from becoming an insider in the American system, but it never quite passed in Britain. Besides English, he learned no other foreign language. In his "European" days, he spoke in English and French, or through a colleague or an interpreter.

The adolescent Monnet set up what must have been a tiny canned food business, "La Bordelaise". How small it was can be gauged from the fact that his mother and sisters helped him find his raw materials and that the *concierge* of his father's business sent him geese for sale in London. Perhaps this should be taken as a sign of entrepreneurial flair, but Monnet's own explanation many years later was that "it made me independent of my father".

Nevertheless, the young man's main occupation from his nineteenth year until the First World War was strictly traditional. He sold cognac abroad for the family firm. He travelled far and wide, to North America, Britain, Scandinavia, Russia and Egypt. North America made a special impact. He tells in his *Memoirs* a story which often came up in his conversation. It happened to him near Calgary. "I wanted to visit some Scandinavian farmers to whom I had an introduction. I asked a blacksmith who was working in front of his forge what means of transport there were. Without stopping work, he answered that there were none. 'But', he added, pointing to his horse, 'you can always take this animal. When you come back, just hitch him up in the same place' ". The conclusions Monnet drew from such experiences were far-reaching. In Cognac, "people are wary of their neighbours and distrust newcomers even more. Here I encountered a new way of looking at things: individual initiative could be accepted as a contribution to the general good. . . . Everywhere, I had the same impression: that where physical space was unlimited, confidence was unlimited too. Where change was accepted, expansion was assured".

North America was not the only mental world Monnet entered. In Egypt, "I accompanied our firm's Greek agent from village to village. We looked in on the wholesalers, who sat us down, drank coffee with us and went about their business. We knew we had to wait a reasonable time. When Shamah, the Greek, decided we could settle, he wrote down the quantity he thought it reasonable for our client to buy, and there was never any argument. He had observed the rites. I rediscovered the importance of time in the Far East. . . . In China, you have to know to wait. In the United States, you have to know how to come back. Two forms of patience to which cognac, itself the fruit of time, is a good preparation". Great stress has often been laid on the American alembic of Monnet's character. In fact, it was only one instance of the practical man's lack of prejudice in adapting to any milieu.

As the elder son, Jean Monnet was being groomed to run the family firm and does not seem to have nursed wider ambitions. His *Memoirs* say that "I was eighteen and negotiating large contracts with the Hudson Bay Company". If a Hudson Bay Company (HBC) report in the 1930s is to be trusted, he was recognised even in those early days as one of his firm's "active heads". The Bay Company had been a customer of J. G. Monnet & Co. since at least 1896. In September 1911, Jean Monnet negotiated an agreement by which J. G. Monnet became the sole suppliers of brandy to the HBC throughout the Canadian West from Fort William (at the western end of Lake Superior) to Vancouver Island. In the correspondence connected with the deal, Monnet indicated that he would probably come "myself" in the following year to "take with your different travellers a thorough trip of Western Canada". This projected trip may have been the occasion when Monnet failed to book a berth on the maiden voyage of the *Titanic*. Had he succeeded, there would have been two chances in three of there being neither a European Community nor a biography of Monnet.

Such episodes apart, the main significance of the relationship between J. G. Monnet and the HBC seems to have been that it was longstanding and cordial and that the young Monnet built on it. The headquarters of the HBC at that time—and until as late as 1970—were not in Canada but in London. Monnet's contacts seem early to have included pillars of the City, such as the governor of the HBC, Robert Kindersley, who was later to become the chairman of Lazards of London and a member of the governing board of the Bank of England. These contacts were to prove very important in Monnet's later business life. He was actually changing trains from London to Cognac at Poitiers on August 1, 1914, when he heard the order for general mobilisation of the French army. He was twenty-five years old.

II
"A REMARKABLY PRECOCIOUS YOUNG MAN"

Monnet's younger brother, Gaston, was called up at once, but Jean was exempted, for nephritis. (His failure to be at the front in 1914 loomed large in Gaullist propaganda decades later.) Wondering what best to do, he decided to promote cooperation on war supplies between France and Britain.

This seems rather banal today. Competition for scarce resources between the British and French was already starting to force up prices, to the profit of traders and neutrals. But the idea implied belief in a long war. Most people expected a short one. "Few believed that a modern nation could endure for many months the strain of a large-scale conflict". Nor did it occur to people that allies should merge economic arrangements. There was little compatibility between a mercantile island and protectionist land power. Government direction seemed natural to a France at war. To free-trading Britain, interference with traders was sacrilege.

In fact, the French (and, once they entered the war in 1915, the Italians) had strong incentives for coordination. They bore the brunt of the losses and were the weaker industrial brethren. Britain, through its navy and merchant marine, controlled the sea-routes to the resources of the world. Yet many of the key figures in Paris would make no commitments. The French were dying at the front. As late as 1917, Louis Loucheur, the Under Secretary of State and later Minister for Armaments, powerful as the friend of Clemenceau, took the view that the British should hand over resources to the French government to use as it saw fit. The idea of active cooperation violated convictions rooted on the one side in blood sacrifice and on the other in the immutable laws of economics. As Monnet remarked in the *Memoirs,* only a very young man could have ignored such biases.

Most young men, however, would have lacked the nerve for Monnet's next move. This was to go straight to the Prime Minister, René Viviani. There were family connections to smooth the way. Monnet's father had a friend, a barrister, Fernand Benon, who knew Viviani, also a lawyer. Benon was Monnet's conduit to the great man. Yet Monnet admits his family thought him "big-headed" to dare to pester the Prime Minister, especially at the height of the battle of the Marne. Still, Monnet did see Viviani in the second week of September in Bordeaux (seventy-five miles from Cognac), whither the government had retired. The timing was good. The costly retreats of August and the "miracle" of the Marne had begun to disperse the first illusions. The importance of the supply train was becoming clear. Viviani passed Monnet on to the Minister of War, Alexandre Millerand. Monnet was sent to London in November to join the liaison mission of the French Civil Supplies Service headed by Quartermaster-General Eugène Mauclère. Ironically, the mission was housed, courtesy of the *entente cordiale,* at Trafalgar House, Waterloo Place. This was located above the Duke of York's steps between Trafalgar Square and Buckingham Palace. (It was also near de Gaulle's headquarters of the Second World War.)

So runs the story in Monnet's *Memoirs.* In fact, it is a highly truncated version of events. It leaves in the shadow a whole dimension of Monnet's activities which may well have helped induce Viviani to receive him. The evidence comes from the archives of the Hudson Bay Company, which, despite its name and operations in Canada—including at one time administrative powers over vast areas—was a British corporation with headquarters in London. At a meeting on March 28, 1922, the deputy governor of the company, Charles Sale, in his own name and that of the governor, Robert Kindersley, credited Monnet with proposing as early as August 1914 that it should become a purchasing agent of the French government for vital civilian supplies. The actual negotiator of the agreement was the HBC's secretary, Frank Ingrams. He arrived in Bordeaux on September 25 and stayed till the first contract laying down the broad lines of the relationship with the French Ministry of Commerce and Supply was signed on October 9. But Sale—though he only joined the HBC in 1915—specified that the deal was due "entirely to [Monnet's] initiative and efforts". He also gave Monnet most of the credit for the agreement of June 1915 to expand its financial base. Monnet's only allusion to this in the *Memoirs* was that his task of buying and shipping wheat for French civil uses "was made easier by the friendly relations I already enjoyed with the heads of the Hudson Bay Company".

Involvement in a major negotiation may help to explain the otherwise surprising ability of a young cognac salesman to capture the attention of key figures in a government evacuated to Bordeaux during a life-and-death crisis. As so often happened later in Monnet's career, crisis itself may have given him impetus. As Sale wrote in 1917:

When war was declared in August 1914, the whole French male population of military age was called up . . . so that within three days every business suffered the loss of the major portion of its staff and the economic framework of French commerce was for the time being destroyed.

The HBC provided an expertise in London and North America that was in desperately short supply in France. It was an important transaction. Correspondence shows Monnet still in Bordeaux and in the thick of relations with the HBC on November 20, 1914. He can only have gone to London at the end of the month, not before.

Monnet's failure to mention all this in his *Memoirs* is intriguing. There seems to be nothing to blush about in having initiated, or helped to initiate, a useful connection that lasted until 1922 and was a precursor of similar deals. The Bay Company "was later to sign agreements with the governments of Belgium, Russia and Rumania. A subsidiary, the Bay Steam Ship Company, was set up and a merchant fleet of several hundred vessels . . . was created. . . . 110 vessels were lost, most of them sunk by U-boats. 145 agencies were involved in running the business, the largest being those in Liverpool, Montreal, New York and Archangel. Thirteen million tons of goods were transported, representing a turnover of £150 million, on which the Company charged a 1% commission". The effort was all the more remarkable in that, before 1914, "while the Company had a very long experience of buying and shipping goods, her little fleets could usually be numbered on the fingers of one hand". Clearly, the HBC was a notable link in the supply chains which helped the Allies win the war.

Why, then, Monnet's silence? One can only speculate. Perhaps he regarded the *Memoirs* as a political testament and did not wish to muddy the waters with his business affairs. They are minimised throughout. He may also have thought in the 1970s that one more piece of evidence of roots in the English-speaking world might alienate a French readership already plied with Gaullist propaganda that he was too international by half. There were rumblings in the French civil service even in 1916–17 of hostility and opposition to the HBC link. "When you think of it impartially", wrote Sale, "it is not surprising that some [French officials] should object to the position occupied by our Company—a British concern entrusted with the operations of probably the most important branch of French requirements from abroad". The machine-gun nests entrenched in the bureaucracy seem to have been neutralised at least in part by Monnet's efforts. As Kindersley wrote to him in July 1916, "Nobody realises more fully than we do that the larger developments . . . between the French government and the HBC have only been made possible by your exertions". This in turn may have produced a certain anxiety on Monnet's part at having his war record associated in any way with capitalist profits. He made a point of taking no commission from the HBC. He also showed reticence about money in the Second World War. He seems always to have been healthily puritan about mixing public service with private profit. According to Sale, "He entirely neglected his own personal interests". Nevertheless, Monnet's lack of personal greed during the war was to stand his family firm in good stead in a later crisis. Monnet's career path in the years between does not suggest advance awareness of this crisis. All the same, he may have been wary about connections being made.

There is a second minor mystery. Monnet's *Memoirs* would lead a casual reader to conclude that once he came to London in November 1914, he stayed there. This cannot have been the case. Correspondence on Christmas Day 1915 and in January and the summer of 1916 with the Bay Company shows him operating from the Ministry of Commerce or working out of a second office or flat at 43 rue de Bellechasse, in short, in Paris, with no sign of being in London. Admittedly, there are wide gaps in the series. But J. A. Mikkelborg, a Norwegian ship's captain sent by the HBC in 1916 to Paris to supervise the Company's traffic, mainly of wheat, into France, describes him as the senior authority with whom he dealt more than once. "The Secretary [Monnet] said that any captain whom I thought well of I should invite him for a quiet *déjeuner*. I did so and it worked wonders". When Mikkelborg went to say goodbye to Monnet, "the day was hot, he was bustling about in his shortsleeves from one workroom to another. . . . When he saw me he took me on one side and we sat down strideways on a seat used to stand on to reach the upper shelves. . . . Jean Monnet was an excellent boss and a hard driver" (terms which were to recur later in many other mouths). Other correspondence suggests a Monnet well ensconced and fairly close to the Minister. In fact, Monnet does not seem to have started transferring to London again till early in January 1917 and really to have settled there until April.

It may be coincidence, but it is interesting that the dates locating Monnet in Paris fall in the period after October 1915, when Etienne Clémentel became Minister of Commerce and Posts. Clémentel was a friend of the elder Monnet. Monnet says that his own efforts in London to achieve greater Allied cooperation, notably over wheat, drew the "Minister's attention to this young delegate in London who was always asking for instructions to negotiate tighter agreements". Either way—or both ways—Clémentel's arrival in office seems, for Monnet, one of those strokes of luck so often encountered in the early years of exceptionally talented people. Clémentel stayed in the job for the next four years through five governments. By the end of the war, he was a one-man band, responsible for industry, transport and supply as well as trade and posts, and the real organiser of the French war effort. He was also an apostle of Allied economic cooperation. Monnet's ascent can really be traced from Clémentel's side in 1916. The elder Monnet could have made the connection or his son have feared posterity would think so. Could unease at owing more than met the eye to family influence have motivated Monnet's failure to record his stint in Paris? There is no other clue, but the lapse of memory is curious.

The previous lack of openings for the Allied economic cooperation Monnet advocated may also explain the obscurity of his first period in London.

Even with Clémentel, a common approach took half the war to begin in crisis and the other half to complete in near disaster. In effect, Monnet's initial appeal to Viviani seems not to have led anywhere in particular and to have had little connection with the real point of departure when troubles and Clémentel began to make innovation possible.

True, an International Supply Commission operated in London from the beginning of hostilities. Despite its title, this was a strictly British organisation for coordinating national and Allied purchases from manufacturers in Britain. Information was exchanged to moderate the scramble for scarce supplies in the world. British ships were passed to the French (and later to the Italians) on temporary lease. The odd refigerated meat boat from Australia or Argentina would be jointly chartered by the French and British. Basically, however, each country fended for itself. As Monnet wrote, "While I spent my first months in London doing the best I could, I was . . . very dissatisfied. I shared the anxiety of my counterparts in the [British] Board of Trade as they watched the various purchasing bodies vying with each other for supplies—to the greater profit of Canadian and Argentinian wheat-growers". No change in these arm's-length arrangements was even contemplated until Clémentel came on the scene.

Clémentel was the first politician to realise France's interest, as a deficit country, in Allied economic cooperation. He seems from the outset to have been aiming at a planned international economy after the war. Even so, he would not have gone far without the cumulative supply crises that occurred as the war ground on. By early 1916, shipping losses began to mount. Tonnage ran short. The result, in a system still dominated by private trading, was soaring freight rates and scandalous trading profits. They bore especially hard on wheat, the staple of civil morale. The British decided to ration bread at home, but this made little sense unless the trade was internationally controlled. This gave their chance to Clémentel, Monnet and their ally, Arthur Salter, the British official responsible for shipping. Salter says the idea of a Wheat Executive originated with Monnet, Clémentel only that Monnet "prepared" the negotiations. Monnet says that a great debt was owed to Salter. He secured the cooperation of the British, who controlled the vital resource, shipping. As it was, it took until November 1916 to establish the Wheat Executive, fully twenty-eight months after the outbreak of war.

The Wheat Executive consisted of three officials, one each delegated by Britain, France and Italy. Their job was to assess the needs of each country and the available supplies, allot the shares by agreement and pass the orders jointly. They were officials and had no independent authority. The bargaining was frequently tense. Yet in practice their conclusions were usually accepted by the governments. The Executive kept wheat flowing, slowed the rise in prices and saved shipping space. The system rapidly proved a success, was extended to all cereals and in the end regulated the supplies even of a large proportion of non-combatant countries. An enormous step towards cooperation had been taken. Even so, it took a further year of disasters to force the Allies to apply the same approach across a broader front.

Shipping was the main bottleneck. In January 1917, the Germans started unrestricted submarine warfare. This soon brought America into the war, which settled the issue in the long run. But in the short, the European combatants had to survive. "In April 1917 the losses were such that, of every four ships which took to sea, only one returned." At times, days separated the Allies from a failure of munitions—let alone of food and raw materials to keep civilian morale afloat and production going.

This gave Clémentel, Monnet and Salter a second opportunity. Monnet seems to have suggested that the wheat regime should be extended to all shipping. Till then, the British, possessing the ships, considered they should control any transport pool. The French aimed instead at joint rationing based on need, not resources. The difficult negotiations lasted most of 1917. Still, at the end of November, a comprehensive supply control organisation, the Allied Maritime Transport Council (AMTC), was formed. It was put to work at once on what was to become Monnet's favourite tool of persuasion, a "balance-sheet", in this case, one of shipping. By the end of the war virtually all military and civil supplies were being rationed by joint Allied control of the item in shortest supply, shipping space. At its climax, just before the armistice, the AMTC was, Harold Nicolson wrote in his biography of Dwight Morrow, who worked in it, "the most advanced experiment yet made in international cooperation".

Clémentel was the ideal chief for Monnet. He had a strategy, listened to advice and was not afraid to take decisions. Under him, Monnet came to the fore. The relationship was in some ways the first of many Monnet was to form with politicians. It is not clear to what extent Clémentel used the young Monnet as an executant or, as Monnet's *Memoirs* imply, was inspired by him. They are not mutually exclusive. Either way, the crux is that the two men were at one on goals and in constant contact on means. Monnet insisted on a direct telephone line to the Minister, and anyone who knew him later will assume he used it relentlessly.

From the end of 1916, when his predecessor, Ernest Vilgrain, went to join Clémentel in Paris as his Vice Minister, Monnet headed the French mission in London for food and shipping, numbering over a hundred officials, and was his country's representative on the four-man Allied Maritime Transport Executive, the hinge of the cooperative system. Still not thirty, he was now in the inner circle of decision-makers, so much so that he aroused opposition in Paris. The Minister of Armaments, Loucheur, an industrialist, an old associate of Clemenceau and a power in the government of the "Tiger", tried to fire him by having him sent to the front. Clémentel appealed to Clemenceau, who personally summoned Monnet in January

1918, and cross-questioned him roughly on his work. A week later, Monnet was confirmed in his post in London by a decree passed in the Council of Ministers and signed by them all, Loucheur included. In 1919, at the peace conference in Paris, American diplomats were reporting back that Monnet was close to Clemenceau.

An incident near the end of the war shows Monnet's ability to get things done in London. The French government was under attack in the National Assembly for failing to prepare for postwar needs and notably to provide extra shipping for relief and reconstruction in the northern provinces freed from the Germans. This extra tonnage could only come from Britain. Clémentel cabled Monnet on October 25 to find it for a ministerial answer to a written question in the Assembly on November 15. Three weeks was an impossibly short time. Yet Monnet arranged a transfer of half a million tons of British shipping to French use just before the deadline. The government's face was saved and Monnet officially thanked.

The speed of the decision shows how well-oiled the Allied circuits had become. Networks of officials were the secret. Salter tells how he, Monnet, John Anderson, then secretary to the Ministry of Shipping, and one other, agreed one evening in September 1917 that an Allied shipping executive could now be set up. When it was, it consisted of Monnet (under thirty), Salter and Bernardo Attolico for Italy (late thirties) and George Rublee for the United States (the senior citizen at forty-nine). The three Europeans were later to join the League of Nations secretariat. Such people formed the nucleus of an international civil service, totally committed, wedded to common goals, holding the initiative and each with considerable influence at home.

The key to establishing an inter-Allied organisation was to feed its views into national decision-making. Even when the system was operating at its height at the end of the war, there was no question of international authority over governments. The system worked in practice not because of its formal powers but as a result of the desperate last stages of the war, the extreme shortages that developed and the "competitive panic" that had to be mastered in the combined Allied executives.

Allied Shipping Control, written shortly after the war by the British chairman of the Allied Maritime Transport Executive, Salter, explained the alchemy of cooperation. Direct access by the members of the Executive to ministers responsible for taking and administering decisions was the first requirement.

> The French member [i.e., Monnet], for example, had long worked in the closest association with the French Minister of Commerce, and . . . was able to secure the necessary action by the French supply departments.

There would only be cooperation if the need was taken into account while policies were being formulated. "If each one of four separate countries

> begins to give [national policy] expression in administrative arrangements, fortifies it with Ministerial decisions and Cabinet authority, adjustment will prove almost impossible.

To avoid this, daily association and mutual confidence were vital between the few players at the crossroads in the Executive in London.

> The position of members of an international committee with a dual personal capacity, international in relation to their own country, national in relation to other countries, is one of great delicacy. They necessarily receive information from their departments (they are useless if they do not) with regard to policy while still in the process of formation. It is a problem of the utmost difficulty to know how much of this can properly be communicated to their Allied colleagues. . . .
>
> Given the proper personal relations, many things can be explained which would never be put on paper or stated in a formal meeting; the limits of concession can be explored. . . . Such work . . . is only possible . . . under conditions of personal confidence and long personal association.

Again and again, in Monnet's life, one heard echoes of the same problems faced and related solutions reached.

WITHIN A MONTH of the armistice Monnet was back in Paris and took part in the peace conference which began in January. Like Clémentel, he hoped to extend war-time cooperation to the period of reconstruction and beyond. Clémentel realised France would be too weak to take on a revived exporting Germany, carving up markets through dominant cartels. He therefore proposed a scheme for the worldwide control of raw material supplies, building on Allied economic cooperation during the war. The aim was not to penalise Germany so much as to create a framework to contain her economic power. There were two main goals. The first was for France to obtain American and British help in financing the transition from war to peace, tentatively put at five years. The second was to use the war-time domination of raw material markets by the Western allies (in fact, by the British and the Americans) to prevent any future German thrust to dominate world markets by cartels or hamper France's growth by rationing basic supplies to her economy, notably of coke to the steel industry. Under the trappings of a world commodity system for the main basic materials, it was a proposal to give France what the French called "Anglo-Saxon" insurance against the superior strength of Germany in any bilateral Franco-German relationship.

It was an imaginative but strange scheme, very French in proposing a political goal as if economics were infinitely malleable. It is true that Clémentel assumed raw material shortages would persist into the peace. Nevertheless an all-embracing commodity agreement could hardly have survived for long even if it had been taken up. It did not articulate any relationship to markets as, for instance, did Keynes's proposals for stabilising raw material prices after the Second World War. Politically, it had no attractions for the British and the Americans. Neither the United States nor Britain was ready to perpetuate a rationing system at "fair" prices in terms of "need" where the relative have-nots, led by France, might acquire a voice in British and American decisions. As the ultimate paymasters, the Americans recognised that postwar relief was inevitable and that they would have to pay most of it. Holding the purse-strings, however, they had no intention of sharing the decisions as to how much should be disbursed, to whom and on what terms. They wanted free trade and a free hand. They turned down Clémentel's project flat at the meeting of the Allies' Supreme Economic Council on April 4, 1919.

The AMTC had been absorbed into the new Supreme Economic Council in February. Monnet represented France on the Council's Supply Section, chaired by Herbert Hoover. In that capacity, he met the Dulles brothers, Allen and John Foster, and John Maynard Keynes, the latter two men serving in other sections. He also sealed his friendship from the AMTC with Dwight Morrow, who was in many ways the conscience of Wall Street. There is too little evidence to suggest how great or small was Monnet's part in the Clémentel plan. But he plainly favoured it. In one document, dated November 2, 1918, he pleads for war-time economic controls to be continued in the period of reconstruction in France and Belgium. He may have had a longer perspective in mind, for his *Memoirs,* over fifty years later, still regretted the demise of Allied planning. "It was to take many years, and much suffering, before Europeans began to realize that they must choose either unity or decline." He quotes Clémentel himself lamenting that "without the altruistic, disinterested cooperation which we tried to achieve among the Allies and should have extended to our former enemies, one day we shall have to begin all over again".

There is a family resemblance between the Clémentel plan and the more successful European schemes after the Second World War: the Franco-German focus, the political use of economics, the decisive American voice. The difference was that in 1950, and against the background of the Cold War and the North Atlantic Treaty, the French and Americans managed to agree on Germany. At Versailles, they did not. Left alone, and ultimately weak, the French adopted policies veering between overinsurance and retreat. Marshal Foch, who seemed to have divine sources of information, forecast in 1919 that the peace treaty would be a "twenty year truce".

In the short term, the hopes dashed in one form in the Clémentel plan were revived in another, in the League of Nations inspired by Woodrow Wilson. The League's Covenant was adopted in May by the peace conference and formed the first section of the Treaty of Versailles. Both Monnet and Salter were deeply involved. They saw the League as "a means to organise peace", but their memoranda show that neither thought remotely in supranational terms. Monnet in his *Memoirs* says that nobody then thought in such terms even if the language people used might now give the impression they did. Monnet seems to have vested his hopes in a mixture of technocracy and propaganda. A quality secretariat with good contacts in the governments would invite the states to "appreciate problems as a whole in the light of the general interest". (The "general interest" was to echo down the corridors of his life.) There should also be vigorous, wide-ranging, popular publicity.

In November 1919 and again in March 1920, the U.S. Congress refused to ratify the Versailles treaty. That meant rejection of the League of Nations, which was part of it. Germany was not a member of the League, nor was the Soviet Union. This left the British and the French in the saddle. When a British diplomat, Sir Eric Drummond, was made its Secretary-General in Geneva, Monnet was appointed his deputy. The British awarded him an honorary knighthood, a KBE (Knight Commander of the Order of the British Empire), usually granted to civil servants at the end of their careers.

At the League, the new knight errant was involved in some major operations. The League was offered the poisoned chalice of all the territorial disputes the Versailles treaty makers had failed to resolve. A first test case was Upper Silesia, a smaller Ruhr of two million people, sitting on coal, belching flame and steel, with two Poles to every German and claimed in its entirety by both countries. France backed Poland and Britain Germany. Bitterness graduated from sullen to belligerent and fighting broke out between well-organised Polish and German irregulars. At a loss, in August 1921, Britain and France decided to entrust the decision to a commission of the League under a Japanese chairman. Monnet produced the report for the commission in three weeks. Published on October 20, the award established two joint bodies to run the basin for fifteen years on both sides of a proposed border-line. One was a mixed Polish-German managing commission, the other an arbitration tribunal whose League chairman held the casting vote. There were many difficulties before a German-Polish convention was signed on May 15, 1922, with 606 articles—easily outstripping the 440 of the Treaty of Versailles. The German Reichstag was. draped in black for the ratification debate. All the same, the system worked for the full fifteen years.

Austria, shorn of an empire eight times its own size, provided the next challenge. Its people were pathetic victims of the war their erstwhile rulers had begun. By the summer of 1922, in Vienna, "people of all classes . . . were visibly starving". Collapse was so complete that there was fear Italy and Czechoslovakia might partition Austria. This in turn discouraged loans to revive the economy. At a picnic on the Lake of Geneva in September 1922, Salter, Basil Blackett (a British Treasury official) and Monnet "concluded that the League could save Austria. . . . Monnet had the brilliant idea that what seemed the worst danger of all, external intervention, might be converted into a massive force for collective assistance". The League's report proposed a "protocol of abstention" by which Britain, France, Italy and Czechoslovakia agreed to respect the independence and territorial integrity of Austria. This made it possible to raise funds and introduce a recovery plan worked out by Blackett. The operation was supervised by the League and set Austria on the road to modest prosperity until the Great Depression. For the first time, an international body had sponsored a programme of reconstruction for a country.

The stir created by the Austrian settlement led to later operations to stabilise the Hungarian economy and to deal with massive refugee crises in Greece and Bulgaria (in which Monnet's hand is not traceable). These operations stimulated hopes that the League might really carry the international system beyond the balance of power and costly breakdowns. But even then limits stuck out as soon as great powers were directly involved. France insisted on detaching the Saar "economically" from Germany in the hope of absorbing it in fifteen years. The policy foundered in the referendum of 1935, which returned the Saar to Germany in a welter of orchestrated Nazi threats. As a high League official, Monnet was an unwilling accessory to the ill-fated policy. It remained a painful memory. As George Ball has pointed out, the reviving quarrel between France and the new Germany after the Second World War over the Saar was a major factor leading Monnet to propose the Schuman Plan in 1950.

In Monnet's *Memoirs,* where the highest commendation for a statesman is that he is "generous" and its polar opposite that he embodies the "spirit of domination", the classic instance of the latter is provided not by a German but by a Frenchman. The issue was German reparations to France. Monnet went along, with one of the grandees of French politics, Léon Bourgeois, and the Belgian delegate on the Reparations Commission of the League, to see the chairman of the Commission, the once and future French Prime Minister Raymond Poincaré. The aim of the visitors was not to persuade Poincaré to rescind reparations, but to put a public limit on them. They thought this vital (as events proved) to avert economic catastrophe. "At this, Poincaré stood up flushed with rage. 'Never, sir. The German debt is a political matter and I intend to use it as a means of pressure' ".

Looking back on the League after the Second World War, Monnet spoke of its "little solutions to big problems" and dismissed it as a "telephone exchange". He remembered being aware even at the time that the national veto was a flaw. But he had no solution. And before Japan grabbed Manchuria in 1931, there was a time of hope for the League. Salter, who joined the secretariat as head of the Economic and Finance Division in 1922, remembered those years as "by far the happiest period of work in my life". When Monnet left at the end of 1922, he gave no sign of disappointment. Nor was any personal failure involved. Louis Joxe, later Secretary-General of the French Foreign Ministry, worked in the secretariat and then in the French delegation to the League. He wrote later that the French, from Foreign Minister Aristide Briand downwards, "swore by Jean Monnet who was their guide and conscience" and that when he left, "the great names of the day, Benes, Titulescu, Politis" (the Czech, the Rumanian, the Greek) "could hardly conceive of life in Geneva without referring to his example". Even Georges Bonnet, the Foreign Minister at the time of Munich, whose tone is more acerbic, wrote that "he enjoyed an extraordinary reputation as a clever diplomat".

Drummond too regretted his deputy's departure. They had become "great friends". But the J. G. Monnet brandy firm was sinking into what was then the disgrace of bankruptcy. The family Wunderkind had to return home. After nine years of public service, he found himself back in business. Monnet would not move back into government for another fifteen years. These years were to land him in a surprising variety of predicaments.

III
COGNAC AND BANKING (1923–1932)

According to Monnet's own account, his father was a traditionalist who believed in a luxury trade of small sales of old brandy to connoisseurs. This tied up a great deal of capital in stock. The firm had already shown signs of strain in the last two years before the war when small losses were posted up. The war stoked up a brief prosperity, but peace, after a first couple of years, soon brought a rude awakening. A doubling of output in Cognac coincided with a near collapse of the main English-speaking markets. Prohibition had a catastrophic effect on sales in North America. British demand fell by two-thirds from pre-1914 levels, with increased duties on spirits and a shift in taste to whisky. All this forced a sudden and radical change of policy in a highly conservative business based at the time on veneration for the product rather than agility in dealing with unpredictable markets. J. G. Monnet & Co. had 9 million francs of debts (about $740,000 at average—but rapidly shifting—1922 exchange rates), with 2 million francs of liquid assets and some 4 million francs in stocks. The younger Monnet decided to sell the stocks—as slowly as possible, to limit loss—and to aim at larger sales of younger spirits, inevitably of lower quality but tying up less capital.

The transition from father to son seems to have been rather painful. It was probably late in 1921 that Jean's sister, Marie-Louise, who later became prominent in Catholic Action, came to Geneva to warn him of trouble at home.[2] Thinking initially in terms of £80,000, he turned to the Hudson Bay Company. The HBC, led by Kindersley and Sale, lent him £40,000 at the end of March 1922 (at that time, nearly 2 million francs or $160,000), the board noting that Monnet had refused, and still refused, any commission on the firm's war profits of well over £1 million from the French connection. It was understood Monnet would repay the loan, but the board decided that if he failed to do so, they would treat it as a gift. With his money in hand, Monnet resigned from the secretariat of the League at the end of 1922 and returned to Cognac.

For a time, J. G. Monnet & Co. continued to face big difficulties. In 1923, Monnet asked the Bay Company to waive the promised guarantees and security on the loan, and the board complied. Recovery came gradually, helped by a fall in production in Cognac, by rising prices and by a partial revival of the British market. The J. G. Monnet firm's deficit of 1.8 million francs in 1921–22 turned into a profit of 2 million francs (or 1.6 million francs at constant prices) in 1925–26, about $65,000 at the falling 1926 exchange rates. The firm was on its feet again. Monnet promptly handed over management to his younger brother, Gaston, who had the misfortune to die of appendicitis within three days in 1927. Cousins, Robert and Georges Monnet, the former of whom had a "nose" for brandy, then took over. Robert bought Jean Monnet's "charming house on the banks of the Charente river". The Bay Company loan was repaid with interest on September 17, 1930, twelve years ahead of schedule. But since, in accordance with the initial agreement, it was honoured in francs, which had by then lost about 60 per cent of their value on the foreign exchanges, J. G. Monnet & Co. really reimbursed less than 40 per cent of the principal and interest in pounds sterling. In short, the Bay Company's help was very substantial and probably saved the business. Monnet kept his shares in the firm and involvement with its policies. Thirty years later, he still travelled fairly frequently between Paris and Cognac to confer with his surviving cousin, Robert.

Jean Monnet was now approached by a New York investment bank, Blair and Company, to set up a joint European affiliate with the Chase National: the Blair and Company Foreign Corporation. The profile of Monnet's father in *Fortune* magazine of August 1944 asserted that the League's Austrian set-

2. The *Memoirs* say autumn 1923, which is impossible, for Monnet had already been in Cognac for most of a year. The most likely time is 1921 because of the loan negotiations with HBC early in 1922. They would have been the obvious first step in any recovery programme.

tlement first brought him to the attention of Wall Street. However, he had already worked at close quarters in the AMTC and Paris peace conference with a good number of rising Wall Street stars. Whatever the origin of his new job, European Blair was set up in Paris in August 1926, with Monnet as vice president and managing partner. Why did Monnet accept? Was he tempted by the money? Did he lack political incentives in Paris? Did he see in the activities of American finance houses like Blair a chance to carry out for profit much the same kind of politico-economic operations he had initiated earlier as a servant of the League? The Dawes loan, which closed the catastrophic German inflation of 1923–24, was followed by five years of rapid growth until the end of the decade. One of the strongest motors of this boom was American investment in Europe. Foreign loans floated in the United States during the 1920s exceeded the total of similar loans floated in all the other capital-lending countries put together. John J. McCloy has called it almost a mini Marshall Plan. There was a widening ripple of reconstruction schemes designed *inter alia* to launch the new countries of eastern Europe carved by the Treaty of Versailles out of the defeated empires. For them, it was the one brief moment of light between birth in turmoil and rape first by Nazi, then by Soviet, imperialists. American banks were much involved in this interlude of hope. So was the French government, busy raising bulwarks against Germany. Blair was one of the leading finance houses and placed many issues for governments and utilities. Monnet himself negotiated loans to Poland, Rumania, Yugoslavia and Bulgaria.

Why did the League not assume responsibility? Salter's view was that "by this time the very fame of the League's action entailed disadvantages. It led to the belief that the appropriate clients for the League were countries that were completely down and out and who both needed, and were required to accept, the same onerous and rather humiliating form of control for a period". In the view of Emile Moreau, the governor of the Bank of France from 1926 to 1930, Poland and Rumania did not want to go to the League because its Finance Committee was dominated by Britain. The economic "adviser" in the American legation in Warsaw in 1927, John B. Stetson, Jr., went one step further: the Poles, he reported, wanted to avoid controls by any of the European great powers. On two points, these views concur: the political nature of loans and the great-power competition in the shadows.

The two major loans in which Monnet was a chief negotiator were for Poland in 1927 and Rumania in 1928. For each, a consortium of American banks occupied the front of the stage. (For Poland, Blair was in partnership with the Bankers Trust, Chase National and Kuhn Loeb.) The consortium was to organise an international issue of bonds in a wide range of capital centres. The proceeds would back an internal economic reform programme, of the classic kind, designed, after a preliminary period of deflation, to set the economy on a stable course of growth. They would encourage foreign capital to invest in the country's development, mainly for railways and utilities. And in each case, though most of the money came from open capital markets, the foundation was the prior backing of the four major central banks (i.e., those of the United States, Britain, France and Germany). It was an early form of the operations the International Monetary Fund has carried out since the Second World War.

Central bank rivalries and nationalism were intense. The Bank of England in the 1920s, while weakened, was still to all appearances much what it had been before 1914. Monnet, though on good terms with Montagu Norman, its famous governor, regarded Norman as an "imperialist". Moreau, at the Bank of France, wanted to bolster his country's protégés in eastern Europe as bulwarks against Germany. Hjalmar Schacht, at the Reichsbank, reflected his government's conflict with Poland. The real power belonged to Benjamin Strong, of the Federal Reserve of New York. It was not, though, fully evident, because in Europe, Strong tended to hand the lead in operations to London.

The Polish loan of 1927 seems to have precipitated a more active American involvement. The year before, Poland's president, General Józef Pilsudski, a prototype of de Gaulle with a flair for the politics of prestige, decided that the time had come for an international loan to set the seal on his regime and his country's prospects for growth. If Moreau's diary does not distort the facts, the first scheme for a loan, promoted by Norman, was the fruit of an alliance between "British financial imperialism and pan-Germanism". It aimed at a "European" solution without the Americans. It contained political conditions, particularly a revision of Poland's borders with Germany in the latter's favour. The Poles were advised that by going to the Blair group and accepting the terms set by the Financial Committee of the League, they could escape these unwelcome attentions. Monnet was duly contacted by his close Polish friend from the secretariat of the League, the head of the Health Department and future creator of UNICEF, Ludwik Rajchman.

During much of 1927, Monnet was on and off in Warsaw in a suite at the Hotel Europeiski. There seems to have been some rivalry with the chief negotiator of the Bankers Trust. Dulles, as the central figure" in the talks, "mediated," according to the source, between the two. At the same time, Moreau's diary suggests Monnet established himself at the centre of the web by becoming a "friend" of Strong. Moreau obviously saw Monnet and Blair as a vital link in a Franco-American alliance to outflank Norman and Schacht. Monnet warned him at one point not to give the impression to Americans, whose aims were economic and financial, that his were political. The issue was settled when Strong decided to come out from behind the Bank of England, take a lead in the loan and compel the two reluctant governors, with some difficulty, to follow suit. Moreau gave Monnet much of the credit for this outcome, "very advantageous to France". The latter was certainly a conduit between Strong and Moreau and may have been much more. It is not clear how much Monnet acted as an American banker or extracurricular Frenchman. The two were compatible. Either way, aligning with Americans to overcome European opposition was prophetic of his later career.

It was finally agreed, over Polish protests, that four foreign directors should sit on the board of the Bank of Poland, one the American resident in Warsaw to supervise the stabilisation programme and three non-residents, British, French and Swiss, but not German. The loan, for $72 million, based on $20 million contributed by the four central banks, was signed in Warsaw at the end of 1927. It was relatively large for the period. The Dawes loan to stabilise the German Reichsmark three years before had been worth some $200 million. Reconstruction worked briefly in Poland till the Great Depression choked off growth.

The Polish loan was barely in the bag when Monnet was to be found, early in 1928, sitting in the Ministry of Finance in Bucharest doing much the same for Rumania and its currency, the leu. Rumania's politics were if anything more turbulent and the economy more backward than Poland's. The strategy of the negotiations was nevertheless much the same. The major difference was the larger sum involved, $100 million, compounded by the sudden loss of the American appetite for foreign securities after the stock market fall of April 1928, a harbinger of the Great Crash of October 1929. Difficulty was encountered in raising the money.

The negotiations were saved by Ivar Kreuger, "the Swedish Match King", who controlled three-quarters of the world match industry. (He achieved this by leasing national match monopolies for a period in return for a capital sum and annual royalties.) He played hard to get until the consortium was on the point of breaking off the talks. He then asked for five minutes, went into a corner and in full view of the exasperated bankers scribbled on his stiff white cuffs. This flourish completed, he agreed to lend the last $30 million against the Rumanian match monopoly for thirty years, on which he promised to pay an annual royalty of $3 million. When Monnet pressed him later, he said: "I worked out that if I put one match fewer in each box, I should make out". The loan was concluded in February 1929. The Depression was only months away.

The Blair period played an important part in the build-up of Monnet's networks. Monnet's main assistant was, as mentioned earlier, the future French Prime Minister René Pleven. Monnet wrote of him in this period as of a tyro whom he trained. Pleven himself has testified, rather more generously, to how much he owed to his early experience with Monnet. Pleven was to remain with Monnet from 1925 to 1929 before joining AT&T in America and working with him again in London during the phoney war. One of the bankers in the consortium was Dwight Morrow, a close friend since the AMTC. The lawyer for the Polish loan was John Foster Dulles, of Sullivan and Cromwell, soon to be the biggest law firm in America. The friendship with Monnet was to last till Dulles's death.

Monnet's activities since 1914, apart from the forced retreat to Cognac, had all been of a piece. Though in detail various, all involved public service with political overtones and international economic reform or cooperation. Now, for the first time, he was tempted, or sucked, into a purely financial helter-skelter. Elisha Walker, the head of Blair, of New York, and the famous Amadeo Giannini, who had from San Francisco built up the Bank of America into the biggest banking network outside New York, with "myriad holding companies" in America and Europe, decided to merge. The idea, in the intoxication of the "bigger and better" 1920s, now nearing climax, was to create the first bank with a worldwide reach. In mid-May 1929, the interests of the two financial houses were fused in a vast holding company, Transamerica, of which Walker, "one of the outstanding financial men of the time", became chairman. In January 1930, three months after the Great Crash on Wall Street, Monnet joined him in San Francisco as vice chairman. The sixty-year-old Giannini, who had frequently talked of retiring, repaired to Austria for an agreed couple of years. Monnet was now in the heart of the American financial establishment. The location was right, the time and partner disastrous.

It soon became apparent to the new management that all was not well with Transamerica. It looked gigantic, but the balance-sheet was swollen by double accounting. Before the New Deal of Franklin D. Roosevelt, American holding companies were not required to produce consolidated balance-sheets. Giannini added the profits of the numerous affiliates without disclosing that these were largely earned off one another and cancelled out. The closer Walker and company looked, the more net assets crumbled. By September 1931, it transpired that Transamerica was worth not $1 billion but under $200 million. The operation was well conducted. "The balloon had been let down from the stratosphere without any serious explosion or any failures". But in banking, as in war, orderly retreat earns few bouquets. The Depression added to the misery. Transamerica shares, which had touched a wild $165 each in September 1929, fell to $2 each by the end of 1931. As shares touched bottom, Giannini re-emerged from retirement, a giant refreshed.

Had he foreseen the crisis and opportunity? Though ill, he converted withdrawal into rout "in the most bitter struggle in the history of American finance", as a contemporary journalist called it. He lambasted the Wall Street bankers for ruining honest Californians. A prospectus distributed by the Blair managers in January 1932 hit back. It accused Giannini of manipulating stock at great cost to shareholders in order to maintain the share price at high levels in October 1929 when the collapse began; of awarding himself over $5 million in three years; and of failing to disclose vital information. Years later, in 1938 and again in 1940, reports by the Securities and Exchange Commission (SEC) again accused Giannini of financial irregularities and misleading statements. Nevertheless, in 1932, the Blair war-cry of "honest banking" proved far too prosaic for the bank's 250,000 small shareholders, four-fifths of them Californian and bred to Giannini's golden touch. For many of them, "honest banking" spelled ruin. Decades later, Monnet would recall an indignant old lady crying, "I don't want honest banking, I want wizardry". The Blair managers were no match for Giannini's populism, and on February 13, he duly wrested back the chair of Transamerica in a proxy fight. Walker, Monnet and most of the other bankers from New York retired hurt, bidding farewell to their own Blair as well as to Transamerica. Monnet, briefly a millionaire, admitted, "I may have been good at making [money] perhaps, but certainly not at keeping it".

IV
CONSULTANT (1932—1939)

To the end of his days, Monnet gave a fair impression of a merchant banker between the wars. He did not go out much, but when he did, ate at Prunier's or another restaurant of settled reputation. He was handsomely stocked with Havana cigars long after he stopped smoking himself. The hairdresser usually came to him. His driver picked up tickets. He crossed the Atlantic by ocean liner when he could spare the time. He stayed for preference at quiet hotels that spoke of wealth in a prewar mode foreign to the virtues of Conrad Hilton. These staging posts had to be as close to greenery as possible, hotels like the Hassler near the gardens of the Villa Borghese in Rome, the Hyde Park in London overlooking Rotten Row where horses and their grand owners once paraded or even the Trianon Palace on the edge of the grounds of Versailles. In the restaurant, he would choose a menu of conservative excellence, like a grilled Dover sole and stewed fruit. His tastes were as sober as his suits and, like them, assumed a quality that came dear. Monnet also retained traces of the 1920s that owed nothing to banking. In the 1950s, he still wore a long racoon fur coat which had been fashionable at Ivy League football games in the Coolidge era.

Nevertheless, the Transamerica débâcle cost Monnet a fortune and he never acquired another. In fact, from 1932 to the end of his life, though he always seems to have spent fairly freely, he was equally never quite on an even financial keel. The *Fortune* magazine profile of August 1944 claimed he enjoyed an "average" annual income of $25,000 from the family cognac firm prewar. If so, by salaried standards, he should have been modestly well off.

Senior international civil servants gladly earned such sums after the Second World War and its inflation. He may also have been lavishly paid for one consultancy in the 1930s. All the same, he finally cleared the debts contracted after the crash of 1932 only thirty years later. More immediately, the fall from the grace of his brilliant early days seems to have been the prelude to the least satisfactory six or seven years of his career. Between the depth of the Great Depression and the Second World War, his numerous activities seem to have been unusually precarious and, when they offered promise, largely to have disappointed it. That he was able to pick himself up at all at first was largely due to a few faithful backers such as John Foster Dulles and Ludwik Rajchman. These also included the leading lights of Lazards of London, none other than Sir Robert Kindersley, the former governor of the Hudson Bay Company, and Robert Brand, also a partner of Lazards, an associate of Monnet's from the supply politics of the First World War. All were active on his behalf beyond the normal call of friendship.

Dulles almost at once steered a job his way. This was to take part in liquidating the empire of Ivar Kreuger. Kreuger shot himself in his Paris flat on the morning of March 12, 1932. His holding company, Kreuger and Toll, was the most widely distributed security in the world. The thefts behind the bankruptcy of his empire of over 250 companies were gigantic. So were some judgements on the man. Galbraith once called Kreuger "a Napoleonic bandit" who perpetrated "the greatest fraud in history". Keynes, on the other hand, thought him "maybe the greatest financial intelligence of his time . . . a canal between countries with an abundance of capital and those in bitter need of it". Either way, the uncovered deficit he left behind was nearly twice the Polish and Rumanian loans combined. In Sweden, the stock exchange was closed for days and flags flew at half-mast. Implicated a little later in the scandal, the Prime Minister, the teetotaller Carl Ekman, fell.

Kreuger, like Giannini and de Gaulle, Monnet used to say in later years, was a large man with a carefully cultivated air of mystery. He needed to be mysterious: "Bonds of the Italian government were found to be forgeries by Kreuger. . . . Assets supposed to have great value were non-existent". When the end came, American creditors held two-thirds of the debentures in Kreuger and Toll. Swedish law provided only for Swedish liquidators. Foreign creditors feared the Swedes would keep the Swedish Match Company afloat at the cost of all the other interests. The American creditors' lawyers were Sullivan and Cromwell, whose managing partner now was Dulles. They imposed two representatives of the creditors on the five-man board of liquidation, one of them a foreigner, who, at Dulles's behest, was Monnet. Monnet was elected on September 10, 1932, after much manoeuvering against Swedish opposition. His subsequent performance earned the admiration of Marcus Wallenberg, the doyen of Swedish bankers, but Monnet withdrew early at his own request on July 11, 1933. The bondholders' settlement in April 1935 provided the creditors with only $2.5 million out of over $100 million. The Kreuger settlement as a whole was not concluded until1940.

THE KREUGER LIQUIDATION was clearly a stopgap, for Monnet hardly began it before edging into his next venture. On November 10, 1932, the finance minister of the Chinese Nationalist government, T. V. Soong, asked him to "organise American-European groups to finance economic developments in China". Soong had been advised to approach Monnet by Rajchman. "Admitted by everyone to be a man of prodigious capacity, enthusiasm and intelligence", Rajchman was an ardent champion of China and close friend of Monnet.[3] There are signs, however, of a further connection. Visiting Europe in 1933, Soong appointed Lazards of London as Nationalist China's sole purchasing agent in England. Lazards, of course, were linked with the Hudson Bay Company, notably through Monnet's old patron, Sir Robert Kindersley. When Monnet went to China soon after, a number of observers thought he was linked to Lazards. At some point in the 1930s, Lazards certainly backed him with what seems, for an individual and the time, a very substantial loan. The date is not stated in the evidence available, which is late, from 1943, but it was already of fairly long standing then. Also, Lord Perth (David Drummond, Sir Eric Drummond's son), whom Monnet employed as his young assistant in China, recalls that the latter could not fly over China in the 1930s because of the terms of the insurance policies on his life. This agrees with the nature of Monnet's debts to Lazards, which in 1943 amounted to some £94,000 secured against assets of only £86,000. Of these assets (which excluded two of Monnet's main sources of wealth, including Cognac), fully £73,000 was represented by life policies and only £13,000 by shares put up by Monnet himself. It seems reasonable to link the restriction on air travel with the life policies backing the Lazards loan and to ascribe it to the early 1930s when Monnet operated in China. The inference is that Lazards, even if they did not regard Monnet as an agent, expected him to generate business in China and channel some to them. Alternatively, it is possible the loan was advanced two years later for a financial partnership Monnet formed in 1935, but that seems less likely.

Monnet now entered the labyrinth of China's frustrated attempts to join

3. Monnet's *Memoirs*, rather short on portraiture, speak of Rajchman with a unique enthusiasm and warmth. He calls Rajchman "this extraordinary man, whose friendship I so much valued" and speaks of "his devotion and his organizing genius. He was a great leader of men and a good friend. . . . Everyone knows how much he did for children the world over, for whom he established UNICEF. . . . When Rajchman died in 1965, in the little village in the Sarthe (north-west of France) where his body is buried, the achievements of his head and his heart survived him, because . . . [he] believed in the generosity of human nature, but he had taken care to establish institutions".

the modern world. He arranged a first meeting with Soong on a train between Chicago and New York, to make sure of a long tête-à-tête before Soong met officials and bankers. It was in May 1933. Educated at Harvard, Soong, the brother of Mme. Chiang Kai-shek, was the foremost modernising capitalist of the Kuomintang. He was, wrote one unconsciously patronising English admirer, "a 'natural' financier who could have made his mark in any country in the world" and struck Salter by the "uncanny rapidity" of his grasp of the most complex issues. Soong turned to the League secretariat, and more particularly Rajchman, for help in his efforts to free China from the financial tutelage of the so-called China Consortium, a cartel of American, British, French and Japanese banks, backed by their governments. The major threat to China being from Japan, which had formally annexed Manchuria in February 1932, he sought, in America and Europe, to form a "Consultative Committee" for investment which would exclude the Japanese and represent Chinese and foreigners in equal numbers. It was an attempt to displace the balance of control from foreigners towards China. Monnet was to be the chairman, clearly because of his association with Rajchman, the League and also Lazards, not a Consortium bank.

Japan sank the scheme on launching by putting pressure on the English and American banks. The Japanese had no interest in China's growth. They wanted China to be ripe for takeover. They clamoured that their "special interest" in China be recognised by the other powers. They harried the Kuomintang to sign a preferential trade agreement. They demanded that in any loans to China, Japan should have "the lion's share", that is, provide the most funds but also have most of the business. They were wholly scrutable. Stanley K. Hornbeck, chief of the Far East Division at the State Department, in one exchange with the counsellor at the Japanese embassy over Soong's committee, was driven to ask

> whether [Mr. Taketomi's remarks] did not amount to a suggestion that
> the world, in deference to Japanese susceptibilities and opinions and / or
> policies, should . . . abandon its wish and effort to be of assistance to . . .
> the Chinese. . . . Mr Taketomi said that it amounted to practically that.

On Soong's return to China in September, the failure of his trip weakened resistance to Japan. Soong lost the Ministry of Finance to the husband of another Soong sister, H. H. Kung.

T. V. Soong remained powerful as chairman of the National Economic Council and head of the Bank of China. He invited Salter and Monnet to China, Salter to report on China's economy, Monnet to propose a development strategy. Monnet arrived in Shanghai by ship via San Francisco in November 1933. In those days, it took three weeks to travel from New York to China, and once installed there, one tended to remain a long time. Monnet stayed eight months. In 1931, there was twice as much foreign investment in and through Shanghai as in the whole of the rest of China, barring Manchuria. Each foreign concession was a replica of the country controlling it. There was a huge contrast between the French concession, which Monnet thought of as "Cognac with Chinese", and the British businesses of the Bund, which gave that street an air of London's City. Monnet and Drummond were set up in a comfortable villa by a local French agent of Soong's, "more Chinese than the Chinese", Henri Mazot.

According to Perth, "When we got [to Shanghai], nobody knew what to do". The problem was the instability of China, made worse by the predations of Japan. The financial expression of the turmoil was the default of the Chinese on the principal and often the interest of their foreign debts. Chinese credit was not so much low as non-existent. Between 1928 and 1933, China failed to raise a single loan.

In Shanghai, nevertheless, Monnet noticed that many of the wealthiest banks were not foreign but Chinese. By the end of February 1934, he reached his basic conclusions. They were the "simple but, for those times, unusual argument" that foreign companies should include Chinese capital in a genuine partnership. Monnet proposed that all the main Chinese public and private capital be brought together in a development bank acting with foreign investors. Involving Chinese banks in investment would give their foreign partners the only solid guarantees. Railways, as Salter wrote, were the core of a development strategy. There was far less track than in India, and "enormous regions like Szechwan" were not served at all. Here too a bank committing Chinese public and private money was the key.

There was then one solution to both issues: a Chinese bank mobilising the Chinese capital driven for safety to Shanghai. Soong dragooned all the main Chinese private banks, some of them highly reluctant, to team up with the four government-controlled ones. The resulting China Development Finance Corporation, or CDFC, was officially incorporated on July 4, 1934.

The CDFC was novel at the time, even if it does not appear so now. No one had thought of making Shanghai's financial institutions the base for a reconstruction program. No one had dared attempt a mixed corporation of the principal Chinese banks, public and private. Chinese individualism was supposed to be far too great. For Westerners, the idea of partnership with Chinese, though germinating, was alien. One British entrepreneur declared he had never received a Chinese in his house "and never would". Without being spectacular, Monnet's solution shifted the assumptions of the day. It seems to have been brought forth unassisted from his imagination. When his thoughts were struggling to be born, he would become "unhappy, physically" and slope off to the cinema alone, much to the chagrin of Drummond, who would have liked a little leisure and to go as well. "He paid no attention to [the film] at all. He was just puzzling over what his thoughts were involved in".

Soong had hoped to bring in foreign capital as well as Chinese. At first, the Japanese again frustrated him. When Chiang Kai-shek also refused to commit himself, it was assumed the CDFC would founder. But the major locally based British banks and businesses, alarmed at Japan's growing influence, and hoping to enlist the Chinese "to fight our battles for us", were won over. The first railway bond issued by the CDFC in 1934 with the Hong Kong and Shanghai Bank was heavily oversubscribed; and from the Chinese point of view, the terms were better than usual. The line, from Shanghai to Ningpo, laid a bridge over the natural barrier of the Fuchun River. With this missing link in place, a broad south-east Chinese rail network came for the first time within sight.

Monnet believed the Shanghai market could subscribe more than half the sums to consolidate China's railway debts and rehabilitate the system. At least one expert in London agreed with him. That autumn, the Foreign Office preferred his proposals for redeeming China's railway debt to earlier ones by the British Shanghai banks. Others too were impressed by the CDFC. Because of it, Monnet, in Washington in October 1934, obtained the agreement in principle of the Export-Import Bank to ingenious credit arrangements enabling China to import equipment for modernisation.

WHEN MONNET LEFT Shanghai for the first time in July 1934, on the Trans-Siberian, he was not simply returning to Europe and America, as he claimed, to complete his financial plans for China. His main interest in Moscow was to conduct perhaps the most important personal transaction of his life. This was to marry, on November 13, 1934, Silvia, née de Bondini, an Italian born in August 1907 and so nineteen years his junior. Photographs of the time show a very elegant woman. John J. McCloy, then a Cravath lawyer working with Blair, thought her the most beautiful he had met. The difficulty was that the future Madame Monnet was married to someone else. Monnet and his wife first met, say his *Memoirs*, at a dinner in Paris in August 1929, "and we forgot the other participants". Her first husband, Francesco Giannini, whom she had wed on April 6, 1929, was, McCloy recalled, a senior representative of Blair and Company in Italy, and was thus an employee of Monnet.[4] Divorce in the 1930s was a far cry from the routine affair it has since become. In Italy, it was not recognised at all. Worse, Silvia and Francesco Giannini now had a daughter, Anna, born in April 1931,

---

4. One has found no evidence he was related to Amadeo Giannini. A Dr. Francesco Giannini was an Italian member of the Programme Committees of the AMTC. The name reappears on the staff list of the secretariat of the League of Nations in 1923. Monnet tended to employ familiar faces.

and in countries of Roman law, including France, custody belonged to the father.

Between August 1929 and November 1934 lay five years and long separations, during which Silvia Giannini and Jean Monnet tried and failed to secure an annulment of her marriage. Salter remembered Monnet's courtship "by cable and transatlantic phone". Monnet finally planned his own marriage like a negotiation between great powers. He "wanted to have the legitimacy of a big country behind us" *(sic)*. The United States was rejected. Even Nevada required residence qualifications, and Monnet and his bride-to-be felt that divorce and marriage Reno-style lacked dignity. This left Moscow. Stalin's Moscow was a surprising venue, but at that time it had two signal advantages. It was possible there to obtain citizenship and residence qualifications rapidly, and to divorce and remarry at once. Rajchman again provided the vital contact, this time with the Soviet government. To the bemusement of Monnet himself, who never found out why, the Soviet government was very helpful. The shift in Soviet policy in 1934 towards the Popular Front against Hitler and the run-up to the Franco-Soviet mutual security treaty of May 2, 1935, may have played a part. In any case, the wedding "cost months of work and a fortune". Monnet as usual roped in influential connections to achieve his ends. The American and French ambassadors in Moscow, William Bullitt and Charles Alphand, appear to have paved the way.

The actual divorce and wedding in Moscow were a lightning operation. Silvia Giannini travelled from Switzerland, where she had been staying with her mother and child as an Italian. In a few days, she became a Soviet citizen. She then divorced without delay. That done, she and Monnet promptly married and left immediately. Meanwhile, Silvia's mother had taken Anna to Paris, where the newlyweds picked her up. The trio then moved to the United States and, in March 1935, to Shanghai.

In Shanghai, there was an attempt by Francesco Giannini, through the Italian embassy, to abduct his child. It failed because, it seems, Silvia Monnet took refuge for a week in the Soviet consulate in Shanghai. There remained a lawsuit for Anna's custody, which was finally settled in Silvia Monnet's favour in the New York courts in the spring of 1937. The settlement was not valid, however, in countries of Roman law, so that Madame Monnet was not able—at least immediately—to return to continental Europe with her daughter. This was a powerful reason for Monnet to work out of New York during much of the later thirties. She did come to Paris, though, on occasion and on June 18, 1939, was naturalised French. She had been long enough in Paris for some of her paintings to be conveyed by a friend to the cellars of the American embassy on the fall of France in 1940. When the whole family came back to France late in 1945, Anna was sixteen. By this time, the Monnets had a daughter of their own marriage, Marianne, born late in 1941. Many years later still, it seems after Francesco Giannini died in 1974, they celebrated a religious wedding in the cathedral of Lourdes.

The Kremlin wedding was the more remarkable because Silvia Monnet was, and became increasingly, an ardent Catholic. Monnet's own mother was "very devout", and his elder sister, Marie-Louise, was prominent in Catholic Action. With Barbara Ward, she was one of only two laywomen summoned by Pope John XXIII to the Vatican II Council in the 1960s. Monnet himself took extreme unction on his deathbed, though it was notable that Silvia Monnet was careful not to propose it. He struck most of those who knew him as closer in such matters to his father, a "radical socialist", which was synonymous in Monnet's youth with free thought and even anti-clericalism. Monnet was no anti-clerical and evinced respect for a church that had weathered two millennia. But this was a secular tribute, and religion never surfaced in his table talk. Adenauer, who might have done, did not regard him as religious. Nor does his daughter, Marianne. Some observers, however, have felt that his outlook in creating the European Community expressed religious values. It has also been rumoured that in his last years he had a series of exchanges with a priest. Monnet was a very private, pragmatic, complex—and also superstitious—man. This was no doubt as true of his attitudes to religion as to everything else.

Anyone who worked with him knew that Silvia Monnet was very important to her husband throughout the forty-five years of their marriage. She was the daughter of the Italian publisher of a French-language weekly, *La Turquie,* produced in Istanbul in the years before the First World War and with a large circulation throughout the eastern Mediterranean. She grew up trilingual in Italian, French and Greek. She was an intelligent, forceful woman and a competent amateur painter. It was fairly characteristic that she took up painting as an adult, probably in New York, because, she said, "she was bored to death by all the dinners and women's lunch parties". Joxe wrote of Monnet in Algiers in 1943 that he "would spend hours writing to his wife, whose opinion mattered more to him than that of anyone else". Monnet paid tribute to her "keen and disinterested mind". He would consult her on key documents and, as successive ghost-writers came to know, take her comments into account. Further than that, it is difficult to assess her influence. As far as observers could tell, he seemed to seek out her views more in order to have an astute lay reaction, a private check on "public opinion", than to tap her for policies. Since Monnet liked the country and had virtually no friends outside work, she lived a rather sequestered life: a substantial price paid for his public one.

THREE MONTHS AFTER his marriage, on February 18, 1935, Monnet set up a financial partnership in New York with George Murnane, who had been deputy commissioner for France in the American Red Cross. From 1928 to 1935 he was a partner in a then famous investment bank, Lee, Higginson and Company, of Boston, which made the fatal error of backing Kreuger to the hilt. He had come on to the Transamerica board under Walker. He and Monnet were, then, among the financial walking wounded. Dulles made their new venture possible. As managing partner of Sullivan and Cromwell, he occasionally invested in people or businesses. Monnet, he wrote to W. N. Cromwell, the aged head of the firm, was "one of the most brilliant men that I know" and "an intimate friend [who] has the full confidence of many of the most important financial people". Dulles and Cromwell duly invested $100,000 in Monnet, Murnane and Company, incorporated in Prince Edward Island, Canada. Dulles furnished Monnet, Murnane with several of their most profitable clients.

Monnet, Murnane and Co., Lord Perth has said, was "a merchant bank without any capital . . . & the Co. was us—that is, David Drummond in London and in Paris Pierre Denis, the son of a French professor who befriended the Czechs in Habsburg days and still has a statue in Prague. Denis, a very skilful drafter of documents, had penned the armistice agreement in 1918. The "and Co." never grew larger. The aim, as Dulles expressed his understanding of it at the outset, was "to engage in work of a consultative and advisory nature to governments and corporations in financial matters". It was, in short, a financial consultancy, something rare before the war. It lived on the contacts, imagination and judgement—the wits—of the partners.

Less than a month after Monnet, Murnane and Company was formed, on March 13, 1935, Monnet wrote an eleven-page memorandum "on the point of leaving for Shanghai". This shows that he saw his end of the partnership mainly as a way of continuing work in China.

All people of importance . . . are interested in China. We ought to be able not only to build up the [CDFC] . . . but also make substantial profits. I see three main lines of our activity: 1. . . . helping the Chinese in the general financial negotiations now starting . . . 2. Develop the [CDFC] as a Chinese entity, sought as their partner by the most important industrialists doing business in China . . . 3. The financial reorganisation of the railways.

Monnet had told a member of the Far East Division of the State Department the previous October that opportunities for the development of China were almost limitless.

His policy was "to base our action . . . in China on British influence, as . . . [Britain] is the one that best understands China and whose actions most benefit it". Britain controlled 56 per cent of the foreign capital invested in

China outside Manchuria. But in 1935, British policy took a turn that dashed Monnet's hopes. This was due to the U.K. Treasury under Neville Chamberlain, which partly usurped the role of the Foreign Office in east Asia. The "sensational step" was taken in September 1935 of sending to China Sir Frederick Leith-Ross, the government's senior economic adviser. Foreign Office sources called him, bitterly, the Treasury's "own ambassador in the Far East".

Leith-Ross wanted to strengthen the prospects of British business in China in response to the Japanese threat and even German competition. He adopted Monnet's arguments for partnership with Chinese investors. But he and the Treasury wanted to appease Japan on the grounds—interesting in the light of Chamberlain's later policies—that war with Germany being inevitable in Europe, Britain could not afford conflict in Asia as well. From this point of view, Monnet, Rajchman, Salter, the Leaguers, all suspect to Japan, were a thorough nuisance.

Christopher Chancellor, of Reuters, mentioned to the Foreign Office unspecified remarks by Thomas W. Lamont of J. P. Morgan, an American Consortium bank,[5] which "gave confirmation of my own conclusion, namely, Monnet is very narrowly removed from adventurer pure and simple. . . . He becomes more dangerous as time goes on and his expenses mount, because his sole motive is the 'rake-off' to Monnet which must come from the importation of capital to China through the channel he hopes to create". He added: "I think Leith-Ross will 'debunk' some of the Monnet-Salter-Rajchman stuff".[6] S. D. Waley, at the Treasury, wrote that he would do anything "to sabotage Monnet". Leith-Ross's judgement was more temperate: "I do not think any British interest would be really well served by Monnet's Corporation", though he added "I only wish that British railway interests were represented here by somebody as active and fertile in imagination as Monnet!" That was in November 1935. Two months later, Monnet decided he would be "more useful in New York" and left China for good. Silvia Monnet acquired residential status in the United States as a Soviet citizen on a Turkish quota.

In one respect, Leith-Ross was very successful. China's currency was based on silver. In 1934 and 1935, Roosevelt, under pressure from the silver lobby in Congress, allowed the price of silver to rise steeply. This precipitated a stringent deflation and distress in Shanghai. Leith-Ross encouraged Soong to move off silver and devalue the Chinese dollar in November 1935. Within weeks, Shanghai experienced a boom. By autumn 1936, China's debts had

5. Lamont and Monnet knew each other from the Paris Peace Conference and the Morrow circle.

6. Monnet certainly hoped to make money, but his memos and letters insisted the real job was railways, and that "this is long pull work with not much money in it for us at the start". This is the language of serious investment.

mostly been cleared. It became relatively easy for the government to raise loans for railway development.

Monnet, Murnane benefitted, or looked like being about to benefit, to some extent. It helped finance the important East-West Lunghai Railway, six hundred miles from the coast to the first imperial capital, Sian, on the Yellow River, opening up the interior. But this was just before the Japanese bombed Shanghai and lit the taper of the Sino-Japanese War. So, as Perth recalls, "the day before I got on the boat, I was worth what seemed quite a lot of money in Lunghai bonds, and by the time I got off the boat two days later, there was nothing".

Whereas Soong had thought of Monnet in 1933 as the manager of China's foreign investment and imports, circumstances, the British, the CDFC and finally the Japanese removed the scope. In so far as the CDFC continued to operate after 1937, on railways outside Japanese reach, from Burma to Szechwan, the managers—T. V. Soong's youngest brother, T. A. Soong, and C. S. Liu—had none of his sense of obligation to Monnet. From 1938, there was a crisis in relations. Monnet was still pressing for arrears of fees shortly before Hitler invaded Poland.

China was really the last of Monnet's ventures for the League of Nations. It was certainly not very profitable. Murnane's verdict, when war broke out in Europe, was: "China once showed great promise—events changed that. We concentrated enormously on it. . . . All of the time we were paid nothing". And again: "I welcome any task, however grim, where someone depends on us to do his side or both sides of any negotiation or other task. I do not welcome tasks where our status is unclear". Perth remembers that, professionally, "it was always a struggle to live".[7]

It is hard to form a rounded judgement on Monnet, Murnane, because so many of Monnet's prewar papers were burned in Cognac by his family during the Occupation. All the same, there is a sense of loss of direction about his activities in the later 1930s. One reason was that the lucrative activities of Monnet, Murnane, those not related to China, lacked Monnet's usual public vision (and probably did not come from him). One can dimly discern

7. One of many existing accounts, less fragmentary than the rest, suggests that the firm earned $960,000 gross during the five years 1935–39, inclusive. Even in the Depression years, that would have been modest for a "finance house". Total income via Monnet from the CDFC came to less than $46,000. Monnet's original contract with T. V. Soong (in 1933, before Monnet, Murnane) provided for a fee of $150,000 to Monnet's office, plus expenses, though there is no account of how much was finally paid or how much Monnet made personally. A U.S. Treasury report on Monnet's income in 1940 put it at $54,000. This was a fraction of Dulles's enormous earnings in the 1930s ($200,000 to $400,000 a year), and two-thirds the salary of the U.S. president. It presumably did not include the $25,000 a year which the Fortune profile of Monnet in 1944 claimed he earned, on average, in the decade prewar (and with wide variations from year to year) on his share of the profits of J. G. Monnet & Co.

important American operations, apparently generated by Dulles. The merger of the Nash Motors Corporation and the Kelvinator Corporation was one of them, a step in the process that led to the formation of American Motors. But other efforts, for instance to release the Italian lira assets of the Belgian chemical giant Solvay, frozen by the Mussolini regime, were purely financial.

In addition, there were Murnane's activities in Germany, it seems in association with Dulles. What seemed legitimate business to a couple of right-wing American neutrals up to 1941 could look very different to others as Hitler's war loomed ever closer. Some of Murnane's activity was constructive. Dulles put Murnane in touch with the Petschek family, one of the great industrial fortunes of Czechoslovakia. Being Jewish, the Petscheks, who had fled to the United States, decided to sell out to the Nazis before their holdings were confiscated. Murnane and Drummond negotiated the sale to Friedrich Flick, representing the Ruhr steel barons and I. G. Farben, the great chemical trust. In normal terms, the Petscheks were defrauded. Their holdings were worth perhaps four times what Flick paid. Nevertheless, they obtained $6.25 million, a large sum at the time, and a huge one from a regime which rationed dollars like desert water. The Monnet, Murnane commission, the biggest they seem ever to have obtained, was $250,000. To salvage a fortune for the Petscheks in their American haven was a feat. In fact, it is not clear why Flick and his backers acted as they did.

The motive may have been that Murnane, in an ostensibly separate operation, undertook, in the event of war, to protect the assets of American Bosch, which was in fact, though not in form, a subsidiary of the giant German electrical engineering firm, Robert Bosch. It is clear from the correspondence with Murnane that Monnet was not a principal in these arrangements. There is a strange letter in which it suddenly occurs to Murnane early in September 1939 that "indirect contact with Stuttgart [the headquarters of Bosch] . . . might be distasteful to you. . . . I cannot myself see that it would have any of the aspect of 'comfort to the enemy' . . . since Stuttgart is not an owner" of the American Bosch company "and cannot become one". This was literally true, because formal ownership was held first by a Dutch company and later by the Swedish Wallenbergs, but they were clearly holding the shares in the Bosch interest. Henry Morgenthau's Treasury investigators in 1942 were told Monnet had negotiated on Murnane's behalf in Amsterdam in August 1939 to prevent the sale of American Bosch to interests inimical to German Bosch. Monnet's papers show this to have been true. This was a natural source of Morgenthau's later suspicion of Monnet.

Monnet polished off the non-Chinese aspects of this period in one paragraph of his *Memoirs*. "In New York, I busied myself with Murnane in a wide diversity of activities of which I have only a sketchy recollection. In short, I was bored with international financial affairs which I would have found large and enriching ten years before". There was almost certainly more to it than that. Towards the end of the war, Monnet told Robert Brand, "for reasons you can well understand", that he had ceased to be a partner in Monnet, Murnane. In many ways, the period after China seems the low point of Monnet's career, the one from which the broad horizons of the rest of his life are absent.

V

INVISIBLE ASSETS

Had Jean Monnet died in 1938, his life, if remembered at all, would have seemed one of unfulfilled promise. He had been "a remarkably precocious young man" in the First World War, a brilliant Deputy Secretary-General of the League at little more than thirty and a millionaire at forty. Ten years later, though admired by influential friends, he was nearer than he had ever been to the "petty financier" that de Gaulle would dismissively call him during the Second World War.

One reason for that was no doubt Monnet's opportunism in the most basic sense. His *Memoirs* said he never groomed himself for a career. The variety of jobs he carried out until his fiftieth year, and their sheer number, bear this out. The longest times he spent in any one occupation were his eight years as salesman for Monnet cognac before 1914 and rather less than seven years for Blair and Company till the expulsion from Transamerica in 1932. Even these were highly mobile and differentiated.

That is not to say the career contained no coherent themes. The simplest was that Monnet was drawn where circumstances and his talent led him. He showed from the first the gifts that make a truly creative official. This is a category full of distinguished names, yet without a label. Two classic instances are Florence Nightingale and Edwin Chadwick (who created basic public services in Victorian England). Another is the novelist Marcel Proust's father, Dr. Adrien Proust, who taught the world to quarantine cholera. Such people are not politicians, because they hold no elected office. Yet they display great political ability. Nor can they be called bureaucrats. They may or may not operate in a formal bureaucracy. They are even anti-bureaucratic to the extent that they are impatient of routine minds. Again, though they are entrepreneurs, they are not people of business. Their imaginations are fired by the public, not a private, interest. They answer needs the citizen recognises as his own once they have defined them. But whereas the creative politician crystallises the public's consciousness, their medium is action ahead of common awareness. They operate at the borders between politics, bureaucracy and business and belong to none. They are, for want of a better term, entrepreneurs in the public interest.

Jean Monnet's history shows that from the very first, and by natural incli-
nation, he belonged to this invaluable but nameless breed. His intuition in
1914 of the need for Allied economic cooperation already bore the seeds of
his work forty years later. His schemes at the League of Nations for Upper
Silesia and Austria, and in China with the CDFC, were not inferior to inspi-
rations of his later life. The tactics behind the Polish and Rumanian loans of
the 1920s already seemed mature. In retrospect, these operations bear the
hallmarks of the qualities that were in the end to give him public standing.

In contrast, Monnet the private man of business and financier does not
carry the same conviction. Too little is known about his operations to be
sure. There may never be enough evidence to paint a full picture. He did
write in his *Memoirs,* no doubt of his first steps in contact with government,
that he had some difficulty in adapting from private to public affairs. And
yet it is where private profit is most evident that his manner of attacking
problems looks least impressive. "Honest banking" was no doubt admirable,
and foreshadowed reforms the New Deal would later carry out, but Giannini
seems to have routed Monnet's chief, Walker, and Monnet himself in the
Transamerica battle. The manner of Giannini's victory was also interesting.
Walker and Monnet were setting up concepts of administration against
Giannini's political arousal of the street. They had no answer to his appeal
to popular emotion. Again, when he was working in partnership with Murnane, Monnet's persistence in what seemed even then high-risk operations
in China suggested he needed an excuse to hold on to public issues rather
than sink back into private ones of narrower scope. Later, he used to stress
the contrast between public service and private profit, pointing out that the
priorities of the two are and must be utterly different. Yet his own insistence
in the 1930s on an unprofitable China hints at a certain half-heartedness in
the pursuit of profit for its own sake.

In short, Monnet until the Second World War was a talent which had yet
to find a policy or vocation. It could have been a formula for waste. Yet even
while he wandered apparently without aim he seems after all to have been
building up capital for his later career. This was less a matter of experience
perhaps—we tend to repeat our mistakes, he said, because our weaknesses
remain the same—than of acquiring a large number of influential friends
impressed by his qualities. He laid the bases of his later networks long before
any public paid attention to them. He had a knack of making his mark with
the most diverse people. Montagu Norman thought he was "not so much a
banker as a conjuror", a tribute wary enough to convey respect. Chiang Kai-
shek thought he would make a good Chinese general, except that he was too
soft with his friends. Salter, within a year of meeting Monnet in the First
World War, decided that he would be "one of the creative men of our time".
Monnet made enemies but, unlike some, rarely among people on his own
side.

The exceptional range of Monnet's international contacts before the Second World War coloured his entire later career. As regards France, the effects were double-edged. He was exceptionally free of the complexes and blinkers of his compatriots, but this very fact cut him off at times from their political reactions. On the other hand, with the United States, the benefits were unalloyed. He became virtually an insider in the overlapping rings that constitute the American establishment. To have been active in business in America before ever encountering Americans in politics or administration, and so to follow their own *cursus honorum,* was particularly important. For all his French accent, it made him one of them. They knew him on their own ground, in their own terms, not simply as a foreign friend. Monnet's entrée into American ruling circles was even more personal than that of the British officials who knew so well how to work the system without ever quite breaching the formality of their own allegiance. Donald Swatland, the Cravath lawyer who would have been a secretary of state had he not refused, said that Monnet had an even better address book in the United States than Churchill. The roster of Americans of importance after 1945 whom Monnet first met in business long before is basic to his later career. Dwight Morrow, who died early, considered him a friend from the closing days of the war at the AMTC. Monnet first met John Foster Dulles at the Paris Peace Conference. He also met around or before 1930 "Jack" McCloy, Dean Acheson, Donald Swatland, Henry Stimson, Averell Harriman and many more. To move in such circles meant that he would be passed on effortlessly to all the other people on the revolving circuits. It was one of Monnet's main sources of strength in and after the war. The years until 1938 appear centrifugal. His later career nevertheless rose out of them in ways that those who did not know what lay beneath were apt to find vaguely incredible, a mystery. It was simply that few appreciated in his later days the depth of his immersion in America long before.

Arsenal of Democracy
1938–1943

Jean and Silvia Monnet were in Paris at the time of Munich. Silvia may have been there in connection with her naturalisation as a French citizen the following year. She would normally have been in New York, in the Monnet apartment at 1158 Fifth Avenue. Monnet, however, was so often in Paris at the time that he used part of the Monnet, Murnane office at 4 rue Fabert on the Esplanade of the Invalides as "his little apartment". Dwight Morrow's daughter, Anne Morrow Lindbergh, who was also in Paris just after Munich, recorded a conversation with Monnet. "He thinks [the ideal] is much over-rated—that children need their mothers all the time. Yes, I say, it is true, neglected children always turn out well. While, says Jean, neglected husbands do *not!*" That same evening Anne Lindbergh and Silvia Monnet talked about "women's struggle to choose between husband and children".

Anne Lindbergh and her husband, Charles, had arrived in Paris on Friday, September 30, the day after Munich, and been driven straight to the U.S. embassy, now presided over by Monnet's friend, William Bullitt.

> The four Powers [Germany, Italy, Britain, France] have agreed! Drive to Embassy [from the station]. Bullitt meets us. He looks white and tired. M. Monnet is in the garden. He also looks rather gray. They have all been through an awful time here—worse than London, I expect. Bullitt wants C. [Lindbergh] to help in organizing some kind of air rearmament for France; talk to people and maybe help them in U.S.A. He wants M. Monnet to organize it.

A few days later, on October 3, Monnet was picked by the French Prime Minister, Édouard Daladier, to go in secret to Roosevelt to acquire American warplanes. This opened his second career in public service.

Daladier, though very short, was known as the "bull of the Vaucluse" (the former papal state round Avignon). His square chin gave him a vague resemblance to Mussolini. He went like Chamberlain to Munich but was not fooled. There is a story, possibly apocryphal, that landing at Le Bourget, the Paris airport, on his way back, he found a large crowd waiting. When, to his amazement, they cheered, he is alleged to have uttered a couple of pungent words, the politer version of which is "idiots".

How Monnet came into the picture is not so clear. His *Memoirs* recall a first contact with Daladier at a dinner to which he was taken by a former League of Nations colleague, Pierre Comert, early in 1938, well before Munich. "From January 1938 onwards", Pleven has said, "I was in a position to observe his desperate efforts to close our gap in air power" with the Germans. Monnet wrote that it was Bullitt who persuaded him to get involved and introduced him "into the group working on these matters", probably around Guy La Chambre, the vigorous young Air Minister. Known to be close to Roosevelt, Bullitt was thought by Daladier to be "as French as the best of Frenchmen". Bullitt advised Daladier that Monnet, with his deep knowledge of America, would be the man to send to Roosevelt. In a cable to the President the day before Munich, Bullitt presented Monnet as "an intimate friend of mine for many years, whom I trust as a brother". An American, in short, initiated Monnet into the French search for American planes.

Or did he? Pleven has said of those days "I never admired Monnet as a man of action more than in the years preceding 1939 and during the 'phoney' war. . . . His analysis . . . was unyieldingly clear-sighted. . . . [He strove] with might and main to awaken the British and French leaders to the need to correct the weakness of their air forces". The dinner to meet Daladier could fit. Monnet did not attend dinners without a purpose. He once said he never acquired a job he had not invented himself. It would be in character for him to have worked his way into Daladier's entourage.

"The whole of my attention was directed to the dangers that were piling up in Europe and threatening world peace. . . . Fear was everywhere." Monnet's *Memoirs* recall a dinner on Long Island in September 1935 when Dulles brought the news of Nazi decrees against the Jews. Monnet says he concluded then that "a man (Hitler) who did such a thing would go to war". He also told Henry Morgenthau in 1942—who thought it suspect—that until 1938 he had hoped for a settlement between France and Germany. These are not mutually exclusive. Pleven is categorical: Monnet was "profoundly anti-Hitler and anti-Munich". The first paper Monnet was involved in, a "Note on the possible establishment of an aeronautical industry abroad out of reach of enemy attack", that is, in North America, was written in spring 1938, six months before Munich.

As Monnet put it in his *Memoirs*, "We had no lack of tanks. . . . But we faced a real and serious shortage of aircraft". Until the mid-1930s, the French enjoyed a lead in the air on the European continent. Then a combination of rearmament and a technical revolution in Nazi Germany, shifting planes from wooden to aluminium structures that sustained higher speeds and heavier weapons, tilted the balance almost overnight across the Rhine. France's air force was obsolete and its aircraft industry not geared to mass production. Lindbergh, returning from a study trip to Germany, concluded a report on September 22, 1938, with the words, "Our only sound policy now is to avoid war at almost any cost".

A real problem, air power was also a fixation of the later 1930s. It had played a very minor part in the First World War. But soon after, the propagandists of independent air forces started claiming, in the wake of the Italian theorist Giulio Douhet, that bombing cities could break the will to fight before the armies had time to engage. The Spanish civil war fed the nightmare with novel terrors like the Germans' bombing of Guernica, well publicised in the fresh medium of newsreels before coming to rest in Picasso's famous painting. The impact on the war was marginal, but it caught the imagination of peoples in the shadow of a greater war to come. "The inevitable tendency", a historian of Britain in war-time has written, "was to magnify the terror of . . . the first 'knock-out' attack in the air". Such horrors came true at the end of the Second World War. In 1939, they owed more to H. G. Wells. Yet Daladier told a French cabinet committee in February 1940 that readiness to "sell every last ounce of gold on the purchase of American aircraft" would make it possible to "destroy the Ruhr in a sheet of flame and force Germany to capitulate". As late as January 1941, Harry Hopkins reported Churchill looking "forward with our help to mastery in the air and then Germany with all her armies will be finished. He believes that this war will never see great forces massed against one another".

With visions such as these, it was not surprising that Daladier said, "If I had had three or four thousand planes at my disposal, there would have been no Munich". Now that war was in sight, the instinct of the French, with memories of 1918 and stimulus from Bullitt, was to find the missing means in the New World. Four days after Munich, on October 3, Monnet took part in a meeting chaired by Daladier which decided to try to buy planes in America. A similar attempt the previous spring had foundered on America's lack of modern capacity. Only a hundred fighters had been purchased. But the need was too urgent for one to be put off by that. It was decided to try again.

Unfortunately, the United States also had memories of the First World War. Isolationism was powerful. The Johnson Act of 1933 prohibited loans for arms to any country which had failed to pay its First World War dollar debts. The French thought one-and-a-half-million dead was payment enough and never stumped up in full. The Neutrality Act of 1935 forbade sales of complete weapons to belligerents. As a result, there was no legal framework or political climate for the French to acquire American arms. The one favourable factor was Roosevelt's growing conviction that Hitler must be stopped. Even he was only just emerging from isolationism.

Monnet was chosen to make contact with Roosevelt as much for his anonymity as for his skills. On October 13, Bullitt telephoned from Washington that Roosevelt expected him. Monnet turned up in New York on October 19 and went straight to Roosevelt's country house at Hyde Park, all classical façade in front and Edwardian balconies behind with cliff-high views of the Hudson Valley. Echoing Daladier, Roosevelt told Monnet and Bullitt that if the United States had possessed five thousand warplanes, there would have been no Munich. He had already asked the Air Corps to make plans to expand aircraft production and directed the State Department to study the removal of the arms embargo from the Neutrality Act. "We estimate that the Germans can turn out 40 thousand planes a year, Britain along with Canada 25 thousand and France 15 thousand. The 20-to-30 thousand extra planes needed to provide decisive superiority over Germany and Italy will have to be found here in the United States". The Neutrality Act could be circumvented by the French setting up assembly plants in Canada and the Americans shipping parts across the frontier. Roosevelt showed Monnet convenient locations on a map. Monnet was deeply impressed. On leaving, he asked if he could keep the sheet of White House paper on which Roosevelt had scribbled his balance of German and Allied warplane output. He never forgot that the President handed him this piece of dynamite without a moment's hesitation.

There was nothing exclusive in Roosevelt's welcome. Two days later, he repeated the performance for Arthur Murray, a Liberal ex-Member of the British Parliament and friend of the Governor-General of Canada, Lord Tweedsmuir (better known as John Buchan, the novelist). But the British did not react as the French did. They thought primarily in terms of their own domestic production. By March 1939, they were turning out six hundred warplanes a month and were reluctant to part with dollars. The French, still investing to turn prototype into mass production, pushed through the chink in America's door as fast as they could.

Roosevelt passed Monnet on to the Secretary of the Treasury, Henry Morgenthau, Jr. A finance minister was, at first sight, an unlikely agent to provide arms. But he was the one senior man the President could trust to fight the opposition to involvement against Hitler, opposition that was open among isolationists and covert in parts of the administration. (The Secretary of War himself, Harry Woodring, was one of the obstacles.) Also, the Treasury had a procurement division which handled war purchases. For more than two years, till Lend-Lease was enacted in March 1941, Morgenthau was the coordinator for all arms sold to the French and British.

Morgenthau saw Bullitt and Monnet on October 22. He jibbed when Monnet said the French government wanted to pass a first order for 1,700 planes worth $85 million. France, Morgenthau objected, did not have that many dollars to spare. Bullitt suggested they could be raised from private French funds deposited in America to escape taxes and inflation at home. Morgenthau approved. "But you will have to put a thousand people in prison". From this dinner till Monnet's return to Paris at the end of the month, the U.S. Treasury busied itself in identifying at least $500 million of French flight capital, and succeeded. This would have been plenty to begin with. Daladier and his Finance Minister, Paul Marchandeau, would have been ready to face the music at home and oblige. Unfortunately, a few days before Monnet saw Daladier in Paris on November 5, Marchandeau was replaced by Paul Reynaud. Reynaud's energetic warnings against Hitler had given him a reputation as a Clemenceau in waiting. He nevertheless refused, in the name of business freedom, to attack flight capital.

Monnet's report of November 14 stated that if orders were placed by the end of 1938, a thousand American planes could be delivered by July 1939 and another fifteen hundred by February 1940. Such a programme would create a large production capacity beyond the reach of German bombers. As insurance against an arms embargo, Canadian assembly plants could be built near Buffalo and Detroit and manned by skilled American labour. America could in particular help France produce more engines, the main bottleneck on both sides of the ocean. French Air Ministry experts were sceptical. They doubted the Americans had planes up to the latest European standards. But Monnet's report and evidence of Roosevelt's goodwill redoubled Daladier's determination. On December 9, in Reynaud's presence, he asked Monnet to go back to Washington to turn his proposals into planes.

Monnet arrived in New York on December 16 and told Morgenthau he could spend up to $65 million to buy a thousand planes for delivery before July 1939. He was also authorised to set up a Canadian corporation. But difficulties soon began to surface. The doubts of the French experts who now accompanied him proved correct. His report, reflecting the producers' claims, had been too optimistic. The United States had no planes in service able to reach the required 500 kilometers per hour (310 miles per hour). The French shopped around for experimental ones instead. The manufacturers were happy enough to deliver. However, the Army Air Corps's forceful chief, General H. H. "Hap" Arnold, was determined the French should not have the first option on his best equipment. Roosevelt and Morgenthau overrode Arnold, who hinted he might expose them before Congress, in the great tradition of the military subverting decisions they dislike. Roosevelt gave Arnold a verbal order on December 21. This too failed to shake Arnold. He forbade all contact between American producers and the French over his favourite Douglas B-7 bomber.

By this time, Morgenthau, though determined to clear all obstacles, was irritated and seriously worried. He was irritated by Monnet's legal counsel, Dulles's firm, Sullivan and Cromwell, suspect to him as quintessential Wall Street conservatives who had represented Franco. He was worried by Monnet's "inability to show us he has got any money" and the French government's insistence on keeping the mission secret. Above all, he was frightened of the proposed French assembly plants in Canada being exposed by the military to Congress. In the end, Roosevelt gave written orders to Arnold to let the French place their orders for the Douglas B-7 bomber, but tried to unload on Morgenthau the political risk of signing it. Morgenthau refused. So, at last, on January 19, 1939, Roosevelt, having warned Arnold that there were places like Guam for insubordinate generals, forced him to give way. Morgenthau told Monnet that "for a month I went through hell".

The apparently open road ahead again proved to be a minefield. On a test flight on January 23 near Los Angeles, a Douglas B-7 prototype crashed with one of the experts from the French mission aboard. He was at once identified and, in Congress, the isolationists raised the hue and cry. The obsessively secret Monnet mission was now front-page news. The revelation almost certainly damaged Roosevelt's campaign for the revision of the Neutrality Act. But he refused to be discountenanced. At a press conference on January 27, he asserted that French orders were good for the aircraft industry and that they would increase capacity for America's own defence. It was still the Depression. The hope of jobs struck a chord with the public. Editorials across the country agreed that America must help the European democracies against Hitler. At last, the Monnet mission was able to operate fairly freely.

On February 5, 1939, Monnet put through firm orders for combat planes and trainers. Taking into account the slippage in delivery dates between July and October, these were less than half of what had originally been intended. Only one hundred American planes were in northern France when the Germans attacked on May 10, 1940. All the same, the French orders quadrupled American monthly production capacity in less than a year. This laid the foundations for the gigantic later expansion of the U.S. aircraft industry.

Late in March, Monnet was back in Paris. Hitler had already paraded into Prague. It was clear that war was only a matter of time. Driven by the sense of crisis, Daladier and Reynaud asked Monnet, back in New York, to contact Roosevelt a third time. The aim was to clear the obstacle of the Johnson Act by a settlement of France's First World War debts, either by part payment or by the cession or lease of French bases in the Pacific or Caribbean. Monnet was received by the President on May 3. Roosevelt was sympathetic but refused to complicate his attempts to secure the repeal of the Neutrality Act. As it was, in July, he failed.

All this time, Monnet was in business. At one point, he hoped Monnet, Murnane might become agents for the French government with American aircraft firms. But events were rushing on. War was only weeks away. The last rites of peace were, for the Monnet family, a private grief. Four days before the Nazi invasion of Poland, the elder Monnet died on August 28 at the age of eighty-three. The founder of a charity, La Fraternelle, he was a popular local figure. The church in Cognac was too small to accommodate the crowd at the funeral. Oddly enough, his son, whom some thought closer to his mother, seems to have been more openly affected by his father's death than he was, seventeen years later, by hers.

II
ANGLO-FRENCH COOPERATION

On July 26, 1939, barely more than a month before Hitler's invasion of Poland, Neville Chamberlain sent a ten-page note to Daladier. He wrote that David Lloyd George's letter to the French Prime Minister in 1917 arguing the need for an Allied joint council with permanent military and "probably" naval and economic staffs was "as true today". Provision for an Anglo-French Supreme War Council was duly made. However, it was primarily military; economic cooperation was not at first included. Though seven French missions were already in London before the war and a joint Allied Food Committee was based on an agreement antedating Munich, there was no general coordination of war supplies.

Daladier wanted to send Monnet off on a fourth mission to the States to buy more planes and engines. This time, Monnet demurred. The day war was declared, on September 3, he produced two memoranda, one for Daladier and the Armaments Minister, Raoul Dautry, the other for La Chambre, in which he argued that American production capacity was now fully exploited. To increase it would require Roosevelt to persuade Congress to repeal the Neutrality Act (he succeeded in November at the second assault). "The programme to be put to the American President after the Neutrality Act has been repealed, but not before, must aim at the prompt doubling or tripling of American production". "It must be achieved by a Franco-British effort, as is plain from the conversations I had with Mr Roosevelt". Roosevelt wanted to keep a firm hand on events. The last thing he needed was competing foreigners trampling over the sensitive terrain of American attitudes to the war. Anglo-French economic cooperation was the condition of a productive relationship with America.

In any case, Monnet argued, cooperation was a necessity in itself. The shortages of war would demand a rationing of supplies. It must be efficient and visibly fair. It would not be achieved by each Ally deciding what it needed and then arm-wrestling with its partner to see how good a bargain it could extract. Again, as in the first war, a failure to act in common would make gaping cracks of the differences in the war efforts of the Allies. The military burden would be mainly France's, the missing resources, particularly of shipping and raw materials, primarily Britain's, through her empire, navy and merchant marine. One should learn the lessons of the earlier war and establish at once the inter-Allied machinery which, the last time, demanded over three years of labour pains.

Similar issues pointing to similar solutions, Monnet proposed more or less the old machinery again. There should be strong inter-Allied executive committees, one for each major sector, capped by policy councils bringing together the relevant ministers. An Economic Council, with one French and one British minister (probably the prime ministers), should give broad directives and referee disputes. A constantly updated balance sheet of Allied needs and resources should be maintained so that priorities could be set by urgency, not bargaining power. Buying abroad should be through joint Allied bodies strong enough to hold down prices and compel neutrals to advance credit. The whole scheme worked towards a pooling of policies and resources.

At the first Supreme War Council in Abbeville on the Somme on September 12, 1939, Daladier proposed that a "Frenchman who is a friend of Roosevelt" (he meant Monnet) might take charge of joint Allied purchases abroad. Three days later, he wrote to Chamberlain urging closer economic cooperation and announced the despatch of Monnet to London. On September 20, he sent proposals almost identical to Monnet's of the 3rd. Monnet attended the second Supreme War Council in Hove town hall by the Channel two days later. Afterwards, he travelled up to London by rail with Sir Edward Bridges, the Secretary of the British War Cabinet, and they discussed his coming tour of the ministries in Whitehall. Thenceforward, Monnet was, as the authors of the official history of the *British War Economy,* W. K. Hancock and M. M. Gowing, put it, "the main fountainhead of the letters, the memoranda, the minutes of official meetings and notes of informal discussions which from late September to early December marked the erection of a logical and genuinely combined structure of economic planning".

The ministries in Whitehall were not ready to go as far as Monnet wanted, by long habit and because economic cooperation implied a greater contribution from the British than the French. As Sir Edward Bridges put it in a letter to the permanent secretaries of the ministries on September 21, "HMG"

> must always retain the last word in deciding what we can supply. . . . A joint committee should be set up . . . of the heads of the French missions and the permanent secretaries of the departments concerned here.

There would be no ministerial councils. It was a system designed to keep decisions in the hands of civil servants while reserving the rights of the home government. The permanent secretaries naturally approved. Only Sir Alexander Cadogan, for the Foreign Office, objected that "I don't quite see why it should be impossible to give a higher committee powers of decision where deadlock has arisen in a lower committee". His tone confessed he did not expect to carry the home departments with him.

Monnet failed, then, to obtain the political balance between ministers he had sought. However, the British did accept that the coordinating committee of civil servants should have a permanent, independently appointed chairman. They thought of Lord Swinton, a former Minister for Air. This was greedy, given that the inter-Allied machinery would be located in London. Paris insisted on a French chairman, and Daladier came up with Monnet. Bridges and S. D. Waley of the Treasury were not amused. They argued—illogically, in view of their desire for an official body—that he lacked ministerial stature. Behind this façade lurked Anglo-Saxon attitudes. Legal experts objected that "this will be the first time since William the Conqueror that any man has stood between God and the king". Bridges told a British meeting that French chairmen should be confined to committees where the "least harm would be done". Waley thought that Monnet "will give us a good deal of trouble before we have finished with him". But they could hardly say no. Bridges tried out Paul Reynaud, the French Finance Minister, when he came to London, in hopes he might be readier than Daladier to drop Monnet. Willing to pass on British objections, Reynaud was not prepared to take responsibility for them. Bridges let the matter drop, particularly as this made it possible for a British representative to become head of the Anglo-French Purchasing Board in America. This was Arthur Purvis, a Scot, who had started his working life with the Nobel Explosives Company in Glasgow, had been sent to the New World by the company and had become a leading Canadian businessman. British reluctance regarding Monnet was matched by Morgenthau's when it was briefly thought Monnet might head the Allied purchasing mission in Washington: "I suppose I can get along with him as well as I can with any other Frenchman . . . but Heaven only knows what all his connections are".

In the event, Monnet exploited his position as chairman of the Anglo-

French Coordinating Committee (AFCOC) to far greater effect than Bridges had bargained for. As its British secretary, W. L. Gorell Barnes, wrote later, "The British negotiators . . . had no idea of assigning a very active role to its Chairman. . . . The French Government . . . and particularly M. Monnet himself, are inclined to think of the Chairman of the Committee as a kind of organiser of Allied action". On November 29, Monnet had himself appointed jointly by the French and British prime ministers, so that his function derived from no individual government or ministry. On December 6, 1939, chairing the first meeting of AFCOC, he unilaterally declared himself an Allied, not a French, official. He now had a structure on which to build, if not in the form intended.

Hancock and Gowing have summarised it. Nine separate executives, for food, shipping, armaments, oil, and so on,

> began operations under clear and rational instructions. Each . . . was expected . . . to make an inventory of . . . resources: to secure the best use of those resources in the common interest: to formulate joint import programmes. . . . Its chairman was given a wide commission to handle all problems of priority and to take the initiative.

The members of the executives enjoyed considerable standing in their own departments. The British were on the spot and the civil service heads of ministries were involved. The French provided a future governor of the Bank of France, Emanuel Monick, finance; two future prime ministers, René Mayer, armaments, and Corporal (sic) René Pleven, aviation; an admired writer, Paul Morand, blockade; and so on. A young statistician, Robert Marjolin, was to become one of postwar Europe's key officials.

Monnet's problem, though he could not know it, was that he had only six months in which to achieve anything. It is the kind of period most bodies assign to teething problems. There were plenty. For, as Hancock observed, "Whereas in the First World War, the late emerging institutions of Allied cooperation had been solidly founded on hard experience and the deep-felt recognition of need, this time the institutions took formal shape in advance, not of the need, but of the experience and conviction of need".

Since imports represented the missing component in British and French supplies, an organisation to manage them was the turnplate of the Allied war effort. It exposed the lack of preparation in both countries. There were the ludicrous episodes which are the usual spice of inefficiency. French agents in Australia drove up the price of tallow against British purchasers buying on France's behalf, and both competed for Belgian silk and Russian flax. Purvis in America had no authority at first to order aircraft or machine tools for the British let alone the Allies, and complained that uncontrolled purchases "destroyed his background" with American industry and government.

In February 1940, the French Ministry of Armaments was still refusing on principle to share its data on production and stocks with London. The French failed to forecast their needs for coal with accuracy and the British to deliver anything like the amounts promised. In March 1940, a major crisis in the French war effort was narrowly averted. The relative shortfall in French imports early in 1940 was nearly 50 per cent on plan against the British 15 per cent. Disparities on this scale were a threat to Allied cohesion.

At the same time, crises stimulated remedial action. The French coal famine was a major factor in the exchange of letters between Daladier and Chamberlain of March 18, 1940, when each admitted, rather late, that civil consumption, hitherto little affected, must be "drastically" reduced. If one regards Anglo-French cooperation as a machine to promote Allied efficiency and mutual support, such developments made its case. As the head of the British liaison secretariat with the French, H. L. Hopkinson, wrote, noting AFCOC's involvement in the coal crisis, U.S. air production and the proposal for doubling the Iraq pipeline, "Similar problems are arising all the time and . . . by the end of the war the Coordinating Committee will be in some way or other concerned with almost every problem affecting the economic and financial life of the two countries".

Monnet's major achievement was perhaps to coax the British to join the French in large joint orders for American aircraft in March 1940. This was a more complex operation than it sounds. A British Cabinet memo thought it part of Monnet's special pleading for Allied centralisation. It was Roosevelt himself in November who had to assure Purvis how "deeply concerned" he was by the lack of Anglo-French cooperation in the States. Another obstacle was the fear, endorsed in the letters of March 18, of being too lavish with foreign exchange. On this point, Reynaud in Paris was at one with London. He resisted the aircraft orders, on the ground that 60 per cent of France's gold reserves would go in 1940 alone on war purchases abroad. It was not Monnet's view, nor Daladier's. They thought, like Roosevelt, that no great war was ever lost for lack of money.

Monnet's instrument to overcome resistance—it became classic with him—was the "balance-sheet". Put simply, the balance sheet was an assessment—often in tabular form—of armaments, supplies, output, and so forth. The method of bringing about and employing the balance-sheet was to ask a deceptively simple basic question, the answer to which conditioned the next round of action. This was in part its own justification, in part a tool of bureaucratic politics. By making administrations face broad priorities, it exposed the satrapies hiding behind red tape and made it harder for them to resist need in the name of precedent or procedure.

As early as October 6, 1939, Monnet sent Daladier a memo arguing that a simple table of Allied and German current air power and actual and prospective rates of production would promote the war effort, Allied purchasing policies in America and institutions for inter-Allied cooperation. It would also "help" the British civil service "to overcome its repugnance for anything in the establishment of these [international] bodies which might seem to limit its prerogatives". In fact, the British were more forthcoming than Monnet assumed. It still took four months to get results, but when these came, they brooked no argument. The Germans outnumbered the British and French together 1.5 to 1 in fighters and in bombers by 2 to 1. This convinced the British government, against the scepticism of the military and the opposition of the Treasury, that there was nothing for it but to dig deep in pockets and join the French in buying American warplanes. On March 29, 1940, the Supreme War Council approved a joint program, massive for the time, to purchase by 1941 from the United States 4,700 airframes and 8,000 engines costing $614 million. No such sum had even been considered before. Added to previous French orders, these again increased U.S. manufacturing capacity.

When Daladier, accused of not pursuing the war with sufficient vigour, fell from power in Paris late in March 1940, Monnet sent his successor, Reynaud, an analysis of the work AFCOC was engaged in. By this time, the balance-sheet technique was reaching conclusions for arms and shipping as well as warplanes. On April 8, Monnet drafted notes on a potentially all-embracing "balance-sheet of products essential for the conduct of the war. Hopkinson thought it "would probably involve a coordination . . . of the Allies in the form of planning of production, pooling of resources, manpower, etc. which goes considerably beyond anything which has been envisaged here".

Gorell Barnes complained as late as April 4, 1940, that apart from aviation, the executives had not yet arrived "at that mutual British and French disclosure of resources, stocks, means of production etc." needed "to undertake any *serious* planning". Bridges thought these "shadows . . . a little over-painted" and the criticisms themselves argued Monnet's case. Hopkinson, though he suspected Monnet would have less influence with Reynaud than with Daladier, felt the cooperation machinery was beginning to relate London and Paris and that its leadership should not be disturbed. In particular, Bridges thought Monnet "very valuable" in his knowledge of "whom to approach and how to approach them" in Washington. The view in Whitehall circles was markedly more favourable than in the previous autumn. Monnet, though, looking back thirty years later on AFCOC, said it "was evident to me that this coordination enabled discussion but did not enable decisions".

III

ANGLO-FRENCH UNION

By now, time was running out for the Anglo-French alliance. On May 10, the Germans launched their Blitzkrieg in the west. Within three weeks, the Panzer divisions broke through the Belgian Ardennes and the French front at Sedan, fanned out across the northern plains of France to the Channel and tied the noose round half a million British and French troops in the Dunkirk pocket. Even de Gaulle judged the battle "virtually lost". Three weeks later still, France had fallen. In this deluge, the proposal of June 16 for an Anglo-French union, in which Monnet was a prime mover, was launched like a lifeboat. In the *Memoirs,* it is placed first, to provide the keynote of unity sought and found. But in fact it was narrowly of its time, a desperate, last-minute attempt of the faction to which Monnet, de Gaulle and even Reynaud all belonged, to keep some part of a fighting France afloat.

Because of deeply different attitudes to Germany, the Anglo-French *entente cordiale* between the wars had been short on both terms. As late as November 5, 1939, Chamberlain wrote to his sister that it would be easier to reach understanding with a non-Nazi German government than it would be with the French, who "do not learn easily from past mistakes", a rich comment, coming from him. However, shortly after, disappointment with the British feelers put out to "moderate" Germans, combined with the establishment of the Anglo-French Coordinating Committee, changed the dynamics of alliance. Economic cooperation was warmly received; and early in December, Chamberlain told Monnet he hoped the new-found Anglo-French cooperation "would continue after the war".

At the end of the year, Daladier speculated in public on some kind of federation as the best guarantee of peace. In a speech at the Mansion House in London on January 9, 1940, Chamberlain tried the thought that "nothing would contribute more to the peace than the extension of Anglo-French collaboration in finance and economics to every nation in Europe". The Foreign Secretary, Lord Halifax, on February 13, wrote: "I am more and more coming to feel that the answer to the [French] Rhine claim is complete unity of France and ourselves". In the Foreign Office, Sir Orme Sargent envisaged permanent machinery which "will for all intents and purposes make of the two countries a single unit in postwar Europe . . . a counterweight to the unit of 80 million Germans". On March 1, Chamberlain approved Sargent's minute.

Strong doubt is cast on the depth of these uncharacteristic commitments by a letter Halifax sent on April 30 to the British ambassador in the United States, Lord Lothian: "Go a bit slow . . . in public speeches . . . over any suggestion that federalism [is] necessarily to be the remedy for our present day discontents". Yet enough was being said in public in Britain, though not in France, for Monnet "to think about some deeper action, political in nature, which would go to the heart of the matter and commit the Allies to face their destinies jointly. . . . I had occasion to broach such ideas with Neville Chamberlain. . . . He was open to them so long as they remained vague".

Monnet's effort to reinforce the Alliance was driven in part by his reading of *Mein Kampf*. He was struck by the divergent fates Hitler reserved for Britain and France. Britain should run her empire and Germany Europe, with France a satellite of the latter. This must be frustrated. Monnet first attempted to unify the Allied effort in the battle of France. On May 25, he sent Marjolin to Dunkirk to organise supplies from Britain, the only possible source, for the surrounded British and French troops, but the idea shrank with the defended pocket. On June 6, helped by Bridges, he saw Churchill, apparently for the first time. He urged him to fuse the British and French air forces and commit the RAF to France. The Allies, with their proven plane-for-plane superiority in combat, could beat the Germans in the air if they combined. Were France lost, American isolationism would feed on defeat to refuse help to Britain. It was a late version of the long-running tussle between the French who wanted Britain's air force in France and the British who wanted it to cover the island. Churchill was not impressed. "He did not receive me well". Yet Monnet was still arguing along these lines when de Gaulle turned up and the three met on June 16. De Gaulle sided with Churchill, and in English (*sic*) said: "I think you are quite right".

As the tragedy unfolded, Monnet wrote later, "we were led to raise our sights and try to recover on the political level the control of events that was escaping us in the field". Pleven was "invited to meet de Gaulle with [Pierre] Denis, René Mayer, Monnet and a few others. We could hardly believe our ears when we heard from him that defeat was more or less inevitable. That's when the idea began to germinate in the minds of Monnet and a number of others, [Sir Robert] Vansittart [Chief Diplomatic Adviser to the British Foreign Secretary], Monick, myself. . . . I cannot say who first thought of the idea. It was more a matter of a group".

Whatever the origin of the idea, which Monnet claims, he certainly made it an issue for the British government. On June 13 and 14, he and Salter, now vice chairman of the Anglo-French Coordinating Committee and a junior minister in the Churchill government, drafted a five-page paper. The means by which unity was to be achieved were vague. A customs union and common currency crept into later versions, but initially the ideas were a "dramatic call for unity", a joint cabinet to run the war, mixed sessions of the parliaments and a promise of common reconstruction of ruined areas. Again, Churchill was not attracted: "I am fighting the war . . . and you come to talk about the future".

On June 14, Major Desmond Morton, Churchill's old friend, private secretary and link with the intelligence services, warned Monnet he would never catch Churchill's ear, because he was not the prime minister of France and could not speak for him. He had better try to persuade Chamberlain, through his private secretary, Sir Horace Wilson, to bring up the issue in Cabinet, in which case Churchill would pay attention. This manœuvre, conducted around midnight, succeeded sufficiently for the theme to be put on the agenda of the War Cabinet the next day. Sir Robert Vansittart, the former civil service head of the Foreign Office, was to draft the declaration.

Early next morning, on Saturday, June 15, Monnet went in search of Vansittart, not an easy task—the weekend was not to be denied and he was in the country. All the same, Morton, Monnet, Salter and Pleven joined him in drafting the text in time to put it to Churchill before the War Cabinet that afternoon. Churchill was not enthusiastic, but to his surprise found that his colleagues were and gave way. It was decided to make a terse manifesto of the text.

The final decision was taken by the War Cabinet on Sunday afternoon, June 16. The proclamation, cast in broad, pungent terms, was telephoned at once around four-thirty P.M. by de Gaulle, "displaying unwonted enthusiasm", to Reynaud in Bordeaux. Reynaud, who had for days shown signs of irresolution, could not believe his ears and had to be reassured by Churchill in person. He then took fire, declaring this would make it possible to fight on.

Reynaud's surprise was understandable. Signals from London until half an hour before had pointed in an exactly opposite direction. On Reynaud's initiative, the Allied Supreme War Council had agreed on March 28 that neither France nor Britain would sign a separate armistice. That was before the German invasion. As the flood broke the dam, Reynaud tried to flee its path, asking the British to state their conditions of release from the pledge to fight. At midday and again at four P.M. on June 16, he had received messages from London insisting that release depended on the French fleet sailing to British ports. Monnet, who heard about them by accident from Vansittart when they had already been sent, had been horrified and immediately pointed out the contradiction with the union plan which was then still under discussion in Whitehall. Now, half an hour after the second message, indissoluble links were proposed instead.

In the French Cabinet, which met at five P.M., the armistice faction, led by Pétain and General Weygand, Foch's former chief of staff, brushed the Anglo-French union aside, claiming variously that it was irrelevant, that it would make France a Dominion of Britain, that Britain would soon be defeated anyway, and even that to continue with it would be like "sleeping with a corpse". It seems Reynaud still had a clear majority in Cabinet, but he failed to find the energy to carry the day. He resigned and was replaced by Pétain, a lapse from which the whole logic of the Vichy regime followed. France had fallen.

De Gaulle and Monnet were among the few who refused to accept defeat. De Gaulle, who had gone to Bordeaux in the night of the 16th, came back to London in a British plane in the early hours of the morning. Major General Edward Spears, Churchill's liaison with the French, recalled that

> We touched down at Jersey. . . . I asked de Gaulle if he wanted anything and he said he would like a cup of coffee. I handed it to him, whereupon, taking a sip, he said, in a voice which indicated that without implying criticism he must nevertheless proclaim the truth, that this was tea and he had asked for coffee. It was his first introduction to the tepid liquid which, in England, passes for either one or the other. His martyrdom had begun.

At six in the evening of the 18th, de Gaulle launched his famous BBC appeal to the French to carry on the war.

> France is not alone. . . . She has a vast Empire. . . . She can combine with the British Empire which commands the seas. . . . She can, like England call to the full on the immense industrial power of the United States. . . . This war is a world war. . . . Whatever happens, the flame of French resistance must not, and will not, be extinguished.

As the reference to American industry suggests, the speech seems to have been discussed with Monnet (and others) on the evening of the 17th. On the 16th, Monnet was the one foreigner due to join Churchill's party on the night train to Southampton, with the intention of meeting Reynaud at Concarneau, in Brittany, the next day. But at the last moment, news came through that Reynaud had resigned. Churchill only learned that Marshal Pétain had requested an armistice when Pétain's voice came through on the radio at half-past midday on the 17th. Monnet, with Vansittart and Pleven, then tried to persuade Churchill to send a telegram to Bordeaux proposing that the French government and as many troops as possible should embark for North Africa under the protection of the British and French fleets, but Churchill refused. On the 18th, Monnet had better luck. He persuaded Churchill to send him to Bordeaux in order to transport to North Africa any members of the former Reynaud government ready to fight on. The Colonial Secretary, Lord Lloyd, went in one plane. His mission was to add force to British pleas to the French to send their large and modern fleet to British ports or, failing that, anywhere out of German reach. Monnet took Monick,

Pleven and Marjolin in the other, the *Claire,* a huge Sunderland flying boat large enough to spirit a government away. Oliver Harvey, of the British embassy, also briefly in Bordeaux, noted on June 19 that "Jean Monnet . . . walked in. . . . Monnet seemed a mixture of gangster and conspirator and wants {*sic}* to get busy collecting suitable men for an alternative Government. I don't care for him and I don't trust him, though in England they think him the cat's pyjamas". But the politicians displayed little will to leave. On the 20th, Monnet and his party returned empty-handed. Pleven, by a miracle, met his wife and children in the street in Bordeaux and brought them back to London.

The whole episode of the Anglo-French union raises many questions. The proposal itself drew support from such an unlikely duo, in Churchill and de Gaulle, the very symbols of national feeling, that one is bound to ask how it was intended. The French government treated it as an irrelevance. They were given no time to consider whether it was or not. This was an occasion when the drawbacks of dramatic coups were more evident than the advantages. As for the British, Chamberlain was crucial in bringing the scheme to Churchill's attention. Yet his judgement, consigned to his diary, was that the proposal (probably the first draft) "was very wordy and obscure but where it was precise it was impracticable". Churchill and de Gaulle clearly regarded it as a desperate throw to keep France in the war (though Monnet has claimed he was less sceptical at the time than later). Monnet himself wrote in his *Memoirs* that "for me, the plan had no federalist overtones".

Would an Anglo-French union have made a major difference had France stayed in the war? Perhaps, with the French fleet and North Africa acting as Allied assets, the Germans would have had to divert a much larger effort in that direction, or the Allies would have saved months lost securing the southern Mediterranean. After the war, the key question would have been whether Britain would have made concessions to French policies in the Rhineland. If so, and ironically, the later Monnet-Schuman policy of integration in the Community might never have emerged.

The Anglo-French union episode was also of interest in Monnet's life because it was the occasion he came into the closest contact with Churchill and it was the first time he encountered de Gaulle. It may seem curious that Monnet, a mere official, was so prominent in the politics of the British reaction to the fall of France. But with the ambassador, Charles Corbin, he was one of the two senior Frenchmen posted in London. As an Allied rather than French appointee, he was in closer contact than Corbin with the higher echelons of Whitehall. It was relatively easy for him to have informal access to Chamberlain and Churchill. On the other hand, it is clear from the details of the event that Churchill, a formal man, indeed regarded him only as a high official and was much more impressed by de Gaulle, in whom he saw a member of the French government, however junior, and what is more—even before the broadcast of June 18—a potential "Constable of France".[1] Monnet was well aware of this. "My relations with Churchill were good" but "my role . . . was not political", and "I often had to find roundabout means of securing his attention". He himself saw Churchill as incomparable, "a true man of war, the legendary incarnation of John Bull". His conversational references to Churchill, limited but favourable, always stressed one cardinal point—that though he was a man of power by instinct and inheritance, "he was profoundly democratic". For Monnet, that was the highest praise after "generous"—a term, however, which he did not apply to Churchill. The clue to this unstated reservation was probably contained in another glancing remark of the *Memoirs:* "Did he see beyond the interests of Great Britain? I think not".

As for the relations between Monnet and de Gaulle, there is a Plutarchan neatness and irony in the fact that the opposed yet complementary embodiments of French postwar policy should have first met over a scheme of union with Britain to prevent the fall of France. To judge by their correspondence at the time, a good part of the first week after their common failure was occupied in discussing what they intended to do and how far they could do it together. De Gaulle's immediate intuition that some part of the French state must continue to fight was, for Pleven (one of de Gaulle's earliest recruits), "his insight of genius". Hence his insistence that he *was* France, whatever the sceptics might say (including Churchill in moments of rage). Perceiving this from the start, he began at once to build his Free French movement. As the senior French official in London determined to fight on, Monnet was a key man to attract. De Gaulle failed. Why?

Pleven, who saw both men at close quarters at the time, believes Monnet "had made up his mind that the General would never share power with anyone". This is persuasive, because Monnet himself said of de Gaulle to one of Corbin's assistants, "he listens to nobody". But that does not exclude discord on policy. Monnet drew from his conversation with de Gaulle on June 17 the impression that the General was thinking primarily of France after the war. He himself thought the war had to be won first. Further, his letter to de Gaulle of June 23, 1940, said that it "would be a great mistake to try to set up in Britain an organisation which might appear in France as an authority established abroad under British protection . . . and which was therefore condemned to a failure which would make further efforts at recovery all the more difficult".

Later, de Gaulle so established the image of French anti-Americanism

---

1. A romantic view, typical of Churchill. The constable (a title and function that evolved over centuries from the Byzantine master of the horse, *comes stabuli*) was the commander-in-chief of the French royal armies in the later Middle Ages and the Renaissance. The overtones, for an English traditionalist, would be of Agincourt and Joan of Arc.

that it is hard to realise that in 1940 rivalry focussed on Britain. British lack of support against Germany between the wars rankled, British imperial ambitions aroused suspicion. America, in contrast, was the hope of last resort. Reynaud appealed in June 1940 to Roosevelt to send "clouds of aircraft", although Monnet had assured him days before that there were no clouds available. In warning de Gaulle against being seen to depend on Britain, and in going himself to the United States to raise the transatlantic juggernaut of victory, Monnet was acting on a perception common among prewar Frenchmen. As we have seen, de Gaulle himself, in his June 18 appeal, gave "the immense industrial power of the United States" as a major reason for France to hope and fight on.

Monnet's initial aim was that France should do that from North Africa. On June 18, General Auguste Noguès, the French Resident-General in Morocco and commander-in-chief in North Africa, asked the Pétain government "with respect but burning insistence" to continue the war. De Gaulle immediately sent him a telegram saying he was ready to serve under him. At the same time, he actively set up his own French committee, the Gaullist National Committee, in London. Monnet's *Memoirs* found it "hard to understand exactly why de Gaulle offered to put himself under Noguès's orders and a few days later formed a French Committee on his own authority and asked Noguès to join it". Monnet believed that every opening should be given leaders in the French Empire to proclaim opposition to the Germans. These leaders were senior to de Gaulle, jealous of their prerogatives and suspicious of the British. To set up a committee in London, dependent on British goodwill, was calculated to discourage them from choosing the right side.

In his *Memoirs,* Monnet repeatedly laments the personal element in de Gaulle's equations. He does not say so, but the inference is that these first contacts convinced him de Gaulle was putting personal ambition above country. This would explain the wariness he displayed ever after. Spears claimed that Monnet, through Halifax, blocked de Gaulle's access to the BBC on June 20 and 21 before the Minister of Information, Duff Cooper, and Spears himself, persuaded Churchill to restore it. It is not clear that this is correct; and where Monnet would have found the time, when he was in Bordeaux from late on the 18th to early on the 20th, is also not clear. It would, however, have fitted his view that de Gaulle had a duty to give the authorities in North Africa time to declare in favour of fighting on. And he did tell both Cadogan on June 23 and Harold Nicolson on the 29th that the French people would never accept a committee made up of mere individuals. The breach with de Gaulle was from the start quite wide. In the democratic or "republican" French tradition to which Monnet belonged, military men in politics are deeply suspect.

The terms on which de Gaulle and Monnet parted in June 1940 were full of portent for the future. Madame Monnet, entertaining de Gaulle while waiting for her husband, who was (characteristically) late for dinner on June 17, asked him why he had been sent to London. "I am not here on a mission, Madame, I am here to save the honour of France". It was clear that if he failed to carry the standard in the grand manner, no one else could or would. The loneliness of June 1940 was his "finest hour", as of the British to whom Churchill applied the phrase, and for all the two men's furious quarrels it was an indissoluble bond between them. Later, Monnet recognised that "only one man in that crisis had the courage to take the decisive step, and that was de Gaulle". By comparison with de Gaulle's quixotic egotism, his own attitude that victory would go to the big battalions smacked of Sancho Panza (and Napoleon). Both were right, though, different facets of reality.

IV
VICTORY PROGRAM

Monnet's last service in London was contained in a telegram to Purvis on June 17: "All further [U.S.] consignments of war materials intended for France should be diverted to the UK". Monnet first hinted at such a possibility to Churchill early in June. Purvis and the head of the French Purchasing Commission in the United States, Jean-Frédéric Bloch-Lainé, rushed the transfer through before the latter lost his authority to act. To have cancelled the French contracts might have led American suppliers to lose all confidence in British ones too. But for the British to pay the required $612 million (of which $425 million was for aircraft contracts) meant throwing financial caution to the winds. It was a big decision either way and for a civil servant like Bloch-Lainé an act of great courage in performing real, as against formal, duty.

On July 2, 1940, Monnet wound up the Anglo-French Coordinating Committee. Even without the French, there was a need for a clearing-house for procurements. So AFCOC was replaced on July 8 by a British North American Supply Committee (NAS), chaired by Salter. Monnet, submitting his resignation from AFCOC to Marshal Pétain, asked Churchill for a job "in order to serve the true interests of my country". He seems himself to have suggested to Churchill that he should continue as near as possible his previous work by joining the British Purchasing Commission (BPC) in North America. Monnet was provided with a passport signed by Churchill and $10,000 a year free of tax on the budget of the Ministry of Supply, which, to its annoyance, was not consulted.[2] On August 8, the small Monnet family flew to America.

A British customs officer, at the stopover in Bermuda, on seeing Monnet's passport, objected. "It just does not make sense for a Frenchman to hold a British job at this point". His attitude was not confined to customs officers. "There was a good deal of blimp talk about him because he was a Frenchman and Frenchmen were not very popular in 1940". In Washington, all the other members of the British Supply Council (as the Purchasing Commission became in January 1941) represented British or Canadian ministries. Monnet was the one "member-at-large". This title of sovereign vagueness meant that any influence he enjoyed depended entirely on himself. He had no other backing. The position was put plainly in a letter from a Lazards friend, Thomas Brand (the nephew of Robert Brand), now handling Supply in the Cabinet Office in Whitehall. It was dated the day the British Supply Council (BSC) was formed and Monnet appointed.

> You may be hurt and are certainly irritated by the way in which we have dealt with personal questions. The Supply Council was only to be composed of heads of Missions. Why have an extra man? If you have an extra man, why have a Frenchman? Therefore our policy was—let him be judged by his actions. In three months you have done great service, this is recognised by all who have any connection with our US problems. . . .
> You have had good friends here, the Secretary [Edward Bridges] and HW [Horace Wilson] both of whom I know are anxious for you to be fully utilised.

The letter also referred to "certain events" which caused Monnet to express his feelings "strongly" in London. This had been "magnified" by some people and not forgotten. Could this have been connected with steps being taken to control his movements in London after the fall of France? Salter protested to Churchill, who put a stop to it.

Brand's letter also admitted that "the US administration, particularly one or two of them, had to accept you as one of us and at first they were critical of your inclusion". Morgenthau told Harry Dexter White later that when Monnet arrived, he had complained to Purvis. "This has completely disappeared", wrote Brand. He was over-optimistic.

The British military in Washington remained suspicious of Monnet, perhaps for no better reason than that he was French and that they could not fathom how he operated. This became significant when the forceful air mar-

---

2. In 1942, Monnet told Morgenthau (and in 1943 Robert Brand) that he had declined the money in order not to be a British pensioner—shades of his argument with de Gaulle.

shal Arthur ("Bomber") Harris—later notorious as the champion of area bombing who ordered the raid which destroyed Dresden in February 1945—joined the British Joint Staff mission in America in the summer of 1941. He viewed with deep suspicion a Frenchman at the heart of Allied war planning who was no follower of de Gaulle. This was communicated to Churchill, who himself began to look askance at Monnet because he was not "sufficiently devoted to the person of de Gaulle". To dispel these suspicions, Lord Halifax, who had become the British ambassador in Washington on the sudden death of Lothian at the end of 1940, asked Felix Frankfurter, the Supreme Court justice, to sound the top Americans about Monnet's usefulness. In reply Frankfurter, using his sources, gave Monnet rave reviews anointing him as "a teacher to our defense administration". Given the channel of approach, Halifax must have been seeking the answer he received. Years later, Frankfurter thanked him for the "decisive share you had at a crucial moment in having Jean Monnet retained for the Allied cause."

Monnet may or may not have been aware of this threat from London. He certainly was of the next, from the American side, in May and June 1942. The new attack was conducted by Morgenthau in person and better based. Monnet later used to say "he thought I was a spy". Military intelligence certainly gave him a negative vetting on one occasion on the grounds that he knew a suspected German spy who lived in the same building. John J. McCloy, the Assistant Secretary of War, who also knew the man, blasted the vetters as idiots. But what Morgenthau said was different. He tried to have Monnet sacked from the BSC for abetting the efforts in 1939 of his partner Murnane to protect the assets of German subsidiaries in America. Oliver Lyttelton, the British Minister of Production then in Washington, questioned Monnet and decided he was "all right". Morgenthau then set the U.S. Treasury's investigating teams on Monnet for criminal tax evasion.

The criminal case soon dropped out of the picture. But on January 23, 1944, talking about the servicing of the Lazards loan from the prewar period, Monnet told Robert Brand that the U.S. Treasury was pursuing him for tax arrears on income earned outside the United States. This referred to Monnet, Murnane and Company, Ltd., Hong Kong, set up in 1937 at least in part to receive fees from non-American operations such as the Petschek sale. If the case went against Monnet, he might have to pay $45,000 in retroactive taxation, which would wipe out all his free assets. That in turn, Monnet told Brand, would make him unable to pay the £500 a year interest on the Lazards loan. Lazards were in any case paying most of the premiums on the life insurance which provided the bulk of the collateral on the loan to Monnet.

The mixture of suspicion and indulgence in their attitude is well caught in a tart letter Robert Kindersley sent to Robert Brand on May 20, 1943.

The papers have reported that our friend (i.e. Monnet) is in Africa, where he seems to have stayed a long time. I have in mind that it is just possible he might return to the United States without coming back to London. . . .

Your letter of 25th March says that [Monnet's] assets [to meet the Lazards loan] outside the National shares now amount to only £5,000. This is even worse than your previous letter [Kindersley was misinterpreting Brand on this point]. . . . Can there be any question of the proceeds of any of these assets, which were definitely earmarked to us, having been used and realised for living expenses?

You may be interested to know that I have taken on my share of the loan but this, of course, does not affect the position with our friend who is concerned with the firm alone.

Six months later, another director of Lazards, G. Tyser, wrote to Brand about "friend Jean", much irritated by failure to contact Monnet, who indeed "did not come through London" on his way back to the United States. Nevertheless, Lazards went on paying the life insurance premiums and refrained from counting in Monnet's collateral his main assets either in Cognac, which were admittedly beyond reach until the Liberation, or in Monnet, Murnane.

This also did not prevent Robert Brand from writing to Monnet, who was then in Algiers, in June 1943 with great affection, adding that "[you] have the complete confidence of the authorities both in London and Washington". This does not seem to have been euphemistic. There is no sign, outside the Morgenthau circle, of tax trouble having left a scratch on Monnet's influence with the Americans, including with the President, whom Morgenthau kept fully informed. Nevertheless, Morgenthau himself questioned Monnet at least twice. The threat, extending over months in mid-1942, must have been, to say the least, distracting.[3]

In a way, the most astonishing aspect of the whole affair was that Monnet and Morgenthau continued till the end of the war to conduct intense official business with one another as if nothing had happened. In private, Morgenthau occasionally voiced dire suspicions. Monnet, in his *Memoirs,* thought Morgenthau "a solidly-built, hard-working man, not very easy to get on with. His main virtue . . . was his total devotion to Roosevelt". The two men were more formal with one another than was customary in Washington, but never broke off relations. This is an extreme example of pragmatism, the refusal to allow resentments to interfere with action. And when, after twelve

---

3. Morgenthau was strongly opposed to "international bankers"—"the J. P. Morgans and the Lazard Frères"—poking their noses into "this war purchasing". He tried to prevent Robert Brand from being appointed chairman of the BSC.

years in office, Morgenthau left government under Truman, he turned up in Paris and got a lunch from Monnet.

This unpleasant background, which could have broken Monnet at any time, has to be fed into any assessment of his activities in Washington. That said, he was sent out on a mission ideally suited to his talents. It was felt in Whitehall that Purvis, who got on famously with Morgenthau, needed the help of one or more advisers, free of administrative burdens, to lighten his load in formulating policy. A small executive committee was formed to offer just the kind of service Monnet could best provide. The lack of specific responsibilities, which might have undermined another man, was for him an asset. It freed him to indulge his forte, looking ahead and clarifying strategies. In fact, Purvis, Monnet and Salter, who was running the NAS in London to which the BSC reported, formed a close policy-making trio. Decades after their association, Monnet spoke of Purvis with exceptional liking and respect.

The distinctive feature of the group was a clear view, summed up and probably originally focussed by Monnet in two propositions: "first that the potential national product in the US was so large there was practically no limit to the value of munitions that could be produced . . . and second that the programming and procurement of munitions should be . . . put in terms of what was necessary to overwhelm the enemy". It was in short a war-winning armaments strategy. In retrospect, nothing less would seem to make any sense. In 1940–41, it was regarded as extreme.

Before Pearl Harbor, the Americans were non-belligerents. Though the fall of France and the Blitz produced growing support for Britain (extended later to the Soviet Union), a broad swathe of opinion wanted to stay out of yet another European war. Others, ready to help Britain, refused to disrupt a civilian economy enjoying its first prosperity in a decade. On the eve of Pearl Harbor, William Knudsen, the industrialist from General Motors whom Roosevelt put in charge of the Office of Production Management (OPM), the bureau handling rearmament, was adamant that civilian output should not be disturbed. A war-winning arms policy was impossible on these terms, but Roosevelt could not, or would not, force the national consensus. The official American guidelines were "hemispheric defence" (a military Monroe Doctrine), based on a two-million-man army; and help to Britain, but very firmly "short of war".

Britain, of course, lacked the power to win the war on its own. Whitehall aimed at military self-sufficiency, based on a fifty-five-division army and paper victory through naval and air power, while in effect waiting for a miracle to bring the United States into the struggle. In short, the United States would not, and Britain could not, adopt a war-winning arms policy. Monnet, Purvis and Salter, in facing the issue squarely, figured as radicals ignoring self-evident constraints. They had to invent ways to persuade the Americans to loosen these constraints when the country was not at war and when few admitted in public it ever would be. They also had to overcome what Monnet considered the stiffly formal relations between London and Washington and to "invent more intimate and open-handed forms of cooperation". A prominent feature of Monnet's epitaph on Purvis in the *Memoirs* was praise for making sure that "London and Washington henceforth spoke the same language in every sense".

The task was complicated by successive layers of obstacles bedded in the nationalist outlook of the establishment on either side of the Atlantic. Each was convinced, naturally, of the superiority of its own weapons (a problem not unknown to NATO since). But Monnet and Purvis had a few major assets. They were at the cross-roads of alliance, pleading for Britain in Washington and carrying conviction in London by their superior access to American decision-makers. Since the fall of France they could rely on the will of the American majority to give Britain all aid "short of war". They knew Roosevelt would help if the right modes could be found. And they had influential allies behind the scenes in Washington, the so-called all-outers of armament against Hitler.

When Monnet arrived in Washington in August, he and Silvia Monnet settled in a house at 2415 Foxhall Road. He had not been out of the country long and easily entered one of those informal Washington networks of people of influence around the White House. Some of them were "already old friends", and they met at his house among others. Monnet's *Memoirs* give pride of place to his "deep friendship" with Felix Frankfurter, but the circle included Henry Stimson, the Secretary of War; John J. McCloy, who was appointed Assistant Secretary of War in April 1941; Robert Lovett; Averell Harriman; Dean Acheson; and the journalists Walter Lippmann and James Reston. Yet another member of the circle, Robert Sherwood, the playwright and Roosevelt speech-writer, has called Monnet "the great, single-minded apostle of all-out production, preaching the doctrine that ten thousand tanks too many are far preferable to one tank too few". Ultimately, the mainspring of the American war effort against Hitler was provided by the "unflagging determination" of this and related groups advising a president who, despite what Stimson called his "artful" hesitations, knew where he meant to go. Monnet's accomplishments in Washington can be understood only in this context.

An important step on the road to American armament had been prompted by the German offensive in the west launched on May 10, 1940. On May 16, Roosevelt's message to Congress called for the production of fifty thousand American warplanes, but without specifying a date. Morgenthau told Purvis the administration was about to assume powers to build arms plant to replace potential that Britain and France had lost in Europe. Monnet (still in London) saw his chance. He wrote to Churchill and Reynaud that financial caution in placing war orders had become irrelevant, because in the last resort the United States would provide the credit. Maximum American capacity for Britain and France should be laid down before American rearmament began to compete for resources.

Action after the fall of France was slowed down by the prospect of the presidential election in November. Nevertheless, Roosevelt released fifty old destroyers in return for leases on British bases in the New World. And in October, Sir Walter Layton, the Director of Programmes at the British Ministry of Supply, visiting Washington, was able to raise the equipment for ten British divisions along with nine thousand planes on top of the fourteen thousand already ordered. This was a purchase, but it was clear it would be the last. British foreign exchange reserves were nearing total exhaustion. Then, in November, Roosevelt was re-elected, against all tradition, for a third term. A new approach could and would have to be inaugurated.

The Purvis-Monnet policy crystallised at this point. On the eve of Purvis's trip to London early in November, Monnet prepared two documents. One, addressed to Salter, stated that it was up to "England to state what she wants from this country [America] and state it in big terms. . . . No account should be taken of Britain's ability to pay". The other proposed, as usual with Monnet, a balance-sheet. The ostensible aim was to focus and dramatise British needs for Roosevelt and his decision-makers. The real one was to stir the United States into action. As Purvis pointed out in London, a full statement of British requirements would show that the United States, even if not officially at war, must have a budget on a war footing and restrictions on civilian manufacturing.

After his re-election, and in face of Britain's dollar famine, Roosevelt in person invented Lend-Lease. In the same fireside chat of December 29, 1940, that he announced the idea, he presented the United States as the "arsenal of democracy". Monnet is usually credited with the phrase. In one version of the story, that of one of Roosevelt's main ghost-writers, Judge Samuel Rosenman, Monnet is said to have used it in talking directly to Frankfurter. In another version, that of John McCloy, Monnet used it in talking to McCloy, who repeated it to Frankfurter. Either way, Monnet was told not to use the phrase again, so that Frankfurter could reserve it for Roosevelt's ear. The process leading to the Lend-Lease Act was now under way. For the first time, there was a prospect of a major United States arms effort—"short of war", of course. This disclaimer was both real, because most Americans wanted to stay out of Europe's conflicts, and a fig-leaf, because on any traditional estimate, the Germans would have been in their rights to take Lend-Lease as an aggressive act. If Roosevelt has often been criticised for moving so slowly, it is remarkable that he persuaded a non-belligerent country, full of isolationist sentiment, to take such a strong stand.

Purvis and Monnet promptly told London to state the total arms Britain would need "to defeat the enemy" without regard to cost. The Ministry of Supply refused to state Britain's "deficiency" in this way, fearing that American rearmament would pre-empt the American machine tools needed for Britain's own war effort. So Purvis and Monnet pulled a figure out of a hat, the apparently astronomical sum of $15 billion, over twice the total of the several successive American defence budgets of 1940.

Purvis presented the request to Roosevelt on December 30. Roosevelt, who had been hoping to be pressed, "took this figure in his stride". By February 1941, the BSC had already revised the estimate upwards to $18.85 billion. This was the figure taken into account in the Lend-Lease bill that Congress passed on March 11, though weapons supply, unlike other items such as food, was cut by 24 per cent. In mid-February, "greatly interested" by the "Purvis deficiency" statement, Roosevelt gave the order that U.S. requirements be drawn up on comparable lines to the British in combined Anglo-American programmes.

Monnet reckoned that a genuine balance-sheet would take four months to prepare. But as late as May, the OPM had not obtained from the American armed services an adequate outline of military requirements projected over a long period. Then, on May 27, came one of those strokes of luck which favour the prepared conspirator. The German battleship *Bismarck* was sunk by the Royal Navy in the Atlantic, but not before causing anxiety in Washington that it might raid the Caribbean. Roosevelt seized the occasion to declare "an unlimited national emergency". The very next day, Stimson instructed the OPM to draw up a combined Anglo-American balance-sheet, including for the first time American civilian plant, and to compare the results with estimated German output and potential.

Obtaining production figures from America, Canada and Britain was complicated enough. They also had to be made compatible. This was achieved only with the visit to London of Stacy May, the chief statistician of the OPM, in August. Inducing the American services to cooperate was a kind of war in itself. The OPM had to make its own assessments for the U.S. Navy rather as Monnet and Purvis had done for the British Ministry of Supply. A British Cabinet memo, probably of August 1941, complained that the U.S. General Staff had blocked progress on the three grounds that (1) the U.S. armed services were authorised by Congress only to arm up to a ceiling of forces of two million; (2) productive facilities were inadequate (in fact, because turning over civilian plant to war production was taboo); and (3) the British would be unable to ship the equipment. And that excluded disputes over priorities between the U.S. Army and U.S. Navy.

During all this period, Monnet can be seen moving to the center of policy-making. In December 1940, he made a vital contact. Roosevelt and

Churchill had never met, but they felt the need to do so, although the President could not risk the symbolism of himself meeting the embodiment of a war leader. So, as second best, Harry Hopkins, Roosevelt's alter ego, was sent to London. Monnet, encouraged by Frankfurter, told Hopkins that in London Churchill alone mattered. This annoyed Hopkins, who was impatient of British aristocrats and of the Churchill legend. When he found that Monnet was right and his trip had been a great success in creating a short line of communication, through himself, between Churchill and Roosevelt, he was impressed in proportion to his original irritation. Shortly after, Hopkins invited himself to Monnet's house one evening. As Hopkins was leaving, Monnet asked if there was anything he wanted. "No, no, . . . I just wanted to get to know you a bit better". "They quickly became buddies", according to McCloy. When the Lend-Lease Act was passed in March, Hopkins took over arms aid from Morgenthau. From then on, as Frederick Hoyer-Millar (Lord Inchyra), who was in the British embassy during the war, told an interviewer much later, "if the British had some insoluble problem with the Americans, it was always Monnet whom they briefed and sent in to see Harry Hopkins: the trick never failed".

In April Monnet came another step closer to the sources of power. Jack McCloy, Monnet's friend, became Assistant Secretary of War under Stimson, who relied heavily upon him. From that moment onwards, as Monnet's archives show, Monnet worked closely with—one might say stuck like a limpet to—McCloy and Stacy May.

All this comes through in a muffled way in the minutes of the British Supply Council. During 1941, Monnet figured more and more as the man in touch with American policy-makers. For instance, at the beginning of August 1941, Wayne Coy, who had been put by Roosevelt in charge of arms supplies to Russia, turned to Monnet at the BSC. It was Monnet who recommended to Halifax that the details of British contracts in the United States should be communicated to Moscow (and then changed his mind). His role as the BSC's house strategist became still more marked when Arthur Purvis, who had just visited London, was killed, with the Duke of Kent, in a plane crash at Prestwick (Glasgow) when taking off for Newfoundland on August 14. At the end of the month, Monnet acted as the main adviser to Lord Beaverbrook, the Supply Minister, when he came to Washington.

The "balance-sheet" for which Monnet was responsible was becoming the spearhead of planning for war supplies. As Hancock wrote, the Anglo-American Consolidated Statement, as it now came to be called,

> was never intended as an end in itself, but was on the contrary always intended to give leverage in shifting the obstructions which impeded an expansion and acceleration of war production.

When completed early in September, and as its promoters expected, the balance-sheet put into sharp focus the limits of American rearmament. On current plans, American arms production at the end of 1942 would barely surpass the combined total of Britain and Canada, despite an industrial capacity four times as large. The ultimate function of the balance-sheet arose directly from this conclusion. As Monnet wrote to Thomas Brand on July 1, this was to lay down plans at once

> for the production some time by the end of 1942 of sufficient weapons, tanks, planes etc to exceed German material strength without any doubt whatever.

On September 25, Roosevelt approved the work on a "Victory Program" to meet the equipment needs of all the Allies, including the Soviet Union. The very name showed how thin non-belligerence was wearing. The OPM statisticians, Stacy May and Robert Nathan, early exponents of national income accounting, made rapid progress in assessing how great an effort the American economy could furnish. By the time of the Japanese attack on Pearl Harbor on December 7, the Victory Program was virtually ready. In fact, the Japanese rendered Roosevelt a service. They prevented any politically inspired delay in launching it.

Monnet made another major contribution in the month following Pearl Harbor. Behind a single label, the Victory Program really consisted of two operations. Monnet initiated the second, which raised the first to a higher level. On December 10, he sent a note to Beaverbrook that "US production schedules at present indicated in 1942 should be capable of at least a fifty per cent increase". The "schedules" were the War Department's programme Stimson sent to the President a fortnight later on December 26 and which already provided for large increases on previous targets.

In fact, the proposals Monnet finally presented raised the quantities of most types of weapons only between a fifth and a quarter—an average between some items (ground and tank machine guns) increased over 50 per cent, all the way to others (anti-tank guns) not increased at all. However, since the original Victory Program already dealt in very large quantities, this represented a massive expansion. It was bold, but it was not arbitrary. Monnet's work, deep in the bureaucracy with May and Nathan, showed that the enlarged Victory Program, though demanding controls on the American civilian economy, would not represent anything like the mobilisation the United Kingdom had already achieved.

With such backing, Monnet had the credibility to carry Beaverbrook. R. G. D. Allen, the distinguished statistician then on the BSC staff, wrote in 1944 that the same data were used on the American leadership as well.

I well remember the meeting in May's office on a Sunday in December 1941 when we [Monnet, May, General Henry S. Aurand and others] actually wrote down out of our heads some goals which we regarded as reasonable. These were passed through Hopkins to the President and were, in fact, very little changed before the latter issued them early in January.

Thus, at the first war-planning meeting of Roosevelt and Churchill and their staffs, the so-called Arcadia Conference, which took place in Washington from December 28 to January 5, the top leaders on *both* sides had been well primed beforehand along the lines of the Monnet-May briefing. It is hard to imagine a benign conspiracy of this kind between a few people, irrespective of office, hierarchy, rank or in Monnet's case origin, outside the ganglionic government of war-time Washington.

Beaverbrook in the Arcadia Conference duly argued for "raising the sights". The American production "warlords", who had been by-passed, thought his new targets beyond reach. Roosevelt overrode the doubters. The result was his famous message to Congress of January 6, 1942, in which he called for the production of 100,000 airplanes and 60,000 tanks with other equipment on the same gargantuan scale. In short, within a month of entering the war, the United States launched the industrial effort to finish it. This is presumably what Keynes was referring to when he told Monick later that Monnet had "shortened the war by a year". Monnet himself has written of Roosevelt's announcement of the Victory Program: "That day, more than at any other time in my life, I felt the satisfaction of having contributed to a decision that would change the course of events".

Monnet seems to have been rich in notions at the time, not all of them dealing with supply. He wanted General George Marshall, Admiral Ernest King and Field Marshal Sir John Dill, the former chief of the Imperial General Staff who headed the British Joint Staff mission in Washington, to form a strategic triumvirate to run the war from there. Not surprisingly, this was vetoed by Beaverbrook and Churchill in London.

Rather more came of suggestions that led on naturally from the Victory Program. There was a difference between announcing barely credible production targets and ensuring they would be the foundation of a coherent and truly allied war effort. As early as December 17, Monnet, backed by other members of the BSC, pressed the idea of a joint Anglo-American board for the allocation of weapons. The same day, Frankfurter sent Roosevelt the revision of a paper prepared by Monnet. The message was that there was no administrative machinery to force through the Victory Program. "Each [plan of production] is under a different authority, none has responsibility for achieving the overall objective".

The problem was settled in theory in January, when Roosevelt created the

War Production Board to coordinate supply programmes in the United States and the Arcadia Conference set up a series of Combined Boards that were designed to share weapons equitably between the Allies. Practice, though, was very different. As Monnet's *Memoirs* gently complain, "The American military authorities, once they had been given an arsenal bigger than they had ever dreamed of or desired, were not very willing to share its output". As the vice chairman of the War Production Board, J. S. Knowlson, put it to his chairman, Donald Nelson, "The idea of combined strategy and combined production receives a good deal of lip service but . . . in many ranks it is considered that . . . anything we give them [the British and Russians] means that it is taken away from our purposes". The U.S. Navy, indulged by Roosevelt, who had been Under Secretary of the Navy in the First World War, managed throughout more or less to ignore Allied claims on equipment. General Brehon Somervell, the aggressive chief of Army Service Forces, was no keener to relax his grip. Monnet therefore suggested a Combined Production and Resources Board (CPRB) to take the major decisions on production as much as possible out of the hands of the American military and shape them by agreement between the Allies.

A British mission, led by Oliver Lyttelton, the Minister of Production, Beaverbrook's successor and a prewar business acquaintance of Monnet's, came over to Washington in May 1942 to establish the CPRB. With Roosevelt's help, it was duly set up on June 9, 1942. But, as a report three months later showed, the board was still failing to overcome military resistance. This led to a second Lyttelton mission, in November 1942, in which Monnet was again much involved and where Roosevelt reiterated his instructions in more urgent and precise language. In fact, the CPRB never achieved the coordination the British sought. However, in 1943 American arms output really began to flow. There began to be such abundance, except in a few items like landing-craft (hoarded by the U.S. Pacific fleet), that the problems of sharing eased. Still, they were not overcome when Monnet left Washington. They were never wholly overcome.

By the time the second Lyttelton mission came to Washington, the Allies had landed in French North Africa. A month later, in December, Monnet was feeling his way to employment in Algiers. The political decisions on the "arsenal of democracy" had been taken. Armament, though gargantuan, was mainly a matter of execution. There was not that much for Monnet to do. It was natural for him to wish to move back to French terrain. Possibly the recent difficulties with Morgenthau were an added incentive. But the evidence (to be noted shortly) suggests they left no smear. Motives for moving closer to home seem enough to explain Monnet's departure for Algiers at the end of February 1943.

V

ARMS AND THE MAN

The four years or so from Munich to Monnet's departure from Washington for Algiers mark a clear stage in the growth of two great themes in his political life, unity in Europe and relations with the United States. His speed in coming forward in 1939 with plans to renew the Allied structures of 1918 suggests not only a like answer to a like need but a man glad of a second chance to revive the cooperation he felt the Versailles politicians had thrown away. The scheme for Anglo-French union was an extreme extension of this. At the same time, Monnet's comparative attitudes to Britain and America came out in a comment in the bleak winter of 1940–41. If, he wrote, French patriots "are of course encouraged by the British resistance, in the last analysis they look to the USA for final hope and guidance". After Munich, he bought U.S. warplanes as the emissary of the French government. The high point of his brief tenure as leader of Anglo-French economic cooperation was when he persuaded the British to join the French in this, and so lay the foundations of America's rearmament well ahead of Pearl Harbor. Finally, in the Washington years, he concentrated with his usual single-mindedness on promoting the huge Victory Program.

It seems he negotiated well in the initial job for Daladier. But he was a temporary agent; the policy was just beginning, the episode was limited, Monnet largely an executant and in part an over-optimistic one. The second achievement was bigger. Though the British were in favour of effective cooperation, they had the resources and saw it in cautious terms against the more radical French, who were driven by need. Monnet had to face initial scepticism, and in some quarters distrust, in Whitehall. As far as the brief record speaks, he was overcoming it when France fell. Had he not, he would hardly have found allies in the British establishment to promote the Anglo-French union, so un-British in its style. Similarly, to join the British Supply Council as a sole Frenchman at the heart of the Anglo-American alliance, and to hold his job against several personal attacks, was a tour de force open only to a man who enjoyed exceptional respect. It also says a great deal for British fairness.

Yet one cannot help feeling that it was in Washington, and working with Americans, that Monnet found his niche. It was there he seemed to find the opportunities for the individual to break through formal layers to the top. Monnet was no megalomaniac, but he leaned to action on the grand scale. Americans were mentally and materially attuned to that. Something in the British establishment's sophisticated scepticism was not, and it discomfited his imagination. America gave Monnet scope.

Even Monnet's growing influence in the British Supply Council in 1941 was related to his American expertise. In the view of General Sir Ian Jacob,

Churchill's military secretary, who came to Washington with the Lyttelton missions of 1942, "The British did not know how to play Washington properly. . . . Monnet was the chap [in the BSC] who really knew how the American government worked" and how to get results. In the autumn of 1941, McCloy said much the same from the receiving end:

> He has been responsible more than anyone connected with the British mission . . . for the orientation of the men with whom he comes in contact in the War Department. . . . Monnet is the only one from their shop who talks and presses to the point almost of irritation the broad picture of the United States obligation. He spares himself no indignity or rebuff but before long he has the Army officers repeating his arguments. . . . He contributes his own method of thinking and working which neither the British nor the Americans seem to be able to duplicate for its effect.

This came from the heart of the system. McCloy probably had more impact than anyone on the formation of American war-production policy.

The word "irritation" deserves comment. In the ten days before the Arcadia Conference, McCloy, at the centre of preparations, was seeing or hearing from Monnet two, three, even four times a day. General Aurand, who was a key man in military logistics, in charge of Lend-Lease, has left transcripts of telephone conversations with Monnet. Monnet is largely telling Aurand what to do, and Aurand takes no offence. There is a later example of the same kind, in the journal in 1943–45 of Oscar Cox. Cox was the General Counsel for and driving force behind the Foreign Economic Administration (FEA), which took over Lend-Lease near the end of the war. His diaries are full of references to Monnet, who turned up so often as to put fear into the stoutest heart.

All this naturally raises the question why Monnet continued to be received by those whose sighs can almost be heard exhaling from the documents. The answer seems to come in comments made by his colleagues on the British Supply Council, when memories were still fresh. Leslie Chance was its secretary and "put a great deal of [Monnet's] drafts into at any rate passable English". Chance wrote of Monnet and Purvis that

> it was the combination of the two and the qualities which they brought to the combination which made it so interesting. Purvis was a remarkable little man. He was full of energy, full of charm, very good looking, dramatized everything that he touched and was a supersalesman. He was not, I fancy, very long-sighted. . . . Monnet . . . had a much longer vision than Purvis and . . . usually saw long before anyone else what was the move after the next one on the board. For the best part of two years, to my certain knowledge, almost every major move in the Anglo-American sup-

ply situation in Washington, that is in the realm of policy, had its genesis in this little French head. The victory programme, the raising of the sights, the famous speech of the President when he told the number of tanks, airplanes and whatnot that were going to be built, the idea of the Combined Boards—all that was Monnet.

R. G. D. Allen added that "the basic idea of the Consolidated Statement of Stocks and Production was Monnet's and that his tactics were to get Secretary Stimson to sponsor the Statement and to use the OPM statisticians (May and Nathan) as his agents". Nathan agrees in an essay on Monnet entitled "An Unsung Hero of World War II". The other "principal supporters of the Monnet thesis" were "McCloy and General Aurand (G4) in the War Department". They were "got by Monnet mainly to shift War Department thinking".

Of course, Monnet harnessed an opportunity. He would have been powerless on his own. Purvis and Monnet formed a partnership. Before Lend-Lease, Monnet may have had many of the ideas, but Purvis had the ear of Morgenthau. Throughout, Monnet could only operate in tune with the convictions of figures like Stimson and McCloy, and it says a lot for them and for an open system that they welcomed him as a pilot. Similarly, if Monnet "raised the sights" in December 1941 and, through Hopkins, prepared Roosevelt, it was Beaverbrook who carried the argument at the Arcadia Conference. Above all, Roosevelt, the procrastinator, always in the end chose the high road against the low.

Nevertheless, until Pearl Harbor, there were difficulties and opposition to the Victory Program at all levels of the American system and even in parts of Whitehall. If action had waited on self-evident need, the United States would have rearmed virtually from scratch in 1942. To see that it was ready once war broke out required action long before. At every point in the previous eighteen months someone had to cut the keys that would open each of the many doors between Aladdin and the treasure. Monnet, more than anyone, appears to have had the intuition of the next challenge and of how to meet it. It is easy to underestimate how many creative acts were required to feed an apparently single result like the Victory Program. After the war, Halifax, not one for hyperbole, wrote to Frankfurter that Monnet "was, with such as Harry Hopkins, one of the real architects of our victory". This achievement against the odds is one of Monnet's most remarkable, even if it lacks the political resonance of others later on.

Algiers

1943

Jean Monnet's stay in North Africa in 1943 was brief. There were barely eight months between his arrival in Algiers on February 28 and his return to Washington before October 27. It could have been an interlude. In the event, it proved a turning point. Algiers was the gathering ground for exiles homing in on the future France. By going there at the crucial juncture, Monnet the longstanding expatriate renewed his passport with the French governing elite. Many coming leaders alighted a while: an American president (Dwight D. Eisenhower), a British prime minister (Harold Macmillan), four premiers of France's postwar Fourth Republic (Henri Queuille, René Pleven, René Mayer, Pierre Mendès-France) and one of de Gaulle's Fifth (Maurice Couve de Murville). Presence there made Monnet a founder member of the postwar leadership in Paris.

Above all, in Algiers, Monnet measured up really for the first time to de Gaulle. (The brief flurry of Anglo-French union in 1940 hardly qualified.) He was one of the few players in the tense game by which, in all but name, a provisional French government under de Gaulle emerged in defiance of Roosevelt. Monnet arrived virtually as Roosevelt's emissary and ended up as a kingmaker for de Gaulle, the last thing Roosevelt had intended. Since relations with America were one of the bases of Monnet's career, and a source of conflict with de Gaulle for decades, Algiers, with its early revelation of their character, is an important item in the file.

ROOSEVELT AND DE GAULLE

Churchill called French North Africa in 1942–43 a "quagmire". Nothing was what it seemed. Roosevelt's agent, Robert Murphy, plotted the Allied "landings" with arch-conservative locals who were no democrats and must be suspected mainly of sensing the way the wind was blowing. The Americans expected to be fêted as liberators. They were stunned when their landings were resisted by the Vichy French troops. After three days, the French laid down their arms and the Americans established a quasi-occupation. But the French officer corps were only willing to collaborate so long as they could square it with their oath of loyalty to Marshal Pétain. Pétain's deputy in the Vichy regime, Admiral Jean-François Darlan, happened to be on hand in Algiers with his son struck down by polio. Whether the coincidence had political as well as family motives has remained a mystery ever since. In any case, Darlan alone had the authority to sign the capitulation and carry the officer corps with him. The American military, none too numerous, and with other matters on their minds (such as reaching Tunis before the Germans, in which they failed), handed over local power to Darlan. So Vichy lived on. The few French generals who had helped the invaders were clapped in jail while soldiers who had fired on the Allies were decorated. Then, on Christmas Eve 1942, Darlan was assassinated, at whose instigation no one is quite sure. General Henri Honoré Giraud, whom the Allies had spirited out of a German prisoner-of-war camp, took over, but nothing else changed. For months, the local French establishment achieved the tour de farce of operating under the Allies while staying loyal to Marshal Pétain, their jobs and their sub-fascist institutions. Charles de Gaulle, the one French leader who had committed himself to the war in 1940, was left deliberately on the sidelines in London.

There were now two French movements in the Allied camp, which was absurd, and one of them was hardly weaned from Vichy, which was a scandal. The watchword, accordingly, was union of the French. But that was easier said than achieved. Like Caesar, Giraud and de Gaulle referred to themselves in the third person on the not infrequent occasions they struck a pose in the looking-glass of history. Neither dreamed of giving way. The Americans tried to exclude de Gaulle, but to their chagrin could not do so, in part because the British protected him. Giraud at first appeared to hold all the cards: North Africa, by far the largest body of French troops, and American support. Yet slowly he gave ground and in a year was eliminated from the political scene.

The causes of these strange proceedings were simple enough. One was the hatred, verging on civil war, between the two French factions, both of which claimed to be sweeping away the vices of the prewar Third Republic. The heirs of Vichy, on the right, were authoritarians who felt they had buried a corrupt Republic. Giraud once asked, "Do you really believe in democracy?" To them, de Gaulle was a rebel officer condemned *in absentia* for treason. He had betrayed his caste and now led a dangerous populist coalition. He could usher in "the dictatorship of the Communist party", Giraud believed.

Gaullist views, relatively on the left, were a mirror image of this. Vichy was a quisling regime which had forfeited all right to represent the French people. To the more sectarian Gaullists—and there were plenty of them—anyone with a touch of Vichy in his make-up at any time was a traitor, irrespective of later service. In the victory parade through Tunis after the German surrender of May 1943, the Free French troops insisted on marching alongside the British in order not to be contaminated by the much more numerous Giraudist contingents. The trump card of the Gaullists was the support of the Resistance inside France. In May 1943, de Gaulle's chief agent, Jean Moulin, achieved the feat of uniting the numerous resistance movements on a declaration recognising de Gaulle as their political leader.

Had American policy been clear, these schisms might have been relatively trivial. But Roosevelt's policy was anything but clear. This could at first be explained by practical considerations. Until December 1941, when unoccupied Vichy France and the United States were both non-belligerent states, Roosevelt tried to keep in touch with, even bolster, Vichy. The aim was to prevent Hitler from gaining control of the French fleet, the fourth largest in the world, and of North Africa, the heart of the empire, with more than a hundred thousand troops. The policy was successful to the extent that the Germans did not lay hands on the fleet and neither sought, nor were given, house-room in French North Africa. In the end, the Germans only landed in Tunis in November 1942 when the Allies were already in Algiers. But when the French fleet scuttled itself in Toulon harbour in November 1942 to escape falling into German hands, and the Germans around Tunis surrendered in May 1943, the reasons for supporting Vichy disappeared. Yet Roosevelt's antagonism to de Gaulle did not abate one iota. Why?

It is tempting, in view of the cast of stars, to reach for personal explanations. It required dedication to be as difficult as de Gaulle, a man who established patriotic credentials by biting hands that fed him. There was also a suspicion that in a war "fought for democracy", here was a general less in fighting than in politics, and in politics no democrat. Harold Macmillan, British and a supporter of the Gaullist movement, confided to his diary, "I'm afraid he will always be impossible to work with. . . . He thinks in his heart that he should command and all others should obey him". On June 18, General George Marshall, the chairman of the U.S. Joint Chiefs of Staff, sent Eisenhower the oath de Gaulle's secret service men were reported to be taking:

I swear on my honour . . . to recognise de Gaulle as the sole legitimate leader of Frenchmen and to devote myself to having him recognised by all Frenchmen; employing to this end if need be the means and methods I would use against the Germans *(sic)*.

De Gaulle's idea of negotiation as a chain of ultimata and walk-outs added fuel to the rumours and misgivings. His most senior follower, General Georges Catroux, warned him his tactics would lead him to be accused of "applying the methods of what is called the technique of seizing power", a phrase bristling with Nazi and Stalinist connotations.

Such irritations helped Roosevelt to conceal his French policies behind sniping at de Gaulle the man. But he said enough behind closed doors to make it plain the basic issues had nothing to do with persons. Receiving Eden in March 1943, he raised a pet project for a new state, Wallonia, to be carved out of the French-speaking half of Belgium, Luxembourg, Alsace-Lorraine and part of northern France. At the Tehran Conference in December 1943, he and Stalin vied with one another in heaping scorn on France. Stalin thought her ruling class rotten to the core. Roosevelt threw in the people as well: "The first necessity for the French . . . was to become honest citizens" and pay taxes.

Why was the guardian angel of democracy so tough with the unhappy "sister Republic"? Disdain for 1940 was undoubtedly a factor. Hopkins virtually said so to de Gaulle before Yalta. But a deeper clue may be contained in an exchange between Churchill, Henry Wallace, Stimson and others in May 1943. To Churchill, the prospect "of having no strong country on the map between England and Russia was not attractive. . . . It was important to recreate a strong France, whatever we might think about French deserts". Churchill needed France despite his reservations.

Roosevelt shared Churchill's reservations but not his need. It was no sacrifice to him to assert that France "would certainly not again become a first-class power for at least 25 years", which in the mouth of a politician was eternity. He told Eden that "after the war", Britain, the United States and Russia "should police Europe. . . . The smaller powers" (i.e., all the rest) "should have nothing more dangerous than rifles. . . . On the future of Germany [he] appeared to favour dismemberment". In such a vision, a clamorous France would be a thorough nuisance. Roosevelt could not stop the French people electing de Gaulle. But he could prevent de Gaulle from turning up on a white charger to harvest votes at the Liberation. In 1944, Roosevelt was still pretending de Gaulle lacked support at home.

Then there were the European empires, which were immoral and a potential time-bomb. Close alliance muffled criticism of the British. Roosevelt was less inhibited about the French. Choice morsels, Morocco, Indochina, New Caledonia, which he viewed as a threat to Australia and New Zealand,

and Dakar, as a rapier pointing at the New World, should be placed under U.N. trusteeship. It suited such motives to deal with "local authorities" in the French Empire, however grimy their past, as in Latin American countries, where rebellion against the central power was rife. Suspicious Frenchmen naturally saw it as a covert way of amputating their possessions.

There was a paranoid streak in de Gaulle but, as the saying goes, even paranoids have enemies. Dismemberment and disrespect were the very threats he was struggling to face down in every quarter. From his embattled standpoint, he was beset by evidence of the Allies' ulterior motives. There were frequent demands in America to take over French bases after the war. Shortly after Pearl Harbor, de Gaulle suggested to Churchill an operation to clear Madagascar of Vichy troops, and Churchill declined, only to send a purely British expedition the following May. To prepare a base against the Japanese, Americans landed troops in New Caledonia without asking leave of the Free French in charge. There was truth in de Gaulle's claim that for the Americans, meaning Roosevelt,

> the horse to back is the one who will give them everything they want. . . . They know de Gaulle will never hand over France's future. So for them de Gaulle will never be the right horse.

De Gaulle, for all his faults, comes out of the clashes better than Roosevelt; and, because he captured the feelings of his people, David beat Goliath.

De Gaulle was strong in standing on a principle anyone could understand: all-out resistance to the invader, and the rejuvenation of his country. Roosevelt failed, in response, to stand on any popular principle at all. The issue was well put in a British note in which Churchill had a hand:

> There is a deep loathing in [Britain], particularly strong among the working classes, against anything which savours to them of intrigues with Darlan and Vichy, which are held to be contrary to the broad simple loyalties which unite the masses throughout the world against the common foe.

Roosevelt had to justify himself even at home. He was driven to admit that the arrangement in North Africa was "a temporary expedient, justified solely by the stress of battle".

It is hardly surprising, then, that for all Roosevelt's fulminations against de Gaulle, his policy was opaque and, when challenged, vacillating. Lip service had to be paid to union. But "union in de Gaulle's vocabulary meant wresting control from Vichy as a nest of traitors". So, from Roosevelt's point of view, union must, if possible, be evaded in practice. If not, union should mean de Gaulle's absorption by Giraud. If that too failed, there could be a two-man regime of equals, Giraud and de Gaulle. What was not acceptable was union under de Gaulle. But few who knew them doubted that union between a personality of de Gaulle's force leading a dynamic movement and a man of Giraud's political naïveté representing former Vichyites must turn to de Gaulle's advantage. Roosevelt's policy was therefore evasive and in the last resort infirm.

How infirm can be gathered from the summit meeting with Churchill in Casablanca from January 14 to 24, 1943. Domestic American criticisms of his policy in North Africa forced Roosevelt, having first excluded de Gaulle from the guest list, to change front on arrival there and invite him to "a shotgun wedding" with Giraud to achieve French unity. This suited British policy, despite Churchill's quarrels with de Gaulle, and led to the highly publicised Giraud–de Gaulle handshake before the cameras. Though neither man's heart was in it, this fixed union on the agenda, the very issue Roosevelt would have liked to avoid. There were to be many examples of such wavering. Roosevelt announced he was "breaking with" de Gaulle in June 1943. Nothing came of it. Petulantly, he retreated step by step until, in October 1944, when it was obvious to all he had no alternative, he recognised de Gaulle as head of the French provisional government. It was not one of the epics of a great presidency.

II
ROOSEVELT'S EMISSARY

This was the ambiguous and difficult background to Monnet's operations in Algiers. It was natural to wish to go there. In his plans in 1940, Monnet showed his belief that the French government should have continued the war from North Africa. Monnet had also given thought to the area when, in May 1941, Stimson and McCloy had consulted him about feelers from the French there for American support to split from Vichy and the Germans. Monnet thought North Africa would be important to the Allies to destroy one of the potential German pincers against the east Mediterranean, keep Spain neutral, and add to pressure on the Axis from the air. Once the American landings had taken place, it was normal, even urgent, for him to play a part in Algiers.

First, however, Monnet had to acquire a base. Neither Gaullist nor Pétainist, he lacked a French constituency. His remaining option was to land on the wings of the Allies, which had advantages but also drawbacks. The Americans, though harried, were the masters in North Africa. Monnet would owe nothing to any French faction. On the other hand, he could become too identified with the Americans. At first, that was not the main risk. The French were more suspicious of the British as imperial rivals. In any case, it could not be helped. It was the price of finding a post which gave him means to act.

In Washington, on Christmas Eve 1942, Monnet sent a memorandum on North African policy to Hopkins and Frankfurter, presumably for Roosevelt's ear. According to one of Roosevelt's senior speech-writers, Judge Samuel Rosenman, a document by Monnet on North Africa was taken into account in preparing Roosevelt's speech on Lincoln's birthday (February 12), 1943. This was presumably the short note of February 5, 1943, in Monnet's archives. (Notes for Roosevelt were best kept brief.) He was laying siege to the White House, and with some success.

This became evident at the summit meeting in Casablanca. Talking to Giraud on January 17, Roosevelt said it would be "splendid" to form a three-man "Committee for the Liberation of France". Giraud should be civil and military head. His military deputy should be de Gaulle. There should be a third man, a civil deputy, for administration. Roosevelt added, according to Giraud, that Monnet "best represented France and the French spirit in North America". Uncharacteristically, he consulted the Secretary of State, Cordell Hull, whom he had left behind in Washington.

> Since there are no French civilians readily available in this area, what would be your opinion of having Jean Monnet come here [to North Africa]? It appears he has kept his skirts clear of political entanglements in recent years and my impression of him is very favourable. I believe that Morgenthau knows and trusts [him].

What Roosevelt meant by the last surprising statement is obscure. Was he trying to forestall objections? If so, he failed. Hull replied that Monnet's connections with Lazards and Pleven, now Free French Commissioner for Foreign Affairs, brought him too close to de Gaulle to be trusted.

Giraud says he had never heard of Monnet. But his political adviser, Jacques Lemaigre-Dubreuil, had. Lemaigre-Dubreuil and Marie-Emile Béthouart, one of the two French generals who had sided with the Allies, and been briefly imprisoned for his pains, arrived in Washington late in December 1942 to obtain arms for a new French army. They found Monnet crucial to their task. As Béthouart wrote later,

> In January, I took part in more than ten meetings with Monnet or McCloy or both together. As a result, my mission, well established and steered onto the right lines, was able to get to work immediately after the Casablanca conference. Thanks to Monnet, I was able to enjoy direct access to McCloy and Harry Hopkins.

From Algiers, Lemaigre-Dubreuil informed Monnet on January 26 that "I have told Giraud of all the help you have given me during my trip". A week later, he telegraphed that Giraud wanted Monnet to come to Algiers.

This time, Hopkins overrode the scruples of Hull. London joked "it is a good idea to have Monnet run North Africa". Roosevelt gave Monnet marching orders on February 20. His letter and telegrams to the Allied commander in North Africa, Dwight D. Eisenhower, on February 22, stressed two reasons why Monnet would be "good for" Giraud. First, he was "in close touch with the activities of all our combined boards. . . . I have discussed all arms matters" with him. Second, Monnet, who was "identified with no French faction . . . could be useful to Giraud, Murphy and Macmillan". Robert Murphy was Roosevelt's personal political representative with Eisenhower. Harold Macmillan, then a junior member of the British government, had been sent by Churchill as Minister-Resident to keep a close eye on developments and on Murphy. The implication was that Roosevelt thought Giraud needed a political adviser. Roosevelt told his son Elliott after the first meeting with Giraud, "He's a dud as an administrator, he'll be a dud as a leader". Monnet was clearly to inject democratic credentials and political nous into Giraud and his regime.

Giraud himself had reasons for wanting Monnet in Algiers. He was driven by the desire for massive draughts of American matériel to renovate his obsolete armed forces, for their own sake and to tighten his uncertain hold on the loyalties of the French officer corps. He had presented Roosevelt at Casablanca with a plan to arm rapidly eleven French divisions, more than 300,000 men in all. Roosevelt, wanting to bolster Giraud, gave his assent without thought to tiresome detail. The American military were horrified. They pointed out that lack of shipping made the promises impossible to honour. Roosevelt's commitments began to blur, through agreement "in principle" to plain postponement. Decoded, Monnet's military assignment was to moderate Giraud's appetite.

Nevertheless, for Giraud, Monnet came as the genie to open the arsenal of democracy for the armies he hoped to lead to France and to glory. Giraud's memoirs leave no doubt that this was the source of Monnet's hold over him in their crucial first days together. Monnet had sent Giraud a curious telegram to announce his arrival. It was completely out of tune with what Murphy has called his "genius for self-effacement". "In view of the importance attached to the re-equipment of the French forces both by General Giraud and the American and British governments, I have been assigned a special mission in North Africa by the Mutual Assignments Board" (which distributed arms to all the Allies) "in order to give all possible fulfilment to the rearming of French forces. This mission has been given me with the assent of the President and of the British government". Normally, Monnet abhorred pomposity. On this occasion, every word pulled rank. Coming on top of the letter from Roosevelt, it established him almost as a presidential emissary with a French accent.

The same impression is given by the memorandum Monnet sent Hopkins and Frankfurter on Christmas Eve, 1942. Hopkins's biographer, Robert Sherwood, not knowing who the author was (though he knew Monnet well), quoted it at length as "an admirable statement of Roosevelt's fundamental point of view in dealing with the French problem". It was a vote of no confidence in both the Vichy-derived and the de Gaulle "groups" and their "concealed competition for power." Darlan had been needed to provide a legal fig-leaf for colonial officers and administrators switching sides in North Africa. But "it is important to prevent the use which Darlan made of Pétain's authority from being developed into a legitimacy . . . fostered by the Allies". At the same time, de Gaulle cannot be recognised on the basis of an "assumed but suppressed endorsement by the French people". Therefore, Roosevelt and Churchill must solemnly declare that only the French people, once free to vote, can produce a legitimate government. It is not said in so many words, but the implication is that no "liberator" must be allowed to rig a plebiscite. Accordingly, there should be no provisional French government outside France, with centralised ministries, as de Gaulle wanted. There should only be a coordinating council of the colonial governors of all factions. This should handle relations with the Allies, including the use of Lend-Lease to raise new French forces. The new-model democratic armies, equipped by the American liberators and identified with them, would restore French pride by helping to free Europe. The "various factions . . . would soon find that if they are to keep any public credit, they must join the French military effort. . . . De Gaulle's forces and possibly himself would join the new French army" (*sic*). To guard against its leader conceiving political ambitions, it must be under the American supreme commander.

How much did Monnet believe in this proposal and how much was it designed to deliver him to Algiers? Some points in it were certainly basic to his views. His acts later confirmed his rejection of Vichy and mistrust of de Gaulle. His views were also affected by his absence from his own country through more than two years of rapid change. In their first days in Algiers, "René Mayer, who had just come from France, informed Jean Monnet, who refused at first to believe it, that the Resistance was wholly tuned in to the messages from de Gaulle transmitted by the BBC". Being clandestine, the Resistance, early in 1942, was an unknown quantity. It had little to show, compared to, say, the Yugoslavs. Monnet seems to have been interested in learning about it, but was sceptical. He took some persuading to accept that it was the trump card de Gaulle claimed.

In truth, neutral in form, Monnet's paper was far from neutral in substance. Giraud's military superiority to the Free French was at least ten to one. If fighting the war, not political union, were the priority, Giraud could simply build up his army with massive amounts of American equipment and take the lead. De Gaulle saw the danger at once when Darlan was appointed. "Darlan . . . can return to France at the moment of victory with, practically speaking, the only French army in existence and perpetuate the Vichy regime". Though de Gaulle asserted that time was on his side, he was probably never confident this was true. What was really in de Gaulle's interest was a merger with Giraud. Thus while Lemaigre-Dubreuil and Giraud soon followed the Americans and Monnet in arguing that French union would come through building up the armed forces, de Gaulle took the line that political union of the French must come first.

In short, Monnet's proposals of late December 1942 were as anti-Gaullist as Roosevelt's entourage. On the other hand, he displayed stirrings already of the emphasis that would make him later lead Giraud towards de Gaulle. A version marked "draft", in Monnet's hand, lays un-Rooseveltian stress on "the unity of the French outside of France . . . unity of sentiment of the French in France, their unity after liberation". This was not the spirit of deals with "local authorities" to pre-empt de Gaulle. It drops out of the text Monnet sent to Hopkins. He was under pressure to tailor his ideas to Roosevelt's if he wanted to land in Algiers. But in a conversation with Hervé Alphand on January 10, 1943, he confirmed his view that the free French factions should unite.

A three-page note by Monnet of January 19 shows no change in policy. However, by this time, the Casablanca conference was halfway through, and it soon changed the situation. The handshake between Giraud and de Gaulle now made it doubly hard to bury aspirations to unity. This was reflected in the two-page note of February 5 that Monnet seems to have contributed for Roosevelt's remarks on Lincoln's birthday. In this note, he added two innovations. First, French territory should not be carved up. He may have been influenced by the visit of Lemaigre-Dubreuil who, on this point, was as firm as de Gaulle. Second, Giraud and de Gaulle should together "form the Coordinating Council" for the French Empire. That was not at all the tone of the December paper, and partly reversed its meaning by hinting at a merger between the two generals.

Frankfurter's diary shows that before Monnet left Washington, he had heart-searchings about the extent to which he must cast in his lot with Giraud. By the time he arrived in Algiers, his mind must have been made up. Murphy has recorded that "in Monnet's first talk with me", on arrival, "he frankly stated that he had come to Algiers not so much to serve Giraud as to seek a solution which would create unity among all French factions." Murphy adds that "this was what all of us were eager to accomplish"—a wild oversimplification, since everything depended on the terms. This is indeed given away in the next clause: "Months passed before we learned that Monnet's idea of French unity challenged Roosevelt's conception". Those few sentences contain the essence of Monnet's part in the Giraud–de Gaulle–Roosevelt imbroglio.

Monnet left Washington on February 23, 1943. At that stage of the war, it took five exhausting days to reach Algiers, via Miami, Georgetown, Natal in Brazil, Dakar and Marrakesh. When he arrived, Vichy still flaunted itself under the gaze of the Allies. A few changes had been made. Jews were now allowed to work in the civil service or join the pioneer corps. Twenty-nine Communist prewar deputies, out of thousands of political prisoners sweating in jails and the Sahara, had been released. For the rest, Nazi-inspired Vichy laws had not been repealed. The press was censored, not only for military operations. Representative institutions from the Third Republic were in abeyance. Portraits of Pétain peered down on public places. The Americans even acquiesced in the appointment on January 19 as Governor-General of Algeria of a former Vichy Minister of the Interior, Marcel Peyrouton. Outrage from abroad came through dimly, muffled by local complacency and the schoolboy indifference of the Allied military. The Vichy colonial establishment, in the name of stability, reigned as if time stood still.

Macmillan and Murphy kept pressing reforms on Giraud. "We made very little progress. We made a number of protests. We received a number of promises. Occasionally, an official was removed, a man was released, an injustice was corrected, a statement made. General Giraud was complacent. He said he must move slowly. It was necessary to pursue *une politique de perroquet*" (i.e., necessary to peck grain by grain like a parrot). He managed almost not to move at all. On February 12, Macmillan wrote to Churchill that "except under extreme pressure from Murphy and me, he does nothing. . . . I see a grave danger of the [Vichy] Cabal around him becoming too strongly entrenched to be removed".

Just before Monnet turned up in Algiers, McCloy came on an inspection tour of North Africa. He and Monnet had conferred several times before leaving Washington, and the McCloys looked after Monnet's family while he was away. Much of McCloy's tour was military, and though he met Giraud twice, the record does not include any basic political discussion. But on February 27, with Peyrouton, he was blunt: Peyrouton was suspect in Washington because of his past as Vichy Minister of the Interior; the supplies for Giraud's army would depend on the "goodwill" gained in the United States from the repeal of Vichy's Nazi-inspired laws; Giraud put far too much stress on gradualism. Peyrouton, McCloy added, was to "have absolute confidence" in Monnet. To Giraud five days later, Murphy added another argument of McCloy's: if Giraud failed to clean up the Vichy stables before de Gaulle's head of mission, General Georges Catroux, arrived in Algiers, de Gaulle would gain the credit for reform whoever was really responsible.

Monnet, however, had assets Allied representatives lacked. Giraud had invited him personally as impresario to an army. And Monnet was French. In communicating with an old-fashioned general who had no knowledge of the outside world, this was a signal advantage. Above all, on Giraud's staff, he had continuous access. As Giraud wrote later,

> From the outset [Monnet] pointed out that . . . I had a reputation in the U.S. as a reactionary and an anti-Semite, without a spark of democratic feeling. This . . . would damage efforts to equip the French army. There was only one way to fight against it. This was to commit myself publicly to democratic principles and restore to the Jews . . . some of the basic rights enjoyed by any citizen in a civilised society. I confess my memory of that first meeting is a painful one".

Giraud adds, "I was to have many other meetings with Jean Monnet. . . . The theme was always the same": no reforms, no equipment.

Monnet was much helped from an unlikely quarter: Giraud's chief of staff, Colonel François de Linarès. Having helped to organise Giraud's escape from a German prison camp, de Linarès had special credibility. He

> resembled a character from fiction. . . . Tall, grey-haired and slender, an officer in the Chasseurs Alpins [elite mountain troops], he had been work-ing with the Deuxième Bureau [the French secret service] for some years. . . . He had both Spanish and English blood and represented the aristo-cratic, Catholic and intensively conservative type of European man. He had left a wife and eleven children in France but brought with him a keen eye for the ladies.

In France, de Linarès had become convinced that Pétain had forfeited the last dregs of popular appeal by failing to denounce the German occupation of Vichy in November 1942. In a long memorandum, he told Giraud he must break with Vichy or lose all popular support.

The arguments of Monnet and de Linarès, from within Giraud's own office and in his own language, day by day, with the lure of American equipment to give them force, packed a punch Allied spokesmen could not match. Monnet arrived on February 28. On March 4, Murphy secured Giraud's promise to sack his chief official, General Jean-Marie Bergeret, as a first step in reforming his administration. On March 6, Giraud informed Murphy and Macmillan that it was proposed to repeal all legislation against the Jews. On March 8, the local Algerian daily, *La Dépêche Algérienne,* published a communiqué announcing flatly that

> The *Official Gazette of Algeria* of March 2 published two decrees of October 19, 1942 issued in Vichy, concerning Jews native of Algeria. . . . A Vichy decree is not valid in North Africa.

In eight days, official relations between Giraud and Vichy had been reversed.

Whether Monnet was responsible for all these changes or not, the pace accelerated immediately after he turned up. On March 8, he sent a long report to Hopkins. He had begun to build a relationship of trust with Giraud, and was, he claimed, making him feel "safer in a framework of principles", a lovely phrase any brain-washer would be proud to coin. To set up such a frame, it was necessary to eliminate all ties with Vichy; any idea that the organisation in North Africa could be a forerunner of that in France; and the suspicions in many minds that Britain wanted to grab bits of the French Empire. Typically, he had told Giraud to deal with the situation "as a whole", and not piecemeal. Giraud had agreed, Monnet wrote, "and I am now to produce a declaration". On March 11, he cabled Hopkins that he was turning the speech into eight decrees.

On Sunday, March 14, Giraud duly gave his address to the Association of Alsace-Lorraine, an important group among the North African colonists. He praised the Resistance as the "true expression" of France, an amazing statement from such a source. He promised to sweep Vichy out of North Africa. Implementing decrees were published three days later, leaving opponents no time to gather breath.

It is unclear how far Murphy and Macmillan influenced the text. A memo of McCloy to Eisenhower of March 8 says that "I urged [Monnet] ahead with the Nuremberg business [Vichy's racist laws] and told him not to await other developments as he was inclined to do". Macmillan and Sam Reber, Murphy's deputy, both felt they had been rather important. But Macmillan has written that the text was produced only on the eve of the speech. This suggests that the Allies had not been involved early on. The impression is reinforced by Lord Sherfield [Roger Makins], Macmillan's deputy at the time. Monnet

> called upon Sam Reber and myself to come round . . . to his flat in the rue Michelet. . . . When Sam and I appeared, we said, "Jean, what's all this about?" He said, "We must turn General Giraud into a liberal". Sam and I, assisted by typists, translated the speech. We then all went over it. . . . We kept it up until one A.M. . . . General Giraud had only to say his piece . . . to become a liberal. He was nearly always prepared to accept any draft which was placed before him.

To judge by his memoirs, Monnet felt he had to overcome more resistance than that from Giraud. "Until the very last minute, under the pressure of his own convictions and of his Algiers advisers, he went on trying to water down my text. The notes with which de Linarès and I bombarded him bear this out".

Made reluctantly or not, Giraud's speech and the decrees which followed three days later amounted virtually to a coup d'état. They annulled all Vichy laws. The democratic laws of the prewar Third Republic and its local institutions, the Conseils Généraux, elected by the million European settlers (not the seven million Moslems), were re-established. Elections by universal suffrage in liberated France were proclaimed the goal. Political, as distinct from military, censorship was removed. All this was more than a reversal of policy. By denouncing Vichy legislation, it undermined the legitimacy, based on the continuity of the French state, of the power structure sustaining Giraud, and therefore of Giraud himself. Several of Giraud's top Pétainist officials, outraged by what they saw as a betrayal, resigned on the spot, followed by Lemaigre-Dubreuil. Macmillan, reporting to Churchill, called the speech the "New Deal" and wrote that "never since the age of miracles, has conversion been so rapid, so thorough or so apparently inexplicable".

The whole operation bore the authentic Monnet stamp. Few people were involved. Much to their fury, Giraud's Vichy high officials were scantily consulted. The speech itself was a dramatic *volte-face*. Monnet might be personally "self-effacing", but one of his hallmarks was theatrical coups.

In practice, liberalisation did not come at a stroke. Sweeping away the authoritarian Vichy inheritance took time. It was the end of April before Monnet told Hopkins that most of the public portraits of Pétain had vanished. A Communist deputy claimed there were still 250 political prisoners in June. In some areas, Giraud would not be budged at all. Despite Monnet's assurances to Hopkins on March 8 that the decision had been taken to restore full citizen rights to the North African Jewish minority, Giraud refused to ratify the decree, on the grounds that it would arouse the seven-eighths Moslem majority. His failure to act produced an outcry in the United States, but the decree was pushed through only in October, when his influence had evaporated. Further, the three top officials—the Governors-General of Algeria and West Africa and the Resident-General in Morocco—all had Vichy pasts. Monnet himself, probably because he thought people less important than the system, did not throw all his weight into the balance to have these men replaced. When de Gaulle arrived in Algiers, their survival played into his hands.

Nevertheless, the New Deal speech cleared many paths, including the one to negotiations on unity between Giraud and de Gaulle. It was obliquely a response to the declaration published by the Gaullist National Committee in London on February 23. This had stated the Gaullists' basic terms: Vichy and all its works and leaders must first be denounced; the civil liberties proclaimed by the United Nations must be endorsed; and "the Republican state of law" restored, which meant setting up a central power with the attributes of a government and a consultative assembly representing French Resistance. Before Giraud's New Deal speech, there was one point only on which de Gaulle and Giraud agreed. This was to fight the Germans and liberate France. In this sense, it was the New Deal speech which, to everyone's amazement and de Gaulle's instant suspicions of a trap, cleared the decks for union between the freed French.

Within a fortnight, then, Monnet was politically as well as physically installed in Algiers. He was to remain in the thick of events for the weeks and months to come. Yet he was more truly invisible than in any of his later incarnations. Later in life, people sought him out, and his "self-effacement" was common knowledge. In Algiers, it was not. The daily diary of Eisenhower's aide, Harry Butcher, fails to mention him once.

This gap is particularly strange for a man sent from Washington as a master of arms supplies. Echoes, but only echoes, of Monnet's involvement are detectable from the records. In his letters from Algiers to Hopkins between March and July 1943, only the first, of March 8, gave much space to his official assignment, the negotiation of American arms for the new French armies Giraud was so keen to raise. It made two points. The first was that he had worked on Giraud to moderate his expectations, but at the same time had started to set up the system to unload and distribute arms and so enhance the French capacity to absorb them. The second was to stress the importance of the Americans carrying out the programme to rearm the French. A revitalised army was the necessary prelude to a political renewal of France—and to an easing of French suspicions, fed for years by German propaganda, of British and American designs on French imperial territory.

On March 25, Monnet chaired a meeting of the American and French supply officials for unloading, assembling and distributing the equipment for three and a half divisions and a hundred aircraft due with a convoy in April. Another meeting followed on April 2 to organise publicity for these Allied supplies. For the rest, there is little trace of activity. The Americans did not follow up on the first convoy till the autumn. Another possible reason for paucity of records is given by Louis Joxe. Joxe, who was, nearly twenty years later, to negotiate independence with the Algerians for de Gaulle, worked for Monnet in the spring of 1943. Monnet, he writes, "gave me the job of arranging the assembly lines for tanks and aircraft for the French forces", but "the task soon fell to the military". Monnet seems mainly to have established the channels for American arms supplies. Once these were opened, the military took over.

If the records are scant on Monnet's contribution to armaments, pen portraits of the political adviser are plentiful. Even in Algiers, where accommodation was almost impossible to find, Monnet managed to operate not from one but from three locales. He had a six-room flat in Algiers, 129 rue Michelet, and six domestic staff, all but one person provided for him by the American military at McCloy's request. Joxe recorded that "everyone who counted for anything passed through this flat". It was not, however, either Monnet's official or preferred workplace. His official base was in the Lycée

Fromentin, a girls' school requisitioned by the Giraud administration and with a splendid view overlooking the port of Algiers. The preferred one, as always, was far from town. Monnet found refuge first at Sidi Ferrush, a small bay west of Algiers, and then at Tipasa, another bay over fifty miles west on the road to Oran. At the latter, he used to sleep whenever he could and disappear to "think". Alphand has described the charms of a place

> beside the soft and shining sea, in a beautiful setting of Roman ruins, scented by wild thyme, under a clear Mediterranean light, with a profusion of flowers and birds. You will find Monnet there, in shorts, with American shoes and socks, talking, thinking aloud, dictating, playing a different part with each of his colleagues, trying his ideas out on all of them, taking care not to limit his options. He lives in a little hotel of a kind one might find anywhere in Provence. There is an abundance of melons, aubergines and mullets to eat, washed down by a fresh local rosé wine.

Monnet loved landscape. It allowed him to pursue public service in private. He could also call on it when necessary to establish a rapport with people. Tipasa was the venue of some of his most important moves. There, in mid-May, he worked out with Macmillan the text which laid the basis for the establishment of the *de facto* French government, the Comité Français de Libération Nationale (CFLN). There again, in mid-June, he worked with André Philip, one of de Gaulle's main Socialist followers, on a compromise for civil control of the military, and by extension of Giraud, so making it possible for the CFLN to operate more or less normally.

Joxe's testimony is particularly interesting coming from a man who was about to become a Gaullist of the inner circle. Monnet's

> charm was enhanced by compulsive little habits he pretended to take lightly, attributing sovereign virtues to a certain mineral water imported by the crate-load from the United States, and claiming to be restored to health after the first sip. To feel at ease and calm in spirit he would, at the right moment, draw on thick red woollen socks. He drank no alcohol, ate little, slept anywhere, spent entire days questioning people or thinking alone by the sea, hours also writing to his wife, whose opinion mattered to him more than anyone else's. Then, abruptly, he would lift the telephone and call Giraud or Bob [Murphy] in Algiers, John McCloy or Robert Sherwood in the States, talking to them as if they were neighbours on the landing.

Monnet's informality is confirmed by a couple of anecdotes told by one of his later collaborators in Algiers, the future ambassador Jean-Louis Mandereau.

Monnet had requisitioned a big summer house on piles near the beach at Tipasa. (It is not clear if this is, or is not, Alphand's "hotel".) On one occasion he was undressing for a swim when the owner turned up, in full fig for a meeting with a government minister, to complain respectfully he had not been paid. Monnet, taking off his trousers and standing in his underpants before the shaken landlord, agreed it was a scandal he had not been paid and gave orders that he should be at once. On another occasion, the aged Lincoln Zephyr which served as Monnet's official car broke down at Tipasa just as Monnet was due to set out for an appointment with de Gaulle in Algiers. North Africa in 1943–44 was an automobile desert, and there was grave doubt a replacement could be found. At this juncture, the local Arab market gardener turned up in his battered old truck, laden with produce, to deliver the vegetables. Monnet seized his chance, induced the man to drive him in his front cabin to Algiers and bounced past de Gaulle's goggling guards to his appointment.

At times, however, the idyll wore thin. A week after Giraud's New Deal speech, on March 23, Monnet was warned that the monarchists, led by two prominent Vichy public servants who had just resigned, with at least passive support from Lemaigre-Dubreuil, were plotting to stage a coup and to kidnap and murder Monnet and de Linarès for a start. Monnet called de Linarès, Peyrouton and two senior officials to a meeting next day. He warned them, and told them to warn Giraud, that rumours of this kind could only delay the rearmament of French troops. There was no further talk of a putsch.

There were more incidents, though. Monnet's chauffeur was Fernand Javel, who later built up an industrial decorating firm in North Africa.

> One of my friends (in French counter-intelligence) came to warn me: "Javel, look out, your boss is in danger". . . . In the weeks that followed, our travelling times became very irregular. . . . One night, around one o'clock in the morning . . . I saw a man lying across the road. . . . Instead of stopping, I accelerated as fast as I could and zig-zagged past him. . . . Once the car had gone by, Monnet looked back and saw the silhouette stand up. . . . One morning, coming back from Tipasa to Algiers, at a place called La Trappe with a crossing at a half-turn in the road . . . a lorry, ignoring the right of way, suddenly bore down on us out of the side-road. . . . I just got by, weaving sharply.

Did Javel read too much into these episodes? Monnet's chauffeurs were usually level-headed, and high opinions of Javel have been expressed. Harry Butcher, Eisenhower's aide, wrote in his diary on June 1, 1943, "There are a lot of hotheads in the de Gaulle–Giraud camps and we wouldn't be surprised if there is at least an attempted assassination". A little later, telephone taps on Gaullist agents recorded boasts of having murdered Darlan and planning to murder Giraud. In 1944, when Giraud was under house arrest, a sniper shattered his jaw. Typically, Monnet failed to mention any near accidents in the *Memoirs*. They were no part of the message he wished to convey.

III
THE HUNDRED DAYS

For the hundred days or so after the New Deal speech, political energies in Algiers concentrated obsessively on the negotiations, or war-games, with de Gaulle that led to the establishment of the CFLN in June. The mating dance of these hundred days was a repetitive and at times unedifying ritual between suspicious wooers drawn together by a force stronger than their repulsion. It fell into three cycles, each divided into a short period of overtures followed by exhausting hostilities. Each time, however, the partners drew closer. The process was so curious that one is bound to ask why they came together at all.

From de Gaulle's point of view this was clearer than from Giraud's. If the Americans built up a large French army under Giraud, de Gaulle could be marginalised. For all his support from the Resistance, liberated France could split between Left and Right, leading to civil war. He could not afford to stand aside. Yet he could not go to Algiers on any terms. From ambition, but also because he symbolised the new France, de Gaulle must come to Algiers as to his own. The stakes for him were extreme. One of the diplomats in the Gaullist mission to Algiers, Guy de Girard de Charbonnières, in much the shrewdest book on those turbid months, has stressed the depression under which de Gaulle laboured most of this time.

Giraud's interest in union was less obvious. Cleaning up the Vichy stables was in theory compatible with pursuing either of two opposing strategies. One, advocated by Monnet when in Washington, would have been to develop the North African regime along democratically acceptable lines, ignoring de Gaulle. This was Roosevelt's preferred outcome. The other strategy was to operate as if purging Vichy set the stage for unity talks with de Gaulle. In effect, the New Deal speech chose the second by calling for French union and singing the praises of the Resistance.

On several previous occasions, de Gaulle had suggested talks on unity, and Giraud had ignored them. Confident in the support of the Americans and, he hoped, of a rejuvenated army, Giraud felt he could manage on his own. He also had no intention of handing over "people whom I consider to be decent Frenchmen to the hatred and desire for revenge of sectarian *émigrés*". The Gaullists could join him, but he had no intention of joining them.

Had he possessed a tithe of de Gaulle's political ability, he might have succeeded. But now, with the New Deal speech, he opted for the alternative and, for him, dangerous, policy of fusion with de Gaulle.

It is not clear how far Giraud realised what he had done with his speech of March 14. The reasons he gave for it were almost childish. As he explained to dumbfounded supporters, "Paris was worth a mass" (a famous comment by the Protestant king Henri IV on converting to Catholicism in the sixteenth-century civil wars). "American equipment is worth a speech". He is even reported to have said, "Of course, I don't believe a word of it", that is, of his own speech. On the other hand, a month earlier, Macmillan had judged that "Giraud (from patriotic sentiment)" was "genuinely anxious to achieve an *accord,* even a fusion" with de Gaulle. But then why wait until the New Deal speech to invite de Gaulle to talks? The inference is that in February his advisers were holding Giraud back and that in March Monnet pushed him forwards.

Uncertainty remains. In his letter of March 8 to Hopkins, Monnet says that "it is only after the transformation of this situation here that there may be a chance" of union between Giraud and de Gaulle. Yet within a week, Giraud issued an invitation. He no doubt thought he could have unity on his own terms and failed to realise what concessions he would have to make. Yet having adopted his new stance, he stuck to it through several provocations from de Gaulle. The combined influences of Monnet, Macmillan, Catroux and at times Murphy may have kept him on the prickly path. His own goodwill should not be under-rated.

The first round of the mating dance started in suitably ambiguous style. Giraud offered talks on unification but, as military and civil commander-in-chief, made de Gaulle no offer to share either authority. All the apples of discord remained. When, therefore, on April 1, de Gaulle informed Catroux, the recently arrived head of the Gaullist mission to Giraud, that he would turn up within a fortnight in Algiers, the cognoscenti were appalled. Catroux, a prewar Governor-General of Indochina, and a five-star general to de Gaulle's temporary two, was an early, and by far the most prestigious, recruit to the Free French. Entrusted with the negotiations in Algiers, he was not ready to have them upset, nor be himself upstaged, by de Gaulle. He also knew de Gaulle had been told by his acolytes Algeria was ripe for Gaullism—which he thought wishful thinking—and that de Gaulle had inquired about "an open car", with the obvious intent of building up a head of popular steam behind what Giraud and the Americans would take for an attempted putsch. The Americans, just about to launch the final offensive in Tunisia, were no keener than Catroux to see this controversial figure turn up in their rear. Amazingly, Catroux seems to have hinted to the Allies that Eisenhower, as Supreme Commander, should ask de Gaulle—which he did on April 4—to stay in London while the offensive got under way. De Gaulle climbed down with furious bad grace. Catroux went to London and persuaded de Gaulle with difficulty to let him hold talks with Giraud in Algiers first. The argument with which Catroux carried the day was revealing: as commander of an American-backed French army, Giraud, not de Gaulle, might have time on his side.

Since on March 15 Giraud had invited de Gaulle to talks and had yet to answer directly the declaration of February 23 of the Gaullist National Committee in London, it was up to him to state his terms. Monnet duly prepared the paper, dated April 1, which Catroux handed to de Gaulle in London on April 9. This was important not for its proposals, which soon dropped out of sight, but for its themes, which persisted through all modulations. The basic issue addressed was how to set up a provisional French administration "by the laws of the Republic", in other words, not by those of a budding autocrat.

Monnet stood his (or Giraud's) ground on two central safeguards. The first was that whatever authority was to be set up should be collegial, take decisions by majority voting and observe collective responsibility, that is, act as an institution, not a screen for one-man or even two-man rule. Monnet dressed this up once again as a council of colonial governors. The second safeguard was that this authority should not have a free hand to organise elections after the liberation of France. This was to "stop attempts . . . for any individual to seize power or for the establishment of an insurrectionary government", clear references respectively to de Gaulle and to the Communists. It followed that the tenure of the council must be limited; and that elections should be organised by an administration drawing legitimacy from whatever grassroots still existed.

A forgotten law, the *loi Tréveneuc,* was dredged up. Passed shortly after France's defeat in the Franco-Prussian War of 1870–71, this act provided that if the legitimate French government were ever again incapacitated, representatives of the elected councils in the unoccupied *départements* (counties) should meet to choose a provisional government. Recourse to this law did not originate with Monnet, but probably around Lemaigre-Dubreuil, who brought it to Washington in December 1942. Frankfurter and Monnet were urging the essence of it in January.

The formal reply of the Free French on April 15 reiterated their view that a central provisional authority for France as well as the French Empire should be established at once and that the men of Vichy must be eliminated from all leading posts. In addition, Catroux told John Winant, the U.S. ambassador in London, Giraud could either be first president, with de Gaulle as the second in charge of the Resistance, or commander-in-chief, but not both. He also said there could be an executive committee of five or seven men, including Monnet, as well as the two generals.

Round two of the mating dance now began. After some twelve days,

Giraud sent de Gaulle a note, dated April 27, again written by Monnet, which stuck to the *loi Tréveneuc* but accepted de Gaulle's idea of a new council of seven people chosen by de Gaulle and Giraud. The council would not be a provisional government but would operate by majority voting. This went a long way from Monnet's club of autonomous colonial governors to de Gaulle's political authority. It also entailed Giraud accepting, most reluctantly, the idea of equal co-presidents. He admitted that his combination of powers as "military and civil commander-in-chief" was unconstitutional, but declined to give it up on the grounds that exceptional circumstances justified exceptional arrangements.

The distance in policy between the two sides had much narrowed, and Catroux thought success was just around the corner. Unfortunately, Giraud invited de Gaulle to meet him at one of two airfields, Biskra or Marrakesh, which were not only at a politically sanitary distance from Algiers but vast American bases. De Gaulle blew up and on May 4, in a speech in London, attacked Giraud personally and woundingly, ignoring his proposals. It was now the turn of Algiers to explode. Monnet wrote to Hopkins that de Gaulle's speech "is in my opinion a straight bid for arbitrary power. It reminds me of the speech that Hitler made before the Czechoslovak affair. . . . This impression is not only mine, Catroux and Macmillan were equally impressed". De Gaulle's formal note of May 3 was more temperate. It stood pat on a central power, that is, a provisional government, which was "an immutable and traditional principle", and on the subordination of the military to the civil power. He was ready to come at once to Algiers but nowhere else.

The mating dance now entered its third and final round. In view of the psychological hostilities at the beginning of May, one may ask why? The Gaullist answer has been that the tide of feeling in favour of de Gaulle in North Africa and in the army forced Giraud to negotiate. This was not the view of Catroux, of Charbonnières, or of Macmillan. They reported that Giraud became harder, not easier, to convince at the time. The cause, they agreed, was the tonic, for Giraud and his popularity, of the victory parades after the German surrender in Tunisia early in May. What seems really to have happened is that the mediators who could bring pressure to bear on Giraud—Monnet, Catroux and Macmillan—decided that the policy issues were now clear and could be settled. Monnet, despite his angry response to de Gaulle's speech, wrote to Hopkins on May 6 that Giraud, Catroux, Macmillan, Murphy and he should now quietly negotiate.

On May 9, Monnet wrote to Hopkins again. Collective responsibility on the executive committee was vital before France's liberation, and the *loi Tréveneuc* after it. "This [last] question will really decide whether personal power or democratic institutions are going to govern France after the war. . . . There can be no compromise. . . . If de Gaulle agrees, there will I hope be unity. If he does not agree, then there will be a break." On one point, however—the men of Vichy in Africa—Monnet stood closer to de Gaulle than to Giraud. "Some as you know have gone, but many remain that must go if the policy proclaimed [is] really to go into effect".

Monnet and Macmillan now prepared a short text to nail down the basic issues and make them as striking as possible for public opinion. "Whatever else was clear about the document", Macmillan wrote in his diary, "it was soon apparent that Giraud was not to be allowed to write it". On Sunday, May 9, "Monnet and I motored off to Tipasa along the coast. We had a delicious bathe in a little cove which we found. . . . We bathed naked, but it was a deserted spot; and we sunbathed afterwards. Then we had a picnic lunch. After lunch we drove on to a little town called Cherchell, where there is a dear little wooden town, and a lovely little harbour—also many fine ruins of a large Roman city. We stayed the night in the hotel". Then "I went out on Wednesday afternoon (the 12th) to Tipasa with Monnet to talk it all over quietly. It was quite lovely out there—hot but not too hot—and we walked in the old Roman city and bathed and talked. I came back on Thursday in time for lunch". And yet again on Tuesday, May 18, by which time the tone has become quite possessive: "At 5.30 I went off with . . . Monnet to Tipasa, to our little quiet hotel, our beautiful little secluded bay, and our Roman city.[1] . . . Wednesday May 19. Up at 7 a.m.; bathed; and breakfasted; took the car up a mountain road; walked with Monnet till noon; bathed; car back to the hotel; lunch. A very delightful morning; and quite a useful one. Monnet is still the *éminence grise* here, and if I can persuade him of the wisdom of some plan or other, he can generally put it over Giraud in time". The diaries tend to imply that Macmillan told Monnet what to do. But since they describe the latter's priorities in exactly the terms of his successive notes, Macmillan may have influenced Monnet less than he thought.

The result of the Macmillan-Monnet collaboration was the final set of terms for the creation of the committee of French union. The text was pared to the bone, and on May 17 Giraud reluctantly endorsed it. De Gaulle should come to Algiers. In return, the familiar principles of Monnet's letter of May 9 were reasserted: the merged committee must work under rules of cabinet responsibility and, on the freeing of France, be limited by the *loi Tréveneuc*. Giraud and de Gaulle could each choose two members and the Council, once formed, co-opt three more. The Vichy Governors-General still in their seats and Giraud's combination of military and civil powers were not mentioned.

By this time, according to Charbonnières, de Gaulle's verbal violence of May 4 had put him out on a limb and he needed to clamber back. He was

---

1. Macmillan later brought de Gaulle to Tipasa for a swim. At least, Macmillan swam. De Gaulle sat on the beach in full uniform.

given an added incentive to reach agreement in the night of May 15 when the news came through that in France all the Resistance groups had formed a National Council and recognised him as their sole leader. The May 17 message from Giraud gave him his chance. Moreover, Catroux warned him the Americans would at best accept only a joint presidency. He had nothing to gain by standing out for more. For his part, Giraud prepared for de Gaulle's likely arrival in Algiers by pushing through a last round of liberalising measures which restored rights to trade unions and abolished the last Vichy laws controlling the press. On May 27, de Gaulle answered Giraud, accepting the *loi Tréveneuc* and collective responsibility in the new executive. As he added, there was now enough common ground for him to come to Algiers. On paper, Monnet had fixed the final terms of union.

It was too good to be true.

On May 30, de Gaulle arrived in Algiers. At the lunch given on his arrival, who should be sitting on his left but Monnet, who "tackled me at once on economic questions", wrote the General with distaste. We do not know what Monnet thought, but through Macmillan we have his reaction to a second, three-hour conversation in tête-à-tête, starting at eleven P.M. that night. Macmillan's note has de Gaulle saying that "Anglo-Saxon domination of Europe was a mounting threat, and that if it continued, France after the war would have to lean towards Germany and Russia. Monnet still finds it difficult to make up his mind as to whether the general is a dangerous demagogue or mad or both".

Next morning, the six members of the still-to-be-constituted CFLN, including Monnet, along with Catroux as a co-opted seventh, met for the first time. Immediately, a crisis erupted. De Gaulle insisted on the three ex-Vichy governors being dismissed before the CFLN was constituted. Giraud refused and de Gaulle stalked out. Macmillan told off Monnet for failing to put a motion formally constituting the CFLN. Monnet ruefully admitted he had mismanaged the meeting.

On top of this, de Gaulle had accepted (and probably provoked) the resignation of Peyrouton, the Governor-General of Algeria, without consulting Giraud. Even Catroux was outraged and briefly tendered his resignation. Giraud jumped to the conclusion de Gaulle was launching a putsch. Since the CFLN still did not exist, he remained in sole command in Algiers. He put in charge of security Admiral Emile Muselier, a recent colleague of de Gaulle who had turned into a bitter personal enemy. It was now de Gaulle's turn to expect arrest: "They are going to pack me off to Colomb-Béchar" in the Sahara. Monnet and Catroux prevailed on Giraud to do nothing rash. In fact, neither side had a coup up its sleeve, and both would have had to reckon with the Allies. Next day they had sobered up. On June 3, the CFLN was formally constituted.

The CFLN now voted five (including Monnet) to two (with only General

Joseph Georges on Giraud's side) to dismiss the two Vichy governors remaining, now Peyrouton was gone. The vote was a vital pointer. It showed at once how isolated Giraud was. On June 5, the CFLN was enlarged to fourteen members, all of whom, including those proposed by Giraud, like René Mayer, were in future to vote with de Gaulle on basic issues. On June 9, de Gaulle attacked Giraud on his unconstitutional coupling of civil and military powers. Giraud refused to budge. Once again, de Gaulle walked out. A week later, on June 17, he came back without formally winning his point. But Monnet, Philip and René Massigli (in charge of foreign affairs) were working on a compromise: Giraud would remain commander-in-chief and be in charge of operations, but a committee of the CFLN—including de Gaulle and Giraud along with their respective chiefs of army, air and naval staffs, eight men in all—would handle defence policy. In short, de Gaulle gained a say he had earlier lacked in military matters.

The same day, Roosevelt cabled to Churchill that the time had come to "break with de Gaulle"; and to Eisenhower that he regarded North Africa as an occupied country and had no wish to deal with de Gaulle or a central French authority. On June 19, Eisenhower simply summoned Giraud and de Gaulle to tell them that the United States would not accept Giraud's destitution from his command in North and West Africa. In the short run, Giraud was shored up. But the feeling among the French that the civil power must take precedence over the military and that the CFLN should decide French policies, not the Americans, was reinforced. Giraud's rapid subsequent eclipse was sealed.

IV

AN INDEPENDENT

By the end of June, de Gaulle was the real head of the CFLN. He had made the perilous leap from being a symbol of French resistance, but materially a pensioner of the British, to president of what was in all but name the French government-in-waiting. A few months earlier, Giraud had controlled the great bulk of resources outside France. Now he was politically obsolescent. De Gaulle had also succeeded largely on his own terms. The programme of his Gaullist National Committee was fulfilled. The CFLN was *de facto* a centralised government with commissioners who were virtually ministers. High Vichy personnel had been purged. On August 27, even Roosevelt resigned himself to recognising the CFLN's authority over the territories it controlled. Recognition specifically did not extend to France or the French Empire as a whole. De Gaulle, though, could now afford to wait. From July onwards, there was a widespread feeling in Algiers that he had begun to relax and become less aggressive. No wonder. His victory had been perhaps the most impressive and difficult of his career and no doubt, secretly, a great relief.

However, to emphasise only the triumph of the hero conveys a false impression. If one compares the evolving positions of de Gaulle and Giraud, there is a pattern in propositions that survived and those that went under. Those that survived reflected the Republican tradition. Those that diverged from it disappeared. The Vichy sub-fascist inheritance and its personnel tainted by collaboration with the Germans; the attempt to maintain the American doctrine of dealing with "local authorities" in the form of a Council of Governors of French imperial territories; Giraud's claim to combine civil and military powers—all went under. On these points, the Gaullist insistence on the primacy of a civil, central power, on personnel identified with resistance to the Germans, on French bodies independent of any tutelage, including American, prevailed. On the other hand, where de Gaulle himself was suspect and where the proposals of his committee in London glossed over the problems of restraints on his own personal authority, he too had to give way. In short, de Gaulle's triumph is less a personal one than an interesting victory of political principle over material power which constrained both victor and loser.

When de Gaulle received Giraud's message of May 17 insisting on cabinet responsibility, he told his aides to find out whether voting had prevailed in prewar governments. In fact, because most of them were loose coalitions, it had not and hardly could have done. Yet collective responsibility did not become a dead letter in the CFLN. The minutes of the CFLN sessions all state that the Committee took such and such a decision. Decrees had to be signed by all the interested commissioners; de Gaulle's signature as its president was not enough. He dominated the CFLN, of course, but as a more or less democratic war-leader, not a plebiscitary autocrat.

This balance might have prevailed anyway. Coming from nowhere, de Gaulle needed to be representative. He wanted to be recognised as a full member of the alliance. He could not afford to confirm suspicions of dictatorial tendencies. The Resistance also threw up three parties, the Communists, Socialists and Christian Democrats, too strong to be manipulated. Nevertheless, during his walk-out from the CFLN in June, he told Murphy, Macmillan and Catroux that he "had no intention of allowing himself to be imprisoned in an executive committee". He tried at least once to rid himself of collective signatures on the characteristic ground that when France was liberated the only name the French would know was his, not those of members of the CFLN. He failed. To that extent, Monnet's persistence in building restraints into the CFLN was based on a correct insight and proved effective. The *loi Tréveneuc,* however, was laid to rest. By the time France was freed, it was an irrelevance.

Charismatic leaders and subordinates with a will of their own seldom get on too well. There was a deep incompatibility between de Gaulle, embodiment of the France of symbol and of high posture in politics, and Monnet, the pragmatist, preoccupied with institutions and limits on personal power. In later years, Monnet often mused on his experience of de Gaulle in Algiers. He recalled they would reach agreements but that subsequently these would emerge subtly changed. Between the agreement and its public presentation fell de Gaulle's historic image. Symbol was both shield and sword to de Gaulle. It concealed the vulnerabilities of the man and the cause behind the powerful projected idea. In the war, when he had so little else to sustain him, it was critical. Whatever one's reservations, his achievement in imposing this image not just on his countrymen but on Stalin and Roosevelt, both potentially hostile, verged on the miraculous.

By comparison, Monnet, who laid no claim to being the soul of France, was part of a sober supporting cast. But as Pleven, a member of this as of so many French administrations, said decades later, "It was a talented team . . . the equal or superior of most regularly constituted governments", and Monnet was one of its leading lights. Drew Middleton in *The New York Times* of July 23 even claimed he was emerging as the leader of the "moderate" group, which was "the chief rival" to de Gaulle. This seems to have been wishful thinking. But as the man with influence in America, the place bursting with resources in a world reduced to beggary, Monnet would have been a key figure even had his character been less resolute. He was enough of a power centre on the committee for Hervé Alphand to note in his diary: "I am to some extent a buffer (is he aware of it?), a peace-maker, between him and de Gaulle".

In Algiers, Monnet and de Gaulle seem to have learned to live together. On most issues their working relations were warily good. But as late as the end of September, Monnet was reported calling de Gaulle "a public menace". Far away in Washington in December, Monnet fumed at rumours that the CFLN might let de Gaulle sack René Massigli, the Commissioner for Foreign Affairs, one of his more independent colleagues. (It was a false alarm.) De Gaulle, referring to Monnet, veered between olympian contempt and suspicions from late Jacobean drama: "The persisting division between Giraud and us . . . is deliberately kept going by Monnet, who sees it as an opportunity to divide and rule. . . . The people we are really up against are the Americans. . . . Monnet is the mouthpiece of the foreigner".

Yet as a mouthpiece, Monnet failed to give universal satisfaction. When Murphy collared him on the decision to expand the CFLN from seven to fourteen members (it was the first time Murphy noticed Giraud had lost power), Monnet said "that he really had no information to impart on French internal affairs. . . . Monnet thus politely declared French independence". Giraud and Murphy both thought Monnet "betrayed" Giraud in failing to back him on the CFLN. Giraud expected Monnet to root for him like a loyal faction fighter. But as Makins noted, Monnet "thinks in terms of principles and programmes". His aim was French unity in democratic conditions, and his objection to de Gaulle that he was not democratic enough. Once that concern was met, he was much closer to de Gaulle than to Giraud on other points, such as the need to purge the men of Vichy or the primacy of the civil power. In addition, Giraud piled blunder on blunder. He put himself in the wrong in July by accepting an invitation from Roosevelt, and in September by invading Corsica, without consulting the CFLN. Such acts were clumsy attempts to reassert his old command and independence. Ironically, he did well in each case. In America, he secured the arms to complete the much-delayed equipment of the French forces. Corsica he liberated. But flouting the civil power, he played into de Gaulle's hands. By October, he was eliminated as a leader.

Politically speaking, it is more interesting, in Murphy's terms, to ask how it was that, "having accomplished what Roosevelt did not want to see accomplished, Monnet returned to Washington later the same year with apparently undiminished influence on the Roosevelt administration". Murphy criticised him very strongly to Roosevelt in July. Yet the French ambassador in Washington, Henri Hoppenot, reporting on the first council meeting of the United Nations Relief and Rehabilitation Agency (UNRRA) in November, stressed it had been widely noted, in the court-like atmosphere of the first quasi-postwar conference, that the only foreign representatives with whom Roosevelt had stopped to have a friendly chat were the Soviet ambassador and Jean Monnet, now representing the CFLN. By this time, the Americans themselves seemed to have lost confidence in Giraud. Eisenhower and the War Department, who were mainly in charge in North Africa, did not share Murphy's initial view of Monnet's performance. Stimson thought he was doing what he sensibly could to moderate de Gaulle's personal rule in the CFLN. Echoing his judgement in January to his son Elliott, Roosevelt at Tehran remarked that Giraud lacked all political and administrative ability. By that time, with the Allies in Italy, Giraud was no longer a factor.

In short, Monnet proved as independent of his White House patrons as of Giraud and de Gaulle. The truth seems to be that, with Catroux, he was above all one of the two main mediators who made French union possible. The Americans did not want unity that put de Gaulle in charge. Macmillan manœuvred masterfully at key moments, but could not himself produce the result. Giraud and de Gaulle were usually the obstacles, not the solution. That left Monnet and Catroux to keep the accent not on persons but on union. They were the moderates, "not candidates for power but volunteers for French unity", Joxe called them. Ten years later, de Gaulle himself, in a bitter personal attack on Monnet, paid back-handed tribute.

The "inspirer" (Monnet) came up with a scheme to confound general Giraud and general de Gaulle in a single government. This time, once again [as in the Anglo-French union of 1940] I accepted the mixture because I had a shrewd idea of the outcome. The fact is, what followed came as a surprise to no-one—doubtless not even to the "inspirer".

In the end, the ill-will only adds to the acknowledgement.

Three key events led to French unification in North Africa on the only terms that were practical, terms that were also the ones Roosevelt would have liked to rule out. The first was when unity was placed on the agenda at the Casablanca conference of January 1943. The second was the dramatic *volte-face* of the New Deal speech, which launched negotiations in mid-March. The third was the memorandum of May 17, which set the frame for the CFLN. Monnet, more than anyone, was behind the last two of these three developments. Given the crippling effects, perhaps a civil war, that a failure to unite could have had during and after the Liberation, France and de Gaulle have owed a great deal more to Monnet and Catroux in Algiers than has been generally noted.

Liberation of France

1943–1945

About the time Monnet became a member of the CFLN in Algiers, back in France the local German general in command in the Charente requisitioned the Monnet home as his residence. In occupied Europe, the worst period of the war was still building up to the ghastly climax of the gas chambers. But round the margins of the Nazis' area of control, the tide was beginning to flow strongly in the Allies' favour. In Russia in July, the gigantic tank duel of Kursk broke Hitler's Panzer armies. The battle of the Atlantic mastered the U-boat "wolf-packs" which in March had threatened to starve Britain. The fall of Tunis opened up what Churchill optimistically called "the soft under-belly of Europe". Many people, de Gaulle and Monnet included, thought they might be facing the last winter of war.

Stimulated by this climate, Algiers in the second half of 1943 was a thriving seedbed of ideas for postwar policy. "One morning," Etienne Hirsch, later his closest colleague, "found Monnet deep in thought"

in front of a map of Europe laid out on his desk and striped with pencil lines. Showing me the regions of the Ruhr and Lorraine, he explained that all the trouble came from that part of the world. It was from their coal and steel that Germany and France forged the instruments of war. To stop another conflagration, it would be necessary, one way or another, to extract this region from the two countries. . . . We had a long discussion. I thought it sheer utopia to think of gouging areas that were such sources of wealth out of sovereign states and, after a gap of a thousand years, dream up a new Lotharingia.[1]

1. In 843, the three surviving grandsons of Charlemagne divided up his empire at the Treaty of Verdun between Neustria (later France), Austria (later Germany) and the middle

Monnet was not the only one to speculate. His own *Memoirs* point out that in his discussions on Europe with Mayer, Alphand, Marjolin and Hirsch, Mayer too "thought in terms of forming an industrial Lotharingia". Alphand, for his part, was cogitating "a European economic union going well beyond a mere customs union". Alphand's ideas had roots in his prewar frustrations with French protectionism as director of foreign trade agreements at the Ministry of Commerce. Like Monnet and many others, he blamed protection for the steep decline of the country in the 1930s. His hopes had already been stirred by contacts with members of the Belgian and Dutch governments-in-exile in London the previous year. They prompted several papers he wrote in Algiers. They were to inspire his attempts, after the war, to set up customs schemes first with Italy and then the Low Countries, which were themselves working towards Benelux (a customs union of *Bel*gium, the *Net*herlands and *Lux*embourg). Leaders in Algiers had their binoculars firmly trained on postwar Europe.

The broadest views were taken by de Gaulle and Monnet. A long, unfinished note of Monnet's of August 5, 1943, hinged on the fear that unless democratic systems were installed at once upon the liberation of Europe, chaos and dire poverty could yield a rash of authoritarian nationalist regimes, the economic face of which would be protectionism. The British, Americans and Russians had worlds of their own to fall back on. France alone, of the larger Allies, was European. With the collapse of Germany and Italy, it would be the only major European power left. It must therefore produce the ideas for a "European new order" (*sic*). The unconscious contrast with Roosevelt's views could not have been greater.

The postwar European order was discussed at a lunch given by de Gaulle and attended by Monnet, Mayer, the Commissioner for Production André Diethelm, and Alphand on October 17. Monnet and de Gaulle were the poles of debate. Monnet laid out his idea of a Europe united on terms of equality between its members. It should be "a single economic entity with free trade". Germany might be divided into several states so long as these were treated as equals. Otherwise, the pressure to reconstitute a single state would be overwhelming. The basic industries, coal and steel, should be placed under international authority. De Gaulle was sceptical. "After a war such as this, it is hard to see French and Germans belonging together to an economic union". He favoured an economic union of France with Benelux, perhaps the Rhineland detached from Germany, perhaps Italy, Spain and Switzerland, in close understanding with the Soviet Union and Britain. This union should not be protectionist. France would take the lead, "a consideration which, as a Frenchman, one cannot treat lightly". While both men

---

kingdom of the eldest, Lothar, from the mouth of the Rhine through Burgundy, the Alps and Lombardy down to Rome, that is, Lotharingia, a memory of which survives in "Lorraine".

focussed on the same questions, Germany, Europe, the future of the nation state and freer trade as a political instrument, their remarks foreshadowed later differences. It was the more striking in that their strategies were not yet coloured by cold war.

At first, little came of these speculations. Urgent issues clamoured for attention. Everything had to be built up, including government.

Like most colonial regimes, French North Africa tended to be "under-administered", by European standards. The civil service, especially in the lower reaches, was settler-dominated and Vichyist in sympathy. But the CFLN included a number of people who would soon prove to be of some stature. With men like Joxe, Alphand and Marjolin to back them up, there were the makings of a talented administration. There was a contrast between the quality of this leadership and the lack of depth below. A few people had to carry a far greater than usual load. Monnet's Commissariat for Armaments, Supply and Reconstruction, set up in the first batch of quasi-ministries a few days after the formation of the CFLN, spanned a vast range of activities.[2] With armaments, Monnet touched on the military. With supply, he controlled the current livelihood of a North Africa short of everything, even of grain. With reconstruction, he had to plan for the liberation of France. These responsibilities, varied as they were, had two characteristics in common. They required loosening bottlenecks by organising imports, and going to the only source to match the need, North America. Monnet, as the one member of the CFLN really well connected in the corridors of power in Washington, held the key to missing treasure.

Though Monnet's influence in Algiers is difficult to document, there is an institutional clue to it. Only two cabinet committees were set up in 1943 to coordinate policy. One was on programs. The other was on reconstruction. Monnet chaired both. When he left for Washington at the end of October, a new arrival, Henri Queuille, Minister of Agriculture, with intervals, from 1924 to 1938 (in a country where over a third of workers were peasants), was appointed chairman of an informal Economic Commission taking over most of Monnet's functions. Queuille failed to make the commission work. So a High Council for Supply was set up at the end of February 1944, still chaired by Queuille, to whom de Gaulle formally delegated his authority. This too, according to an official memo, "rapidly ended in resounding failure". The various commissioners were too jealous of their independence. From April 1944 onwards, de Gaulle himself chaired a new Economic Committee. At last, this worked moderately well. For a time, the committee became a centre of economic policy coordination. It is striking that Monnet

2. Because the CFLN was not a recognised government, its *de facto* ministries (and ministers) could not call themselves that, and so were set up as commissariats (and commissioners).

a year earlier had met none of the difficulties Queuille encountered. It would probably be an exaggeration to say he was, in a term occasionally used in Britain, an economic overlord. But he was in effect a minister for external economic affairs at a time when all the components of economic vitality had to be syphoned from abroad.

Though Macmillan, seeing him at a gathering in August 1943, thought he looked "bored", Monnet was active in his few months as a commissioner in Algiers. The least of his activities was probably in the arms field. The system to absorb the huge supplies from the United States had largely been set up in his period with Giraud before the CFLN. The last big transfusion of equipment, to fit out three divisions, had occurred in April, after which followed a substantial pause. The next major event was not due to Monnet but to Giraud, who in his visit to America in July, persuaded Roosevelt and Marshall to complete the supply of eleven divisions promised at Casablanca. Transport remained a major headache. Hirsch, who worked with Monnet, believes that "without his constant chivvying of his friends in Washington" the American arms programme for the French would not have been carried through. But this was routine. Early in September, Monnet dropped arms, it seems spontaneously, from his empire. He concentrated on planning for France's future liberation.

This was complex, and the least of the problems were material. The main one, seeping into everything, was the difficult political relationship with the United States. There was a constant tension between negotiating practical agreements—every one of which was a step towards *de facto* recognition of the CFLN—and Roosevelt's refusal to countenance recognition as the final outcome. As long as he could, he sustained the view that France should be treated as an occupied country, like Italy. De Gaulle's attitude was, of course, diametrically opposed. The CFLN turned itself into the Provisional Government of the French Republic (GPRF) in May 1944, three weeks before D-Day, without asking anyone's say-so. In the end, the audience that mattered to de Gaulle was the French public, not Roosevelt.

These tensions came out immediately in Monnet's negotiation, in tandem with Massigli, of the so-called modus vivendi with the Americans on Lend-Lease. Signed on September 25, 1943, this agreement was mainly a codification of recent practice in North Africa. It was called a "modus vivendi" to minimise the connotations of recognition. The CFLN was to pay cash for its "civil" imports, that is, those not directly tied to the military. No Lend-Lease agreement with any other authority or state had such a restrictive clause. It could be construed as another sign of disfavour. On the other hand, the American forces in North Africa did spend enough dollars on the spot to provide the CFLN with the means to pay. The trouble was that this was temporary and there was a risk, which materialised, that the Americans would regard it as a precedent when conditions were not so good. The CFLN had to swallow its pride, but the clause was an omen of arguments to come.[3]

Lend-Lease agreements were about war. Monnet's longer-term concern was the Liberation. A committee in London chaired by Leith-Ross had been planning for the return to Europe since barely six months after Pearl Harbor. A year later, proposals focussed on setting up a United Nations Relief and Rehabilitation Agency (UNRRA). The first meeting of UNRRA's "Council"—in reality, a conference of governments to set up the organisation—was initially scheduled for July 1943. The CFLN was too new to be ready for this. Monnet asked for the meeting to be postponed till August. He need not have worried. It was put off more than once, ultimately to November, as a result of the resistance of the governments-in-exile of the smaller nations, especially the Dutch. There were two conflicts. First, relief was withheld from any area "the government of which is in a position to pay in suitable means of foreign exchange". This would in particular have hit the French, who had managed to store most of their gold reserves out of reach of the Germans. Second, the system was so centred on the American Director-General and on Washington that they feared for their domestic authority once they were liberated.[4]

As it happened, Monnet and Alphand, who were entrusted with the negotiations, had had an almost accidental conversation on these matters in Washington long before, on January 10, 1943, and had reached similar conclusions. Alphand, as the economic planner of the Gaullists in London, had come over to discuss "relief". He found Monnet ill in bed, but the two had concurred. Relief should be confined to bare necessities. It should be organised at the supply end by the Combined Boards and financed by Lend-Lease; but the governments of the liberated countries should administer distribution themselves outside the immediate war zones.

This was a political priority, though when the time came, Monnet clothed it in purely practical arguments. Since "relief will take time, it is urgent for France to benefit by aid before UNRRA and outside UNRRA". Giving a lead to the governments-in-exile of the smaller countries (Belgium, Holland, Norway, Czechoslovakia and Poland), Monnet and Alphand won the assent of the first "Council" of UNRRA, held in Atlantic City from November 9 to December 12, 1943. More precisely, Dean Acheson, for the Americans, accepted, glad to be rid of an opposition which could have grounded the organisation itself.

By the mere fact of being there, and making a mark, Monnet and

3. Lend-Lease also had its funny side. When the CFLN applied for help for the important wine-growing industry of North Africa, they were told that funds could not be given to encourage the consumption of alcohol.

4. Leith-Ross wrote, rather surprisingly, in *Money Talks,* that Monnet expressed interest to him in becoming Director-General of UNRRA.

Alphand advanced another priority of their talk of January 10: asserting the presence of France in the emerging "United Nations". Wishful thinking or not, Henri Hoppenot, the "delegate" of the CFLN in Washington (that is, the ambassador without the name), reported they had made a strong impression on the conference.

II
RELIEF AND RECOGNITION

Since aid was not to come through UNRRA, the key to French strategy lay in Washington. Monnet was still in Algiers on Wednesday, October 20. By the following Wednesday, he was in Washington as commissioner-at-large, still a full-fledged member of the CFLN, with Alphand as deputy and Marjolin in tow, a small but strong team.

Monnet was to handle the entire range of issues raised by the expected Allied landing in France. These included the administration of France by a French authority in the lee of the Allied armies; emergency relief to a starving people; currency arrangements in the transition from German occupation to sovereignty; and, implicitly, *de facto* recognition of the CFLN as the prospective government of France. Monnet was really to negotiate the total Franco-American civil relationship. This by-passed diplomatic channels to the point where McCloy checked with Massigli that Monnet really had so much authority from the CFLN.

The key issue, as ever, was the political one. When Monnet arrived in Washington, "the British and Americans had agreed that they would determine the Civil Affairs arrangements for France among themselves and instruct the military authorities without reference to the CFLN". This opened the way to the ultimate humiliation, from the CFLN's point of view, of being treated like the ex-enemy, Italy, and "occupied" by military government. It was the very danger Monnet had been sent to avert. Bad was made worse by the fact that the British and Americans had already reached agreement. Reversing it would be an uphill task.

Yet at first all went well.

As a quasi-insider, Monnet could exploit at least two favourable factors. The first was that he knew where decisions were really made and who made them. He dealt directly with the Combined Boards on which he himself had sat in 1942. He was in effect talking mainly to old cronies: McCloy at the War Department, who chaired the Combined Civil Affairs Board and its subcommittee for France; Oscar Cox, formerly of the Lend-Lease administration and now the General Counsel and main force in the new Foreign Economic Administration (FEA); and Dean Acheson, who had become Assistant

Secretary of State for economic affairs. Though he was also in close and constant touch with the British ambassador, Halifax, Monnet's concentration
on this inner circle tended to cut out London. There was suspicion of his
motives in Whitehall, relayed to Algiers by the CFLN's representative in
London, Pierre Viénot. It was only allayed when the British conceded that
basic supply decisions should be taken in Washington and only execution
handled in London, where General Eisenhower, the Supreme Commander,
had set up his headquarters.

The second favourable factor was the logic of the situation on the ground.
Eisenhower, who had to face the practical problems of fighting through
France, was convinced by mid-January 1944 that operations there would
require the CFLN to administer all but the combat zones. As Alphand
reported later to Algiers,

> military factors led Messrs Stimson and McCloy as well as General Eisen-
> hower to this view. . . . During a short trip to Washington, General
> Eisenhower stated them to the President. After several meetings which M.
> Monnet attended unofficially (at no time did the French representatives
> raise the matter officially), it was decided that Mr. Stimson should
> approach Mr. Hull [Cordell Hull, the Secretary of State] . . . who stated
> that the State Department would not oppose recognition . . . but that the
> matter must be put to the President by the Secretary for War. . . . For
> the first time, the State Department displayed benevolent neutrality
> towards the Algiers Committee. . . . Mr. Stimson saw the President; who
> asked that a draft of a joint Anglo-American declaration be prepared. . . .
> The draft was drawn up by Mr. McCloy . . . and handed to the President
> around February 10. A telegram from Eisenhower in London backed it up.
> . . . All the British ministries and the Prime Minister, all the technical
> American departments, including Mr Hull's office, wanted a prompt set-
> tlement of the question.

In short, by early February 1944, the whole Anglo-American establishment
below the President, including Churchill, was recommending that the
CFLN be treated in the planning for the invasion of France in a way that
implied *de facto* recognition. In three months, the huge Anglo-American
decision-making machine had been turned round one hundred and eighty
degrees from the original preference for handling France like the ex-enemy
Italy to the CFLN's vision of relations between Allies. Alphand, who took
part in the process and observed it at close quarters, wrote in his diary for
January 23: "Jean Monnet amazes me. It is he who drafts the memoranda
handed to the President of the United States, he who incites Eisenhower to
send telegrams to shift the balance in our favour. . . . I will be the only
Frenchman to know how much we owe him in this phase of the war".

Monnet unwisely concluded the time had come to read de Gaulle a lecture on the way to handle Americans. On February 12, he announced that

the negotiations on the recognition of the CFLN are on the point of succeeding. . . . By discussing purely technical problems, such as those of supply, the currency and credits, we have been able to make the American administration understand the necessity of recognising the authority of the CFLN in France; never by asking formally for recognition as such. . . . A journalist has just asked the President in the most inopportune way, in his last press conference, if he can envisage any revision in the American attitude to us. The President answered that "one cannot talk of a revision, only of an adjustment" . . . This instance illustrates the anxiety of the administration not to appear to be eating its words. . . . These results are due in large part to the will displayed, both by the CFLN and by the Consultative Assembly, to restore democratic institutions in a liberated France.

This was a scarcely veiled sermon on the superiority of Monnet's "low posture" approach to the General's "high posturing" confrontations. Democratic innuendo was thrown in for good measure. What de Gaulle thought of it all the record fails to say. In any case, the deaf ear to be wary of was less in Algiers than in the White House. Monnet had over-rated Roosevelt's goodwill, or his readiness to be cornered, or both.

The months of Purgatory now began.

Quite simply, the President refused to follow the advice of his administration and the British. He never actually said no. Desmond Morton "told me"—in London—"on March 7th", Alphand wrote in Algiers in his review of events of March 21, "that the famous draft was floating on the President's table in a sea of papers, and that every time it surfaced, the President, without a word, plunged it back under the layers, a game which could go on for ever". The whole episode is an instance of the extent and the limits of Monnet's power to influence American administrations. By his contacts, he could swing the government machine around. But if the President was determined not to listen, there was nothing he, or his American friends, could do.

By March 10, Monnet's tone had changed completely. He addressed a wail of anguish to Hopkins. "When we last talked on the telephone, the French question seemed on the way to be solved. Well, since then the situation has deteriorated. I am at a loss to understand the reasons. In fact, very soon I will not know what to do. I am wondering whether I have not made a serious mistake in not seeing the President myself. The reasons were that I did not want to bother him and also did not want to discuss the problem with him without your guidance". No reply is recorded.

A week later, Roosevelt took refuge in one of those half-measures so typical of his dealings with de Gaulle. He left it to Eisenhower to decide what civil administration he should deal with behind the fighting zones in France. Algiers passed through anxious moments, but Eisenhower had no practical alternative to dealing with the CFLN. The result was a statement by Cordell Hull, recently the most anti-Gaullist voice in Washington, that the Allies would deal with the Comité as the civil authority in France "under the control of the commander-in-chief". Monnet, who kept in close touch, demurred at the last clause, but was told it was not the end of the process. Though the *i*'s were not dotted, nor the *t*'s crossed, this was all but recognition. In reality, Algiers had won its tortuous struggle with Roosevelt. But there would still be a price to pay.

Hostility at the top of the pyramid of power was bound to filter down. McCloy was almost dismissed at one point by Roosevelt because he was not hard enough on the CFLN. On another occasion, he felt he had to defend himself from the charge of being "too subject to the blandishments" of Monnet. Monnet's own attempts to negotiate the terms of emergency supplies for the French part of the so-called military Plan A for liberated areas were frustrated by the refusal of the Combined Boards to let him know what they were prepared to supply. He had put in a proposal on behalf of the CFLN in January. In mid-April, he had still received no schedule of possible deliveries. The reasons alleged were plausible enough. Monnet understood the stumbling block had been a British refusal to envisage Allied supplies to civilians outside the combat zones. In fact, the Combined Chiefs of Staff feared, not for Monnet's ear, that the French might leak information and give the Germans vital clues to the landing in France. At the receiving end, and even without knowing all the private conversations, it was all too easy to see this as one more form of discrimination. On April 21, Oscar Cox and Eugene Rostow (then at the State Department) talked to the head of the Foreign Economic Administration (FEA), Leo T. Crowley, "about Jean Monnet's threatened resignation. Monnet apparently feels that adequate supplies are not being obtained for us in metropolitan France upon liberation". At last, on April 28, after a talk with James Dunn, who was in charge of the European desk at the State Department, Monnet reported to Algiers that it was "now possible to establish plans". A great deal of time had been lost, and little remained.

In the end, the storm broke on D-Day over the currency issued to the Allied troops in France. It had been agreed long before not to issue pounds or dollars, to spare French feelings, but that left plenty of room for trouble with francs. If the apparent authority on the bills was French, this would imply recognition of the CFLN. If it was the Allies, it would seem to proclaim a military occupation as in Italy. When Monnet arrived in Washington, the State and War Departments were proposing to issue a military currency without reference to the CFLN.

Persuading Stimson, the Secretary of War, to persuade the State Department and Treasury, Monnet began to turn the situation round. In a telegram dated December 8, 1943, he reported that the U.S. Treasury had prepared two designs for the currency, the one bearing the inscription "Interallied military currency" with a French flag flanked by the British and American ones, the other labelled "French Republic" on both sides and making no mention of the Allies. On January 8, 1944, Morgenthau and McCloy submitted the design labelled "République Française" to Roosevelt, who was ill in bed. Roosevelt quibbled vigorously. "How do you know what kind of a government you will have when the war is over? Maybe it will be an empire; maybe we'll have an emperor again". FDR even claimed that "de Gaulle is on the wane". Morgenthau and McCloy came back to Monnet. He repeated that "République Française" was crucial to differentiate Allied from Vichy bills. The issue was fundamental. They said they would try again, "but we are subordinates".

On January 15, in a telegram addressed to Mayer for de Gaulle, Monnet reported that the first order for bank-notes was being placed. They would bear the amount in francs and the words (in French) "Issued in France, series 1944" on the face; a tricolour with "Liberté, Egalité, Fraternité" on the reverse; and a blank square to add "French Republic. Public Treasury" (in French) *if* the CFLN became recognised. The bills made no mention of the Allies. They leaned to the French side of the argument, but Eisenhower was to issue the currency. As Edward Stettinius, the Acting Secretary of State, wrote later, "While the representatives of the [CFLN] . . . were not pleased with the decision that General Eisenhower was to issue this currency, they nevertheless accepted it". The "representatives" included Pierre Mendès-France, the CFLN's Commissioner for Finance, who came to Washington in May 1944. This seems to have been the one time Monnet and Mendès-France worked seriously in tandem.

Characteristically, it turned out that de Gaulle did not feel bound by his ministers' menial commitments. Called from Algiers to London on June 4, only two days before the landings in Normandy, de Gaulle was asked to broadcast a statement in support of the Allied currency being put into circulation behind the lines. Outraged, he refused. He alone had the right to issue such a proclamation. The Allies' bank-notes he referred to contemptuously as *vignettes* (labels) and as "counterfeit". Churchill and Roosevelt exchanged suspicions that "this currency issue is being exploited to stampede us into according full recognition to the *Comité*. . . . Prima donnas do not change their spots". Massigli told Murphy that if Monnet had approved the Allied currency, he had exceeded his authority. Mendès-France told Murphy that if he had seen de Gaulle, he could have moderated the response. De Gaulle reproached Mendès-France for failing to deny the Roosevelt version of the money quarrel and wanted him to instruct clerks in French banks to refuse to honour the Allied notes. Morgenthau said that "if this man de Gaulle throws us down, then . . . Jean Monnet . . . should be kicked out of Washington. . . . And I don't give a God-damn what the State Department or the War Department says".

Everyone behaved in character, and equally in character, de Gaulle won the battle. The event which transformed the situation was his brief but triumphant visit to the Normandy bridgehead on June 16. The rapturous response from the crowds relieved him of any anxiety that his popular support inside France might be less complete than he claimed. He seized the opportunity to appoint prefects in the French tradition and snatch the local administration from under the noses of the Allied command. The needs of the invading Allied forces also worked in his favour, as Eisenhower, McCloy and Stimson had foreseen they would. As early as June 26, three weeks after D-Day, negotiations on the civil affairs agreements had reached a stage where the French were recognized as the issuing authority of the Allies' "supplementary francs". In early July, de Gaulle paid Roosevelt a superficially cordial visit at the latter's invitation. He forbore to raise the issue of recognition. Nevertheless, on July 11, the day de Gaulle left, Roosevelt, in a press conference, conceded the *de facto* authority of the "French Committee" in liberated mainland France. This was confirmed by the civil affairs agreement signed on August 25, the day Paris was liberated. Even this was grudging, though. Roosevelt still refused to note that the CFLN now called itself the Provisional Government. It was only on October 22 that fear of independent British recognition induced him to rush in and recognise it before the British did.

Despite his airs of injury, de Gaulle knew all along what was in the wind. Cables on the monetary issue had been going back and forth between Monnet and Mayer for months, many of them for de Gaulle's personal attention. Mayer had given several reports in sessions of the CFLN. It is clear that de Gaulle, seeing he could not win by orthodox means, bided his time and made the loudest possible fuss when he knew it would most embarrass Roosevelt. It was the riposte of his "high posture" to Monnet's premature sermon on the "low" one four months earlier.

The difficulties in Washington seem to have sapped Monnet's position on the CFLN. Already at the end of March, Alphand, now back in Algiers, noted that

> the disappointment here, in the wake of the hopes raised by the press, by our friends and by our telegrams from Washington, is pretty deep. The General shows the greatest indifference. . . . I explain at length the discussions we have had to de Gaulle, Massigli, Queuille, Gouin [Félix Gouin, the socialist chairman of the Consultative Assembly], the Russians

and the British. I point out to them how justifiable it was for Monnet and myself to reach the conclusion the issue had been settled.

There are signs of irritation with Monnet in Mayer's journal at this period. At the end of June, de Gaulle sent Monnet a curt summons to return to Algiers "to give account".

Monnet stayed in Algiers for two months. During that time, Alphand accompanied de Gaulle to Washington; Alphand negotiated the agreement on civil affairs in France with Eisenhower and the British in London; and on September 9, when the Provisional Government (GPRF) moved to Paris, Monnet was dropped from the only French government of which he was ever a member. So were eight others, and the ministry was widened to bring in people from the Resistance in France. Nevertheless, when Monnet went back to Washington in September, still as commissioner-at-large, he was no longer a minister in government. Mendès-France, though also implicated in the currency row, was kept on. Soon after, Monnet was also dropped from the Economic Committee.

It is tempting to see this as what in royal courts used to be called "disgrace". It was clearly a setback. Yet Monnet's failure, if such it was, had been relative compared to his long list of successes in drawing the Allies away from initial policies that really would have been disastrous from the French point of view. Had de Gaulle been lying in wait for the chance to make him a scapegoat? Monnet had shown his independence, which was in itself provocative. He compounded this with ties to the Americans and the presumption to lecture de Gaulle. The chance to cut down to size a man who was no liege may have been too good to miss.

At the same time, one discerns limits to the fall. De Gaulle's laudatory letter of dismissal can perhaps be discounted as the art of sacking people. More substantially, Monnet's plans for carrying on talks with Washington on civil imports into France were endorsed by the GPRF. He was also sent to negotiate these and Lend-Lease with the Americans, on terms which made him more than an ordinary high official. He was appointed, largely (and as usual) at his own suggestion, chairman of a Committee for Imports. Administratively dependent on the Ministry of Economic Affairs under Mendès-France, then Pleven, this was responsible for keeping a continually updated "balance-sheet"—again!—so that import needs could be reassessed as circumstances required. In fact, during the last year of the war, the label "Monnet plan" did not have its current significance, but referred to his import schedules. In November, he dropped the chairmanship of the Committee for Imports to concentrate on negotiating Lend-Lease with the Americans. But neither his function nor his degree of independence seems to have been much affected by these variations. As we shall see, he still had de Gaulle's ear. In short, the year from autumn 1944 to autumn 1945 saw a distinct sag in his career. It would strain the evidence to present it as a fall.

Monnet also continued to have an exceptional entrée to the top decision-makers in Washington. When Mayer, then Minister of Communications, came to Washington in January 1945, Monnet arranged for him meetings with Hopkins and McCloy and offered dinners for him with the Morgenthaus, Frankfurters, Claytons (Will Clayton was the new Under Secretary of State for Economic Affairs) and Robert Patterson (McCloy's colleague as Under Secretary of War). The wary respect of the Morgenthau diaries confirms his location at the heart of things. Presenting Mendès-France to Morgenthau in May 1944, Harry Dexter White wrote, "He is sincere; he has a rather simple mind you know, compared to Monnet. Monnet gives you the impression of being very shrewd—one of the fellows you want to nail down everything while he is around". Morgenthau said, "There isn't a smarter fellow in town than Jean Monnet". Clayton added, "You know Monnet, how freely he circulates, and how quickly. . . . It's extremely difficult to keep anything from him because he gets around and talks to so many people".

III

IMPORTS AND LEND-LEASE

By the time Monnet reached Algiers, at the end of June 1944, the Allied bridgeheads in Normandy were established. Events were moving beyond the political issues of the previous year, even recognition of the GPRF. The main issues now were material: supplies for the civilian population in countries weakened successively by defeat, the pernicious anæmia of German occupation and the fighting to free them; and the means to pay for emergencies and reconstruction France could not finance itself.

These too had been the subjects of long and sometimes hard bargaining since 1943. In Algiers, the French, following up on work by the Gaullists in London, had prepared quite elaborate plans for emergency supplies to the liberated areas. The motive was as usual partly political, to display self-reliance and maximise American help while minimising American tutelage. In practice, though, plans were difficult to draw up. The main problem was to predict the conditions in which the Germans would withdraw. Would they collapse or resist a long time on French soil? How much of it might they control? Would farms and factories be left relatively intact or would the victors find "scorched earth"?

Despite all these uncertainties, by early October 1943 Monnet's Commissariat for Supply and Reconstruction, as it had become by then, had drawn up a notion of priorities. First should come pump-priming to make the best of the production capacity that existed; then longer-term reconstruction. A month later, it became clear that, as indeed the CFLN intended, UNRRA would not be the source of emergency aid for France. A prior category—relief (*secours* in French, which also means "first aid")—was slipped in ahead of the other two, to make henceforth three stages. This fairly obvious frame was realistic enough to persist. In fact, the whole of French reconstruction, from the depth of Algiers to the edge of the economic miracle of the mid-1950s, can be quite neatly fitted into it.

On the first point, civilian relief, Monnet's team had drawn up a precise shopping list before he left Algiers late in October 1943. They aimed at basic imports for a three-month emergency program from "November 1943 to January 1944" of about 900,000 tons a month (a rate about 30 per cent of prewar imports). The bargaining with the Allies in Washington finally produced a slight cut in total supply, drastically stretched out over six months, in effect halved. However, the Allies would take care of port, road and rail repairs needed by the military and guarantee water and sewers for towns over ten thousand people and gas and lighting too for those over thirty thousand. At this low level of expectations, the supplies were supposed to meet the basic needs of the population in the worst case, assuming the Germans left only "scorched earth" behind them in their retreat.

In fact, the Allied breakthrough in 1944 was so rapid that France's industrial and agricultural potential was left largely intact. Instead, there was an unforeseen collapse of transport. As Monnet put it in a report, "The Germans prepared for a long defence and occupation of all the major ports of France; and in this they largely succeeded". Without the pre-fabricated Mulberry jetties, which provided temporary docking space, the Allies could never have launched their offensive. As it was, the Allied breakneck advance in the autumn of 1944 came to a halt at the German borders in part through lack of petrol.

According to Mendès-France, Monnet convinced de Gaulle it was necessary to clear the ports. De Gaulle immediately saw this as a chance to launch a strictly French military operation where the new armies could win their spurs. But the forces besieging the "Atlantic pockets" were poorly armed *maquis* fighters, and the ninety thousand Germans held out until the 2nd Armoured Division (also French) turned up in April. Between the Allied landings in Normandy in June and the following spring, the total imports of non-military supplies for France, of all kinds, including coal and oil, averaged about one-fifth of the Allies' planned levels, at a starvation rate of 4 per cent of what they had been prewar.

The railways and roads inside France were largely destroyed by Allied bombing and sabotage by the Resistance. Most of the bridges over the Seine and Loire rivers were down. Ninety per cent of lorries were out of action. Only one in six locomotives worked. It was impossible at first to move enough wheat from north to south, where the shortage was most acute. The most vulnerable areas, mainly Paris and the south, were kept going, but the winter was very severe. Material conditions became worse than under the German occupation. In the towns, the average food supply fell to 1,500 calories, a little over half what is usually estimated necessary for health. Incidence of infantile mortality rose, and almost forgotten diseases, like typhus, diphtheria and dysentery, made a reappearance.

Since the near-vacuum for imports lasted nine months, the six-month programme lost all point. Monnet absorbed it in a new "Emergency Programme", negotiated with the Allies, which became known as the "eight-month plan". Drawing on bitter experience, this was based on the gradually growing amounts that the Allied Supreme Headquarters (in full: Supreme Headquarters, Allied Expeditionary Forces, or SHAEF) calculated the ports would be able to process after the military had helped themselves. Unfortunately, the German Ardennes offensive in the dead of winter made military demands soar again. Docking-space became free on the required scale only when the eight-month programme was supposed to be past midway. By that time, in April 1945, the French had managed, with some difficulty, to shake off the military controls over shipping and imports, as well as the SHAEF bureaucracy, which Monnet condemned as "ineffective and irritating". Communications now improved rapidly, because the German pockets at the ports were cleared and military needs began to wind down.

Significantly, the "eight-month plan" had a rather different focus from its six-month predecessor. Its aim was not just to provide basic sustenance and health. It was to acquire a minimum of raw materials to keep industry and workers employed. This was proving a major social problem. One fifth of the prewar workforce off the land was partly or wholly unemployed, even though a second fifth was in Germany. The plan provided for imports on average of 20 per cent of prewar levels, composed (apart from coal and oil) one-third of food, one-third of raw materials for industry, and one-third of items for production on the farms. Lacking all provision for machinery, this was designed to prevent economic and social breakdown, not to initiate reconstruction. All the same, it clearly moved over part of the way into the area that Monnet, in the tidier expectations of Algiers, had called "pump-priming" *(remise en marche)*. It was therefore a natural progression that, well before it was completed, it was largely superseded by the major economic development of the winter of 1944–45, the signature, for the first time and in the nick of time, of a full Lend-Lease agreement between the United States and France.

The "modus vivendi" agreement of 1943 only applied to the imperial territories administered by the CFLN. Since the United States did not recognise the CFLN as a provisional government, there was no precedent for Lend-Lease to France itself. This was what one might call the Roosevelt obstacle to an agreement. There was also a second one, from the U.S. Treasury. This turned on the fact that the Bank of France had managed to keep its gold and foreign exchange reserves out of the hands of the Germans. The visible part of this treasure was in Dakar. The invisible part was held as private deposits by Frenchmen in the United States. Together, the amounts were estimated to total some $3 billion to $4 billion. Paul Leroy-Beaulieu, the French financial attaché in Washington reported that Morgenthau and Harry Dexter White "consider this hoard of gold rather shocking". What Leroy-Beaulieu did not know was that they also thought "it would be easier for the President around the peace table if they [the Allies] were broke". The British had had to exhaust their reserves before being accorded Lend-Lease. Why should the French escape? While they had all this money, they would have to pay cash on the nail for civilian goods. The French could hardly subscribe to this puritanism at their expense. Their store of gold and foreign exchange was large in a ledger and a drop in the ocean of need. By 1943, the principle applied to no one else. They felt it was one more proof of ill-will to the CFLN.

When Monnet first arrived in Washington from Algiers in late October 1943, he found that the administration had already taken a decision that in any new agreement the CFLN should pay from its gold hoard, even for military items. As with all similar cases, Monnet managed to have this giant backward step reversed. But, he reported early in April, "the attitude of the Americans to Lend-Lease is becoming increasingly restrictive. . . . They have already made the British pay for the greater part of their industrial equipment". The prospects for what he was really after, American help in funding an investment program, seemed poor.

However, late in April 1944, they were transformed by provisions inserted into the Lend-Lease agreement with the Russians to make it possible to supply industrial equipment on long-term credit on easy terms. Acheson hinted to Monnet that similar loans might be made available to the French. On the eve of returning to Algiers, at the end of June, Monnet informed the CFLN that the State Department and the FEA were about to recommend to the President a $2.5 billion Lend-Lease agreement with the French, of which the core would be credits for industrial equipment. Such equipment could be delivered at any time until three years after the expiry of Lend-Lease. This was an important concession. Lend-Lease was due to end with the war, which might mean the war in Europe, and this was patently near.

Roosevelt himself read the main terms of the agreement to de Gaulle when the latter came to Washington in July 1944, or so Alphand claimed. American sources denied it, and the War and Treasury Departments still had to speak up. De Gaulle had hardly left when, on July 20, McCloy handed Alphand, who had stayed behind, a new text of the Lend-Lease agreement. This cut industrial credit on easy terms by three-quarters and required that the French should pay cash for non-military supplies, including relief. The Treasury had shown its hand.

The French refused to discuss these terms. In the civil affairs agreement signed in London the day Paris was liberated, they obtained an American promise to negotiate a Lend-Lease pact. On September 8, back in Washington, Monnet saw Roosevelt and rolled the rock up the hill once more. He pleaded for "industrial items to get French production going again for the maintenance of the civil population". Three days later Hull sent Roosevelt a memorandum saying that the official U.S. position of July 20 meant "in effect a rejection of Monnet's program" and that he did "not think you intended, nor would I recommend, so flat a position". His conclusion was that a list of items deserving long-term credits should be negotiated.

Unfortunately for the French, this was the period of Morgenthau's peak influence with Roosevelt. At the Anglo-American summit conference in Quebec in September, which Morgenthau attended but not Hopkins, the Morgenthau Plan for Germany and the Lend-Lease agreement with France were both raised with Churchill. Churchill took strong exception to the latter on the grounds that it would give France better terms than were being discussed in the negotiations with Keynes on a long-term postwar loan for Britain. Morgenthau suggested that Lend-Lease for France should be "indefinitely postponed", and Roosevelt concurred.

The prospects looked bleak for the French. The end of 1944 was very late in the war, and since Lend-Lease was to cease with the fighting, the chances of getting cheap industrial credits for reconstruction looked dim. However, experience of the lamentable state of France in the winter of 1944–45 made an impression on SHAEF and in Washington. SHAEF realised that "this situation" had "in it the seeds of the greatest difficulties, not only for France but for the war effort of the Allied armies on the front". The State Department became anxious about the political stability of the country. The German Ardennes offensive also made it possible for the FEA, handling Lend-Lease, to argue that France was "the great advanced base of the Allies in the war against Germany". Recognition was no longer an issue. On January 8, 1945, Oscar Cox for the FEA, at a meeting with Will Clayton, now the Economic Under Secretary of State, and Harry Dexter White, promoted the thesis that a "master-agreement" on Lend-Lease should be signed with France on terms similar to those for Britain and the Soviet Union. By mid-January 1945, the War Department took the same line. On January 19, Roosevelt, in a Cabinet meeting, approved negotiations.

On January 26, Monnet reported a "long, very cordial and frank" talk with Morgenthau in which Morgenthau said he "fully understood our difficulties" and asked Monnet to stay a few days more to complete the details. Even then, though, the Treasury held up the agreement to make sure that French cash payments were tied up first. On January 31, 1945, the *New*

York Herald Tribune carried an accurate story based on contacts with "several high [U.S.] government officials". This was that Monnet had booked his air passage home to Paris to report the failure of his mission over "differences on whether France should pay part cash for civilian Lend-Lease goods" and over the unwillingness of the military to release ships for civil supplies. This does not suggest Monnet meant to walk out; rather that he realised his bargaining position had greatly improved and that a forcing bid could at last produce a breakthrough.

And so it did. On February 28, 1945, a Lend-Lease agreement was signed. It provided $2.575 billion, a sum far in excess of the $1 billion for all American supplies previously made available to France. It was qualitatively much more favourable as well. $1.675 billion in current supplies of food and raw materials, which France had previously paid for in dollars, now came under Lend-Lease. The remaining $900 million consisted of equipment and machinery for reconstruction, officially for prosecuting war. As Monnet had made clear to the GPRF the previous July, this was a legal fiction to provide France with funds on concessionary terms. The French had to pay 20 per cent of the price on delivery, but the rest was to be reimbursed on very favourable terms, over thirty years at 2.375 per cent interest. It was pointed out by Paris critics that the agreement provided only 70 per cent of the industrial credits asked for. But Mendès-France, now Minister for the National Economy, after some hesitation, pronounced the agreement "fully satisfactory", and Pleven, the Finance Minister, called it "unhoped for". After about eighteen months of hair-raising negotiation, the search for American aid for civil supplies to metropolitan France had reached a substantial conclusion.

Agreement came just in time but produced a powerful reaction in Congress, which it "struck . . . like a bombshell". The Republican and conservative Democrat minority were fiercely critical of "the blank check era" which "ought to end with the cessation of hostilities". An amendment introduced into the Senate to prohibit Lend-Lease agreements for postwar reconstruction, that is, of the French type, was only rejected by the casting vote of the vice president, Harry Truman. Congress did not want to be "taken for a ride" by wily foreigners with a begging bowl. It demanded more and more visible returns on largesse. Suggestions that loans should be made against bases became more insistent. Pressure for free trade to open foreign markets to American exporters was exerted.

Moreover, in May, only three months after the French Lend-Lease agreement, the war in Europe did end. The French were lucky that the new president, Harry Truman, did not annul Lend-Lease there and then. But when Japan fell, Truman, as a recent ex-senator highly sensitive to congressional opinion, cut off Lend-Lease abruptly with effect from September 2, 1945, six months after it had come into operation for the French. The risk was known and Monnet had warned the French ministries to put in their orders quickly. Still, the advantages of Lend-Lease were not enjoyed to the full. On October 29, only $1.465 billion of contracts were in the pipeline or could be paid for on deferred terms. New money would have to be found for goods not formally ordered by September 2. Recognition in Washington of the difficulties resulted in a $550 million loan from the Export-Import Bank which Monnet obtained on Lend-Lease terms in December.

IV
LEND-LEASE AND THE MONNET PLAN

The sudden end of Lend-Lease did not stop the need for dollar credits to ravaged Europe but threatened to turn off the tap of supply. That the emergency was not a surprise hardly reduced the problems posed.

A minor consequence, but one which immediately occupied Monnet, and for at least two months, was rather odd in light of the record. This was the reorganisation of the French Supply Council in Washington, which had been built up since autumn 1943 and now had five hundred officials. Monnet, though the effective chief of French economic diplomacy in America all that time, had steered well clear of administration and had used the Council but had not run it. Indeed, the Council had been set up in October 1943 as the joint emanation of six of the Algiers commissariats, including Mendès-France's for Finance, Mayer's for Transport and Monnet's own for Supply. The man who established and led it till the end of the war was the financial attaché Christian Valensi, who, like so many others, had briefly worked with Monnet at the beginning of the war and for him in Algiers. But when, with the end of Lend-Lease, the Council had to switch from dealing in the bureaucratic mode with the U.S. administration to direct commercial contacts with American suppliers, Monnet (clearly still the authority though no longer a minister) stepped in. He may well have been helped by Pleven's taking over from Mendès-France as Minister of Finance and Economic Affairs. Valensi concentrated on representing the Ministry of Finance. In his place at the Council, Monnet put Léon Kaplan in charge, one of his close collaborators since the Liberation, who later became a director of French Shell. The most striking decision was to assign three of the main operational posts immediately beneath Kaplan, economic planning, communications and the legal counsel, to Americans. The legal counsel was George Ball, whom Monnet had first met as the legal assistant to Oscar Cox at Lend-Lease and then the Foreign Economic Administration. Ball came fresh from the survey he had carried out, with John Kenneth Galbraith, Paul Nitze, the poet W. H. Auden and others, to assess the effects, or lack of them, of

Allied strategic bombing on the German war effort. His appointment was supposed to be temporary before he set up his own law firm. But Monnet, anxious to keep Ball's services, arranged that he should have a retainer from the French government. It was the beginning of a long, varied and close association between the two men, culminating under Kennedy.

The basic issue, though, was that the money which flowed so freely for war through Lend-Lease would have to be raised for reconstruction by entirely new means. In late August, just before Lend-Lease was shut off, de Gaulle turned up in Washington, invited by Truman. Monnet did not accompany him to the White House, but on August 23, the two had a long talk. This is the occasion when Monnet's *Memoirs* recount he told de Gaulle: "You speak of greatness . . . but today the French are small. There will only be greatness when the French are of a stature to warrant it. . . . For this purpose, they must modernise—because at the moment they are not modern. Materially, the country needs to be transformed". According to Monnet, de Gaulle was deeply impressed by the power and prosperity he saw round him in America and did not try to conceal it. "You are certainly right", de Gaulle said. "Do you want to try?"

Whatever had been in Monnet's mind before, this was the genesis of the Monnet Plan. It was not devised for its own sake, but for strictly practical purposes. The aim was to draw up a large prospectus to justify access to more of the dollars that Lend-Lease no longer provided. There is no record of Monnet's conversations with Americans on the subject, but there is evidence that some of those with whom Monnet was close thought along similar lines. Will Clayton told the head of one of the French purchasing commissions in America, André Armengaud:

> Be liberals or *dirigistes*. Return to capitalism or head toward socialism. . . . But in either case the government must . . . formulate a precise program proving its desire to give France an economy that will permit it to reach international production costs calculated in man hours. If it . . . demonstrates to us the seriousness of its program, we shall help your country, for its prosperity is necessary to peace.

Monnet's main proposal was no hand-to-mouth expedient. On September 23, 1945, *The New York Times,* reporting a Monnet trip to Paris, stated that de Gaulle had specified to correspondents in August that two programmes, one immediate, the other long-term, were intended.

This is confirmed by a number of documents of September and October 1945. They show Monnet distinguishing clearly between a stop-gap like the loan from the Export-Import Bank and much larger credits to deal, as he put it in a letter dated September 24 to Clayton, with the "longer range problems of reconstruction and modernisation". However, at this stage, while his aims clearly foreshadowed the Monnet Plan to come, there was no hint of a plan as such. The search for funds arose as a natural extension of the emergency aid for France he had been negotiating ever since he first went to see Roosevelt before the war. In fact, the Monnet Plan before Marshall aid in 1947 was an extension of the politics of Lend-Lease at least as much as Lend-Lease was a preface to the Monnet Plan.

Just as striking as Monnet's motives was his convergence with de Gaulle. For all their temperamental incompatibility, the embodiment of French nationalism and the roving internationalist both now agreed, explicitly that France must have a plan of rejuvenation and implicitly that only the United States could furnish the means. It was perhaps the purest note of harmony Monnet and de Gaulle ever struck. They started the plan together and de Gaulle sponsored it as a major national effort. It probably fitted his image of himself as the spiritual heir of the kings, who cared for all their subjects above party. The irony is that the closest identity of purpose the two men ever reached should have been over a scheme inspired by the need to raise dollars.

Rebirth of France
THE MONNET PLAN
1945—1952

Monnet brought his family back to Paris early in November 1945. He had not been there much for over a decade. But from now on, apart from three years in Luxembourg, the long, low, thatched house, Le Carrefour des Buttes (The Crossing on the Mounds), set at the top of a field with a few trees, was the settled family home. He bought the house from Ivar Bratt, the prewar director in France of SKF, the Swedish ball-bearing firm. With franc inflation, the payment in Swedish money melted away: "just enough to buy a grandfather clock", according to Bratt years later. The hamlet of Houjarray the house stands in is at the edge of the forest of Rambouillet, twenty-seven miles west of Paris. In the late 1950s, Brigitte Bardot came to live on the farther side of the green, much to the alarm of the seekers after quiet already installed there. They need not have worried. She wanted to be alone even more than they and erected a skyscraper palisade against cameras in trees.

Although in retrospect the sequence of Monnet's self-imposed tasks seems entirely natural, there are hints that as the war ended he passed through a period of uncertainty about his future. How to re-enter French life was a problem. The conversation with de Gaulle at the end of August settled the issue favourably. But had it not, the options could have been quite different. Monnet refused at least one tempting offer from Wall Street and clearly had no intention of going back into business, least of all with his old partner Murnane. But his late, brief assumption of the presidency of the French Supply Council could have been a safety net. He himself stated that "because of his preoccupation with the future of France in Europe", he toyed with the idea of standing as a parliamentary candidate in his native Charente. He was approached by Léon Jouhaux, the veteran Socialist Secretary-General of what was then the single General Confederation of Labour (CGT). But he soon gave up the thought. He reflected a little ruefully that he lacked the temperament. "I should have liked to be an orator; I was not. As a young man I longed to be a boxer. . . . My temptation to engage in politics at this late stage resembled my youthful ambitions. . . . At the same time, . . . I was beginning to see quite clearly what I could usefully do. . . . If there was stiff competition around the centres of power, there was practically none in the area where I wanted to work—preparing the future". This was an earthy version of de Gaulle's remark that one should make for the heights, as it was less crowded there. It was also shrewd in terms of the Fourth Republic after the war. The most famous of its twenty-four premiers in twelve years was probably Pierre Mendès-France, and the most powerful perhaps Guy Mollet. They held power for eight and sixteen months, respectively. Monnet the planner had the ear of government for at least seven years.

For an office, Monnet first took a couple of rooms in the Bristol Hotel, in the rue du Faubourg St. Honoré, between the Elysée Palace and the British embassy. He called for help on his recent associates, Marjolin, Hirsch and Félix Gaillard, a budding politician from his own region of Charente. They used even the bathroom as a workplace, with a wooden board spread out on the tub. This was less eccentric than it seems. The hotel was requisitioned by the government. It was also heated, and most ministries were not. "The three of us", Hirsch has written, "produced the report in a month". It was not a plan as such but a concept and procedure for producing one. "We worked literally night and day. We consulted a host of people, but above all we talked among ourselves". Thus began the feverish improvisation and debate that were to mark much of the First Investment Plan, better known as the Monnet Plan.

It is not clear how Monnet's partly focussed preoccupations of mid-October 1945 turned into the framework for producing a plan in early December. There was plainly a logic of events pushing in that direction. But one of his distinguishing marks as a pragmatist was a reluctance to miss possible options by rushing to supposedly obvious conclusions. At first, his main concern was to make the most of as many dollars as he could get. This could well have led to the type of general loan Keynes was then negotiating in Washington for the British. On the other hand, the British economy, though run down as a result of the war, was a going concern. The French, which had suffered a longer depression in the 1930s, and now had fewer resources and greater need, was largely obsolete. This, and the intellectual influence of Robert Marjolin, Monnet's main technical adviser and a planner at the time, certainly favoured commitment to a plan. Unfortunately, the point of crystallisation cannot now be determined.

At this distance, November 1945 looks like peace-time barely hatched. In fact, Monnet turned up in Paris rather late in the day. Though he had planned urgent imports since 1944, he had not taken part in the broader debate on planning the economy before, during or after the war. Mendès-France, who saw him in America in the summer of 1945, said that "the odd thing is he did not like plans". And by the time he came on the scene, the idea of a plan had already been rejected once and was on the point of dying. Indeed, the first question which has to be asked about the Monnet Plan is why it was not the Mendès-France Plan.

In the war-time debate over the future, the idea had emerged of a giant ministry to mobilise the material energies of the nation. It would be focussed on the real economy, not on money like the traditional Finance Ministry. Reformers, during and after the war, held the Finance Ministry in great suspicion as a bastion of the conservative policies on which they blamed the economic decline of the 1930s. When the first post-Liberation administration was set up in Paris in September 1944 (and Monnet was dropped), de Gaulle appointed Mendès-France Minister for the National Economy (Economic Minister). Two months later, on November 23, 1944, the Interministerial Economic Committee approved Mendès-France's proposals for the ministry, which gave it very wide powers. A sketch for a plan was presented to the meeting. This looked out across a vast eleven-year panorama. In 1945, the economy should be allowed to pick up as it could. The next two years, 1946 and 1947, should work to fairly precise targets taken over from the Vichy technocrats. The time gained would then be used to perfect the eight-year sequel, the plan proper. These ideas were never fully taken up. Still, a plan was on the agenda a year before Monnet became involved.

Why then did de Gaulle encourage Monnet in August 1945, having let Mendès-France resign as recently as April, a month before the war in Europe ended? One reason was certainly that Monnet concentrated on a single objective, his plan. For Mendès-France, it was part of a triple programme of monetary reform, industrial restructuring and nationalisations. The most controversial panel of Mendès-France's triptych was monetary reform to soak up the latent inflation in the country. This risked, amongst other things, alienating the peasants, still a third of the workforce, who, for once, had had the economic whip-hand of France under the Occupation and prospered on the black market. No one cared to offend them. When de Gaulle stalked out of government in January 1946, it was the Left, the Socialists and Communists, who vetoed Mendès-France's return as Finance Minister, for fear of his austerity policies. De Gaulle could have weathered such opposition in 1945. But there was still no constitution and the state had no formal basis. De Gaulle was more concerned with the war, with establishing the authority of the state and with popular legitimacy than with risking complications. Mendès-France went, and the prospects of his plan went with him.

Second, Mendès-France pressed his programme as something desirable in itself, which invited controversy. Monnet stifled doubt by putting up his plan to meet a crisis. This was Truman's abrupt termination of Lend-Lease.

France had lost more than a quarter of national wealth in the war, and its infrastructure was barely functioning. In such circumstances, dollars were a blood transfusion. They were necessary to keep the economy going and to reconstruct the country and beyond that to reverse the economic decline that seemed a fitting prelude to the collapse of 1940. None of this could be achieved in anything like an encouraging time-scale without dollars. Neither de Gaulle nor the Communists, later notorious anti-Americans, disputed it. By arguing that the only way to persuade Congress to part with dollars would be to present a good long-term programme, Monnet took the plan out of the area of ideology into that of crisis management. It is significant that his first act once the plan administration was set up in January 1946 was to leave for the United States to raise a loan. He was still months away from a finished plan.

The relatively late timing in the winter of 1945–46 is also explicable in terms of the priorities of the regime. It had no formal or legal title until the elections of October 21, 1945, to elect a Constituent Assembly empowered *inter alia* to draw up a constitution. The major economic reforms of the postwar period, the nationalisations of banks and insurance, energy agencies and basic utilities, as well as the investment plan and the extension of social security, all came between October 1945 and May 1946. The Monnet Plan, in short, came in its place in the definition of the political and economic system after the Liberation.

Third, Monnet's pragmatic attitude to planning allowed him to side-step the bureaucratic traps sprung on those who preceded him. His covering letter to de Gaulle for his proposals in December referred to his "method" in a way which suggests it was central to the two men's talk back in August. "I have tried," he wrote, "to express the ideas we discussed". The contrast with previous approaches could not have been more striking.

The draft decree presented by Mendès-France to the Economic Committee of the Council of Ministers on October 9, 1944, a month after the return from Algiers to Paris, typified the approach before Monnet. The Economic Committee, presided over by de Gaulle, was to propose all economic decisions to the government (the established procedure). The Economic Minister, Mendès-France, was to be the vice chairman and economic overlord (an innovation). His ministry, responsible for the overall direction of economic policy, of preparing the plan and of supervising its execution, was to have authority over all the sectoral economic ministries. It was even to overlap with the Ministry of Finance on monetary policy, credit, prices and exchange rates. The minister could also establish any interministerial committees he thought fit. As a marginal comment on a note prepared for the Economic Committee pointed out, this gave the minister the potential to short-circuit the Economic Committee and by implication the head of government himself.

Naturally, this assumption of power aroused general resistance. François Tanguy-Prigent, the Socialist Minister of Agriculture, wrote a letter which was no doubt solemnly meant but reads like parody. "Personally" convinced of the need of all the functions the Economic Ministry claimed to fulfill, he proceeded to extract, with care, every tooth which might have made the plan bite. "Agriculture cannot agree to be treated as a minor ministry". Years later, Mendès-France wrote that his plan had been "killed by the opposition of the Ministries of Finance, Industry and Agriculture". If one is to believe a letter of Monnet's, this was an understatement: the Ministries of Transport, Posts and Colonies all rejected the authority of the Economic Ministry. As Monnet wrote

> I have had occasion in the past eighteen months since the Liberation, during which I have worked with all [the ministries], . . . to note how much time and energy have been frittered away in sterile disputes . . . over questions of competence, areas of authority and powers to act.

There was to be no economic overlord.

Authoritarian assumptions ran too deep for the lesson to be readily assimilated. In September 1945, the Ministry of Industrial Production, under the Socialist Robert Lacoste, published a brochure asserting that it would henceforth seek "to implement a truly directed economy". Yet as *The Economist* pointed out, "even the most elementary facts and statistics are not available". In January 1947, Monnet sent a letter to André Philip, then Economic Minister, pleading with him to withdraw a decree to "enforce" production goals. "To publish such a threatening regulation will again antagonise the producers. . . . They will drag their feet, and the administration, having delivered itself of a verbal broadside, will be unable to follow through".

Monnet took a different line. "Do you think anyone will ever hand you power on a plate?", he asked someone who wanted the backing of a formal decree. "What you have to do is convince people. If you do, you will have produced a plan. If you don't, there won't be one". He side-stepped competition with ministries by not making claims. The High Commissariat he first proposed (renamed a month later the Commissariat General of the Plan) was to be an agency and its chairman not a member of the government. It was to have no operating or administrative powers or investment budget. It was simply to draw up the classic Monnet "balance-sheet" in consultation with all the relevant interests, and to produce a plan. Nothing was said about life beyond the document.

Monnet's proposals of December 6, 1945, duly rested on a broad consultative approach. "All Frenchmen" were concerned, so that "all the vital forces of the nation should take part in elaborating the plan". Employers, cadres, workers and experts should sit on "modernisation commissions" along with the bureaucrats, and there should be the widest diffusion of results. There should be one such commission per economic branch or function judged to merit the plan's attention. The Monnet Commissariat would prepare the guidelines for these commissions and draw the overall conclusions from their work. It would recommend priorities to the Council of the Plan, which was to consist more or less of the government in its economic guise, along with experts and representative employers, cadres and workers. There was to be no plan decreed from above, but a "concerted" effort of the responsible parties. This was felt and proclaimed to be democratic—as indeed it was, given the practical alternative of state centralism.

Monnet's approach succeeded in launching the plan. In the Economic Committee of December 14, the Economic Minister (another one!), the Communist François Billoux, noted that "the cooperation between all the interested parties is safeguarded by the temporary character and structure of the commission" whereas "competition between the ministries would certainly lead to failure". On January 3, 1946, a decree established the Commissariat General of the Plan (CGP) to produce the plan in six months. Monnet claimed a short while later that he had no difficulty obtaining from the departments the data stubbornly withheld from the Economic Ministry.

However, he was not naïve. Careful not to tread on ministers' toes, he was determined they should not step on his. His frequent criticisms at this period of the incapacity of ministries to plan were designed, amongst other things, to repel any efforts to control him. The decree of January 3 put the CGP directly under the head of government. Monnet's *Memoirs* stress that he insisted on this through many a threat to resign.

Gaston Palewski, the head of de Gaulle's staff, has testified that he himself first suggested the CGP should be attached to the head of government. The aim was to provide a counterweight to the Communist, Billoux, at the Economic Ministry. A French historian, Philippe Mioche, has drawn the conclusion that Monnet's independence of ministries was an accident due to "the progress of the Communist party" at the general elections of November 1945. However, the background favoured such a solution in any case. Queuille's difficulties in Algiers were fresh in the memory. A note, written probably by Alphand, pointed out that "constant appeals to the authority of [de Gaulle] alone made it possible to introduce . . . a tolerable working discipline". The need to rely on the head of government was familiar to anyone in the field. Georges Boris, Mendès-France's main planner, argued the case publicly in September 1945. Such arrangements were also nothing new to Monnet. He habitually stuck as close as he could to the source of power.

The result was a supposedly self-effacing approach perfectly tailored to Monnet's strengths. The understated manner was a sign of self-confidence, not of modesty. His independence protected his access to the top. He did not seek the trappings of office, because so long as he could talk to ministers, he could count on his powers of persuasion. For the rest, he relied essentially on giving a lead and on having a strategy when tactics absorbed others. In reality, he not only believed that action matters more than status, he knew that it generates greater momentum.

He also picked an exceptionally able team. Monnet's main helpers at the CGP included Gaillard, a future "youngest prime minister" (at the age of thirty-eight); Marjolin, later one of the founders of the Common Market; and Paul Delouvrier, who was to become de Gaulle's Delegate-General in Algiers during the Algerian War. All these had moved on by mid-1948. Hirsch, who took over from Marjolin, stayed and became Monnet's successor as head of the CGP. Prewar, he had been a manager in a large chemical firm. He was (and is) a short man of calm exterior, dry humour and passionate convictions. He played quartets in the family circle. From early 1947, there was also Pierre Uri, the economist, a brilliant analyst and unfailing source of ideas for the CGP and later for the Schuman and Common Market treaties. He too stayed on. All these and their colleagues formed probably the most creative team in Paris, "the envy of the ministries". As for Monnet, Delouvrier has remarked, "he barely had a school certificate and dominated the lot of us".

The CGP was ostentatiously unbureaucratic, set up in an informal townhouse unearthed by Palewski. It had belonged to Ambroise Vollard, the art dealer and friend of Cézanne. It stood at 18, rue de Martignac, on one side of a quiet square almost closed at one end by the church of Ste. Clotilde, where César Franck was once the organist. Around the corner was the Prime Minister's office, the Matignon. The way the CGP's apparently inconvenient corridors and staircases wandered in and out of each other positively encouraged contact between the inmates. It was also impossible to expand in it, and most of the staff worked in quasi-attics. To this day, the CGP has remained tiny. Under Monnet and Hirsch, it never acquired more than a hundred people, down to the last secretary and chauffeur, a fact in which both took enormous pride. Monnet's desk was a large trestle table. All this was flaunted as a badge of initiative, speed of response and hard work. The contrast could hardly have been greater with the Ministry of Finance, where the size of the Louis XV–style bulbous green ormolu clock on the mantelpiece was a joke—one key status, two keys better—but not one to laugh at too heartily.

After the war, according to Delouvrier, there was "a kind of exhilaration at being liberated and at the same time an intellectual void". Another young reformer of the time, Libert Bou, has contrasted the "enormous clouds of hot air at the Liberation" with Monnet, "who knew precisely what he wanted . . . and when he needed to know more, listened". A third, his chief of staff,[1] Jacques Rabier, has said, "We knew how rich his imagination was and how determined he was to finish anything he started. He did not have subordinates but members of a team". Bou added that "they were a disinterested bunch, which was rare in the bureaucracy". Monnet made them feel they were plugged in to reality at a higher level than their peers elsewhere. As Uri noted, "I had direct access to ministers". The senior staff of the CGP operated as policy commandoes, revelling in improvised responses to one urgent problem after another, often ahead of the ministries supposedly in charge. They were not overawed by technical expertise, and they advanced by a dialectic of trial and error and debate. They did not win all the battles. But they had the morale of a corps of trouble-shooters who despise uniform.

Inevitably, this created tensions. Robert Lacoste, the Minister of Industry for over three years in seven governments, at one time forbade his staff to go to Commissariat functions. On one occasion, he burst out, "Monnet takes the decisions and I have to pick up the pieces". Pierre Pflimlin, one of the Ministers of Agriculture, a kingdom in its own right, sought to launch a domestic French Green Plan at least in part to recapture ground from the CGP and because he thought the proper place for planning was in the ministries. Jules Moch, an important Socialist who was Minister of Transport for a couple of years, suspected Monnet of dark political ambitions. These two were leading lights in the parties supposedly most committed to the plan. The planners in their extra-territorial station never went unchallenged.

Monnet was correspondingly careful to keep on close terms with successive incumbents of the key Ministry of Finance. With an old associate like René Mayer, relations were relaxed. With Robert Schuman, they were not at first so free. In fact, Georges Bidault, who was Foreign Minister when he was not Prime Minister in most of the earlier years of the Fourth Republic, has claimed there were considerable strains when Schuman was at Finance. Monnet nevertheless built up a relationship through Schuman's chief of staff, Bernard Clappier. He got on well with Queuille, though Queuille, a Radical (i.e., conservative), was credited with the remark, worthy of the young Queen Victoria's adored Lord Melbourne, that "no problem is too intractable to resist an absence of decision". Relations were more variable with the long-lasting Maurice Petsche, a Moderate (even more conservative than a Radical). Even these, François Bloch-Lainé has claimed, consisted of "laughable fallings-out followed by mutual seduction scenes".

The rapport with Bloch-Lainé—the son of Jean-Frédéric Bloch-Lainé, who helped transfer France's arms orders in America to Britain in June

1. The French title rendered here and elsewhere in this book as "chief of staff" of a minister's private office is *directeur de cabinet*. *Chef de cabinet,* which might seem to correspond more closely, is in fact only the administrative head of the office.

1940—was just as important as with any minister. Ministers (even Petsche) came and went. Relatively, Bloch-Lainé went on for ever. As Director of the Treasury, the holy of holies in the Ministry of Finance, he was the *primus inter pares* of the top officials. The plan attracted Bloch-Lainé because, uniquely, it offered a lead on a vital issue facing the country. Disillusioned with nationalisation, Bloch-Lainé came to feel close to Monnet's team instead. They for their part regarded him, one of them has said, as "not always an easy friend *{long pause}*, a friend, nevertheless". This was crucial. Tensions between the CGP and Ministry of Finance were inevitable. Bloch-Lainé could have created endless trouble. His support often tilted the balance.

Finally, great weight was laid on the twenty-four Modernisation Commissions (eighteen set up in 1946 and six more in 1947) dealing with the sectors and functions covered in the plan. Monnet agreed with the authors of the report of the Commission for Steel that "however carefully a plan has been worked out, it will be effective only to the extent that it has been thought through and adopted as their own by a broad enough swathe of the people involved". The "main credit" for the plan, the CGP claimed,

> must go to the method employed. Collective effort, and consultations before all decisions, overall views constantly brought up to date and known to all, these are the essentials.

CGP documents constantly drew attention to the "thousand people" drawn into planning through the Modernisation Commissions.

In April 1962, Sir Robert Shone, who had been appointed chairman of the National Economic Development Organisation (NEDO) in London, came to pick Monnet's brains on planning. Monnet made three points of which two are relevant here. "The key to success", he said, "is to get Labour on your side. When you then proceed to influence government, industry is isolated and has to follow. . . . Moreover, an industrialist, or politician for that matter, behaves better when a trade unionist is present, even if the trade unionist never opens his mouth". The other trick of the trade concerned appointments to the commissions. It was necessary, he said, to have men of standing in their industries or unions who had no formal mandate to speak on the latters' behalf. Instead of being the advocates of an interest, they then became genuine instruments of communication between government and practitioners. "I spent at least half my time finding the right people".

The effect of such sophistications is hard to assess, but it was not all myth. At one session of the Steel Commission, the deputy rapporteur, who was the deputy director of the steel division in the Ministry of Industry, resigned. His director asked that his successor should take his place as if this went without saying. But the commission chairman, a steelmaster himself, pointed out, with finality, that Monnet chose all the rapporteurs. It could be argued that Monnet's right of appointment fell down when it came to the ministries because the relevant directors appeared in all the commissions. But the ministries too had to compromise. Claiming implicitly that planning was their prerogative, they wanted to chair the commissions. Monnet refused. It was agreed that ministerial directors would be vice chairmen, but the chairmen and rapporteurs would be appointed by Monnet, and the secretaries would be members of his staff. So long as the chairman and rapporteur were worth their salt, and had good relations with the planners, authority was diffused, with the CGP to some extent a referee.

Together, the end of Lend-Lease, the need of dollars to reverse the economic decline that seemed a fitting prelude to 1940, and finally Monnet's methods, may seem sufficient, even pressing, reasons for launching the Monnet Plan. The timing too seems natural in the light of other events. However, a second view has been expressed by Frances Lynch in *The Political and Economic Reconstruction of France 1944–1947, in the International Context.* She argues that planning, which failed to attract a consensus when promoted by Mendès-France in the war, was suddenly made acceptable to the establishment by Truman, Churchill and Stalin at the Potsdam Conference of July 1945.

> The French became painfully aware that . . . the Allies were preparing to reconstruct Germany along lines which could endanger French security. . . . An effort had to be made to ensure that the French economy would not only be reconstructed before that of Germany but would also be assured of resources which had formerly been controlled by German industry.

This prompted the view, the argument runs, that French steel (as the supposed key to all industrial power) must expand on a diet of Ruhr coke till it largely replaced German steel. Even the Versailles treaty had not hoped to reverse roles like that. However, Mendès-France himself wrote in March 1945 that replacing Germany as a manufacturer of steel was a French war aim. The idea clearly lay behind his own plan. It was nothing new several months later. Potsdam may perhaps have given it fresh urgency. Alphand, now Director of Economic Affairs in the Foreign Ministry, gave it an airing during the conference. But an ambition of such scope could hardly vanish and revive within weeks. Monnet's proposal cannot have depended on it. By the winter, other needs had become just as urgent and closer to hand.

II
THE PLAN

France at the Liberation was, as J.-C. Asselain has written, "animated well beyond the parties of the left by anti-capitalist feelings the intensity of which is hard to conceive today". Private enterprise was widely felt to have failed the country before the war. Employers had lost "all sense of creative risk", as Philip put it. Many had collaborated with the Germans under the Occupation. De Gaulle in person told the "privileged classes" they had "disqualified themselves". The investment everyone recognised was needed "had to take place on the initiative and under the control of the state". In any case, at first, the authorities alone had the capital.

Sectoral plans galore were being hatched in Paris at the end of 1945. Raoul Dautry, the Minister of Reconstruction, complained that each ministry and industry was preparing one as an excuse to demand as much material, credit and labour as possible. Georges Boris, the chief planner under Mendès-France soon after the Liberation, caustically suggested that "one of these days the silk manufacturers will announce a five-year plan to furnish every Frenchman with half a dozen silk shirts". Coal, power dams, railways, merchant shipping, machine tools, cars, agriculture and the war damages authority, all had plans. The trouble was, Monnet pointed out, they "are incompatible as soon as one adds them up". The Monnet group's function was less to invent a plan than to fix priorities and focus scarce resources, relate partial targets to general needs, encourage necessary programmes not emerging of their own accord, and clear the obstacles to action—in a word, coordinate. Otherwise, given France's recent history of economic restriction and lack of self-confidence, the risk was, as Monnet stressed, of the French economy prematurely "crystallising at a low level" once again, with the lobbies agitating "not to renew the instrument of production but to be protected".

For Monnet, indeed, the plan was above all "a method" of mobilising people for collective effort. He had to be argued into a specific target by Marjolin and Hirsch. He wanted to launch a process, not to be nailed down to a figure or to prophecies. "The important thing is to make a solid start". In the end, he reluctantly accepted that people had to have an apparently precise goal. Marjolin defined this as the output needed to propel the country into self-sustaining growth by 1950. The planners told the first session of the Council of the plan on March 16, 1946, that this would be attained with a national output in 1950 a quarter larger than that of the champagne year of 1929 and a half over that of the depressed last full year of peace prewar, 1938. These were orders of magnitude. There was no true plan as yet.

Such aims could be presented as fairly modest. Even if they were met,

France would still lag far behind Britain. In fact, they were immensely ambitious. They required a qualitative change from the patterns of the previous fifteen years. Since 1930, the economy had failed to provide the investment even to renew equipment. Then had come the war. Material damage had been far greater than in the first war and income from investments overseas had fallen steeply. To get growth going meant compensating for all these failings and losses while finding fresh resources for exports and investments, all this in a setting of dire consumer shortages. Achieving it in five years implied investing some 30 per cent of national income per annum for an annual growth rate of about 11 per cent. East Asian countries have touched such levels since. At the time, there were no precedents.

Significantly, the first activity of all, in the period from January to March, was to prepare a bid for the third loan from the United States in little over a year. This was to be the largest. Monnet told Clayton that France would matter as much to American policy in Europe as Britain. Its needs would justify a loan on the lines of the one Keynes had just signed in December for Britain. He informed the American financial adviser in Paris, Ivan White, that he wanted some $3 billion for three years, or some three-quarters of the projected uncovered deficit. Since the deficits were assumed to fall steeply thereafter, he hoped in effect to secure the dollar needs of the plan-to-be virtually for its entire span.

The French sent a strong delegation to Washington for the talks, which began on March 25. The political head was the veteran Socialist leader and premier of the Popular Front government of 1936, Léon Blum, whom Monnet much admired, but the latter handled the negotiations. Unfortunately, whereas both the British and French were riding a rising tide of need, they found the Americans on an ebbing tide of willingness to lend. Keynes complained that he could have obtained $5 billion without difficulty at the beginning of the U.S.-British talks in September 1945 (having asked for $6 billion), but by December he was having a hard time holding the line at the $3.75 billion he finally obtained. With the end of the war, the U.S. Congress was reverting to type, as a political market-place where favours are exchanged, not doled out. It was becoming increasingly economy-minded. Why should American taxpayers subsidise Allies to win markets from American traders? Polls in June 1946 showed the American public 48 per cent to 38 per cent against the British loan. Congress took seven months to ratify the loan agreement and then only on condition it set no precedent.

The U.S. administration was acutely aware of Communist parties in France and Italy, near-starvation in Germany and refugees stranded in central Europe. Lessons from the First World War were absorbed. Allied debts run up under Lend-Lease were virtually cancelled. But the United States designed the postwar loans to put Europe on its feet so that it could fairly soon run itself. Everyone, Europeans included, under-rated Europe's difficulties not so much of recovery as of adaptation to new circumstances. There was certainly not the sense of crisis that propelled Lend-Lease before and Marshall aid a year later.

Reacting to its own prewar protectionism, the American government insisted on an open world economy the Europeans were not strong enough to face. The loan to Britain was made conditional on the instant convertibility of sterling. This was a major factor in the crisis of 1947, when Britain ran out of loan dollars that were supposed to last till 1951. France accepted the principle of free trade, but Monnet won the key concession that this would follow, not precede, "modernisation". The French did not seriously begin to lower trade barriers until the Common Market, thirteen years later.

On the other hand, Monnet brought back from Washington nothing like the money he had hoped for. Britain was to be unique. The Sterling Area coloured a quarter of the globe a non-Soviet red. It was a pillar of a free-trading dollar world. All that and 1940 deserved a premium. The Secretary of the Treasury, Fred Vinson, stressed that "with no [other] country . . . [are] we attempting to supply funds . . . to meet a pluriannual deficit", which was exactly what Monnet had hoped to obtain. The French loan would have to be settled in the routine way from the funds Congress had voted for the Export-Import and World Banks. These were limited, and the competition was stiff, including the Soviet Union and Nationalist China. Clayton and Jefferson Caffery, the U.S. ambassador in Paris, told the French they might get better loan terms if they modified their German policies which cut across those of America. The French ignored the hint, and it is not clear that Congress would have paid much for the concession.

American officials seem to have been impressed by the texts Monnet put before them. The experts suggested no major modifications. But they offered no endorsement either. They were nervous of the emphasis on investment, feeling political stability required more for consumption and housing. They feared the plan would be inflationary. They argued that the French had overestimated the foreign exchange required. They whittled down the net dollar deficit from the French figure of $3.3 billion to $2.2 billion. They then refused to fund the whole of the gap thus redefined. In a complex formula, clouded by uncertainties, such as the value of cut-price surpluses, the agreement of May 28, 1946, provided perhaps $1 billion of new money along with the prospect of a loan of $500 million from the World Bank the following year. (In the end, only $250 million was lent.) The French told the Americans all these funds together would be exhausted by the end of 1947. The talks which the French had expected to last a fortnight had taken over nine weeks.

Monnet returned early in June from Washington with only 30 to 50 per cent of the funds he had led Paris to expect. Schuman, as Minister of Finance, feared aloud in cabinet that the plan would be too inflationary to work. At least there was enough to start with. Characteristically, Monnet argued later (and at the time, according to Delouvrier, his Finance Director) that "once [the plan] was set in motion, its own impetus would create the internal and external conditions that were essential to its success".[2] In any case, there was little alternative. Investment was needed with or without the plan, and it made more sense to order priorities. "We were disappointed . . . [but] we carried on", Alphand has said. In any case, as Marjolin (briefly in hospital) informed Monnet early in June, "We now have all the elements of a five-year plan". Yet it took another seven months before the plan was effectively launched at the third Council of the Plan on January 7, 1947. Understanding of what happened in the interval suffers from the disappearance of most of the early archives of the CGP. Clearly, though, there were difficulties, and important developments occurred.

The key decision seems to have been to concentrate funds on a narrower front. The "basic activities", in retrospect so characteristic of the first Monnet Plan, were now officially singled out as such for the first time—coal, power dams, railways, steel, cement and tractors. The resulting programme was theoretically ill-balanced, but it restored credibility in the face of reduced resources. Monnet has been praised, by Billoux at the time for being practical, and recently by historians for a resilient response to setbacks. Members of Monnet's team remember the decision in different (not necessarily incompatible) terms.

> Marjolin laid on Monnet's table a fine report, summarised in tables which interlocked neatly. The logic was perfect, it was a real study in planning. Monnet read it. A week later, he summoned us. "My friends, this is a textbook. Send that to a politician and he will not make head or tail of it. . . . [Y]ou'll have to throw that into the waste-paper basket. We will have to think again about the points where we can get the process started. You will have to explain to the politicians and public opinion what the priorities are in ways they can understand".

Delouvrier believed "Monnet could have had twice as many dollars and he would still have chosen" the basic activities. "On that occasion", Jacques Van Helmont, then a young recruit, has said, "I learned the difference between an intellectual idea and one geared to action".

In fact, the priority for "basic activities" had really existed from the outset. The previous May, the Americans in the dollar loan negotiations noted that "the investment figures for coal mining, electric power, railroads, mer-

---

2. He wrote in the same vein later of the Marshall Plan that the five-year aid gap the Europeans estimated in 1947 at $29 billion was "artificial. . . . Forget the later years . . . the first year is the crucial one".

chant marine and the steel industry, representing about 40 percent of the total, are firm investment programmes for the industries concerned". These were the bulk of the "basic activities". The real point was that the manufacturing and consumer industries were now relegated down the queue for scarce resources. A little over half of all investment went in 1947 to the nationalised sector (energy and transport). The far larger transforming industries did not catch up in capital spending till 1951 and then only through the revival of private capital markets.

An even more drastic decision was to sacrifice housing to the infrastructure for production. This was really stringent, as anyone who recalls the antediluvian housing in France in those days will appreciate. Ironically, the draconian measure was possible because the minister in charge of housing was none other than Billoux. The Communist party was so wedded to the "battle of production" that in February 1946, it had backed a law subordinating the forty-hour working week to the needs of recovery. A *de facto* forty-eight-hour week was admitted in the dollar loan talks. This was an enormous concession, as the forty-hour week had been the sacramental working-class prize from the Popular Front government of 1936. The Communist now made another. The postponement of housing was settled with Billoux and never even went to Cabinet.

The support the Communists gave the plan in 1946 was crucial. Monnet's personal relations with some Communist leaders were good, notably with Billoux and with Benoît Frachon, the Secretary-General of the General Confederation of Labor (CGT). These went back to Algiers. Billoux and Frachon had led a group that had come to thank Monnet for freeing them along with other political prisoners, and Monnet had taken them out to lunch. Until the Cold War broke out, they came occasionally to his country house, which was almost unheard-of in relations between Communist and non-Communist leaders.

In November 1946, the CGP finally drew up its general report for decision by the government. There appeared now a four-, not a five-, year plan. One year, 1946, had already elapsed. There was no talk, as in the spring, of investing 30 per cent of national income a year. The proportion was now around 24 per cent a year. Moreover, firm appropriations existed only for the first year, 1947. Spending on the "basic activities" in this year fitted well into the supposed four-year timetable. But for others—agriculture, engineering and other manufacturing, distribution and housing, together demanding three times as much investment—the rates implied completion only in six or seven years. Had all the targets been held in the four-year time-frame, the budget would have been about 25 per cent higher than it was. One can take this as a rough measure of the shrinkage reality forced on the abstract aspirations of the spring.

The Monnet Plan, as revealed by its funding, aimed at a strong national base in energy and steel, seen as the foundations of industrial power. Ostensibly, this was not ideological. Several countries without basic industries, such as New Zealand or Switzerland, were held up as models of high living standards achieved by technical progress. Higher productivity must therefore be the supreme French aim. It was also stated that "our country is tied to international trade". Nevertheless, the argument that whatever happened the country would need fuel, steel and cement, was used to promote as high a self-sufficiency as possible in basic industries. The idea was put explicitly for steel. "All the big modern states (the United States, Britain, the USSR, Germany) produce all the steel they need". It followed that France must do so as well. So in the Monnet Plan, coal and hydro-electric power—French resources—were stressed against imported oil, and railways using electricity against cars running on petrol.

Mainly nationalised, the basic sectors tended to be ones where the managers had most initiative. Remarkable similarities have been noted in the targets for coal and electric power in the four general plans from that of the Vichy technocrats in May 1944 to the Monnet Plan in November 1946. Harold Lubell, an American economist in France at the time, stated that the coal and railway lobbies had at first over-estimated the demand for their products, while the power generators had been too cautious. This implies they more or less set their own targets. In such cases, this left the CGP mainly an enabling role. This did not have to mean an empty one. The industries' plans could be derailed by economic anarchy and lack of foreign exchange. Or the managers, who had a production not a marketing bias, could corner more resources than made sense. Either way, the CGP was a countervailing force. There was truth in the comment of a consultant that "the plan provides potent means to make a success of the recent nationalisations".

The plan had less direct impact on sectors outside the "basic activities" and investment industries. The CGP's relations with other branches were very variable. At one end of the spectrum, it never tried in any direct way to hold back sectors such as oil, pharmaceuticals and cars, which spontaneously found markets and capital to grow fast. At the other end, machine tools, with a host of small, often backward firms, none too happy to be caught up in anyone's planning process, failed to produce a report and protested when the CGP did it for them. A number of Modernisation Commissions lived up to their names and strengthened reformers against traditionalists. There was a touch of a generation gap. In the Steel Commission, there were several confrontations between the cautious leaders of the industry and their critics, including their own (relatively) Young Turks. The Monnet Plan, followed five years later by the Schuman Plan's common market in steel, began to press restructuring on the industry. One of its later leaders, a member of the Steel Commission, considered that the "impulse for change" came "from Monnet in particular and government in general". Ultimately, the emphasis of the CGP on growth and productivity contradicted the initial bias to self-sufficiency. In France, as in other countries, the attempt to build up protected home production required so many imports that attention soon had to turn to exports. This was to lead to common markets in Europe and ultimately much freer trade with the world.

A striking feature of the plan, implicit in its bias to self-sufficiency, was its fifth priority on "security". The defeat of 1940 was related to France's industrial weakness. Henceforward, Monnet argued, a country's war potential depended on its heavy and engineering industries. This might seem to be a form of obeisance to defence. On the contrary, it was used to claim that military spending should not be allowed to interfere with investment. Clearly, the military were a prime rival of the plan for public funds. Both in 1946 and 1947 Monnet pressed for cuts in the defence budget. At the same time, in the bargaining, he either came to share, or was driven to adopt, the French bias in favour of heavy industry for motives of industrial power. At the time, of course, the idea was fashionable in much of the world as a result of Soviet planning and of the Soviet victory over Nazi Germany.

In practice, this led to an emphasis on steel, the significance of which has first been emphasised by the economic historians Alan Milward and Frances Lynch. The basis for it was an equation summarised in 1950 by Monnet himself: "The core of the superiority French industrialists have traditionally conceded to Germany is its production of steel at a price with which they cannot compete. They conclude that the whole of French industry is handicapped by it".[3] Put like that, the Franco-German problem was stark, because French steel was dependent in at least one key respect on Ruhr supplies. The region of Lorraine, where two-thirds of French steel was produced, had been largely German between 1871 and 1918 and built up by the Ruhr barons. Lorraine had large reserves of iron ore, the Ruhr of coking coal, the two bulk materials of the steel industry. A partnership was natural. Nevertheless, whereas Lorraine had little alternative to Ruhr coking coal, the Ruhr increasingly used scrap and higher quality Swedish iron ore. Thus, in normal circumstances, the Ruhr had the upper hand in bargaining with Lorraine. But with Germany down and out after the war, France was almost bound to use its chance to haul out coke and coal from the Ruhr. Either way, abuse of power was virtually built into the situation, so long as nationalist assumptions prevailed.

3. The strength of German steel was (as now) the width, depth and quality of engineering, which gave it a massive domestic outlet. As early as 1950, German domestic steel consumption was 40 per cent higher than French. In France, engineering was weak. As late as 1955, official reports lamented that, far from being a motor of the French economy, it was lagging behind the growth in manufacturing as a whole. This tends to suggest that steel really served as the symbol for a wider sense of weakness.

Strong emotions were bound up in this. Normally, the Ruhr "barons" had only to ration exports of coke or raise prices and freight rates to establish a competitive advantage or even ration rivals' output. To the French bureaucrats in charge of steel, like the forceful Albert Bureau, it was axiomatic that the prewar cartel had operated in this way; and that the French industry had acquiesced in a subordinate position and low output because it had been allowed to milk high prices from its restricted home market. Ruhr coal and steel had been the engine of French weakness as much as of German strength. History must not be allowed to repeat itself. French supplies from the Ruhr must be secured.

"Supplies" meant coal in general and coke for the steel industry in particular. Prewar, France had been the world's biggest importer of coal. The Plan, looking back to prewar experience, relied on coal (along with hydro-electric power) as the fuel of postwar growth and on prewar rates of import of around 20 million to 25 million tons of coal a year. However, conditions changed after the war. Of the four main sources of coal prewar, Britain, Belgium and eastern Europe largely dried up as exporters, and Ruhr production lagged well behind target. The result was that the Plan's hopes of annual supplies of 10 million to 15 million tons from the Ruhr and 5 million tons from the Saar in effect meant forcing the Ruhr and Saar to disgorge. This did not seem strange in 1946, when the policy of America, as of every other Ally, was that Germany, having destroyed Europe by the war, should provide the resources for its reconstruction. But it was predictable that with every year the strain would grow. The Monnet Plan carried seeds of renewed conflict between France and Germany.

Despite that, there is no evidence that Monnet or the CGP shared the Foreign Ministry's ideology of turning France into the heartland of western European manufacturing by treating Ruhr resources as its own. There is no statement of Monnet's to compare with those of Alphand, Couve de Murville or Bidault, the longstanding MRP (Catholic Party) Foreign Minister. As late as July 1947 Bidault stated that "France, with the aid of Belgium and Luxembourg, can, if it receives enough coke from the Ruhr to increase its steel production substantially, meet all the needs of western Europe, including those of Germany". The nearest Monnet came to anything like that was in reply to a leading question from an American negotiator in the loan talks in Washington. He answered that "if France is to take the place of Germany as a supplier, it must have an adequate steel industry". He added that after 1950, the goal was 15 million tons of steel (against a rate of output of only 6 million to 8 million tons just before the war and 10 million tons in 1929); and that the French "would be in a position with modernisation and lowered costs of production to take a substantial part of German markets". That was commercially aggressive. It did not add up to supplanting the Ruhr. An official negotiator in 1946 could hardly say less.

In fact, being practical, the Monnet Plan for steel was comparatively moderate. The authors were aware of the limits the weaknesses of French engineering placed on steel. They aimed mainly to fulfil the industry's existing theoretical capacity (of around 12 million tons a year in 1946) by modernising its antiquated plant and structures. Talk of output of 15 million tons specified no dates (and was not achieved till 1959). Though *"grandeur"* was mentioned once, the effective goals of the steel plan were realistic, to supply the home market at competitive prices and exploit the industry's traditional export networks as an important item in foreign trade. Twenty-five to 30 per cent of production had been exported prewar. Postwar plans implied a similar proportion. From 1950 onwards this was consistently attained, mostly on overseas markets. The report was also fairly pragmatic in foreseeing that steel's dependence on the Ruhr could principally be reduced by technical innovation and by the railways and industry using less French coal, including potential coking coal. As early as 1948, coal production targets were cut to take account of competing fuels. By 1950, the advance of fuel oil and radical changes in coal consumption were beginning to ease the strain on the coke supplies to Lorraine.[4]

The policy of the Monnet Plan was, in short, to secure supplies of coke and coking coal from the Ruhr to underpin the promotion of France as a "normal" industrial power on the British or German model. Even this aim could conflict with a reviving Ruhr's own heavy industries using the same basic materials. The main reason was the failure of coal production everywhere in western Europe (except in France) to return to prewar levels, while steel plans all aimed at rapid growth. Moreover, perceptions lagged well behind any signs of new trends. Green shoots were small, and no one could count on their growing. So French efforts to hinder the revival of the Ruhr were fuelled by steel as the symbol of Germany's industrial potential. Yet the Monnet Plan's steel targets, if only because they were much closer to economic reality, never squared up to the diplomats' airy talk of France displacing the Ruhr in manufacturing. Interestingly, Hirsch, who worked closely with the authors of the steel plan, has denied firmly that this was an active CGP priority.

When the Monnet Plan appeared, six months late, the CGP had become

4. The plan of 1946 envisaged coal consumption in France of over 86 million tons in 1950. That year, because of slower growth than the plan had initially envisaged, recession in the first six months, and the shift to alternative fuels, coal consumption was only 58 million tons, a shortfall of 28 million tons, or more than total coal imports forecast in 1946. Average annual coal imports into France from 1948 through 1951 (excluding the Saar) were 13 million to 14 million tons, of which about 40 per cent came (expensively) from the United States. Imports of coke, mainly from the Ruhr, at 3.5 million tons to 5 million tons a year, were large but pretty stable. This was to be the case throughout the 1950s, while steel production rose two-thirds.

almost by default a permanent and autonomous body. The Economic Ministry made one last effort to absorb the Commissariat. Monnet parried it with one more threat to resign. On January 14, 1947, a government decree finally launched the plan, "the first attempt in postwar Europe to draw up a balance-sheet and overall programme for the future". It was a considerable achievement to have come even that far.

The plan was still an enormous gamble. About half the proposed investments for 1947 were funded only on paper. This was due not to a lack of dollars but of domestic French capital. Whatever (no doubt insufficient) capital there was had been driven by inflation into bolt-holes like Geneva. "While we propose to launch the greatest investment program in our history, real savings have fallen to zero", commented *Le Monde*. The formal reliance on "savings" in the plan for 1947 was window dressing. Short of a miracle, the plan would fuel inflation or have to be cut. Bloch-Lainé has remarked that "we jumped in with our eyes shut. Would anything have happened had we not?" This is almost certainly correct. Yet the Monnet Plan's very first months were to demonstrate just how feeble and exposed its financial flank was.

III

MARSHALL TO THE RESCUE

Everything came together in 1947. The Cold War came to a head with the failure of the Four Power Council of Foreign Ministers in Moscow in March and April. The main immediate cause was the Soviet-American clash over reparations from Germany, but the underlying one was control of its future. In April, too, in France, strikes flared up in the Renault car plant, the bellwether of labour relations. They spluttered on, like forest fires, unpredictably, all round the country for eighteen months, with one climax in November and another in June 1948. In May, the Communists were expelled from government. At first surprised themselves by the strikes, they gave some later ones an insurrectionary bite. Though the outbreaks never fused in one conflagration, external events were bound up in domestic turmoil.

The main symptom of disruptive forces and cause of chaos was inflation— as Van Helmont has said, "*the* problem for the whole of government and in every field". This went deeper than shortages. Most countries in Europe faced shortages, yet French inflation (like Italian till mid-1947) was on another scale. The special feature was weak government with strong roots. It suited a partly pre-industrial society, with relatively few wage-earners and many independent workers, peasants, shopkeepers, artisans, professionals of all kinds. Farmers, 30 per cent of the workforce, were virtually tax-exempt. Evasion in the rest of the population was estimated at a quarter of taxes actually raised. This was compounded by political tradition. In the later 1870s, there had been a struggle between the supporters and opponents of a strong executive, which the latter won. Government ever since had been dominated by a Parliament which embodied the politics of patronage. The effects on long-term planning may be imagined. In 1948, Harlan Cleveland, one of the authors of the Marshall Plan, concluded that "the French society and fiscal system do not now seem able to carry out a really large investment programme".

Inflation took off in the second half of 1946 and built up to a rate of 60 per cent a year in 1947, when drought dried up hydro-electric power. Factories went on a four-day week. Two hundred million dollars went on imports of wheat, against the plan forecast of $30 million. In August, the bread ration was reduced to two hundred grams a day (seven ounces), less than under the Germans. Prices of food, the purchasing of which represented over 40 per cent of working-class spending, shot up, and real wages failed to follow. Inflation sucked in imports and withheld exports. In America, too, dollar prices rose 40 per cent in fifteen months, eating into the purchasing power of the dollar loan of the year before. By summer 1947, France could only cover half of minimum dollar imports to the end of the year.

Monnet wanted a national government to tackle the emergency. There are letters of Monnet's in the summer trying (and failing) to keep relations going with Billoux and Frachon. In September, John Snyder, the U.S. Secretary of the Treasury, visiting Schuman, his French counterpart, to assess France's urgent dollar needs, was none too pleased to hear that Monnet was telling any American who cared to listen, including a visiting delegation of congressmen, that the Communists had been constructive in economic policy and should come back into government. Paul Ramadier, the Socialist Prime Minister, even had him investigated for being too close to Moscow! Some French officials still held this against Monnet when the Schuman Plan was launched. In fact, Monnet was beginning to realise the Communists were not to be wooed. The idea was dead by the time of the November strikes. Yet his sense of deep crisis lasted into early 1948, when he told the powerless but influential President of the Republic, Vincent Auriol, that "we must give this people [the French] some reason to hope. Otherwise they will die of lassitude and fear".

The factor which dissipated the gloom was of course the Marshall Plan, announced at a commencement address at Harvard by the Secretary of State, General George Marshall, on June 5, 1947. It came in the nick of time, for it took till the following May before shipments began to flow. With Italy and Austria, France was one of three countries unable to wait. They received "interim aid" from December. All the same, for planners and politicians, the worst was over by August, when sixteen West European governments attended the Conference on European Economic Cooperation [CEEC] in Paris. They no longer faced the abyss.

However, the Marshall Plan did not simply provide a smooth road bridge across the chasm. Being addressed to western Europe as a whole, it raised a number of uncomfortable strategic issues that had been largely ignored by countries, each working on its own account and remarkably ignorant of what neighbours were doing. For one thing, it threatened to fill the gaping hole in postwar Europe, the place of Germany. Western Europe's recovery was impossible without recovery in western Germany. At the end of July and beginning of August, Monnet held numerous discussions with the senior American in Europe, Will Clayton. Their intensive review of German policy led in the end to the Schuman Plan and is best considered in that light (see Chapter 6, below). But that was not the only issue. Since the United States saw western Europe as a whole and believed that the solution to its troubles lay in union, there was a year-long political debate over whether the system of allocating aid should be centralised in Europe or settled bilaterally between the individual European capitals and Washington. The whole question of sovereignty and integration was raised actively for the first time. Further, since Marshall aid needed a criterion, and the politically urgent as well as most practical one was the balance of payments deficit of each country, the issues which lay behind deficits had to be addressed. In particular, inflation, as an engine for creating such deficits, came under much fiercer scrutiny than before. These issues—Germany, centralised planning and inflation—were more explicit and acute in France than anywhere else, and Monnet was involved in all of them.

The Americans insisted that the west Europeans should agree among themselves on the amount of their collective request for aid to Congress. On July 18, 1947, Monnet sent Bidault a note arguing that to squeeze practical results quickly out of a rushed negotiation of so many states, the CEEC should set up a small five-man group, working together full-time, isolated from everyone else, with a tiny staff, until the conference report, a balance-sheet of aid requirements, was completed. This characteristic advice was followed in so far as a restricted executive body was established. The monastic rule of work was not. Bidault wanted Monnet to chair the executive group, but he refused. He said it would blur his responsibilities to the French plan. The CGP did, however, coordinate the ministries in Paris to prepare the French submissions for aid.

The same institutional issues came up in a more acute form in March 1948, when the Americans, in an attempt to sustain the political momentum of Marshall aid, insisted that the CEEC should be turned into a permanent Organisation for European Economic Cooperation [OEEC]. George Ball, brought in to help Monnet in this period, says that Monnet "heavily influenced" the French proposals for the OEEC conference opening on March 15, 1948. These do read like an uneasy compromise between national vetoes on general policy decisions and a more Monnet-style "constitution which will enable [the OEEC] to act with speed and effectiveness". The basic decision-making body was to be an "assembly" of government representatives deciding under the unanimity rule. But there were also to be a small executive committee of five national officials and an executive body headed by a Director-General. This two-headed leadership would act as an intermediary between the Americans and Europe in the fixing and sharing of aid and examination of investment plans. The Americans would have wanted to go further and limit national vetoes. If the scheme had gone through, it could perhaps have produced a dilute European version of a Monnet Plan. Most European countries, led by Britain, wanted neither planning nor limits on sovereignty nor middlemen meddling in their relations with the United States. The OEEC that emerged was predictably intergovernmental.

In March, Paul-Henri Spaak, the Belgian Foreign Minister, suggested to Monnet that he should chair the OEEC executive committee, and again Monnet refused. In the end, Spaak himself chaired the committee. Monnet did, however, suggest that his recent deputy, Marjolin, who became the first Secretary-General of the OEEC when it was formed on April 16, 1948, should have the *ex officio* right to initiate proposals. This prefigured one aspect of the European Community a decade later. But it was not much on its own and seems never to have been exploited to any effect in the OEEC.

The issue of the powers of the OEEC came up a last time in July 1948. The Americans, once the emergency of the first year was over, wanted the Europeans, for the second year, to produce a "long-term program" for Congress. The idea was to show they really planned to become self-reliant as aid tapered off from 1949 till it ceased in 1952. Here again, the Americans and Monnet wanted stronger institutions than the European governments would countenance. The Americans wanted the OEEC to allocate aid. Monnet wanted it done by a "panel of distinguished Europeans with no official governmental connections". Failing this, he proposed a small, high-powered executive committee of the representatives of the three major countries (France, Britain, Italy). In his mind, this was almost certainly meant as a spur to action. The French and British governments accepted it, with the addition of one small country, probably because it maximised their influence in an intergovernmental OEEC. After this last flicker, Monnet lost interest either in European planning or the OEEC. In later years, whenever he said of something that it was "an OEEC affair", he meant nothing would come of it. The verdict of Hirsch, who was much involved, is that failure to build a strong system "led to unrestrained competition . . . for as large a slice of the cake as possible". If that was the game, France would be no loser. "The existence of a [French Monnet] plan was a major asset".

This was true but with a proviso. French inflation was widely taken as a sign of the inability or unwillingness of the regime either to risk monetary reform or to tax the non-salaried classes adequately while fighting a colonial war in Indo-China and launching ambitious investment plans. If the French government failed to display better control of the economy, the plan itself would be penalised. Accordingly, Monnet took the initiative in tackling inflation. For a while, the CGP became a source of action across the whole range of French macro-economic policy. The second half of 1947 in particular was one of those periods when Monnet went into overdrive, with activities so diverse and far-reaching that it is amazing he kept a grip on them all. As one of the recurrent Ministers of the Fourth Republic, Pflimlin, referring to 1947–48, has written of an incident that concerned him: "I rapidly realised I had to convince Jean Monnet, who was the key man. Without participating in government he inspired its economic policies". On the occasion in question, "his influence was so great that the decision was taken without discussion".

Originally, Monnet thought inflation would cure itself once new output began to come on stream. Uri recalls him repeating (in American) "we'll railroad it through". The American emphasis in the dollar loan talks of 1946 on reducing inflation seems to have cast the first seeds of doubt. On his return, to double-check on Marjolin's work, he asked his old war-time associate Robert Nathan to assess the emerging Monnet Plan. Nathan was encouraging, but repeated the warning on inflation. Early in January 1947, the published plan stressed that prices must be "relatively" stable, budgets balanced and foreign loans not wasted by plugging holes in current spending. (Everyone would have been aware of the war in Indochina.) Monnet repeated the message in a covering letter sent to each member of the Council of the Plan. In February, he wrote to the Finance Minister, Schuman, that the current budget must be "on the road to a balance" to safeguard investment. In March, as he had done the year before, he tried to engineer defence cuts. But inflation had taken hold. Forty per cent of the 1947 plan was postponed, although the basic sectors were exempted. Inflation had now become a direct threat to the plan. As Monnet wrote in his *Memoirs,* "We had to fend off the criticisms of classical economists who regarded investment as the source of inflation, while winning over members of Parliament who would have preferred to give the public short-term satisfactions".

Monnet plied Schuman with proposals during the summer of 1947, and in the autumn the next Minister of Finance, René Mayer. As he wrote to the latter, "A substantial revival [of the economy] has already been achieved. . . . The essential [now] is to stop inflation". This resulted in October in the establishment of a National Balance-Sheet Commission to define the "inflationary gap". According to Uri, the source of the idea was Edward

Bernstein, a former U.S. Treasury official who was now the chief economist at the IMF and whom Monnet consulted. Monnet chaired the commission.

The normal procedure would have been to entrust an initiative as basic as this for macro-economic policy to the Ministry of Finance. But Monnet "had flair and good advisers", and was the first with ideas on how to tackle inflation. Some CGP staff were familiar with newfangled "Anglo-Saxon" techniques of national income accounting; the rest of the establishment were not. The CGP also possessed, in Uri, an economic one-man band eager to play a new tune. In less than two months, he ran up the first French national accounts, imperfectly, critics in the Finance Ministry later claimed, but as a pioneer, which no one contested. The report, delivered in December, duly defined a large "inflationary gap" of some 5 per cent of GNP, proportionately equivalent to the United States budget deficit of recent years.

The core of Monnet's proposals to Mayer of November 21, 1947, was to impose on the higher income groups a "levy", bringing in about half the "inflationary gap". Mayer, a decisive man, took over this and most of Monnet's suggestions in his stabilisation package. The privileged swallowed their medecine with much less fuss than had been feared. Unfortunately, the impact was frittered away in further political instability and strikes in the summer of 1948. The real turning point came in the autumn, when the Americans forced the Queuille government to raise taxes and the prices of nationalised services and openly threatened the National Assembly with loss of American aid if it failed to vote the taxes in. In the second half of 1949, to general surprise, inflation suddenly stopped. It was real ill luck, for once, that a year later the Korean War started it off again.

Though there were times, as in 1948, when investment was partly financed by inflation, in general it created debilitating uncertainty. Governments were always tempted to cut investment rather than current spending. Marshall aid became a protection against this, for a number of reasons. For one thing, it provided the foreign exchange Monnet had tried and failed to obtain through the loan of 1946. He admitted to Schuman in a letter from Washington in April 1948 that "it has now become possible to achieve the Monnet Plan thanks to Marshall credits", which said as clearly as possible that it had not been before. Marshall aid was also structurally biassed in favour of France. It was based on the dollar deficits of recipients. France had the largest. Indeed, the Monnet Plan's ambitions ensured that imports would remain high. France obtained even more American net aid from 1948 to 1952 than Britain, which had a much larger economy.[5] It accounted for more than a quarter of dollar deliveries of equipment to the whole of western

5. Net aid took into account not only direct dollar aid but also intra-European drawing rights.

Europe. Last but not least, a week after the Harvard speech, Marshall quoted the Monnet Plan as a possible model for the whole of Europe.

This was an invaluable endorsement. For it was not a foregone conclusion that Marshall aid should favour investment. Treasury Secretary John Snyder considered that counterpart funds should be used to reduce national debt and that to channel them to investment was inflationary.[6] Many policy-makers in Europe agreed with him. Further, in 1947, Washington thought the best way to fight communism in Europe was to flood the region with consumer goods and provide housing. On these assumptions, the Monnet Plan's determination to postpone the good life seemed socially and economically risky. Its rather Soviet concentration on basic sectors was not orthodox either. However, pushed by Monnet, the French negotiators in Washington succeeded in linking Marshall aid to the Monnet Plan. It dawned on the Americans that hindering French aims would create more problems than it solved. This was reluctantly recognised first on a provisional basis in the attribution of interim aid. Then after Monnet spent a month (March 20 to April 20) in Washington, trying (successfully) to raise the French daily bread ration from 200 grams to 250 grams—a key issue at the time—it was confirmed in the bilateral Franco-American agreement on Marshall aid of June 28, 1948.

At the working level, a telling factor in favour of the Monnet Plan was William ("Tommy") Tomlinson, the top Treasury official working with the Marshall aid mission in Paris. This was led by David Bruce, who was now embarking on what would be a career of great influence over American policies towards Europe. Tomlinson, an inspired bureaucrat, often outspoken and even rough, built up a unique relationship with Monnet. As Raymond Vernon has said, "The two of them were so central to the aid allocations, the special terms, the bilateral negotiations, everything else, that everyone watched with a mixture of envy, admiration and disconcertment. . . . The U.S. bureaucratic structure—the autonomy of the various agencies, the absence of a cabinet and not even the pretence that you can get consensus within this sprawling machinery—made people like that terribly powerful in policy-making". Tomlinson was a persistent influence in favour of the Monnet Plan in Washington. When he died in his mid-thirties in 1955, the French government, in a virtually unheard-of gesture, gave his American widow an official French pension. Tommy's photograph was the only one of a younger colleague Monnet kept on his desk. One sometimes felt he had almost been a son.

There was in effect a triangular alliance between Bruce and Tomlinson,

6. Governments acquired materials and machinery from Marshall aid. They sold them to their nationals, for which they received in return large quantities of pounds in Britain, francs in France, lire in Italy, and so forth. These sums which governments accumulated were the Marshall aid "counterpart" funds. Many experts held that they should be withdrawn from circulation by repaying government debt.

Monnet, and a few key officials in the Finance Ministry, especially François Bloch-Lainé, who saw to it that Marshall aid was used directly or indirectly to maintain basic investment. According to Arthur Hartman, later the U.S. ambassador in Moscow, who worked at the time with the Economic Cooperation Administration (ECA) mission in France, "The deal struck between Monnet and Tomlinson was that the Americans would not give their approval to any proposal which Monnet didn't feel fitted in with his plans. . . . People in the French Treasury were aware of it, and also used it to make sure that the funds were not used in a way they did not approve of. . . . We would insist on those conditions and in effect force the politicians to accept them".

In the end, the bulk of Marshall aid was channelled into the Monnet Plan. Marshall aid represented only 20 per cent of French investment from 1948 to 1952, but it was a crucial margin. In 1949, the peak year, when it became evident the policy was on balance succeeding, state funding influenced two-thirds of France's manufacture of investment goods, about a quarter of all industrial output, and Marshall aid was the larger part of this. It greatly loosened France's main external bottleneck, the inability to earn dollars. And aid offered a key to changes which France on her own might have taken far longer to achieve. For instance, large-capacity steel rolling mills, which only the United States produced, demanded plant and firms much in excess of the French norm, as well as broader markets. Only a reformed industry could tackle them. Without Marshall aid, the French, starved of dollars, could probably not have carried their intentions through.

The limit on Monnet's success in capturing Marshall aid was an institutional defeat at home. This too was related to inflation. The plan was barely launched early in 1947 before he told a meeting that "our aim" is to see the basic decisions "should not be called in question every year" in the budget debates, but "should be put in train quickly for the four-year period". This was not just technocratic. The Fourth Republic's domination by Parliament injected a permanent bias to clientelism, patronage, zeal for spending and reluctance to vote taxes, in brief, the shortest of short-term policies, which made it somewhere between maddening and impossible to pursue long-term goals.

Monnet wanted, therefore, an autonomous funding agency for the lifetime of the plan, to escape the annual manœuvres over the budget. He had a second motive, expressed to Shone in 1962. Planners must have a grip on the distribution of public funds to nationalised or subsidised industries. Since Treasury control of spending was poor, that was the only way to know what they were doing. The decree launching the CGP on January 16, 1947, gave the CGP the task of "seeing to" the plan's execution. Monnet soon complained he lacked the means.

The idea of a fund under CGP control (but not administration) cropped up in CGP memoranda in 1946 before the plan was launched. In a note of May 12, 1947, to Schuman as Finance Minister, Monnet pleaded that the counterpart of foreign loans should be fed, with other credits, into an autonomous fund. (This was before Marshall aid, but the French had of course already contracted dollar loans.) The aim was relatively modest, to guarantee investment in the basic sectors, which covered about a quarter of all prospective spending on the Monnet Plan. Monnet tried again in the autumn of 1947, when Mayer became Minister of Finance and took the CGP's Finance Director, Delouvrier, as his chief of staff. Early in January 1948, Monnet thought Mayer was ready to accept the independent fund and that he was home and dry.

In the end, though, probably because of the opposition of Bloch-Lainé, Mayer turned Monnet down. Bloch-Lainé either suggested to Mayer, or Mayer developed his own conviction, that Monnet and the CGP was one of the "baronies" which it was his mission, as a "strong" minister, to put in their places. The controversy dragged on throughout Mayer's tenure, towards the end of which Monnet uttered one of his periodic threats to resign. When Mayer left in July 1948, a decision had still not been taken.

As so often in the Fourth Republic, a settlement required the advent of a new government. In October, the Fund for Modernisation and Equipment was set up "provisionally" under the tutelage of the Finance Ministry. The Minister of Finance chaired the committee taking the investment decisions. The Planning Commissioner, however—that is, Monnet—had a right of initiative and counter-signature of decisions. Given the commitment of Marshall aid to investment, this was favourable enough. But it was not Monnet's idea of an "autonomous" fund, insulated from the annual budget battle and allowing the CGP to follow the use made of credits.

Monnet did not give up. He proposed in March 1949 to present the plan formally to Parliament (it never had been, though it came up each year with the budget estimates). A note by Tomlinson makes it plain he was trying to achieve by a new route the pluriannual commitment of funds and powers of oversight denied him the previous October. He even contemplated resigning so that personalities should not confuse the issue. This too came to nothing. Still he came back to the charge in November 1949 in a letter to the latest Prime Minister, Bidault. He complained that the ministries failed to provide the information the CGP needed to judge the use producers made of credits. This seemed reasonable enough, but he was rebuffed, this time in formal session, by the whole Council of Ministers. He was covered with laurels the better to bury his request. The CGP was not to be allowed to elbow its way through the ministries.

In short, as soon as Monnet tried to behave as Mendès-France and others had done, he ran into the same immovable barrier. This strongly suggests that any planning where the planners had more direct authority than Monnet initially sought would always have failed. The institutional modesty of the plan was the condition of its success. The price—*sub specie asternitatis,* perhaps not a high one—was that the CGP was congenitally vulnerable to digestion by a powerful ministry as soon as its purposes lost urgency. In 1954, Mendès-France, now Prime Minister, placed the CGP where Monnet had least wanted it, under the Ministry of Finance, which had in the meantime swallowed the Economic Ministry as well. Monnet had long gone and tradition reasserted itself.

IV
LAST YEARS OF THE FIRST PLAN

The OEEC Long-Term Programme of 1948 had several effects on the Monnet Plan. For one thing, it gave the CGP an opportunity to rejig targets towards further modesty without admitting the fact too openly. A couple of years were added to adjust to the Marshall aid terminus of 1952 in such a way as to make the fit with the original Monnet Plan as opaque as possible. Peering through the smokescreen, ECA experts estimated that it amounted to a cut of about a third on the targets for investment of late 1946.

For the rest, the temporary nature of Marshall aid, while easing the dollar famine and immediate dangers of inflation, actually increased the need to deal urgently with both. French minds turned for the first time to foreign trade. As a CGP note put it: "The organising idea of the Monnet Plan in 1946 was the mobilisation of basic resources. Now [it is] the balance of payments". Priority switched to exports, notably of wheat and steel, which OEEC discussions suggested were most in demand (though not necessarily at French prices). The targets for sectors dependent on imports, such as ships and civil aircraft, were sharply cut.

The search for markets, in a period of bulk buying and little free trade, took Monnet frequently to Britain, France's principal partner in the OEEC. He did not register much success with the trade agreements that were his formal purpose. France was not, in London's view, a competitive producer of wheat and still less of other farm products. On the other hand, the visits increasingly became opportunities to discuss Germany (see Chapter 6).

At home, in Paris, the last years of the first Monnet Plan were dominated by a struggle to preserve investment from the shears of successive Finance Ministers. The plan entered an endless round of tough annual bargaining sessions on investment funds. Contrary to what one might expect, Monnet did not defend the plan's estimates at all costs, but stuck to the disinflationary posture he had taken up in 1947. It was a way of retaining credibility in defence of core funds at the cost of proposing cuts himself. He sometimes went to surprising lengths. In 1950, he shaved the requests of the ministries passed to the CGP by a full 20 per cent. Early in 1952, when Antoine Pinay became Prime Minister, Monnet, almost alone in the establishment, advised him he could afford to launch what was to prove his politically successful programme of budget retrenchment. Pinay felt duly encouraged. This seems to have sealed a relationship between the two men which, like so many in Monnet's life, was put to use later on.

Every late summer, the ministries would make their investment bids for the coming year. The CGP would cut them. They would then go to the Investment Commission, where the CGP, ministries, and departments of the Ministry of Finance were all represented. The Investment Commission would marginally reduce the requests of the CGP. The Minister of Finance would then grant the force of all the arguments against further cuts but insist he had no alternative. The appropriations would be cut again, often quite heavily. The final credits could be as little as half the initial bids. There would be protests, mainly from Monnet, and few concessions in reply.

Relations seem to have been particularly difficult with Petsche. Petsche was a stout fiscal conservative. For him, the only healthy investment was through a capital market. He recognised this did not exist, but, as between low taxes and high investments, he chose low taxes. There is a letter from Alphand protesting against the fact that the French had barely put their Long-term Programme to the OEEC before Petsche was telling the Americans he feared it could not be carried out. Monnet had some tense encounters with Petsche, particularly over the latter's first budget at the end of 1948. One comes across the minutes of a meeting where Petsche repeats about half a dozen times that the government has already decided on the ceiling for investments while Monnet insists that these are unacceptable. A few days later, Hirsch announces that the CGP and the spending ministries are appealing to the Prime Minister. Matters were not helped by the fact that Petsche, who was reputed to have the finest table in Paris, seemed to resent Monnet's spartan working meals.

On the whole, the impression conveyed is of an investment budget under great pressure. Yet it is not at all certain that appearances gave a true picture. François Bloch-Lainé is adamant that it was a charade and that the establishment were determined to protect the core of investments. Certainly, levels of investment, expressed as a proportion of national output, fell only slightly from 1947–49 onwards, though there was a natural shift from public funds to reviving capital markets. In this light, Monnet's launching of major projects as early as possible in the life of the plan paid dividends. A frequent argument in the papers is that it would cost more to halt operations than to carry on. Most of them seem to have been completed, somewhat late, but not disastrously postponed.

Around 1949, the Monnet Plan was turning to routine, and its eponymous hero began to show signs of finding it stale. He played with dry runs for initiatives that did not mature. In one case, he worked with the political scientist Maurice Duverger on plans for constitutional reform of the Fourth Republic, which certainly needed one, but was not likely to get it from the main beneficiary of the system, Parliament. At the same time, the German problem was looming ever larger. Though he could have stayed near the centre of French politics for years to come as head of the CGP—and in fact did remain till August 1952—he was clearly ready for a change of diet.

V

BALANCE-SHEET

Great surges of economic growth tend to be international. The "glorious thirty" years after the war, the longest, steepest, most widespread boom in history, were certainly that. No one, except a few pot-holers in the footnotes, might ever have heard of a Monnet Plan without this general buoyancy. If one compares with other countries at the time, the results were not outstanding. In 1954, for instance, the growth of French industrial output relative to prewar (1938) was well below that of West Germany, Italy, Scandinavia and the Netherlands, and only marginally above that of Belgium and Britain. The plan fell short of its own admittedly ambitious goals. When it was launched at the end of 1946, investment was plotted at a rate of 23 to 25 per cent of GNP a year. In the event, the level attained was 18 to 20 per cent of GNP a year. This was middling to low by contemporary European standards. France itself had achieved similar rates in the years before 1914 and in the late 1920s. Energy goals were virtually achieved, but only because oil, which the planners had played down and which was more than able to fund its own operations, vastly outperformed expectations. For the rest, the only sectors to come in shouting distance of their targets were electric power and railways. Steel output grew at two-thirds of par, coal, cement and tractors—the other basic activities—at a third or less.

Other reservations have been, or could be, expressed. Warren Baum, a former U.S. aid official, reached the conclusion thirty years ago that "there has been little systematic planning in the sense of a set of specific and internally consistent goals". More recently, a French economist, Patrick Messerlin, has objected that the plan, too skewed to basic industry, would have been better suited to a country with Germany's natural endowment. "The conclusion is hard to avoid that the Monnet Plan was in fact copying the German model". A French expert, Christian Stoffaës, has argued that French industrial policy has been driven by security goals, such as energy self-sufficiency, rather than competitiveness. In short, the Monnet Plan lacked economic criteria beyond a spirit of expansion vaguely blessed by the mark of Keynes. Even that was not its monopoly. The nationalised industries had laid abundant plans of their own in 1946 and were eager to carry them out. Monnet's Plan, as he himself explained, aimed to order priorities, to prune rather than invent.

But all such criticisms pale in comparison with what the simplest narrative shows, the enormous difficulties which had to be overcome to keep to any long-term goals at all. Most of them were rooted in a regime for which weak government and short-term considerations were a way of life. To establish investment as a priority in such a system was an endless struggle. And until the Marshall Plan, there was a delay, which could have proved fatal, in obtaining guarantees of dollar aid. The will-power needed to complete the journey can hardly be exaggerated. In any case, the general economy's 6 per cent per annum average growth for the six years was respectable, even for a period of reconstruction. Monnet preferred momentum to figures. He saw statistics mainly as incitements to effort. For him, the plan was "like life" a "continuous creation", not a blueprint.

His opportunism, which may seem a shortcoming in retrospect, was a positive advantage at the time. As Bloch-Lainé has remarked, "The genius of [Monnet] and his lieutenants was to avoid ideology at the political and theoretical levels and demarcation disputes at the bureaucratic one; then to produce good papers and have good conversations to present their views and convince people; in short, to exercise, as the phrase goes, 'the dictatorship of services rendered' ". There was, of course, an obvious need. Nothing less could have brought aboard such a motley crew as the U.S. government, the Communists, the Third Force parties of the regime, the nationalists behind de Gaulle and the Labour Unions. The fact remained that others besides Monnet had tried and failed. He it was who gradually mobilised a political coalition on both sides of the Atlantic behind investment in France, and he who gradually fixed the plan and its slogan of "modernisation or decadence" in French consciousness.

He side-stepped the political and ideological controversies of the day. He did not commit himself on nationalisation. He was a planner impressed by large markets. He exploited the temporary monopoly of the state over capital and credit, while denouncing protectionism and preaching the growth which ultimately forced the economy to open up. This seemed self-contradictory at the time, yet foreshadowed the development path of most successful industrial economies since the war. He eschewed the bureaucratic claims of Mendès-France and Lacoste. He finessed potential confrontations with the ministries. He built up credibility by widespread consultation, while, thanks to the Americans, keeping his hand near enough to the till. He offered a practical programme to the Fourth Republic that was in dire need of one. He helped create a relative consensus behind what used to be called the "mixed economy".

While operating within norms the French bureaucratic tradition could recognise, he also provided a conduit for Anglo-American intellectual influences on a ruling Parisian elite which had been conservative before, and lost touch during, the war. Marjolin spent much of the war in America and Britain. Uri went to Princeton after the war. Nathan in 1946 and Bernstein in 1947 were instrumental in the CGP tackling the inflation crisis. Ball came to Paris in the summer of 1947 to produce papers for Monnet for the CEEC and to be "a punching bag for ideas". The productivity missions to the United States from 1949 onwards were inspired by their Anglo-American counterparts. Monnet and Hirsch credited the Modernisation Commissions to Sir Stafford Cripps and the British working parties. The borrowings were almost as frequent as Monnet's transatlantic telephone calls to his old acquaintance, Captain Granville Conway, who controlled the American coal-tankers for Europe. Even serving the salad with the cheese at the CGP seemed "American".

Had Monnet not insinuated the plan into the system, the most plausible outcome of previous trends would have been a rapid erosion of long-term goals and investment quite in the style of the Fourth Republic and even of the economic leadership, or lack of it, of de Gaulle in 1945. The return of the Right to power at the Ministry of Finance in 1948 might well have led to investment being sacrificed to balanced budgets, without any loosening of trade barriers, the protectionism in "mediocrity" of which Monnet had warned in 1945. Marshall aid would have been tied to containing inflation. Instead, Monnet produced for the first time in a France regarded as the sick man of Europe some premonition of robust recovery.

It was not an illusion. The first Monnet Plan, by laying an economic foundation, lastingly expanded the range of options open to all future French leaders, of whatever stripe. It could not on its own determine, but it favoured, the emergence of an expansionary mentality among politicians, employers and labour unions at just the right time, on the threshold of a great boom. Similarly, it encouraged an at least partial shift of the mandarins—crucial in the French context—from the pretensions of a moth-eaten great power to the realism of a medium-size but ambitious economic one. It made possible (though no more than possible) the settlement with Germany launched through the Schuman Plan. It has been an important force in the transition of France from the perils of backwardness to the confidence of an industrial society. Above all, it came at the start, the hardest time and the crucial one, when small variations of angle most change the course downstream.

Monnet was no natural leader for the French, even for bureaucrats. Mendès-France was much better equipped. He had a feel for the State, a touch of its puritanism, of its nationalism also, and an ideological edge, all of which made him the natural "conscience" of high-minded mandarins itching to reform a regime that was not so much inept as intolerable because humiliating. De Gaulle had yet greater prestige, but especially at this period was felt not to be a reliable "Republican" (i.e., democrat). Monnet, in contrast, operated in the margin of the state in a system where the state was everything. He had lived for years outside his own country, in which a resentful nationalism was never far below the surface. In many ways, the Monnet Plan was an interlude in his international career. Yet it was also a return to the roots that made the next phase possible. Through the Monnet Plan, he came nearer to the heart of the French establishment than ever before or after. Without it, he could hardly have proposed the Schuman Plan.

Europe's Breakthrough
1950

Monnet could have stayed on indefinitely at the Planning Office as its prime mover. But in the spring of 1950, French relations with the new Germany became critical. Monnet responded with a plan for a European federal authority in coal and steel round a Franco-German core. In so doing, he laid the cornerstone of today's European Union.

Every decade that passes confirms this event as one of the landmarks of the century. The implications go well beyond Europe. Many reforms were introduced after the war. But of all the international bodies invented to correct the weaknesses that led to war, none addressed the fragmentation of authority in the hands of numerous states, which arguably had been one of the greatest flaws. The Schuman Plan alone, as Monnet's scheme was called once the Foreign Minister, Robert Schuman, took political charge of it, broke the mould by daring a federal experiment.

To the casual eye of a later age, federation might seem a natural response of former great powers to a catastrophic decline in fortune. One of the effects of the second European war was indeed to purge old hatreds by sheer excess and to open minds to union as the only way out of the old vicious circle of violence. This outlook was a precondition of the Schuman Plan. Had it been sufficient, though, one would be entitled to ask why the birth of Europe had to wait a full five years after the end of the war and take the limited form it did?

Of course, reconstruction was a factor. There was little room for anything else till it was well under way. But the deeper reason was that a specific stimulus was needed to turn a latent disposition for change into active reform. It required choices governments could not avoid. This came only with the gradual revival of Germany in the wake of the Marshall Plan.

At first, after the war, the United States banked on an international system based politically on understanding with the Soviet Union and materially on a dollar standard replacing sterling and the *pax britannica* as the foundation of an open world economy. This vision broke down in less than two years. Growing competition with the Soviet Union over Germany—the Cold War—was an obvious reason. Another, less conspicuous, was that early assumptions about the effort the United States would have to make to ensure rapid recovery in Europe proved, in the crisis of 1946–47, too optimistic. Fear of a material and political collapse in western Europe, with Stalin as residuary legatee, took over. The result was that from Marshall aid onwards, the United States began to see the economic recovery of Germany and later its military contribution to Western defence as vital to the European, and by extension world, balance. Once the United States moved in that direction, it had to reckon not only with the opposition of the Soviet Union, discounted as beyond the pale, but with that of an ally which also saw itself as a prime victim of German aggression: France. How to satisfy Germany without alienating France became a major American dilemma.

The issue for France was the obverse of the American. Taking the total defeat of Germany in 1945 as their first opportunity to shape Europe since the botched Treaty of Versailles, the French started the postwar years by seeking a fragmented Germany of "regions". When that proved a pipedream, they tried to have the Ruhr neutralised, restrained or otherwise controlled. But this policy had three basic flaws. It depended on German weakness, and Germany, even truncated, was potentially stronger than France. It relied on America to achieve what France alone could not. And it fuelled the reciprocating engine of hostility between French and Germans. Once Western Germany acquired a government in September 1949 and all three reactions became critical, a new policy grew urgent. It was this that made Monnet's old ideas for European unity spring to life in May 1950 and not before.

II
WESTERN APPROACHES

In his memoirs, Paul-Henri Spaak remembered his first meeting with Monnet in war-time Washington in 1941 for two reasons. One was the meal of Gallic quality served up by Monnet's cook, something beyond the dreams of war-time London, where Spaak, as Belgian foreign minister–in–exile, had sadly to ply his fork. The other was the postprandial walk, with Monnet expounding something like the Schuman Plan for coal and steel he launched a decade later. In Algiers, in the conversation with de Gaulle and others of October 17, 1943, Monnet was the champion of a Europe united by free trade, within which Germany's successor states should be "on terms of equality" with other members. Otherwise, the urge to re-create a single Germany would be too strong. In the thick of war, the most unconventional aspect of the eccentric map Monnet showed Hirsch in Algiers of the steel areas of France, Germany and their neighbours torn out of their parent nations and put under common authority, was that it roped in parts of France as well. A year later, on July 7, 1944, he told Macmillan that the whole future of Europe turned on Germany and that a full United States of Europe was out of reach, but that a strong League of Nations enhanced by interstate trade and monetary arrangements might be feasible. England, he thought, should take the lead, backed by France. In August, *Fortune* magazine published a profile, "Mr. Jean Monnet of Cognac", by John Davenport. In Europe, said Monnet, there would have to be "a true yielding of sovereignty" to "some kind of central union". There should be a big European market without customs barriers, to prevent the nationalism "which is the curse of the modern world". The Ruhr should be internationalised under a European authority with its own powers. "But where to begin? And how far to go? And could England be brought in? For without England . . . the concept of a unified Europe turns all too quickly into a Germanized Europe all over again".

These shifting speculations were well within the wide range of ideas aired on all sides as victory approached. But on one point they fell into a distinct category. They accepted that in the long run punitive measures would not work. This put Monnet in opposition to the plan for Germany Morgenthau presented to Roosevelt and Churchill at Quebec in September 1944. The idea was to erase German industry and, after subtracting the extensive eastern territory handed to Poland and the Soviet Union, divide the centre and west into three agricultural states, a northern one, a southern one and the Rhineland under international rule. It was consonant with Roosevelt's views put to Eden eighteen months before (see p. 101). Stimson led the opposition in Roosevelt's entourage, arguing that the ruin of industrial Germany would be the ruin of Europe too. Thinking Monnet's views an antidote, he invited him to lunch. Monnet largely repeated what he had said to Davenport. He "could speak only for himself and not for his French colleagues" (who would, as Stimson interpreted him, "probably be hell-bent to have France get this asset", i.e., the Saar-Ruhr area).

There were resemblances between the Morgenthau Plan and the first French postwar policy to Germany, inaugurated by de Gaulle. De Gaulle accepted the need for Germany to have industry, but sought the fragmentation of the country into regional states and the dismantling of plant as reparations. It was the spirit of François Mauriac's grim Cold War joke that he loved Germany so well he preferred two of them. Initially, the French wanted several. Their diplomats voiced the idea that France should fill the industrial void left by Germany's defeat and become the manufacturing core of continental western Europe.

Monnet and the CGP never seem to have invested in such ideas. The steel targets of the Monnet Plan of November 1946, though with an appetite for Ruhr coal and coke, were not consonant with ambitions to replace its heavy industry. The discarded Mendès-France Plan had proposed to nationalise French steel and machine tools, which would have fitted into a strategy to displace the Ruhr. The Monnet Plan did not. When, on July 30, 1947, Will Clayton said he had no sympathy with French ambitions to curtail heavy industry in the Ruhr in order to build it up in France, Monnet answered that while individuals probably did have such ideas, he did not think they were entertained by the French government or people. Right, wrong or disingenuous, this was not at all Georges Bidault's language at the time.

In any case, from the first half of 1947, the Cold War and Marshall Plan between them changed the entire context of French policy to Germany. Together, they placed West Germany in the front line of the West. There was no point in America pouring aid into West Germany with one hand and dismantling industry or restricting output with the other. To borrow a phrase, West German recovery was implanted in the Marshall Plan like the yolk in the egg. Any hopes of supplanting the Ruhr now had, at most, to make way for the search for insurance against its revival.

On July 22, 1947, shortly before the Marshall Plan conference opened in Paris, Monnet sent a long paper to Bidault. He pointed out that, given the breach with the Soviet Union in Moscow in April, France was now committed to agreement with the Anglo-Americans. In Marshall Plan diplomacy, the recovery of France and western Europe, and the future of Germany, were all bound up together. France had bargaining power for the moment because it was crucial to the success of the Marshall Plan conference. This must be used. The key would be "the statute of the Ruhr, which the French consider essential to their security and the peace of Europe. [They] can only have confidence in [the Marshall Plan] if the development of German resources is coupled with safeguards to ensure that they will not, one day, be used again by the Germans to make war".

Clayton, the leading official on the American side, said of the ensuing weeks, "I conferred often with Jean Monnet who came several times to Geneva to see me and whom I saw often in Paris". At a quiet dinner they had in Paris on July 29, Clayton proposed "that the Ruhr should not be internationalized or detached from Germany", but that there "should be an overriding international authority of which Germany would be a part, clothed with power of allocating [German coal] production as between domestic and foreign" consumers. This would ensure the flow of Ruhr coal to Lorraine steel. There followed four meetings from August 6 to 14, all including Clayton and Monnet, three with Bidault, and two with Couve de Murville and Alphand as well. Out of the process came, on August 14, a Franco-American agreement on "an international board, made up of representatives of US, UK, France, Benelux and Germany, with power to allocate Ruhr output of coal, coke and steel between German internal consumption and exports". It was the initial sketch of the International Ruhr Authority (IRA), which came into operation, after enormous travail and much diluted, nearly two years later. The August meetings in effect inaugurated France's second postwar policy on Germany.

These changes were not just ordinary events. They were psychological upheavals. For once, in speaking of early postwar attitudes to Germany in France, that grossly overworked word *trauma* is justified. Individuals might view the situation relatively calmly; the body politic as a whole could not. There was a furore in Paris in June 1948 when the three western Allied governments agreed at the London conference to create a German Constitutional Assembly pointing to a German republic; and the ceiling on German steel production was raised to 11 million tons per annum, much like French medium-term goals. There was intense fear in Paris that the "Anglo-Saxons" were taking the first steps to free West Germany of all control. Emotions ran high. The French National Assembly approved the "recommendations" by a majority of only fourteen votes on June 8. That was after the "Anglo-Saxons" had given public warning they would go ahead anyway. It was one of the crises in French postwar policy to Germany. When the government fell six weeks later, much more significantly Bidault, the perennial Foreign Minister since the war, went with it. He was felt to have given too much away.

Concurrently with these developments affecting Germany, the Cold War and Marshall aid gave rise both to the first official proposals on European union and to the first pacts on collective security, European and Atlantic, all of which interacted with one another.

The American Marshall planners were very anxious to promote European "integration" (at first a vaguer euphemism for "union"), by which they mostly meant free trade throughout western Europe. True, Monnet, wrote Clayton later, "convinced me that western Europe was too weak in 1947 to accept conditions of regional free trade". All the same, customs unions were in the air, and in August, Alphand, at the Paris conference on the Marshall Plan, committed the French government to discussing one with any partner ready to consider the offer. Only Italy took up the idea at first. This was ironic, because France and Italy were the two most protectionist countries of a protectionist bunch. It was the beginning of complicated and protracted parleys which the Benelux countries later joined. The resulting scheme was then anointed with the ludicrous sobriquets of Fritalux, Finebel and even at one point Fritnebel. It became significant for a while two years later.

The rift between the West and Soviet Union of 1947 froze into Cold War in 1948. The first major date was the Prague coup of February 24, 1948, when the Communists, with Soviet backing, seized power for the first time in a democratic country, Czechoslovakia, and sent a *frisson* of dread through the rest of democratic Europe. This gave new force to the Treaty of Brussels, setting up the Western European Union (WEU), which was signed by Britain, France and the Benelux trio on March 17. The Treaty, in which the five pledged themselves to mutual armed assistance against the Soviet Union and Germany, was the greatest British commitment in Europe at the time and encouraged hopes of further European integration.

Fear of Stalin also led to the Congress of The Hague in May 1948, chaired by Winston Churchill (out of office), which launched the European Movement. This in turn led to government negotiations on a Council of Europe, which was to match the military cohesion of the WEU on the political front. For the first time, European union became a fashion.

Monnet was unyieldingly absent from these festivities. Apart from Konrad Adenauer, he was the one major "European" figure of later years not to attend the Congress of The Hague. Nor, though the two men were close, did he join in Alphand's customs union schemes. One could have concluded that, absorbed in his investments, he had lost all interest.

In fact, though few hints have leaked of his European activities in 1948, he seems to have been active along other lines. Robert Murphy, then the U.S. political adviser for Germany, told the French historian Pierre Mélandri many years later that Monnet was arguing in the spring of 1948 for a future international Ruhr authority to be a body of European scope. If so, he was anticipating many suggestions a year later. Mainly, though, he turned to Britain. Ernest Bevin, the British Foreign Secretary, alarmed by the Prague coup, seemed for a few weeks early in 1948 open to federal initiatives. Monnet was in London in February and in March for bilateral discussions to reduce France's trade deficit with Britain. He caught Bevin's aberration on the wing, and told the French president, Vincent Auriol, on March 11 that partial delegations of sovereignty to a European body on an Anglo-French foundation might be possible.

Monnet's remarks on this occasion were revealing. He was convinced, noted Auriol, that war was on the way, because people were resigned to it. If nothing was done, there would be a catastrophe. He thought the British were hesitating between Europe on the one hand and the United States and the Dominions on the other. Their anxiety about the state of France, because of the instability of its governments, was a factor in the balance. If things went on as they were in France, social unrest would grow worse and the Communist party "would have to be eliminated". The French would be forced into one or other camp. The only way to escape from such a dilemma was a Franco-British federation. A federation of this kind, "with a partial pooling of sovereignty and completely independent of the United States and Soviet Union" would change the political climate. But how could something on this scale be handled when French governments were so unstable? There had to be a constitutional reform in which the National Assembly, elected for four years, voted in the Prime Minister but was dissolved when he was overthrown. Characteristically, Monnet asked Auriol not to breathe a word to the British ambassador, Sir Oliver Harvey. "He repeats everything". "An interesting conversation", Auriol noted. "An intelligent man, but sometimes a trifle systematic".

A month later, on April 18, Monnet wrote to Schuman, then Prime Minister. He did so from Washington, where he was negotiating on wheat for France. He argued that the states of western Europe must make "a genuine European effort which the existence of a Federation of the West alone will make possible". Refusing Spaak's offer of the chair of the OEEC executive committee, he added that working for "a real Federation of the West" was the only job he would be ready to take on apart from the Monnet Plan. He did not explain what he meant by a "Federation of the West". The nearest clue is that in 1950, writing about the "so-called Atlantic" political framework fashionable then, he singled out "western Europe, Britain, the United States and British Dominions" as the units of a Western Federation. This idea was to survive in different guises.

The threads all came together in 1949. In April, agreements on the Atlantic treaty and the International Ruhr Authority were signed. In May, there followed the Basic Constitution of the German Federal Republic and the Council of Europe. In the summer, the Finebel negotiations sprang to life. Among these, every one of the European initiatives failed in its larger purpose, with the signal exception of the emergence of the Federal Republic of Germany (FRG) as the alarming guest at the feast.

The Council of Europe at first evoked some wild hopes. A romantic even as pragmatic as Spaak believed for a short while, when the Council of Europe's Consultative Assembly was set up in 1949, that it was a *"constitu- ante"*, meaning, in French revolutionary jargon, an echo of the Third Estate, which in 1789 seized power from the limp hand of Louis XVI. In fact, the British insistence on the national veto in the Council of Ministers left the limp hand to the Consultative Assembly, not the governments. Though the assembly attracted glittering names, it soon became a byword as a talking-shop.

The most interesting failure in some ways was that of Finebel, Alphand's "pet scheme", as Marjolin called it. It was a result of the accumulation of three factors, all significant for the future. One was that though Finebel was presented as a scheme to liberate trade, it was in practice so imbued with French and Italian protectionism that it was touch and go whether a deal could be reached with the Benelux countries (or indeed between the French and Italians). Another was that when the French government really had to take a decision, in the first ten days of February 1950, they could not brace themselves to include West Germany in the scheme without Britain. And finally, the British, when forced to come off the fence, made it as plain as their determination not to commit themselves would allow, that they would not look kindly on any plan which included the Germans and not them. In any event, Finebel itself had become so tortuous that it was easy in March 1950 to turn an Anglo-American preference for a general European payments union into an alternative which duly came into operation in September 1950 and proved one of the most important of OEEC's achievements. It fell short, however, of any formal delegations of sovereignty.

Monnet did not take an active part in Finebel, but Germany increasingly occupied his anxious thoughts. "It was axiomatic" to Monnet, George Ball has written, who saw a great deal of him in 1949, that "lasting peace could be achieved only by bringing France and Germany together and exorcising the demons of the past". Monnet at that stage was still trying to approach German policy through Britain. In March 1949, the British and French were much exercised with the OEEC's Long-Term Programme, so that Monnet, between March 4 and 7, had four talks with Sir Edwin Plowden, the head of the Treasury Planning Staff. Monnet argued that western Europe was a vacuum between the dynamic forces of communism and American capitalism. He thought Britain, which had combined the redistribution of wealth with freedom of the individual, was the only dynamic force in western Europe. The OEEC had no capacity to meet Europe's problems. These could be dealt with only if England and France "were to consider their problems together as one nation, always recognising that they had separate political and fiscal systems". He wanted informal talks without an agenda. He was sure they would soon turn on the relationship of Germany and western Europe.

> Neither England nor France now had any positive policy towards Germany. . . . [U]nless they soon developed a common one, they would find themselves disputing about the line to be taken.

A weekend followed at Monnet's country house, reluctantly on the British side. Monnet, Hirsch and Uri acted as hosts to a trio of British Treasury officials led by Plowden. The exchanges came to nothing.

Nearly a year later, on February 1, 1950, in Paris, Monnet tackled Plowden again on Germany. The background this time was the Finebel issue, which was in its decisive stage. He said that "any French government would be most reluctant to the inclusion of Germany in Finebel unless the UK were also to join". He added that French enthusiasm for Finebel had "markedly declined", since it had been realised that France, with few unemployed, would be tying itself to three of the countries—Germany, Italy and Belgium—which had the most unemployment. He was exasperated with the American pressure, presumably for free trade, and "wondered whether it would not be better if there were to be no further [Marshall aid] appropriations". His key point, however, was that

> if the resurgence of a hostile Germany were to be avoided, the UK and France should have not only a common economic but a common political policy. . . . Neither country has really thought out . . . policy towards Germany and . . . little time was left. . . . He returned to this theme again and again.

and again there was no response. Monnet's failed wooing of the British strongly coloured later events.

By 1950, Britain was widely believed to have a veto on European integration. Spaak at the end of 1949, Charles ("Chip") Bohlen, the U.S. minister in Paris, in January 1950, Alphand on April 29, all pronounced integration with Germany and without Britain impossible. David Bruce summed it up on April 25: "(1) . . . there will be no real European integration without whole-hearted participation by the UK, (2) the UK will not whole-heartedly participate . . . (3) ergo, there will be no purely European integration. . . . Instead we" (he meant the Americans) "should advocate . . . an Atlantic Treaty Community". April 1950 produced a rash of Atlantic schemes. Americans, British, Germans, Italians all thought up proposals for different kinds of political umbrella organisations under NATO. On April 17, Bidault suggested an Atlantic "High Council for Peace". Rather like planning in France just before the Monnet Plan, European union on the eve of the Schuman Plan seemed to be on its last legs.

As regards Monnet personally, his activity in the years before the Schuman Plan leaves at least two impressions. One is that his involvement in areas that put the widest, even wildest, interpretation on his duties at the Investment Plan was taken more or less for granted by French and foreign policy-makers alike. The other is that what Monnet was seeking need not, as far as he personally was concerned, have been the Schuman Plan. He ranged widely—Britain in 1940, and from 1948 to 1950, as well as the "West" in 1948. In retrospect, the European Community looks like an end in itself. It may, to Monnet, have been a lucky strike when other prospectors had given up.

III
THE PLAN IS LAUNCHED

All this left policy on Germany up in the air. And the problem was growing more and more urgent. The American-sponsored Federal Republic and the Soviet-sponsored Democratic Republic both emerged with their own governments in the autumn of 1949. The competition between "East" and "West" through these two proxies made it only a matter of time before Allied restrictions on West Germany were sloughed off. France's would-be safeguard, the IRA, was hardly inaugurated in May 1949 before it began to bear all the marks of mortality.

The Foreign Ministers of the Western occupying powers, Acheson, Bevin and Schuman, began to meet every few months after the North Atlantic treaty was signed in April 1949. At their second meeting, in New York, from September 15 to 19 (the week Adenauer became chancellor in Bonn), Acheson put Schuman on notice that at their next meeting, he, Schuman, should propose the broad lines of a German policy for the Three. It was a polite way of saying that Paris could not stand pat on the status quo. According to Schuman's chief of staff, Clappier,

> Bevin gave a grunt which could have signified that he was unprepared or none too pleased, but which Acheson chose to interpret as assent. As for Robert Schuman, the bald top of his head went red as always when he was embarrassed. . . . Back in Paris, hardly a week passed without Schuman pressing me: "What about Germany? What do I have to do to meet the responsibility put upon me?" It became an obsession with him.

Acheson did not let Schuman off the hook. The promised Foreign Ministers' meeting, in London, fell on May 11–13, 1950. The timing of the Schuman Plan, scrambled through on May 9, was no accident at all.

French relations with the new West German government added to the pressure. They began well but soon turned sour. Shortly after Adenauer was elected chancellor, Schuman visited Bonn. Both men were devout Roman Catholics, Adenauer a Rhinelander, Schuman from the German-speaking part of Lorraine, Lotharingians to the manner born. In fact, since Schuman's part of Lorraine was annexed by Germany between 1871 and 1919, he had served in German uniform during the First World War. The two men had a cordial meeting of minds, in German, on European good intentions. But there was no follow-up. On the contrary, Schuman's first official visit to West Germany in January 1950 was a disaster. The trouble was the Saar.

The Saar is the small German region on the northern border of French Lorraine rich in coal and with significant steel capacity. The population of a million is German. Despite this, the French thought, after the Second

J. G. Monnet & Co., Cognac, 1994.

The "big house", Cognac, 1994.

The salamander trademark, J. G. Monnet, Cognac, 1994.

Jean Monnet and his parents. CREDIT: Fondation Jean Monnet pour l'Europe, Lausanne, Switzerland.

Jean and Silvia Monnet. CREDIT: Fondation Jean Monnet pour l'Europe, Lausanne, Switzerland.

Trip to the United States, probably before the war. CREDIT: Fondation Jean Monnet pour l'Europe, Lausanne, Switzerland.

Washington, the British Supply Council, December 30, 1941. CREDIT: Fondation Jean Monnet pour l'Europe, Lausanne, Switzerland. All rights reserved.

Robert Schuman, *left,* and Jean Monnet. CREDIT: Fondation Jean Monnet pour l'Europe, Lausanne, Switzerland. All rights reserved.

Jean Monnet visits Bonn at the penultimate stage of the Schuman Plan negotiations, April 4–6, 1951. *Left to right:* Walter Hallstein (head of the German delegation to the Schuman Plan conference and State Secretary for Foreign Affairs; later chairman of the EEC Commission, 1958–67), Jean Monnet and the Federal German Chancellor, Konrad Adenauer. CREDIT: Bundesbildstelle, Bonn.

"From now onwards there will no longer be French, German, Belgian, Dutch or Luxembourg steel, but only European steel". CREDIT: Fondation Jean Monnet pour l'Europe, Lausanne, Switzerland, Pol Aschman.

Monnet's speech at the inauguration of the High Authority in Luxembourg town hall on August 10, 1952. Seated are the members of the High Authority. *Left to right:* Paul Finet, Léon Daum, Enzo Giacchero, Franz Etzel, Albert Coppé, Dirk Spierenburg, Heinz Potthoff, Albert Wehrer. CREDIT: Photographic department, Information Directorate-General of the European Commission, Brussels.

The High Authority at work in the early days. *Left to right:* Paul Finet, Franz Etzel, Ursula Wennmakers, Enzo Giacchero, Albert Wehrer, Jean Monnet, Dirk Spierenburg. CREDIT: *Life* magazine Farbman.

World War as in 1919, that they could shift the balance of power in steel partially in their favour by controlling the territory. De Gaulle talked about it to Truman in August 1945. In December 1946, they erected a tariff frontier around the Saar inside their zone of occupation in Germany. In April 1947, at the dawn of the Cold War, the Americans and British recognised France's "economic" annexation of the Saar ("pending a peace treaty"). It was the price of France giving up opposition to the Anglo-American Bizone as the first (unacknowledged) step to a new West Germany. The French began to set up a *de facto* protectorate in the Saar.

Early in 1950, the French government was preparing a dozen conventions with the Saar. These were intended as a slight relaxation of terms to give the puppet regime greater standing, but confirmed economic fusion with France. *The New York Times* called them "a return to the policies of Richelieu". To the Germans, the Saar was German. Worse, if the French succeeded, they would undermine the case for German reunification in the East. Adenauer blew hard on the nationalist horn. The puppet Saar government "would have to answer for its actions before the German people. . . . *Protectorate* is too good a term for such a regime", and so on. He then tried to compensate in interviews on March 9 and 23 with Kingsbury Smith, of the International News Service, by proposing a "complete Franco-German union", starting with integration of the two economies. Far from being gratified, Paris snubbed his presumption. The one favourable, though vague, response came from de Gaulle.

Monnet knew the danger signals all too well. George Ball, who spent three and a half months in Paris in 1949, has testified that

> we spent hours talking about the Saar. . . . During his League of Nations days, Monnet had played a role (albeit a reluctant one) in working out a settlement that left the political responsibility for the Saar with the League of Nations but gave France full ownership of the coal that was its principal wealth. He had quite accurately noted at the time that "the Saar cannot remain independent. If the population insists, it will sooner or later return to Germany". Though he proposed a referendum, the French objected; they were clearly bent on a takeover of the Saar's economic resources. Now he saw history repeating itself.

The reciprocating engine of hostility could spring to life again at any time. Monnet's own *Memoirs* state that the need for a "daring act" in 1950 "owed a great deal to the timidity of the Saar settlement in 1922".

It was also becoming clear that the system of restraints on German steel production by which the French sought to protect themselves was coming under terminal pressure. As Monnet wrote to Schuman on May 1, 1950,

Germany has already asked to be allowed to increase its output from 10 to 14 million tons [French output was 9 million tons at the time]. We will refuse but the Americans will insist. Finally, we will make reservations and give way. . . . There is no need to describe the consequences in any detail: German export dumping; pressure for protection in France; a halt in the freeing of trade; the revival of the prewar cartels; . . . France back in the rut of limited protected production.

Pleven, the Defence Minister in May 1950, told his British counterpart, Emanuel Shinwell, that French recovery would be blocked if the problem of German industrial production and its competitive capacity were not rapidly resolved.

There was another complex of factors contributing to the sense of crisis in Monnet's eyes. The alarm he had expressed over the drift of the Cold War to Auriol early in 1948 had not abated. His memorandum to allies in the French government at the beginning of May said:

People have latched on to a simple and dangerous aim: . . . The Cold War, the basic aim of which is to make the adversary yield, is the first stage in the preparation of war. This is breeding a rigidity of mind characteristic of fixation on a single goal. . . . We are already at war.

In mid-April, he told a visitor when asked how things were going, "Badly, my friend. . . . They are going to drop it, the atom bomb, and then . . ." This was before the Korean War. Monnet, a man of passionate imagination, tended to pile on the agony in formulating an idea, almost as part of the nervous energy of conceiving it. A month later, when the Schuman Plan was launched, he had simmered down. A French diplomat noted that he "does not believe a war is likely". Then in mid-June the Cold War theme came up in a new form. In London, Monnet met the editor of *The Economist*, Geoffrey Crowther, who had worked with him at the British Supply Council in Washington. Shortly after, Crowther told David Lilienthal, the hero of the Tennessee Valley Authority, a friend of both, that Monnet "in this very room" had said the Schuman Plan

has as its purpose [the] setting up of a neutralized group in Europe—if France need not fear Germany, she need have no other fears, i.e., Russia. That they were tired of the cold war, which was something we here said Russia was engaged in, but which is now something America is pursuing.

Across all these moods and variations, one theme was consistent. Monnet saw European integration as an effort to order peace. Though often tactically convenient, this was always more than a slogan.

In short, in late spring 1950, Schuman faced the toughest dilemma confronting any French Foreign Minister since the war. As Robert Mischlich, a member of his personal staff at the Quai d'Orsay, has put it, "The system of domination of Germany, through the Saar and the Ruhr, could not be maintained for ever, but no one [in Paris] wanted to be responsible for the decision to bring it to an end". It seemed political suicide for Schuman to give ground on German recovery like Bidault in 1948. Anything he could do—including doing nothing—was risky for his country and career. Suddenly, European integration, hitherto a vision in speeches, served an urgent need.

Yet, as Monnet rather pointedly remarks in his *Memoirs,* Schuman had no idea what to propose to Acheson and Bevin in London in May, "although he had pondered deeply and consulted many people". The minister did ask his civil servants for proposals, but according to Mischlich, these "seemed to him inspired by a tradition of mistrust and to have little chance of changing the course of events". It was here that Monnet came in. He was able to fill the void for several reasons. He had access to any member of government at any time. He was freer to give attention to whatever he judged important than were leaders consumed by the game of musical chairs. Above all, he was recognised in the small circle of harassed men at the helm as someone to turn to in trouble.

Monnet and Schuman are an odd couple, paired by history rather than by any personal compatibility. Their first connection, a distant one, seems to have been through Mendès-France. A tart telegram of his from Algiers in 1944 asked Monnet in Washington why he had not answered an earlier request about job prospects for Schuman. It was also Mendès-France who, refusing the Finance Ministry from Bidault in 1947, suggested Schuman, whom he had noted in the Finance Committee of the prewar Chamber of Deputies. Schuman then became Prime Minister for a turbulent eight months before replacing a resentful Bidault as Foreign Minister in July 1948 and staying put. Throughout, Monnet, as was his wont, kept in touch, directly and through Clappier. Monnet and Schuman, says Clappier, "became friends, but it took a long time. Schuman was still wary in May 1950. In the first place, he was wary on principle. On top of that, he and Monnet were not at one on supranationality. For Schuman, the plan existed to solve the immediate Franco-German problem. For Monnet, it was the first step to a united Europe. Schuman accepted supranationality for the plan because there was no alternative, but was not committed".

Schuman was very different from Monnet. Stooping, a deeply religious bachelor with a tonsured head and a long nose that was a gift to caricaturists, he was modest in manner, with shrewd eyes. One recalls him in profile in a railway compartment, alone, peering hesitantly into a battered old attaché case filled with little parcels wrapped in newspaper, presumably food his housekeeper had prepared. He and Monnet were nevertheless similar in two respects. They were men of the marches. Schuman, from Lorraine, became a Frenchman only at the age of thirty-two. For Monnet, it was not a matter of birth—nowhere could be more French than Cognac—but of long life among the "Anglo-Saxons". They also both convinced most people of their integrity. The British ambassador, Sir Oliver Harvey, who had so distrusted Monnet in 1940, had changed his mind. Schuman, Monnet and Clappier, he wrote home, are "men of goodwill, sincere, disinterested & patriotic". Dirk Stikker, the Dutch Foreign Minister, at first hostile to the Schuman declaration, was won round in a week by Schuman because he "had the impression these were honest people. . . . It was not a French trick", he added, in good Calvinist style. At one of Schuman's lunches with Monnet and his associates in the tiny dining-room of the plan office, Monnet suddenly said, "You have a great asset. You look honest". Schuman smiled gently in his clerical way: "Do you mean to say, M. Monnet, that you are not sure I *am* honest?". "No, no", said Monnet, "I am not joking. You *look* honest. It is a priceless asset in a politician. People will believe what you say". Schuman, for all his gentle airs, earned an international respect never accorded to the erratic Bidault. Monnet wrote later that he and Schuman built up a friendship. Some associates felt they were never really that close. But they certainly came to trust one another. Schuman said once of Monnet, "He is very obstinate, but plays fair".

As Monnet tells the story of how the third postwar French policy to Germany was launched, he went off to Switzerland in the second half of March on one of his meditative walking holidays in the Alps. He came back primed not with a plan but with a focus for action and contacted Clappier to let him know. There was a gap for Easter, and then, on April 12, he called in Paul Reuter, a law professor at Aix-en-Provence who was a consultant to the French Foreign Ministry (the "Quai d'Orsay"). Reuter was passing by on a quite different errand and barely knew Monnet, but seems to have been pushed into his office because Monnet wanted to see an international lawyer. At first, Monnet thought that the border regions between France and Germany might be pooled on his Lotharingian lines of 1943. But after two further meetings, with Hirsch, and then with Uri as well, it was agreed by April 16 that all French and German coal and steel should be included. On April 17, the first two (of nine) drafts of the Schuman declaration were discussed.[1]

The proposal was passed to Clappier on April 20. Then, because he heard nothing from Clappier, Monnet passed it to Pierre-Louis Falaize, the chief of staff of the Prime Minister, Bidault. Monnet had received no response

---

1. Though there is no reason to doubt this version, Monnet's diary says he was in the Alps from March 5 to 16. March 17 to April 3 is a blank. Monnet used to chop and change appointments shamelessly and at times his diaries gave up.

from that quarter either, when Clappier popped up again, on April 28, and assured him of Schuman's interest. The plan was then handed to Schuman, who, over the weekend at home in Lorraine, decided to adopt it. From then on, Schuman took over the plan. He mentioned the matter with consummate obscurity at a first Cabinet meeting on May 3. The next Cabinet session of May 9 was brought forward because Schuman had to be in London next day for the meeting of the three Foreign Ministers. Schuman broached the subject at the end of the morning, after Adenauer had assured Schuman's secret envoy, Mischlich, of his backing. This time, there was more discussion. But Pleven, Mayer and Antoine Pinay, all of them contacted by Monnet or Hirsch, and all in favour, had been well primed, and no one else (except possibly Bidault) was familiar with the issue. Schuman's proposal went through. Early that evening, Schuman announced the proposal to a press conference crammed into the heavily gilded mirror-and-chandelier salon of the Quai d'Orsay, the salon de l'Horloge ("of the Clock"). Adenauer, in his enthusiasm, had to be restrained from jumping the gun with the press in Bonn.

The whole operation was conducted with a secrecy and speed totally foreign to the Fourth Republic. As the British ambassador wrote, "shock tactics" ensured the Schuman Plan "could not be strangled at birth". The steelmasters, potential stranglers, proud of having eyes and ears in every ministry, were deeply shaken to have detected no hint of the coming earthquake. Acheson, who happened to stop over in Paris on May 7 to see Schuman on his way to London, seems also to have been taken by surprise.[2] Tomlinson, meeting Hirsch on May 9, told him, "with tears in his eyes", that at last the French had taken a major decision without turning to the Americans first. London was not informed, and Bevin, meeting Acheson and Schuman on May 11, accused them of plotting behind Britain's back. His fury was comprehensible. He had already insisted in the recent Finebel affair that no decisions involving Germany should be taken before the meetings in London now about to start. It was equally comprehensible that Schuman could not comply.

The Schuman declaration proposed that France and Germany should enter

2. Here again, things may be less simple than they seem. David Bruce's diary says that Monnet told him on April 28. Harold Callender of *The New York Times* reported on May 4, 1950, that Schuman would soon be proposing the unification of British coal, Ruhr steel and Lorraine iron ore. Armand Bérard, the French Deputy High Commissioner in Germany, wrote that Clappier had told him "six weeks" before that something was afoot. Monnet's relations with Bruce and Tomlinson were such that it is just possible he told them without their passing it on. This is made plausible by Acheson's first reaction, which hurt Schuman, that the plan was a cartel. Nearer home, Hirsch, with Monnet's permission, told the chairman of state-owned French Coal and Alexis Aron, the most respected expert in the Steel Association, both of whom encouraged him to go ahead.

talks to "pool" or "fuse" their markets for coal and steel. (The term "common market" was not used.) The pool should be regulated by a High Authority with independent powers to act. Any democratic European country ready to accept these principles could join them. This offered a simple solution to a raft of problems. Pooling coal and steel, the real or supposed sinews of war, dramatised the will to peace and to "common growth in competition but without domination in a European Union". It met France's fear of the Ruhr while dropping attempts to control it from the outside. Now France tried to solve the problem by putting an end to foreignness between the two countries in the two industries.

Monnet did not demand French quotas or guarantees in the Ruhr. He asked for equal competitive conditions as in a single country. Likewise, France laid its own resources and markets open to Germany. The logic of the Schuman Plan required that all limits on German output should be lifted. The whole scheme was based on the principle of the equality of the participants before laws jointly made. Territorial and control issues became (in theory) irrelevant. Shrewd old Adenauer did not bother to ask Mischlich about the Saar and Ruhr. They were replaced by promise of a common future. In these conditions, a common authority with true powers was vital—in order to be effective and impartial and to take the first step to a European federation (mentioned twice in the proposal). Accepting the principle of a High Authority with real powers was the entry ticket to the Schuman talks.

The Schuman Plan also had the practical advantage of being relatively focussed. The Council of Europe, in its political approach, and the customs union, in its economic one, had been too broad too soon and aroused the maximum opposition. Coal and steel were more manageable. They sidestepped the bulk of the French lobbies. And if Monnet could show that it would give French steel equal access with German to Ruhr coal and coke, he had an unanswerable argument in the National Assembly. He no doubt believed it himself. He still had an interest in dramatising the idea.

Seeing how theatrically the Schuman Plan was sprung on the world, it is curious to record there was nothing original in the idea, "an old dream" as William Diebold noted long ago. As far back as 1926, the steel cartel had been welcomed as a healer of Franco-German hatreds. There was Monnet's own Lotharingia mapped in Algiers. During the long gestation of the International Ruhr Authority, variations on the theme popped up all over the place. Ten have been counted in France alone. On New Year's Day 1949, Karl Arnold, then Minister-President of the German *Land* of North Rhine–Westphalia, which contains the Ruhr, asked: "In place . . . of this one-sided . . . control of the Ruhr area, could one not erect an association . . . [to which] Germany would bring the Ruhr, France the ore resources of Lorraine, both of them the Saar, Belgium and Luxembourg their heavy industries" on a "basis of equality"? The Westminster Conference of the European League for Economic Cooperation suggested on April 25, 1949, that European "public institutions" for steel, coal, electricity and transport should be set up. On August 25, Adenauer offered to internationalise Germany's largest steel plant, the Thyssen works, as a first step to a European coal and steel organisation. In September, a journalist, Jacques Gascuel, after selling Monnet the idea of a coal and steel community, or so he thought, published an article in the magazine *Perspectives,* which made a stir. McCloy, now the American High Commissioner in Germany, suggested in *The Times* on October 18 that the International Ruhr Authority might be extended to the whole of western Europe. Monnet's own *Memoirs* refer to speeches of André Philip, Edouard Bonnefous, Robert Boothby and Paul Reynaud in the Consultative Assembly of the Council of Europe late in 1949. This list is far from complete. In retrospect, the Schuman Plan seems to have been launched on a thousand lips.

Yet it came as a shock. One reason was that the conversion of a French government had a force no foot-loose politician could muster. As Dulles told Acheson, this was what Marshall and he had talked about in Moscow in 1947 but assumed the French would never do. Yet the real novelty lay elsewhere. The resonance of the Schuman Plan was due to its braving its own choices. A senior State Department official, Edwin Martin, had complained of Finebel in October 1949 that "France had not tackled any of the basic issues". The Schuman Plan remedied that. It attacked sacred cows and outraged their owners. But this also gave it the mobilising power of what the French call an *idée force.* It was popular with the public.

Of course, the obvious break with the past concerned the commitment with Germany. Five years after the war, the very idea was threatening. Sir Oliver Franks, the British ambassador in Washington, observed that the French "have seen the hopelessness from their point of view of the Ruhr Authority and are now willing to stake the ore of Lorraine and the future of the French steel industry in the effort to secure an international control of the Ruhr on which France is represented". There being no hope of preventing the Germans from achieving their superior potential, the Schuman Plan gambled instead on a partnership to common ends. Adenauer had already stated that the citizens of the new Germany wanted to contribute to a new Europe, but as equals, not slaves. The Schuman Plan took him at his word. It provided the frame Adenauer needed to be reconciled with France and integrate Germany into the West. Further, for all the recently dwarfed Europeans, it provided hope of one day perhaps talking to superpowers on less unequal terms.

Many French politicians had talked of something like a Schuman Plan. But words were one thing, actions another. In practice, most French leaders found the logic of the Schuman Plan almost impossible to swallow. Even strong "Europeans" were schizophrenic. Pleven amazed Hirsch one day by approving European controls on German coal, but asking why they need apply to French iron ore (a much less strategic asset). Mayer, as Prime Minister in 1953, received Adenauer and told him he regretted the Saar had not been settled with the Schuman treaty. He meant that France's economic annexation should have been recognised.

The Schuman Plan's second leap was to abandon the safety net of the *entente cordiale* with Britain. Even Acheson, prodding Schuman to action, had been ambivalent about this.

> Any proposal for western European integration without the UK would revive fears of German domination. . . . Therefore, British participation is necessary. . . . This might require special arrangements for continentals to proceed faster without full UK participation.

Having Britain in (and necessarily vetoing) European integration, and out (so that the latter could go ahead), hardly resolved the dilemma. In contrast, Monnet and Schuman struck out boldly. The lessons they drew from Monnet's earlier explorations with the British and from the experience of Finebel were firm and realistic. Decision-making powers for the new bodies came first, Britain second. In May in London, Monnet told Cripps, "We waited on you for a decision when Hitler entered the Rhineland in 1936 and the results were disastrous. We shall not make that mistake again". He told Makins and Plowden on May 16 that the French government had decided to go ahead with Germany, alone if necessary. This was much bolder than it sounds today. Britain in 1950 stood head and shoulders above its European neighbours. It had been neither violated nor shamed by war. On top of its empire, it was much the biggest economy in the region, larger than West Germany's. Hirsch recalls the Whitehall mandarins, and Cripps himself, saying flatly that without Britain the Schuman Plan could never succeed.

In retrospect, however, raising anchor from the *entente cordiale* was not as risky as it looked. The Schuman Plan, though a shift from Britain to Germany, was in fact a transfer of insurance from Britain to America. America was far more of a counterweight to Germany than Britain could be. By its mere presence in Europe, it created a safety zone. The Schuman Plan was presented as a plan for peace between France and Germany. Politically, this was true. In the old military sense, the Atlantic pact had already removed the danger. And unlike the British, the Americans backed European unity. After initial suspicion that the Schuman Plan was the prewar steel cartel in fancy dress, they became enthusiasts. As Acheson wrote, "The more we studied the plan, the more we were impressed".

On the other hand, in French opinion, American patronage was a liability as well as an asset. There was an undertow running right through the Fourth

Republic of restiveness with the American alignment. In the eyes of the anti-American Gaullists, Communists and neutralists, Europe suffered from guilt by association. It could be argued, and was, that European nations were so dwarfed, only union would restore their influence with America. But this grail was very remote. From day to day, a policy close to Washington could always be presented as subordination. Nationalist feelings abhor the humility of pragmatism. Even for pro-Americans, there was no certainty the Americans would stay in Europe. Eisenhower supported European integration a little later in part because he thought it might speed the day the "boys" could "come home.".

Yet the Schuman Plan's greatest violation of conventional wisdom was bound up with Monnet's third break with the past, "supranationality". The irritant was not the principle as such. It was widely accepted that no collective could work if each member state were free to reject joint decisions. The League of Nations, the Council of Europe, were object lessons. The Schuman Plan was not to repeat such mistakes. The difficulty was in the corollary, that France lost its freedom to do as it liked along with everyone else.

For France's neighbours, this was precisely what made the plan serious. J. van den Brink, the Dutch Minister for Economic Affairs in 1950, has recalled that "Holland was normally rather suspicious of any proposal from France. We always thought there was some ulterior motive. . . . But when I heard that the French were ready to bring their own coal and steel industry in[,] . . . this had body, flesh and blood". French politicians and officials brought up in a great-power tradition had enormous trouble seeing it this way. As Harvey observed on June 24, "Though French public opinion is almost unanimously in favour of the general idea of a pool, Monnet has not apparently succeeded in selling his own particular proposal for a supranational authority with delegated powers to any French politician other than Schuman". If one is to believe Clappier, even this overstated the case.

In fact, the unsolved mystery of the launching of the Schuman Plan is how Monnet and Schuman persuaded the rest of the French government to endorse their decision, when Finebel had been rejected only three months before because Britain was not willing to take part. Certainly, the increasing pressure of the German problem concentrated ministers' minds. Schuman was able to argue that he had to present something to the Anglo-Americans in London. The Cabinet also seemed to be taken by surprise. Petsche told Cripps on June 10 that he, Bidault and Mayer all "had grave misgivings about placing French industry under a supranational authority. [He] fulminated in very bitter terms against M. Monnet's successful attempt to rush ministers into decisions without adequate time for reflection". The whole episode—"bizarre" as Diebold has called it—could no doubt be taken as an object lesson in the peculiarities of the Fourth Republic.

It is no accident that the Schuman treaty conference was the one French negotiation of this century taken out of the hands of the diplomats. All the other delegations, from Germany, Italy and Benelux, were orthodox. The French were led by Monnet. This anomaly cannot have been due to the Foreign Ministry's incapacity to conceive the strategy. A note of December 13, 1948, proves it could:

> We still . . . have a hope of settling the German problem in a . . . European steel pool in which French and Germans would be equally represented, and would together exercise joint control over steel production in Europe".

This is the reasoning of the Schuman Plan itself. Why did the initiative not come from the Quai d'Orsay?

In 1948, of course, there was no German government to talk to. But in any case, the chain of command to the minister went through Maurice Couve de Murville, then Political Director, and Jean Chauvel, the Secretary-General, or civil service head, of the ministry. Couve, later de Gaulle's Prime Minister and Foreign Minister, was more or less a Gaullist. Chauvel, like his successor, Alexandre Parodi, belonged to the middle-of-the-road *entente cordiale* tradition, which regarded Britain as France's irreplaceable partner against Germany. The Gaullist and *entente cordiale* schools both tended to regard community with Germany as suicidal or a betrayal of France's great-power prerogatives. According to Mischlich,

> An opposition grew up inside [Schuman's] own ministry. . . . France had to keep a free hand. . . . If there were to be a military or economic alliance, it should in no way foreclose France's political freedom, notably to withdraw from any alliance. This was already [General de Gaulle's] *l'Europe des patries*. . . . [Schuman] was criticised, even his patriotism was cast in doubt.

An ambassador once remarked of Schuman: "To think that nobody has attacked that man for having fought in German uniform". Adenauer saw the Schuman Plan as a "victory of the minister over his officials". It was strange language to use, but realistic. Some diplomats "considered they were paid to fight against giving up elements of national sovereignty", as François Seydoux de Clausonne, later French ambassador to Bonn, once said to Monnet. It would have been against nature for the Quai d'Orsay to sponsor the Schuman Plan. Monnet wanted to run the talks. Schuman knew he would produce results. That an interloper negotiated the most long-headed French initiative in foreign policy of the century shows how far the Schuman Plan flouted tradition.

IV
NEGOTIATION

The Schuman invitation, with its emphasis on subscribing to an agency with effective powers to act, forced governments to make basic choices from the start. Adenauer had in effect already given his assent. Monnet and Clappier duly visited Bonn on May 23. But there was a contradiction between Allied occupation controls and the Schuman Plan promise that the new German government would take part in talks as an equal. Symbolism dictated that the Allied High Commissions, as occupiers, should not sit at the conference table. Monnet had to obtain their assent to this. It was formally dependent on a majority vote among the Three. He had the French vote. McCloy did the rest in smoothing the way to the Allies' absence from the Schuman negotiation.

There followed a remarkable first encounter between Monnet and Adenauer. During the drive to the chancellor's office, Monnet was tense, but the meeting proved a decisive success. Adenauer endorsed the two basic points: a High Authority with its own powers; and negotiations solely to set it up— meaning that political institutions came first and material issues could be worked out later. Monnet recalled later that Adenauer at first was "unable completely to conceal a degree of mistrust. Clearly, he could not believe that we were really proposing full equality". Gradually, he relaxed. Armand Bérard, the French Assistant High Commissioner, who was present, was struck by the high-flown terms in which the two old men talked. Their task was political, not technical; they had a "moral" duty to their peoples, and Adenauer would not let detail interfere with the European goals he had entertained all his life. In the end, he even volunteered to send the prospective head of the German delegation to be vetted by Monnet, who subsequently, in dinners at Houjarray, turned down one candidate, the industrialist Hans C. Boden of the electrical firm AEG, before endorsing Walter Hallstein, a lawyer who was rector of Frankfurt University. There is irony in Bérard's account, understandable in view of the hard bargaining that followed. Yet major innovations are not possible without some agreement on the aims and values behind them. Throughout the formative years, the understanding reached so quickly between Adenauer and Monnet operated as a shadow court of appeal. "I can say of Adenauer what he said in his memoirs about me", Monnet recalled: " 'After that, we were friends for life' ".

Dealings with London were more complicated. Monnet and Hirsch spent the week of May 15 to 19 explaining their ideas to Cripps and senior officials at the Treasury and the Foreign Office. A tense negotiation ensued from May 25 to June 3. The British refused to commit themselves to a supranational

High Authority—to "buy a pig in a poke", "sign a blank cheque" or "commit ourselves in the dark"—but wanted to join the talks. On two occasions, Schuman "went some way to meet us", Harvey reported, and "produced extempore suggestions" that Petsche and the French diplomats would have preferred, but which he "later repudiated". In fact, on May 23, Schuman told the Foreign Affairs Commission of the French National Assembly that he was "virtually certain" the United Kingdom would be a full member of the projected authority. There is little doubt the restraining hand was Monnet's. He argued simply that if the British were not committed to anything, the Germans would not be either, and the point of the Schuman initiative would be lost.

Why the British were so resistant to European union is a bottomless pit of a question. Reticence was more obviously natural in 1950 than later. As the then Labour government put it: "A political federation limited to Western Europe is not compatible either with our Commonwealth ties, our obligations as a member of the wider Atlantic alliance, or as a world power". This was a powerful if slanted list. However, behind it a long litany of other factors could be cited: the British instinct for the English-speaking world; the psychology of a victorious power fresh from the special war-time relationship with Washington; a worldwide empire and by far the strongest economy in western Europe; pride in the Mother of Parliaments and in the newly minted welfare state; an island with a deep sense of security quite alien to much-defeated Continentals, yet at the same time living in a Paradise Lost rather than one to be gained; an establishment incredulous of any straying from the balance of power as the norm; not to speak of an almost Chinese condescension which goes before a fall: a member of the U.K. delegation to the CEEC argued in March 1948 that "if the UK does not lead the movement [to European integration], it will not occur. For no other country in Europe has the moral authority and the organizing capacity". Yet the active reason may have been less all these, strong as they were—and some of them still are—than that Britain, unlike France or the United States, had no overwhelming cause to reorder its policies around Germany.

Makins, suggesting that "the underlying motive for the [Schuman Plan] was French unwillingness to see Germany associated in any way with the Atlantic treaty", added that "British policy was to bring Germany into a more general framework than the European one". Given the facts of power, that meant leaving decisions to the Americans. In most ways, France had even greater emotional reasons than Britain to resist ties with Germany. These were not decisive, because fear compelled a choice. Necessity made "Europeans" of the French. The United States was frequently more "European" than Europeans, because it saw integration as cardinal to its German policy and Germany as the fulcrum of the world balance. The British had no

German top priority and so were not driven like the others to curb their insularity to meet it.

On June 12, an interministerial committee of the French government decided there would be no French delegation in the normal sense, only a single delegate, Jean Monnet, who would be free to choose his advisers. The talks began on June 20 with France, West Germany, Italy and the Benelux trio represented, all of them ostensibly paying Schuman's entry fee of accepting supranationality as the basis of the talks. In fact, the Dutch were openly shopping on approval. The Belgians were covertly uncommitted. The process by which the Schuman Plan became the European Coal and Steel Community can only be understood as an "exploration". Monnet and his team had been operating for years at the French investment plan by trial and error, chipping away at the rough block of a policy until it began to assume a viable shape. If one angle of approach failed, they tried another. Their eagerness now to try anything for size could be seen even in tiny points, such as the suggestion that if the states could not agree on a president for the High Authority, the job should devolve on the *youngest* candidate. It was an adventurous and youthful approach, full of energy and zest.

Monnet's first ideas in 1950 showed no marked advance on those tried on Hirsch in Algiers. What, Monnet asked of Reuter on April 12, did he think of a Franco-German Parliament? The Belgians, Dutch, Luxembourgeois, Lorrainers, Saarlanders, Alsatians and Swiss were neither German nor French: could a revived Lotharingia contribute to a united Europe? Even after the Schuman Plan was launched, the Belgian Foreign Minister, Paul van Zeeland, and on another occasion Plowden, having heard Monnet, thought it "so vague on essential details it was impossible to speak definitely about it". Macmillan called it "a plan to have a plan".

Monnet had other ideas. McCloy, whom he rang "several times a week", noted on May 23, that though he had "not yet advanced very far in his thinking on implementation of the plan and realizes that some technical points of difficulty will be fundamental, he is seeking to avoid delay in furthering the main design through preoccupation with what he terms technical details". The same day, Monnet told Adenauer that what the German chief negotiator would need was "not so much expertise. In all political problems, the approach is the difficult point". As late as mid-October, the German trade union leader, Ludwig Rosenberg, was complaining of Monnet's insistence on "agreement in principle" and dismissal of all material issues as "secondary".

On June 12, Monnet amazed Bérard by saying he wanted to complete the treaty by the end of the month, to prevent the opposition getting its breath back. The treaty was to set up the new European bodies. Working out the "technical" issues would then be left to them. The political framework was what mattered. "Technical details" could wait. Not surprisingly, Monnet was not allowed to invert normal bargaining in this way. As Max Suetens, the chief Belgian delegate, told him at the opening of the treaty conference on June 22, "You see the solution to our problems through the [supranational] High Authority. We see the High Authority through our problems and their solutions". The Benelux trio were determined to work out the small print before signing on the dotted line. The conference which Monnet had hoped to tie up in one month, and Adenauer in three, finally took ten months.

However, Monnet and Adenauer having agreed on May 23 that the heads of delegation, chaired by Monnet, should concentrate first on the framework of institutions, they did so. After the opening session on June 20 to 22, Monnet's team put up a forty-article draft treaty, as a "working document". Monnet "did not for a moment expect [it] to be accepted in full", a British observer reported. He himself reserved the right "to suggest substantial modifications". All the same, it offers a marker for gauging the changes the conference made to the initial concept.

The draft treaty, sketchy in most respects, made clear provision for a single market in coal and steel of all the member states—in other words, the basis of one Community. Customs duties, subsidies, discriminatory and restrictive practices were all to be abolished. The single market was to be established and supervised by a High Authority, with powers to handle extreme shortages of supply or demand, to tax and to prepare production forecasts as guidelines for investment.

The day after the Schuman declaration, Monnet told a British diplomat that he had in mind a European Monnet Plan office. The High Authority would be small. That being so, it would work through regional associations (reminiscent, one may interject, of the Modernisation Commissions of the Monnet Plan). The regions would follow natural lines, such as coal basins, regardless of frontiers (article 20), "in order to avoid national groupings which are camouflaged cartels". There were no anti-trust articles. The High Authority—a name turned down for the International Ruhr Authority— would, of course, consult governments, but no formal relationships were mapped out. Recourse in disputes would be through *ad hoc* arbitration tribunals, possibly presided over by a judge from the International Court in The Hague (article 8). Monnet seems to have had in mind the arbitration tribunal which he had created for the League in 1921 and which had "worked successfully in Upper Silesia". To meet the charge of technocracy, there was, at the suggestion of Philip, a Common Assembly, elected from the national parliaments. But it was to meet like an annual shareholders meeting once a year, to debate the High Authority's report, and it had only the shareholders' power to throw out the management (articles 11 to 13). Once, Schuman actually compared the High Authority to the supervisory board of a firm. Of the political concept of a balance of powers there was little sign.

The Dutch government, attracted to the Schuman Plan for its approach to the German problem, but not to France, Germany or a High Authority as Zeus, insisted that a committee of ministers should be set up with power to give the High Authority orders by majority voting. For a while, Monnet suspected the Dutch of subversion. But the chief Dutch negotiator, Dirk Spierenburg, soon convinced him that since coal and steel interacted with the rest of the economy, governments must join the circuit. Monnet consulted Schuman and agreed, so long as the ministers took majority votes on policies proposed by the High Authority. The Dutch accepted. This turning-point came as early as July 8 in a conversation in Monnet's office with Spierenburg and a few others. By mid-August, the broad institutional pattern was set. The initiative still lay with the High Authority; decisions affecting the member states would involve the Council of (national) Ministers. Accountability to parliaments would be vested in the Common Assembly and to the law in the Community's own Court of Justice. Although the Council of Ministers brought into the open the latent tension between the High Authority and governments, it was the contrary of a defeat for the Schuman idea. A body as divorced as the original High Authority from the give-and-take of politics could hardly have survived.

The institutional rebalancing and tempering of the Schuman Plan before the summer holidays was followed by an economic one in the last months of the year. Though each delegation had a national point of view, the main forces in play can be reduced to three. Leaving aside differences in broad political approach, from the federalism of the Germans and Italians to the very reserved stance of the Belgians and Luxembourgeois, the economic approaches of all five of France's partners played variations on a fairly predictable tune of industrial interests. The Luxembourgeois, with a steel industry accounting for 80 per cent of national income, like the Belgians, with coal and steel representing 16 per cent of national income, were totally innocent of grand designs. As Alan Milward has written, "it is impossible to find in the papers of the Belgian delegation the slightest hint of any aspirations to 'make Europe' in the sense in which federalists used the term".

The second attitude, that of Monnet, was more complicated. He not only put heavy emphasis on institutions and politics, but he refused the French steel industry a place in his delegation. Monnet had read the Sherman Act as early as 1944. In October 1949, when many observers feared the long-expected postwar slump was about to break, Monnet "expressed great concern over the danger of the recrudescence of national and international cartels", especially as regards Germany, which occupied "a key position in the cartel movement". Acheson's first reaction to the Schuman Plan was suspicion it might be a cartel. Monnet hurriedly got Uri to produce a document to refute such a heinous idea. Producers would have access to each other's markets, the opposite of a cartel, in which each home market was a national preserve.

Combined with his belief in the large market, this might make Monnet seem a free-trader. In fact, he was more of a planner with a strongly expansionist outlook. Free trade was an excellent means to encourage growth and to lower political borders. It was not a decisive criterion on its own. The ultimate sin of cartels in his eyes was to set up private interests against public ones, economic restriction against expansion and protectionism against union between peoples. Monnet told a British diplomat that "in order to prevent the revival of the prewar cartels it was desirable to erect a public authority which would not have the vices of a cartel". When a German mentioned the danger of too much international planning, Monnet retorted that the issue was "not between international *dirigisme* and free enterprise, but between competition and cartels". He was determined that private power should not subvert what he saw as the general interest. He also wanted American support.

The third group were indeed the Americans. They were not in the negotiations but a major force behind the scenes. This was partly because they held the ring between France and Germany, partly through the close personal links with Monnet via Tomlinson and McCloy. Tomlinson was a key figure. But so, in the shadow of the shadow, was Raymond Vernon (of later fame for his studies on industrial policy at Harvard). He was passing every clause of successive drafts of the treaty under his microscope down in the bowels of the State Department and coming up with exegetical commentaries of Biblical abundance. He stressed the importance of *(a)* the powers of the High Authority, *(b)* the freedom of the projected common market from restrictive practices and *(c)* a Community open to foreign trade. Vernon's telegrams were treated as instructions by Tomlinson whenever he felt so inclined.[3] Vernon thought he was making quite an impact, and so he was.

Monnet concentrated in the first half of September mainly on German rearmament. He turned back to the Schuman conference in the second half. Meanwhile, the material issues of the single market for coal and steel were being discussed in expert working groups. These resulted in a synthesis

---

3. Tomlinson was credited with two techniques for enjoying maximum room for manœuvre. One was to contact and impress figures at the top of the pyramid. The other was to send enormously long telegrams, as complete and complex as possible. The length would mean they passed at the end of the queue; the completeness ensured he could not be faulted; the complexity would keep Washington busy for a long time, so that when instructions came back he could always claim, if need be, that the situation had changed. This technique was open only to a workaholic who was supremely well informed, which was why he had no imitators.

which centred the system on the High Authority working through the regional associations on the Monnet Plan pattern of Modernisation Commissions. But it did not follow that what worked inside a parliamentary regime in a single country was acceptable in an international organisation with no deep-rooted, long-established political frame and loyalties. The dangers were underlined by the Belgians, who argued the regional associations should be national, that is, precisely the "national groupings" Monnet had so recently denounced as "camouflaged cartels" (see p. 210). This alarmed both him and the Americans.

On October 2, Bruce cabled Washington that in the previous few days his team had pressed with the French "the major preoccupations of [the State] Department" by criticising the Schuman treaty drafts so far. They had stressed the need for greater price flexibility and competition, the danger that regional associations would be cartels and the risk that "excessive caution . . . will lead to compromising permanently basic principles of [the] proposal". Bruce added that "our ideas on major points are shared by Monnet and other leading delegates".

At the negotiating session of October 4, Monnet suddenly launched into a diatribe against cartels and regional associations. Suetens, apparently reeling, reported home that the tone was quite unlike the Monnet he knew. On October 10, Monnet took all the major issues out of the hands of the experts and concentrated them in the steering group he chaired. In October, too, Robert R. Bowie, a Harvard anti-trust lawyer and McCloy's chief adviser in Germany, became a frequent visitor to Paris. Monnet asked him to draft anti-trust articles for the Schuman treaty. The texts of the two articles he prepared (on cartels and the abuse of monopoly power) became the basis of the Schuman anti-trust regime. Anti-trust laws were not a European tradition. Monnet's alliance with the Americans had swung into motion.

To some extent—certainly on cartels—the negotiations were now fought out between the Monnet-American alliance, stressing a competitive regime run by the High Authority, and the Five in different degrees representing the European national and cartel traditions. The conflict of approaches was brought to a head by the French draft treaty of November 9, which raised protests from the Five. They accused it of going back on agreements in order to claw back powers for the High Authority. As Suetens reported home to Brussels, on cartels, "the French . . . went back on their [experts' assent]. More serious still, Mr. Tomlinson . . . having hesitated a long time, strongly backed [them]". The Americans were active in the mêlée that ensued. Telegrams poured in from Vernon in the second half of November pushing views on cartels, monopolies, production quotas in crisis situations, trade, prices, Belgian coal and the powers of the Council of Ministers. For instance, on cartels (article 41 at the time), the "French" draft (i.e., largely Bowie's for Monnet) presumed agreements guilty until proved innocent, while the Germans considered they should be permitted unless forbidden. Vernon considered the German approach had failed between the wars and was a cloak for the cartel lobby. His telegram concluded, "Request you give strong support to French". On another occasion, at a lunch where Tomlinson was asked by Monnet to comment on the plans for the Community (in practice, the Germans and Dutch) to subsidise Belgian coal during a five-year transition period in return for a yearly reduction of up to 3 per cent in production capacity, Suetens protested that "he could not agree that Americans should be interested in whether Belgian coal was a full member of the single market".

Nevertheless, the result of the flurry of bargaining in November was that the bulk of the treaty instituting the European Coal and Steel Community (ECSC) was completed by early December. The lineaments and tone of the original Monnet concept were clearly visible in the finished work. In some respects they were even fleshed out. His first narrow, technocratic view of relations between the High Authority and the industries and governments had become a political system, which is still substantially that of the European Community today. The common market for coal and steel was to be opened at once, free of customs duties and other trade restrictions; discriminatory practices were outlawed; and firms were obliged to post their prices and could be heavily fined for cheating. The High Authority could administer Europe's first strong anti-cartel law, subject to appeal to the Community's own Court of Justice. It could raise its own taxes on coal and steel up to 1 per cent of "average value" of output. It could contract and extend loans and give public "advice" on investment plans. It could aid labour to adjust to technological change in the industries in its charge. In a complex balance with the Council of Ministers, it could introduce production quotas to meet "manifest crises" caused by extreme swings in the market. As far as paper agreements could go, the treaty delegated major powers to the new circle of European institutions and to their proposed centre-piece, the High Authority, in particular.

At the same time, when one looks at the treaty in detail, it is evident that the states and industries too made their weight strongly felt in the negotiations. On prices, Monnet himself assumed in May that "it would probably be necessary to fix prices by zones in relation to fixed pricing points", which was an approach associated with planning or price leadership or cartels. In June, Tomlinson expected steel prices to be quoted ex-works in the most competitive way. Monnet's view was much closer to the final outcome. On cartels, concessions were made to the Germans and Belgians. Certain kinds of specialisation and joint sales agreements had to be authorised (unless proved guilty). The interdict on agreements also applied only "within the common market", an open invitation to an export cartel. The Americans were also not particularly enamoured of the arrangements to deal with "manifest crises". Typically, all these choices reflected a European preference for public (or private) regulation of the market. Further, the High Authority's powers were fuzzy where coal and steel touched fingers with the rest of the economy. The High Authority had virtually no powers over foreign trade, transport and the free movement of labour despite the fact that all three areas warranted whole sections of the treaty (chapters VIII, IX and X).

The treaty, of course, could be no more than a pointer to the future balance of powers between the new High Authority and the established governments and industrial associations inside the ECSC. Even so, as Miriam Camps, a State Department official at the time of the Schuman negotiations, concluded a decade later, "Although the articles as finally agreed . . . are all somewhat more qualified than American officials in touch with the negotiations would have wished, they are almost revolutionary in terms of the traditional European approach to these basic industries".

As for timing, the mystery is that the treaty was in essence complete by mid-December 1950 yet only signed the following April. The fact was that one of the central dramas of the Schuman negotiation was not played out in the conference at all but enacted elsewhere. This was the power struggle over the deconcentration of the Ruhr. It was not the only clash between the proposed priorities of the new regime and the ambitions of member states. There were difficult negotiations above all with the Belgians determined to insulate terminally inefficient coal mines and to a lesser extent with the Italians intent on expanding high-cost steel capacity. (Both were successful, the Belgians only in the short run.) But important as these were they did not have the impact of the Ruhr.

V

HIGH OR RUHR AUTHORITY?

Properly speaking, the deconcentration of the Ruhr was the responsibility of the Allied High Commissions in Germany and no concern of the Schuman conference. But the future of the Ruhr was, or seemed to be, at the root of relations between France and Germany. The formal link with the Schuman Plan was that the anti-trust articles of the draft treaty affected the Ruhr. Shortly after Bowie finished his draft, Hallstein telephoned Monnet from Bonn to say that it was not acceptable. Meetings of heads of delegations were suspended. Early in December, the Germans formally reserved acceptance of the anti-trust articles of the treaty until the terms of deconcentration in the Ruhr had been agreed. Thenceforward, everything hung on the Ruhr negotiations. The struggle lasted until March 1951, postponing signature of the treaty by a good three months.

In 1950, deconcentration was a relic of the early postwar policy of breaking up the industrial and other structures presumed to be behind Nazism. The Americans' practical problem was to allay France's fears that the oligarchy controlling German steel and coal might dominate western Europe, without giving the new Germany a lasting grievance; in short, to give both parties the feeling that the "equality" promised by the Schuman Plan was not a sham. One firm, the Vereinigte Stahlwerke ("United Steel-Works") had an output in 1938 one and a half times that of the whole of France. Yet the Germans regarded the concentration of coal and steel as one of the bases of their economic efficiency and a right. The steel barons were a formidable lobby because they embodied a national tradition.

The issue surfaced on September 21, when the Allied High Commission, under its Law 27, required the deconcentration of the German steel and coal combines. Within a week, on September 28, Ludwig Erhard, the German Minister for Economic Affairs, turned up in Monnet's office with a message from Adenauer. There was a radical incompatibility, Erhard explained, between the Schuman Plan, which promised Germany equality, and the Allied plans to reorganise German heavy industry. The Allies had not consulted the German government and their plans discriminated against Germany alone. Adenauer was worried about how to defend the Schuman Plan before the Bundestag (the lower house of Parliament in Bonn). Hallstein asked the French to press the Americans to desist.

Monnet sympathised in part with the Germans. He wrote at once to Schuman that "we must not give [them] the impression that we are trying to take away with one hand what we are giving with the other". It had been agreed from the start that the IRA and ceilings on German steel production must be abolished as soon as the Schuman Plan entered into effect. This was confirmed in a conversation between Monnet, Hallstein and the Americans on November 21, which found the first two in full agreement. A month later, a letter covering these and related points was drafted, "in very generous terms to alleviate the political difficulties of Adenauer", by Monnet and the French Foreign Office. Schuman was to send it publicly to Adenauer at the time of the signature of the treaty.

Production ceilings were one thing, however, and deconcentration was another. The French were determined to cut the umbilical cord between German coal and steel. With giants like United State's Steel three times the size of the Vereinigte Stahlwerke, the Americans were underwhelmed by the power of German steel and its ownership of coal. In contrast, their anti-trust tradition was shocked by the German coal sales monopoly, the Deutscher Kohlenverkauf (DKV), in their eyes a flagrant restraint on trade. The irony was that the French, with a coal import monopoly of their own, the Association Technique de l'Importation Charbonnière (ATIC), found the DKV rather convenient. Europeans, burdened with deep mines, discontinuous narrow seams and high overhead costs, were more easily convinced of the virtues of planning in coal than Americans, used (amongst other factors) to better geological conditions.

On the German side, the Ruhr industrialists played for time in the plausible belief that it was on their side. There are signs they intrigued to some effect with the French steelmasters, who stopped expressing anxiety about German competition in November 1950 and concentrated their fire instead on the "excessive powers" of the High Authority. There is little doubt that the steelmasters would have preferred, as the chairman of the Vereinigte Stahlwerke, Hermann Wenzel, put it frankly, to negotiate a "Schuman Plan" among themselves. The French steelmasters, Wenzel claimed, "desired neither the deconcentration of steel nor the separation of steel and coal". There were reports in December that Monnet was having trouble obtaining the French government's assent to the anti-cartel provisions of the draft treaty. Informal moves were made in the French Parliament to discuss the treaty clause by clause so as to throw out only the anti-cartel articles.

Adenauer's position was complex. Albert Bureau, the head of the French section of the Steel Control Group in Germany, noted the steelmasters crowding round him. Adenauer's closest adviser, Dr. Robert Pferdmenges, was a former member of the supervisory board of the Vereinigte Stahlwerke. In mid-October 1950, Adenauer appointed as Minister of the Interior Rolf Lehr, another member of its board, who had given a speech the week before lambasting the Schuman Plan as a protective screen for inefficient French steel and offering the prewar cartel as a model. Monnet took the speech as a "declaration of war" by the Ruhr barons. In the end, Adenauer was to show that he was ready to stick to his policy in face of the industrial lobby. But for much of the winter of 1950–51, it was not clear he could impose this line even if he wanted to.

In a series of meetings from October to the end of the year, Monnet, McCloy and their associates set up a common Franco-American front. They agreed that deconcentration would not be viable if the Bonn government failed to commit itself and accept it. Formally, it must propose the final settlement. The Bonn government was ready to do this, but for the opposite reason: to take matters out of the hands of the Allies. On November 9 and again on December 27, it presented arguments and proposals to handle the Ruhr itself. It was clearly playing for time.

The French themselves, as Monnet informed Schuman, "were held up throughout October" by the reluctance of their own coal representatives in Germany to accept a package with the Americans. Finally, a series of meetings in Monnet's office with Bowie and Leroy-Beaulieu, now the Economic Director of the French High Commission in Germany, resulted on December 19 in a joint line. In essence, this combined the American determination to break up the coal sales agency with the French one to split German coal from steel.

On December 28, McCloy told Acheson that the Schuman Plan would be a "dead duck" without action by the United States. In the New Year, things began to move. Adenauer agreed on January 15, 1951, that the coal sales agency might be dissolved by the remote date of April 1954. Two days later, Bowie met Erhard, who said he was ready to work for a compromise, and at the end of the month Erhard sent a draft which provided one. All this was too good to be true. In mid-February it was duly reported that "Erhard has been blocked by the industrialists' last minute counter-offensive". On February 17, in a three-hour talk with Adenauer, Erhard, and Pferdmenges, McCloy said that the "insistence" of the Ruhr industrialists "on their full demands supports [the] French and our own fear that [their] purpose is to attain artificially preferred position for German steel which will enable its growth at expense of normal growth of competing European industry". On February 19, he came to Paris to see Monnet. He hesitated to act, he said, because he was not sure of the firmness of the French government. Monnet assured him it stood firm. On February 22, at a meeting in Frankfurt, after a call to Monnet, it was decided the Americans should tell the Germans no further concessions could be made on the link between coal and steel. "Adenauer's goodwill was not in doubt, but who held the power?" wrote Leroy-Beaulieu. McCloy was depressed and "more or less certain of failure in the Schuman Plan because of the Germans, which alarmed him".

In fact, the tide was turning again. Adenauer spent the whole of February 22 and 23 in a kind of seminar to persuade the industrialists to give up opposition to the Schuman Plan. Finally, on March 14, he sent a letter to McCloy accepting terms. The Vereinigte Stahlwerke was to be divided into thirteen firms and Krupp in two. (Even so, all seven steel plants producing over one million tons each in the ECSC in 1952 were German.) The steelmasters' control over coal output was reduced from the prewar level of 55 per cent and from the 25 per cent the Germans were seeking to 16 per cent (against a French demand of 8 per cent). The DKV was to be broken up into four sales agencies by 1952. This was the decision which aroused most German protests, especially from the labour unions concerned with unemployment, still sizable at the time.

Less than a week after Adenauer's letter, on March 19, 1951, the Paris treaty setting up the European Coal and Steel Community was initialled and on April 18 signed. Monnet confessed to Bruce that "without the firm assistance" of the United States, there would have been no treaty.

In Paris, Monnet had been given a remarkably free hand by the government. Pleven, now the Prime Minister, and Schuman backed him on all the main issues. At last, on December 15, 1950, the first cabinet committee on the subject since June required Monnet's team to discuss the nearly completed treaty in detail with the ministries. The process lasted much of the next two months. The ministries raised a large number of questions and suggestions, with criticisms notably of the supranational powers of the High Authority. Most of these, however, were parried or absorbed with surprising ease.

The really big issue between the initialling and signing of the treaty was, as so often, the Saar. When, early in December in the Schuman talks, the Dutch raised the Saar in relation to the powers of the High Authority, Hallstein said, "If you raise that now you will sink the Schuman Plan". To Monnet, the electricity in the air was palpable. The Gaullist French proconsul in the Saar, Gilbert Grandval, was a forceful character. He lobbied hard in Paris for the Saar to be made a seventh full member of the Community, autonomous from both Germany and France. These manœuvres were fended off, with some difficulty, by Schuman, but the substitute on which the French fell back, that the government sign on behalf of France and the Saar, was such, Hallstein said, that Adenauer might "be forced to refuse even to sign". In the end, Schuman and Adenauer published letters attached to the treaty specifying that it affected the claims of neither country on the Saar. Both men were criticised at home for conceding too much. When Monnet visited Bonn on April 4–6, he proposed that France and Germany should have equal representation in all Community bodies, irrespective of the Saar or of German reunification. Adenauer, whose experts had proposed voting weighted by output, which favoured Germany, agreed at once.

After all the *Sturm und Drang,* it is intriguing that the impression left on a battle-scarred negotiator like Spierenburg was that the Schuman talks were "of a cordiality unequalled in [his] experience". Monnet had originally intended to cut down formal sessions to a minimum and to hold as many "direct conversations" as possible with the other chief delegates. Suetens complained early in September that it was less a negotiation than a conversation, and agonisingly slow, but that it helped bring the Dutch along. Max Kohnstamm, the Foreign Office deputy to Spierenburg in the Dutch delegation, has recalled the amazement and suspicion of Spierenburg when he first saw Monnet arguing with Uri and Hirsch in a conference session. "How can I negotiate if they do not know their own interest?" But openness quite quickly made its mark. At the end of term, Hallstein praised Monnet as "a leader in whose person was incarnated the spirit of European solidarity" and quoted Suetens's joke that "we have lived in the House of the High Authority". Bowie, who dealt closely with both, believes that Monnet and Hallstein "developed a remarkable rapport. . . . [Hallstein] was intellectually very honest. At bottom, so was Monnet. He could dissemble, but basically, he really did want to get down to what the reality was. . . . Obviously, [Hallstein] had to represent the German point of view, and Monnet to bring along the French, but both were coming at it like people trying to create something".

The conference wound up in schoolboysterousness. "While Schuman and the Quai d'Orsay looked on in wonder, the Belgian delegation led the others in singing a ballad of its own composition on the Schuman Plan". Hallstein, not usually one for levity, led in a parody of the Nazi Horst Wessel hymn:

Die Preise hoch
Kartelle fest geschlossen,
Monnet marschiert
mit ruhig festem Schritt!

("Prices high, cartels shut down, Monnet marches with calm firm tread.") When one considers postwar feelings in Europe, this was of more than anecdotal interest. A divide had been crossed. Much of the later resilience of European policy was rooted in the corporate feeling developed in the Schuman conference. The British later talked of a "Euromafia". The core first met around the Schuman table. To have been of the small band of begetters of the first Europe conferred battle honours. An epic had been shared.

VI
RATIFICATION

Fourteen months elapsed between the signing of the treaty and the last ratifying vote in Italy on June 17, 1952. This was normal enough, and success was never seriously in doubt. Yet the reasons for the passing time were not only procedural. The British, for instance, held up the adjustment in the Occupation Statute to the Schuman treaty—a condition of German ratification—in order to compel the Bonn government to honour its promises of supplies of scrap to the British defence effort in response to the Korean War. The British had remained deep in the shadows during the talks on Law 27, probably for fear that they might be accused of trying to sabotage the Schuman Plan. This may well have produced a build-up of resentment, because the largely irrelevant dispute over scrap was conducted with unusual bitterness in London. Agreement was reached only in October 1951. The Allies were then able at last to confirm that the International Ruhr Authority and ceilings on steel production would disappear once the European Coal and Steel Community, as it now was, entered into force.

In many ways, the striking feature of the ratifications in both Germany and France (where the National Assembly passed the treaty on December 13, 1951, by 377 to 233 votes) was the failure of the steel interests to exert greater influence on the outcome. Even in Germany, where commitment to the Ruhr system was so deep-rooted, the German Federation of Trade Unions (DGB) backed the Schuman treaty despite the opposition to it of the Social Democratic Party and despite its own doubts about the break-up of the DKV. The Schuman Plan and co-determination for workers, trade union leaders said, "were the only means effectively to strip the German coal and steel owners of the tremendous economic power which was misused twice in the past".

In France, the steelmasters were used to thinking of themselves as the aristocracy of the employers. Their association, under government authority, fixed supplies to firms, output quotas and deliveries to customers. The balance of production between plants had hardly budged since 1918. The Schuman Plan, therefore, threatened the Steel Association not only with competition but with loss of power. It came out publicly in opposition on July 17, 1950. Subsequently, it refused to provide data on industry costs to Monnet's negotiating team. The President, Jules Aubrun, complained that Monnet excluded the steelmasters from the talks, whereas all the other governments kept industry in close touch. Monnet responded in terse, sarcastic letters.

The details are less important than the fact that Monnet—still ensconced at the CGP—won with ease. His team argued in parliamentary committees that the French industry could compete (an argument helped by the Korean boom) and that the ECSC would help by guaranteeing coking coal supplies at competitive prices. Monnet even claimed (optimistically) that with "the achievement at last of transforming industries, Lorraine could become a second Ruhr in a united Europe". The government did not cave in to the Steel Association's noisy campaign. "We found it easier to deal with the steel industry than we had expected". The unpopularity of the steelmasters was certainly a factor. They were also divided, because a minority backed the Schuman Plan. Their failure came as a great shock to men used to getting their own way behind the scenes, and affected employer reactions to the Common Market later on.

The ratification was in some ways most severely contested in Germany. It was not just that the Socialists (SPD) in opposition were preparing to vote against the treaty under the influence of their vehement leader, Fritz Schumacher, who regarded integration of the ECSC Six as a flawed distraction from the reunification of Germany itself. The impending vote improved the bargaining position of those who wanted to claw back concessions on the Ruhr and the DKV in particular. McCloy wrote to Adenauer on August 27, 1951, that he was "amazed" the German representatives dealing with the DKV had "in effect repudiate[d] the position taken in [Adenauer's] letter of March 14". Nevertheless, on January 11, 1952, in the name of Europe and the greater equality offered Germany by the ECSC, Adenauer rang up a majority of 232 to 143 for the treaty in the Bundestag. Yet the struggle around the DKV was still not over. In June 1952, the German coal trustees again refused to plan for new sales agencies on the grounds that the Federal Republic had not accepted the Allies' regulation. McCloy dealt this time with Ludger Westrick, the new Under Secretary for Economics, brought in as a representative of industry and beyond Erhard's control. After some sparring, McCloy reached an "entirely satisfactory" agreement with Westrick, and Monnet obtained the assent of the French government in the first week of July. Only then was the final conference of Foreign Ministers held to set up the ECSC.

This meeting took place on July 25, 1952. The ministers had to nominate the members of the various ECSC bodies and decide where the latter should be sited. The Interim Committee to prepare such questions had recommended one of Monnet's favourite ideas, then and later, that there should be a European District, an embryo "federal capital", containing all the institutions. In the meeting, Schuman surprised everyone, Monnet included, by proposing Saarbrücken, the capital of the Saar. This sudden manœuvre to confirm the separation of the Saar from Germany infuriated Adenauer. Failing to reach agreement, the ministers instructed Monnet and Hallstein to prepare a communiqué saying that the entry into force of the Paris treaty, and therefore of the ECSC, would be postponed. The same day, however, Luxembourg, the last country to do so, deposited its instruments of ratification of the treaty, which thereby entered into force. The effect was to abrogate all Allied Occupation controls on the Ruhr without the new ECSC being in a position to take over. The conference went back to work. In the general confusion, the ministers proposed Turin as capital. Monnet and Spierenburg warned that they would not take up their High Authority posts if the Alps screened them from the industries. Van Helmont, who was present, has described what followed.

Italy was offered the presidency of the Court instead of the District. Brussels was then accepted all round. Van Zeeland, the Belgian Foreign Minister, went to the phone, and came back. He did not want Brussels. He wanted Liège and claimed the presidency of the Court for Belgium. I can still see one of the two Dutch delegates, a tall, big, blond man, stand up, put his bursting briefcase on the table, shut the lock with a click, turn round to Van Zeeland, say "You disgust me", and walk out. In the end, around four o'clock in the morning, Joseph Bech, the Luxembourg Prime Minister, proposed that operations might begin "provisionally" in Luxembourg. This was accepted.[4] . . . Adenauer left the meeting first. Down-

4. Actually, Van Zeeland insisted that Luxembourg's hold on the institutions should not even be "provisional" but "precarious". According to a report from the U.S. embassy in Paris,

stairs, the journalists clustered round him. His only comment, as he climbed into his car, was *"arme Europa, arme Europa!"*—"poor Europe, poor Europe".

Monnet told the number two of the British embassy in Paris, William Hayter, that he had been "driven by Van Zeeland's behaviour to resign three times in the course of the evening from the position of President of the High Authority to which he had not yet been appointed". It was perhaps the first, and it was not to be the last, of such scenes of confederal confusion and byzantine dealings. Two weeks later, on August 10, 1952, the High Authority of the European Coal and Steel Community set up headquarters in Luxembourg with Jean Monnet as its president.

VII
A LEAP IN THE DARK

The art of the Schuman Plan was, as the then editor of *Le Monde,* Jacques Fauvet, pointed out, "to extract a policy from a need", that is, powerful positive energy from potentially destructive ingredients. It was a gamble, a "leap in the dark", as Schuman himself said. But it drew strength from the popularity of "Europe" with the public. And it turned a lost cause, which could have become a rout, for Schuman himself and for France, into a new world of opportunity.

The conflicts beneath the surface were perfectly rendered by the fierce struggle over the Ruhr which the Americans and McCloy settled (at least provisionally), not the French or Monnet. It was argued by Ruhr spokesmen at the time that the Schuman Plan was only promoted to protect the Monnet Plan. Certainly, Monnet sold the Schuman Plan to the French Parliament in part on the strength of its preventing the Ruhr from crushing the life out of French industry by its quasi-monopoly of coke for French steel. It was a key argument for ratifying the Schuman treaty.

Nevertheless, steel was more the occasion than the cause of the Schuman Plan. A clue is that Monnet and Schuman made no effort, as other French leaders would have done, to make a condition of guarantees for the Saar. In so doing, they discarded the mirage of a balance of power in steel. They replaced it by a new approach to relations. An anachronism is relevant here. In 1956, the year the French government agreed to return the Saar to Ger-

---

the "entire question" should be "re-examined" at subsequent meetings of the ministers. Bech thought of Luxembourg as the potential headquarters of the ECSC at least as early as July 1950.

many, German and Saar steel production, at over 26 million tons together, was already twice as large as French. If power in steel had really been the key, the French should at this stage have dropped the Community. It was in fact the year they accelerated toward the Common Market. Steel was too narrow for a European policy which is very much alive today, long after postwar French motives in the Ruhr have been forgotten. With or without steel, the French would have had to face Germany as a state with greater potential than their own.

Monnet thought of a European coal and steel authority as a source of peace when he showed Hirsch his map in Algiers. All five clauses of the preamble to the Schuman treaty deal with peace in one form or another, and only two turn on economics. He was trying to ensure against German dangers as the French saw them, but his vision was of a new Europe. Adenauer was seeking to regain sovereignty and power for his country, but he was determined to integrate it in the West, reconcile it with France and make it a respectable member of a community of nations. Both were trying to make the old rivalries alien to the new political process. The Schuman Plan, as most participants knew, was about turning around the psychology of relations between states and peoples. When at their first meeting Adenauer and Monnet talked of "moral duty", it was neither hot air nor hypocrisy, but the core of necessity in the calculations.

Perhaps the most extraordinary feature of the Schuman conference was the enormous, almost internal, role the Americans played. Without them, the conference would have failed and the foundations of the European Community never been laid. This proved that while France might be able to give a lead, it could not, even in 1950, set the terms of a relationship with Germany. Throughout the Cold War, the minimum as well as sufficient force for the progress of European unity was, as Van Helmont has pointed out, the triple alliance of the United States, France and Germany. One of the historic merits of the Schuman Plan was to mobilise this passing convergence to lasting ends; and one of the strengths of Monnet to be able to raise American support in a way no other European could rival.

Monnet, at this stage, showed great sureness of political touch. He himself said, many years later, "In 1950, I was at the top of my form". He made many controversial judgements hindsight shows to have been correct: the narrowing of focus to coal and steel; the sudden announcement to catch the expected opposition off balance; the insistence on powers for the High Authority; the daring move to slip the moorings with Britain; the stress on equality and non-discrimination; marginalising of the Saar; ties with the United States. It is also probable that his superior feeling for the politics of innovation made the Schuman Plan and the ECSC possible where routine strategists and tacticians would have lost their way. The contrast between the conception and launching of the Schuman Plan and the failures of Finebel and of Pierre Pflimlin's stab at an agricultural community suggests that a good part of the difference between their respective fates lay simply in Monnet's more expert and determined generalship, from the choice of ground to the exploitation of it.

It is ironic, then, that Monnet's prime invention should bear another man's name. That was the price of being the architect, not the politician. It is difficult to apportion roles between Monnet and Schuman. Monnet was the driving force, the more fertile in imagination, the clearer in strategy, the stronger in will. The British ambassador in Paris noted at one point: "A contrast to the woolliness of French politicians generally, and even of M. Schuman . . . is of course provided by M. Monnet whose views seem to be quite clear-cut and determined". Yet Schuman, who had shown firmness as prime minister in difficult conditions in 1947, provided the political space for Monnet. Pressing forward, the latter was in constant danger of losing touch. Schuman took responsibility for the difficult manœuvres over the Saar; he carried the policy inside the Fourth Republic governments, never the most cohesive of groups at the best of times; he beat off the steelmasters. For the best years of the two men's careers, Schuman bore the final burden and delivered. For that alone he deserves the misleading label of his plan. Monnet, though, rapidly and rightly came to embody the European policy in an active sense Schuman never began to match. By the time the European Coal and Steel Community was set up, he had already established the reputation as "Mr. Europe", on which he capitalised for the rest of his life.

The First Europe

1952–1954

The Sunday after the Schuman conference opened, North Korea attacked South Korea in what the American historian Thomas A. Schwartz has called "the Pearl Harbor of the Cold War". George Ball was at Houjarray. "Monnet saw the implications . . . almost faster than Washington. The Americans, he declared, would never permit the Communists to succeed with such naked aggression. . . . Yet for America to intervene in Korea would not only jeopardize the Schuman Plan, it might well create panic in Europe and increase American insistence on a larger German role in defense of the West".

Monnet's insights proved extremely accurate. America engaged its own forces in Korea to block the victorious advance of the North. It was able to carry this out under a United Nations umbrella, with small contingents of allies, because the Security Council condemned North Korea as the aggressor. This would never have happened had the Soviet Union not blundered and temporarily lost its ability, as one of the five permanent members of the Security Council, to veto Security Council decisions. It had rashly walked out because America systematically vetoed the claim of Mao Tse-tung's Communist regime, in complete control of mainland China since September 1949, to replace the Nationalists, who had fled to Taiwan, in China's permanent seat on the council.

The parallel between a divided Korea in Asia and divided Germany in Europe haunted Western leaders. If Stalin exploited weakness in Korea, what might he not do in Germany? Germany, not Korea, was the fulcrum of the balance of power. But America would only bring troops to prop up Western Europe's sense of security if the locals contributed to an adequate defence against the Soviet armies. Such a defence, all the military agreed, the French included, was inconceivable without German troops.

Pressure began to build up straightaway. On July 22, 1950, Acheson asked the NATO allies to indicate by August 5 how and how much they proposed to rearm. On August 11, the Consultative Assembly of the Council of Europe, led by Winston Churchill, called for "the immediate creation of a unified European Army, under the authority of a European Minister of Defence". On September 9, McCloy leaked American proposals for "a fully armed German force of ten divisions integrated into a west European Army". When Schuman turned up in New York on September 12 for the regular tripartite meeting of foreign ministers with Acheson and Bevin, he found Acheson making the despatch of more American forces to Europe conditional on the Europeans equipping sixty divisions, ten of them German.

This was a nightmare, five years after the war. In Germany itself, the attitude of many was *ohne mich* ("without me"). The rejection was most acute in France. Not that the French had suffered even more than other occupied peoples, but their pride as a traditional great power had been much more deeply battered. Alone at the meeting of the whole Atlantic Council in New York in September, Schuman held out against German rearmament in NATO. When the defence ministers met in October, the Frenchman Jules Moch, whose son had been tortured and executed by the Germans, yielded not an inch. Madame Moch sat straight behind him, dressed from head to foot in black.

All the same, stonewalling was not a policy. A draft note, dated August 1, in Monnet's papers argues that rearmament in the Atlantic alliance should be a common effort, not a "juxtaposition" of national ones. "Central" bodies should run it, and there should be a common defence fund. Costs should be shared in the light of each country's per capita income. Germany should contribute materially but not be allowed to manufacture weapons. There was no mention of German troops. The French note of August 5 reflected all this less than Petsche's concern for defence dollars from America. However, the next one, on August 17, arguing for coordinated arms production, showed greater Monnet influence. There was no response to it either. On September 6, Schuman complained to Bruce that there had been no American reaction to the French notes of August 5 and 17. In fact, the Americans were determined that these "far-reaching" proposals must "not delay [the] urgent efforts" needed. According to Irwin Wall, they saw the French ideas as "a transparent scheme to 'spread their inflation' among all the allies, collectivise the cost of the Indochina War, and make the United States underwrite the military budgets" of the Europeans. The first French line of approach was blocked.

On August 23, Monnet drafted a handwritten letter from Silvia Monnet's holiday house, the Old Mill on the Île-de-Ré, a bean-shaped island in the Bay of Biscay, to his old associate, René Pleven, now Prime Minister.

Decisions are imposed by events and each is taken in isolation. We are soldiering on in Indochina. Why? . . . The movement in Asia is Asian, against the foreigner whoever he happens to be. . . . How can our military effort in Indochina succeed? . . . In my opinion, all this is absurd and dangerous. . . . We are operating with partners. These partners happen to be the most powerful in the world, they have helped us, and without them we could not have resolved our "material" troubles after the war. But their help, which has been so great, has seduced them and us into bad habits. Their help has been *material*. They continue to think in material terms. What they need, and we need with them, is a political concept, that is, a spiritual and ethical one. . . . I propose you bring to the partnership a strong, constructive concept as well as a determination to build up a stout external defence[,] . . . the establishment of a structured Atlantic free world, accommodating the diversity of its three constituent parts, the United States, the British Empire, and continental Western Europe federated around an expanded Schuman Plan. . . . [We] would transform our archaic social conditions and come to laugh at our present fear of Russia.

The hope . . . lies in the fact that the team leader is the United States. Of all the countries of the West, it is the readiest to accept change and listen to strong straight talk, so long as one throws a constructive idea into the ring. The United States are not imperialist, they are efficient. . . . Alone, they will not develop the political vision of which the world stands in need. I think that is our task.

There is a striking concordance between these words and Monnet's acts in the following decade. They show that, for him, union looked not only east to Germany, but west to Britain and America.

Monnet finally sent his letter to Pleven on September 3. On September 5, he was struck by a press conference of Schuman's on defence which failed to mention the Schuman Plan. He drafted a note to Schuman stressing the links between the two. He did not send it. Instead, he saw Schuman on the eve of the latter's departure for New York. France must regain the initiative. If the Germans obtained through national rearmament the "equality" on offer in the Schuman Plan, they might drop the latter and France would be bereft of a German policy. A few days later, he wrote to Schuman claiming the Germans were indeed becoming more nationalist in the talks. Two days later still, he sent Schuman in New York a memo he proposed to give Pleven that afternoon. It was really the same draft, ending on three options: to do nothing; to back German national rearmament; or to widen the Schuman Plan to defence. Put like that, there was little choice. Because of these communications or not, Schuman and Alphand in New York concluded at the end of the Atlantic Council in September that there must be a French defence proposal on Schuman Plan lines.

During the first half of September, Monnet redeployed his small team, with Clappier, Reuter and Alphand, wholly on a "European" plan for defence. Not one of the group was a military man or anything near; and the only diplomat was Alphand, to the annoyance of critics in the Quai d'Orsay. Monnet's *Memoirs* do not apologise. "We had no more need of military experts than we had had of specialists to Europeanise steel. . . . Essentially, it was a political question"—to provide a scheme which could attack the problem and pass muster with the French National Assembly, as interpreted by Pleven, the most circumspect of tacticians. Monnet later believed he had been the one to convince Pleven there must be a European Army. This was Pleven's own impression. It is not the same as saying Monnet "invented" the Pleven Plan for a European Army. The idea was palpably in the air, as the Council of Europe demonstrated. What Monnet did was to take it up, put it into shape for the more or less willing group at the heart of government in Paris, and push it through.

No one was enthusiastic. At the last minute, Pleven seems to have had cold feet at what he was taking on. Delouvrier lunched with René Mayer, himself an uneasy supporter, on October 24, the day Pleven was due to announce the plan in the Assembly. The telephone rang. It was Pleven, wondering if he was not committing a blunder. Mayer gave him short shrift. "If you don't know now, it's too late". Even Monnet was far from in love with the scheme. Several people working near him at the time had the impression he regarded the European Army as at best premature.

Pleven's speech was duly delivered that afternoon, and the Assembly endorsed its ideas by 343 votes to 220. The proposal provided for a European Army under the Atlantic umbrella run by a European Minister of Defence and Council of Ministers, with a joint commander, common budget and common arms procurement. But negotiations were not to be broached before the Schuman Plan had been signed; and, for all but the Germans, it was to be *an* army, not *the* army. The French, Belgians, and so on, could keep national forces apart from the European Army for colonial and other purposes. Only the Germans would have a European duty but no national option at all.

The Pleven Plan was received abroad with a suspicion quite unlike the welcome given to the Schuman Plan. Germans attacked it for being "discriminatory" and denying them "equality", and as "a German foreign legion under a flimsy European coating". Those views were close to Adenauer's own in private. Two items especially stuck in German throats. One was the condition that the Schuman treaty should be signed first. The other was that German troops should be integrated into the European Army "at the lowest level of unit possible". This turned out to be the battalion, which the military (including the French) considered unworkably small. Acheson welcomed the scheme in public but in private wrote to Bruce that it "postpones a solution for many months" and that the Germans "will not participate in a plan where they are . . . blatantly labelled as inferiors". To the French ambassador, Henri Bonnet, he even spoke of a "hopeless situation" unless the scheme was changed.

Three days after Pleven's speech, McCloy came with Bowie to see Monnet at Houjarray.[1] To his "surprise, Pleven and Schuman arrived and in the course of a four hours' conversation" explained that the Pleven Plan was not intended to evade the issue. They hoped the Schuman treaty would be signed in a month. The terms "were only drawn up in [the form they were] so as to secure the necessary parliamentary majority". For political reasons, McCloy already leaned to a European approach. Having heard Pleven and Schuman, he concluded they were sincere.

There were now two plans for a "European" defence force.[2] One was the American NATO solution, pursued by everyone, including Adenauer, bar the French. This allowed German national rearmament (but no General Staff) within an Atlantic command under an American commander. The other was the French plan for a unified European Army, still under Atlantic command, but run by a European minister (i.e., no German Defence Ministry, no German General Staff, no full divisions). The military—Allied, German, even French—were impatient of the latter. The diplomats were more aware of the political minefields. Priority was given to the negotiations on the Atlantic approach, which began in January 1951 at the Allied High Commission offices on the Petersberg above the Rhine; but talks also opened in Paris a month later on the French scheme for a European Army of the six Schuman Plan countries.

Schuman asked Monnet whom, of Pierre-Henri Teitgen (a leading Christian Democrat politician and colleague of Schuman) or Alphand, he would prefer to see chair the European Army talks. It was *inter alia* a way of saying the chairman would not be Monnet. Monnet opted for Alphand. The French continued to stall in the Atlantic talks. They also suggested there should be a new four-power conference with the Soviet Union to see if rearmament was really necessary. There could have been a major complication if the Soviet Union had responded as it did a year later and put forward a proposal for the reunification of Germany. On this occasion, Moscow took no initiative. The

1. Like Spaak in Washington, Bowie vividly remembered the food: "One of the most magnificent soufflés Grand Marnier I've ever had".

2. There was great vagueness over what constituted being "European". Lewis Douglas, the able U.S. ambassador in London and McCloy's brother-in-law, wrote at one point, of the "prerequisites . . . of a genuine European army", that the first was "the assumption of command . . . by an American".

fruitless Palais Rose negotiations dragged on from March to June 1951. The European talks were also held up by the French general elections due on June 17. There was, in short, a six-month virtual standstill. Time was passing by.

Acheson and, the evidence suggests, Adenauer also, despite paying lip-service to European integration, would have preferred to follow the Atlantic tack. It offered a shorter route to the target and for Adenauer hope of the special German-American relationship familiar later. At the same time, it too smacked to the Germans of second-class citizenship. A major reason was the French veto in the Petersberg negotiations. The Americans were reluctant to ride roughshod over it. The impasse was broken by a reassertion of the old Schuman Plan alliance between Monnet and the American proconsuls in Europe, Bruce and McCloy.

Bowie, who believed, like McCloy, that a European Army was the only way to reconcile the French and Germans to German rearmament, suggested, and McCloy took up, the idea that Monnet and Eisenhower should meet. Eisenhower had been appointed Supreme Commander in Europe the previous December and had enormous prestige. He was beginning, for political reasons, to lean to the European Army, which he had initially dismissed on the military grounds generally shared in the Pentagon. McCloy and Bowie visited him in his office as, restlessly, he practised golf putts on the carpet. On June 21, Eisenhower and Monnet met for the first time since Algiers at a lunch with Harriman, General Alfred Gruenther, the chief of staff, and others. Monnet insisted that the Franco-German tangle over rearmament could be resolved only in a European Community. Eisenhower agreed with him that this was a political rather than a military problem. According to Monnet, when Gruenther, with some irritation, interjected that Franco-German reconciliation and common European uniforms would not provide the necessary divisions, Eisenhower retorted that the real issue was relations between peoples and that on this he agreed with Monnet. Monnet was never one for full-length portraits of those he encountered. But Eisenhower earned Monnet's ultimate accolade of "a generous spirit" and, more particularly, in connection with this meeting, Monnet added that Eisenhower's "political sense overrode his military instincts when it came to defending the peace". Several years later, David Bruce expressed the opinion that Eisenhower's conversion "was really not such a difficult task. A man of very simple ideas, he had been earlier sold on the unification of Europe. And Monnet rose to great heights in defending something he didn't really believe in".

The June 21 encounter was a turning point in the short history of the European Defence Community (EDC). On July 3 Eisenhower gave a speech to the English-Speaking Union in London publicly espousing the European Army. In the State Department, a parallel decision was taken to support "a real European federation even though the membership be restricted and even though there was the possibility that Germany might eventually become . . . the dominating element". Pentagon opposition was overcome.

Change from the American side was only half the story. The French had to purge the Pleven Plan itself of the more glaring discriminations against the Germans. The political pre-conditions for such a shift were met when, as a result of the general elections, the Socialists left the second Pleven government, formed on August 8, and Moch went with them. At one point in the long iterregnum between the elections and the new government, Monnet brought together Alphand (for the French government) and Bowie (for McCloy) in a three-day session at Houjarray with Hirsch and Uri. This was his first major initiative on the European Army since his successful siege of Pleven the previous autumn. The principle of equality was reaffirmed and the size of unit was left to Eisenhower to settle, who (in October) plumped for "groupings" (divisions under a blander name, to save French face). Pleven and Schuman now assented. For the first time, the French scheme for a European Army became negotiable.

Monnet took no official part in the negotiations on an EDC which followed. A comment he made to Alphand, "your team is not good", suggests a certain dissociation. But Paul van Zeeland, the Belgian Foreign Minister, who tended to see Monnet's hand in everything, complained to the American ambassador in Brussels, Robert Murphy (the Murphy of Algiers), early in 1952, that Monnet and Hirsch were "forcing the pace apparently in hope of achieving European unity by the back door, and loading down the European army proposal with [a] top heavy political super-structure borrowed from [the] Schuman Plan". At this stage, before they found by experience that common institutions advanced their interests, the Benelux countries were not at all their later federalist selves. They tried hard to turn the EDC into a NATO-style coalition army against the federal views of the French, Germans and Italians. They successfully resisted the original idea of a single European Defence Minister, which was inherently federalist, in favour of a board, whose powers were divisible and therefore negotiable.

Monnet could follow the EDC talks through Hirsch (they both still worked from the Monnet Plan office) as well as through Alphand. In October 1951, Hirsch became chairman of the conference's Committee for Armaments. This placed him at the heart of the bargaining on a Community for Arms Production, fully comparable in scale to the military flank of the EDC or the Schuman ECSC. Given later failures to standardise armaments in NATO, it is far from certain the EDC could have succeeded. However, in the 1950s, the options could still seem open. The defence industries were barely reviving and Germany had none. The EDC might have influenced their rebirth. One side-effect, invisible at the time, suggests it was already too late in some areas. The EDC treaty applied collective controls on all nuclear output. The French Atomic Energy Commissariat, with strong Gaullist sympathies, suddenly awoke to the implications for its own covert steps to develop nuclear weapons. Henceforward, it was alert to all European threats. This was to have consequences later on.

Monnet and Hirsch were also drawn into a matter well outside their usual range. In September, the Atlantic Council decided to ask "Three Wise Men" to recommend the size of forces it would make political, financial and military sense for NATO to aim at in Europe, the original Pentagon goals being plainly overblown. Averell Harriman was chosen for the United States and Edwin Plowden for Britain. Schuman and Alphand prevailed on Monnet to complete the trio. He made up his mind in a strange way. Normally a man who took his own decisions, this time he consulted a crowded meeting of associates. All but two favoured acceptance. He took on the job, although ratification of the Schuman treaty was looming, the EDC talks were starting in earnest, he still ran the Monnet Plan office, and NATO was apparently peripheral to his main concerns. His motives remain a mystery.

He may have felt an obligation to Schuman and Alphand. There is at least one later instance of his turning aside in this way. Perhaps he hoped to make an indirect contribution to the EDC. Politically, the French would not accept larger German than French forces in the EDC. But the Indochina War was an immense drain on the French army and economy.[3] Monnet told the newly appointed American consul to Hanoi in March 1952 that "France had no alternative except to withdraw from Indochina on pain of failing to meet its commitments in Europe". A letter he sent to Schuman the previous month suggests he possibly wanted to force the issue and hoped the Wise Men's report would help achieve that. If so, Tomlinson, for one, did not understand the motives. He attacked Monnet bitterly for inadequate commitment to the EDC. Hirsch seems to have done most of the actual work in the six months allotted. The riddle remains.

The European Defence Community treaty was finally signed on May 27, 1952, as a less than federal instrument. Van Zeeland had managed to subject the budget in part to national vetoes. Even so, the French government, now under Antoine Pinay, signed the treaty on the tacit condition that no immediate attempt should be made to ratify it. The EDC was rotting before the ink was dry. Schuman was coming under steadily growing attack. The French president, Vincent Auriol, who had more influence than official power, noted that Schuman was "tired", that "the diplomats complain of Monnet's influence on him" and wondered whether he should be replaced at

---

3. The Indochina War killed each year the equivalent of an entire class of St-Cyr, the French West Point. A French official memorandum of 1950 claimed that since 1945 it had cost as much as the value of the counterpart funds from Marshall aid.

the Foreign Office. Reports filtered through to the Belgian government that there was opposition in the French government to Monnet being nominated to the presidency of the High Authority.

If the EDC was to be ratified by the French National Assembly, the demands of the Socialists would have to be met. They wanted a more "democratic" EDC, with a European Assembly elected by universal suffrage. And so, once the EDC treaty was signed, the European Political Community (or EPC, not to be confused with the EDC) came on to the agenda. Monnet and Guy Mollet, the Secretary-General of the Socialist Party, saw the EPC more as a way of reasserting civilian control over the military than as a step to a federal union.

Like most European ideas, this one had been ripening for some time. Bruce recorded Monnet speaking of the need for a "political community" over a year before, when the Schuman treaty was signed. There were desultory exchanges during 1951 between Monnet and Pleven on a "constitutional conference" to raise a common political roof over the prospective Coal and Steel and Defence Communities. Schuman told Acheson in the early autumn that he had a political Community in reserve "wider than the ECSC and EDC", and that Adenauer and the Italian premier, Alcide de Gasperi, were both pressing for one. In the controversies with van Zeeland, de Gasperi proposed that the future EDC Assembly should prepare a draft European constitution for the governments to negotiate.

The French duly proposed in June 1952 that the EPC should be put on the official agenda. The aims were both strategic, to give the Communities, and particularly the EDC, a political cohesion they lacked, and tactical, in order to win over the French Socialists. Monnet also told Acheson that the EPC was needed to repair the failings, in particular the financial failings, of the European Army treaty, which, thanks to van Zeeland, had become a "cartel of generals". To lose no time, Monnet and Schuman decided to hitch the EPC to the Common Assembly of the ECSC and not wait till the hypothetical moment when the EDC Assembly came into being. The decision was to be taken at the meeting of Foreign Ministers at the end of July. The haggling over the seat of the ECSC was so acute on this occasion there was no time for anything else. But in September, at the first session of the Council of Ministers of the ECSC, it was agreed that the Common Assembly of the ECSC should be asked to change its numbers to those of the EDC Assembly and set itself up as an "*ad hoc* Assembly" to propose a draft EPC treaty to the governments.

This was the context for the inaugural ceremony of the European Coal and Steel Community in Luxembourg on August 10. In the autumn of 1952, there were not one but three prospective Communities, two pillars and the roof of a potential European union. Covering coal, steel, defence, arms production and perhaps elements of foreign policy—that is, economic and political functions close to the core of the state—they provided the outline of a federation in the classic style. To achieve so much would be extraordinary three or four years from a standing start and less than a decade after the war. On the other hand, there were disturbing signs that all this might be a house of cards resting on the fate of the European Army. It was all the more important, then, to prove, by making the first Community for coal and steel work, that Europe was alive and practical.

II
EUROPE'S FIRST GOVERNMENT

Monnet, whose entire membership in government had been confined to the CFLN in Algiers, now, as president of the High Authority, had, in coal and steel, to establish one from scratch. He presented it as "Europe's first government" and certainly in the ECSC treaty, it was designed to give the lead. As Tomlinson's assistant, Stanley Cleveland (a brother of the Marshall Planner Harlan Cleveland), reported on the eve of Monnet's move to Luxembourg, "He is anxious to make clear in [the] public mind that [the] High Authority is not just another international 'coordinating' organisation, but a group endowed with real authority and the intention to exercise it without reference to national governments". Monnet, in short, had a strong sense of the need for a new policy framework to create a new political system producing new patterns of behaviour from old rival states. The success or failure of the European Coal and Steel Community in particular, as of the whole European experiment, has to be judged in this light.

Monnet set the tone in his inaugural address on August 10 in the town hall of Luxembourg City, drenched in flowers. International organisations, he said, were "incapable of eliminating our national antagonisms". But now six parliaments had established "the first European Community, merging part of its members' national sovereignty and subordinating it to the common interest". He stressed the High Authority's "mandate" to take "in full independence" decisions binding throughout the Six. He pointed to its "direct relations with all firms"; its power to levy taxes; and its political responsibility to a European Assembly and, as regards the law, not to national tribunals but to a European Court of Justice. "All these institutions can be modified and improved in the light of experience. But there is one point on which there will be no turning back: these institutions are supranational and, let us not shrink from the word, federal".

The supranational theme was balanced, however, by a promise not to rely on formal powers. "It is not our task to direct the production of coal and steel: that is the role of firms. . . . We shall immediately establish links with governments, producers, workers, consumers and dealers and with the associations they have set up. . . . we shall base the working of the Community on constant consultation. . . . We shall submit our decisions to the test of debate". Shades of the Monnet Plan stirred.

Having laid these foundations, the speech stressed three points for the initial programme, all fixed by the Paris treaty setting up the ECSC. First, the High Authority would, in a few months, open "a single market for coal and steel throughout the Community". Second, the High Authority would submit a balance-sheet of the Community to the Common Assembly in five months' time. (Again, shades of the Monnet Plan. But this time the balance-sheet, an administrative concept, was stillborn. Politics took precedence.) Third, immediate steps must be taken to establish an association with Britain and close cooperation with the United States.

Significantly, perhaps, Monnet moved first on the last and least technical of these, the political issue of relations with the major English-speaking powers. His aim was to obtain from them what they alone could confer, international recognition of the new Community as an independent player in the world. Both obliged, though in characteristically different ways.

On August 11, the day after the inaugural ceremony, Acheson assured the Community of America's "strong support. . . . the U.S. will now deal with the Community [i.e., not the nations] on coal and steel matters". A mission was appointed, led by none other than Tomlinson. Three months later, the American presidential election was held, and Dwight D. Eisenhower, running on the Republican ticket, defeated the proposed Democratic successor to Truman, Adlai Stevenson. Eisenhower replaced Acheson with Monnet's old friend John Foster Dulles as Secretary of State, and David Bruce became U.S. representative to the Community, still with Tomlinson as his chief deputy. The family relationship between Monnet and the old American Paris team lived on. The latter also followed the EDC and EPC. Dulles himself descended on Luxembourg on February 8 in a migrating swarm of journalists.

With Britain, matters were more complex. Britain could be a member of the *European* Community, the United States could not and would not, and this lay always in the background. Monnet's first public act in his new role was to travel to London on August 21, where he was greeted by Makins at the Foreign Office, so he later recalled, with the words, "Now that you are a fact, we shall deal with you". It was decided that Britain should send to the ECSC in Luxembourg a permanent delegation, which put up its sign within a fortnight.

This was the simple part of the story. There was a more contentious one. In March 1952, the British had marketed the Eden Plan. This was named after Anthony Eden, the Foreign Secretary and heir apparent to Churchill in the Conservative government which had taken office in October 1951. It was

a bizarre attempt to subordinate the federal Community to the intergovernmental Council of Europe. The ECSC Council of Ministers and Common
Assembly were to become subdivisions of the Council of Europe's Committee
of Ministers and Consultative Assembly, all to be served exclusively by the
Council of Europe secretariat. Members of the Council of Europe (representing fifteen states, nine of which had not signed the Schuman treaty) would
sit in on the affairs of the ECSC Six. The ostensible aim of these manœuvres
was to break down barriers in Europe. In France, it appealed to government
inter alia because any link with the British attracted the deeply divided
Socialists, on whom EDC ratification depended. Schuman, under ever-
increasing pressure from the anti-EDC lobby, encouraged the Eden Plan.
According to the British, he told Eden on September 15, 1952, that "the
[E]CSC had only a limited function" and that the French government did
not want it "to become . . . the hub of the European movement". Less than
two months later, the British thought they detected signs of Monnet's loss
of influence in Paris following his departure to Luxembourg.

Monnet, for his part, told Acheson the Eden Plan was "a most dangerous
suggestion". It seemed to him another British gambit to influence the Community without paying the membership fee. His suspicions would have been
confirmed had he known that Macmillan was urging Churchill to make Britain, through the Council of Europe, "the leading power in Europe as well as
in the Commonwealth, [able] in this dual capacity . . . [to] cooperate with
the United States on more equal terms".

The issue came to a head over the inaugural session of the Common
Assembly of the ECSC. The treaty required that the High Authority should
organise it within a month of taking office. (The Assembly, naturally, was
thereafter to look after itself.) The obvious venue, for political reasons and
for the sake of efficiency, was Strasbourg, in the chamber of the Consultative
Assembly of the Council of Europe. (The names are, unfortunately, all too
similar and unmemorable, one of the banes of the international circuit.) But
Jacques Camille Paris, the French diplomat, Secretary-General of the Council of Europe—and son-in-law of the poet and playwright Paul Claudel—
refused to provide hospitality unless the Common Assembly handed over all
its servicing to his secretariat in the spirit of the Eden Plan.

Monnet, with the backing of his High Authority colleagues, wasted no
time in brushing aside these procedural cobwebs. He contacted Emile Blamont, the clerk of the French National Assembly, and persuaded him to
bring together the clerks of the parliaments of the Six. The aim was to
arrange the Common Assembly's first session in Strasbourg, but at the
Chamber of Commerce not at the Council of Europe, should the latter prove
stubborn. This paid off very quickly. The night that Enzo Giacchero, the
Italian member of the High Authority, and Max Kohnstamm, its Dutch
secretary, drove away from the meeting where matters were settled with

Jacques Paris, they passed the alternative venue where refurbishing was proceeding under the floodlights. On September 10 and on time, the ECSC Common Assembly held its first session in the Council of Europe chamber on its own terms and with its own secretariat.

On the larger issues of the Eden Plan, Monnet warned Anthony Nutting, Eden's parliamentary private secretary (a political post), that if the plan were imposed, he would appeal to the Court of the ECSC to declare it unconstitutional. As for Schuman, he seems to have realised, as he delved deeper, that to mix ECSC and Council of Europe bodies would produce endless confusion. He began to back-pedal. The battle was over, bar a few minimal face-saving compromises.

It was now incumbent on Monnet to prove that he too could promote the link with Britain. He gave the British delegation to the ECSC in Luxembourg a warm welcome. The members were encouraged to make contact at all levels of the High Authority, with "direct access . . . to Monnet", who "has already given proof . . . of a great capacity for informal discussion". If anything, the British had more informal access to Monnet than did members of ECSC governments. A Joint Committee of the High Authority and the delegation was set up, ostensibly to explore the scope for a bilateral Anglo-Community "association", and held its first meeting on November 17.

From Monnet's point of view, such an association would confer on the Community recognition by a major state. It would exclude the small countries of the Council of Europe, which he saw as clouding the main issue of relations with the English-speaking powers. It would leave the door open for the ultimate aim, Britain's joining the Community without changing the latter's ground rules. In short where the British hoped through the Eden Plan to define the Anglo-Community relationship from London, Monnet proposed through the association to shape it from Luxembourg. By blocking the Eden Plan, he in effect began to steer the relationship down his, not the British government's, channel.

Still, in the end, Europe's foundations had to be laid in the Community itself. To keep to the schedule of the Paris treaty, Monnet had, in eight months, to build up the High Authority from scratch, set the tone for relations between the ECSC institutions and open the common markets (for there were in fact five different ones, from iron ore, scrap and coal to steel and even, a year later, special steels). These added up to a large programme in a very short while.

Monnet had a vivid sense that Europe's infant institutions must be nurtured in the right way. They had to live up to the enormous European ambition of changing relations between states. The early years would be the test. The civilising role of institutions began to loom large in his utterances. "The tragic events we have lived through . . . have perhaps made us wiser. But men pass on and others take their place. We will not be able to hand on our personal experience. It will die with us. What we can hand on are institutions. . . . Institutions, adequately structured, can accumulate and transmit the wisdom of successive generations".

Monnet's personal prestige with the men of power, from Adenauer to Eisenhower and Dulles, gave the High Authority considerable political presence. In the view of Jelle Zijlstra, for many years Minister of Economics, Minister of Finance and finally Prime Minister of the Netherlands, "He was very powerful". He certainly had easy access to many leaders on both sides of the Atlantic. He was also in many ways an inspiring leader, who managed to impart a strong sense of service to a cause, even a pioneering spirit, to the officials who came to the High Authority from six diverse and even mutually suspicious backgrounds. As Edmond Wellenstein, the Dutchman who later succeeded Kohnstamm as secretary of the High Authority, has put it, "Everybody agreed that nothing [Monnet] did was with his own career in mind or with France. . . . That really set the tone". The atmosphere of permanent emergency he generated (and to which quite a few strongly objected) drove people of different and stubborn traditions to overwork together and, almost without knowing it, to develop a corporate identity and pride. And he put everyone who had something to offer on the same footing, irrespective of rank or nation. "All opinions were allowed. Everybody in the rather large circle around Monnet could suggest things, and they were even taken up". When he announced his departure, "there was an extreme unease in the staff. . . . Not only because he left, which was a very emotional matter, [but] because he *was* the High Authority". On this point, even a member of the board of the High Authority with whom Monnet had had fairly frequent differences, the Belgian Vice President and former Minister of Economic Affairs, Albert Coppé, agreed. Monnet, Coppé said at one critical moment, "is the personification of the High Authority".

In short, Monnet's regime had a strong personality, and as usual in such cases, the advantages were bought at a cost. One charge often made against him, especially by opponents like the head of the French Steel Association, Pierre Ricard, was that he was far too involved in the politics of Europe—code at the time for the EDC—and far too little involved in coal and steel. There was truth in this. Monnet told David E. Lilienthal in April 1952 that coal and steel were "the least important part" of the new Community. What mattered was that "the people of Europe" were ready "for a deep change". Monnet and a good proportion of the staff of the High Authority had certainly not gone to Luxembourg out of fascination with the scrap market. Ricard's criticism was echoed by those members of the board of the High Authority who felt that their first priority must be coal and steel. The two most articulate of these, Spierenburg and Coppé, who complained that Monnet tried to monopolise decision-making, came from the Low Countries. They were particularly suspicious of the threat to the smaller countries they divined in Monnet's emphasis on the Franco-German relationship. Monnet and Franz Etzel, previously chairman of the Bundestag's Economic Policy Committee and regarded as Adenauer's man, met several times before going to Luxembourg and cultivated their relations, which ripened into real friendship. It was all the more remarkable in that Etzel's French was very sketchy and his English poor and Monnet's German was non-existent. Admittedly, they were helped by an interpreter of great quality, Ursula Wennmakers, who sadly died young. The bond between Monnet and Etzel was widely admitted to be of basic importance, but it created tensions. When Coppé found they were meeting before sessions of the High Authority, he organised meetings of his own. Monnet complained and both were, at least formally, dropped. Earlier, Monnet, appalled by a board of nine (he had wanted five, to make it plain members were not representatives of the six states), had tried to persuade Etzel and Spierenburg to join him in an informal leading trinity. Spierenburg, wary of being drawn into a Franco-German directorate, refused.

These tensions were compounded by a radical and at times almost comic incompatibility of humour between Monnet and routine administration. He was so suspicious of bureaucratic routine that he insisted all officials should remain on temporary contract and refused to commit himself to an organisation plan. He regarded time, weekends, his immediate staff, even his colleagues of the High Authority as totally at the disposal of whatever priority he considered overriding. "He really didn't care very much [to structure an organisation]. He wanted to be able to call on people left and right, whatever their jobs, whatever their particular responsibilities". For similar reasons, he was an unapologetically bad time-keeper. His sense of the need to persuade rather than outvote the minority in the High Authority led to endless late-night sittings which were very unpopular. At first, the atmosphere of permanent crisis generated a certain creative tension, but it was not possible to run a major institution like that for long. In November 1953, on the votes of the High Authority members from the smaller countries, and against Monnet's wishes, it was decided that working groups of High Authority members must prepare decisions for the full board. Monnet held on to the purely political areas of information, and relations with Britain and America.

Relations developed well between the High Authority and the potentially "federal" institutions of the Community—the Common Assembly and Court of Justice. During the Schuman conference, Monnet was a technocratic minimalist on the Assembly. France resisted the supranational kind of Assembly favoured by Germany. But once in Luxembourg, he realised the High Authority and Assembly were natural allies. The head of the British delegation, Sir Cecil Weir, reported that "it has become the practice for the High Authority to hold frequent sessions with the Assembly's Commissions covering a wide variety of subjects". When Monnet announced he was leaving the ECSC, the Assembly passed a resolution thanking him "for his contribution to . . . the effectiveness of Parliamentary supervision". This was particularly important over the years in cementing relations with the German Socialists who had voted against the ECSC treaty. As for the Court, Monnet's attitude can best be gauged from his reaction to one of its first major rulings. The High Authority had changed the steel pricing rules to make them more elastic. This did not suit the French government, which appealed to the Court. Shortly before Christmas 1954, the Court found against the High Authority on the grounds that it had exceeded its powers. Monnet's comment was "good. That shows the institutions are working".

Relations were much stickier with the two bodies which, in Monnet's eyes, belonged to the old order in the new: the Council of Ministers representing the governments, and the Consultative Committee, only advisory but dominated by industry. There is little doubt that throughout Monnet's tenure of the presidency of the High Authority, and beyond, there was a basic tension with both the governments and industry. To some extent, this was the normal process by which a governing body, whatever its theoretical powers, has to reach a modus vivendi with its constituency. One of the first decisions the High Authority had to take was to fix the levy on which its funds were based by virtue of the Paris treaty. As Monnet stressed when the first discussion in the Council of Ministers took place on December 1–2, 1952, the High Authority was *consulting* the Council, but the *decision* on the tax was its prerogative. This did not deter the ministers from trying to influence the rate. At first, the High Authority got most of what it wanted, a tax of 0.9 per cent of the value of coal and steel production reached in three steps, instead of the 1 per cent at once it had originally sought; and the system lasted until the end of 1955. But once the High Authority had largely achieved its initial fiscal aim—mainly to secure its credit as an international borrower—it was not able to ignore the clamour for cuts of the industries which paid the tax, backed up by the governments. On January 1, 1956, the rate was halved to 0.45 per cent.

All this was natural enough as part of a political process. The High Authority could not operate in a vacuum. But the difficulties went deeper than that. Both coal and steel were in fact, if not in theory, highly regulated, with governments in the background. The power struggle arose not just with the industries but with the governments as well. It became clear on frequent occasions that the governments were most reluctant to concede the supranational powers Monnet asserted in the name of the Paris treaty. For instance, article 93 of the Paris treaty stated that the High Authority "shall maintain whatever relationships appear useful with . . . the OEEC". But Van Zeeland, true to form, refused it the right to speak for the Community in the OEEC. In the GATT, there was the bizarre spectacle of the United States insisting that the ECSC should act as a "contracting party" or member of the organisation, while the Belgian ambassador, Max Suetens, representing the Six, denied there was any such need because the High Authority had no responsibility for trade policy. The United States won, but the omen for supranationalists was less than reassuring.

The immediate challenge was the opening of the common markets, first on February 10, 1952, for the raw materials—coal, iron ore and scrap—and then, scheduled for April 10, steel. Customs duties and discriminatory prices were abolished overnight in the Community and not, as in the later general Common Market, gradually over many years. The only significant customs duties were on steel, but other barriers and distortions were considerable. For instance, export prices charged for Ruhr coal (exclusive of transport) were about 10 per cent above those to German consumers. In addition, discriminatory freight rates came on top of such double pricing on some major rail traffic in raw materials to the steel industry, such as iron ore from Lorraine (France) to Belgium and the politically crucial coke from the Ruhr to Lorraine. In the latter case, the cost of transport, a major item in the delivered price, was cut by some 15 per cent. These changes were quite substantial and were made at once.

Nevertheless, it was no mere formality that the door was opened on a five-year transition to the full common market. One function of the transition period was to press and help uncompetitive sectors, such as Belgian coal, to adapt to new conditions. There were also others. The coal-mines in the member states were either state-owned (as in France and in part in the Netherlands) or cartelised (as in Germany and in Belgium); that is, one way or another prices were not free. This condition was revealed by the fact that though the coal market was already weakening at the end of the Korean boom early in 1953, the High Authority felt it had to place ceilings on coal prices to prevent them from rising, particularly in the Ruhr. Monnet argued that "it would be mistaken to think that the common market can be set up from one day to the next and without any restriction". More time was needed to deal with the structures which underpinned prices. The High Authority really began to discuss coal policy only at the end of 1953.

The technical problems of opening the common markets were compounded in the next case, that of steel, by a sudden and (amazing as it may seem) unforeseen political squall. This concerned the impact of turnover taxes on competition, in particular between France and Germany. The issue was not important for coal, but discussing coal brought the problem to light for steel, for which it mattered, or seemed to matter, much more. When exporting goods, the French, like all the member states except Germany, followed the practice, endorsed by GATT, of withdrawing the turnover tax levied on sales at home. But they had invented a new turnover tax, the now widely practised VAT, or value-added tax, which was totally unfamiliar at the time and the rate of which seemed extraordinarily high. This meant that when it was removed from exports, the Germans could only see that it allowed French steel to undercut German prices in Germany, and cried foul. Most of them were convinced it was a French cheat. At the Council of Ministers of February 7, 1953, even before the coal common market, the issue was so explosive that Erhard, not normally a belligerent man, walked out. The two main states of the Community were locking antlers even before the new system had begun to function.

Monnet reacted instantly. He persuaded the High Authority to postpone the opening of the steel common market by three weeks to May 1, though some feared this would be seen as a sign of weakness. Since the Germans at the time, and quite mistakenly, saw Uri (whom Monnet had brought with him from Paris and whose intelligence they feared) as the evil genius of all "plots", Monnet told him to cut all connection with the issue. The High Authority then appointed a trio of internationally distinguished economists, a Belgian and Englishman, chaired by the ultra-scrupulous Dutch planner Jan Tinbergen—in short, anyone but a Frenchman or German—to pronounce on the extraordinarily arcane and technical ins and outs of the dispute. After several weeks of intense consultation with economists nominated by the governments of the member states, the panel found that there were indeed a number of "imperfections" in the way the prevailing systems of turnover taxes worked, within nations as well as between them, but that these could be mitigated and in any case were as nothing to the distortions that would result from applying the alternative favoured by the Germans. The High Authority decided to stick to the existing system but to study and remedy its "imperfections" to save German face.

The crisis lasted some three months. The extreme political dangers lurking just below its surface can be gauged from Monnet's brief remark in his *Memoirs* that if the German thesis, which was sincerely, even passionately, held, had prevailed, it would have given "an immense tax advantage" to German sales of steel in the ECSC, exactly what the Germans claimed the current system did for the French. Luckily, the experts' report was the beginning of the end of the dispute. It did not seem so when the German Bundestag voted a compensatory tax of 12 per cent on French steel imports, which would have violated the Paris treaty. But Monnet persuaded Adenauer not to apply the tax. The German government issued a conciliatory communiqué. The French steelmasters obligingly raised their prices in unison. The tax row, which at one time threatened to produce an earthquake, soon ceased to be even a talking point. Senior German officials, like Hans von der Groeben, in charge of the Schuman Plan division in the Ministry of Economics under Erhard, had themselves reached the conclusion it was irrelevant. Something new was cemented in the Community. In Luxembourg, it was felt as a great victory, the best possible send-off for Europe. Monnet and Etzel, the latter of whom had wavered under unbearable pressure from the Ruhr, celebrated with champagne.

The tax crisis had barely blown over when Dulles informed Monnet, who was planning an informal trip to Washington, that Eisenhower proposed to make an official visit of it. On June 3, Monnet, accompanied at his insistence by Etzel and Spierenburg, was housed like a head of state at Blair House, and Eisenhower welcomed the three as the representatives of the new Europe. Monnet testified before the Senate and House Foreign Relations Committees. He worked hard to dissipate the congressmen's ignorance of the Coal and Steel Community, which so struck Etzel and managed briefly to damp down their growing doubts over the ratification of the EDC treaty. Apparently without precedent, the White House and both houses of Congress exchanged messages of support for the nascent Europe.

Monnet stressed he was not in town in search of dollar grants and adopted the pose of a man simply introducing the new Europe to good friends. This was novel coming from a European at the time and duly impressive, but disingenuous. He wanted loans, and his allies in the State Department favoured them. A large part of the rationale for the High Authority levy was, in Monnet's eyes, to feed its loan guarantee fund. With this, he hoped, the High Authority could raise large loans outside Europe on favorable terms for the industries in its charge and obtain a hold on investment policies. This was still the psychology of Marshall aid and of the influence on policy it had given the Monnet Plan.

At the end of summer 1953, the High Authority could look back on a seminal year. It had set up "the first government of Europe"; opened the common markets for coal, iron ore, scrap and steel pretty well on time; come through a tax crisis which could have been lethal; and been recognised as a new entity in the world by Britain and the United States. Most of the problems of making the system work still lay ahead. Nevertheless, whatever might ail the EDC, the ECSC had given the new Europe a foundation.

III
COMMON MARKETS IN PRACTICE

When the new political season opened in September 1953, Monnet laid before the Common Assembly the High Authority's priorities for the year to come. The top two slots again involved the English-speaking powers, the negotiation of a dollar loan and a formal association with Britain. Whatever their other merits, these were now part of the politics of ratifying the European Army treaty, indirect assurances to France. In practice, the association with Britain failed in this purpose. There was interest in Whitehall in a common market in steel with the Six. But the British steel industry was strongly opposed. Moreover, there was no sense of political urgency to help any EDC "tomfoolery", as Churchill called it. Association materialised only later and in different circumstances.

The American loan, however, like the third of Monnet's announced priorities, cartels, was, or was thought to be, crucial to the High Authority's capacity to govern. In fact, the American loan proved much more difficult to land than Monnet expected. Averell Harriman had given Monnet the impression as early as June 1950 that substantial U.S. loans would be made available if the Schuman Plan materialised. In March 1951, Monnet raised the issue again. He was told by both the State Department and the ECA that a specific proposal would be received with "sympathetic" interest. Nothing loath, he fished for a very large sum, $500 million. With a fund of this size, borrowed on better terms than those in Europe, the High Authority could have influenced three-quarters of all Community investment in coal and steel for five years.

However, by 1953 conditions had changed. Marshall aid had in effect ended. Eisenhower had replaced Truman. Though he and Dulles were ardent supporters of the new Europe, the Republican administration was "not in the banking business", and policy was to cut the budget deficit not add to it. Further, the American coal and steel industries were beginning to suffer from falling demand. And a vocal school of thought, led by Clarence Randall, chairman of Inland Steel and the Foreign Economic Policy Board, argued that the ECSC was only the latest guise of the old European cartel. Congress was hardly going to vote money to help competitors in Europe. When Monnet came to Washington to negotiate the loan in April 1954, he was met by two complaints: the restrictions on sales of American coal in Germany and Belgium, and cartel behaviour in the ECSC. Dulles had a real struggle with the Treasury Secretary, George Humphrey, to extract any funds at all. Luckily, the $100 million loan for twenty-five years at 3.875 per cent secured on April 23 and hints of possible further loans later on were still enough to make an impression in Europe, not least, as Dulles stressed, as "an exceptional political act".

Monnet played the loan for all it was worth as proof of U.S. commitment to European unity. Even $100 million on competitive terms was far from negligible. It also laid the basis for further borrowing by the High Authority. By 1958, it had become the largest foreign issuer of bonds on the New York market. Although High Authority loans accounted only for some 4 per cent of all ECSC investment from 1954 to 1957, they were relatively much larger than that in the priority sectors—pithead power stations and the processing of iron ore—and facilitated investments two to three times as large again. Nevertheless, the outcome was a far cry from Monnet's original vision of the High Authority as the hub of Community investment. The very idea had in fact been rooted in postwar shortages. Capital markets in Europe were beginning to recover. The High Authority was not to be a Monnet Plan office for Europe's basic industries.

The question of where power lay in the nascent common markets for coal and steel was even more tightly linked to Monnet's third priority, cartels. In his speech at the initialling of the ECSC treaty on March 19, 1951, Monnet had placed the elimination of cartels on a par with supranationality and the common market as one of the holy trinity of the new Community. Now, he was taken at his word. Complaints that the High Authority was too slow to act became audible even before the common market for coal was opened. In September 1953, for motives that are not wholly clear, Monnet invited his old friend René Mayer to address the nine members. Mayer told them they were beginning to lose face on cartels. Monnet thanked him for a serious warning. Monnet himself repeatedly inveighed against cartels, promising "energetic action" to a host of audiences. What actually happened was quite different.

In coal, the Community had only one major supplier, the Ruhr. The problem of the Ruhr, as seen by Germany's neighbours (not just France), was to buy the coke basic to steel production on the same terms as the Germans themselves. Otherwise, in the postwar world of shortages, the Ruhr quasi-monopoly of coking coal could handicap competitors by favouring Germans on price and quantities. In a world of shortages and on national assumptions, such behaviour was normal. The French did the same with their iron ore, the British with their coal. The difference was that the Ruhr controlled the key resource, metallurgical coke. In addition, recent memories injected raw emotion into the brew. Outsiders tended to see the Ruhr as a bunch of potential Nazis, while the Germans thought they were being penalised for their superior efficiency. They argued they had to have a single coal sales agency to protect the higher-cost coal-mines, employment and economic supply.

Throughout the period between Adenauer's letter of March 14, 1951, formally proposing, and in reality reluctantly accepting, McCloy's imposition of Law 27 and the opening of the common market for coal in February 1953, the whole German body politic, including the labour unions, stubbornly resisted every effort to break up the coal sales monopoly, the DKV. The German trustees supposed to implement the Adenauer programme refused to do so on the grounds that they had never been consulted. Finally, three days before the opening of the common market for coal and the transferring of responsibility for the DKV from the Allied High Commissions to the High Authority, the Germans suddenly set up a new coal sales system for the Ruhr, consisting of six sales agencies but also a central coordinating body. This new organisation was called "Georg" (*Gemeinschaftsorganisation*), and even experts had difficulty telling the new central arrangements from the old. This started the long official scrutiny all over again and wasted more time. Would the High Authority succeed when the American superpower had passed the buck?

In summer 1953, the High Authority issued regulations requiring cartels to seek authorisation or risk violating Community law. Georg, with sixty-two other associations (thirty-three French), duly applied. Monnet opined that once the case had been investigated, Georg must be liquidated and given six months to replace itself with a body which could be authorised. In May 1954, Georg was indeed refused authorisation, but negotiations were opened between the High Authority, or more precisely Etzel, chairman of the High Authority market working group, and the German government. The talks crawled forward for months. The Dutch official in charge of anti-trust policy in the High Authority talked to an American diplomat of changing his job. A first result was obtained only under Monnet's successor, René Mayer, in 1956. Georg was reorganised, but the central functions of the agency, although formally reduced, were not eliminated. Whether the new arrangements would have made any difference will never be known, because falling transatlantic freight rates from 1957 to 1958 made American coal lastingly cheaper in Europe than Ruhr coal.

Georg was an interesting case. On the surface, the High Authority, like the Allied High Commissions before it, failed to decartelise Ruhr coal. But the enthusiasts for breaking up the DKV had been the Americans, not the French. At a meeting in Essen in December 1954, the head of the official French coal importing agency, ATIC, expressed his support for Georg. It is not sure that the High Authority itself was intellectually convinced of the case for free trade in coal. Monnet certainly was not even though he strongly objected to "domination" by Georg.

As for the original French purpose in all this, to loosen the near-monopoly of the Ruhr on coking coal supplies, the 1950s eased and then eliminated the problem. The French increased steel output by two-thirds from 1949 to 1959, while net imports of coal and coke from the OEEC area remained steady, in the case of coal at levels far below prewar. There were several causes for this. As coal consumption fell in France, freed indigenous supplies shifted to the coking ovens, whose output nearly doubled. Technical advances raised the proportion of coal used for coke in the blast furnaces and cut the amount needed per ton of steel. Then, in 1953–54, Friedrich Flick, who had bought out the Petscheks in 1938, was forced to sell off one of the best and largest coking coal mines in the Ruhr, Harpener Bergbau. He sold it, in what seems a kind of peace-offering by the Ruhr, to a French consortium led by the lords of Lorraine steel, the de Wendels. An enthusiastic report from the French Ministry of Industry claimed that Lorraine would now be free of German heavy industry. Finally, from 1958 onwards, European coal went into permanent decline under pressure of much cheaper coal and oil from overseas. Ruhr mines were as anxious as others to make any sales they could. By the 1960s, the French fixation on coking coal was a thing of the past. The age of the Ruhr was over.

Steel was supposed to be another matter, but it is not clear that it was. An export price cartel was formed by the Community producers in March 1953, just before the opening of the steel common market. On September 8, 1953, when markets and prices were weakening, the cartel tried to prop itself up by introducing sales quotas and fines for exceeding them. It covered about 19 per cent of Community production and half of world exports. It was a clear violation of the spirit of the Paris treaty. Monnet wanted to act promptly. But the treaty was at its weakest on export cartels. A major reason for this was that in America itself the Webb-Pomarene Act exempted export cartels from anti-trust provisions. The High Authority's lawyers argued that action depended on proof the internal market was affected by the export cartel, in theory a logical inference, in practice one that was very difficult to prove in court. The High Authority itself was wary of confronting the governments and industries on grounds where it had so little treaty support. Albert Wehrer, the member from Luxembourg, which was heavily depen- dent on the steel firm Arbed, argued in a lecture in September 1954 that world market conditions and the inability of the cartel to enforce quotas made action unnecessary.

In fact, there were quite independent signs that the steelmasters were colluding *within* the common market, where the treaty powers of the High Authority were in no doubt whatever. For instance, as already recorded, at the end of the tax crisis France raised steel prices to reduce the impact of the VAT rebates at frontiers which the Germans had found so objectionable. A more obvious case of collusion would be hard to invent. Monnet told his American listeners on April 9, 1954, that he hoped to erode the cartel gradu- ally through flexible, public and transparent price policies. In fact, the pub- lic price lists published in July 1953 led the High Authority itself to conclude, in private, that this was "proof positive that international agreements are carving up the market". Public price lists, one of the main anti-cartel devices of the Paris treaty, were proving to be not enough. The High Authority then decided to take advantage of the weakening market in late 1953 and early 1954 by making the price rules more flexible. Producers could vary their prices by up to 2.5 per cent or more to meet (but not undercut) the cheapest competition, without changing their published price lists. The French government, however, was not amused and appealed to the European Court against the "Monnet margin", as it was called. In a ruling on December 21, 1954, the Court found against the High Authority on the grounds that flexible pricing, by allowing producers to discriminate between customers of different nationalities, violated the Paris treaty. There was no third system in Monnet's time.

On mergers also, the High Authority came close to laissez-faire, though in this case the issues were more ambiguous. The Paris treaty gave it the right to forbid concentrations which conferred potential powers in restraint of trade on those who controlled them. In fact, as William Diebold showed thirty years ago in his admirable study of *The Schuman Plan,* the High Authority, "in over a hundred cases" in its first four years of active mergers policy from May 1954 to April 1958, "found no reason to forbid any merger or other measure of concentration". At the end of 1952, Robert Schuman, speaking to the Foreign Affairs Commission of the French National Assembly, had claimed that the High Authority's responsibility would not be to inhibit mergers as such but to see that the allied deconcentrations in the Ruhr were maintained. In fact, by the end of 1954, the High Authority specifically concluded that Allied Law 27 was not relevant, its only yardstick being the Paris treaty. In June, it had already authorised the purchase by Mannesmann of a major coal-mine and an engineering plant, thus virtually re-creating one of the prewar trusts and providing a precedent for others. Werner von Simson, the agent at the time of the Ruhr steelmasters in Luxembourg, has stated that there was a tacit agreement between Monnet, Etzel and the German firms that the latter could gradually reconcentrate. The only limit was that there should be "no Vereinigte Stahlwerke again".[4] True, in 1954, the biggest concentration, Thyssenhütte, represented well under 10 per cent of Community steel output. But this begged the question whether the common market had truly replaced the national markets as the most relevant criterion for dominant economic power.

Why Monnet acquiesced in policies so contrary to his rhetoric is not clear. He certainly had little time to act. The experience of the United States has shown that anti-trust policy can only be built up slowly, case by case. His first year was fully taken up with establishing the High Authority and the various common markets, with the tax crisis and with the state visit to Washington. In the summer of 1954, he fell ill. At the end of the summer, the EDC treaty was struck down, and Monnet, the personification of the rejected policy, became a lame-duck president. He was really free to deal with the power issues collected together under the heading of "cartels" only in the nine months from September 1953 to the end of May 1954. It was a very short time to dig into such tangled roots.

However, this is not enough. The dominant fact about Monnet's presi-

4. Prewar, the Vereinigte Stahlwerke, with 8 million tons of steel in 1938, accounted on its own for 40 per cent of German steel output and (in the same year) for 25 per cent of the production of the area included in the 1950s in the ECSC.

dency was probably that it was hobbled by the EDC crisis in France. Most of the major power problems in the Community arose with the French and German governments. In France, from early 1953 onwards (at the latest), every issue was bound to be sucked into the EDC obsession. The deputy head of the British delegation to the ECSC in Luxembourg, James Marjoribanks, thought in September 1953 that Monnet was so much absorbed by it that it was hard for him to give his full attention to coal and steel. The trouble in France gave added importance to the relationship with Germany. This too was not easy. Zijlstra says flatly that "there was a power struggle with the Germans". To deal with the industrialists, the High Authority had to have German allies. These could only be Adenauer and the "Europeans" behind him or the labour unions (the Social Democrats came later). When McCloy left Bonn in June 1952, Adenauer turned largely to Monnet for advice, but primarily on the "high" politics of the EDC, not coal and steel. Monnet in return was loath to complicate Adenauer's task on matters that were not at the top of the political agenda. Adenauer at one point warned him that "premature" efforts to deal with the cartel problems of the Ruhr could endanger the ratification of the EDC treaty in the German Parliament. In addition, on coal, the German labour unions were strongly attached to the existing system. That left no local support to lean on.

Once he had to face realities, Monnet seems to have put other priorities higher than control of the Ruhr. Though in the early days in Luxembourg Monnet seemed to be willing to risk confrontation with the Council of Ministers in asserting the High Authority's right to lead, some observers were struck rather more by the lengths to which he was ready to go in seeking a consensus. Wellenstein "never saw [Monnet] press a decision. Everything was talked out". When an investment questionnaire was sent out to firms, Monnet insisted on tact to enlist the voluntary cooperation of managers. At the height of the Georg affair, Monnet told the High Authority it had to convince the government "of a country as directly affected as Germany of the rightness of its decision". He was specially concerned to allay any fears of the labour unions. A week later, when a range of coal subsidies in Germany were eliminated, he emphasised that "this is the common responsibility of the High Authority and of the Federal Government as well as of the interested parties" (the trade unions and producers) and expressed "particular satisfaction" at "the unanimity achieved".

Further, under pressure, the planner in Monnet came to the fore again. After a few months of the common market for coal, he said that "contrary to steel, where real competition must be introduced, coal requires some form of organisation". The same tendency was evident as regards scrap for steel production. The Italians had virtually no coal or iron ore and their steel industry lived on liberal drafts of scrap. A common market, as Monnet and the treaty-drafters agreed, implied that Italians should not be discriminated against. But if the Italians were to have free access to scrap from the north (mainly France and Germany), prices would shoot up. Scrap is speculative and prices always exaggerate the market trend in either direction, high or low. The High Authority, the governments and the expert consensus all wanted to keep steel costs down. On two separate occasions, in March 1953 and in December 1954, the French government violated the treaty by slapping controls on exports, essentially to Italy. Gradually, however, the High Authority managed, with the acquiescence of the governments, to define the rules and assert control over a highly managed market, which kept scrap prices relatively cheap and ensured that Italy (the great beneficiary) was treated on a par with everyone else. Free-market critics pointed out that this reduced incentives to invest in the long-term solution, increased supplies of pig-iron. But the consensus regarded it as a useful corrective to high prices.

In fact, the major aim of both the High Authority and the governments most of the time was to keep steel costs and prices down. This was rather successful. The 1950s brought booming steel output while, as Monnet's *Memoirs* emphasised, prices rose more slowly in the common market than in other markets. This did not square with the conceptions of a cartel carried over from the interwar years of stagnant production and high prices. Nor was the Community unique. Price leadership ruled in the United States, where output was far more concentrated on the three largest producers. The British steel industry was tightly regulated by the state. One of the reasons why *liberalisers* in Britain wanted a common market in steel with the ECSC was its more flexible pricing rules. Moreover, the common market induced just the kind of restructuring (through mergers) which the Monnet Plan had struggled with limited success to produce in France. By the time Monnet left the High Authority, well over half of French steel was grouped in five firms. Of course, German steel was reconcentrating too, but so was Belgian. The sharp prewar contrasts in capacity between German and other European steel firms were moderating. They were also soon to be reduced by the advantages of coastal plants (notably in the Netherlands and Italy) using iron ore and coking coal at world prices well below European ones. The "thirty glorious years" of the long postwar boom made cartels seem relatively innocuous and blurred the distinction with public planning. Looking back, the general impression is of a move in the Community from the quasi-American, antitrust tone of the Schuman treaty to a more European kind of regulated coal and steel market, but in a very expansive environment.

The beginnings of the great boom undoubtedly freshened up the results of the first Community under Monnet. But the new political framework it introduced also changed the picture. In the first place, it led to a number of specific changes. Blatant discrimination by nationality was greatly reduced in coal pricing and transport rates. Trade across frontiers in the common market for steel doubled as a proportion of steel consumption in the Community in a decade (from 7 per cent in 1952 to 15 per cent in 1962). Second, the political emphasis on European integration made compromises possible that would not otherwise have been reached. Adenauer, for instance, gave instructions to his negotiators to find common ground with the French and institute rail charges inter-country on more or less the same basis as intra-country. The Ruhr behaved as a steady (though not expanding) supplier of coal. Third, the new system forced the member states into constant negotiation with one other. They were less able to act unilaterally than in the traditional system, though they sometimes tried. Even in intergovernmental organisations, governments tended to act first and consult afterwards. Despite exceptions, the normal practice in the Community was that consultations and compromises came first. As Louis Lister noted thirty years ago, "Far from rolling the individual states back, economic union thus has increased rather than reduced the need for intergovernmental negotiation and agreement". Fourth, since joint decisions were necessary, the High Authority enjoyed a practical as well as legal initiative. It was not as great as Monnet would have liked, just as some of the members of the High Authority, under pressure from their governments, were far less independent of them than their oath of office required. Nevertheless, on most occasions and policies, from loans to scrap or the abortive "Monnet margin", the High Authority was expected to give a lead. Fifth, the rule of law applied. As Monnet wrote in his *Memoirs,* "I have never known a ruling of the Court to be challenged or ignored". There is little doubt that, on balance, the new Community represented a major shift in relations between the member states towards a confederal norm. It gradually lowered tension all round, raised trust and in this sense laid the foundation of a new Europe.

However, the changes fell far short of the federal revolution Monnet had envisaged. The High Authority failed to take firm hold of its field. The managers of the twenty major steel firms into which the common market was resolving were left largely undisturbed. The governments controlling the general economy continued to condition coal and steel. The French government gave up controls on steel prices, but from 1952 maintained those on all the major industrial consumers of steel, with virtually the same effect. At least one initiative by the German government probably violated the Schuman treaty. By this arrangement, the whole of German industry paid a levy to help steel with investment, which had fallen behind in the days of dismantling and production ceilings. It was not effectively challenged. In June 1956, Gerhard Kreyssig, on behalf of the Socialist Group in the Common Assembly, declared that the "High Authority has weakened its position . . . because it has failed to use some of its powers, allowing national governments and producer groups to exercise functions which belong to it". Monnet was no longer there, but cannot escape his share of responsibility.

IV
EUROPE'S FIRST DEFEAT

The immediate challenge came not from coal and steel but the mounting nationalist campaign in France against the European Army. Though the storm in Paris had been brewing during the whole of 1952, it only burst with the fall of the Pinay government just before Christmas. Pinay fell basically because he was about to bring the EDC treaty to the National Assembly to ratify. The EDC was therefore at the centre of the formation of the new government, under René Mayer. Mayer supported the EDC, but to become Premier, he needed the votes of the Gaullists, who had split during Pinay's tenure of office and one section of whom were ready to play the parliamentary game. The manœuvre was a paying proposition in internal politics. The trouble was that the one Gaullist credential these heretics clung to was opposition to a supranational Europe and particularly a European Army. To buy Gaullist support, Mayer set a series of "preconditions" for ratification of the EDC, including a Saar settlement, British association, American guarantees and the negotiation of a series of "interpretative" protocols of the treaty. After all that, Mayer too was toppled on a side issue in May when he showed signs of taking the EDC to the National Assembly. The tide was demonstrably turning against a supranational Europe.

Above all, Robert Schuman lost the Foreign Ministry, to which Mayer appointed Bidault. From the European point of view, this was a disaster. Bidault was a near-Gaullist on Germany. He had also regarded Schuman ever since 1948 as an interloper and was not going to plait the laurel crown for the other man's programme. Finally, he wanted to be elected President of the Republic at the end of the year and needed Gaullist votes. Bidault spun out time, tangling up the threads behind him as he went.

He exercised this talent with brio on the EPC. When the *ad hoc* Assembly presented its moderate draft of an EPC treaty to the ministers of the Six— on time, in March 1953—he made plain he would ignore it. "There is an inevitable division of labour between men with bold and independent minds and governments whose honour and burden it is to bear the responsibility". He added an ironic "salute to adventurers".

Monnet had, in Schuman's last days, hoped the failings of the EDC treaty might be remedied by the EPC. If anything, the negotiations between the ministers, which began after another long interval, in Rome in September, and ended at The Hague in March 1954, made the structure still more intergovernmental. As one of Bidault's senior advisers remarked, the French view would be decisive, and Bidault gave a free hand to his diplomats, now openly against the EDC and all supranational schemes.

The key issue was the election by universal suffrage of the EPC Assembly (covering the ECSC and the EDC as well). "A genuine political authority under democratic control" (i.e., a popular assembly) conditioned the French Socialists' acceptance of the EDC. Given their hinge position in the French National Assembly, satisfying this need and ratifying the EDC were, or were believed to be, identical. Bidault, however, somehow managed to sow doubt as to whether the Socialist leader, Guy Mollet, really meant it. Finally, when the EPC came out of the hands of the negotiators, the whole question had been postponed till after the EDC was ratified. The condition for the EDC was now conditioned by the EDC, a perfect whipped cream of diplomacy. After eighteen months of effort, the EPC was back in the limbo from which de Gasperi had tried to rescue it in July 1952.

Monnet, like all insiders aware of the parliamentary arithmetic since early 1952, working through political friends in Paris, tried, but in vain, to meet the Socialist conditions. He also seems to have thought an attempt should be made to reshape the EDC-EPC complex, but his allies, considering that matters were complicated enough as they were, resisted any would-be simplification. In his *Memoirs,* Monnet ascribes his lack of impact on the later phases of the EDC to the fact he had too much on his plate in Luxembourg. True; but this hardly inhibited him on other occasions. The real blocks were in Paris: Bidault; and a government of coalition politicians, bred to constant compromise, paralysed by a campaign against the EDC which fed on raw emotion. (Interestingly, surveys showed that the voters were less stirred up than the establishment.) In particular, with Bidault at the Quai d'Orsay, Monnet was disconnected for the first time in years from French foreign policy.

Monnet himself became a target for *odium theologicum.* In a press conference on November 12, 1953, de Gaulle launched a personal attack on "the inspirer", without naming him directly. Monnet replied in an interview in *Le Monde* on the 17th. The "Europe of Jean Monnet" now became the ritual red rag to the more militant opponents of the EDC. Originally, the main opposition had been to German rearmament. Increasingly, revulsion against the disappearance of the army of Turenne, Napoleon and Foch in a "stateless" hotch-potch, a "monstrosity," as de Gaulle called it, seemed to take over. The EDC became the enemy as much as the German rearmament it had been meant to sterilise—for Gaullists, even more.

In the end, events were precipitated by an apparently unconnected crisis which, however, had this in common with the dithering over the European Army: both were widely taken as symbols of the unwillingness or inability of the reigning politicians of the Fourth Republic to measure up to unpleasant decisions. In Indochina, the guerrilla armies of the Communist-led Vietminh were slowly but steadily exhausting France's postwar efforts to reassert the control over its rich colonies there, which it had lost to the Japanese in the Second World War. In fact, by 1954, the Vietminh, supplied from

Communist China, had graduated from guerrilla bands to a formidable regular army. The French commander-in-chief, General Henri Navarre, made the fatal mistake of deliberately challenging the Vietminh to an infantry battle in the inland hills of Laos, at Dienbienphu, in the hopes of destroying the adversary by a major blow. The French armed camp turned into a trap for the defenders, who lacked the air power to break the artillery concentrations that pounded them from the surrounding heights. The last strong-points of Dienbienphu fell to the besiegers on May 7, 1954, after fifty-six days.

The Dienbienphu disaster discredited not just the government but the whole parliamentary class. Political stormwinds, filled with angry energy, brought Pierre Mendès-France to power. He was no ordinary premier of the Fourth Republic. The hunger for reform he captured was nationalistic and in some respects proto-Gaullist. Symbolically or not, it was at this moment, on Saturday, June 5th, that Monnet, in his sixty-sixth year, contracted a mysterious illness which kept him away from all activity for three months. It was announced as flu, but was in fact a stroke, which seems to have involved brief paralysis of one side. The doctors ordered complete rest, which he took first in the Jura Mountains, then the Alps. He recovered remarkably quickly. There were no obvious subsequent signs, and he had no recurrence in his active life. This in itself suggests the exceptional strain he was under at this time. He was incapacitated when he would normally have been in the thick of the mêlée. It is hard to believe that the frustration of the period had nothing to do with an uncharacteristic moment of physical frailty.

Mendès-France, having extracted France from Indochina, did grasp the nettle of the EDC, at least in the sense that he presented it to Parliament for ratification, the first French premier in over two years to do so. Declaring that the European Army treaty could no longer be ratified in France as it stood—even though all of France's five Community partners had already ratified it—he faced the Five in a conference in Brussels from August 19 to 22. He put forward yet another French protocol, which would have weakened the EDC still further, in effect turning it at least for the eight initial years into a cooperative, not integrated, organisation and opening the door to a possible further complete renegotiation within the year. By now, the patience of France's partners had run out. The conference duly failed. Mendès-France then presented the treaty to the French Parliament, but his attitude, which was formally neutral, conveyed a hostility which is not concealed in his later interview deposited in the Monnet archives in Lausanne. He underlined the gulf separating him from Monnet and the Community Strategy in a single phrase, when he told the National Assembly that "the axiom of French policy must be to stick to Great Britain".

Monnet in his high Swiss valley played little part in the final drama. Still, at the end of his convalescence, from mid-August, he exchanged several letters with Mendès-France. It was a vain attempt to persuade him to come out in favour of the EDC. Monnet also seems to have been in touch with Spaak and advised him towards the end of the Brussels conference to make no further concessions to Mendès-France's protocol. In later years, he regretted this. "One should never break off". He returned to politics by sitting in the public gallery of the French National Assembly for the decision to "pass on to the next item on the agenda", and in effect reject, the EDC treaty by 319 votes to 264 on August 30, 1954. The triumphant majority burst into the *Marseillaise*.

The EDC was Europe's first great crisis and defeat. A battle had been lost. Had the war itself? Certainly, a kind of Europe had been eliminated. Nobody after the first two years of Monnet's presidency at the High Authority would again talk of it or its equivalents as a "European government". The watering down of the initial Schuman Plan concept had in fact begun during the negotiation of the EDC treaty and been accentuated in the EPC talks. This shift hardened after the French rejection of the EDC. Awareness that the French would have to be coaxed into further progress introduced caution into the European vocabulary. The word *federal* was reserved as the political equivalent of Latin for the rare religious occasion. Even *supranational,* itself a fig-leaf at first and a word Monnet disliked, tended to be used only when another fig-leaf could not be found. The idea of a Europe in some sense above the nations was no longer stated in the open.

The first Europe was in many ways a security Europe, not an economic one. This was more than the accident of the raw material of the EDC. The shared characteristic both of the ECSC and the European Army was that they were primarily addressed to German power. Each had economic aspects, but neither was economic in essence. Yet, by a paradox, the EDC proved that it was dangerous, even impossible, to pursue further European union by direct security or political means. Monnet, never very fond of military questions, despite his record in the war, became more wary of defence than ever. "Mental processes in that field are not normal", he told Jean-François Deniau, many years later, when Deniau was a member of the Commission of the European Economic Community (the Common Market). Approaches henceforth would have to take more oblique—meaning, in practice, *economic*—avenues.

Monnet himself could not escape unscathed from the wreck of the EDC. It was largely a reaction against the federalism he personified. He was weakened most in Paris. This came in three stages. First, he vacated his own post there in the corridors of power to go to Luxembourg. Second, there was the departure of Schuman from the Foreign Office. During the Luxembourg days, Monnet was already without the hold on government he enjoyed when Schuman ran French foreign policy. Third, the personal attacks on him in the heat of the EDC hardened into habit by the defeat of the treaty. As a result, Monnet became for the first time a publicly controversial figure, that is, a political one, which he had not been in 1950. The situation was different in the five other Community countries, which had all ratified the EDC. But even here there was a reaction in government. According to Zijlstra, Monnet "was at the peak of his influence when he was President of the High Authority. . . . [He] had an enormous authority over the national governments. . . . And one of the reasons why the [later Common Market] did not have a High Authority, but a European Commission, was to try and avoid any misunderstanding that even traces of that situation would be repeated". The governments rejected anything or anyone that threatened, like Monnet, openly to compete with their monopoly. The opposition had been mobilised, and he never again held the initiative quite as he did in 1950. He would still draw on astonishing reservoirs of support and there would be achievements to come, but none to match the partnership with Schuman. It is true that in the short time available to them, they switched the points of European statecraft traditional since the late Middle Ages.

The Most Hazardous Straits

1954-1955

I t is difficult today to convey the blow for its supporters of the EDC's rejection. Many observers thought it had put paid to European integration for ever. Adenauer had never seemed to one of them "so embittered, so depressed". Baron Robert Rothschild, the chief of staff and friend of Spaak, retired to Nyon on the Lake of Geneva, very quietly, in effect to convalesce. "There was a period of apathy, of lethargy, as in concussion". Bruce and Tomlinson, as Americans not officially involved at all, went to the office like automata and did not address a word to each other for a week. Tomlinson's stroke and early death in April 1955 may well have been hastened by the shock. Monnet reacted differently. When Delouvrier told him a few days after the vote that the way the EDC had collapsed was "dirty, frightful", Monnet looked at him "very calmly" and said, "you know, the EDC was a bad business", in a tone that buried the past and moved on.

"Anyone who had then predicted that the Six would soon be actively engaged in the creation of two new Communities might reasonably have been dismissed as a light-headed visionary", Miriam Camps has written. While Mendès-France was in office, British-style cooperation was possible, but federalism was not. He was reported to have told Michel Rasquin, the Luxembourg Minister of Economic Affairs, that "the French government is pursuing a policy of balance in Europe and not a European policy". Even when he fell, the advisers of the Dutch Prime Minister and grand old man of the Labour Party, Willem Drees, thought Mendès-France might well return to power. Others were less sure. They knew French politics for the volatile matter they were. The European party remained strong despite the EDC.

The first priority for Atlantic treaty governments was to complete the job left unfinished by the EDC. West Germany was still not rearmed four years after the idea had been launched. To complete the process required recognition of its sovereignty, the end of Allied occupation and its entry into the Atlantic military alliance—in fact, the original American intentions of 1950. The opponents of the EDC in France had fondly claimed they had buried all this. What they had actually interred was the French veto. The British, who had foreseen the EDC debacle, seized the initiative. The London conference of September 28 to October 3, turned the Federal Republic of Germany into a full Atlantic ally under a NATO integrated command headed by an American. French anxieties were allayed by bringing Germany and Italy into a reformed version of the Brussels Treaty Organisation of 1947, renamed the Western European Union (WEU). Britain gave the WEU a guarantee it had withheld from the EDC—that British troops would not leave the Continent without a concurring vote of the other member states. Arms controls were devised, in fact if not in form, for Germany. These arrangements were experienced as a triumph of intergovernmentalism. Ratification took priority throughout the winter of 1954–55. European Community schemes, if any, would have to wait.

Admittedly, when Dulles visited Adenauer on September 17, the joint communiqué went out of its way to underline

> complete agreement that European integration was so vital to peace and security that efforts to achieve it should be resolutely pursued and that this great goal should not be abandoned because of a single setback.

Defiant statements of this kind are often swan-songs.

One European bastion remained: the European Coal and Steel Community in Luxembourg. Spaak had confided to Macmillan in October 1952 that if the EDC failed, the ECSC too would collapse. In the event, this did not happen. If anything, fear that it might do so heightened the determination to recapture the initiative. Monnet's colleagues on the High Authority thought the ECSC offered the only possible base of future operations. He disagreed. In his eyes, the EDC crisis had proved that the sources of power lay in the nations, channelled through the governments, not the Community in Luxembourg. He must raise coalitions of support in the member states. On November 11, he announced he would resign when his initial term of office expired on February 10, 1955, in order to be free to work across the board for European unity. After two or three telephone calls from Monnet, McCloy told Frankfurter that "Mendès-France had given the impression that a certain return to nationalism was in the air and Jean felt this should be counteracted". Heinrich Sträter, the German steelworkers' leader and one of a trio of German trade union leaders Monnet met on either side of Christmas 1954, reported that he wanted to found a committee to exert "all possible pressure" on those, "like Mendès-France", standing in union's way. In retrospect, this seems common sense. At the time, it was controversial. The Common Assembly urged him to stay on. So did Adenauer. So, more surprisingly, did the Council of Ministers, though chaired by the French. In the High Authority, there were mutterings about his abandoning his brainchild and his colleagues in their hour of need.

Whatever the future required, the first priority was to keep the ECSC going. The High Authority, as the one supranational citadel, was weakened but had to manage coal and steel as if the ground beneath it had not shifted. Paradoxically, Monnet's last months in Luxembourg were positive for the Community. Agreement was reached, for instance, on charging coal and steel rail freight across frontiers on a degressive basis, from end to end of a journey, as within countries. Lack of this had handicapped traffic across borders, and big interests were vested in the status quo. The reform was a success. Most of the credit was due to Spierenburg.

Monnet's involvement was more direct in the association agreement with Britain. Significantly, this was important for the future of European integration rather than for the ECSC as such. As a model for relations between Europe and Britain, "association" answered (in part) some difficult questions on the Continent. The reluctance of the French and German Socialists and of the Dutch and Belgians in general to commit themselves without Britain had been a constant drag on plans for European integration. Britain's refusal to be committed to the European Army had, after all, prompted the split among the French Socialists which broke the EDC. As Tomlinson told Washington, association with Britain was "considered necessary for political acceptance on the Continent of European federation".

The mental reservations holding up an association agreement on all sides were in effect confessed by the snail's pace of progress on the issue and long pauses for rest. The start was brisk enough. The British government announced the intent to establish "a close and lasting association" with the ECSC as soon as it opened in August 1952. Monnet echoed this in his trip to London towards the end of the month. A Joint Committee of the High Authority and British delegation to the ECSC in Luxembourg was duly set up and first met on November 17. Confidential talks followed, but only in February 1953, between Monnet, Etzel, Spierenburg and the head of the British delegation, the businessman Sir Cecil Weir, and his deputy from the Foreign Office, James Marjoribanks. Further action then waited on a working party of the relevant ministries in London which, for the second time since 1950, was studying relations with the new creature in continental Europe. The chief influences on the group were, first, fears that British steel might not be able in the long run to compete with a continental cartel led by Germany and, second, the belief that the highly regulated system governing British steel since the war should be liberalised. The dominant voices felt that close association with the ECSC might answer both anxieties. The report, in July, recommended to the U.K. government that there be a single U.K.-ECSC market in steel, free of tariffs and quotas, and that Britain observe the Community's steel pricing arrangements. However, in June, Monnet announced impending High Authority proposals, so the British waited. He made soundings in London which despite the July report discouraged his original aim progressively to establish a common market with Britain. His ideas finally materialised only on Christmas Eve. By this time, he thought negotiations urgent to influence French politics on the EDC. His letter to Weir spoke of cuts in tariffs, of "joint formulation of policies" and of "common rules", notions in effect watered down from the Whitehall report. All the same, the British took another four months to declare their readiness to negotiate, on a political framework but not on material substance, late in April 1954. An association agreement of this kind was concluded only in December, after the EDC's collapse, when supranationality was in the doldrums.

As *The Times* of London put it on December 20, 1954, "the main reasons" for the slowness of proceedings and exiguity of the result "lie in the reluctance of two of the chief interested parties . . . to an encroachment on their activities by M. Monnet's High Authority with all its pretensions to sovereign power". One was the British Iron and Steel Federation. "There . . . was a trend of thought represented within the British Government which was prepared to commit this country to a very intimate partnership with the ECSC. . . . [T]he Iron and Steel Federation felt sufficiently disturbed . . . to deliver an unusually sharp public counterblast on the subject. There was no attempt at diplomatic equivocation: association was condemned root and branch". The other critic was Mendès-France. The difficulty (as an exchange of long letters with Uri published much later makes clear) was his dislike of the High Authority, a non-state, reaching an agreement and managing relations with a real state, and a large one.

All this was true as far as it went, but *The Times* could have cast its net still wider. On the British side, the Iron and Steel Federation, and its powerful spokesman in the British Cabinet, the Minister of Supply (and Churchill's son-in-law), Duncan Sandys, would not have had their way so easily if attitudes had been more positive. There was little or no political desire in London to promote the European Army treaty or become entangled with the ECSC. As the Italian scholar Ruggero Ranieri has written of an earlier phase of the association saga, "the higher the level of discussion, the firmer the resolve not to to act" on the more committing aspects of the civil servants' proposals of July 1953.

As for the Six, there was some fear in the Council of Ministers of opening up the common market to British steel, which practised (indirectly subsidised) lower prices than the continentals. There was also general resistance to the High Authority encroaching on trade policy through arrangements with Britain. Monnet's hopes of negotiating tariff cuts were ruled out. The Council of Association that remained was one more political framework, a shell, for further talks. Its only achievement, from Monnet's point of view, was that it placed the High Authority, the spokesman of the Six, on the same level as the British government.

In the end, Monnet travelled by boat-train to London to sign the agreement (with Etzel and Spierenburg for the High Authority), over two months late, on December 21, 1954. On arrival at Victoria station at seven A.M., and as he was still framed in the doorway of the *wagon-lit,* he was confronted, three inconveniently deep steps down on the platform, by a slender, blond young man in top hat, tails and striped trousers who announced, "I am Government Hospitality, Sir". Monnet, somewhat taken aback, stumped after him to the ponderous Humber of State.[1] The agreement of association was signed the next day with Sandys. Monnet, asked his view two months later, professed himself well satisfied. He saw the agreement as "a pattern for association in other fields" with Britain. It fed the claim that the Six, by going ahead with integration, did not repel the British but drew them in their wake. It partly squared the circle of how to reduce Whitehall's mortgage on new Communities while encouraging closer relations with Britain. And though nobody, of course, put it so crudely, in hard times it affirmed the international presence of the new Europe.

II
MONNET AND SPAAK

By resigning "to be free to act", Monnet made it plain his eyes were set on the future. In fact, he and Spaak had already taken the politicians' equivalent of an oath over the open grave of the EDC. The story is told by the only witness, André de Staercke, for many years the Belgian permanent representative to NATO, then in Paris.

> Spaak, downhearted, left with me the evening [of the EDC vote] for my house on the Italian shore of Lake Maggiore. My mother was alive then. . . . She was extremely interested in politics, and Spaak liked her very much. She listened to Spaak's tale of desperate efforts to save the EDC. . . . Then she said, "But from what you tell me, it was predictable. . . . Now is just the time you should look for something else". We went out on the lake in a small boat and Spaak said, "She's right, you know. We

---

1. The Humber was a portentous but otherwise unremarkable car, which has long since vanished. It was patronised (amongst others) by the British government.

must go back to Paris tonight. Telephone Monnet that I would like to see him". . . . We took the train to Paris and reached my flat in the Île de la Cité at eight o'clock in the morning. Monnet turned up at once. I received him in the downstairs sitting-room. He must have waited for a time . . . because he had picked some books off the shelves and was reading the *Maxims* of Lao-tse, and pronounced them excellent. Spaak then turned up and his first words were, "Obviously, it's a disaster. . . . Can we do anything in the economic field?" And they were off. . . . Monnet said, "Yes, we must try".

This seems to have been around September 3. The Monnet diary is not clear, though there are traces of contact with Spaak by telephone. A long lunch with Spaak in the Ardennes ending at four-thirty P.M. followed on September 12. The two men seem to have agreed that Monnet should prepare proposals and Spaak take the diplomatic initiative. Although the omens were poor, Spaak had found his Monnet, Monnet a second Schuman. Benelux, recently the weak sister of Community Europe was now, with the shift in foreign ministers to Johan Beyen in The Hague and Spaak in Brussels, its shining light.

Monnet started exploring the ground for a new European campaign before 1954 was out. His plans started from the idea of delivering a manifesto upon leaving the High Authority. They then divided into two streams that gradually dug separate beds: (*a*) new European initiatives for when the time was ripe; and (*b*) the creation of a power base for himself when out of office. Each in turn broke down into a variety of ideas taken up and dropped or tempered and revived. Themes rose and fell. There was a gradual flow from texts emphasising principles towards specific plans. There are not far short of fifty drafts in the archives covering one or other of these aspects between, it would appear, the latter half of December 1954 and April 18, 1955. Most seem to have been written by Van Helmont, a few by Uri, one, a rarity, by Monnet himself.

The first drafts were prepared for the "declaration of February 10", the date of Monnet's presumed departure from the High Authority. The idea was that politicians and trade unions would endorse it publicly. Then he must have realised he would have no opportunity for a formal statement to Community institutions. By mid-January, drafts relate to a "declaration in Paris" on February 15, that is, the Tuesday following departure from Luxembourg. All the early texts, say, from December to mid-January, tended to be cast in high principle and generalities. They spoke of a Franco-German declaration of common European intent, an elected European parliament, a U.K. association, the extension of the ECSC to energy and transport, and a supranational arms pool. The French had proposed the arms pool. The governments never took it seriously. Beyen called it "fake integration". But

Monnet, like the politicians of the ECSC Common Assembly, thought he saw the thin end of a supranational wedge. The idea cropped up in drafts in January 1955. After February 3, it disappeared, no doubt because he realised it was a mirage. In a manner prophetic of the later frustrations of all would-be rationalisers of arms industries, every country wanted to keep control of its own. Even the Germans, with none, hoped to grow one on a diet of American licenses.

The extension of the ECSC to other forms of energy and transport figured in nearly all these drafts, but rarely with much definition. Monnet was less of a supporter of this line than members of the High Authority like Etzel, Spierenburg and Coppé. Uri's memory was that they said,

"After such a defeat, we will have to be modest. We should try to extend the powers of the High Authority. . . . We have the coal, why not take on oil, gas and electricity? And transport, as . . . it plays a major role in coal, iron ore and steel". I must say I came out against that straight away. . . . "Oil is international. . . . As for transport . . . it would contribute nothing politically and raise insurmountable technical problems".

These ideas staggered on in the communiqués but by 1956 dropped out of the procession under the experts' withering scrutiny.

Monnet did not reject such suggestions but plumped more and more for a new Community in a new sector, civil nuclear power. Max Isenbergh was the man who first impressed it on his imagination. Isenbergh, the deputy legal counsel of the U.S. Atomic Energy Commission (AEC), was in Europe on a Rockefeller Senior Fellowship. He was studying the control of civil nuclear power to prevent military proliferation. He was also out of sympathy with the new chairman of the AEC, Lewis Strauss. He seems not to have been on a mission in any way, rather to be enjoying Europe in self-imposed exile and playing the clarinet. He had an introduction from some of Monnet's friends in Washington: Frankfurter, who had been Isenbergh's mentor, and Philip Graham, the owner-consort of the *Washington Post.* Isenbergh met Monnet for the first time in January 1955. Almost at once, Monnet was keeping him for day-long sessions, in his usual style when an idea caught his imagination.

The earliest dated draft to contain the civil nuclear-power Community, later called Euratom, came on January 21. Once the theme was introduced, it remained in all drafts, steadily taking on life and detail, until in the end its roots took virtually all the room in the pot.

Given the assumptions of the time, nuclear power had enormous attractions. In December 1953, President Eisenhower had made his "Atoms for Peace" speech to the United Nations General Assembly promising to make nuclear materials available for civil power programmes. Civil nuclear power, claimed the AEC, would be so cheap there would be no point metering it in the home. It was also thought (as with micro-electronics since) that the technology would transform the whole of industry and ways of life. Uri slipped into an early Monnet draft a phrase about a "new industrial revolution . . . on a scale without precedent in the past hundred years", which percolated into many a text and communiqué.

The superpowers and Britain were blazing the trail. Britain had announced a commercial nuclear-power programme in February 1955. It seemed the then classic case of continental Europe lagging behind. To carry out the enormous research and development needed to know what reactor types would be most economic demanded resources on an American scale. Clearly, here was an area for collective effort if Europe were to climb the steep ascent to industrial parity with the competition. The Atoms for Peace policy aroused hopes of tapping American technology and know-how. Nuclear power also demanded public regulation, because there were no hard-and-fast barriers between civil and military activity. The very home of free enterprise, the United States, regulated it. It was, then, a natural field for regulation in Europe by a supranational body. It was easy to see nuclear power as God's gift to integrators.

Joint regulation could also ensure that Germany's nuclear development would remain strictly civilian, and on terms acceptable to the country. In bringing Germany into NATO, Adenauer unilaterally renounced the manufacture of nuclear weapons. But Mendès-France thought the self-denying ordinance could not last more than fifteen years, and some American diplomats feared it would be even less. At times, in private, Adenauer himself talked as if the renunciation might be temporary. European controls could reinforce the safeguards. Further, France's nuclear effort, tiny by superpower standards, was larger than those of all its Community partners put together. Here was one sector where the inferiority complex which had played havoc with the EDC ought to be irrelevant. This was a major factor in Monnet's choice. Finally, since the industry was new, there should be no lobbies ready to spring to arms against change, like the defence industry of Marcel Boussac, the textile magnate and racehorse owner, against the EDC. In a radio talk Mendès-France gave on October 25, 1954, he pointed out that "European integration" (integration was a vague word) "should be greatly helped by the fact . . . that nuclear power is only just beginning". Coal and steel had provided the material for the great symbolic burial of old feuds. Nuclear power could provide the basis for Europe's great symbolic entry into the modern world. Given such expectations, failure to act might in retrospect seem unforgivable.

In short, by February 1955, Monnet had elaborated a view on new steps towards "Europe". His recipe was fresh sectoral integration of the kind already embodied in the ECSC, but separate from it; the basic ingredient was nuclear power. However, if plans and ends were fairly clear, means and timing were not. Then he had a stroke of luck. Four days before his expected departure from Luxembourg, on February 6, the Mendès-France government fell. It was not as if opportunity had suddenly opened up. Great uncertainties remained, epitomised in Paris by the centre-right government, headed by Edgar Faure, which took over at the end of February. On Europe, one of the great fault-lines of French politics, this was a cabinet of opposites, with nine ministers, mostly Catholic, who had voted for the EDC, six, mainly Gaullist, who had voted against, and none who had changed his mind. Riven on every essential except domestic economic policy (which proved rather successful), the government held on, as Van Helmont has put it, "by grace of the Holy Ghost" and of Faure's talents as a conjuror. Still, uncertainty was better than an impasse. Suddenly, there was room for manoeuvre.

Mendès-France had proposed a Socialist former Prime Minister, Paul Ramadier, to replace Monnet as High Authority president. Ramadier had been sceptical about the ECSC and hostile to the EDC. A little black book of his un-European sayings was circulating in Luxembourg. Monnet was horrified and spent a whole evening pleading with Pleven to step forward. Adenauer and Spaak also disapproved. Ramadier might not have been chosen anyway, though Faure (who was Foreign Minister for the last three weeks of Mendès-France's government) made an effort to woo Spaak. Ramadier's chances vanished with Mendès-France. A replacement would have to be found and it would take time. The Foreign Ministers' meeting called to name Monnet's successor on February 8 was postponed.

It may have been at this point that a curious little incident occurred. Monnet was just about to leave Luxembourg, with luggage piled high in the courtyard of his house of Bricherhof. The members of the High Authority came to see him in a body, and as if seized with shyness pushed forward its legal counsel, Michel Gaudet, to point out that the President could not leave till his successor had been appointed. In fact, in February 1955, Monnet was happy enough to remain, blocking Ramadier while someone more suitable was found. Because Adenauer and Spaak wanted Monnet to stay at the High Authority, he could also pose a few conditions. He would remain if the governments committed themselves to negotiate treaties on new Communities. In any case, choosing a successor would require a Foreign Ministers' meeting, the first since the rejection of the EDC. Here was a chance to introduce fresh schemes of integration. The succession stakes became entwined with manoeuvring over a new set of European Communities.

In short, the fall of Mendès-France opened a new phase. Yet it was still not easy to chart a course. There could be no movement on Europe until the Paris Agreements defining the new German defence arrangements had been ratified in Paris and Bonn. It was clear that, having left no palatable alternative, the French Parliament would be forced to swallow the agreements at a second bite, having choked on them a first time in December. This would now take place in the form once regarded as the least palatable of all, a German national army, or at least most aspects of such an army, in NATO. Among Frenchmen, only the Gaullists were consoled, amazingly in view of their rhetoric, but logically: rather that, de Gaulle affirmed, than the "lamentable surrender" of the millennial French army into some sort of European porridge.

If many continued to regard European integration as vital, it was primarily due to the anxiety generated by German national rearmament. The fears of a German national army in 1955 may seem overblown nowadays, when a crisis is caused in Bonn by the prospect of sending a naval craft into the Adriatic for peace-keeping. But then the Federal Republic was fewer than six years old. No one could guarantee the lethal combination of Ruhr magnates and German military would not reappear. Adenauer himself expressed the gravest misgivings. That was the burden of a famous midnight chat with Spaak and Joseph Bech, the simultaneous and eternal Prime Minister, Foreign Minister and Sylviculture Minister of Luxembourg, one of the characters on the postwar political circuits. They all sat on one side of a partition in the lobby of Claridge's Hotel during the London conference of September 1954 and were overheard by the correspondent of Der Spiegel, Lothar Ruehl, sitting on the other side. Because Spaak spoke no German and Bech interpreted, Ruehl, who knew French well, got the message twice over. His report was never denied. German Social Democrats, who had launched the ohne mich ("without me") campaign against rearmament, had even less reason to feel safe. They had suffered too much in the Nazi past to be anything but anxious. "German labour", Monnet told Dulles on December 17, 1954, "considers that European integration is the only way to keep their liberties for the future". When such views were held in Germany, those in France can be imagined. As Van Helmont has recalled, "The French had rejected the EDC, they were being forced to swallow the Paris Agreements, what was happening was very bad, very dangerous, and what it would finally result in was anyone's guess". Integration seemed more than ever the way to harness Germany to safe purposes.

Failures like the EDC usually lead to realignments of forces. In this case, there were no defections from the European camp in the six Community countries. A remarkable instance was Mollet. He was a classic party boss, for whom the unity and strength of the Socialist Party he controlled were sacrosanct. The EDC had split the party down the middle, fifty (including Mollet) voting for the EDC and fifty-three against, in the midst of much personal animosity. Following such a disaster, he was bound to be obsessed with party unity. Yet his support for new European proposals never wavered.

At the same time, the opposition to European schemes and to Monnet in person was very strong in some quarters, much stronger than before the

EDC, mainly but not only in France. "In recent years", as the Dutch free-trade and anti-supranational paper, *Nieuwe Rotterdamsche Courant,* put it, "European integration has come to be more identified with Monnet than with any other politician". "Once Monnet's mind is made up, he pursues his convictions relentlessly", wrote Weir. "This obstinate streak is at once his strength and his weakness. . . . While he has never deviated from his principles, his methods in achieving them have made him many enemies". The Belgian ambassador in Paris reported that French industry did not want "to hear a word of new schemes under the mantle of the Coal and Steel Community or of M. Jean Monnet. . . . [There is] a personal animus against M. Monnet". Bech remarked that "Erhard . . . dislikes M. Monnet and his schemes even more than do the industrialists of the Ruhr and nearly as much as French Gaullists and industrialists". On the other hand, as one British diplomat reported from Paris, "Faure himself is not one of the 'Europeans', but he has Pinay, Pflimlin, Teitgen and André Morice in his Cabinet. These latter are undoubtedly keen on seeing some new initiative taken by France in the direction of European economic integration. . . . Monnet is their man, their spearhead if not their leader".

This was the complex background to the Monnet-Spaak preparations to launch a new European campaign. According to Monnet's diary, he and Spaak saw each other on four occasions early in 1955. Monnet's first proposals were handed over at a meeting on February 21 when he brought with him Hirsch, Uri and Van Helmont. Spaak was already making use of their themes in conversation with Edgar Faure on February 7. According to Baron Rothschild, speaking probably of the February 21 meeting, Monnet's visit triggered the European *relance.* "He said, 'We must act. If we do not, we will lose the initiative' ". However, active moves were still held up by the ratification of the Paris Agreements. At last, on March 29, the Council of the Republic (the Senate) completed the painful and at times doubtful process in France. The European floodgates opened. Two days later, Spaak reported that "the French were again thinking about European unity, a new situation existed and its effects would be seen in the shape of new proposals". A British diplomat reported, "Everybody is bursting with new ideas".

Monnet and Spaak met on March 27. There is no record of what they said. But on April 4, a week after French ratification, Spaak wrote a letter containing the Monnet proposals to the German, French and Italian Foreign Ministers (Adenauer, Pinay and Gaetano Martino). He proposed that a conference be convened to negotiate treaties to extend the ECSC to all of energy and transport (including airlines) and to create a new Community for civil nuclear power. The conference should be chaired by Monnet, who, in these circumstances, Spaak "had good reason to believe" could be persuaded to withdraw his resignation from the High Authority. Spaak, in short, was proposing Monnet's programme for a further round of sectoral European integration on the pattern of the Schuman Plan and, again somewhat as in the Schuman Plan, that Monnet should take charge of negotiations from his supranational eyrie in Luxembourg.

III
COMMON MARKETS AND FREE TRADE

The conspicuous gap in Spaak's letter was any mention of a general common market. This was not an oversight. A version of February 19 on the eve of Monnet's first proposals to Spaak envisaged a common market for "consumption goods" at a "later stage" than energy, transport and nuclear power. Then it faded from view. In the final presentation to Spaak, on April 22, 1955, it reappeared. Again, it was left to a later stage. The significance of this is heightened by a meeting on April 6, when Monnet sounded Carl-Friedrich Ophüls on Euratom. Ophüls, the chief German lawyer in the Schuman talks, was now head of the Political Department in the new German Foreign Office.

> To [Monnet's] great surprise, Ophüls said the German government would not be interested [in Euratom] and that Erhard would be against. Monnet was completely nonplussed. At this point, I [Uri is telling the story] butted in and said: "I understand the Germans. . . . If I were they, I would be interested in America, in Britain, because [they have] a lead in this field, in Norway for heavy water, in Switzerland for precision instruments. But the Schuman Plan was two things at once. One was a common basis of development, the other was a prototype for general integration. What if we developed both approaches at the same time, Euratom on one hand and a general common market on the other?" . . . Ophüls said at once, ". . . The German government would agree completely and Erhard would not hold out against it". Afterwards, Monnet, looking rather depressed, said to me, "There's nothing for it but that".[2]

This meeting established the basic fact of the coming negotiations: at no time were the Germans willing to swallow Euratom without a general common market. This and Monnet's parting words to Uri make doubly striking the fact that his later texts, written after the Ophüls meeting, still relegate any general common market to a second stage.

Monnet seems to have had two reasons for postponing a general common market. The first was that he feared it would be the EDC fiasco all over

---

2. Monnet and Ophüls (and Van Helmont) met again in Paris on April 19.

again. "We started with Euratom because we didn't dare go to a Common Market". That was a good enough reason, but the second went deeper. At the end of November 1955, Delouvrier reported a conversation with Monnet and Uri, the gist of which was, in Kohnstamm's diary: "Is it possible to have a Common Market without federal social, monetary and conjuncture policies? . . . Monnet thinks it is not".[3] By implication, Monnet felt any likely common market would be so near free trade lacking institutions as to undermine his political purposes. Conversely, federalism adequate to make a common market work his way was out of reach after the EDC. Adenauer too, feared a common market might be too complicated to be feasible.

This was also Spaak's initial view. He wrote later of Monnet and himself:

> Our ambitions were modest. So were our hopes. It seemed important to us to advance on solid ground where we had real chances of success, leaving bigger plans till later. Above all, we had to avoid another rebuff.

Spaak had suppressed several attempts in his own country to revert to intergovernmental schemes in the OEEC. Two weeks after the rejection of the EDC treaty, the Belgian Economics Ministry convened a meeting of Benelux civil servants to examine alternative policies. Dutch sources show that by November the argument leaned towards discussion of a Free Trade Area in the OEEC,[4] that is, including Britain and Scandinavia. Later, a senior minister, Jean van Houtte, made the suggestion publicly. Victor Larock, Spaak's own deputy, as Socialist Minister for Commerce and Vice Minister for Foreign Affairs, proposed in November (and again in March) sectoral Free Trade Areas in the OEEC as economic branches became ripe for the treatment. These ideas in effect wove variations on the theme of customs-free areas, which had been the main focus of European integration schemes in the 1940s before the Schuman Plan.

A note of urgency was introduced into all this by Adenauer and Mendès-France. Meeting in the margins of the conference over German rearmament in NATO, on October 26, 1954, they announced an agreement between the Industrial Confederations of Germany and France on bilateral economic cooperation. There was to be close consultation by the two governments; coordination of investments; a "division of labour" in industry; government-

---

3. Max Kohnstamm was still secretary of the High Authority. He formally joined Monnet at the Action Committee for the United States of Europe in September 1956.

4. A Free Trade Area, like a customs union, eliminates frontier obstacles to trade between member countries. Unlike a customs union, each nation keeps its own tariffs towards countries outside the union. One could imagine free trade areas that were more committing than some customs unions, but in practice they are the minimalist solution favoured by governments unwilling to be entangled in tighter regimes.

industrial commissions to rationalise some sectors, especially the aircraft industry; cooperation in the French union; and regular meetings of the chairmen of the two confederations. Nothing came or was likely to come of such notions, which indeed were not new. Beyen, for one, was unimpressed. The last thing Erhard and German industry wanted was exclusive economic relations with France.

Nevertheless, the mere prospect produced great agitation in Luxembourg and Belgium. The Luxembourgeois were alarmed, *inter alia,* that the institutions of the ECSC, "precariously" housed in Luxembourg, might be wafted off to Saarbrücken to sweeten a deal on the Saar. As for the Belgians, special relationships between French and Germans touched a raw nerve. They still referred in the 1950s to the so-called Benedetti treaty, named after the French ambassador in Berlin at the time of the Austro-Prussian War of 1866. This document, carefully leaked by Bismarck, connived at France annexing Belgium as the price of neutrality in the war. Nothing had come of it except red faces in Paris and recurrent nightmares for Belgian diplomats.

Spaak, however, ignored the pressures for a Free Trade Area in the OEEC, with Britain but possibly without a hyper-reluctant France. He preferred collusion by France and Germany to conflicts between them. He also agreed with Monnet that the priority was to integrate Germany and that only supranational Communities could achieve this. His consistent attitude was a key to the continuity between the ECSC of the first round of Europe-building and the second round now about to open. Without him, the issue might perhaps have gone another way.

Spaak's letter to the foreign ministers of April 4, then, with its largely Monnet content, expressed a deliberate choice of sectoral integration, ignoring the alternatives of a Common Market or Free Trade Area. His covering note to the French Foreign Minister, Pinay, sounded confident that "the ideas . . . are identical with those we discussed in my last visit to Paris" and that "we must now act on the general lines we agreed". Pinay's reply, then, must have come as a shock. Only a verbal message through the Belgian ambassador, it feared that proposals to "supranationalise energy and transport might produce another EDC in France" and added that "Edgar Faure, far from wishing to extend Monnet's powers, [is] against maintaining him at the High Authority". The ambassador added, "Take care! Edgar Faure does not like Monnet", who was suspected of "politicking" against him. Faure told the Italian ambassador that if foreigners "intrigued" to maintain Monnet as president of the High Authority, he himself would ask to leave the ECSC and "become the most popular Premier of France". The other recipients of Spaak's letter were hardly more encouraging. Adenauer was evasive, counselled delay and argued that the governments should form a group to make proposals on what to negotiate, which more or less ploughed up the Spaak-Monnet agenda. Gaetano Martino was opaque.

The only positive note in this dirge of muffled negatives was struck by Beyen, who, independently it seems, in a letter also dated April 4, came up precisely with the Common Market idea Monnet and Spaak had rejected. Benelux notwithstanding, Beyen and Spaak do not seem to have consulted at all. Beyen, a banker and æsthete, was an individualist who wrote—with some intellectual force—his own speeches and memoranda. He was not absorbed in politics as a Spaak or a Monnet was. He had been brought in from the executive board of the International Monetary Fund late in 1952 as part of a political deal between the Labour and Catholic parties in The Hague. He was thought by some who were close to him to be interested in his job only to the extent that he could introduce a European Common Market. If so, he succeeded in his brief political life more than most professionals ever do. He was, until recently, one of the unsung heroes of European integration.

After the EDC's demise, Beyen's first response had been that "we should not place much hope on further supranational organisation in western Europe". A little later, he had entertained Snoy's idea that the Benelux countries might propose Free Trade Area discussions in the OEEC. But after the fall of Mendès-France, his tone changed. He moved to the idea of a common market. Far from being incompatible with supranationality, a common market, he argued, required it. He rejected "the general opinion that [a common market] would only be possible on an intergovernmental basis, and cooperation on a supranational basis only . . . for specific sectors". In short, he took the opposite view to Monnet's.

Though the Netherlands had been one of the countries most in favour of customs unions in the OEEC before 1950, Beyen's line was not a standard rationalisation of Dutch trading interests. He encountered doubt verging on opposition at home. There was a strong body of opinion in Dutch government, civil service and industry that was wedded to worldwide free trade as an overlay to a long tradition of neutrality. In the nineteenth century, the Dutch Empire depended ultimately on the British navy. This reliance on a tutelary power was transferred after 1945 to America and Atlanticism. People with this outlook wanted nothing to do with France or plans for a "little" Europe. As Charles Rutten, then in the European directorate of the Dutch Foreign Office, has recalled:

> The official secretary of the Chamber of Commerce in Rotterdam, a very powerful figure, van der Mandele, fought a violent campaign . . . because he said, "If we get into a customs union with the French, it will be high tariffs, it will be the Continental system all over again. Where Napoleon did not succeed, Mollet [the French Premier in 1956] will succeed, and grass will grow on the quays in Rotterdam".

The Prime Minister, Willem Drees, was not far from such a view and suspected the Community of being a Popish plot. (So too in 1950 had Bevin and Mollet.[5]) At the other extreme, many Dutch decision-makers thought, like Spaak and Monnet, that sectoral integration was the only solid route ahead.

Still, there was a Dutch tradition behind a common market with supranational elements ("general integration", as it was called, to distinguish it from "sectoral integration"). In 1949, a working group, including Tinbergen, Spierenburg, Kohnstamm, and others, and set up to consider the measures needed to make economic integration work across the board, had reached such conclusions. Some Dutch thinking had also been influenced by the failure of Benelux to engender economic union by intergovernmental means. The members, the three small trading nations of Belgium, Holland and Luxembourg, should have been better equipped than anyone to succeed along such lines. If *they* could not, who could? The experience had bred a conviction, among some influential decision-makers, that a customs union must involve elements of common policy if it was to go any distance. Beyen, in 1953, had inserted an article on a common market into the abortive EPC treaty.

The memorandum Beyen sent to Spaak on April 4, 1955, was a vigorous reversion to this line of thought.

> All partial integration tends to settle problems in one sector by measures which harm other sectors or the interests of consumers and to exclude foreign competition. That is no way to increase European productivity. Further, sectoral integration does not reinforce the sense of solidarity and unity in Europe to the same degree as general economic integration. To strengthen these sentiments, it is vital that a feeling of joint responsibility of the European states for the common welfare should be embodied in an organisation which follows the general interest, with an executive which is answerable not to the national governments but before a supranational parliament.

Soon after, Beyen told the British ambassador that "the OEEC does not offer the degree of control western European countries need to make sure their economies are not at loggerheads". Later still, he was emphasising the Community's role in linking Germany to the West, in the style of Spaak.

5. The British ambassador to Luxembourg, Sir Geoffrey Allchin, reported that "M. Bech later told me that M. Drees had startled the party by making a 'European' speech. M. Bech, a 'European' when it suits him, had congratulated him on this and said that he had not known that he was 'one of us'. M. Drees had replied that, if he were M. Bech, he would not count on it".

Beyen, in short, despite widespread scepticism in his government and his own initial leanings to a Free Trade Area, introduced two new ideas into the integration debate among the governments in 1955. The first was economic integration across the board, not in sectors. The second was the thought, foreign to the conventional wisdom at the time, that this could and must be supranational like the ECSC in order to work and also to fit Germany into a stout European frame. Beyen overcame the resistance of his colleagues partly because of strong backing in the parliamentary parties, and partly because he exploited with skill the free hand each Dutch minister then enjoyed in his own field. His personal responsibility for launching the Common Market was very great.

The "daring" of Beyen's vision "scared me", Spaak confessed in his memoirs. He wrote Beyen on April 7 to say, "Basically, I agree with you. But I wonder if the policy you propose has much chance of success . . . in particular if the French government can accept it". But there is another version. Rothschild remembers that he and his colleague, Albert Hupperts, along with Baron Jean Snoy, the Secretary-General of the Economics Ministry, were sent by Spaak to present his sectoral ideas to Beyen, who, of course, rejected them in favour of his own scheme. They came back fully expecting Spaak to turn Beyen down. They were surprised when Spaak replied, "He is right, you know". When Spaak and Beyen met on April 23 to settle the joint approach they would take with Bech, they simply cobbled together the two approaches, the Beyen "general" and the Monnet "sectoral" (a last version of which had been handed to Spaak the previous day), and worked them up as the Benelux Memorandum. "The sectoral approach was put into it because, Spaak said, if we fail with the overall approach, we have to have a fall-back position".

The decision of the Benelux ministers to force the European issue in April and May after the dim responses to Spaak's letter of April 4 remains a minor mystery. Where did they dredge up the confidence not merely to go ahead but to raise the stakes with a general common market? There are no signs of covert encouragement from Adenauer or of cross-border consultations. One can only speculate. The need to meet to nominate a successor to Monnet at the High Authority provided a possibly unique opportunity to launch new European schemes. The Benelux countries may have felt the need to take the initiative in order to block bilateral ones between the French and the Germans. Beyen and Spaak, however, were possibly less influenced by such fears than were any of their compatriots.

The combination of an official Benelux memorandum and of an impending conference forced the remaining ECSC governments to define their own positions. In Germany and Italy, the main lines of debate were similar to those in Benelux. Only in France were they radically different.

Though Beyen proposed a common market, the commitment of Germany to one was the decisive factor. Throughout, the French and Germans were preoccupied primarily with one another. The negotiations between the six Community states were shadowed by a bilateral one between the Two, which surfaced at critical junctures. In the end, it was the Germans who took the French to market. For the first time, in 1955, they in effect seized the initiative. The "economic miracle", the *Wirtschaftswunder,* and restored sovereignty were already making their weight felt.

Adenauer himself displayed the caution of a sapper clearing a minefield during the first half of 1955. He was sceptical of Monnet's sectoral supranational approach—indeed, for a while, rather sceptical of Monnet himself, after the EDC debacle—doubting it could decisively shift power from the national capitals. He wanted a political union but increasingly kept his options open on ways to achieve it. The EDC and EPC would have begun to give it him, so that the EDC collapse came as a great shock. He briefly inclined to Britain early in 1955. The uncharacteristic mood passed, but he continued to fear European schemes so long as the Saar conflict had not been settled. In general, at this stage of wary minimalism, Adenauer was not ready to move anywhere too far out of step with the French government.

He sent a message to Pinay on April 3 to the effect that

> on the German side there were hesitations about proposing a new European round of schemes along the lines suggested by M. Monnet . . . handing over to the ECSC new Communities for transport, energy and nuclear energy. This would be to go ahead too fast. . . . The Chancellor therefore proposed to put off a meeting of the Six until May and would first like a tête-à-tête with M. Pinay.

Two weeks later, Adenauer told the French ambassador, the veteran André François-Poncet, that

> he in no way excluded the thought that there might be salvation outside the ECSC, though he remained attached to M. Monnet and hoped he would remain President

of the High Authority. Pinay duly came to Bonn, on April 29–30, and the two men mostly discussed the Saar. The communiqué called for new steps in "European cooperation" and singled out transport, civil aviation, aircraft production and research on civil nuclear power—that is, Monnet's programme without the supranational commitments.

Adenauer was a man of power rather than ideas, and German attitudes to a European revival were mainly fought out at the level below him. There were a few German supporters of sectoral integration, but not many: mainly Etzel at the High Authority and Hallstein, the head of the nascent Foreign

Ministry. Hallstein argued, in a long letter to Erhard, that if the Community failed to establish the core of a political union within five years, disintegration would set in. In general, however, there was a strong reaction in Germany, fuelled by the steelmasters, against sectoral integration of the ECSC type. Critics attacked it as a French "dirigiste" heresy. The Germans, the argument ran, had accepted European controls as the price of political integration. If that prospect failed, they would look on them as "the policy of Richelieu", in other words, of French hegemony.

With sectoral integration squeezed out, the main contenders, as in the Netherlands, were free trade and common markets, and in much the same way, common-marketeers gave more weight to political and institutional factors than did free-traders. The initial impulse for German proposals for a common market seems to have come from a meeting, before the failure of the EDC, in which von der Groeben faced the criticisms of the advisory but official Scientific Council, which dismissed sectoral integration on practical and theoretical economic grounds. Even a common market was suspect to Erhard, the Economics Minister credited with the *Wirtschaftswunder,* who was crown prince to the unadmiring Adenauer and, like most crown princes, a figurehead for more or less loyal opposition. Erhard wanted OEEC-style cooperation as training for world free trade. A common market designed to produce a structured Europe pointed away from the goal, he felt, not towards it.

Two key bureaucratic battles took place towards the end of May. The common market idea promoted by von der Groeben prevailed in both, but not to the same degree. On the first occasion, when von der Groeben met Etzel in Bad Bertrich on May 20, each of them accompanied by several officials, he persuaded the vice president of the High Authority of the advantages of the general over the sectoral approach widely favoured in Luxembourg. Two days later, von der Groeben and Etzel met again, in Eischerscheid. But this time, Erhard, Westrick and Wilhelm Rust (who was close to Adenauer) from the Ministry of Economics were there. So was the Foreign Minister–designate, Heinrich von Brentano, and Ophüls. In short, it was a confrontation between the spokesmen of all three salient views: institutional integration, common markets and free trade. The resulting compromise settled firmly for "general" as against sectoral integration, and for a customs union of the Community countries rather than ubiquitous free trade, but was almost wholly non-committal on the forms and scope of common decision-making. As a result, the German memorandum somewhat resembled the Benelux one except that it was even vaguer on institutions.

German indecision masked the conflict between Adenauer, committed to European integration for political reasons, and industry and the economists in the wake of Erhard, who preferred free trade if not a free hand. Erhard was no match for the wily Adenauer, who despised him as unpolitical. Adenauer always won in a showdown, but avoided one till sure of victory. In between, Erhard's ability to obstruct and confuse was considerable; and Adenauer was not, on his own, able to devise the details of policy, especially on economic issues. The result was an amazing spectacle in Bonn for much of the European *relance* (1955–56). The Chancellor was more or less openly contradicted by his free-trading Minister of Economics and heir presumptive, who in turn was by-passed, more or less openly, by his own ministry's representative in the European negotiations, the common-marketeer, von der Groeben, the Chancellor's man. Von der Groeben is another person of considerable importance in the emergence of the European Community as it is today.

The notion of a customs union as a political matrix was nothing new in German history. The *Zollverein* formed by most of the numerous German states under the leadership of Prussia (but excluding Austria) between 1834 and 1871, was a cherished memory as a forerunner of Bismarck's empire, though in fact it had been a prelude to rather than a cause of it. In the Wilhelmine and Weimar periods, Ministers of Foreign Affairs, politicians and economists like Kiderlen-Wächter, Walther Rathenau, Gustav von Schmoller and Friedrich Naumann (the latter the author of a book, *Mitteleuropa*, famous in its day), all considered the possibilities of various kinds of customs unions, in part as a means of providing a larger market for Germany, in part to reach a settlement with France. Before 1914, the imperial chancellor Theobald von Bethmann Hollweg had pondered "a German-Austrian-Hungarian customs union, flanked both west and east by secondary partners such as France and Turkey". In the middle of the First World War, in November 1915, a congress was held in Dresden with Austria-Hungary, Turkey and Bulgaria to set up a customs union as a first step to a political one. Agreement was actually reached on the eve of the armistice of 1918, which, of course, cancelled it.

If one regards attention to the needs of exporting industry as one of the constants of modern German history, there was no break in the postwar years. The resistance to deconcentration of the Ruhr; the distrust of publicly supervised sectoral integration of the type of the ECSC and Euratom, which threatened industrial structures of control; and the championship of a common market; were all explicable in these terms. Indeed, there was so much consistency that the German historian Hanns Jürgen Küsters has denied there was any revival of European integration after the failure of the EDC, only continuity. This is an interesting view. In the French context, it would seem incomprehensible.

In Italy too the choice was Community or OEEC. In fact, at one point, in May, the official Italian position leaned to action in the OEEC or WEU, that is, in touch with Britain and on non-supranational terms. This seems to have been imposed by the technical departments on a divided Foreign

Ministry. Nevertheless, Italy, the poorest Community country at the time, wanted investment capital, outlets for surplus manpower and regional aid for its less developed south. The Italian memorandum in response to that of Benelux featured a series of requests, for investment and other funds, which implied strong institutions. Beneath the anti-supranational mood of the moment, it offered a hint of things to come. The Italians did not commit themselves. They kept "an open mind".

France was the odd man out. Proposals began to surface there too, under pressure from the "Europeans" in the Cabinet. But to champion a common market in public in Paris in 1955 would have been political suicide, and a Free Trade Area was unthinkable. As for supranationality, it was too controversial for polite society. That left room only for sectoral integration with decision-making powers wrapped in enigma. On April 5, Edgar Faure made a speech in favour of a Europe "perhaps" focussing on transport and energy, including nuclear power (the Monnet agenda) but "without dogma, . . . flexible and evolutionary". The Belgian ambassador noted that "the Schuman [ECSC] treaty seems to [Faure] a 'legal straitjacket'. . . . He feels much happier in a grouping of fifteen nations such as the OEEC or the European transport conference". In this, Faure reflected the bureaucratic temper in Paris. The Atomic Energy Commissariat (CEA) was on the road to nuclear weapons and, since the EDC had threatened to block the route, alert to the slightest hint of outside control. It appreciated the advantages of cooperation on research, but these led to Britain and the OEEC rather than to a Community of nuclear have-nots. In a related spirit, the proposals prompted by the Quai d'Orsay, which Pinay put to Adenauer on April 30 under the grandiose title of a European Confederal Council, provided for a "standing conference" of foreign ministers, to which Britain and even Franco's Spain could have been welcomed.

Given the family resemblance between the Monnet and Faure positions, despite the contrasts, the question arises as to who, if anyone, influenced whom. It seems reasonable to conclude that Faure's suggestions, intergovernmental and non-committal, were primarily meant as a vaccine against the virus of integration. He had to keep his government afloat and was under pressure from his "European" ministers, especially those of the MRP, whose congress launched the same themes, but in Community-style, the same day, April 5. The themes in turn were being fed from two sources. One was Louis Armand, a hero of the Resistance and chairman of the nationalised railways, who saw nuclear power as the key to the industrial future. He was a "European", in the sense that for him "big industry" must be multinational, but agnostic between cooperative and supranational means. The other was Monnet, whose campaign was less public but more political. He was much in Paris between February and April, seeing the leading "European" ministers, Pinay, Schuman and Teitgen, as well as Mollet, half in and half out of opposition. Almost certainly, Monnet and Armand provided versions of the sole European idea acceptable in Paris. They also knew one another from Monnet Plan days. Yet, strangely, there is no sign they worked in concert at this stage.

IV
MESSINA

With the Adenauer-Pinay meeting over, it was possible to fix the conference of foreign ministers to choose the successor to Monnet in Luxembourg and discuss new European Communities. Messina and June 1–2 were chosen, to help the Italian Foreign Minister, Gaetano Martino, with his electioneering. What the French would accept was anyone's guess, and no one expected it to be much. French objections to freer trading, on which new initiatives turned in all the other Community countries, were well known. Meeting in the margin of the NATO Council in Paris on May 9–11, Spaak, Beyen and Bech toned down the Benelux Memorandum they had considered together on April 23. They substituted "an organism" for a "common authority"; instead of "drawing up treaties" they decided to "propose studies"; and all reference to turning the "Common" Assembly of the ECSC into a "European" Assembly was dropped. On May 18, they sent their revised text to the other governments.

Three days later, on Saturday, May 21, Monnet wrote a letter to Edgar Faure. In fact, he did more than that. He delivered it in person to the prime minister's office to make sure that Faure could not claim he had failed to receive it, like Bidault in 1950. Then he published it on Tuesday, May 24. In this letter, he said that in view of the Benelux Memorandum he was ready to stay at the High Authority. Monnet had long made it plain that "if a conference with positive objectives were to be set up by the governments, and if he were asked to take charge of it, and it were felt he could undertake the task more effectively while retaining the presidency of the High Authority, he would feel obliged to accept". The conditions were numerous and testing. On May 2, he said he would decline to chair a European conference if it was committed only to study further integration schemes. But the May 21 letter "finds sufficient justification if the Foreign Ministers' meeting is expected to consider the Benelux Memorandum". Almost all the conditions had vanished. Why?

Some, including Bech and the Americans in Luxembourg, thought that Monnet simply wanted to hang on. This is also the view of his daughter, Marianne, to whom he said much later that he had made a mistake in leaving the High Authority. The premier N told François Valéry, a French diplomat closely concerned with the Schuman Plan from the beginning, that he had decided to leave the High Authority "several months ago". That could have referred to the obvious political date of the rejection of the EDC treaty, but also to an older and more personal one, such as his stroke in June. He never liked the High Authority much. His resignation might have been more personal than met the eye. But when he saw the prospects held out by the Benelux Memorandum, partly his own creation, his appetite could well have returned for a part in the action.

However, this cannot have been the whole story. Bech almost certainly told Monnet on May 17, four days before Monnet wrote his letter, that Edgar Faure had vetoed him. Kohnstamm told the British before Messina that Monnet knew the French government was preparing to bury the Benelux Memorandum under pious resolutions. To force Faure into making an issue of rejecting Monnet made it harder for the French to withhold concessions at Messina on the Benelux proposals. The other interpretation, that of Van Helmont, is similar, except about the target, which in his view was Spaak. Monnet tended to suspect Spaak of being too apt to compromise. Spaak had talked recently with Edgar Faure in the wings of a WEU meeting and been discouraged by the encounter. To express readiness to stay on at the High Authority on condition Europe were relaunched would make it embarrassing for Spaak to fail to push for progress on substance. Another sign Monnet's motive was to promote the Benelux memorandum is his letter of May 31 to Adenauer that he could not accept the High Authority presidency if the German memorandum were substituted for the Benelux one.

Monnet was under a double French veto: as president of the High Authority and (more important) as chairman of any intergovernmental conference on new initiatives. He did not go to Messina. Kohnstamm was sent by the High Authority as an observer.

According to the [ECSC] treaty, the members of the High Authority must be consulted when a new President is nominated. . . . It was purely formal. We were in this marvellous hotel, the San Domenico, in Taormina, an old convent. I felt like a leper. People did not want to talk to me. . . . Monnet was on the telephone all the time. . . . The communications with Luxembourg were impossible. . . . You had to shout, "Pronto pronto", and then there was nothing. Then you got his voice and then it went again, and then it came back, and said, "Go and see Spaak and tell him to do such and such", "Go and see Hallstein and tell him to do this". In the end, this drove me mad and I said, "M. Monnet, please understand. They are not here to make Europe. They are here to bury *you*". Then there was a pause on the end of the line, and a chuckle, and he said, "Then they are very much mistaken' ".

Expectations ran low when the Messina conference opened on June 1. Adenauer did not attend, for fear of failure. Indeed, when the moment came for drafting a communiqué on the evening of June 2, the conference virtually was a failure. True, René Mayer, a strong candidate, had been chosen to succeed Monnet at the High Authority. Many, including Bech and Beyen, thought Monnet had become so controversial in France that the changeover would greatly benefit the ECSC. But no progress had been made on new European schemes. The Benelux ministers and the Germans wanted general integration measures, Pinay, for the French, sectoral ones. Benelux wanted negotiations led by a "political figure" (a transposition of Spaak's idea of Monnet's chairing a treaty conference). Pinay, echoed by the Germans, talked of a permanent consultative body working under the foreign ministers, which would have given civil servants an open licence for obstruction. One American diplomat, the young Arthur Hartman, who was a political-military officer in the Paris embassy at the time, believed that only the personal intervention by Monnet with Adenauer induced the German delegation to switch from their own minimalist proposals to those of Benelux.

In fact, the French were not as free to dictate terms as their partners no doubt feared. On the plane to Messina, Pinay summed up the French position by saying, "So it's yes to Euratom and no to the Common Market?" Olivier Wormser, the Director of Economic Relations at the Foreign Ministry, no supranational zealot, replied: "Minister, it is not quite like that. France has already said no to the EDC. It cannot cast an outright veto a second time". There was, then, a narrow path through which a passage to the only kind of deal the Germans would accept, linking Euratom and the Common Market, might be opened. But the gap in the defences of the French was well screened. Even their notion of Euratom was full of reservations. It was to have decision-making powers, but none to take over bilateral national agreements with the USA, none to pool information and none to replace or coordinate national policies. What was left after that was none too clear.

Yet in the early morning of Friday, June 3, Kohnstamm (who had gone down with a temperature) was woken by Winrich ("Teddy") Behr, his colleague from the High Authority and Etzel's chief of staff, with the news that the outcome was much better than expected. During the last night something happened which still remains opaque. It involved a crisis meeting between Spaak and Pinay. According to de Staercke,

> I thought we had lost. I told Spaak, Pinay has made up his mind not to give you what you want. Spaak said "Well, I will go and see him alone". And he convinced him at eleven o'clock at night. . . . When Spaak finally returned to his room [after the final session of the conference] . . . it was

early morning, with the sun coming up, and he was so pleased he ordered
a bottle of champagne. . . . Then he began to face the dawn [on the
balcony] and sing "Sole Mio". Pinay occupied the room above. He opened
the shutters and said: "Look here, Spaak. You have been pestering me all
night, can't you give me a chance to sleep?" I've got the photo of Spaak
singing "Sole Mio".

Whatever transpired between Spaak and Pinay before this final scene of *opera
buffa,* the Messina communiqué laid an initial base for the European *relance.*

Even that was far from evident at the time. The one agreement on substance was readiness to continue "exploratory" talks between the governments on how one might implement the Benelux Memorandum, including
the Common Market. Wormser emphasised the French had only agreed not
to oppose a continuation of the talks, and that this was very different from
assent. However, they had given way on procedure, because the Messina
declaration provided for a "political figure" to animate the inquiry. Spaak
won this battle, because, having first proposed van Zeeland, a distinctly
unpopular choice, he became the "animator" himself and turned the talks
into the beginnings of a real *relance.* But that was settled only a week later.
As yet, appearances were far from exciting. Press coverage was meagre. The
scepticism was so deep it muted all the echoes.

Wormser told the British that the "aim at Messina had been to keep the
idea of Europe alive, but to take the sting out of the Benelux proposals. This
had been achieved". Perhaps he thought there was a good chance of talking
the *relance* into the ground. That had been the technique to drag down the
EPC; and was to be used again for the British Free Trade Area scheme. The
treaties of Rome could have gone the same way. That they did not was due
partly to vital changes in the political context later, and partly to the vigour
Spaak imparted to the post he had once proposed for Monnet and now taken
on himself. Later, Wormser argued that "Spaak deceived Pinay". But it was
none other than Pinay, the cautious "European", who proposed Spaak as
chairman of the "exploratory" talks. Shortly before Messina, Spaak wooed
him in several private meetings in the Paris town house of a rich American,
Mrs. Margaret Biddle. Spaak brought along Rothschild and de Staercke, but
Pinay came alone, which suggests he had no wish to broadcast the contacts.
No record was kept, but European integration was the theme. To this day,
Pinay (a centenarian) expresses the warmest regard for Spaak.

A number of vital steps were taken in the depression between the fall of
the EDC and the Messina communiqué. Monnet and Spaak ensured that a
Community agenda was launched in the spring of 1955. Their initial insistence, inspired by Monnet, on a nuclear-power Community, much aided by
Armand's advocacy in Paris, gave the "Europeans" in the French government
the chance to involve it in the process. This would not have been the case

had the Common Market, launched by Beyen, been the only scheme on offer. France's partners all placed more weight on the latter. Yet it too marked a victory for a system with independent decision-making powers over pure free trade. The victory was weakest in Germany, where Adenauer's French connection and Erhard's preferences blurred any "European" commitment. It was strongest in the case of Spaak, who choked all efforts in Belgium to turn from supranationality to intergovernmentalism in the British style. At Messina, Spaak and Pinay agreed, if only tacitly, to give the European option its head under Spaak, the most unequivocally "European" leader after Monnet himself.

Messina was thus both a turning point and a confirmation. It was a turning point because, thanks to Beyen, general integration, a common market, was injected into the process. Monnet the personification of the supranational, sectoral principle was partially eclipsed. The French removed him from the official scene by rejecting him as chairman of a European conference. Yet, *sub rosa,* the institutional core of his approach was confirmed at Messina. The Community of the Six was reasserted as the matrix for further plans, even though other groupings might have seemed, in nuclear power especially, to make more sense. It was admitted, if only implicitly, that new Communities must have the means to take decisions. A new round of Communities—should there be one: on that a French question-mark remained, even if the powers were diluted—would be in line of descent from the Schuman Plan. Probably the most hazardous straits in the whole European journey had been navigated, but narrowly. The prospects remained uncertain.

The Second Europe

1955—1957

Jean Monnet handed over to René Mayer the presidency of the High Authority on June 10, 1955, and returned to France, but not home, three days later. The family house in Houjarray was rented out till the end of the year. Silvia Monnet went to Cognac. Monnet lodged in Paris with his sister, Henriette Chaumet, who was married to a well-known jeweller. He set up office in the large and handsome flat of Silvia's brother, Alexandre de Bondini, at 83 avenue Foch on the edge of the Bois de Boulogne. He worked there for the next twenty years. Bondini, who admittedly travelled a great deal, seemed confined more and more to the rear quarters of his own apartment. Edgar Faure lived on the floor below. He and Monnet would bump into one other in the hall or elevator and vow to meet and rarely lift a finger to do so.

The return to private status was a turning-point. Monnet had been in public service since 1939. His achievements had been linked to his locations in or near government. Now, he had little chance of coming back. He was sixty-six, he personified "supranationality", he was a symbol, too international, too controversial and too senior for any likely national office. As for Europe, it did not exist outside the ECSC he had just left. Monnet had been extruded from the system at the top. He stood poised over what was, for one who hoped to shape events, the abyss of elder statesmanship. "Mr. Europe" now had to build a political base or fade away.

Monnet took time to make up his mind, consulting even junior associates. But old friends themselves did not sway him. Frankfurter wrote to McCloy that "I have me doots. Jean's great talents seem to be in the wings, not the stage. What are the wings for him as a promoter without a post for Federated Europe?" But when McCloy shared his own "doots" with Monnet, he reported that he failed to carry conviction.

Monnet's thoughts seem to have crystallised when, on two occasions either side of Christmas, the heads of the German trade unions for coal—Heinrich Imig—and for steel—Heinrich Sträter—and the president of the German Federation of Trade Unions (DGB), Walter Freitag, came to state their concern that integration should continue and their readiness to follow his lead. Sträter said later they had told Monnet he "enjoyed the confidence of the trade unionists in the ECSC, that he had shown himself to be a true European in spite of their fears that he would prove himself to be basically French in attitude, and expressed their concern that Monnet's successor might not be European-minded". Monnet must already have been mulling over a committee consisting of organisations, not individuals. His *Memoirs* recall they said yes when he asked if they could commit themselves as delegates of their federations, with or without the German Social Democratic Party, the SPD. He clearly hoped they would give him a line to the latter. Under Kurt Schumacher, who died in 1952, the SPD had voted against both the Schuman Plan and the European Army on the grounds that they hindered German reunification.

Many of the near on fifty drafts reflecting Monnet's evolving intentions between January and April 1955 dealt with his committee, or lobby. A note in his diary for January 4 envisaged a committee of leading individuals from political parties and trade unions, with first priority on the "free trade unions of the West", but not organisations as such. A draft of January 21, shortly after the second meeting with the three German labour leaders, envisaged a Committee for the United States of Europe, this time of organisations. However, it comprised several to which Monnet never really took, such as employers' federations. It also anomalously included an individual, Altiero Spinelli, the federalist, whom Monnet respected but with whom he did not agree. Then it became a "Front". Gradually it settled down to a stable concept, a committee of the leaders of political parties and trade unions, and no one else, as delegates not individuals. It also acquired a standard name, the Action Committee for the United States of Europe. "Action Committee" crops up in a conversation before February 12, but was not canonical on February 21, when a draft still spoke of a "Front". After that, it prevailed. *Action Committee* was not a new term. There was one in Algiers dealing with the Resistance in France. But memories are short. The name felt fresh and true to the founder's personality. It made an impact.

For Monnet, an action committee's resolutions had to commit member political parties and labour unions and so have institutional force. He drew the line at European movements (not representative) and employers' federations. He thought employers incapable of distinguishing the general interest from their own. The labour unions, he felt, because they represented broad masses, had a better sense of it. He had also been helped by the French unions in the Monnet Plan, and the German unions were helping him now.

His experience of French steelmasters or Ruhr magnates was mainly of trouble.

Until Messina, and despite the fifty drafts and the one-in-four working days—on top of all weekends—Monnet spent in Paris, Bonn or Brussels, his diary suggests he was not primarily forming his committee. Manœuvering for Messina took priority. Once Messina provided a programme, the other effort accelerated. Monnet could be sure of the backing of the Christian Democrats and of the non-Communist trade unions. The key targets were, therefore, the Socialists, especially those of Germany and France, the two groups having posed problems in the past. Adenauer was old and it was vital to secure bipartisan support in Germany for "Europe" beyond his reign. As for the French Socialists, their splitting in half had condemned the European Army. To gain their united support was the *sine qua non* of laying the EDC to rest and making a fresh start.

Though voting against the Schuman treaty, the SPD had nominated most of its leaders to the ECSC Common Assembly. Monnet secretly but assiduously wooed them on the side at the sessions. The SPD and labour unionists also said they obtained more information through the ECSC than from government and employers in Germany. At one of the Common Assembly sessions, in May 1955, the SPD announced its "wish" to be "involved in all studies for the extension of the ECSC". On June 24, Herbert Wehner, the deputy leader, backed a new supranational agency for nuclear power supervised by a European Assembly. The SPD strongly opposed nuclear weapons. In total contrast to governmental Germany, the SPD switched to Europe over Euratom and not the Common Market.

On July 5, Monnet visited Erich Ollenhauer, the SPD leader, in Bonn. In his diary, Monnet scribbled a note saying that Ollenhauer told him all the Socialist parties in the Community states, including the French, agreed on the need for economic integration; and that three years' experience of the Common Assembly of the ECSC had made this possible for the SPD. On July 26, Monnet visited Ollenhauer and Wehner in Bonn, and a letter from Ollenhauer the next day confirmed the SPD's readiness to join the Action Committee as a party. Ollenhauer sent a note to Monnet at his hotel thanking him for asking them to join at that juncture. The SPD leadership seized this chance to take a first step out of sterile opposition towards Adenauer's integration policy, which was popular with the voters. It was the first step also to the Bad Godesberg programme of 1958. This turned the SPD officially from a Marxist party to a social democratic one, accepting the neo-capitalist economy while stressing the redistribution of income. It is hard to believe such perfect timing, so important for Monnet's purposes and for those of the SPD, can have been altogether an accident. Without firm evidence, one has to assume that the labour unions, and especially their international secretary, Ludwig Rosenberg, who was fluent in English, provided

Monnet with a more likely channel of discreet communication than did the French Socialists.

As for the latter, the relationship between Monnet and Guy Mollet was decisive. The Communists apart, the Socialists were the one strongly structured political party in France. Mollet's authority as Secretary-General soon recovered from the EDC schism. The main reason, apart from party discipline, was that the Paris Agreements discredited the anti-EDC faction by creating a German national army. This was exactly what they had claimed an anti-EDC vote would prevent. The effect was evident at the party congress in March 1955, which discussed the ratification of the Paris Agreements. After that, integration, focussing on economic measures, quietly regained the high ground. There was in any case nothing like the opposition to economic integration there had been to the European Army. Monnet's Community for strictly civil nuclear power was rather attractive to the Socialists, since it implied planning, a renunciation of weapons by the French and nuclear controls on the Germans.

Further, Mollet's anxiety to keep in touch with Britain was weakened when the British government made concessions to the WEU, which it had withheld from the European Army. During 1955, he progressively accepted Monnet's thesis that the one way to draw Britain into Europe was for the six Community states to forge ahead until Britain felt it could not afford to be left behind. The two men became close allies. Early in 1955, Monnet's agent in Paris, Van Helmont, was asked to consult Mollet on draft after draft prepared for Monnet. He only had to telephone to have an immediate appointment. Mollet's adviser on European integration, Emile Noël, has said that during this period Monnet became Mollet's "mentor" in this area.

The presence of the SPD in itself made the establishment of the Action Committee for the United States of Europe, on October 13, 1955, a strong political act. European integration was now bipartisan policy in Germany. Across the Community, only the Communists, Italian Nenni Socialists and French Gaullists did not belong. All the other political parties and trade unions were represented by their leaders. Monnet also asked Mendès-France to join. Mendès-France refused so long as the British were not represented, but delegated the Secretary-General of his Radical party. In sum, all this extended the parliamentary support for integration well beyond the spectrum of 1950. The name of the Action Committee alone was a programme and, greatly daring, the prospectus slipped in the taboo word "federal" for a rapid airing. The membership held out the promise of large majorities in every parliament for supranational European treaties.

In practice, the realities were more complex. No one knew how the French Parliament would react to treaty texts. In a paradox true of much of Monnet's European career, the weak link in his Action Committee was France. Communists and Gaullists apart, much of the political centre and right, the Radicals and conservatives, though generally pro-European, were a quicksand of clusters of influence and isolated *notables*. One could never be sure how committed they were and to what. For all that, the Action Committee created an imposing lobby which was more than façade. To form such a committee at all was a tour de force and gave Monnet a permanent visiting card to any head of government. It would have been beyond the powers of any conventional politician tied to party.

The task the Action Committee set itself in its inaugural manifesto of October 13, 1955, was "to ensure that the Messina resolution . . . should be translated into a genuine step towards a United States of Europe. . . . Mere cooperation between governments cannot suffice". The key problem was to coax France into a more "European" mood and, since all its five partners put more weight on "general" than "sectoral" integration, to nudge it to the Common Market as well. In 1955, this looked remote. The turning point was the French general elections of January 2, 1956. These threw five-sixths of the Gaullists out of the National Assembly. The stalemate between pro- and anti-European forces was broken. The balance was now held by the Socialists, led by Mollet, who became Prime Minister.

In addition, Mollet's arrival coincided with the rise of the Algerian rebellion to the top of the political agenda. The disastrous Indochina War was still a burning memory. As a result, the undeclared but armed conflict of ever increasing intensity with the Algerian independence movement was recognised from the first, late in 1954, as the greatest potential crisis in the French retreat from empire. It was even a threat to political stability in France itself. The main reason was the adamant opposition of the European-settler minority to any transfer of power. As early as the Second Republic (1848–1852), Algeria had been turned in most respects into an administrative part of metropolitan France and given equal representation in Parliament with other parts. But this "integration" was virtually confined to the settlers, over a million strong in the 1950s. (Only a tiny fraction of the Moslem seven-eights of the population had any political rights.) The shifting government coalitions between many parties in the Fourth Republic gave almost endless leverage to determined minorities. The European settlers in Algeria exercised a quite disproportionate influence on politics in Paris.

Because, as Prime Minister, Mollet placated the European settlers in the Algerian War, the conservatives were unwilling to unseat him. This made him unassailable on other issues. As Maurice Faure, the Vice Minister for Europe in the Mollet government (and no relation to Edgar), has pointed out, "Political passions were entirely soaked up by Algeria. It is in the nature of passion to be able to concentrate only on one thing at a time". So the coming two years of governments led by Mollet, in person or by proxy, though all of them powerless to settle the Algerian War and a terminal disaster for the Fourth Republic, were a unique opportunity for Europe.

Mollet's arrival in power in Paris was, Van Helmont has pointed out, more truly the "relaunching" of Europe than Messina. Mollet slowly but firmly redirected France onto the European path. European unity owes a great deal to his determination in exploiting a temporary dominance, rare in the Fourth Republic, to advance integration.

Before the French elections, talks between the six ECSC states were confined to the "Intergovernmental Committee" in Brussels, chaired by Spaak. Because of French reservations, the negotiation masqueraded as an inquiry. Spaak wisely explored Euratom and a Common Market without any irritable hankering after commitments. A large part was played, now and later, by officials who, either in the governments, in the secretariat of the Council of Ministers or, like Uri and the lawyer Michel Gaudet, in the High Authority, had experienced the ECSC at first hand and, in many cases, worked close to Monnet. Uri in particular, suggested by Monnet to Spaak, acted as Spaak's architect of solutions. He invented most of the original devices in the Community system. He seems, for example, to have fashioned the ostensibly simple voting arrangements in the Council of Ministers, which nonetheless met the tight specifications of preventing a veto on action either by the three small Benelux states together or by a single one of the Big Three (France, Germany, Italy), backed by tiny Luxembourg.[1] In general, Uri, more than anyone, reduced the complexities of the Common Market, which originally daunted everyone, to manageable working propositions. There were strong personal links between the first Community and its successors and even, in Uri's or Delouvrier's cases, with the Monnet Plan.

Once the Mollet government took over in Paris, early in 1956, the stream of negotiation split into a kind of delta. One stream was the official talks in Brussels. Another, the main one in many respects, was the bilateral exchanges between the French and Germans. And a third was constituted by the efforts of Monnet, using the Action Committee and the Americans as supports, to steer the governments in his preferred direction.

Events moved rapidly in 1956. In April, Spaak's Intergovernmental Committee published its conclusions embracing the Common Market (eighty-four pages) and Euratom (twenty-four pages), the so-called Spaak Report. Uri dictated it during a hectic fortnight in purdah in a hotel on the French Riviera shortly before the season opened. Von der Groeben provided the check of the German view, and Albert Hupperts, a Belgian official, reported to Spaak. The text had a sweep and force rare in official documents. Taking the report as their starting-point, the Six agreed in Venice at the end of May

1. The Big Three had four votes each, Belgium and Holland two each and Luxembourg one. Twelve out of seventeen votes formed the "qualified majority" to decide on most Commission proposals. In 1950, Luxembourg had 300,000 people, Benelux as a whole 19 million, West Germany and Italy 47 million each and France 42 million.

to begin negotiating officially. The French government had still not decided whether it was committed or not to the Common Market.

Bilaterally, between the French and Germans, the striking feature was the importance still assumed by the Saar. In autumn 1953, the Council of Europe developed a scheme to "Europeanise" the Saar under a Council of Europe commissioner. The French were to keep their customs union with the Saar, but it would gradually open up to Germany. In October 1954, Adenauer and Mendès-France agreed to put this European Statute to a popular referendum in the territory. This referendum, held in October 1955, after a campaign with strong nationalist overtones—deplored in Bonn—produced an overwhelming vote in favour not of the statute but of a return to Germany. Edgar Faure and Pinay greatly impressed Bonn by accepting the result at once, without question, subject only to economic compensation for France. This compensation had to be negotiated to complete the transfer of the Saar to the Federal Republic. When the Mollet government came in, Maurice Faure spent the whole of the first half of 1956 negotiating with Hallstein not on the new Communities but the Saar. In June, the decisive outline agreement was reached. The French and Germans had at last buried an issue which had poisoned relations since 1919. "Without a Saar settlement, there would have been no Common Market". Equally, without the political climate created by European integration, there might have been no Saar settlement. With France and Germany rivals, the Saar was a bone of contention. Once they were partners, it became irrelevant.

France had still to decide on accepting new Communities. The Mollet government tested the waters with Euratom first. As Christian Pineau, the new Foreign Minister, told the American ambassador, Douglas Dillon, on February 7, 1956, a "Common Market would not be possible . . . without . . . a great deal of education in France". Here too the summer brought change. In July, a major debate on Euratom in the French National Assembly was held. Armand, invited to speak as an expert witness, electrified the parliamentarians with a brilliant speech and was said to have swayed the debate Euratom's way. The vote proved there was a potential majority for new economic Communities.

The time had come to risk the Common Market. The German government would swallow neither Euratom nor a European *relance* without it. The linkage, the *Junktim,* between the two, as it came to be called even by non-Germans, was basic to its position. But for anyone to promote a Common Market in France required nerve. Marjolin, the top civil servant negotiating the European treaties under Maurice Faure, recalled that the bureaucracy could barely be brought to contemplate the idea. Like Mendès-France, they wanted to keep industry protected until it grew strong enough to meet German competition. Yet a small, crucial minority were beginning to argue that opening up was not the problem but the solution, that French industry would never compete without competition. Marjolin and Pineau had both taken part in a Socialist seminar group the previous year which concluded the economy must be opened up. Further, as Alan Milward has pointed out, bilateral exchanges between France and Germany suddenly shot to the top of each country's trade in the mid-1950s. In August, Marjolin persuaded Mollet to negotiate the Common Market in earnest. The caveats were still so numerous that Faure had to assure France's partners they were not designed to sabotage the treaty.

Ironically, France's political conversion to the Common Market had little to do with competition or with industry, which was divided and wary after the fiasco of the opposition to the Schuman treaty. Faure and Marjolin concentrated on convincing the farmers' leaders in the first half of 1956 that it could offer them a protected outlet for their growing surpluses of grain and sugar beet. The farmers still accounted for more than a quarter of the working population and were over-represented in Parliament. Their support was politically decisive. Monnet was first moved to believe the Common Market might succeed when Marjolin brought the farmers' leaders to see him in October 1956. The other Faure, Edgar, meeting Monnet one day downstairs in the hall of 83 avenue Foch, said he would back the Common market because "the farmers are in favour".

With the intellectual underpinnings of the new Communities provided by the Spaak Report, with the Saar out of the way, and with the French government edging towards the Common Market, negotiations began in earnest, at last, in September 1956. They coincided with one of the most dramatic seasons of the entire Cold War. It was heralded earlier in the year by premonitory rumblings in Eastern Europe and the Middle East alike. The publication in March of Khrushchev's "secret" report on Stalin's excesses, denouncing the "cult of personality", precipitated the anti-Russian feeling through much of eastern Europe into upheavals in both Poland and Hungary. In the Middle East, growing tensions between the nationalist Egyptian leader, Gamal Abdel Nasser, and the West—extremely diversely represented by Israel, Britain, France and the United States—crystallised, on July 26, in Nasser's nationalisation of the Suez Canal, Britain's alleged lifeline once to India and now to Persian Gulf oil. Late in October, both crises erupted at once. From October 25, in Hungary, insurgents with whom large swathes of the national army identified fought successfully with the secret police and local Soviet garrisons until, on November 4, an invading Warsaw Pact force led by Soviet tanks quelled all resistance. In the night of October 29, after a period of rising tension with its Arab neighbours, Israel attacked Gaza and Sinai, both then parts of Egypt. Next day, the British and French governments announced they would intervene, ostensibly to separate the combatants and protect the Suez Canal. Their real aims were to reassert control over the canal and inflict a politically lethal defeat on Nasser. Nasser's fall, the

French chose to believe, would dry up the rebellion in Algeria. On November 5, French and British paratroops landed along the canal. On November 6, the day Americans went to the polls, as it proved to re-elect Eisenhower president, Khrushchev and Bulganin, in letters to the British, French and Israeli governments, brandished Soviet "rockets" at them. Eisenhower, endowed with more usable means of influence, forced a cease-fire on all three colluding powers the same day.

It was at the height of this political typhoon, on November 6, that Adenauer, ignoring many of his advisers, came, as previously arranged, to Paris to settle with Mollet the main Franco-German differences over the European treaties. This living theatre amply dramatised his comment to Mollet that only unity could spare Europe such humiliations in future. He and Mollet reached enough agreement on the European treaties for success in the negotiations to be no longer in doubt. This was a key moment for Germany as well as France. In coming to Paris, Adenauer put a firm end to the divisions which had rent the German Cabinet on both the Common Market and Euratom since the ambiguities of Eicherscheid a year and a half before (see p. 276).

II

EURATOM

Monnet, for his part, in the third stream of the *relance,* concentrated exclusively on Euratom. Until 1957, he and the Action Committee paid only lip service to the Common Market. Work began at once on his return to Paris after Messina on June 10, 1955. He and Louis Armand now formed the working alliance which had been lacking earlier. Armand was the chairman of the nationalised railways, of the supervisory board of the Commissariat à l'Energié Atomique (CEA) and above all of the Council of the Corps of Mining Engineers. This last was perhaps the most important. It made him the senior alumnus of the French state's oldest school for mandarins, Polytechnique, and the dean of an informal but tight-knit *nomenklatura* permeating government. He also had a golden tongue, and could infuse technology and science with romantic appeal. Together, he and Monnet became the driving force for Euratom. Monnet's diary says they first met on Euratom as late as the end of August 1955. After that, there were nearly fifty recorded meetings till the end of 1956.

It is odd they did not meet earlier. Armand seems to have come to Luxembourg on April 22, 1955, for his OEEC report on nuclear energy. Monnet visited Spaak in Brussels that day. The OEEC may be the clue. Anything to do with that temple of intergovernmental cooperation irritated Monnet. He may well have taken evasive action. However, in October 1955, as chairman of the Euratom working group in the first, exploratory phase of the Spaak committee following Messina, Armand wrote the report on a possible Community approach to the same issues. (He introduced the nickname Euratom, taken from an obscure technical group, by which the European Atomic Energy Community has come well-nigh exclusively to be known.) If all this suggests a certain eclecticism, Armand's interest was in promoting a strong European industry rather than in politics. The main points he brought out were that nuclear electricity was becoming competitive, as shown by the substantial British production programme launched in 1955, and that the costs of development were so great the laggard Europeans could not meet them unless they combined.

In contrast, Monnet pursued political goals even through technical ones. He was in a greater hurry for results than Armand. He wanted a massive nuclear-power programme not merely to ensure Europe's energy security but to strike the popular imagination. This new "industrial revolution" would be uniquely European, in the sense that none of the nations individually could achieve the same results. Further, the high road to development ran through America. America's huge lead was based on the military, but civil nuclear power would come late there because the competing conventional forms of energy were so much cheaper than in Europe. Nuclear power, then, gave unusual scope for the potentially "equal" association between Europe and America so dear to Monnet's speculations.

In practice, Euratom had to walk a tight-rope. On the one hand, the United States was the only source from which it could expect the fissionable materials and know-how on the required scale. On the other, nationalism had destroyed the European Army in France and could not be ignored.

Monnet started, at the American end as it were, from the premise of a purely civilian Euratom, with the member states renouncing nuclear weapons. According to Isenbergh, the option of a common weapons programme was raised and promptly dropped. During the autumn of 1955, Van Helmont drafted a framework for Euratom closely patterned on the McMahon Act of 1946, revised for civil power in August 1954, which regulated nuclear policy in the United States. Euratom must be so similar to the American system that critics in Washington could not find fault. It would in fact be a "single AEC" for six countries. As such, it could inspect the nuclear cycle of production to prevent all diversion, open or clandestine, to military purposes in all the member states. To make this policing effective, it should, as Armand stressed, have the ownership and monopoly of the purchase and sale of all fissionable materials on the territory of the Six. It was at this point that Euratom turned its face to the nationalists. A system incorporating six states could provide its own collective controls. It need not submit to those of outsiders. Monnet saw a chance for Euratom to strike free of either direct

American inspection or an indirect one through the United Nations. If this could be achieved, Euratom would trump the ace of nationalists in Europe, for no individual state could aspire to do the same. Talking to Americans, he insisted on the "compulsion . . . of the Europeans to achieve atomic independence". Thus, what was a purely civilian Euratom at one end of the spectrum was an independent inspection agency at the other.

These priorities were adopted by the Action Committee at its first session of January 18, 1956. The able Italian Liberal leader, Giovanni Malagodi, wanted to insert a strong plea for the Common Market into the resolution. Mollet and Monnet answered in unison that any commitment to the Common Market was premature in view of the political balance in France. "Our Committee wants to attain the goal which can and must be reached most rapidly . . . atomic energy". Euratom would have its own mandatory system of controls, to prevent any diversion of fissionable materials to military uses. Other countries than the Six could become members, meaning Britain (mainly to satisfy Mollet). It was also decided to introduce resolutions in favour of Euratom into each legislature of the Six to spur on the governments. These were introduced by the political parties of the committee into all the legislatures of the Six, except in Italy, during the spring and summer.

The main short-term asset of the Action Committee resolution was that Mollet signed it. He became French Prime Minister a fortnight later. His investiture speech in the French National Assembly emphasised that setting up "a [general] Common Market in Europe will be a long haul", that is, it would be postponed to a later stage. He opposed "the creation of a European industry to produce nuclear weapons, which is virtually impossible nationally". In the February issue of *Les Cahiers Républicains,* he specified that "we will ask the member states of Euratom to make a solemn commitment to renounce the use of the atom for military purposes". In other words, the member states as well as Euratom itself would be non-nuclear-weapon producers. Monnet could not have wished for more. His concept of Euratom was now to all appearances in the saddle. He had committed himself to it in the belief that nuclear power had a vast future and no past. The rest of the story of Euratom is a long recital of imaginative feats to reach the goal in face of the gradual revelation that neither assumption was valid.

The prime political obstacle was that all six Community states, but particularly France and Germany, were already latching on to national nuclear ambitions. As Van Helmont has observed, Euratom, like the ECSC, was promoted against the industries concerned. Encouraged by American firms, the powerful German chemical industry expected, with their cooperation, to catch up on Britain and France in six years and become a major nuclear exporter. However, French ambitions, centered in the state agency, the CEA, surfaced first. They took the initial form of a secret drive for nuclear weapons as a short-cut to great-power status. Had the superpowers alone possessed nuclear arsenals, perhaps France might not have trodden this path. But it was not prepared to defer to Britain. The other problem, common in some degree to all of the Six, was industrial nationalism. Here were the first stirrings of the policy of "national champions" of the 1960s, by which states strove to expand the market shares and exports of top firms favoured "at court". Looking back, it is evident that all this industrial nationalism was strong and healthy in the 1950s. It was less clear at the time, when the emphasis was on formal frontier barriers to trade.

In France, Mollet's and the Action Committee's statements in favour of purely civil nuclear policies produced a near relapse into the furor of the EDC. A campaign "of great violence", orchestrated from the Right, broke out against any renunciation of the right to nuclear weapons. "Europe was accused of mutilating our national defence . . . and of placing France . . . on an equal footing" with Germany. "Were it not for Algeria, Euratom would be in the forefront" of conflict, the Belgian ambassador reported. As Dillon, his American colleague, put it, "Poujadists and Gaullists [and Communists] . . . oppose giving up the right to manufacture as . . a derogation of national sovereignty. . . . the chances are almost zero of obtaining [the] required 300 favourable votes out of the remaining 375 members of the Assembly". Well before, at the meeting of Foreign Ministers at Noordwijk in September 1955, Pinay had taken Spaak aside to warn him that Euratom could never be ratified in France if the impression were given that it would stand in the way of nuclear weapons.

None of this surfaced in public. The Socialist Party and the MRP were both against "the Bomb". Edgar Faure as Prime minister in 1955 made a brief effort to drop the nuclear weapons programme on budgetary grounds. For the rest, in government, this was a façade for *raison d'état*. Early in May 1955, Pflimlin, the Minister of Finance in Faure's Cabinet and a leader of the MRP, declared that France should not acquire atomic weapons. A fortnight later, he assigned defence funds to the CEA for a third reactor to furnish plutonium to the military and to conduct studies for a prototype nuclear weapon. The CEA, a state within the state under Pierre Guillaumat, who was close to de Gaulle, had already begun its phased programme moving towards a nuclear explosion by 1960 (when it actually occurred). The more one probes the period, the clearer it becomes that most of the French political establishment were determined to acquire "the Bomb".

Within a fortnight of Mollet's coming into office, the Foreign Ministers of the Six met again, in Brussels. Pineau, for France, argued that his country's renunciation of nuclear weapons would depend on the progress of disarmament between the superpowers. Spaak, who "had long favoured" the renunciation of nuclear weaponry by all Six, wondered (without explanation) "if it was still politically wise". All the rest similarly resigned themselves to clearing the road to French nuclear weapons. Soon after, an exchange of letters with Spaak provided that France need not renounce nuclear weapons but that there would be a four-year moratorium on tests pending disarmament agreements between the superpowers. This was no constraint. The French technicians were four years away from a nuclear device. The Fourth Republic, not de Gaulle, created the French nuclear arsenal.

The only surprise is the apparent source of the moratorium idea. On February 6, 1956, a week before the Foreign Ministers of the Six met in Brussels, John Foster Dulles gave a small dinner for René Mayer, on his first visit to Washington as president of the High Authority. Mayer said that France "could never give up the right to atomic weapons". Dulles "suggested that . . . there might be an agreement that [non-nuclear] countries would not make atomic weapons for a period of time—say five years—during which an effort would be made to eliminate those weapons by agreement between the US, the Soviet Union and the UK". Given the very low risk of disarmament, Dulles in effect told the French that the United States would not make a fuss about the Bomb. For anyone inclined to go ahead, this was virtually a green light.

Mollet told Monnet in secret in late February or early March that he "could not take the responsibility for a unilateral renunciation of nuclear weapons". Monnet neither informed anyone of this nor changed his own stance. The Mollet government's shift became public in the three-day debate on Euratom in the French National Assembly early in July: France would not renounce its right to manufacture nuclear weapons, though it would accept a four to five year moratorium on tests. It would be represented in its own right in the International Atomic Energy Agency of the United Nations, not only through Euratom. Euratom would be open to member states of the OEEC. It would control no more than 20 per cent of France's nuclear energy programme. These were all positions of the national nuclear lobby. Mollet also put Guillaumat in charge of the French team negotiating Euratom because, he said, he did not want to have the CEA free to snipe at him from the sidelines. Who finally controlled whom is a subtle question.

The primary purpose of Euratom controls, to preclude nuclear weapons, had lost its point. There was still a secondary one, to stop any diversion of fissionable materials earmarked for civil use to the military. But this was binding only on horses which had no intention of bolting from the stable. Euratom could now be presented as a hypocritical device of the French to control Germany while evading all obligations themselves. Franz-Josef Strauss, the brilliant, nationalistic German Minister for Atomic Affairs, had denounced Monnet's proposals for Euratom as "discrimination" from the start. So long as the system was wholly civilian, it was easy enough, not least for the German Socialists, to answer back. Now it had ceased to be. When Monnet and Kohnstamm went to Bonn on September 11 and 12, 1956, a glowering Herbert Wehner left them in no doubt of the SPD's anger. A week later, Heinrich von Brentano, the new German Foreign Minister, warned Maurice Faure that the Bundestag would not ratify a treaty which discriminated too glaringly against Germany. Franco-German distrust was rearing its head again.

It was a golden opportunity for the anti-Euratom lobby in Germany. Strauss denounced as "socialism" Monnet's cardinal points of exclusive ownership of fissionable materials and controls by Euratom and denied they were necessary. The danger loomed of an alliance between industry and Strauss in Germany and the CEA in France to unwind the Euratom treaty. Monnet wrote to Robert Schuman on October 24 that "Strauss is making Euratom impossible".

Monnet responded in a variety of ways to this crisis. First, he moved to reassure the SPD. The Action Committee resolution of September 20 stated that it would still be possible "to maintain leak-proof controls. . . . [A]ccording to the French position, Euratom control and property should also apply to materials destined ultimately for military use". Via Emile Noël, Mollet's adviser on Europe, Monnet arranged an exchange of letters between Mollet and Ollenhauer, as heads of Socialist parties and members of the Action Committee, to confirm the point.

Second, Monnet made a supreme effort to achieve priority for the Euratom treaty over that for the Common Market. In Bonn, on September 12, he told Adenauer that the French Parliament might not ratify the Common Market and that Euratom should be completed first, and soon. Adenauer was half-converted, which was amazing in view of the opposition of much of his Cabinet to any such thing. Then von der Groeben rallied Hallstein and Etzel to change his mind again. The Action Committee resolution of September 20 asked that the Euratom treaty be submitted for ratification before the end of the year. This failed when Adenauer and Mollet met on September 30, and Mollet accepted the *Junktim* between progress on the Common Market and Euratom treaties.

Third, Monnet campaigned to make sure the Euratom treaty would provide a base for American help on a nuclear-power programme in Europe. This meant ensuring, *pace* Strauss, that Euratom should, on the model of the United States' AEC, own all fissionable materials of whatever origin in the Community and have a credible system of controls over their use. The key period was the run-up to Adenauer's climactic meeting with Mollet of November 6. Kohnstamm and Winrich Behr, Etzel's aide, drafted papers, through Etzel, for Adenauer. According to Hallstein, these were exactly what was needed for the discussions on Euratom in the Cabinet in Bonn. The German Socialists were also important in the background, because they would have attacked the Bonn government had it tried to water Euratom down. The decisive intervention, though, was that of the American ambassador in Bonn, James B. Conant. He was "authorised" by Dulles to impress on Adenauer the importance of Euratom's monopoly ownership of fissionable materials and controls over use. Adenauer confessed it did seem absurd for German industry to complain of these as "socialist" when the United States, the haven of free enterprise, applied them. This was on October 29. He overrode Strauss before meeting Mollet. "Without the constant involvement of Adenauer, the whole business would be lost", Kohnstamm confided to his diary. The Americans, through Adenauer, had again proved the ultimate weapon in Monnet's armoury.

There were parallels between this and the struggle over the Ruhr in the winter of 1950–51. In each case, there was an alliance between Monnet and the Americans on a European vision clashing with the ambitions of industry in Germany. In each case, the Americans, through Adenauer, settled the issue in the short-term. And in each case, the long-term prospects remained open.

The *i*'s of the treaty still had to be dotted and the *t*'s crossed. The principle that Euratom owned all fissionable materials without reservations was only confirmed, at Mollet's insistence, influenced by Monnet, at the final conference of heads of government of the six Community states on February 20, 1957. (This meeting almost unthinkingly set a precedent: it was the first of what would later become many Community summits.) The Euratom treaty signed in Rome, along with the Common Market, on March 25, 1957, was good for Monnet's purpose of a major programme with the United States. Euratom owned all fissionable materials, could inspect their use and had the right to negotiate foreign agreements. In addition, the funds for the first Five-Year Research Programme were ample. Monnet thought the Euratom treaty fairly solid. His one regret was that the Executive Commission lacked the High Authority's taxing powers.

At the same time, the treaty had retreated a long way from the original idea of Euratom as a kind of AEC, initiating and supervising nuclear-power programmes. The Germans and the Dutch, who did not want a centralised system, as well as the French, restricted Euratom's powers in all sorts of ways. Euratom's supply monopoly was subject to exceptions. The Commission had no power to authorise nuclear-power stations. The rules for pooling technical information were weak. Inspection, specified article 84, stopped short at the doors of military "sites". The French also emasculated the treaty in one final and important particular. At the Foreign Ministers' meeting of January 28, 1957 in Brussels, one of the French negotiators, Félix-Paul Mercereau, was surprised to hear Maurice Faure suddenly change his line on nuclear research. Until then, Faure had come down on the integration side of the fence and backed majority voting for the budgets to fund Euratom's research programmes. Now he reverted abruptly to cooperation between sovereign states by announcing he would "concede" unanimity in decisions on these. Hallstein and others told him, "as friends", that they were not seeking such "concessions". He declined to retract. His move reflected the views of the CEA.

Monnet seems to have had no prior knowledge of this *volte-face,* nor to have accorded it much importance when he was informed. From his point of view, a research Euratom was not "very exciting", as Kohnstamm wrote. Yet given the costs of development, the competition from other forms of energy, and the inherent uncertainties of a new sector, Euratom research could have fulfilled a vital if more modest function than Monnet envisaged. The chance to do that was snuffed out by Faure, perhaps to buy the neutrality of the CEA in the ratification debate in Paris.[2]

The story goes that when Guillaumat showed the Euratom treaty to de Gaulle, the latter said, "Is this all it is?" Jules Guéron, the distinguished chemist who was first director of research in the Euratom Commission, believed that it still gave ample scope for a dynamic leadership working on the principle that anything not expressly forbidden in the treaty was allowed. But to achieve this required—even more than dynamic leaders—that the current of events should flow Euratom's way.

III
TARGET FOR EURATOM

Monnet's next efforts were intended to generate that current. He had always seen Euratom in terms not of research but of a big nuclear-power programme. From this point of view, the events of 1956 could hardly have been better staged. The story ran that in April, Khrushchev and Bulganin, when in London, had told Eden they would do everything short of war to interrupt the West's supplies of oil. (This is not confirmed in Eden's memoirs.) Monnet told this story frequently to visitors. The Suez Crisis itself, with its "grave warning" of the dangers of growing dependence on vulnerable Middle East oil, was a miracle of timing. As Kohnstamm has put it, "We had set everything on Euratom. The French had pulled the rug from under our feet [with the Bomb]. . . . Suez came as a godsend". Of a sudden, in autumn 1956, it seemed possible to give Euratom production goals and momentum even before there was a treaty.

Monnet came off the Alps at the end of the holidays with a note in his

2. There is a view that the CEA initially wanted a Euratom research programme to share the costs of a gas diffusion plant to enrich uranium 235. American civil reactors used U 235, French ones did not. Thus the CEA could only want it for the military. France's Euratom partners had no reason to help in this. They certainly aimed to build American-type reactors themselves, but it was cheaper and quicker to buy the U 235 in America. The CEA seems to have plumped for the national veto ("unanimity") as soon as it lost hope of tempting them.

diary saying, "Must introduce new Euratom element". Guidelines emerged in a single day, on September 2, with Kohnstamm. In fact, in June, that is, a month before the Suez Crisis broke out, Monnet's office had set down nuclear-power targets very similar to those published a year later. The Action Committee resolution of September 20 proposed a "Wise Men's" group to consider nuclear-power production. (It was a vintage year for Wise Men. They had already wandered into NATO's manger.) The aim was to secure Europe's energy independence. Euratom's Magi were to define a programme, specify targets, and state the shortest time and the means to put them into effect. After some hesitation, Mollet endorsed the idea when he received the Action Committee the same day. The foreign ministers of the Six, meeting on October 20–21, nominated Etzel, Armand, and Francesco Giordani, the head of the Italian Atomic Energy Commission, as the Wise Men. On December 10, 1956, Dulles invited them to Washington. All this in six weeks, a tour de force for someone like Monnet with no official status

Monnet kept a discreet hold on the operation that followed. The Wise Men's secretary was Kohnstamm. The technical adviser was another of Monnet's English-speaking freelances, Campbell Secord, a Canadian and one-time official in the U.K. Ministry of Fuel and Power, introduced by a member of the British delegation to the High Authority in Luxembourg, Charles de Peyer. Monnet first met Secord in May 1955 before leaving the High Authority. Secord gave him a paper which proposed a nuclear authority with three aims: the initiation and development of reactors, their financing and their strict control. Secord had been his main source of expertise ever since. Secord was a colourful character. "We couldn't get a scientist from the Atomic Energy Commission in France, because they were opposed. . . . We couldn't have had an official Englishman. There were very few experts in Europe. . . . And Monnet liked Secord. . . . He was a genius . . . [and] did a great job. In many ways, a very lovable man. He had some difficult qualities. . . . And Secord was a Canadian, living in Britain, not talking French . . . [who] did not suffer fools gladly." In his attitude to Armand and to others, "there was no respect" (i.e., deference).

For Euratom to have a major production programme, it would have to tap the one great well of resources, the United States. Monnet visited Washington in January 1957 to pave the way for the Wise Men. He saw Dulles a couple of times and also saw Lewis Strauss, the chairman of the AEC, and arranged for Kohnstamm to have urgent access to them in case of need. The Wise Men followed early in February and were received by Eisenhower, who reportedly told Dulles that "if these fellows tell the experts to go to Timbuctoo, they must go to Timbuctoo". Lewis Strauss made available a number of his top technicians, including the AEC's deputy general manager, Richard Cook, to help Secord and Kohnstamm draft the report.

The Wise Men were very nervous lest all this momentum should carry them way beyond where they really meant to go. According to Kohnstamm, "The more we came to the meat of putting their names under the report, the more they hesitated". Monnet virtually forced Armand to fix a target for the nuclear-power programme when the latter returned from America in February 1956. Armand was himself uneasy—not surprisingly in view of the CEA waiting in ambush—over the collaboration with experts from the American AEC.

Costs were a basic uncertainty. Most of the authorities on the matter—in the United States, Britain, the Electricity Committee of the OEEC in January 1956, and the authors of the Dutch White Book of 1957—argued that the costs of nuclear power would soon fall (as those of conventional electricity rose) and become very competitive. Cautious voices pointed out that nuclear energy was still in the exploratory stage and that it was impossible to say when commercial operation could begin. As so often with political exploiters of a new technology, Monnet, Kohnstamm and their American allies like Robert Schaetzel, in the office of the Special Assistant to the Secretary of State for Atomic Energy Affairs, were in effect bent on creating facts that would prove the rosier version right.

When it was published in May 1957, two months after the Rome treaties were signed, the report, A Target for Euratom, stated that the Community countries, unchecked, would be importing by the mid-1970s more oil than their entire production in 1957 of coal, which then provided most of their energy. This seemed gigantic (but was in fact only half the reality by the first oil crisis of 1973–74). Such dependence on the volatile Middle East could produce "an economic calamity". Nuclear power offered the only safeguard. It was coming well within the range of conventional power costs in Europe and should fall below them in the 1960s. There should, therefore, be a massive, joint American-European programme in Europe. The report posted a target of 15-million-kilowatt nuclear-power capacity within ten years, larger than the combined electrical output of Germany and France in 1957. This should stabilise fuel imports at the level they would otherwise reach by 1963. It was not excessive in view of the fact that Britain's programme, already under way, aimed at 6-million-kilowatt capacity by 1965 for a population a third as large.

It would have been impossible to produce either a credible Euratom treaty or the Target for Euratom without massive support from the United States, which, as René Mayer put it, "would be decisive for . . . integration in the atomic energy field". On December 17, 1955, Dulles told Monnet for public consumption that the United States would be ready to give Euratom fissionable materials and technical information so long as it was supranational and could prevent the secret military use of nuclear fuels. A month later, Dulles added that "the US does not attach to the Common Market the same immediate security and political significance as we do to Euratom". A month later still, President Eisenhower announced that twenty tons of uranium 235, equivalent to 40 million tons of coal, an enormous amount by the standards of the time, could be released for countries meeting American conditions of sale and use. Euratom grouped the only nuclear novices who could use anything like such quantities. Next day, Monnet wrote to the members of the Action Committee that Euratom controls could replace the American ones envisaged in bilateral nuclear agreements between the United States and individual countries. In order not to undermine Euratom's claims to take over from national policies, the Americans held back as long as they could on the bilateral nuclear research and power agreements they would normally have concluded with Euratom's member states. They could not hold out altogether, but wrote provisions allowing for a transfer to Euratom in bilateral agreements with governments. In October 1956, they were decisive in persuading Adenauer to squash the German opposition to the Euratom treaty. In February 1957, Eisenhower went out of his way to receive the Wise Men and let them into secret installations, such as Shippingport and Oak Ridge, that only a handful of continental Europeans had visited. The AEC provided top technicians to work on the *Target for Euratom*. Eisenhower and Dulles could not have helped more.

Historians have naturally sought the self-interest behind this insistence. It followed on Eisenhower's Atoms for Peace policy. This had two aims, to discourage military nuclear proliferation and to promote American civil reactor exports. What could be more logical than for these motives to find expression in American policy to Euratom?

The very low price at which the United States was willing to sell enriched uranium was indeed equivalent to an anti-proliferation policy. The fuel was offered at prices half those a European undertaking could meet, and they were again lowered in November 1956. This made economic nonsense of any European gas diffusion plant with military potential. The Six duly gave up their gas diffusion plant early in 1957. Backing a supranational Euratom with independent controls was also a form of non-proliferation policy as regards France's partners, especially Germany. But Dulles's suggestion, on February 6, 1956, of the "moratorium" on the French nuclear weapons programme, shows that non-proliferation policy had its limits. Robert Bowie, who, as Director of Policy Planning in the State Department, worked closely with Dulles, thinks that nuclear non-proliferation, at least to Britain and France, had nothing like the importance for Dulles and Eisenhower that it was to assume in the next decade under Kennedy and Johnson.

This is the conclusion to which Henri Teissier du Cros has come on technical grounds in his *Louis Armand, visionnaire de la modernité*. He has argued that non-proliferation may well have been the original American intention, but that it cannot have been the guiding one by the time Euratom was formed. Article 84 of the Euratom treaty exempts materials which are being "specially processed" for "defence requirements" from controls on fissionable materials. Theoretically, that would still make it possible to ensure American fissionable materials did not leak into defence establishments in Europe. But Armand, at a press conference in the United States on the Wise Men's trip, confessed that the sheer mass of fissionable materials in a nuclear-power programme aiming at electricity-generating capacity of 15 million kilowatts would make certainty impossible. Teissier has concluded that the Eisenhower administration was resigned to the French nuclear weapons programme.

The same policies could, of course, have been intended to favour the development in Europe of nuclear reactor types based on the American fuel, slightly enriched uranium. But long-term export promotion cannot have been the sole or even the main driving force in helping Euratom. Both the AEC and the main U.S. nuclear producers were trying throughout the period of negotiation of Euratom to conclude bilateral licensing agreements with the European nations, especially Germany. They were baulked by the State Department. Moreover, help to Euratom could create a large-scale European industry when equivalent output in America was still uneconomic, and shift the balance of production to Europe. This was actually demonstrated later, when Siemens and Framatom cancelled the licence agreements which had tied them at first to Westinghouse. While American aid to Euratom would never have emerged had the American corporations been on the defensive, it gave the Europeans a chance to become major, "equal", even senior, "partners" and competitors.

The message that shines through all this is the determination of a small State Department group around Dulles and Eisenhower to give every possible politically efficient help to the revival of European integration after the EDC defeat. Siege was laid to the AEC, which was no spontaneous sponsor of Euratom. Lewis Strauss was fanatical about security, as his role in the misfortunes of Robert Oppenheimer amply demonstrated. He was initially dubious about Monnet. He regarded the French as dire security risks and suspected Euratom of "socialism". The AEC had constantly to be restrained from pressing ahead on bilateral agreements with the individual European Community countries. It had doubts about the wisdom of giving up direct American controls on fissionable materials, which bilateral agreements sustained. In many of these attitudes, it reflected the preferences of industry. Beyond the AEC and industry, there was a large body of opinion, including many liberals—Isenbergh for one—who believed it was dangerous to breach the universal inspection system of the IAEA in favour of Euratom. Lewis Strauss himself was in favour of the IAEA. Europe was by far the biggest prospective producer of nuclear power. The exception not only breached the principle of a universal system and created a precedent; Euratom was likely in practice and all on its own to generate activities far larger than those supervised in the rest of the world (outside the military nuclear powers) by the IAEA. It blew a great hole in the regime of inspection being laboriously constructed with the Russians in the United Nations and to which the Atoms for Peace policy tended. All these varied objections, the "Europeanists" at the heart of the administration steadily overrode.

They did not put major obstacles in the way of the French bomb. They accepted the Euratom controls insistently and openly presented by Monnet and others as a statement of political self-reliance. They sponsored a joint programme the aim of which was to raise the European nuclear industry to a level comparable with the American. They used all the influence they could to suppress opposition in the Six to Euratom. They even shared Monnet's scepticism about the Common Market until late in the day. It is hard, in the face of all this evidence, to reach any conclusion but that the American priority, at the top, in the Eisenhower years, was the political one, to help Europe unify. It also gives the strong impression that the specifics of support for Euratom did not come primarily from American nuclear priorities. They came from general policy, from the Europeans and to a marked extent from Monnet.

Monnet's own priorities and motives in pursuing Euratom raise questions too. His insistence on Euratom and the member states being "pacific" at first sight seems very natural. He never much liked the military. He belonged to a broad civilian-minded strand in French as in other European opinion which thought nuclear weapons best confined to the superpowers. But it is also hard to believe that a man who knew well so many French politicians most in favour of nuclear weapons—Gaillard, Pinay, Mayer, Pleven and others— had no inkling of what was in the wind. He warned Dillon on February 6, 1956, before the row over the Action Committee's stance broke in public in France, that the United States should stand well clear of the flying debris. If he knew, or suspected, the real situation, what light would that throw on his intentions? Did he realise the system might end up with controls on Germany but not on France?

Monnet certainly put a high value on controlling the German military and industrialists, whom he thought of at this time as a nationalist menace. This was, of course, a French objective, but not only French. It was shared, to a greater or less degree, by the Americans and by the German Socialists. Rosenberg told Monnet and Kohnstamm in the autumn of 1956 that the SPD would not accept the Common Market without Euratom, an inverted *Junktim*. Monnet once said that if he failed to get Euratom ownership and strict controls on fissionable materials written into the treaty, "the Action Committee will disintegrate". He was thinking of the SPD. Even had he wished to move off a strictly civilian interpretation of Euratom himself—and this would have been most unlikely—the crucial importance of the relationship with the SPD would not have allowed him to do so.

The central thrust of Monnet's Euratom policy, which aimed at "equality of rights" amongst Europeans and "partnership" with the United States on power reactor programmes, ran spectacularly counter to the ambitions of the French CEA and its supporters. A *Target for Euratom*—reflecting the conclusions Armand reached in the United States—implied that the American light-water reactor, miniaturised for nuclear submarines, was inherently superior to the more primitive natural uranium type; and on economic grounds dismissed a European gas diffusion plant. The CEA saw this as an American bid to colonise European nuclear power and thwart the CEA's own ambitions. Production programmes based largely on American light-water reactors, not French natural uranium ones, undermined CEA hopes for a preferential market in the Community. Stressing "European" inspection and controls was also anathema to the CEA. It is very hard to credit even tacit collusion between goals and attitudes as incompatible as those of Monnet and the French nationalists. The truth is probably that he was trapped in a situation he could not fully control.

By the time A *Target for Euratom* was published in May 1957, the treaties establishing the Common Market and Euratom had already been signed, on March 25, with heavy and not wholly appropriate symbolism, on the Capitol in Rome. Euratom was poised on the threshold of life with a treaty of variable sufficiency which nevertheless gave plenty of room for Monnet's pet project of a massive civil nuclear-power programme underwritten by the United States. On the whole, it was remarkable Euratom had come as far as it had. As Zijlstra has remarked, it did not really come "from the ground up". Close observers of the process by which it was born tend to agree that its determined backers "could have fitted in a small room". This small group included Armand, Mollet at crucial times, the SPD leaders, Eisenhower, Dulles and a cadre in the State Department led by Schaetzel. Without these, there would probably have been no treaty nor any target for Euratom. The core of the political will behind it was provided by Monnet himself. To put Euratom on the agenda and keep it there; then, when it contracted fissures at the epicentre of French bureaucratic nationalism, to relaunch it with the Wise Men's operation; fused tenacity and imagination. A *Target for Euratom* was the first policy proposal based on a clear view of the risks of overdependence on Middle East oil.

After Messina, as before, Euratom provided a vital bridge from the first to the second Europe. It continued to offer time and chart a route for the French to adapt to the idea of a Common Market. Pineau has suggested that Euratom was a "smokescreen" for the Common Market. It may have been for him, but politically, in the first half of 1956 as in 1955, the latter was out of the question. It was no accident the Mollet government led with Euratom in presenting its European plans to Parliament: otherwise, the dangers of an upset would have been too great. Euratom also gave the German Socialists the chance they needed to reverse their initial postwar stance, under Schumacher, of placing German reunification before and to some extent against Western European unity.

IV
RATIFICATION

Once the Common Market and Euratom treaties—the Treaties of Rome—were signed, Monnet stopped discriminating between the two. He threw himself into the campaign to have both ratified together and quickly. He was not unique in this. Speed was the hallmark of the governments' approach to ratification. All were still haunted by the fiasco of the EDC. The debate on the Common Market in the French National Assembly in January 1957 and the support of the farmers' organisations had stacked the odds in favour of ratification. Yet having burned their fingers once, the French and German governments in particular were determined not to let the moment slip. Mollet laid the treaties before the National Assembly within a week of signature.

Monnet was not invited to the signature of the treaties in Rome, which took place on March 25, 1957. Instead, he had a talk in Paris with the clerk of the National Assembly. Emile Blamont was a technical, not political, figure, but he operated the drawbridge to legislation. There is no reason to believe he was much interested in European integration. Nevertheless, Monnet had already turned to him for help in fending off the Eden Plan when the ECSC was set up. Blamont had helped then and he helped now. He may in fact have been the source of a procedural simplification which greatly streamlined ratification. Usually, all the French parliamentary committees reported individually on treaties of major importance. Now only one did, the Foreign Affairs Committee. The twenty or so other committees merely delegated rapporteurs for oral contributions to the debate in the Chamber. Though the Mollet government fell on May 21, 1957, the committees continued to work on the treaties during the interregnum. This again, though not unprecedented, was uncommon. When the next government was installed on June 12, there had been no delay.

On May 7, the Action Committee, with a characteristic tone of urgency, called for ratification before the summer holidays. Monnet seems to have developed four topical arguments for speed. First, the negotiations had lasted two years, and even short delays in ratification could, as experience had shown, result in long delays in implementation, with an increase in the "difficulties and risks". Second, Euratom must be put in place in time to launch a nuclear "association on a truly equal footing" with the United States before the American mid-term elections of November 1958. These required ratification in the U.S. Senate to begin next March. That in turn implied the need for Euratom to start negotiating well before. Third, there was the Free Trade Area scheme which Harold Macmillan, as U.K. Chancellor of the Exchequer, had proposed on October 3, 1956. The new Communities must come into existence as soon as possible to start the talks with the United Kingdom and, by implication, not be "diluted" by them before they could solidify.

The essential argument, however, was the fourth, the importance of rapid, simultaneous ratification in the French and German parliaments before the German elections in September. With Frenchmen, like Pleven, Monnet stressed the need to avoid any temptation for the German Social Democrats to abstain on the treaties. Adenauer was old. The SPD could one day be the majority party in a Germany seeking national reunification. Ollenhauer had indeed announced a new reunification plan on May 23. It was vital to tie the SPD into the European strategy. But Europe was traditionally Adenauer's policy. It raised problems for the Social Democrats, against their own past record, to vote in favour of the treaties only a few weeks before the elections. Yet to postpone matters till after the elections in September could create uncertainties. The French must ratify soon to close the door on an alternative to Europe in Germany.

The argument for the German Social Democrats, Ollenhauer and Wehner, was the mirror image of this. Given worsening conditions in France as a result of the Algerian War, it was vital to put pressure on the French to ratify at the same time as the Bundestag before the holidays. Ollenhauer had first considered holding off his party's assent until the elections were over. Monnet persuaded him without real difficulty to do so before.

In the event, both the Bundestag and Assemblée Nationale ratified the Rome treaties in the first week of July, within three and a half months of the treaties' being signed.[3] The last ratification, the Italian, came in December. The whole process lasted nine months, compared with fifteen for the ECSC and twenty-seven for the EDC. As at so many points of the *relance de Messine,* the willingness of one and all to press ahead, even when the arguments might not seem decisive, appears in retrospect to have made the differ-

---

3. Allowing for the different compositions of the French National Assemblies elected in 1951 and 1956, the voting for the Rome treaties (EEC and Euratom) and Paris treaty (ECSC) was very similar. The odd man out was the EDC treaty.

ence between success and failure. Oddly enough, the one argument nobody seems to have thought of using was the risk that General de Gaulle might come back to power in Paris. Yet by the autumn, the Fourth Republic was already beginning to fall apart. Whether the Rome treaties could have by then been fitted into the agenda of a Parliament obsessed with Algeria is a moot point. To ratify them before de Gaulle returned to power the next year was a tightly timed insurance against "renegotiation", or worse.

TEN

Europe in the World
1958–1979

On New Year's Day of 1958, the governing bodies of the European Economic Community (EEC)—that is, the Common Market—and Euratom started work.[1] Since it was widely expected that the Common Market would soon lead to economic and then political union, their fragile beginnings carried high hopes of the new Europe to come. One aspect of the establishment of the EEC Commission, almost *because* it passed virtually unnoticed, was felt by Monnet amongst others to be particularly significant. As soon as Walter Hallstein made it plain he was a candidate for the presidency of the Commission, his appointment was accepted without question, including by France under the Gaillard government. This was remarkable only twelve years from the end of the war. The very lack of a sense of drama in the choice of a German for the most important of the new posts was not only a tribute to Hallstein's achievements and reputation but proof of giant progress since the Schuman Plan. The seed of the Franco-German reconciliation at the root of today's European Union was planted and began to emerge

1. There were now, therefore, three European Communities—the old European Coal and Steel Community (or ECSC) and the new European Economic Community (EEC or Common Market) and European Atomic Energy Community (or Euratom), each based on a unique treaty (treaty of Paris for the ECSC and separate treaties of Rome for the two others). In 1967, there was a partial fusion of the institutions of the three Communities (p. 332 below). Since the ratification of the Maastricht treaty of European Union in 1993, there is one European Community embracing all three economic Communities, still based on separate treaties but with a single set of institutions; and the European Community itself is part of the European Union, the other part of which consists of intergovernmental regimes covering monetary union, foreign policy, security, and law and order. Throughout this chapter, the Community or European Community (or EC for short) is used whenever one refers to the three European bodies collectively.

well before de Gaulle and Adenauer together dramatised—and thereby enhanced—its growth in the early 1960s.

The Messina programme, which the Action Committee had assigned as its objective, was now fulfilled. The assumption that it had completed its task was so strong that Monnet's two closest advisers went to Euratom in 1958. Kohnstamm, who largely handled German and Benelux affairs, decided to negotiate the United States–Euratom agreement. Van Helmont, Monnet's drafter of texts and French political counsellor, went to set up Euratom's nuclear safeguards system.

Monnet asked the members whether the committee should be wound up. They decided to carry on for a couple of years. At the end of that time, Monnet tested the waters again and talked of leaving for a year "to think". Once more, the members demurred. Ludwig Rosenberg, the "foreign minister" of the German Federation of Trade Unions (DGB), and Otto Brenner, the president of the powerful Metalworkers Union, told Kohnstamm the Action Committee was "unique". Its proposals were "concrete and precise" and it offered a venue for confidential exchanges that "existed nowhere else". It must continue.

This left the question of the scope for action. It was obvious that the EEC would assume vast areas of responsibility. Monnet was hardly involved in many issues which swallowed Community time and energy in the 1960s, such as the common agricultural policy, nor did he wish to be. Instead, he concentrated on the political frontier. In practice, this meant the new issues which hove into view ahead of the Common Market. Ironically, it now became his mainline station for onward journeys. This fact alone transformed the landscape through which he travelled. Hitherto, he had sought to establish European bases in major but specific areas: sectoral integration. Even the Political Community he had pushed for the control of the European Army more than for its own sake. Now, however, when he had a choice, his plans were steps to one of Europe's presumed final goals: monetary union, political union and the Union's place in the world.

The "European District", an idea already proposed for the Coal and Steel Community in 1952, was a good example of the new reach, and also of the difficulties. Now that there were three Communities, it made sense, the Action Committee pointed out in a resolution of November 25, 1957, to concentrate them "on a single site under a European statute". This was presented as good administration. In reality, it was politics. "We are building Europe brick by brick", Monnet wrote. "No doubt, this is the only way open to us, but it is not the best. . . . Europe . . . needs a focus to make it tangible and real to people". A European District, a District of Columbia housing all the European institutions together, would give the Community the magnetism of a nascent capital.

To Monnet, the principle of a District came first. Still, the location could not be ignored. For a while, lobbied by its mayor, he favoured Compiègne. The attraction was the famous rail coach in the forest where two armistices were signed, in 1918 and again in 1940. Etzel and Kohnstamm convinced him that Compiègne was too near Paris. It would be too much like a French takeover. The French and Germans then envisaged Strasbourg and Kehl, on opposite banks of the Rhine, for the same symbolic reasons as Compiègne. The other states objected. This looked too much like a Franco-German takeover. Etzel and Kohnstamm favoured Luxembourg and, by December, Monnet agreed. Unfortunately, Bech refused either to allow any more Eurocrats into his tiny country of 300,000 people or to let go of those already there. His motive, apart from holding on to the revenues of playing host to the ECSC, seems to have been reluctance to oppose Luxembourg's big brothers, the Belgians, bent on capturing the new Communities for Brussels. Whatever his reason, he made a single site impossible. On such matters, national vetoes applied in the Community, and that included Luxembourg.

The foreign ministers of the Six met on January 6–7, 1958. Victor Larock, the Belgian, told his Parliament that "several governments" (not his own) "took very much into account the views of the Action Committee". The Six assented readily to the principle of a European District. They failed, just as readily, to agree on the site. They set the new Communities "provisionally" in Brussels and left the ECSC at its supposedly "precarious" post in Luxembourg. There might still have been some kind of European District in Brussels, with its own postal arrangements, security guards, and so on, on the model of the United Nations in New York, but even this fell foul of municipal politics and of a change of Belgian government. Monnet's frustrated attention turned late in 1959 to the idea of one European Commission for all three Communities, which was achieved in 1967. There is still no European District.

Monnet never forgave Bech. Monnet in turn was publicly attacked by Max Buset, who charged him with acting as a French nationalist by opposing Brussels for the new Communities. On January 16, 1958, Buset and Théo Lefèvre, the presidents, respectively, of the Socialist and Social Christian parties—the Belgian equivalent then of the Democrats and Republicans—resigned from the Action Committee. Monnet was in Washington. He waited till March 8 before returning the accusation back to sender: "I did not use the idea of the single District to stand in the way of Brussels. The people who promoted the idea of dividing the institutions between Brussels and Luxembourg set up a conflict between Brussels and the single District". The row soon subsided with Lefèvre. He attended the next Action Committee meeting in October and soon became a "highly committed" member.

The leaders of the Belgian Liberal party and labour unions stayed on as if nothing had happened. But the Socialists only came back with a new president, Léo Collard, two years later.

The District was a natural issue once the new Communities had been created. It has even been argued that Monnet was rather slow—as a would-be pioneer—in waking up to it. The case for the District would have been strengthened perhaps had there been an article in the Rome treaties to sanction it. On another issue, however, he was far ahead of the field. This was monetary union. As he wrote late in 1958 to C. P. M. Romme, the president of the Catholic Party Group in the Netherland's Second (popular) Chamber, the States-General, he thought "the current Communities should be completed by a Finance Common Market which would lead us to European economic unity. Only then would . . . the mutual commitments created by the Communities make it fairly easy to produce the political union which is the goal". It was the first bow of an issue over which Europe is still agonising today.

The development that triggered Monnet's interest in it was the French financial crisis, which was due to the Algerian War. This threatened the country's ability to take the first material step to the Common Market on January 1, 1959. Gaillard, Monnet's former assistant, first Finance Minister and then Prime Minister, asked Monnet to help on a crisis strategy and on a dollar loan to gain time while remedial measures were introduced. Monnet's characteristic response was that the French problem could only be solved in the European framework. He turned to Uri, Marjolin, Delouvrier and above all Marjolin's Belgian friend, the Yale professor of finance Robert Triffin. With them, he produced a draft in August 1957 which suggested a "European stabilisation fund". "Via money, Europe could become political in five years", he told Kohnstamm in September.

In January 1958, Monnet went to America on his purely French mission to raise a loan for the Fourth Republic (one reason why he took so long to answer Buset). The aim was to reschedule France's debts to the United States on the loans Monnet himself had obtained at the Liberation. After a month in Washington, he returned with $655 million (including about two-thirds of new money), postponing the repayment of the instalments for 1958 and 1959 on the old loans till 1981. In the circumstances, it was a notable success.

Back in Paris, he reverted to his habitual European priorities. On March 6, he proposed to Gaillard a European Reserve Fund, the free movement of capital in the Community and a common financial policy. To manage the fund, the member states would have to pursue common policies. Whether Gaillard would have taken this up was never tested. In April, he fell. The Algerian War was reaching a paroxysm.

In fact, the first achievement of the new Communities arose from a more predictable area, the agreement between Euratom and the United States on a joint nuclear-power programme. Kohnstamm negotiated this. Monnet took a back seat. He intervened only when asked to clear obstacles out of the way. The effort nevertheless followed so naturally from the Wise Men's report as to be part of the Monnet strategy.

The U.S.-Euratom agreement was doubly important because of the initial void at the heart of Euratom. There was a long hiatus after *A Target for Euratom* in May 1957. It was hardly possible to act before the Euratom Commission was set up and its president appointed in January 1958. Armand, the prophet of a nuclear Europe, was the automatic choice. Unfortunately, he was not a happy one in any sense. Monnet virtually propelled him into the job, despite doubts about his temperament. It was a serious mistake. Weaned from Paris and his beloved railways, Armand proved unable to build an institution from scratch and suffered a severe breakdown. For the whole of its first year, a period of rapid growth for national nuclear programmes, Euratom lay flat on its back.

The U.S.-Euratom agreement provided the missing spark of life. It was negotiated—*concocted* might be a better word—by the same group who had drafted *A Target for Euratom*. Only Secord, apart from the brief appearance here and there, was not of the party. Kohnstamm ran the Euratom end, working with one or two around Schaetzel at the State Department and a handful of experts from the American AEC, led by Cook. Kohnstamm and Schaetzel seem to have taken the first step in Luxembourg on October 13, 1957. Agreement with America, Kohnstamm said, would make all the difference between a research Euratom and a power-producing Euratom. The plan must be born in Armand's trip to America immediately he was appointed president. If Armand turned initially to the Euratom governments, nothing would happen. American acceptance in principle must come first. Armand himself could not prepare the programme without the governments knowing. Therefore the Action Committee and the informal group must prepare it for him.

A week later, from October 17 to 20, Kohnstamm attended an American Assembly conference on Atoms for Peace at Arden House, about forty-five miles from New York, the Harriman mansion donated by Averell Harriman to Columbia University in 1951. He then spent a week in Washington meeting his partners in State and the AEC. Detailed preliminary work began when the Americans came to Luxembourg in late November. They and Kohnstamm rapidly turned into a single team. Contacts were so informal and friendly that when Kohnstamm went to Washington he virtually had an office in the State Department. In December, he asked Monnet, then in Washington for the French loan, to stress the importance of the Euratom power programme in talking to Dulles and Eisenhower. Monnet obliged. In January, Kohnstamm pointed out to Schaetzel that Euratom's condition meant the United States must take the initiative but not appear to do so. Formal talks began in Luxembourg on February 14, 1958. Four months later, on June 12, the two parties signed a memorandum of understanding. On the 23rd, Eisenhower presented it to Congress.

It might be tempting to ascribe the State Department's zeal to American interests. In fact, once again, these nearly all went the other way. In June 1958, a storm of opposition blew up in the AEC. Why should Euratom have its own regional controls, when global ones were being worked out in the United Nations? What if Comecon were encouraged to set up its own multilateral controls? In July and August, the agreement came up before the Joint Committee of Congress for Atomic Affairs. But it got tangled up in feuding between the chairman of the AEC, Lewis Strauss, and the dominant personality on the committee, Senator Clinton P. Anderson. As a result, the Euratom agreement itself became controversial. George Ball, Monnet's lobbyist, reported that Anderson wanted to know why, if the administration was so keen not to subsidise American industry, it was so determined to subsidise Euratom's programme instead? A strong group in the AEC itself echoed the objection. Despite this, Congress endorsed the memorandum and Eisenhower signed it on August 18. But a detailed agreement of cooperation had still to be negotiated, and before it was signed on November 8, the American reactor industry, waking up rather late in the day, tried hard to insert "Buy American" clauses.

Control over fissionable materials was high politics and highly charged. For the United States, Euratom controls constituted a "revolutionary" change in non-proliferation policy. For Euratom, it was vital to show that Europe was "more equal" than any member state in bilateral dealings with the AEC. There was a crisis. In July, Kohnstamm asked Monnet to contact Dulles to advise Eisenhower to send a message to Congress to press for ratification. This the President did early in August. It helped, but infuriated Anderson. Anderson in turn was nobbled through Walter Reuther, the president of the powerful United Automobile Workers union. In the end, Kohnstamm had to concede some "mutual" inspection. It was a polite fiction. The Americans supplied fissionable materials to Europe. Europe supplied none to America. So only Europe had anything to be inspected. Yet for years the AEC took on trust the merely oral reports submitted by Van Helmont, running Euratom's inspectorate.

In mid-June, Monnet wrote to the members of the Action Committee that the Americans were going to help Euratom build six prototype power reactors, double the rate of development of nuclear power in the Community, and pave the way for a major effort to improve energy independence by 1968. They would provide a third of the funding, guarantees for the supply of thirty tons of nuclear fuel (equivalent to sixty million tons of coal), and technical assistance. In return, Europe, with higher energy costs than the

United States, would be the proving ground of the new technology and would pool with the United States the knowledge gained. This would be a first association "of equals" between the new Europe and the United States in a sector that could determine the future of industry.

In 1958, the agreement with the United States was not merely a hope, it was the substance, of Euratom. The first year had not been wasted, despite the crisis in the Euratom Commission. The agreement was patently not an arrangement between current equals. Subsidies proved that. But it inverted the usual assumption that in an association between the strong and weak the strong must grow stronger and the weak weaker. Yet the whole programme was also, like the half-funded Monnet Plan of 1946, a gamble. The prospects depended on costs proving favourable to nuclear electricity. If they did, Euratom would be a political power-house. If not, it would be a house of cards.

II

GAULLIST MUTATION

The new Communities were only five months old when an event occurred which changed the rest of Monnet's career. On June 1, 1958, a legal coup d'état in France, fomented by hints that the Fourth Republic was about to treat with the Algerian independence movement, brought Charles de Gaulle back to power. The Fourth Republic, unable to produce a stable or realistic majority in Parliament on colonial issues, collapsed under a threat of revolt, with army support, in Algeria. A strike by the police in Paris showed the government no longer had authority over its own agencies. De Gaulle, whom the politicians were still discounting a few months before, now seemed the only recourse, both for the rebels, to prevent a "sell-out" to the Algerian liberation movement, and for the political parties, which feared the rebels might install a sub-fascist regime.

It was a profoundly ambiguous situation, which ended only in the summer of 1962 when, after many twists and turns, including a settler and army revolt against him in 1960, de Gaulle and the French public acquiesced in Algerian independence by the Evian Agreements. De Gaulle's return to power, however, was clear enough in other respects. One was that it eclipsed the old political parties and their leaders who had backed European integration. De Gaulle told Hirsch, with some hyperbole, in March 1961, "We are no longer in the era when M. Monnet gave orders". His first Prime Minister, the fanatical patriot Michel Debré, so detested Monnet's policies that he would pass him with averted gaze. The European reformation had scarcely begun, and the counterreformation was installed in Paris.

From June 1958 onwards, a defensive element entered integrators' plans.

They knew they had lost the initiative. They could manœuvre to persuade, they could indirectly constrain, they might mobilise deterrent coalitions and stonewall or lie in wait for opportunities, but they could not win by superior political fire-power. This had also been true of Mendès-France's tenure of office, but it had been on a lesser scale, conditional and brief. None of these limits fenced in de Gaulle.

As always, Monnet adjusted coolly to the new realities of power. In October 1958, he came out publicly in favour of de Gaulle's constitution for France on the grounds that it met the need for stronger government while respecting minimum democratic safeguards. Monnet voted "yes" in the referendum on Algeria of January 8, 1961, convinced that de Gaulle alone could grant independence and outface an army coup. Delouvrier, now the Delegate-General in Algiers, found on his trips to Paris that only Monnet gave him serious advice, warning him to vet appointments in the army. Monnet kept in touch with the new Foreign Minister, Maurice Couve de Murville, whom he knew well from war-time Algiers and before. As ever, his feelers were out for any path that could be cleared.

The omens for European integration, at the outset of de Gaulle's second period of rule, were mixed. Pessimists contemplating the change in Paris and fearing an assault on the Communities, could feed their forebodings on the miseries of the High Authority. The issue which precipitated its troubles was the disproportionate impact of the slight recession of 1957–58 on the demand for coal. It was the beginning of the long, terminal decline of European coal. The Schuman treaty's prescription in such a case was for the High Authority to gain the assent of the Council of Ministers to "manifest crisis" measures. But these required the unanimous vote of the Council. The member states were too divided between coal-producing and coal-consuming countries to agree. The High Authority, which had fallen into weak hands after René Mayer's departure in 1957, took no line till late in the day. When it did make up its mind, the German and French governments refused to accept the "Community nature" of the problem and flagrantly impeded its attempts to work out a solution.

Monnet, as the household god of the High Authority, was asked by its members to counsel them in their distress. He thought it should "calmly continue to carry out its job", issue a white paper to pin the responsibility for failure on the governments and take the lead in launching a European energy policy. In May 1959, the Action Committee requested the High Authority and the new Common Market and Euratom Commissions to set up a joint group to propose one. The three duly set it up in October, and the Council of Ministers turned down its recommendations in January. The rest was silence.

In another political climate, there could have been mileage in claiming the fault lay with the national vetoes frustrating compromise and that the

Schuman treaty should in this respect be strengthened. That was not the mood in 1959. Gaullism in Paris was matched in Germany by ill-will towards sectoral integration. Etzel told Monnet that the basic industries, used to cartel planning under government patronage, wanted to break the High Authority. Erhard, speaking to Behr, prophesied that "in three years, they"—the High Authority as a group—"will be up in heaven". In these conditions, a defeat for federalism of the style of the First Europe, Monnet's own, was an accident in waiting. The conclusion drawn in a note in the Kohnstamm archives was "not to cling to the forms of a discredited ECSC. If necessary, one might sacrifice this advanced patrol which has fulfilled the essence of its mission by acting as pathfinder [and] fall back on the strong points of the Common Market."

For de Gaulle's attitude to the Common Market was much more favourable than to the ECSC. This became plain on the eve of the first step, on January 1, 1959, in the elimination of frontier obstacles to trade required to institute the Common Market. In November 1958, de Gaulle wooed Adenauer by taking a strong line in defence of Berlin against the threats of Khrushchev. At the meeting with Adenauer and his ministers at Bad Kreuznach of November 26, he stated that though he had been against the Rome treaties, he was willing to draw the political and economic consequences from them. This statement was not wholly clear, of course. But his reform of the franc on December 28, which permitted France's full frontal entry into the Common Market on January 1, contrasted with the warning of the last leaders of the drowning Fourth Republic that, because of inflation, they might not be able to take such a step. De Gaulle's choice was a tonic for integration, a potentially decisive commitment. The Common Market was about to enter its spectacular initial progress, driven by the zest with which business took to it, and in effect made it happen, as the "thirty glorious years" of postwar boom climbed to their apogee. De Gaulle's partners remained very wary, but were encouraged to work on the premise that a strategic compromise with him might be possible. Monnet was one of the most assiduous of these explorers. He knew de Gaulle would have his own agenda, but thought it a mistake to assume it had to be all negative.

The ambiguities of the early days of de Gaulle's reign were displayed around Euratom. Around August 25, 1958, the day the joint committee of Congress approved the U.S.-Euratom agreement, Monnet wrote to Kohnstamm that Armand was about to resign as president of the Euratom Commission. There was talk of Monnet, who saw de Gaulle on November 11, succeeding him. This was not Monnet's idea. Through Guy Mollet, Minister for Europe in de Gaulle's first government, Monnet secured the post for Hirsch. This seems surprising, since de Gaulle knew the close links between Monnet and Hirsch. Perhaps, as some thought, he was glad to winkle Hirsch out of his strong position in the French bureaucracy. Perhaps he was trying to cultivate Monnet. The latter had few illusions. Van Helmont says that before de Gaulle, Monnet concentrated on Euratom, after de Gaulle on the Common Market.

The third volume of de Gaulle's *War Memoirs,* published in 1959, showed that he still held much the same views expressed in his conversations with Monnet and others in Algiers. The aim would be to persuade

> the states along the Rhine, the Alps and the Pyrenees to form a political, economic and strategic bloc; to establish this organisation as one of the three world powers and, should it become necessary, as the arbiter between the Soviet and Anglo-American camps.

On June 26, 1959, at the end of a visit by de Gaulle to Rome, the Italo-French communiqué referred to political cooperation of the Six and a permanent secretariat to serve it. On November 24, the foreign ministers of the Six agreed to hold quarterly meetings on political "extensions" of Community activity. In reality, the welcome of France's partners was at best subdued. The Benelux countries, now the most integrationist and Atlanticist were particularly suspicious. Monnet was more forthcoming. He found de Gaulle's dreams of power "obsolete". But he was ready to be a fellow traveller while it served European unity. On September 16, 1959, he saw de Gaulle. According to him, de Gaulle said he agreed on European union as an aim, but not on moving too far ahead of opinion. He was held up by the Algerian War. Could the Action Committee pave the way for steps on political union on which de Gaulle could agree and Monnet take "a more active role"? When Monnet replied he was committed to the supranational approach, de Gaulle replied, "That is no obstacle". Monnet remained wary. He said later he did not see himself joining a government headed by Debré, "and in any case that's not what de Gaulle said". The Action Committee resolution at its seventh meeting, on November 20, carried no mention of political union, even though the previous meeting, a year earlier, had done so.

On May 31, 1960, de Gaulle announced that "France would work to build western Europe into a political, economic, cultural, human grouping, organised for action, progress and defence". Spaak, not in government at the time, discussed the situation with Monnet. "We were both surprised. . . . However, we agreed that we must not oppose an initiative which might bring movement in a direction where there had been none since the Treaty of Rome". In July, Monnet tried to inflect de Gaulle's plan. He suggested to Couve a European Confederation with a Supreme Council of heads of government observing in many cases Community procedures. Couve made it clear this would not pass. Still, on August 10, Monnet wrote to Action Committee members that "a political authority at the level of heads of state would be an important step forward".

In his press conference of September 5, de Gaulle said: "To imagine that something can be built which is efficient in action and approved by peoples, above and beyond states, is a delusion". Undeterred, on November 21, Monnet wrote to Adenauer. He was ready to envisage a "privileged" Franco-German agreement if this would give the European Communities a new lease of life. His greatest fear today, he said,

> is that we risk halting our progress . . . in order to hold long debates about questions which, although important, must not become preconditions for action. Must the question of NATO be settled before we continue the unification of Europe? Must Britain take part in our political discussions? Are General de Gaulle's proposals merely for "cooperation", and not "supranational"? It is only by advancing that we shall find answers to these questions, primarily on the political plane.

The next day he wrote to the Action Committee on similar lines. Their replies were deeply dubious. In his anxiety to draw de Gaulle into the European mainstream, Monnet was less Monnetist than they.

One of his motives was fear that Adenauer's lease might be running out and that German support for European integration might fray. He also seems to have seen political cooperation as necessary to confirm European integration at a time when enlargement to Britain and a new relationship with America were looming up. All the same, there was a limit to pragmatism if Monnet were not to renounce his life's work. This was expressed after two summits of the heads of government of the Six—the first in Paris in February 1961 and the second in July in Bonn—resulted in the establishment of a committee, known from its French chairman, Christian Fouchet, as the Fouchet Committee. Its job was to investigate, then to negotiate, a political cooperation agreement. The Action Committee in its ninth session, on July 10–11, came out in favour of "political cooperation" but stressed that it was "vital to define the links . . . with the existing European Communities". De Gaulle's Council of the Heads of State must not become an intergovernmental court of appeal from the decisions of the supranational Communities and put them in doubt.

These precautions were amply justified. In a secret note of September 30, 1960 to his Prime Minister, Michel Debré, de Gaulle put his position in exactly the terms his wary partners suspected. "If we manage to produce a cooperative Europe of States, the Communities will *ipso facto* be reduced to size. Only if we fail to produce such a political Europe will we need to deal directly with the first fruits of integration". In the same spirit and the same month, he told Jan de Quay, the Dutch Prime Minister, that the Rome treaties should be revised to subordinate the Commission to the Council of Ministers.

Naturally, the first French memorandum presented to the Fouchet Committee on October 19, 1961, reflected these views. In the talks that followed, France's five partners dug in their heels. By early December, the draft Union of States contained safeguards for Community institutions and for relations with NATO. The Germans and Italians were satisfied, but the Dutch and Belgians subordinated agreement to British entry into the Common Market. Going ahead without Britain, they said, made sense for a supranational Europe, but not for de Gaulle's British-style "Europe of States". Faced with this opposition, the French came back on January 18, 1962, with a revision of the Fouchet proposals—written it was rumoured by de Gaulle himself—which scratched out virtually all the painfully inserted guarantees. The Italians led some broken-backed efforts at repair. The Dutch and Belgians vetoed these too. De Gaulle's attempt to conduct a concert of Europe through the Community was frustrated. On May 15, he gave a scornful press conference: only the Europe of States had any meaning "outside the worlds of myth, fiction and appearances". As Anthony Hartley has suggested, the failure of the Fouchet Plan probably decided the next route he chose, less than a year later, of revolt against Western orthodoxy.

III
EQUAL PARTNERSHIP

De Gaulle's revolt may also have been precipitated by the rapid flowering, fertilised by the Common Market, of others' vision of a more developed Western community. Monnet was in the thick of this efflorescence. Its immediate roots lay in the British response to the shock of realising that the Common Market, contrary to all previous expectations in London, might succeed. The British scheme for a Free Trade Area (FTA) emerged in the OEEC in July 1956, a year before the Rome treaties were ratified and two years before de Gaulle's return. It proposed free trade in manufactures throughout western Europe, without integration, and without agriculture.

For champions of closer ties with Europe, the FTA was a genuine attempt to adapt Britain's interests to the Common Market. There were so many untidy joins between the two, from agriculture to the Commonwealth, that a special arrangement was understandable. But there were also undertones of *Realpolitik*. The Common Market would "melt" in the FTA "like a lump of sugar in a cup of tea". Far from English understatement, Macmillan wrote that if the FTA failed, "we would fight back. . . . We would take our troops out of Europe. We would withdraw from NATO".

Before de Gaulle, the reluctance to exclude Britain from the Community was such that no member state had the will to oppose a British plan of substance now that one had at last been put forward. Marjolin, the old OEEC hand, told Monnet that the FTA would succeed because "everyone wants it". Monnet himself wavered. He told the Anglo-American Press Association in Paris on June 5, 1956 (i.e., on the eve of the launching of the FTA), that he had changed his mind about the need first to create a European Community and then to seek Britain's participation or association. Neither Britain nor the Six could solve their problems independently, and it was "neither natural nor wise" for Britain to stay out of the efforts on the Continent. However, four months later, the first response of the Action Committee to the FTA, in a communiqué of October 16, reverted to Monnet's usual position. It welcomed an FTA as "an association of Great Britain to the Common Market" but reiterated previous calls to the Six to speed up their negotiations on the new European Communities. In effect, Monnet stuck to a superficial view of the FTA as a new form of the "association", the halfway relationship he had long advocated for Britain short of full membership. Basically, like others, he was none too clear about its implications. Perhaps, as with the Common Market when it was only an idea, he feared ramifications he could not calculate.

De Gaulle transformed the situation. A British-dominated FTA—this was before the first steps to a customs union in the Common Market—did not fit his plans of conducting a Community concert. In November 1958, a French spokesman simply pronounced the tortuous FTA negotiations dead. Though unilateral, this was decisive, in part because, as the talks had dragged on, anxiety about the FTA's effects on the Common Market had spread in the Community. It was no accident that the ambush of the FTA, the meeting with Adenauer at Bad Kreuznach and France's embrace of the Common Market followed hard on one another in a single month. In essence, de Gaulle gained German assent to cutting down the FTA in the name of Community Europe. *The Times* thundered at "France the Wrecker", but to little effect. The FTA was defeated by an alliance of de Gaulle and European federalists increasingly suspicious of Britain's motives.

The British tried tenaciously to resuscitate the corpse. Monnet turned his back on it. A paper circulated to the members of the Action Committee, dated January 22, 1959, shows that he now wanted to leave the FTA behind. It was, however, the new Common Market (EEC) Commission, under Hallstein (probably devising the arguments Monnet now used), which took the first political step forward. Its paper on external economic relations adopted by the EEC Council of Ministers on March 16, argued that there should be no regional association of the Common Market with the FTA. Instead, the EEC should pursue a liberal trade policy to the world. This was bold, because it deflated the OEEC in which Britain was dominant; farsighted, because it took account of the global impact of the Common Market; and shrewd, because, in satisfying American aspirations, it minimised Britain's chances of mobilising an effective coalition.

Everything now depended on the United States. The Americans faced a new situation on their own account. In 1959, Washington abruptly awoke to the strange problem, for those reared to postwar conditions, of the United States no longer being able to earn a foreign-currency surplus with other industrial economies. This radical shift of perspective seemed symbolic. Economic "miracles" were making competitors of America's erstwhile protégés in Europe and Japan. The Common Market even promised a "second America". It was a problem, but also the triumph of Marshall aid policy. Economic concern mingled with political optimism. Though Congress was in no mood to go far in freeing trade or coordinating anything which might dilute its own sovereignty, the Eisenhower administration was becoming keen to involve the other industrialised market economies, including Japan, in a framework of cooperation.

The Americans, like the British, were anxious not to pay in lost trade for the Common Market. Unlike Britain, they were committed to European integration. On balance, they were ready to pay a commercial price for the EEC so long as it adopted liberal trade policies. They were not willing to do so for an FTA dreamed up to avoid integration. As Ernst van der Beugel, then Dutch Vice Minister in charge of European negotiations and a free-trader, has written, "By their own conviction and through the influence of Monnet and his entourage, the Americans . . . fully supported the . . . primacy of the Six".

Monnet, though, took some time to make anything of the new situation. On May 11, the Action Committee's resolution at its sixth session called only for a Round Table of the EEC Commission (for the six Community states) and Britain, on a European Economic Association. Then, on May 27, he went to Washington as the only foreign pall-bearer at the funeral of his old friend John Foster Dulles. He saw Douglas Dillon, now Under Secretary of State for Economic Affairs, and next day lunched with Eisenhower. Back in Paris on June 9, he had a long talk with John ("Jack") Tuthill, the Economic Minister at the embassy. He now suggested that the United States and Canada should become full members of a reformed OEEC. The stress would be on a triangular relationship of North America, the EEC and Britain to discuss the economic problems of the "free world": trade, aggregate demand, money, and aid to developing countries. Monnet led the conversation all the way.

A week after the talk with Tuthill, Monnet sailed again for New York. He lunched with Dillon and on June 23, with the help of McCloy, revised a paper for Dillon under the title "A New Era in Atlantic Relations". On July

1, he rang Dillon at his holiday house at Bar Harbour, in Maine. The United States and Canada were to join the OEEC as members. An Action Council was to be set up in the OEEC with the United States, the Community, the United Kingdom and Canada as permanent members, and one or two other countries in rotation (echoes of Monnet's ideas for OEEC in 1948). There was to be majority voting in this new Action Council. What attracted Monnet, clearly, was the chance for the Common Market Commission to be the "single voice" of an EEC taking decisions with the United States. A completely new form of cooperation could open up between the two shores of the Atlantic. The politics of Western organisation would be wafted away from the sterile "dialogue of the deaf" over the Free Trade Area. And once all hope of outflanking the Common Market had vanished, Britain might feel forced to join it. Here were vast possibilities.

Back in Paris, Monnet saw Tuthill again, who proposed a new organisation to replace the "discredited" OEEC. On July 27, Monnet handed a modified French version of his paper to Pinay, the French Minister of Finance. There was no mention of the OEEC but of "permanent consultations including the Common Market, the U.S., the U.K. and some representation of small and developing countries". The proposal could be made jointly by de Gaulle and Adenauer.

On the surface, nothing further happened till Tuthill returned to Washington and the State Department in October, and wrote a paper proposing a new economic organisation, including Japan. Monnet, however, was busy preparing plans to address the substance of American-European cooperation. The aim, as in the Wise Men's report on Euratom, was to focus on areas where the Community should act as a unit, not as a collection of states. This would strengthen the Community institutions, bind the member states together and help to deal with Washington on "equal" terms. The Rome treaty already empowered the Common Market Commission to negotiate on behalf of the member states on trade. Monnet now sought to add money and resurrected his European Reserve Fund. In September, Kohnstamm explained to Schaetzel that it was "the crucial element" in Monnet's plans. The fund should be "made up of 20 per cent of the reserves of each member state" (of the EEC). This would force the Six to coordinate their monetary policies. Further, the Fund, "*qua* central bank, would be a first step toward a fully effective international reserve system" (*sic*) . . . "Pinay and Etzel [the French and German Ministers of Finance] could probably pull this off."

On November 13, 1959, Monnet wrote to Adenauer stressing the change produced by Washington's sensitivity to its newfound dollar deficit. On November 20, the Action Committee stated that EEC-U.K. relations must be seen in a Western context, now that the limits of America's ability to support the system were in sight. There should be a Round Table Commission of the EEC, the United States, United Kingdom, and one other OEEC state to clarify the issues. The resolution also pressed for the European Reserve Fund.

Everything came together in December. Dillon came to Europe for a week at the beginning of the month (the 7th to the 12th). After the NATO Council meeting in Paris (the 15th to the 19th), the leaders of the four major Western powers—Eisenhower, de Gaulle, Adenauer and Macmillan—held a summit of their own (the 19th to the 21st). Monnet wrote to Eisenhower, on the 19th: "Europe is now a full partner conscious of US concern regarding its balance of paiement *{sic}*" and stressed the "great importance that the Common Market Commission . . . be included in the . . . Committee which will study" how to establish the new Organisation for Economic Cooperation and Development (OECD). The four duly decided to turn the OEEC, hitherto European only, into the organisation of all the industrial market-economy states. A committee of four experts was appointed in January 1960 to work out the details. The European, however, was Clappier, Schuman's old chief of staff, who was a French official, and not Marjolin, who was the vice president of the Common Market Commission and whom Monnet had wanted to speak for the EEC. He was annoyed with Hallstein for not lobbying with more vigour. He was disappointed but scarcely surprised when the decisions on the new body came through. These were intergovernmental. It took another twelve months before the OECD convention was signed, and nine more before it began work in September 1961, but the die was cast.

Monnet won and lost in these manœuvres. His bid for a joint American and Community management of the Western economy, with the Common Market Commission as the European "voice", was thwarted—predictably, given the balance of forces. After that, he lost interest in the OECD as he had before in the OEEC, and for the same reason: he regarded it as another intergovernmental talking-shop. His monetary proposals were also shelved. But his other objective was achieved by the mere fact that a Western economic organisation including the United States had been set up: any hope of Britain dealing with the Community on British terms was foreclosed. It must now look to entry to solve its Common Market problem. And though Monnet had little influence on the form the OECD took, he surprisingly emerges as its most probable "inspirer". Before he stepped forward, no one seemed to have a view on the matter.

Once the Free Trade Area had been interred, and the British government had lost hope of a halfway house, its decision to seek entry into the Common Market was only a matter of time. Monnet could not claim direct influence on this decision. He conferred with Edward Heath, the Lord Privy Seal and Macmillan's Minister for Europe, in the London house of David Drummond, now Earl of Perth and Colonial Secretary. But these meetings were lubricants of policy, rather than determiners. All the same, indirectly, Monnet was more responsible than anyone else for Britain's choice. Having sowed the Community, he was the main influence preventing Britain from stunting its growth. In France, until the failure of the EDC, the leaders of the parties most favourable to European integration were also those most tempted to let Britain pick its terms. Schuman had almost conceded the British case in May 1950. Until 1955, keeping close touch with Britain was the main priority for Mollet. Free-traders throughout the the Six regarded Britain as the key to alternative strategies. Monnet had to struggle to make his view prevail that the British would be convinced by facts, not argument, and that the locomotive of integration must roll on.

Once that basic choice was made, the two crucial factors were the existence of the Common Market and the policy of the United States. Fear of exclusion from the Common Market—not Monnet's creation—forced Whitehall into Europe. As for the United States, Monnet was a potent influence. He made the most of the Americans' bias in favour of the Community.

He intervened on numerous occasions. One such episode happens to have been caught on the wing. In March 1960, the Common Market Commission published proposals to accelerate the steps to be taken towards tariff-free trade within the Common Market while reducing duties on imports from the outside world. No one objected to that. The controversy came in the corollary, that no special concessions would be made to Britain and its FTA allies. The British government had not reached a consensus on entering the EEC yet and was strongly opposed to the latter forcing the pace. Christian Herter, who had succeeded Dulles as Secretary of State, informed Eisenhower at the end of February that "the United Kingdom still hopes for an eventual Free Trade Area". (This was a full fifteen months after the breakdown in the FTA negotiations.) At this juncture, Adenauer came to Washington. The joint statement after he met Eisenhower on March 15 endorsed the Commission policy of accelerating the completion of the Common Market. The British did not know it, but Monnet had rung up his allies, Dillon and Tuthill, the previous Friday, March 11, to ensure they put the "right" words in the statement. These roused Macmillan to a high rhetorical state. Visiting Eisenhower a week later, he threatened to withdraw British troops from Germany if the United States continued to support the Commission proposals. Selwyn Lloyd, his Foreign Secretary, had issued similar threats in a more veiled but public fashion to the Council of Europe.

These efforts in the gentle art of persuasion had no effect. So Macmillan waited for a new president and came to see Kennedy a year later in April 1961. Ball, Monnet's old friend, was now Under Secretary of State. Kennedy listened to him and urged Macmillan to join the Community. As Miriam Camps has remarked, "There was a 'Monnet effect' on Ball and then a 'Ball effect' on Kennedy and then a 'Kennedy effect' on Macmillan". As a result

Macmillan, despite his earlier threats, announced Britain's application to enter the Common Market on July 31, 1961. It was a triumph for Monnet. In June, he walked side by side with Macmillan to the Senate House when Cambridge University awarded them both honorary degrees. They had come a long way since Tipasa.

Once Macmillan applied to join, Monnet championed British entry through thick and thin. He refused to entertain the doubts felt by many in the Community, such as Hallstein and Marjolin, over Britain. The British, he told Heinrich von Brentano, the German Foreign Minister, "will be good partners . . . on one condition: that there will be no exceptions for them in the rules". He finessed any doubts by his usual optimism of action. Many years later, in an interview on BBC television, he said, "You've heard many people say 'if England comes into Europe, she will not accept to delegate certain power'. My conviction is contrary to that."

British entry was more than an end in itself. It laid the foundation for a potential restructuring of relations in the West. Ideas for this were in fact brewing before the British change of front. Between February and July 1960, Bowie prepared for Herter a massive policy paper, "The North Atlantic Nations", on the future of the Atlantic alliance. The main political idea was that the revival and integration of Europe

> has greatly modified the power relationships between western Europe and the United States. . . . Still greater unity is likely to be achieved [in Europe] in the next decade. . . . Such a Europe could join in a genuine partnership of equals [with the United States].

Bowie came to Europe while preparing the report and saw Monnet. The Action Committee declaration at the eighth session, of July 11, 1960, announced that "the economic union which in Europe paves the way for political unity is proving externally the ferment of change for the West as a whole". The Western powers, in an "equal association of the US and Europe", must work together as the "motor" of the world economy. They must help the developing countries as one of the conditions of the gradual emergence of a "real dialogue" between East and West.

When George Ball was asked to prepare the programme for the Kennedy administration during the presidential campaign of 1960, the Bowie experience was largely repeated. Ball consulted Monnet, claiming that his function was "known to only four or five people in the United States". His report included a twenty-page paper outlining a Policy for Partnership. It was no accident, then, that the themes enunciated in the last year of Eisenhower's presidency were exactly the ones repeated two years later in Kennedy's famous speech of July 4, 1962, proposing an Atlantic "partnership of equals" between the United States of America and the uniting states of Europe. The

Action Committee voiced them on this occasion too (June 26, 1962). The one difference was that Kennedy left out the idea of a dialogue with Moscow. That came only after the fright of the Cuban Missile Crisis in October.

In one sense, partnership clearly was a strategy to prevent de Gaulle from splitting the West between the English-speaking powers and continental Europeans. In Bowie's eyes, it "was essentially put forward as a way of making a graphic retort [to de Gaulle] that if only Europe continued [to] do the things necessary to achieve integration, at the end of the line [it] could have a self-respecting role". The Americans also thought Britain in the Community would buttress their influence in the new Europe. At the same time, the seeds of a "partnership of equals" long antedated de Gaulle's return to power. They went back to the Marshall Plan. Monnet was preoccupied with the "Federation of the West" in 1948 (p. 187). The Acting Secretary of State, James Webb, wrote in 1949 to David Bruce in Paris that

> the world today requires . . . new and probably radical methods [of] dealing with economic and political problems which respect no national frontiers. . . . The ultimate objective is the provision of machinery for dealing effectively with such problems on a worldwide basis. In the near future, progress depends upon developing means for dealing with specific problems among a small number of nations most directly concerned and gradually building outwards from such nuclei.

In the winter of 1954–55, when nothing seemed more remote, Van Helmont inserted in a draft for Monnet a short paragraph about a relationship of cooperative equals between the Europeans and the United States.

According to Bowie, Kennedy had "nowhere near the interest in the [EC] which either Dulles or Eisenhower had". But Ball steered him to Bowie's concept and more than once to Monnet the man. Kennedy was taken with Monnet and impressed by the Community. With Britain in the process of joining it, an Atlantic partnership "of equals" seemed attractive. In the margin of the Library of Congress copy of a short book, *The Grand Design*, on the Atlantic partnership written by the well-known syndicated columnist Joseph Kraft some reader has written "Phew! was this to take six months or a year?" For Ball and Monnet, the stakes were more concrete than that. The partnership was a licence to develop the Community in cohabitation with America.

Monnet was aware that equality was a norm to aim at between America and Europe, not a current fact of life. Similarly, the Americans had the psychology of a very senior partner indeed, and their support had limits. The Community must develop as an ally. Ball was the main author of the Trade Expansion Act of 1962. This led to the "Kennedy Round" of talks and the agreement in 1967 to cut tariffs on trade in manufactures worldwide by about a third. It was a sign of American fear of being cut out of the new Europe. But it was also basically creative and forward-looking. Americans such as Ball were ready to open the door on a gradual Community accretion of influence in the West. In Bowie's words,

> Our basic analysis was that it was not awfully healthy for the United States to be so predominant and the others to be such small fry. . . . They would feel themselves as not having a voice in what happened, and we would feel them as not doing their share. . . . We were assuming that the basic interest was such that we would have to cooperate, and that it would be probably more enduring if there were something nearer an equal relationship.

Just how much this stood on the liberating wing of American opinion can be gauged from later attitudes. In 1973, Henry Kissinger explained to the European Community that while America's role was global, that of Europe was only regional. Over ten years later, the Assistant Secretary for Europe, Richard Burt, wrote a letter requesting the governments of the Western European Union to consult the United States before reaching any decisions among themselves.

In retrospect, Kennedy's partnership speech was the high-water mark of the ideology of integration. Nuclear stalemate, collective security, the success of the Marshall Plan, a worldwide boom associated with dollar strength and leadership, fuelled a belief as the 1950s developed that new forces were taking over from nationalism. The irruption of the Common Market in world consciousness around 1960 focussed this feeling. The postwar collapse of Europe was becoming a memory. The West was finding a quite unforeseen and politically powerful response to Leninism. The Atlantic partnership was a logical further step in an exploration that had already proved its worth. Ahead lay the beacon of collective management of the major problems of the world.

In reality, as is the way with high tides, it was already on the turn. For all sorts of reasons—including the Vietnam War and the worldwide boom itself, lifting many states from the postwar nadir—the 1960s brought nationalism back into fashion. The first agent of the unthinkable was de Gaulle. He saw international relations in terms of power: someone must gain and someone lose. Monnet once suggested to him that there should be a Franco-German union (of "equals", of course). De Gaulle's answer was that "if the Germans are determined to become Frenchmen, I do not see why not". From such a standpoint, integration and partnerships were flimsy masks for American empire. The process had to be stopped. Britain's attempt to enter the Common Market was a necessary point where this could be done and dramatised.

Monnet proclaimed British entry into the Community to be inevitable. When Robert Kleiman of *U.S. News and World Report* told him in May 1961 that Geoffroy de Courcel, the Secretary-General of de Gaulle's presidential staff, had said de Gaulle had no intention of letting the United Kingdom into the Common Market, Monnet replied, "He can't stop it if the English put their case right". He insisted, as in launching the Schuman conference, that "the negotiations must be pressed quickly to avoid confusion": Britain should enter the Common Market first and negotiate her special problems after. That was what Community institutions were for. There "must not be a traditional negotiation of the FTA kind". At lunch on Sunday, October 8, 1961, Macmillan told him obstacles to entry were rising in Britain. The two agreed the talks must go forward rapidly. On October 31, Monnet sent the British ambassador in Paris, Pierson Dixon, a paper suggesting that "broad decisions" before entry be distinguished from details after. Yet the talks were both detailed and slow. He tried to speed them up. Late in 1962, he affirmed that they were sufficiently advanced for everything to be wrapped up without delay. He was irritated when Hallstein denied that they were. All this probably concealed fear of a de Gaulle veto, but that he never actually voiced.

On Sunday, July 3, 1961, visiting Metz, de Gaulle did say that "Britain must enter the Common Market without posing conditions", rather in the Monnet style. However, by March 1962, he was freeing himself from the Algerian War. The British embassy in Paris began at once to suspect he would veto British entry into the Common Market and in June warned Macmillan. Macmillan had burned his boats, and pressed on. When de Gaulle's veto was finally pronounced on January 13, 1963, the shock was violent. Couve has said that he never saw Monnet in such a rage. It was different from the veto on the Free Trade Area, when Community and American interests had been quietly served. Now the long-feared Gaullist assault on Western mainline policies had materialised. The British were outraged by the brutal blackball. The Community was violated because the veto was unilateral. The Americans knew they were the target, for the British were rejected as their "Trojan horse". That Germany was just as good a "Trojan horse" was widely noted. De Gaulle chose to ignore it.

IV
LAST BATTLES

De Gaulle's veto on Britain marked the watershed between the first half of his reign, when others found it expedient to make the best assumptions about living with him, and the second half, of political trench warfare.

The way Germany went, the system would follow. The nightmare was that de Gaulle might infect the Germans with the nationalism he personified but could never practice with Teutonic potential, and tempt them into playing off the West against the Russians. This was not all paranoia. One of Khrushchev's last acts before his fall in 1964 was to send his son-in-law, Alexei Adzhubei, the editor of *Izvestia,* to Bonn on what looked like a fishing expedition for a special relationship. The fear was deeply felt by Monnet himself. His gravest charge against de Gaulle was that he was playing fast and loose with Germany. European union was the key to Germany's future. Monnet's duty was to do all he could to ensure that Germany's bipartisan commitment to European unity should survive. This was the main thread running through all the Action Committee's operations during the decade of de Gaulle.

On January 23, 1963, only ten days after the veto, Adenauer came to Paris to sign the Franco-German Friendship Treaty. This was the fruit of Adenauer's visit to de Gaulle the previous July and of de Gaulle's visit to Germany in October. De Gaulle had received an ecstatic welcome from crowds intoxicated by reconciliation with France. But now the timing of the signature looked like provocation. Just before the signing, Monnet had a long talk with Adenauer and Hallstein at the German embassy. At this point, he was still doing all he could to revive the talks on British entry. He told Adenauer, in no uncertain terms (which shocked Hallstein), that he could not possibly sign the treaty without reopening the negotiations. "The efforts you have made and the glory that will be yours are in danger of being tarnished and destroyed". Adenauer did not take offence—or the advice.

The Americans now put enormous pressure on the Germans to dissociate from de Gaulle's aims. Since the American security guarantee was even more important to the Germans than the link with France, the pressure did not shift their priorities. It simply forced them into the open. On May 16, the Bundestag in Bonn, which had to ratify the treaty or seem to reject friendship with France, prefaced the text with a long rambling preamble, not part of the original document. This welcomed the pact in terms so tied to Atlantic and European orthodoxies that it amounted to moral separation before the wedding was even celebrated. De Gaulle greeted the rebuff with a verbal shrug, "Treaties are like maidens and roses, they each have their day". Adenauer paid the price. He was felt to have been too easily seduced and to be at last, at eighty-seven, too old. He was forced out in October and, gall to his spirit, had to make way for Erhard.

Debré and Couve have both affirmed that Monnet was the author of the preamble. His own *Memoirs* do not claim so much. He surely wanted to block de Gaulle's schemes. At lunch on February 23, Couve de Murville claimed that "the Six no longer exist", only the Franco-German relationship. Monnet, for all his own stress on the Franco-German link, was horrified. Like others, he tried to use the Bundestag ratification of the Franco-German treaty to stop the rot. But the draft he took with him to Bonn at the end of February shows he was thinking only in terms of a Bundestag resolution. In the case of the preamble, it was the form not the substance that required inventing. He did not find it, nor did Americans like Ball and Acheson who pressed the Germans hard. This proves the flattering place Monnet held in the demonology of Gaullist leaders. A letter to him of March 16, 1963, from Kurt Birrenbach, a Christian Democratic Union (CDU) politician, member of the Action Committee and friend in the thick of the parliamentary manœuvres in Bonn, conveys the impression that German constitutional lawyers may have found the device. The Free Democrats (Liberals) first gave it an airing.

However, Monnet did strongly urge another response to de Gaulle. This was Kennedy's journey to Germany in June 1963, which culminated in the "ich bin ein Berliner" speech at the Berlin Wall. Monnet also endorsed the NATO Multilateral (nuclear) Force (or MLF), including the Germans but under American control, which Bowie first suggested and friends in Washington were promoting. The motive was to scotch any temptation of the Germans, supposedly driven by resentment of British and French nuclear ambitions, to develop their own. With great difficulty, Monnet persuaded the Action Committee on June 1, 1964, to give conditional endorsement to an MLF directed to an ultimate "equal relationship" with the United States. But the Germans, as in Euratom, proved indifferent to the politics of nuclear pretension. Six months later, President Lyndon Johnson, who had stepped into the murdered Kennedy's shoes, quietly dropped the scheme.

Despite, or because of, the struggle over the soul of Germany, Monnet and Couve continued to meet for private lunches. The Common Market was still making spectacular progress, but the new distrust between member states directed Community decision-making towards political barter, or "package deals". De Gaulle extracted the Common Agricultural Policy (CAP) from Germany by threats of boycotts. The Germans in return exacted high farm prices (the source of today's European farm surpluses) and insisted on French commitment to the "Kennedy Round" and freer world trade.

This ambivalent but dynamic period came to an abrupt halt in mid-1965. The EEC Commission, led by Hallstein, was tempted by the establishment of the CAP to assume that de Gaulle had committed himself beyond recall. It therefore proposed that the EEC should receive the income from farm levies and all customs duties as its own revenue. The European Parliament should therefore have the last word on the budget unless five out of six governments in the Council of Ministers voted against its view. This implied a limited but clear transfer of powers to the centre in the Common Market. De Gaulle may well have decided to act before the EEC passed the mythical "point of no return" so often invoked in its history. On July 6, 1965, the French delegates walked out of the Council of Ministers and all Community meetings and so launched the "empty chair" crisis. A long boycott by one of the main founder states threatened the Community's very existence.

At lunch on July 6 and 10, Couve de Murville said that France was not in principle opposed to the Community having its own revenues or to an increase in the Parliament's powers. Monnet was emboldened to write to Hallstein on July 13 suggesting that a compromise postponing most of the thorny issues till 1970 might pass. Hallstein took this advice on July 29 only to face another French rejection. The crisis dragged on.

The French presidential elections fell due in December 1965. De Gaulle's attacks on the European Community generated far more opposition in France than expected, especially among farmers. Stressing that he had voted for de Gaulle on constitutional reform and an elected presidency in 1958 and on Algeria in 1960, Monnet announced he would now vote against him. He did more than that. French presidential elections are held in two rounds, the first involving all candidates, to give expression to every view, the second only the top two from the first round, so that the final winner enjoys an absolute majority of votes cast. Since neither Pinay nor Maurice Faure was willing to stand against de Gaulle, Monnet first tried to persuade a Catholic MRP leader, Joseph Fontanet, to do so. When this failed, he fell back on Jean Lecanuet, the MRP mayor of Rouen, and endorsed him. De Gaulle was placed in the humiliating position of winning under 44 per cent of the vote in the first round. In the second round, Monnet endorsed François Mitterrand, the remaining opposition candidate. This time, de Gaulle won by a margin of 55 to 45 per cent, again far short of the massive plebiscites he favoured.

It was a setback for de Gaulle and, on January 29, 1966, led to a political settlement in the Community known as the Luxembourg "compromise". This was a misnomer both in form and in substance. In form, France and her five partners agreed to disagree on the key issue, France insisting on national vetoes on all "vital interests", the Five sticking to the Rome treaty, which frequently envisages qualified majority voting. In substance, or practice, however, the French managed to introduce national vetoes on all issues bar the budget. This infection of the Community by the very styles of decision-making it had been created to overcome, more or less froze progress for the next twenty years. The system was workable because the interests involved were now so huge that governments were driven to frequent "package deals". It was nonetheless one of the prime sources of the stagnation and "Europessimism" which spread insidiously in the 1970s.

Shortly before the "empty chair" crisis, it had been agreed, on April 8, 1965, that the bodies running the three Communities should merge, with one Commission and Council of Ministers (in addition to the existing single Parliament and Court) operating all three treaties. This was the idea the

Action Committee first launched in 1959 when the European District failed. But even here ambiguity reigned. One reason the French government supported the move was as a chance to sink Euratom in the merger. The Euratom treaty remained and so did the more important technical functions, like the inspection system, the standards authority and health regulations. But all pretence of policy initiation disappeared. It was not just three Communities that were merged in 1967. It was sectoral integration, Monnet's kind, that was more or less swallowed up by the general Economic Community, that is, the EEC or Common Market.

Two factors had already undermined Euratom. The first and most potent was that contrary to the good wishes around its cradle, the problems of nuclear power, notably regarding safety, proved so daunting that the price rose steadily while that of conventional energy (again contrary to the received opinion) fell. The turning point came in 1959. The British had launched their nuclear-power programme in 1955, tripled it in 1957 and cut it back to the original target as early as 1960. When de Gaulle asked about the U.S.-Euratom agreement in March 1961, Hirsch answered that it was out of date. Though Euratom contributed to five power reactors, there was little incentive for industry to go ahead.

In these circumstances, it was fairly simple for the second factor, French hostility, to take effect. De Gaulle told Hirsch in March 1961 that he would forbid Euratom inspectors entry into any French defence installations. Actually, inspections continued long after, but the campaign seeped into everything. Almost the first act of Pierre Chatenet, the French Minister of the Interior who replaced Hirsch as president early in 1962, was to announce that the Euratom Commission would no longer invoke majority votes even when the treaty provided for them. He formally abandoned the U.S.-Euratom programme. Even so, Euratom's research retained some vitality for another five years, and might have flourished, but in the merger of the Communities in 1967 it was dropped. When the energy crises of the 1970s brought nuclear power back into fashion, development was national. Ironically, much of the ability of European firms to respond to the demand, notably in the two countries with relatively the largest programmes, France and Belgium, was rooted in the few reactor orders under the U.S.-Euratom agreement. Meanwhile, France had to give up the CEA's favoured natural-uranium reactor type, in whose name the CEA had so obstinately sabotaged Euratom. Euratom itself was no longer there to seize the opportunity.

Shortly after the empty chair crisis, de Gaulle announced that France would be leaving the NATO integrated military command. He had now, in quick succession, attacked both the European Community and NATO. The veto on Britain in 1963 had created severe strains in relations with France's neighbours. The empty chair crisis of 1965 and withdrawal from NATO's integrated military command in 1966 created a complete rift. From now on, everyone adjusted to stalemate with de Gaulle. Opposed governments and political forces basically played out time.

In 1967, the British government, to make sure the country's claims to enter the European Community could not be ignored, revived the request to join. De Gaulle vetoed again. But the initiative was shifting. Monnet had given up all contact with de Gaulle or Couve since 1965, and Action Committee meetings took place in Bonn, West Berlin or Brussels. Monnet himself was in internal exile, his phone, he suspected, tapped. Not that he cared much. The Action Committee now proposed a resolution to be laid in all the parliaments in favour of British entry. This was ignored in Paris, but in the Bundestag on October 17, the resolution was passed unanimously. Monnet, who was in the visitors' gallery, was given a standing ovation, and the then chancellor, Kurt Kiesinger, came up from the rotunda to sit with him for half an hour.

This was gesture politics, of course, but with a serious function. The Action Committee had become the keeper of the European conscience. In this, it was very successful. There were no defections. On the contrary, recruits joined. The "left-wing" Nenni Socialists from Italy came in 1967. A year later, so did the French Independent Republicans, non-Gaullist junior partners in de Gaulle's governments, led by Valéry Giscard d'Estaing. It was a sign of the times. The three major British political parties followed (but not the British trade unions). Monnet himself said, "It is amazing. We lead them from defeat to defeat, and still they come to our meetings and sign our declarations". The unfamiliar multinational context obscures the fact that in essence the Action Committee was operating as a loyal European opposition biding its time.

In the end, its time came, as so often, unexpectedly. The student pseudo-revolution of May 1968 in Paris shook de Gaulle to the core, even though the June elections, in reaction to the disorders of the previous month, gave the Gaullists and their political allies a huge majority in Parliament. The climate had changed. The spirit of the times, radiating from the Berkeley free-speech movement and the student revolt over Vietnam in America, gave a *fin de régime* tinge to specifically French signs of weariness with a decade of de Gaulle's personal rule. The near-general strike and wage increases that followed the student demonstrations lit the fuse of inflation. The franc, to which de Gaulle attributed sovereign powers second only to nuclear arms, had to be devalued, and Gaullist "grandeur" looked naked beside the economic power of Germany. De Gaulle, in a final fling, hinted to the British through their ambassador in Paris, Christopher Soames, Churchill's son-in-law, in February 1969, that Britain and France might perhaps run a directorate of two in a loosened Common Market. But he had played this kind of hand too often. The British ignored the offer. His policy terminally isolated, he abdicated in April, after a gratuitous referendum in which he almost courted a majority of "no" votes. It was a confession of failure in the great game, the only one he really cared for.

The departure of de Gaulle seemed the occasion for another of European union's periodic revivals. Monnet slipped back into his old role of "inspirer". Willy Brandt and Edward Heath, both of them staunch political friends for a decade, now led the governments in Germany and Britain. Georges Pompidou, de Gaulle's heir, talked of building up the fragments of a European government and the triptych—"completion, deepening and enlargement" of the European Community—became the official goal of the governments of the Six member states. The unfinished business of British entry into the EC, and of monetary and political union, stood much as it had a decade earlier. It was tempting to carry on where the old agenda had left off. In 1969–70, at The Hague, the EC countries duly relaunched European integration. By 1970, the customs union at the base of the EEC was fully open, ahead of time. The moment seemed ideal.

Yet the world had changed. De Gaulle's decade at the helm had legitimised the state bureaucracies in their visceral rejection of outside interference. The economic miracle years were drawing to a close. Inflation, rising everywhere, with widening variations from country to country, was beginning to drag European societies apart. Monnet himself, almost exactly two years older than de Gaulle, was an octogenarian now.

Monnet, with Triffin, revived their old idea of a European Reserve Fund for Brandt. Karl Schiller, the German Minister of Finance, vetoed it. For several years, Monnet wrote the fund into Action Committee resolutions. In his eyes, it would force EC governments to manage their foreign reserves together. This in turn would compel them to concert their domestic policies; and economic union would follow. But the Germans distrusted a fund run by politicians. They regularly amended Monnet's resolutions to say that monetary union could only be set up *after* the economic policies of the member states had "converged"—in effect on their own model, where the central bank is insulated from direct political influence. This inverted Monnet's approach. Helmut Schmidt, Brandt's successor as chancellor, has pointed to Monnet's *Memoirs* as a source of his proposal of the European Monetary System in 1978. But this was for the political approach not the financial substance, because in fact Monnet's fund was rejected. The rejection was a harbinger of the German-led monetary Europe of today.

The summit of European heads of government of October 1972 issued a call for a European Economic Union by 1980. No action followed. The tensions on the ground and disagreements between governments were too great. Monnet concluded that only regular meetings of heads of government might provide the missing dynamic. Unlike de Gaulle's old proposals, his plan, drafted by Van Helmont in August 1973, meticulously respected the existing rights of EC institutions. He presented it to Michel Jobert, the French Foreign Minister, then to Brandt and to Heath. It was transformed, finally, by Pompidou, into something quite different—regular summits to discuss "political cooperation", meaning little more than diplomatic consultation.

The one major change was due to Pompidou's lifting of de Gaulle's veto on British entry into the Community. In fact, thinking in Gaullist power terms within the EC, but less confident than the General, he welcomed it as a make-weight against Germany. Britain duly entered, with Denmark and Ireland, on January 1, 1973. It was a long-delayed fulfilment for Monnet, though he would have preferred Britain to join alone. In 1972, Heath made him a Companion of Honour, Monnet's fourth, last and rarest British distinction.

Suddenly, on October 6 1973, the Yom Kippur War broke out, the result of a new, concerted and more limited strategy by Nasser's successor as ruler of Egypt, Anwar Sadat, and King Faisal of Saudi Arabia. Their aim was no longer to eliminate the Jewish state, nor even to reconquer the territories lost to Israel in the lightning 1967 War, but to force negotiations on the territories' return, or partial return. The means were to be restrictions on oil exports, largely monopolised by the Arab Middle East. These were applied almost immediately the Egyptian army achieved surprise by crossing the Suez Canal, thinly defended by Israel, into Sinai. The hope was that they would force the West to put pressure on Israel. The calculation failed. But the oil embargo of 1973–74 did precipitate a recession which brought the thirty years of postwar world boom to an abrupt and, as it proved, lasting end.

Monnet suggested, and the German Finance Minister, Helmut Schmidt, took up, the idea that the EC countries should establish a common scheme of allocation of oil. But the French and British acted unilaterally, ignoring their European partners. Then, between March and May 1974, Pompidou died, Brandt and Heath (the one British premier in whom the Continentals recognised a kindred "European" spirit) both fell—Heath because of losing elections in the wake of a major coal-miners' strike. The whole issue had to be raised again with a new trio: Helmut Schmidt, Valéry Giscard d'Estaing and Harold Wilson *redux*.

On September 19, 1974, Monnet put his scheme for regular meetings of heads of EC governments again to the new French president, Giscard. Giscard and his Foreign Minister, Jean Sauvagnargues, seem to have been thinking along similar lines, and Giscard has said that Monnet's arguments finally convinced him to go ahead. Whatever the balance of inspiration, Giscard, at the Paris meeting of heads of government in December, made three proposals. The grandest was to regularise summits as a "European Council".

The others were reversions to devices of the Rome treaties: direct elections to the European Parliament (as the Assembly came increasingly to be called) and majority voting in the Council of Ministers. The aim was to give the EC a new and more political lease of life. In practice, however, the British prevented majority voting from becoming the rule, and the new European Council injected little vitality into the system. The sum of internal changes in the European Community between 1969 and 1974 was, apart from the European Council, to introduce something not very different from the proposals of the Hallstein Commission, which had set off the crisis of 1965. In the event, the impact they made was so modest that it was hard to understand why they had once precipitated such a storm.

The key to the paradox was probably the Gaullist success in marginalising majority voting, which was a symbol of revived state self-assertion, and the switch from boom to recession, slow growth, rising unemployment and what Keynesian theory would have thought impossible in the circumstances, inflation. Nationalism and mercantilism flourished. This left little room for integration and set the tone for fifteen years after de Gaulle left the stage. It gradually became the tone of bankruptcy. As European economic performance, even German, compared more and more poorly with American and above all Japanese, Europessimism spread. In fact, it prepared the ground for the reaction of the mid-1980s when the EC countries were persuaded to make a real effort to achieve the ambitions of the Treaty of Rome. This meant really introducing the joint regulations needed to make the customs union a true single market, which it still was not; and for this purpose reviving majority voting as the treaty had initially intended. The result was a European Community which from 1987 to 1992 worked perhaps for the first time as it was originally designed to do; with a renewed sense of progress, dramatised in 1990 by the contrast with Soviet collapse in Eastern Europe.

In 1975, the Action Committee could look back on twenty years of effort, many of them over arid terrain. The Action Committee's influence, indeed that of Monnet, had gone through several stages. In the first years, from its formation to de Gaulle's return to office, it operated in the environment which had produced the European Communities. Monnet was still treated almost as a quasi-government on issues like Euratom or the European District. But when de Gaulle returned to office, his power of persuasion fell radically in Paris. He still had influence elsewhere, but one of the poles of the field of action was gone. Monnet's principle was that "for action to succeed, the goal must be limited". Before de Gaulle's return, Action Committee resolutions concentrated on one target at a time. Afterwards, each sprayed four or five targets like buckshot.

Because it held the flag of Europe aloft and because of Monnet's networks, the Action Committee remained more than a conventional political lobby. But after de Gaulle's return to power, its main achievements were in declaratory rather than active policy. The chief innovation was the idea of Atlantic partnership, enunciating an aim beyond the tired old alternatives of nationalism or submission to empire. The most important continuity, after de Gaulle's veto on Britain and the empty-chair crisis of 1965, was keeping European integration alive, not least in German policy. It was a political achievement in itself that a German politician as powerful as Herbert Wehner (with whom Monnet and Kohnstamm had a special affinity) wanted the Action Committee to live on. Although the members came from divergent, even opposed, points of the political compass, Wehner saw it as "a circle of friends . . . serving the same cause. . . . Young people had not lived through the crises and tragedies of the past and Jean Monnet's thinking and the work of the Action Committee were a treasure that could not be allowed simply to sink into oblivion".

When de Gaulle went, Monnet still had easy access to heads of government. But postwar establishments had become too deeply embedded for him to have the old impact. Even in the United States, his influence waned. His last significant intervention was in the nuclear non-proliferation negotiations of 1964. It was proposed in the negotiations with the Soviet Union—and without consulting Euratom—that the individual Euratom countries (except the weapons state, France) should be inspected directly by the United Nations IAEA. Monnet managed to prevent the United States agreeing to this and to steer matters towards a negotiation between the IAEA and Euratom as a whole. Despite this success, America's gaze was straying, via Vietnam, from Europe. Also, the American special relationship with Germany in resistance to de Gaulle indirectly devalued European union in Washington by showing that Bonn would stay in line with the United States, in the short-term anyway. Europe itself was stalled. None other than George Ball told "good Europeans", "You complain we are not interested, but what are you doing that is interesting?"

The fact was, Monnet's war-time generation was retiring from the scene. He himself was growing old and frail. By 1975, he was in his eighty-seventh year. His phenomenal mobility and energy had been waning for some years. Even in 1969, he did not respond with vigour to semi-overtures from Pompidou. True, he wrote, "I was concerned with the role of Europe in the world and he was interested in the place of France in the Common Market". Still, Monnet would never have let such chances slip when younger. He realised his mind was not as sharp as it had been. He fell seriously ill in February 1975 with pneumonia and took weeks to recover. On May 9, the twenty-fifth anniversary of the Schuman Plan, he dissolved the Action Committee. He hesitated a long time on whether to hand on the torch or not. He thought of Brandt, but that would not have been acceptable to the Christian Democrats. In the end, there was no last meeting. He simply wrote round to the members.

Monnet now concentrated on his *Memoirs* for two strong reasons. One was that he wanted to convey his message to posterity. Despite this basic urge, his attitudes were such as to make the task almost impossible. He could not write himself and was deeply suspicious of anyone doing it for him, wanting the result to improve on Shakespeare. He did not want to tell his life for its own sake but to leave a political testament. Nor was he interested in sketching pen portraits of contemporaries. He even asked why one could not write "memoirs of the future". Matters were particularly held up by his obstinate refusal to use the word *I*, as being egocentric. (He had to give way.) Composing the book was a labour of angelic patience by one of his longstanding assistants, François Fontaine, who had to start with a pretence of doing it in secret. Monnet acted as if he knew nothing of what was going on so as to deny all responsibility if it suited him. Fontaine managed frequently and remarkably to capture Monnet's tone of voice. But Monnet only decided to go ahead after David Bruce praised an early chapter with great conviction, knowing (whatever else he thought) that nothing would happen until he did.

The second and even stronger reason for the *Memoirs* was that Monnet badly needed the money. After he left Luxembourg and employment, he continued to live in the soberly expensive way to which he and his family were accustomed, but lacked the income. He had been president of the High Authority only for three years, which limited his pension (he had others, including from the CGP, but not enough). The Action Committee was funded in principle by its members, especially the ever supportive German trade unions. In the end, they paid all arrears, but he covered the deficits over long periods and received nothing as chairman. The Ford Foundation, under McCloy, and through one of its most active and clear -sighted officials, Shepherd Stone, once a *New York Times* reporter and head of public affairs in the American High Commission in Germany in McCloy's day, helped fund some of the committee's activities, but not Monnet himself. He would not have had it otherwise. He turned down directorships or soon dropped them. He cherished his financial, and therefore political, independence. But the price was a severe strain on his finances. From the annual accounts which remain, he seems in most years to have spent about twice his income. In 1960, he and his childless cousin Robert began to sell the family's controlling interest in J. G. Monnet & Co. to a French bank which from 1963 onwards sold it to the big German drinks concern Asbach. In 1961, he deposited some $250,000 after paying the claims of the other shareholders, who included his sisters and André Meyer and a large unnamed partner, who may have been his old creditors at Lazards of London. Robert continued to manage the firm till his death in 1971. Then, in 1992, Asbach sold its share to Hennessy and the wheel came full circle. J. G. Monnet & Co. was absorbed by one of the giants it had once been formed to resist, an episode in the steady drive to concentration in the industry.

By the mid-1970s, the transfusion of funds from J. G. Monnet no longer sufficed. Silvia Monnet once remarked: "Jean wanted to sell Houjarray but I refused. It would have gone in restaurant and telephone bills". Thus the fees and royalties of some $150,000 for the book in 1976–78 seem to have provided a lifeline at just the right moment. This did not prevent him from playing the publishers like fish on a line.

To mark Monnet's retirement, the European Council, prompted by Schmidt, proclaimed him (one and only) Honorary Citizen of Europe on April 2, 1976. But Monnet had lived in the mêlée, had no other deep interests and felt the isolation of retirement keenly. "What use are friends one never sees?" He came to question his life's work. Was European union too narrow for a changing world? Had the Common Market really added to growth? Talking to Tuthill, he hoped Europe had "at least secured peace between France and Germany". Tuthill replied that this was enough for any man to have achieved. But even there, one could argue the American presence in Europe had mattered more than a European Community reduced, it seemed, to a customs union. Monnet was not one to repine. His grandchildren gladdened him. Two days before his death from a general physical breakdown, when Kohnstamm said, "They have been marvellous years", he replied, barely able to speak, "Yes, more than one could have hoped". Despite the impending first general elections to the European Parliament, the new dawn of the mid-eighties was still well out of sight.

Jean Monnet died on March 16, 1979, aged ninety years and four months. Four days later, Chancellor Schmidt turned up from Bonn by helicopter and, in a buzz of outriders, joined President Giscard at a crowded funeral in the fifteenth-century church of the nearest country town to Houjarray, Montfort l'Amaury. It was a last tribute from the Germans, who had long paid Monnet special honour. It was also a gathering of the "European" clan from both sides of the Atlantic. McCloy, Ball and other American friends came. At one point, "The Battle Hymn of the Republic" rang through the nave. Giscard wrote later, with a touch of asperity, that a Frenchman almost felt left out.

After a few months, Silvia Monnet repaired to Rome and, though nearly a generation younger than her husband, died there little over three years later. The family house in Houjarray was bought by the European Parliament and turned into a museum. In 1983, Kohnstamm set up a new Action Committee for Europe. From 1985, it worked in alliance with Jacques Delors, the president of the European Commission, in the process leading to the Maastricht treaty of European Union. In 1988, President François Mitterrand, himself in origin a man of the Fourth Republic Monnet had illumined, celebrated the centenary of the latter's birth by transferring his ashes to the crypt of the Pantheon in Paris, a vast echoing sarcophagus of Republican

saints and statesmen.[2] Mitterrand addressed a torch-lit (and flood-lit) ceremony on the broad steps and crescent arena beneath the massive classical
façade. A large orchestra played Beethoven and Messiaen through imperious
loud-speakers. The German president, Richard von Weizsäcker, and chancellor, Helmut Kohl, and other dignitaries from Community member states
attended. (Margaret Thatcher pointedly did not.) Monnet would no doubt
have been flattered and glad for Europe. Personally, he had chosen his rustic
grave to face the sun.

2. Mitterrand would have liked to do the same for Schuman, but his family declined
the offer.

PART II

Legacy

A Citizen among States

K ennedy's remark that Monnet did more to achieve unity in Europe by an idea than all those who tried to impose it by force is true enough. Yet isolated thinkers have had an idea of European unity for centuries. For all the impact they made, they could have spared themselves the trouble. Nearer to the relevant time and to practical politics, the Schuman Plan in 1950 spawned a bunch of imitations, all French. The Minister for Agriculture at the time, the experienced Pierre Pflimlin, tried to launch an agricultural "pool". Another well-known politician, Edouard Bonnefous, got his ministry to produce a vast memorandum on a transport "pool". A third minister, Paul Ribeyre, proposed a health "pool" in 1952. All of these fell at once into the hands of the professional associations and of the governments in the OEEC and disappeared from sight. If the Europe of Jean Monnet represents an idea, it is in part because he dared promote one, which few professionals do, but even more because he had sharper strategic and tactical insights than the competition.

Monnet had a nose for action, and his behavioural intelligence was probably his decisive asset. In the end, the test of leadership is the capacity to bring ideas down to earth. If he had not already been a virtuoso in moving bureaucracies and governments long before he stepped onto a political stage, Monnet's views would have had no more impact on decision-makers than the worthy proselytising of a Coudenhove-Kalergi or a Clarence Streit.[1]

1. Count Richard Coudenhove-Kalergi, whose father was Hungarian and mother Japanese, founded the Pan-European Union in 1923–24. The PEU held congresses and was prominent between the wars. It brought together some famous people, including Aristide Briand and Albert Einstein. But it neither had mass support nor was organised for action. In 1939, a former *New York Times* reporter, Clarence Streit, made an impact with *Union Now,* a book which argued that the League of Nations had failed because it had lacked decisive, federal

His ideas were usually in the air at the time, yet failed to materialise till he came along. The novelty was not the ideas but that he put them into effect. His plans were original because practice was not just their goal, but was, so to speak, in their genes. As a result, they never emerged in quite the form prevalent in the general debate. That was true of the way in which they were designed in the first place. It also applied to the implementing tactics which were normally sharp, in contrast to the routine moves so frequent with other operators, even experienced ones.

While Monnet became that rarity, a statesman, he never grew into a conventional politician. This peculiarity was built into his decision to propose policies to harassed leaders rather than dissipate his energies in the endless fight for power. His choice may have had personal roots, or perhaps cultural ones, given the social background of the France of his youth, long on peasants and artisans and short on factory workers. His memoirs say, "How can one affiliate to a system over which one has no control? . . . To belong, to a [political] party, the very phrase repels me". This smacks of peasant individualism, almost of old-fashioned southern anarchism. It is hard to imagine urbanised Nordic Europeans expressing such sentiments. At the same time, Monnet was clearly also protecting his creative independence. He did not want his gift for innovation occluded by the endless struggle to keep political head above water or by the formal ladder of officialdom.

Even if Monnet's choice was a rationalisation of his lack of talent for, or fear of, the political life, he undoubtedly found a solution well suited to his gifts. In particular, it left him free to concentrate on his own agenda. "What I had undertaken, at every important turning-point in my life, had been the result of one choice and one choice only; and this concentration on a single aim had shielded me from the temptation to disperse my efforts". Monnet, in contrast to most politicians, chose his own objectives, and was not to be distracted. "I have never taken a job I did not myself invent". Jean-François Deniau has rightly emphasised his "ability to select. . . . There is nothing harder in the modern world than to see what is self-evident. It was perhaps one of Monnet's rarest strengths".

If seeing "what is self-evident" means detecting through the endless babble an action which can transform the ground rules for everyone, this was perhaps Monnet's speciality. But, of course, what is "self-evident" is what has emerged from the political maelstrom of competing tomorrows. It is the consecration of success. It needs a keen eye to focus ahead of time on what

---

powers. Late in 1940, when preparing *Union Now with Britain,* published in 1941, he had exchanges with John Foster Dulles and, through Dulles, with Monnet on a scheme of his devising for a Union of Democracies (to start with the USA and those of the British Commonwealth, but looking forward to subsequent European and Latin American adherents). Monnet thought the public should be educated in the general approach first and that to publish specific proposals at such an early stage would be a "mistake".

will be crucial and possible. Monnet considered he had the required antennae. Take the moment when proposals for the Victory Program, in which he had played a big part, reached Roosevelt:

> On the basis of what I had told him, Beaverbrook produced figures which to the American experts seemed fantastic: . . . Only Roosevelt listened to those requests without demur. . . . "It's not a matter of what we *can* do, but of what we *must* do", he replied. I recognized in his attitudes and decisions that same philosophy of action that I myself had acquired. . . . [T]his philosophy, which concentrates on what is necessary, is more realistic than one which takes account only of what is possible.

This is always the reformer's cry. But there have been hecatombs of "necessities" which proved unrealistic. The art is in detecting those which might be viable and then in making them so.

Originality in a collective activity like politics is unlike that in individual arts, where the composer is more or less dictator of his material. To have a truly original idea is a waste of time for an active politician, because there will be no constituency for it. The first quality for political originality consists in having a nose for an idea marginalised in the current ethos and round which nevertheless a coalition can be built to carry the day. It is not the idea that matters so much as the way it is tailored to mobilise the potential support.

To recognise a relevant issue and opportunity demands a sense of timing. The right idea at the wrong moment cannot be concrete. "Events that strike me and occupy my thoughts lead me to general conclusions about what has to be done. Then circumstances, which determine day-to-day events, suggest or supply the means of action. I can wait a long time for the right moment. In Cognac, they are good at waiting. It is the only way to make good brandy". Monnet had a version of the Schuman Plan in mind as early as 1941, but put it aside for nine years until France's German policy was about to collapse.

For Monnet, a crisis was an opportunity. In a crisis, ministers, who are far too busy to act unless forced to do so, face choices which are as unpleasant if they fail to act as if they do. They are temporarily open to, even eager for, advice. "When ideas are lacking, they accept yours with gratitude—provided they can present them as their own".

Monnet rarely had difficulty in envisaging a step which, in complex situations, might change the flow of action. He once said, without undue self-deprecation, "In crises most people do not know what to do. I do know". This attitude had the signal advantage, over generalised propaganda for "Europe", of being geared to life as politicians lead it. He promoted ideas through specific solutions to specific problems. He showed no interest in the

Council of Europe, which promoted European union as a good in itself. On the contrary, the Monnet Plan was precipitated by the end of Lend-Lease, the European Army by German rearmament, and so forth. Euratom, which failed, was not tied to a generally felt need of this kind.

In later years, Monnet's knack of producing relevant schemes could be explained by his being near the seats of power. But he was nowhere near them in 1914 and at the stripling age of twenty-five, when he conceived the notion, outlandish at the time, that the British and French should organise their war effort in common. He displayed a brand of imagination then in which ideas came to him intuitively—raw talent.

This capacity to detect a ford across the rush of current affairs required him to stand well back from the flood of trivia which overwhelms ministers. Monnet had a regimen to protect his privacy. He took no part in the cocktail round of politics, and he shunned conferences. He paid great attention to his health. People laughed at his hypochondria and his sesame seeds, his press-ups in the garden at sixty-nine, but it was part of keeping a balanced detachment. Much of his working life was taken up in long, often solitary walks. The habit started before 1914 in the Rocky Mountains and became systematic in Rock Creek Park in war-time Washington. In Houjarray, he would stump off early every morning, nosing through the woods around his house, walking sometimes as much as fifteen kilometres (nine miles); and turn up rather late at the office, electrically charged with priorities and ideas which fell like hail on subordinates' desks. Whenever he was brooding on a major move, he vanished into the Alps. The idea that emerged from such self-communings was nearly always more of a focus for action than technical or detailed. When he went to see Viviani in 1914, "I had no proposals, properly speaking, but a conviction to express which must, if accepted, result in action". The initial Schuman Plan was a lump of rock to work on, not a finished statue.

If choosing the stone was a lonely business, the next step, carving it into shape, was social. Monnet's proposals were hammered out in intense debate with his office family. In Kohnstamm's words, "You put your head through the door, you were called in, and you were kept there for the rest of the day". Anyone with something to offer might abruptly be added to the group. The Schuman Plan and Euratom, respectively, began with men with whom Monnet had in one case only casual acquaintance (Reuter) and in the other (Isenbergh) none at all.

Monnet had a confidence in dealing with experts which was quite exceptional in a virtual autodidact. He made no effort to appear clever and never talked down to anyone, but sooner or later would be quietly laying down the law. Like many who enjoy the aristocracy of their gift, he was indifferent to diplomas, age or rank. In youth, he said, he could never bring himself to utter the compulsorily deferential "monsieur le Président". His respect went simply to anyone who interested him or might be useful to his constant process of prospection.

Once in Monnet's circle, nationality—French, American, less often Dutch, British, German, Belgian or Italian—was irrelevant. An American, Stanley Cleveland, one of the talents in the Marshall aid mission to France, has left the most graphic picture of Monnet hammering out a scheme. Monnet

never wrote anything in his life, as far as I know; he developed the ideas and let other people write them up for him.[2] But whenever Monnet attacked a new problem he would gather a bunch of people around him. Some of them would be his intimates—Hirsch, Uri—people who were close to him, Tommy [Tomlinson] when he was alive, and others. Some would be people he hardly knew but had somehow laid his hands on. They knew a lot about the particular subject. He would begin a sort of non-stop *Kaffeeklatsch*. It could go on sometimes for a period of one or two weeks—hours and hours a day. It generally started out with a rambling discussion of the subject in which relevant facts would be brought out. People would begin to argue (these were a very argumentative bunch). Gradually two or three approaches and positions would develop in the group. Monnet would remain silent, occasionally provoking reaction, but not saying much. . . . Then gradually, as the conversation developed—and it often took several days or even a week before this happened—he began venturing a little statement of his own. Usually it was a very simple statement, just a few words, almost a slogan. It distilled, out of all this argument among highly verbal, brilliant people, a couple of kernels of an idea. These he would throw into the conversation. Then people would react to him. Gradually, Monnet would begin to expose a little more in a few sentences, then in a couple of paragraphs. The process then was that people in the group who had been arguing against each other would all turn against him. They would argue with him, indicating all the things that were wrong about what he was saying. Monnet would listen, reformulate his ideas—taking into account what somebody had said, refusing to heed what somebody else had said. . . . At this point, he would begin to come out with a formulated concept, an idea. It was usually action-oriented and contained all of the necessary elements. Then he would go through what was, in some ways, the most excruciating part of the process. Yet it was the ultimate refinement. Monnet would go on saying the same thing, over and over again, in practically the same words, occasionally modifying a detail

---

2. A very slight exaggeration. Monnet wrote rarely, and even rarer was a finished draft from his hand. One of his collaborators just before the war, Jean-Louis Mandereau, says that in particular, Monnet at this time "had real difficulties in writing French".

to take account of a legitimate criticism. People would still argue with him but . . . the arguments would die out because he would have taken into account all of the legitimate arguments. . . . In the end, there was . . . in Monnet's head, and ready to put on paper, a perfectly formulated idea.

Cleveland's account will ring true to anyone who helped prepare the versions—six to twelve, sometimes thirty—of a Monnet memorandum, speech, declaration, proposal, note for another politician's use or even modest letter. In each case, Monnet was trying to distill what Ball has called "the vivid aphoristic summation he habitually sought". The aim, as Uri put it, was "to simplify not the problems but the solutions". The resulting pseudo-simplicities had many uses.

One was to convince Monnet himself, the better to convince everyone else. Bowie thinks that "he was trying to be absolutely confident . . . first, that he had really identified the right point of entry, the right place to put people together; and second, to be sure . . . he would be convincing in getting Adenauer, and so on, to see it through his eyes. . . . [His] persuasiveness was based on the fact that he believed . . . he had seen more clearly into the situation and into the potentialities, and was therefore able to help the leaders, who did have power, to see both his conception and why it fitted into their purposes". Monnet would have felt vindicated by a remark in one of Frankfurter's letters after a dinner with him: "What an expositor Jean is. . . . He goes to the essentials in problems".

Another use of simplicity was to forestall the criticism that must arise when a scheme was held up to public gaze. Once an idea had been streamlined, simple though it might seem, it had been through the wind tunnel and was designed to resist friction. The Monnet Plan seemed simple enough, but long ago, Henry Ehrmann made the point that Monnet and his collaborators sought "a flexible institutional setting to which neither 'liberals' nor 'interventionists' could easily object". Ehrmann added a footnote which showed this was no accident. "The same point", it read, "has been made in regard to M. Monnet's latest creation, the Schuman Plan, by Horst Mendershausen". The Schuman Plan was "interventionist" by the very fact of being sectoral, but a single market in place of many was "liberal"; the crisis powers of the High Authority to deal with "lack of sales" and "penury" were "interventionist", but the anti-cartel provisions were "liberal"; prices were fixed by zones, which smacked of cartels, but had to be published, which was "liberal"; and so on. Quite often, these were paradoxes in terms of the shibboleths of the day. They are one measure of the care taken to circumvent rehearsed responses. The same was true of the political aspects of the plans. Each of them drew support from the most unlikely fellow travellers, from Americans to Communists in the case of the Monnet Plan. The ability of both Monnet and Schuman plans to stand in high relief and yet be many things to many groups had much to do with their being implemented.

Simplicity was needed in order to address all of Monnet's audiences in the same way. Misunderstanding could be a potent weapon in the hands of opponents. John Leddy, a trade policy-maker in the State Department who was Dillon's main adviser in launching the OECD, has noted that

> he kept all his presentations clear of complications. It's like a piece of music, a repetitive theme. . . . He did not care about the minor detail, so long as the central theme was there.

Of Montagu Norman, the interwar governor of the Bank of England, Monnet said: "What he failed to understand was the power of simple ideas explained plainly and unvaryingly, over and over again". In the same vein, he stressed to David Lilienthal the "power of an idea" if "concretized . . . made real, specific, with content". He often said, "If it's worth saying once, it's worth saying a thousand times". He relished his grandmother's nickname of "Marie la Rabacheuse", or "Monotonous Mary".

The same principle covered Monnet's relations with the media, especially the press, his main channel for broadcasting his views. His relations with journalists would warrant a study in themselves. He was very succesful, though the means were not showy. As Leonard Tennyson, the head of the Washington Information Service of the Communities, has said, "The press found in Monnet someone whom they felt they could trust and rely upon. It's that simple and uncomplicated". He was seen by many journalists, especially Americans, as a source of innovation and optimism from a continent where attitudes were often depressing. The early Cold War was an age of anxiety. Monnet was a shining exception. It was rarely that he felt a journalist had traduced what he had been at pains to simplify. The American and British media in particular tended to see the European Community through his eyes.

The relationship was unaffected rather than Machiavellian. Monnet respected good journalists as vital sources of information and political weather-gauges. In the early 1950s, the one world-class French daily, *Le Monde,* was vaguely neutralist and became strongly anti-EDC, and so a thorn in Monnet's flesh. He nevertheless remained a close friend of its editor and moving spirit, Hubert Beuve-Méry, and helped save it from takeover. He believed, simply, that France needed a serious paper with integrity. That Monnet cumulatively obtained the kind of press politicians dream of was largely a tribute to the service he provided. He enjoyed publicity, especially good photographs of himself.[3] At the same time, *exegi monumentum* was his

---

3. He had to be caught unawares, though. He would be full of life, then he would catch sight of the camera and freeze as in a Victorian family group. He had no idea of acting informally when on show.

wager with fame, and he was content to rest his reputation on his works. The publicity was for them. If the monument was solid, it would provide pedestal enough for him.

It followed that simplicity was a way of imposing categories on the collective debate. As early as the negotiations on the Schuman Plan and the early days of the High Authority, Monnet's terms tended to be taken up and become common currency, not only with those in close contact with him. Phrases like "non-discrimination", notions such as the importance of institutions, or that Britain will "accept facts", not arguments, became categories in which many thought and moved.

Finally, simplicity was an instrument for building trust. It helped Monnet to address all audiences in virtually the same language. This was prudent in a multinational adventure. René Pleven, twice Prime Minister of the Fourth Republic, has stressed that Monnet

> never went and told X something different from what he said to Y. He . . . never used against people what they had said to him. That is how he gained the confidence of . . . [politicians] who are on the whole mistrustful, devious, inclined to intrigue and keenly alive to having enemies.

More striking still, as it comes from an opponent, is Couve de Murville's

> Monnet . . . never tried to deceive people. . . . [H]e used the same arguments with everyone, Frenchmen and foreigners alike.

Monnet was proud of German trade union leaders telling him they accepted his lead because he "did what he said and said what he did". Mollet, on Emile Noël's account, had a similar view, judging Monnet "disinterested . . . reliable, steady in his views . . . clear and precise". Monnet thought he had learned in China the absolute necessity of making one's actions coincide, and be seen to coincide, with one's words. There is little doubt that over the years Monnet established a moral authority over a wide range of people who themselves had substantial responsibilities. The one-off accusation of nationalist ulterior motives from the Belgian Socialist leader, Max Buset (p. 311), came as a shock because it was so unusual.

Simplicity came at a price. Schuman, in 1950, thought Monnet's approach to the Schuman Plan rather "simplistic". According to Teissier du Cros, Armand fell in with Monnet on Euratom "despite his misgivings about the slightly superficial side of Monnet's thinking". Marjolin, in contrast and despite reservations, acknowledged a debt:

> For ten years . . . I had tried to embrace all the social sciences and found it difficult to ignore the complexities of things. . . . But I rapidly learned

that Monnet was right and that to succeed it is vital to simplify. I have often noticed that in a conversation where one is trying to convince someone of something, it is necessary to harp on a simple, apparently self-evident, idea and blot out the complications which would inevitably invade the exchange if the door were not kept tightly shut on them.

Monnet was more the political entrepreneur than were some of the critics. Armand, a huge success at the head of the French Railways, failed when he had to launch Euratom. As the brilliant Panzer commander Heinz Guderian said of a colleague: "He was a clever man. . . . He could recognize problems but could not find the point of departure from which to set about solving them". Monnet was a virtuoso precisely at finding such points of departure. He went late in life to the Vatican, and returned saying, "Those people have no idea how to engage an action"—not, as Van Helmont has stressed, action in general, but *an* action in particular.

Once the idea had been polished, it had to be sold. Monnet, who was weak in large meetings, had an acute talent for carrying conviction in small groups or in a conversation with one or a few people. Salter said of him, "He can't write, he can't read, he can't speak, but he always persuades".

Stories used to circulate. Werner von Simson, a lawyer who represented the German coal and steel firms in negotiations with the High Authority, has told an anecdote about a director of one of the largest of these, who went in to lecture Monnet "in rather forceful terms" on everything wrong with the ECSC. At the end of half an hour, he emerged "thrilled. Yes, he agreed, he was the man to fight side-by-side with Monnet for a greater and more enlightened Europe". Matters were not always that simple. But some thought, half-jokingly, they detected a whiff of hypnosis. Possibly it was a mixture of the "power of the imagination" Kohnstamm has stressed in Monnet and of the discipline that came of the latter's obsessive efforts to synthesise and simplify, to impart vision while being practical. For Marjolin, "he was a man who believed in ideas and in whom ideas did acquire great force". Wellenstein has suggested why: Monnet had a "sense, even in a very complex situation, for identifying an opportunity to make things move forward . . . to show a direction . . . in extremely simple, even simplified terms. . . . Very often . . . the situation was much more complex. But it mobilised people out of the confusion into a new clarity of thought". Whatever the explanation, this vital link in the chain should not be passed over simply because it is intangible.

This gift largely took the place of what from a distance tends to look like a bent for intrigue. True, Monnet did sometimes give rein to a "mania for secrecy". Those who knew him well were amused by his offices with two doors, the first to let a person in, the second to bundle another out. He could be conspiratorial and hush-hush in an amateurish way. Monnet's conversations when he thought that his telephone was being tapped by the Gaullist government were hilarious and in the end more explicit than if he had simply made his point. Yet basically the web, if there was one, was imposed by the situation. As Sir Ian Jacob has written, Monnet

> knows what he thinks should be done, and his ideas are usually correct and far in advance of those of other people. But he has to rely on other people to push them through. This leads him into a maze of telephoning, lobbying, interviewing and indirect pressure which is not always successful, and makes slower and more direct people regard his activities with suspicion. Not being in an executive position prevents him acting otherwise.

When allowance is made for this predicament, Monnet went about mobilising support for his schemes in the simplest possible manner.

His approach was based on gaining and maintaining direct access to the source of power. He went straight to the place where what he wanted could be obtained, and walked in. The only mystery was his success in by-passing channels. The pattern seems to have been established from the first in 1914 in his approach to the French Prime Minister, Viviani. In essence, he did the same with de Gaulle on the Monnet Plan, with Bidault and then Schuman on the Schuman Plan, with Spaak on the *relance de Messine,* with Mollet on the Wise Men's operation for Euratom, and so on. He always stuck close to the key man. There was Clémentel in the first war, T.V. Soong in China, Daladier in the phoney war, McCloy and Hopkins in war-time Washington, Giraud in Algiers, successive prime ministers at the Monnet Plan, and so forth. He was able to gain, and retain, a hearing for the most basic of reasons: he had something to say and services to offer.

Monnet worked through very few contacts at a time, a small circle nearly always at the highest level. That did not necessarily mean the obvious people. For instance, in the Netherlands in the 1960s, his main contact was C. P. M. Romme. At the time, Romme was more or less pope, if one may put it that way, of the Roman Catholic Party, which had (and has) been in every Dutch governing coalition since the war. Romme was not in office himself but indispensable to the party indispensable to government. In some ways, the extreme instance of Monnet's influence was to be found in the United States of the Eisenhower-Dulles period. As Ernst van der Beugel, the Dutch Vice Minister for Foreign Affairs during the Common Market talks, has written,

> There was a very thin line of communication . . . which ran either from Monnet through the Paris embassy or the United States Representatives in Brussels and Luxembourg through one or two officials in Washington,

directly to Dillon [Under Secretary of State] or [Dulles] and through them to [Eisenhower], or it originated in the State Department—mainly in the Policy Planning division [Bowie]—and followed the same direct and short road. Under the Kennedy and Johnson Administrations, Under Secretary George Ball served as a direct link between Monnet and the top of the American Administration. . . . If Monnet thought a particular country made difficulties in the [Rome treaty] negotiations, the American diplomatic representative in that country approached the Foreign Ministry in order to communicate the opinion of the American Government which, in practically all cases, coincided with Monnet's point of view.

Over the years, Monnet built up tentacular networks of individuals, powerful and not-so-powerful, on whom he could almost invariably call as occasion demanded. In the United States, the list of trusties was particularly long. Only a few were used at any one time. George Ball, like many others, has noted that when Monnet needed him, he would ring up three times a day and that months would pass without a word when he did not. It was rarely resented. It was part of the rhythm of work. Monnet always valued and respected anyone who had ever been useful to him, and relations, though often hugely elastic, almost never broke.

Yet the striking point about Monnet's dealings with the great was how circumspect they were. His technique was to offer a service and in general try to make the politicians feel they needed him more than he did them. The essence of the service to be rendered was, of course, to propose and carry out policies because, as an acerbic passage in the *Memoirs* remarks, "Men in power are short of new ideas; they lack the time and the information; and they want to do the right thing so long as they get the credit". Monnet was at pains to avoid any appearance of competing for jobs or glory. This paid off. Rothschild has pointed out that Spaak was never wary of Monnet, because he was "not a rival anywhere. That was one of Monnet's great strengths. He never tried to take other peoples' jobs". He abstained from, and was even impatient of, the gossip that seems a substitute for a bloodstream in politics. Thinking ill of others detracted from the job in hand. This was discipline, not innate goodness, as the odd tart comment would betray at very long intervals indeed.

Monnet liked to quote a remark of Dwight Morrow's that "there are two kinds of people—those who want to be someone, and those who want to do something".[4] In this spirit, he often conditioned the great by working

4. For reasons that will appear below, it is possible that this maxim is as much Monnet as Morrow. Harold Nicolson's biography of Morrow quotes a letter of Morrow to Monnet in December 1925 which says something slightly different: "I fear that I am in danger of getting out of the class of which my son considers you one of the most conspicuous members—that small group which tries to get things done for which other people get the credit".

through their subordinates. As a man of discreet power, he had a nose for others in similar situations. He was adept at locating unknowns behind the government façade, irrespective of their age, status or experience, who exercised influence over crucial holders of power, provided a route to them, or simply conveyed important information. He had no snobbery. A useful contact would be cultivated as carefully as a prime minister or president, and with the same respect. Although in his last three decades he could walk through the door of virtually any head of Western government more or less when he wished, most of the time he preferred to lay indirect siege to the men of power and not to overtax his welcome.

Everyone who experienced these blandishments comments on them. At the simplest level, it was a matter of picking up information. As Berndt von Staden, later Germany's ambassador to Washington, has observed:

> Monnet was able to make a distinction between people of influence, and people who were well-informed. If it came to information, he did not hesitate a moment to call a very junior man and question him.

Sir Michael Palliser, in Harold Wilson's private office at 10 Downing Street in the late 1960s, and Rothschild, with Spaak, had much the same experience. It applied to others, such as Léo Tindemans (later Belgian Foreign Minister and Prime Minister) in the early sixties when he was on Prime Minister Lefèvre's staff, or Katherina Focke in the Chancellery when Willy Brandt was chancellor. There is a long roll-call of workers in the vineyards of the great enlisted by Monnet—Clappier with Schuman, Delouvrier with Mayer, Noël with Mollet, and many more.

The method could only work if the great man was well disposed. Monnet achieved wonders for the Victory Program because, in the last resort Roosevelt, "artfully" hesitant as he was, always overruled the opposition. In 1944, he got nowhere on the recognition of de Gaulle's French National Committee, despite the backing of virtually the whole establishment, because Roosevelt was hostile. When, however, the great man acquiesced, the subordinates were as productive as he could be. They provided continuity of presence and attention. They could be roped in to help Monnet prepare plans in full knowledge of the great man's views. Before seeing Kennedy in 1961, he told Henry Owen, then Director of Policy Planning at the State Department, "You're talking of what interests me. What I want to know is what interests him". They made it easier not to see the Great Personage too often and exhaust good will. Their knowledge could ensure optimal timing for initiatives. They were close associates, substantial players.

This approach may well have been influenced by Monnet's encounter with war-time Washington. His memoirs speak of the inner circle round Roosevelt in admiring terms.

This was a quite informal group, united by mutual trust. . . . Problems
of prestige had no place. . . . Frankfurter, like the others, was completely
disinterested. He was not seeking any political position, and those people
who had taken official jobs, like Stimson, McCloy, Harriman and Dean
Acheson, saw themselves as on active service on behalf of the United
States. Their true career was in the service of law . . . members of that
characteristically American profession, in which ability and technical skill
are carried to the highest degree that I have ever seen. . . . No one who
was not disinterested, in fact, would have given up his lucrative practice
and answered the President's call as these men did.

In fact, these are terms which, with very little change, might be, and have
been, applied to him by those close to him in action. The ring is familiar.

Of course, Monnet's networks were an "elitist" phenomenon. It is hard to
see how a more "popular" approach would have worked. The populist tactic
had been tried in the Council of Europe. The result had been virtually nil.
The situation was not revolutionary, and voters were neither a motor nor a
brake. "Europe" enjoyed, as Ehrmann wrote of France, "a general though
not very alert sympathy in public opinion". Integration was rarely, if ever,
the top political priority. There was always some issue, often evanescent,
nearer home. The only feasible strategy was to work on governments from
within, or through party leaders. Party leaders were particularly valuable,
sometimes decisive, allies. For the rest, establishments tended to be where
the opposition hid, in the bureaucracy and industrial lobbies. All this necessarily meant going over the sappers' heads to the leaders. With them, personal networks were the key to effective action.

At this stage, preparations crossed the dividing line into action and Monnet changed gear. Marjolin has pointed out that

> his life consisted of two different phases, one in which he struck the nail
> on the head again and again to drive it home and the other when, laying
> down his hammer, he was open to criticism and the thought that perhaps
> the procedure he had chosen might not be the right one.

This may explain why outsiders sometimes thought him peremptory and
little inclined to views not his own, while close associates thought of him as
more open to argument than most. Joxe wrote that he stood out among his
talkative compatriots in Algiers because "he listened". Léon Kaplan, with a
little more nuance, said that "he listened—not to everyone and not all of the
time—but he listened". One of the lessons Uri learned from Monnet was to
ask at every step, "Where is the snag?", a phrase Monnet used in English.
There is no neat equivalent in French.

The balance in all this may be found in the distinction between strategy and tactics, though tactics in this context can take on broad connotations. Where Monnet sensed basic opposition, he sought almost military means to contain, outflank, or overrun it. The function of the shock tactics used to launch the so-called New Deal in Algiers in 1943 and the Schuman Plan in 1950 was plainly to catch the opposition off balance, before it could mobilise. The emphasis on the role of labour in the Monnet Plan was in part to isolate the employers, seen as the vested interests among whom the main dangers lay. The insistence on making the supranational principle the condition of taking part in the Schuman Plan talks was to block from the start any possible sapping tactics by the British. Monnet, in launching a proposal, was never trapped, like Pflimlin, Bonnefous and others, into letting the profession negotiate for him, or allowed himself to become dependent on governments hostile to his purposes.

While, in the Schuman Plan, Monnet was adamant that the British must accept the basic supranational principle, with the Dutch, who had agreed to negotiate on that basis, even provisionally, he was flexible. J. van den Brink, the Dutch Minister for Economic Affairs, noted, "You had the feeling he understands our problem and is willing to look together if there is a solution to be found". In general, Monnet was open to discussion. One must not exaggerate this. Unorthodoxy on basics was not particularly popular. But given agreement on the broad direction, there was great freedom to express views and argue back. Monnet was not frightened of debate. In fact, he felt very uneasy without it. He was also not a man to let vanity stand in the way of substance. Hirsch remembers that when he first put Philip's idea of a parliamentary assembly for the Schuman Plan, Monnet pooh-poohed it. Two or three days later, he came back—"What about that idea of yours on an assembly? It's a good idea"—and it entered the Schuman declaration. There was no such thing, in his entourage, as a patent on an idea, or of complaint if a "good" one were unceremoniously dumped.

Informality was essential to this dialectical approach.

> Monnet had a tiny dining room installed under the eaves (at the Monnet Plan office), with an adjoining kitchen. . . . The meals were of a Spartan simplicity, but there was Monnet's "Anniversary" cognac, Havana cigars and Cantal cheese fom the cook's contacts. . . . If the negotiations on the Schuman Plan unfolded without major trouble and engendered a sense of complicity between all the participants, the credit must go in large part to that dining-room. An invitation to lunch had a higher rating than one to the Tour d'Argent

—or so Hirsch has claimed. The only parallel to Monnet's success in giving cohesion to the Schuman talks was when Spaak, a little later, gave much the same sense of creative purpose to the delegates negotiating the Treaties of Rome. In both cases, it was not for lack of clashes of interest between the participants. It was because the chairman managed to convince the participants of his leadership in a common cause.

The sense of common cause lived on and broadened after the Schuman conference. Sufficient numbers of those who negotiated the Schuman treaty went on to the High Authority and then to the Common Market and Euratom to create a community of Europeans. Strong bonds were woven between people across frontiers, secure channels for rapid communication, and in time of need means for the decisive pulling of strings. It helps to explain how the Treaties of Rome were possible so soon after the traumatic rejection of the EDC and why the British Free Trade Area proposals a little later made so little impression on the founding states of the European Community.

While Monnet could be imperious, most of the time he was above all untiring. Hirsch, and more surprisingly de Gaulle's chief of staff, Gaston Palewski, have both praised his "determination to achieve results". He himself stressed "the final effort, the one that carries the decision". Von Staden has stressed his exceptional mobility until he was well into his eighties. "He had to move about", Van Helmont says. This was true on the large scale and the small. He wrote as if surprised in 1948 that "I had not during all my life excepting my younger days stayed as long a time in France as I did during the last two years". And from day to day he would travel anywhere at the drop of a hat to advance a point. He was also ready to work at most hours of night or day. "I have never sat down to discuss anything without having a draft before me. . . . Generally, people come to the table empty-handed, out of either circumspection or sloth. In their hearts, they are pleased to find that a paper has been produced overnight. To produce it means staying up late". These are not matters of detail, he wrote. It was not quite as rational as he made out. He behaved in exactly the same way to make sure his luggage had been placed in the boot of the car.

Partners, from McCloy to Adenauer and Schuman and many others, commented again and again on Monnet's persistence. Adenauer once said of him that "he concealed beneath a benign exterior an invincible obstinacy". One French diplomat remarked, half in jest, that he suffered from "obsessional psychosis". As Rothschild sees it, Monnet was

> one of those rare men who want something very very strongly, not for personal gain, but for an idea, and are ready to spend enormous effort and energy to attain it. . . . He seemed a man possessed.

Felix Frankfurter, comparing Monnet and Chaim Weizmann, said they both had "blinders on".

For the things that [Monnet is] interested in he doesn't dissipate his energies, or doesn't take time off, or doesn't listen to anything else. They are very much alike, powerful wills. . . . That's the difference between statesmen who matter and statesmen who don't—resolution, pertinacity, patience and persistence, and in Weizmann, as in Jean Monnet, the central quality that I call resolution, will, was manifested in an extreme intensity.

One of Monnet's favourite stories celebrated endurance. He had read it in Jacques Benoist-Méchin's biography of Ibn Saud and repeated it to all and sundry. "A Western visitor asked Ibn Saud the secret of his success. Ibn Saud replied, 'God appeared to me in the desert when I was a young man and said something which has guided my actions throughout my life: He told me: "For me, everything is a means—even the obstacles" '."

Monnet's optimism was notorious. Recalling him trying to sell the EDC, Acheson wrote, "Sometimes it seemed to me that Monnet forgot . . . Justice Holmes's admonition that certainty is not the test of certitude". Monnet defended himself: he was "not optimistic, only determined". As George Ball put it, "optimism to Jean Monnet is the only serviceable hypothesis for a practical man or woman with a passionate desire to get things done". At heart, Monnet was not such an optimist. He came from too old a culture for that. Sometimes, when he was weary in his later years, his face carried the burden of the ages. Basically, he seemed a stoic, pre-stressed to take enormous strain. Optimism was his prophylactic.

II
ENDS AND MEANS

The key to Monnet's approach was creative individualism. A man who went for regular walks in the countryside or the Alps, looking for inspiration in nature, that is, in his own; who paid compulsive attention to every detail that could advance his cause of the moment and ignored everything else; who displayed anxiously tireless tenacity in handling the resistant matter he was operating on, but grew bored and restless at once with the routines he covertly despised; who always protected his privacy and independence, subordinating all other activities successfully to his own; and who sought fulfilment not directly in status but through the work he was laboriously constructing ("doing", not "being")—this man was patently not a politician or bureaucrat in any normal sense, but obsessed with the creative act, like a researcher, an inventor or an artist.

In old age, Monnet denied he was a lone wolf. "On his own, a man can achieve nothing. I have never been alone, contrary to what people may think". He cherished the memory of some sycophant expatiating at a dinner on Churchill's having saved Britain in the war till Churchill erupted, "You bloody fool! Without the Conservative Party, I couldn't have done a damn thing". For all that, Monnet never enjoyed firm institutional support. As Bowie has said, "He never really had any political base. The only thing he had was persuasiveness". The one time he was a member of a cabinet, it was a self-selecting provisional administration, the Committee of National Liberation in Algiers. The High Authority of which he was president was so much outside the traditional state circuits that when he resigned from it he never regained, never even sought, an official post at home.

With the exception of his years at the High Authority, Monnet in effect always behaved as a one-man consultant to governments. He worked with a small family of advisers, to whom he was attached, and this family changed only gradually as individuals moved in and out. Usually, those who did move out remained country members of the club for the rest of life. Institutions for which he was responsible operated around him as disguised private secretariats. It was not possible to behave in quite this way at the High Authority, and the complaints which arose about his administrative methods came directly from the fact that he tried to do so. Tactical shifts that seemed required—and they were frequent, often abrupt and sometimes acute—had to be followed by the whole institution, down to the exhausted translators struggling through the early hours. He was quick to say that "there could be no progress without a certain disorder, or at least without disorder on the surface".

With priorities such as these, he rarely observed formal disciplines. An anecdote told by one of his war-time collaborators, Jean-Louis Mandereau, is characteristic.

Every one of Monnet's flights [from Paris to Washington towards the end of the war] raised difficulties which he majestically ignored. "I shall leave tomorrow. Get me a seat on the first flight to Washington". All flights were controlled by the American military. Monnet told me to ring Eisenhower's chief of staff, [Walter] Bedell Smith himself. The reservation was provided without delay. The same night Monnet would ring me. "I can't leave tomorrow. I'm too busy. Get me a seat for the day after tomorrow", and I would. When the postponements multiplied from day to day, matters became a little more difficult. But Monnet's prestige with the Americans was such that finally Bedell Smith's assistant, though somewhat irritated, said, "Tell M. Monnet not to bother to reserve. If necessary, we will dislodge a colonel, a general or an admiral . . . but he can go when he wants", and that was that.

In such respects, Monnet was ruthless. His justification, as he told Kohnstamm and the Belgian-American journalist André Visson, on one occasion, was that "creating things and renewing things are not administering things. [They] are very difficult, tiring and energy-consuming tasks, which make it necessary to look at every detail".

Individualism made Monnet an outsider in the ordered hierarchies of government. For such a man, relatively open political systems offered the best chance of wielding influence. The dishevelled French Fourth Republic was one. Coalition governments, the norm of the regime, involved complex party political networks through which a determined individual could always exert pressure on a minister who was otherwise unimpressed. The United States was even more open. Monnet's unique success as a foreigner in America was a tribute to his gifts, but owed at least as much to the opportunities that always exist in the interstices of decision-making in Washington.

Even there, such influence would have been virtually unthinkable without the Second World War. A foreigner in peace-time Washington could not have hoped to gain the standing Monnet acquired—as a British civil servant, another extraordinary war-time feature—through the Victory Program and the Combined Boards. Equally, in France, without the war, Monnet could never have accumulated the unique influence he exerted from the Monnet Plan office. In normal times, there is no civil service more impervious to lateral entry than the French. For a short while, the discrediting of former cadres, the upheaval in generations and outlooks, all the fluidity resulting from defeat, occupation and resistance, made the French administration as soft as a hermit crab that has cast its shell. The carapace soon hardened as administrative empires like the CEA asserted themselves, even before de Gaulle's return to power. After that, there was little place for an outsider, however talented.

An easy entrée into government is not normally available anywhere in Europe, where the state tradition is far older and tighter than in the United States. This was masked to the extent that a man, as influential as Monnet was in Washington, could open many doors with American help. Adenauer, the Dutch and in the last resort the British, were always open to American blandishments. The resistance to European integration in the Netherlands and Britain looked to the American connection—free trade and NATO—as the alternatives to Community commitments. If Washington failed to endorse, or even discreetly hindered, such resistance, there was nowhere for the opposition to go. American indifference to the Free Trade Area and hints of scepticism about the "special relationship" more or less forced Britain into the arms of the Common Market in 1961.

Still, there were at least two situations where an outsider like Monnet was parlously weak. The first was where his strategies came up against domestic patronage. That was demonstrated by the Luxembourgeois and the Belgians on the European District. The second case was in dealing with closed hierarchical systems with uncommitted or hostile leadership. The example which leaps to mind is the elective monarchy of the Fifth Republic under de Gaulle. But it was just as difficult in the "normal" case of Britain. Despite influential contacts, Monnet had little or no direct impact on British policy to Europe. He more than made up indirectly. Going ahead with the Community (his decision) and the Common Market (which was not) finally forced Britain to enter the game. But this was not achieved by the kind of private influence which was supposed to be the hallmark of Monnet the international *éminence grise*.

At the centre of his far-flung networks, Monnet cut a redoubtable figure almost to the end. After de Gaulle vetoed British entry into the Common Market in 1963, his Foreign Minister, Maurice Couve de Murville, frequently lunched with Monnet. Couve's job was to forestall the impact on foreign governments of outright opposition by Monnet to de Gaulle's policies. It was one of the sincerer forms of flattery. But for all his reputation as a mysterious mover of many governments, Monnet clearly reached his maximum influence in the years when he could sway his own national government of France. His international circuits greatly amplified his ability to achieve results when the basic French condition was met. They were not a total substitute when it failed.

Monnet's individualism was as marked in his goals as it was in his methods. His civilian approach was much closer to the outlook of the citizen than that of the servant of the state, bureaucrat or otherwise. It was the psychology of the private contract, with its assumption that all the parties will benefit. It was the language of business, but also of community and civil politics, the reverse of the social Darwinism of states. His insistence on treating as a source of wisdom what he had just been told by the postman, the labourer or the hotel doorman had a touch of coquetry about it, but also arose from a feeling that the final yardstick was the "individual", whom he appears to have associated with the upright citizen of Cognac. "We are uniting people, not forming coalitions of states". He defined the word *power,* without glorifying overtones, only as the capacity to act.

This was perhaps the essence of his conflict with de Gaulle. As Van Helmont has pointed out, "For de Gaulle, the defeat and impotence of the French State, which he had lived through, were the ultimate misfortune and never left his thoughts. For Monnet, the great evil was the recurrence of wars, and what caused them, the instinct for power of nation states reined in neither by laws nor common institutions". For de Gaulle, the State was the embodiment of a country's tradition. Monnet was too practical to be against the state. He used the state. But he never observed its rites, except at the High Authority when trying to set up a counter to existing ones, and then in an idiosyncratic way. The state had no romantic connotations for him, only specific uses and abuses, of which one, "domination", was intolerable. This attitude went back a long way, right back it seems to Cognac: "I have never been able to tolerate domination", he said late in life.

This was, and remains, a quietly but firmly nonconformist position to take in a world of nation states. It was odd then that he was often criticised for being too technocratic, that is, for evading basic clashes of values. In fact, his commitment to European union had deep emotional and political roots. For him, as for many of his generation, the policies pursued after the Second World War echoed directly the hopes of building the peace frustrated after the First. For virtually the whole of his adult life, Monnet worked in expectation of war, the conduct of war, or recovery from war; and release from these left the Cold War still to come. His moderation was post-tragic, soaked in the awareness of catastrophe. As he told the first session of the Common Assembly of the ECSC in September 1952, "When one looks back a little on the past fifty, seventy-five or hundred years, and one sees the extraordinary disaster the Europeans have brought upon themselves, one is literally aghast. Yet the reason is simple. It is that each country, in this century, pursued its destiny, or what it thought its destiny, by applying its own rules". Late in life, Monnet daydreamed of writing a book in two parts, the first entitled "Yesterday, Power", the second, "Today, the Law".

The main reason it was possible to argue Monnet lacked political values was that in most of the twentieth century, until the internal collapse of the Soviet Union, these have been conceived as of one kind only: struggles over economic equality springing from the French and Russian revolutions. All others were treated as peripheral. The conditions such conflicts assumed had little in common with those which plagued international society. They presupposed civil traditions of open debate. These were precisely what international society lacked. International relations were, and are, closer to the feudal anarchy before the imposition under the Renaissance monarchies of the order from which civility and open debate within nations ultimately sprang. The international problem was, and is, in effect to achieve between nations what has already been achieved within them, to tame anarchy at the borders and remove frontiers as barriers to the operation of domestic laws and values. In these terms, Monnet stated the issues with more consistent and articulate feeling than anyone else, certainly in Western Europe.

At the League of Nations, Monnet saw salvation, as one might expect of an international civil servant, "through underlying agreement among men who enjoyed widespread influence in their own countries". His attitudes at the time were technocratic. He told an interviewer in 1971 that "I did not understand the politics of Versailles, only the economics". He was then of an optimism that would have done honour to the eighteenth-century Enlightenment and even Dr. Pangloss. "The selfishness of men and nations is most often due to imperfect understanding of the problem". But the subsequent failure of cooperation between the wars left a deep scar.

> It is astonishing how little the word "alliance", which people find so reassuring, really means in practice if all it implies is the traditional machinery of cooperation . . . where national sovereignty is ultimately vested in points of prestige and solutions are compromises between them.

States can speak only for themselves. Yet their egocentricity, multiplied by all the members of the international system, ruins the collective climate which governs each one's individual health. If problems transcend frontiers, and nation states only recognise their primary duties within frontiers, no one can see the issues whole. International bodies have the field of vision, but not the power; national governments have the power, but not the field of vision. The priorities become the individual anxieties of the parties to the problem: no one feels bound by the consequences for anyone else of a botched arrangement, and all sense of general gains or losses is dissipated in squabbling over relative ones. There is a premium on power and the abuse of power, and everyone becomes wary of his neighbour.

The practical problem was to change this psychology of action. Monnet agreed with Edward Gibbon "that a permanent interest very frequently ripens into sincere and useful friendship".

> I have never lacked friends; but friendship, to me, is the effect of joint action rather than the reason for it. . . . [It] grows up naturally between men who take a common view of the problem to be solved.

If the destructiveness of international politics was to be outgrown, a structure had to be built up to induce people to "take a common view. . . . One can only achieve a common effort by fixing on common goals". In a folksy but vivid phrase to which he was much addicted, most bargaining sets people on opposite sides of the table, confronting each other, with the problem never addressed. Instead, the people should be brought round to the same side of the table, with the problem by itself on the other side.

The key to breaking the vicious circle was to give political force to the sense of general gain or loss. There must be a body with powers to inject the "general view"—another favourite Monnet phrase—into the international process. The function of the general view is to assess the optimal outcome for all the members of the group ahead of the relative ones between them. It had an interesting history in Monnet's development. At first, it was an expression of a synthesising mind's need of intellectual control over any issue it confronted. He had long been a devotee of the "balance-sheet" (he often referred to it in English). His *Memoirs* take it back to "those great account books that my father taught me to read in Cognac when I was sixteen. . . . Balance-sheets . . . have been milestones in my work: the strength of our fleets in 1916, of our air forces in 1940; of Allied and Axis military power in 1942, of the French economy in 1945, and of the six-nation European Community in 1950". At their simplest, balance-sheets were an obvious tool to order priorities. At a higher level, they were also a weapon of reform. To reduce any task to bare essentials was often to uncover the life hidden beneath the rocks. According to the *Memoirs*, the mere attempt to state simple and coherent targets for the Anglo-French and later the American war production programmes during the Second World War challenged the authority, the zones of influence and operative habits of unacknowledged fiefdoms. Because of these real but covert obstacles to clear statement, the bureaus were initially unable to provide necessary answers. Channels had to be unblocked and hierarchies shaken up. Asking a clear question became the first step in restructuring the power networks on which an active response depended.

Little by little, as Monnet's reformist activities widened, the technical notion of the balance-sheet merged into the political concept of the "general view", itself with antecedents going back to the First World War or, perhaps, to Monnet's instinctive reactions. The strength of the Commissariat-General of the Monnet Plan was rooted less in its formal powers, which were minimal, than in the "general view" which it enjoyed and which other bodies lacked. In the case of the High Authority, the general view was not at first explicit, because the stress was on "delegating sovereignty". But it was already in the proposal of 1948 that the Secretary-General of the OEEC should have a right of initiative; likewise it was in the compromise agreed to by Monnet and Spierenburg on July 8, 1950 (p. 211). Monnet seems to have used the phrase increasingly in the early days of the High Authority, which is significant. It was probably developed in response to the nascent attacks on supranationality as the anti-EDC campaign warmed up in France. It was the origin of the Commission's right to initiate policy proposals in the EC today for qualified majority decisions by the Council of Ministers. This was devised in the Rome treaty negotiations, not by Monnet, and the drafters perceived it as a derivation from ECSC practice rather than theory, but the system adopted nevertheless remained faithful to his "general view".

There were ethical depths beneath this conception. For one thing, all partners must be equal before the law. "I always have felt, ever since the beginning," Monnet said late in life, "that equality was absolutely essential". For another, the law itself had to be equitable. Any body charged with defining policies based on the "general view" must be responsible to the group as a whole and not primarily to any single member of it. A group carrying out joint tasks must accept common responsibility for the effects of its collective decisions upon each member. No state can commit itself to joint bodies if the obligations it owes its own citizens are not taken over by the wider group. If the parties are to trust one another enough to accept "a common view", they must also enjoy equal rights before the rules. In short, the establishment of the "general view" or "general interest" is the core of the Community system. It governs every stage of decision-making: the formulation of proposed common policies, trust in their equity, and the exercise of common responsibility for the effects on the member countries. It was, in Monnet's view, the engine of common action. Everything else in the Community system—the Council of Ministers, the Assembly and the Court—provided checks and balances.

Checks must not be absolute, of course. One that had to be limited was each member state's veto on the action of the whole Community. This is in some ways the most dramatic aspect of the delegation of sovereignty to common institutions, because it is where the shoe pinches the national sense of self. But it would be inconceivable without the less visible changes which give the Community organs the capacity, and duty, to assume on behalf of all the members the responsibilities to citizens which each of the states had hitherto exercised strictly on its own account.

In principle, all this is federalism. Monnet, in the heady early days of the launching of the Schuman Plan and before the crash of the EDC, often talked like a federalist. He also spent most of his last years trying to promote a political union. Yet even in May 1950, he told Armand Bérard that Europe was too diverse to federate like the United States. He also said much later that "when I do not know how to implement something I cannot proclaim it as if it were real". Monnet's approaches in his last years, with their emphasis on councils of heads of government, were largely heretical from a federalist point of view. Hirsch, who believes he introduced the notion of federalism into the Schuman declaration and was very close to Monnet from 1950 to 1952, does not believe that Monnet ever really was a federalist.

Certainly, Monnet's stance, in behavioural as distinct from declaratory terms, fell well short of anything so full-blown. It was rooted in two needs. One was to reshape group psychology so that governments should shift from unilateralism to working together. The other was to make sure that cooperative institutions had the power to take decisions, a power that was lacking in neutered ones like the League of Nations or Council of Europe. These two elements would, of course, be prime pieces of any federal mosaic. But of themselves, they did not add up to federalism. They merely ensured that collective bodies could actually perform the tasks assigned to them. Monnet's method was molecular federalism rather than the generalised variety—up to a point open-ended and empirical. It was interested less in perfected constitutional blueprints than in shaping human patterns of response to induce a change of process.

It in no way diminishes the sincerity of all this to point out that Monnet's good sentiments for society did not always chime in with his individualism. He was too impatient to reach his goals to be entirely happy in his own relations with institutions. He made the High Authority run in circles like a horse being broken in at the end of a rope every time he took a tactical turn. He was very quick to criticise the Commission of the Common Market for being bureaucratic. He was not too keen when it was proposed that the presidency of the European Political Community should control the High Authority.

Despite such tensions between life and ideas, there was an exceptional congruence between Monnet's style of action and policies. Both turned around the instinctive bias to civilianise, or turn into relations between people, the impersonal traditions of relations between states. It was an attitude shaped by the passion to outgrow war. It was determined to set the standards of law of domestic politics in place of the balance of power of the interstate system. This was simple, but enormous, and challenged a whole tradition. Monnet was applying on his own account de Gaulle's profound epigraph, ascribed to Hamlet, of *The Edge of the Sword*: "To be great is to be identified with a great cause".[5]

5. One would be hard put to find anything like this in the supposed original. "Greatly to find quarrel in a straw" is almost the reverse of de Gaulle's meaning. It should comfort those who fear national quirks may be lost in the electronic global village that the British and French, twenty-one miles apart, are unable or decline (bar the rare exception, like P. G. Wodehouse) to quote one another without wilful or grotesque misunderstanding.

Changing the Context

The seeds of Monnet's vocation to replace international power politics by a civil order can be detected early in his career, but these seeds grew and matured very slowly. It took a long time for the League of Nations civil servant after one war to become a supranationalist after the second. Monnet thought in retrospect that he did not cross the dividing line between his first cooperative-pragmatic approach and the later quasi-federal one until as late as the Anglo-French union scheme of June 1940.

Continuity and evolution can be traced through Monnet's career in other ways. The most important was the deep underlying unity between the Clémentel Plan of 1918–19, in which the young Monnet played a part, and the Schuman Plan, which produced the European breakthrough a generation later. In both cases, the goad was France's need for security in dealing with a Germany which had a much larger population and industry—in other words, a Germany which had greater power. In both, salvation was sought in a collective system placing Germany and France in a wider frame. In both, economic means were manipulated to political ends.

Granted the family likenesses of the two schemes, all the advantages lay with the Schuman Plan, which drew the lessons of the bitter experiences in between. For one thing, in 1945 Germany's defeat came home to roost as it had not in 1918. Though no one could be sure at first after 1945, the structures of militarism were broken as they had not been before. For another, the United States, which washed its hands of Europe and killed the Clémentel Plan the first time round, gave strong support to European integration in the Schuman Plan. The latter itself was more solid than its precursor by reason of its attacking only a relatively narrow sector. Finally, it faced up to the need in any Franco-German arrangement for a common purpose, the cutting edge of which was supranationality. To invert a distinction made by

Mendès-France, the Schuman innovation was a European policy, not just a balance-of-power policy in Europe. Clémentel and his contemporaries, like Mendès-France himself, had plumped for the latter.

Nevertheless, the family likeness between the Clémentel and Schuman plans remained. For all his belief in large markets and dislike of protectionism, bred in the American environment, Monnet never seemed at ease with policies shaped around trade. He paid little or no attention to Finebel. (Admittedly, few did take it seriously.) Initially, he was suspicious of the Common Market. He was slow to see the implications of the Free Trade Area. This seems to have amounted to a pattern. Though his approach with the years became increasingly institutional and political, the base was always administrative rather than commercial. In short, though Monnet was close to the Americans, and seen as such by the French, in retrospect his policies, like his personality, have a strikingly French air.

The same observation has been given a political status by scholars who have followed the economic historian Alan Milward in arguing that Monnet's European policies were much more deeply rooted in the postwar aims of the French establishment than had previously been assumed, and even that they carried on French national and bureaucratic ambitions by other means. Monnet, who returned to France from the background of Washington and the end of Lend-Lease, does seem to have been influenced by the ethos in Paris at the end of 1945. Indeed if, as he claimed, the investment plan was to be in any real sense representative, he was bound to be. In 1946, he emphasised France's need to draw on Ruhr coal for the economy in general and steel in particular with the best of them. In February, he regarded 20 million tons a year of Ruhr coal as more urgent than a dollar loan. (France was not to import that much—even including coke—at any time postwar.) The mood changed fairly soon on that point. But Monnet seems to have feared for the better part of a decade that the Ruhr barons might choke the whole of French industry by starving the steel industry, seen (a common view at the time) as the key to manufacturing power. Monnet was orthodox French in his analysis of the problem for much or most of the immediate postwar period.

Solutions, however, were another matter. During the war, Monnet had a European vision of the postwar system. There would have to be a "strong" League of Nations, Continental free trade "to prevent nationalism" and "equality" of the various political entities, including the (several) German ones. (Interestingly, this looked back to the League more than forward to the European Community and, when it looked forward, more to the Common Market than to Monnet's later sectoral schemes.) Above all, in Algiers, Monnet's map of Lotharingia showed that he did not put France on a special footing. Though such ideas went into eclipse immediately after the war, they re-emerged, in a different form, with Marshall aid and the Cold War in 1947. At first, they were on a high level of generality, focussing on the

Atlantic "federation of the West", not the pan-European perspective of the war years. However, when Monnet brought them down to earth in 1950, they still embodied some of his old basic principles. The most important of them was the notion of equality with Germany, the lack of which had been the original sin in France's Versailles policies, repeated at the Liberation. Further, the Community placed France on the same plane as everyone else and committed it like the rest. It was a decisive parting of the ways between the former international civil servant and the bureaucratic and national tradition of the French state.

Supranationality was a common idea in the French political parties and popular with the public, before and after the Schuman Plan. But the closer one came to the heart of government, the less enthusiasm it evoked. Schuman himself seems at first to have had reservations about supranationality. There was scepticism verging on resistance even in the Bidault government, which gave Schuman and Monnet their head. The most rooted suspicion in France was situated in the lobbies, especially the Quai d'Orsay and industry, the former wedded to the balance of power tradition, the latter to protection and cartels. The Quai d'Orsay, whilst not against the Schuman Plan in the ferocious way it opposed the European Army, proved incapable of spawning a supranational scheme. The idea of committing the state to a system in which it was not in sole control was too big a leap for the scions of the great-power tradition, even when the tradition was drained of great power.

Monnet's own attitudes to Germany were clearly complex and at the least dualistic. He was "haunted", as a British diplomat put it in the early 1950s, by German nationalism. He loathed the "will to dominate" he ascribed to the Ruhr industrial "barons" and German General Staff and was alive to the slightest hint of their possible revival. On the other hand, he was not tempted by any French "will to dominate", either. He was the "anti-Poincaré", as Alphand called him; the man who wanted to reach out to a more liberal, pacific Germany and build a common future with it. As a former official of the League, he was far more critical of French interwar policies than were most Frenchmen. "We lost the peace in 1919 because we introduced discrimination and a sense of superiority. . . . Equality is absolutely essential in relations between nations, as it is between people". He was ready to play to the hilt the Community game of the rule of law, non-discrimination, and "equality" (or genuine reciprocity). Simply, he was not a nationalist. True, French attitudes survived in the midst of his non-nationalist policies. It would have been strange if they had not, and it was legitimate that they did. Only, nationalism was the demon to be exorcised. Monnet was a European with French roots, but a European nonetheless.

The Schuman Plan began to break the circuit of the old rivalries not only by treating French, Germans and their partners as equal before the rules, but by distracting attention from all too familiar grievances to the new aim

of Europe. Specifically, it reduced the conflict embedded in the steel economies of France and Germany so long as the traditional norms of national
economic policies prevailed, that nationals always took first place and foreigners always the hindmost. The dilemma was resolved by the expedient,
simple in principle, of treating the coal and steel of both states as much as
possible as if they belonged to a single country.

In practice, of course, the transition was far from easy. The power of the
Ruhr continued to be a problem or at least a fixation. Monnet's experience
at the High Authority implies either that he lacked the capacity to control
the Ruhr industrialists, not least because of the European Army crisis, or
that he realised the policy of reconciliation with the new Germany was more
important than the particular issue of the Ruhr. There are hints of both in
the record. This may be the real meaning of the support from the German
trade unions with which he emerged from the years in Luxembourg. They
were attached to the German coal monopoly for employment reasons. The
fact that Monnet did not attack it or seek to prevent all reconcentration of
German steel deserved in their eyes the certificate of "Europeanness" as
against "Frenchness" they delivered after the EDC fiasco. It was a beginning
in the gradual dissociation of the industrial balance between France and Germany from the much larger and more important issue of the quality of relations between the two countries and peoples. When they were potential
enemies, the industrial balance and the control of the Saar were part of the
count of competing strengths. If they became partners, competition took on
a different meaning and disappeared in the old territorial sense.

Two later pieces of evidence are interesting in the demythologising of the
Franco-German industrial balance. The first, concerning Monnet, was that
he was just as suspicious of the German industrialists and generals at the
time of Euratom as he had been in the Schuman Plan and European Army.
The difference was that on Euratom and nuclear weapons he had the support
of the German Left and unions. In fact, initially, for the SPD, Euratom as a
bulwark of a non-nuclear Germany was the condition of their commitment
to the European Community. Almost certainly, he could not have had their
support if he had tried to use the ECSC to break the Ruhr coal-selling
agency. The other, which shows that the evolution in attitudes was much
wider than Monnet, is the response of the French government led by Edgar
Faure and Pinay to the referendum in the Saar in October 1955. This produced a two-to-one majority for a return to Germany. Faure and Pinay
accepted the verdict at once, without fuss. This finally buried the use of the
steel balance as the yardstick of relations between France and Germany. Yet
it did not prevent the Common Market from becoming negotiable the following year. By the 1960s, steel had ceased to be a central Franco-German
political issue. "Europe" had taken over.

The ultimate test of "European" attitudes in a mainstream Frenchman was the prospect of German reunification. This aroused not one but two fears: of a revival of German power, and of a massive swing in the balance of power to the Soviet Union. German reunification was a theme of several Soviet proposals. That of March 10, 1952, a couple of months before the signature of the European Army treaty and the linked Contractual Agreements ending the Occupation in West Germany, was particularly sensitive. There were frequent suspicions among Germany's Western neighbours of a new "Rapallo", the German-Soviet agreement of 1922, symbolic of a German balancing act between "East" and "West". Monnet regarded it as a defeat, Van Helmont reports, when the negotiators of the Contractual Agreements granted the Federal Republic the right to review its membership in the EC if the two Germanys were reunited. When ecstatic crowds greeted Chancellor Willy Brandt as he met the East German premier, Willy Stoph, in Erfurt in March 1970, Monnet felt a dam was about to burst. But he faced the issue fairly and squarely at least as early as April 30, 1952, when he told the National Press Club in Washington that the only reunification of Germany "conducive to lasting peace would be unity in a united Europe".

This claim was partly tactical, to ensure that German reunification and European unity should not become entrenched alternatives, and to meet Communist and neutralist charges that Europe was a Cold War gambit. But it was also in the logic of the European policy. The collapse of Soviet power in east-central Europe has since proved it was not just propaganda.

Of course, in crude power terms, the weakness of a united Europe as a frame for any real or supposed hegemonial power was and is that the force may be too great for the container. But that ignores the more important question of process, or the way in which the motives of member states are shaped. The basic issue is not who is dominant—some groups always will be—but the quality of relations between them and others and their mutual perceptions. Will these be as in Switzerland, with its German-speaking and non-German-speaking cantons, where the German-speaking majority take careful account of strongly defined cantonal rights? Or at the other extreme, will they be like those of occupied countries under a conqueror? And if neither, then in what situation in between? The justification of European integration has always been, and is, that it raises a body of law and operating rules which apply to every member of the union, from the strongest to the weakest. So long as the rules are themselves felt to be reasonably equitable, a united Germany and its partners can all fulfil themselves within a united Europe. Monnet could not have foreseen that German reunification would turn out as his projections claimed. But the intuition that the Community provided an appropriate framework has so far been justified by events. Considering the crisis there could have been if the traditional conventions had held sway, the lack of one is striking.

Monnet's willingness to contemplate "equal" Franco-German relations in a Community was far from typically French. In fact, it is doubtful that a Frenchman of his generation who had not spent the larger part of his career outside the country could have believed enough in such a policy to ram it through. For the Schuman Plan simultaneously took risks and demanded the same commitments of France as of Germany. This violated centuries of great-power attitudes. Even Aristide Briand's reconciliation with Germany did not contemplate such a solecism.

The novelty was so great that French governments have never steadily accepted the constraints of Community. They created it initially to safeguard themselves from a more-than-equal Germany. Assent to the second Europe after German rearmament in NATO was an instance. Later European *relances,* or relaunchings, have tended to coincide with signs of better German-Soviet relations, as during Willy Brandt's Ostpolitik (1969–72). On such occasions, the Germans have been anxious to reassure their West European partners of their fidelity to the Community. The French have been keen to reinforce the European framework to prevent a "Rapallo". But in between such phases, the French have tended to presume on their privileges as initiators of the Community to pursue unilateral ambitions or claim more-than-equal status themselves. As usual, de Gaulle flaunted what others discreetly practised. It was the pro-European Mollet and Gaillard governments of the Fourth Republic which took the basic decisions to make France a nuclear weapon state. Frequently, French foreign policy within the Community has been reminiscent of nothing more than of British outside. The similarities of France and Britain explain almost as much of postwar European history as do their differences.

The Schuman Plan, then, did not once and for all displace the old French policies. Ever since, there has been a pendular swing between more and less Community-minded phases. The old and the new have been competing and alternating, or even neutralising one another, as in defence until the 1990s. At the same time, the dynamic imparted by the Schuman, or Community, policy has never evaporated. A new option has been permanently added to the palette of policies. It has added a whole new dimension of possible answers to crises which the old policies could not provide. And both in terms of the internal effects inside the Community and of the magnetic attraction on outside powers, it has introduced a series of pressures that did not exist before.

This dynamic was inherent in the original initiative. The problem posed by Germany's postwar revival could not be met by the usual incremental caution dear to policy-makers. "We must not try to solve the German problem in its present context", Monnet wrote on May 3, 1950. "We must change the context by transforming the basic facts". As a bilateral problem, Franco-German relations were insoluble. The Schuman Plan broke out of the impasse not by reaching a deal between France and Germany but by pointing

beyond them both to a common goal and larger context, that is, a united Europe. "Europe" has been, by all the usual standards, a successful policy to deal with the German problem, from the point of view of Germany's neighbours as well as of Germany itself. This has been largely due to the extent to which the energies of policy-makers have been diverted from the old channels into new.

This mode of action was one of Monnet's hallmarks. The method was quite consciously to switch the landscape in which a conflict was viewed in order to break out of a current impasse and release a new course of events. The earliest instance was perhaps the collective protocol of abstention, or "non-interference", as regards Austria in 1921. Supervised by the League of Nations, this was signed by the very countries which might have asserted competing claims to Austria's territory. Monnet attempted many more. The China Development Finance Corporation of 1934, which sought to commit Chinese and Western financiers for the first time to joint ventures, was one. The efforts from 1938 onwards to bring the New World in to correct the balance of the Old, in the form first of buying airplanes from America and then of making it the arsenal of democracy, constituted another. So was the Anglo-French union of 1940. So was the European Army project to finesse German rearmament in NATO. Much later, Monnet tried again, with the proposal of the OECD, to outflank British attempts to revive the Free Trade Area and make the European Commission the "single voice" of the new Europe in a broad range of policy.

It is doubtful that Monnet was aware of the analogy between "changing the context" and the invention of new hypotheses which theorists treat as central to scientific discovery and creative work. He had little interest in theory not suggested to him by his own experience and insights. Yet he had clearly found for himself a principle of great force. To change the context can transform the way in which people experience closely related kinds of behaviour, to the point of obliterating the family likeness. For instance, the economic competition between individuals and firms can be an instrument of conflict and even war among mercantilist states; divorced from state competition, and as free trade, it becomes one of the bases of the division of labour and of prosperity. Or take the balance of power. Between rival states, subject to no laws, it long ago invited the bitter gibe of Alexander Pope:

> Now Europe balanced, neither side prevails;
> For nothing's left in either of the scales.

Once, however, it has been domesticated under a single government and law, it becomes the countervailing powers in politics which are the main guarantees of civil tolerance and freedom. The same transforming idea underlay Monnet's own magnum opus, the European Community.

Changing the context was not a once-for-all transformation but the launching of a process: "One change begets another. The chain reaction has only begun". The idea was already built in to the Monnet Plan. One of Monnet's parables was about the industrialist who came to him and said, "Now I have modernised". Modernisation, to Monnet, was "continuous creation", never ending. This idea of change became ever more central with European unification. Europe was far too large an ambition to achieve at a single sweep. It had to be encompassed over time. The first step could only point to a final goal. But it would create the conditions for the next step, and so on, step by step, in constant exploration. There could be a broad goal but no pre-set programme.

Monnet believed, like the poet W. H. Auden (of whom he had certainly not heard), that "men are changed by what they do". He frequently used the image, from his own alpine walking tours, of the view modified step by step as one climbed the mountain. The perspective shifted minimally but inexorably all the time. It followed that it was a fallacy to extrapolate from the present. Down in the valley, the view was the one offered by a valley, with all the particulars of the enclosed scene. Only when one had moved out of the valley, or rather when action had created a new context, would new options heave in sight and stimulate new views. They would have little in common with those at the outset on the chalet terrace.

In this dialectic, the crucial step was always the first one, that is, in any given situation, the next step to be taken. On its success and accomplished fact every later effort would depend. Hence the obsessive care Monnet lavished on whatever he was addressing at the time: it was the key to keeping on the move a campaign he was pursuing. As George Ball has written, "not to lose momentum: that was Monnet's constant preoccupation". Another consequence was that anything but the most general statement of final ends was meaningless. To quote Ball again, he was "masterful in responding to events and thus he never thought in terms of frozen progression".

"Europe will not be conjured up at a stroke", announced the Schuman declaration of 1950, "or by an overall design; it will be attained by concrete achievements generating a community of interest" ("*solidarité de fait*"). Monnet and his entourage used to talk in the early days of "dynamic disequilibrium". All this really meant at first was that the European Coal and Steel Community was not viable on its own in the long run and so would create tensions with national processes which would become unmanageable unless there was progress to new Communities. The assertion was vague and the possibility of an unwinding of the Community was ignored. There have been times when one could wonder whether the dynamic was real. But after forty years, it seems the intuition was fundamentally correct. A dynamic has emerged within the European Community. It has expressed itself in three closely interrelated ways.

The first has been negative but powerful. Any failure of Community tends to bring back to the surface the problems it was designed to settle. Opponents of the European Army project learned this to their surprise when they vetoed the scheme and found that German rearmament was determined by others. Similarly, the failure of the European Political Community, with its Dutch suggestion of a customs union, once again in 1955 brought up the choice of a Free Trade Area or a Common Market with roots in the Marshall Plan period.

Second, every move to Europe has tended to create vested interests in the new system. In the Common Market, this has been obvious. But even the ECSC made a limited political and administrative routine of Europe and to that extent injected elements of an active community of interest in the working life of the member states. In so far as the Community has gathered support, or encouraged new relations, as in trade, a built-in lobby has been formed. It may not always have been strong enough to force further movement forward. It has usually been more than adequate to prevent movement back.

The result has been to produce the third pressure for change. It has often been claimed, in the Community's rhetoric of alarm, that what cannot move forward must sooner or later fall back. Yet the corollary, that what cannot fall back presumably at some point has good chances of moving forward, has in practice been more in evidence. It has proved easy on a number of occasions to make the Communities mark time; it has never been possible to nullify altogether the power of attraction of "European options", as the shrewd title of Van Helmont's book has called them.

To the extent that the analysis underpinning the European strategy is well-founded, sooner or later a moment comes when national solutions disappoint. At that stage, European proposals, which in effect provide a permanent alternative, exert a strong attraction. The sense of the need to make fresh efforts in unison reasserts itself. Environmental policy is an instance. Once an effective demand for action imposes itself, powers have to be given to the European bodies to produce results. Each time a European solution is adopted in this way, Community roots strike deeper. The dynamic is therefore powerful, if not necessarily fast-flowing. The European Community has frequently been in the doldrums, especially during the twenty years from the empty-chair crisis of 1965 to the Single Act of 1986. But even de Gaulle was unable to dissolve the system, because he needed parts of it; and so at least to some extent all have been saddled with its operational logic.

Significantly, European union as a broad idea has proved more resilient than individual Communities. The Schuman Plan was voted a success as the lone standard-bearer, only to suffer a major reverse when the second Europe came along. When Euratom was ingested in 1967, the demise seemed to be that of sectoral integration as a whole. But in the following years, the mercantilist behaviour of governments cast serious doubt on their commitment to large or free or common markets. Once, however, "Europessimism" spread—due to poor economic performance compared with Japan and America and to the threat of impotence inherent in the weakening of the decision-making rules by de Gaulle—alarm at the dangers focussed in a giant corrective step forward. A programme was approved to make the Single Market effective by 1993, requiring agreement on nearly three hundred regulations—laws, some of them of broad sweep—covering every aspect of economic activity. It was given teeth by the curiously named Single Act of February 1986, which restored majority voting in the Council of Ministers. The Common Market from the mid-eighties began at last to put into effect, a generation late, most of the economic union imagined by the founding fathers thirty years earlier.[1]

However, the assent to the Single Market still falls well short of political union. Monnet always thought ultimately in terms of such a union. The letter he wrote to Romme in November 1958 was typical. It argued that a "finance common market" would lead to economic unity, and economic unity in turn would make political union "relatively easy" (p. 312). On the other hand, his concept of the approach to union as a dialectical one, step by step, was so pragmatic that at the margin it was always possible it might lead to another destination.

II
FERMENT OF CHANGE

During four decades of existence, the Community's dynamic has been at least as evident outside its frontiers as within. This has been the unforeseen result of two settled enemies like France and Germany suddenly unsettling everyone else by becoming partners. The ripples of the seismic shock to the old landscape have spread far and wide.

Monnet, when baulked in the 1960s, sometimes claimed that European unity should have begun as a purely Franco-German affair. This, he thought, would have given it greater momentum. At the time of the Schuman Plan, however, he realised the Benelux trio and Italy were necessary to ratification

1. The title *single market* is significant. There is no real difference with *common market*. (Indeed, *single market* was the term in use in 1950.) Except the common market, through the failures of the intervening years, had become associated with the mere customs union to which the EEC had been confined. By the time it was decided to implement the common market in full, the term had been devalued. A new name was needed to convey the full force of the old idea. Nowadays, the "common", or "single", market (however called) includes regional and environmental policies no one catered for in the 1950s.

by the French Parliament. Reciprocally, the very fact the French and Germans proposed to come together put these four states under immense pressure to join. It would have been inconceivable for them to stand aside, for trading and political reasons. Others, though, led by Britain, did stand aside. So a "two-speed" Europe separating the maximalists from minimalists was created from the start. It was in fact a condition of anything being achieved. Yet originally it was almost an accident, a by-product of Monnet's determination not to allow Britain to veto a Community with powers to act.

For a few years, the result seemed a relatively stable division between players and abstainers. But once the Common Market extended the Community system across the whole range of the trading economy, the British were forced from the side-lines. Reluctantly, they acknowledged that if they did not join, a Euro-American link might, and probably would, push into second place Britain's "special relationship" with Washington as entertained in London. Macmillan tried and failed, from 1961 to 1963, to enter the Common Market, and Edward Heath succeeded only a decade later, after de Gaulle's abdication. The doubling of membership of the European Community since 1972 from six members to twelve has been the most obvious, but neither the first nor certainly the last, evidence of the EC's almost embarrassing attractions for every conceivable European country (and even some, like Israel and Morocco, which are not eligible because they are not European). Such magnetism is, of course, a form of power with little precedent in history. But it can also overwhelm the centre of attraction. The avalanche of prospective candidates has become a potential threat to the cohesion of a Union which aims to work at all.

Monnet never thought of the Community as confined to the original Six.[2] "Our Community", he told the Economic Affairs Committee of the Council of Europe Assembly on March 28, 1953, "is neither a little Europe nor a closed Community". This was implicit in his treating European union as the only solution for German unity. This could hardly have taken place without changes affecting the whole of central Europe—which has proved to be the case. On a few occasions, in private, he tried to be specific. At the time of the Polish and Hungarian crises of 1956, he wondered whether long-term contracts with Poland for coal might not help it while insuring the Community against failures of oil supply from the Middle East. On October 18, 1956, in a conversation with Kohnstamm and Visson, he argued that "we have to get England in, later the Scandinavians and then maybe Poland". But these were hardly typical. Apart from Monnet's suspicions about the insularity of the Scandinavians and small countries in general, the Iron Cur-

---

2. The various Community treaties all provide that European states may apply to join. However, to enter, candidates have to be unanimously accepted by the member states (treaty articles ECSC 98; EEC 237; Euratom 205).

tain, however rusty, seemed an insuperable barrier to thinking of Europe as a political whole.

In reality, he gave little detailed thought to Eastern Europe and, like everyone else, saw the Soviet Union largely as an external power. His first concern (as with Britain) was that European union should not be disrupted. "As regards the Soviet Union", he told the ECSC Common Assembly on June 15, 1953, "the basic question is whether we have faith in ourselves". Like the State Department and Adenauer, he was anxious to prevent Soviet proposals for reunifying Germany from tempting Bonn into a balancing act between East and West. Yet he was no more a Cold War zealot than he was prepared to let the Kremlin dictate the agenda. About a year after the thaw in the Cold War began at the Geneva conference of August 1955, Gerard C. Smith, who ran the Office of Atomic Energy Affairs in the State Department, and much later negotiated the SALT I agreement, was impressed by a lunch to which Monnet invited him. Monnet questioned him at length on American nuclear policies, probing to see whether they might appear aggressive viewed from Moscow. In the speech he gave for his honorary degree at Dartmouth on June 12, 1961, Monnet said that

> when it has become evident to everyone that it is impossible to divide the West . . . Mr. Khrushchev or his successor will accept the facts. The conditions will then exist at last for transforming so-called peaceful coexistence into genuine peace.

The same idea was expressed in the Action Committee declarations of July 11, 1960, and June 26, 1962, which asserted that "a lasting peaceful settlement between East and West" would then become possible. This was before the Cuban Missile Crisis of October 1962 completed the switch in the Kennedy administration from the imaginary missile gap to superpower detente.

Nevertheless, Monnet paid attention essentially to relations with the major English-speaking powers. He had lived all his life in a world revolving round Europe, the British Empire and America. In his own way, he believed as much as Winston Churchill in the latter's "three circles". For him too, Britain played a pivotal role. Its entry would give "Europe" the critical mass to transform relations with America. The big difference was that where Churchill and Macmillan meant to take the lead of Europe and the Commonwealth, Monnet saw Britain very much as one among equals.

From the outset, there was heavy pressure to welcome Britain into the Community on London's terms. At first, it was a struggle to hold Monnet's line that there should be no clouding of the distinction between a Community with powers to act and foggy international bodies, like the Council of Europe, which Whitehall deployed like a gladiatorial net to confuse the issue. Britain should be welcomed only so long as it accepted the basic rules.

The pressure wore off during the 1950s as its lack of European zeal sank in. By the time of its request to enter the Common Market in 1961, there was a general belief that Monnet had been right all along. By the same token, however, once his policy had prevailed, it was inconceivable to think up new conditions, even had he wanted to. His position never varied during the years of de Gaulle's veto on British membership. Britain must be welcomed into the Community now it had accepted the basic rules.

Yet presuming on how the British would operate once inside the Community was a gamble. Their position was buttressed by de Gaulle, when he re-imposed the national veto through the misleadingly named Luxembourg "compromise". For twelve years, they treated it as their charter of membership. Ironically, they changed when Margaret Thatcher, of all people, signed the Single Act of 1986. This reinstituted majority voting across a wide front. She had to accept that otherwise there would be no Single Market or, worse, that it might go ahead without her. But since then, the Major government's emphasis on the Maastricht treaty of February 1992 as a charter not of union but of intergovernmentalism, has reinforced the view that Britain mainly joined the Community because, as one ambassador to it, Sir Con O'Neill, used to say, "the smallest country inside has more influence [upon it] than the largest outside". In basics, Britain's attitude in Europe seems to have changed very little since 1950. On such evidence, Monnet's view that, once within the Community, Britain would be captured by its dynamic could not have proved more mistaken. He might seem more prescient in the long run. But the reasons for believing that have so far been fewer than those for doubt.

Monnet himself quite often had private misgivings. Such incidents as the Labour leader Hugh Gaitskell's famous reference in 1962 to the "thousand years of [British] history" being threatened by European Union were hardly calculated to allay them. Whatever his fears, he never wavered in his public support for Britain's membership in the Community. He had long admired Britain's democratic traditions, steadfastness and freedom. He belonged to a generation in whom the City of London inspired deep respect. Before the war, he thought that British bankers and civil servants best understood China. Later, he contrasted the support a man in trouble could expect in the City with the Wall Street tendency to drop such a man and move on (a comparison all the more striking because some Americans stuck with him through thick and thin). He had a number of old and very good friends in the City, like Perth and the Brands. In March 1949, he told Plowden that Britain was the only dynamic force in Europe, having uniquely succeeded in redistributing income while preserving the freedom of the individual. He worked with the British in two wars and even as a British official in part of one. He could not conceive of a democratic Europe without Britain.

For all that, his *entente cordiale* was with Americans. He distrusted the imperial streak in the British establishment. He told David Lilienthal during the preliminary exchanges of fire with London on the Schuman Plan in late May 1950 that "we are not dealing with a Labour government but with a Foreign Office that got its instructions a hundred years ago". He often said the British should never be allowed a "privileged position" in any form of cooperation. His *Memoirs* said he formed this opinion as early as the First World War.

He was also more at home in the loose American system of government than in the tight-lipped disciplines of Whitehall. A small incident just after the launching of the Schuman Plan seemed typical enough. Monnet rang Plowden at the Treasury in London, complaining that now dealings had got into the hands of "the lawyers" there was serious risk of failure and asking him to come to Paris for a talk. That, from a British point of view, was a recipe for total confusion. Makins choked it off in favour of the "recognised official channels". Despite Monnet's success in Whitehall in war-time, some episodes, as Miriam Camps has pointed out, make one wonder whether he was that much in tune with the British official mind. He grossly overrated the chances of Bevin endorsing European federal schemes in 1948. The conversations with Plowden in April 1949 assumed an influence Monnet enjoyed in Paris but not Plowden, or any other official, in London. Some British at some periods were apt to distrust Monnet. Even as old and close a friend as Thomas Brand said of him, "Monnet is naughty, you know—always has been". This may have been prompted by the experience of the Lazards loan to Monnet. Whatever the reason, there were notes from time to time of mutual reserve rarely, if ever, heard in relations with the other side of the Atlantic.

Still, there is no doubt of the importance Monnet attached to British membership of the Community. Part of this was intrinsic, but not all. He saw it also in addition as a chance to change relations with the United States. The danger of these, from a European point of view, was a comfortable settling into dependence. Monnet thought such an evolution bad for both parties to a relationship. As early as April 1948, when Marshall aid was young, he went on record, for the separate benefits of Schuman and Frankfurter, with the view that "it is not possible . . . for Europe to remain dependent for very long and almost exclusively for her production on American credits and for her security on American forces without undesirable effects both here"—he was in Washington at the time—"and in Europe". The solution was for a uniting Europe and the United States to join as potential "equals" in managing Western prosperity, tackling the development of the Third World and laying the bases for stable relations with the Soviet Union. The United Nations had failed to reform a flawed international system, because of the Cold War, if for no other reason. The effort could now be revived in a new form, empirically, from the ground up, by a West whose self-confidence was riding high on the "second America" of the Common

Market. By 1960, Monnet was talking of Europe as the "ferment of change". It was ironic that this was thanks to the Common Market he had at first studiously ignored.

The relationship with the United States was probably the central fact of Monnet's career because it was also the central fact in the situation of Western Europe. George Ball's opinion is that until the mid-1960s, Monnet had closer, because more personal, access to the upper reaches of U.S. government than did any other foreigner, including the British. This was so well-known that it was exploited even in Paris under de Gaulle. Jean-François Deniau has recalled an occasion when the Germans were digging in their heels in one of the difficult negotiations of the early 1960s on the Common Agricultural Policy. Clappier, with the agreement of the French negotiators, asked Monnet to contact the "Secretary of State" (in fact, Ball), who rang the Chancellor (at that point, Erhard). The next day, the negotiation resumed as if there had never been a problem.

In the immediate postwar years, the United States accounted for over half the manufacturing output of the world, a dominance never matched before or since by any power, including the United States. To have influence in Washington was an enormous advantage almost everywhere. In Paris, however, it also carried costs. De Gaulle is reported to have said, late in his second reign, that "Jean Monnet is not a Frenchman in hock to the Americans; he is a great American". This view was not confined to Gaullists. At a meeting in Rome in March 1987, Christian Pineau, the Socialist Foreign Minister who signed the Rome treaties, said that "Monnet and the Americans were always of a mind". It is a safe bet he did not mean the mind was Monnet's.

There is no doubt that Monnet's world view was centred at times closer to Washington than to Paris. His window tended to be that of a metropolis of the West looking out on the world. This was quite unlike French views set resentfully at the receiving end of someone else's hegemony. American insistence on lifting the production ceilings for German heavy industry and on rearming Germany pushed the French to act in 1950. Was the United States then the parent of Europe? This assumes France would have had no German problem without the United States. It was hardly the lesson of the years between the wars and of the desperate French efforts from 1938 to enlist American aid. After the Second World War, relying on the United States to hold Germany down, as de Gaulle did, was unsustainable, an unacknowledged confession of weakness. Sooner or later, the French would have had to face Germany's potential anyway. It was far safer with America holding the ring.

In fact, the French, West Germans and Americans had converging political interests in the Community. The French needed it to influence the evolution of Germany. Germany needed it to be accepted as a member of international society and to deploy economic power without disturbing neighbours. America needed it to buy off France while reviving West Germany in order to secure the balance in Europe. As Van Helmont has pointed out, the necessary and sufficient condition for the European Communities has been the triple alliance of France, the western part of a divided Germany and America. Britain was marginalised because she was neither willing to be involved nor central to the action.

Nevertheless, need of America in dealing with Germany could be the starting point of a "protectorate". How to handle relations with the United States has therefore been the litmus test of attitudes to integration in Europe. Unhistorically minded integrators like Monnet took American support for Union at face value and built their policies on it. A historicist of the balance of power like de Gaulle assumed America would never relinquish control over Europe. One of the most basic debates in postwar Europe has probably been between de Gaulle and Monnet over relations with America.

For de Gaulle, the assumption of Monnet's European policies that relations with the United States could evolve was pure delusion. The European Community could never cohere. It lacked a "federator", by which he meant a superior force, a Prussia to a Germany, compelling the merger the parties would never achieve of their own free will. The only "federator" could be Europe's "protector", the United States. The Community had to be a fig-leaf for American domination. Consciously or not, Monnet was an agent of American empire.

Yet when de Gaulle came back into office, his policies signally failed to shake the foundations of the system he deplored. He tried to join America and Britain in a Western "directorate", excluding Germany; to dominate the Community by a special relationship first with Germany and Italy, then with Germany alone, excluding Britain and America; next to put a wedge in the American protectorate in Western Europe by a special relationship with the Soviet Union, excluding the British and the Americans and holding down the Germans; and finally, when all else failed, to fall back on a British alliance in the Community to close the hatch on the Germans; all "Machiavellian" tactics in the supposedly central tradition of European statecraft. Yet there was a crippling disparity between ends and means which a Bismarck would have scorned. So long as Germany regarded the United States as the guarantor of its security, it would never choose France against America.

De Gaulle's policy prolonged the neuroses born of France's humiliations between 1870 and 1945 and in the end may have reduced its real control over events. His insistence on re-establishing French rule in Indochina was responsible for the gravest colonial crisis before the Algerian War. His revival of the Versailles gambit of the economic fusion of the Saar with France could have poisoned relations with Germany for decades to come.

Had Bonn paid any real attention to his manœuvres in the 1960s, they could have ruined the main achievement of postwar Franco-German relations, the Community. The usual emphasis is on the weaknesses de Gaulle had to repair. This has ignored his own legacy of misjudgements, some of which he dumped in the lap of the Fourth Republic in the first place.

For Monnet, all this was theatrical and very dangerous. It jeopardised everything the Community represented in relations with France's neighbours, and the Germans in particular. Gaullist policies, obsessed with casting European neighbours in subordinate roles to France, could have no appeal to them. If they had to be subordinate to someone, the United States was less shaming. It was a superpower not a local rival, it was more predictable and helped provide a frame for Germany. In many ways, Monnet's approach to relations with America was nearer to that of the Germans or Japanese than of his own countrymen. This was to cast off inferiority as much as possible in real terms, and then, and only then, judge the use one could make of one's freedom of choice. He was critical of the "Third Force" arguments peddled by European neutralists in the early days of the Atlantic alliance on precisely these grounds. Without "force" there would be no "third". With "force" the entity would be itself and not defined uniquely in relation to the policies either of the United States or of the Soviet Union.

The second difference with de Gaulle was the underlying attitude to the use of freedom to choose, when and if acquired. For Monnet, there was nothing to be gained from the Gaullist antithesis of a one-sided wedding or divorce as the only possible relations between Europe and America. A middle way was required between the unquestioning support so common in NATO circles and nationalism which undermined precious collective achievements. This could only be provided by an association, or partnership, "of equals" between the already United States of America and the newly uniting states of Europe.

Partnership resolved, at least verbally, the abiding tension of apparently contradictory forces: the European need to take a real part in decisions and the fact that transatlantic ties were immensely powerful. It mattered little that equality did not currently exist overall, so long as it began to appear in some areas (of which the first was trade) and it offered a goal, a norm, to aim at. De Gaulle excepted, the partnership commanded a consensus. It reconciled European self-respect with Alliance priorities.

However, if a partnership of equals took the West off the horns of de Gaulle's dilemma, it re-created it in the new one of whether partnership and equality were compatible. The party of "interdependence" on both shores of the Atlantic realised that "partnership" was not integration. Yet the fear of serious conflict was largely discounted. As Monnet remarked in 1953 about American policy:

It is the first time in history that a great power, instead of basing its policy on ruling by dividing, has consistently and resolutely backed the creation of a large Community uniting peoples previously apart.[3]

Why did the United States feel that European integration was in its interest? The Russians did not think that way. In terms of the past, they—not the Americans—were orthodox.

The anomaly of America's behaviour has usually been glossed over by stressing its interest in balancing Soviet power in Europe. This was true as far as it went, but did not explain the lack of broad-based opposition to, or fear of, helping a potential rival, however remote and theoretical. The support for union in Europe had roots in America's own myth of genesis and in America's being relatively so powerful at first that rivalry seemed rather abstract. But the risk of conflict, if Europe really revived as a major power, did not call for much imagination. Dulles admittedly brushed aside the possibility that European union might create problems. But in the main, American leaders did not ignore it. They simply judged that they should have more in common than in rivalry with West Europeans. They were all democracies, therefore pacific, and rich, with a stake in stability. Better a reviving Europe than a "fortress America" in an alien environment. Moreover, the need for common control of "interdependence" overrode traditional competition between states. Difficulties could be handled. In sum, American policy to European union expressed a conception of interest in which confidence in compatible social and economic processes carried more weight than traditional statecraft. The sense of kinship with Europe weighed in the balance. Latin America did not bask in the same benevolence. The American attitude nevertheless marked the entrance of a new theme.

Monnet went further. He stood on its head the assumption that equality contained the seed of conflict by arguing, as he did with Adenauer, that "cooperation on an equal footing between the United States and a divided, fragmented Europe would be impossible". The latter would suffer from "an unadmitted inferiority complex, which takes the form of discontent with others, when in fact we are discontented with ourselves". Only unity could qualify Europe to undertake with the United States—another of Monnet's relentlessly reiterated phrases—"the common management of common problems".

Whatever the force of these arguments, they were very different from the ones Monnet used for European integration. If institutions taking the "general view", plus majority voting by governments, were vital to achieve collective action in the European Community, it was difficult to see how the

3. Napoleon III helped Cavour unite Italy, while exacting a proprietorial fee, the transfer of Nice and French-speaking Savoy to France.

same results could be obtained merely by "interdependence". If, on the other hand, as the Atlantic "partnership of equals" implied, interdependence was sufficient to evoke unity of purpose between democratic societies with common values, then the forces of unity between them were organic and not institutional. The partners were living in a kind of *de facto* confederation, a common economic and political texture, more like the familiar domestic than an international regime. The success of the Community itself might really be due to these forces. If so, the problem ceased to be the social Darwinism which Community institutions existed to domesticate. Rather, it demanded countervailing powers à la Montesquieu to improve political balances, as in all self-respecting domestic and democratic regimes. The Community could be seen as one of these countervailing powers vis-à-vis the United States. Such powers, of course, have been regarded as the *sine qua non* of good government inside countries by a long line of thinkers, from the classical Greeks to Galbraith.

Beneath a surface unity, then, Monnet was working both sides of the street: first, European unity through institutions with powers of their own; and second, through Europe, improved international common management by a directorate.

Since institutions were Monnet's great theme, the sub-theme of directorates has tended to be lost to sight, but it was always there. In his anxiety to achieve grand designs Monnet tended to reduce the actors to the few key players of whatever combination he was trying to mount. Egalitarian in many respects, he was privately impatient of small countries. Changing the priorities of the sharks was hard enough without the pilot fish putting in their pennyworth. He used to quote with cheerful assent an anonymous pre-war American who complained that in international conferences, and whatever the agenda, the Norwegian delegate rose to talk of fish. For these practical reasons, and from the OEEC to the OECD and from the Community to the Atlantic partnership, Monnet tried (always without formal success) to limit decision-making groups to what was in effect a directorate.

Monnet the practitioner and optimist of action was probably not interested in these conceptual difficulties. He saw opportunities to be exploited and two distinct problems calling for separate solutions. Institutions were necessary to provide a stable base for a democratic Germany in a Europe of many nations. The United States was more powerful than the whole Community put together. The two situations were too alien to allow of a single answer. The important thing was to move ahead. At the same time, at least one anecdote suggests that, while he appreciated the obstacles, he saw supranationality along the spectrum from partnership rather than in opposition to it. Shortly after de Gaulle's veto on British entry into the EC, he and Kohnstamm shared a glum breakfast with Heath at Monnet's hotel in Brussels, the Astoria. Monnet escorted Heath to his car and came back smiling. Kohnstamm asked him what was so amusing. "I was just thinking what difficulties we will have when the United States are forced to recognise they cannot exercise sovereignty on their own." As early as 1959, when America's new-found dollar deficit emerged, he began to claim in a telegram of July 8 to his young agent in Rome, Renato Giordano, that the Community "method" could have "unlimited" *(universelle)* application.

In the abstract and from a distance, it is possible to see Monnet's duality as a sign of a hidden agenda. His refusal to be a European nationalist, and yet determination that a uniting Europe should achieve "equality" with the United States, has been interpreted in just that way. Gaullists saw Monnet as a pawn of the Americans. They ignored his cherished goal of association in equality. Henry Kissinger, in his *Years of Upheaval,* drew the opposite conclusion from Monnet's success in calling repeatedly on America to over-come opposition to his schemes in Europe. He saw Monnet as a kind of European Gaullist proposing to obtain from America by stealth what de Gaulle hoped to wrest by force. He ignored Monnet's stress on interdependence. And yet what de Gaulle and Kissinger wrote off as camouflage, because neither would, nor could, bear to believe it, was in fact the clue to his strategy and values. Through partnership, he was seeking in the world the same effect as through the Community in Europe, to "civilianise" international relations.

Whether partnership could have worked as Monnet assumed is another matter. Any accumulation of power creates a potential for conflict with other centres. However, in the European Union, the risk is probably minimised. It is not just that interdependence is real. The Union is more like a regulated market place for a number of stallholders than a single corporation. Centralisation is limited, the premium on consensus high and the propensity for taking risks consequently low. Another is that democratic "trading states", as Richard Rosecrance calls them, that is, ones in which economic interests are in the driving-seat, are not likely to play fast and loose with the orderly environment that keeps them on the road. The problem for, and with, the Union in the immediate future is more likely to consist in getting it to move decisively.

In practice, because of the historically predictable obstacles to the emergence of a European political union, the reality has not been a partnership but a modified extension of postwar American leadership. This has been diluted by the relative growth of other economic centres, in East Asia and Western Europe. This has put more of a premium on collective action than in the immediate postwar years of the American near-monopoly of power. Practice has leaned to a limited hegemony of America over the industrial powers and of the industrial powers over the world. The hegemony has the virtue of existing and in theory of flexibility. But when countries pull in different directions without means of drawing them together, it is inefficient and potentially divisive. Common management has so far been honoured as much in the breach as in the observance and, in consequence, has bred limited expectations. Moreover, unilateral or oligarchic definitions of the general interest lack legitimacy. These shortcomings raise more or less permanently in a wider context the issue Monnet first tackled in a new way for Europe in the Community: can one carry international cooperation very far without rules to ensure decision-making in the service of common goals? As the world shrinks relative to the growth of human power, the question of the "common management of common problems" comes to roost ever nearer home.

Transforming Leader

Monnet's achievement is best understood in terms of James Mac-Gregor Burns's distinction between "transactional" and "transforming" leadership. Transactional leadership is the art of tying up compromises between political forces in the normal operation of a settled system. Transforming leadership requires a much rarer capacity—to renew the terms in which the political debate are conducted. Burns identifies it with people such as Gandhi or Roosevelt. Monnet cannot compare directly with either. He had none of their contact with the masses. Yet his view of changing the context by injecting a new vision, through a new entity, into the status quo, a "ferment" of change, puts him in the same category. "We are starting a process of continuous reform which can shape tomorrow's world more lastingly than the principles of revolution so widespread outside the West." It would be hard to find a purer expression of the idea of transforming leadership.

David Drummond observed as early as the 1930s that Jean Monnet had been "involved in one reorganisation or another ever since the war." The sheer number of initiatives in which he was a seminal figure, over half a century, is hard to parallel. Few in the time and field come to mind with anything like the same fertility of innovation.

Politics being highly competitive, there was naturally a high wastage rate. If few of Monnet's schemes between the wars left lasting traces, the fault lay less with them than with world slump and the evil genius of Hitler and the Japanese militarists. There was no obvious qualitative gap between Monnet's early and later plans. It would also be wrong to suggest that his early career was narrowly technocratic. The Upper Silesian and Austrian settlements were primarily political. The difference was that after the Second World War Monnet operated at a higher level, had a more sharply defined view of the means to achieve his ends and above all benefitted from a more benign environment.

From the Second World War onwards, Monnet's efforts bore more obvious and in general lasting fruit than before. For nearly five years, in effect from 1938 to the beginning of 1943, he strove to bring America's industrial power to bear decisively on the defeat of Hitler. If Keynes was right and Monnet shortened the war by a year, that was a life's work in itself by most standards. Even if he did not, it was extraordinary that a lone Frenchman in exile should have played a major role in the ultimate recesses of the Anglo-American war effort. Then in Algiers in 1943, Monnet and Catroux between them did more than anyone else to unite the warring Free French factions. This brought Monnet close to the heart of French government for the first time since the Treaty of Versailles. He stayed there for a decade, during which he launched the two great postwar schemes which have made his name, the Monnet and the Schuman plans.

These were of a different order from the usual reform. They were not specific initiatives so much as generic ones, affecting broad economic and political processes. The first plan laid the foundations for the renewal of a fallen great power, France, as a medium-sized but modern industrial society. The second, on a far larger scale, launched Europe on the road to a transformation of interstate relations. In both cases, the achievement was closely associated with processes of renewal.

Renewal, the creative harnessing of energies which seem exhausted, is in some ways the hardest and perhaps most important of all operations in a society. Britain, Dean Acheson said and wrote in the 1960s, to much resentment in London, lost an empire and failed to find a role. France lost a catastrophic war and almost lost her soul as well, yet discovered a vocation. Moreover, it was not confined to one scene, France, but applied to two, embracing Europe. When one considers how often failure and "decline" exert cumulative force and thrust a once great power like Spain onto the sidelines for centuries, or left a society like Britain bewildered by persistent failure to perform to expectations, it is plain that reversing a slide is a victory against the odds.

The Monnet Plan was certainly not the only postwar factor in the economic revival of France. There was a diffuse spirit of expansion before Monnet came on the scene. But morale in France, given massive defeat, was probably more fragile than in any other European country. The confusion of spirit was great. There was an inferiority complex towards Germany seventy-five years deep. When Monnet turned up, de Gaulle's government had failed to adopt any economic policy to inspire an electorate. After de Gaulle stalked out, it became clear that the prewar republic—designed to frustrate aspirant dictators—would be restored, with weak governments subject to a capricious National Assembly. It was a regime calculated to sacrifice long-term goals to short-term patronage. The anti-parliamentary parties, the Communists and soon the Gaullists, had the biggest votes and best organisation. In these circumstances, to pursue a consistent investment policy at all was a remarkable achievement. It stood out even at the time.

It succeeded by a kind of political judo. Monnet mobilised an effective coalition behind his plan, not least in the Finance Ministry, by disclaiming all political or bureaucratic ambitions. Political pretensions had aborted Mendès-France's plan. Monnet too was rebuffed later on when he sought to acquire major powers for the Planning Office. His initial self-denying ordinance was the condition of success. His plan would still have failed without Marshall aid. Yet there is little doubt that he maximised American support and funds. Because of a benign conspiracy between Monnet, top officials of the Finance Ministry and the Marshall Plan administrators, France managed to concentrate more aid on direct investment than any other recipient country.

This achievement underpinned all later progress. France had a foundation for growth when economic "miracles" began to break out all over Western Europe in the middle 1950s. Although protectionism was still rife when the Rome treaties were negotiated, and observers talked of France as a "farmcart stuck in the mud", the growth mentality had taken sufficient hold for optimists, including de Gaulle, to conclude against the pessimists, led by Mendès-France, that a Common Market would be salutary. The Monnet Plan began the shift from a depressed to an expansive view in a country whose prospects remained a source of anxiety for years until de Gaulle ended the Algerian War in 1962.

To initiate this shift in expectations was a major achievement. Building on a renewal already begun is one thing. It is another to find and sustain a formula for rejuvenation when appearances are at their worst, proposals of reform themselves are tainted by the misperceptions they set out to correct, and the angle of novelty, at the narrow starting point, has yet to convince a disillusioned public that it offers better prospects than earlier false starts. The much derided Fourth Republic was responsible for just such a feat of medical clarification, and Monnet largely inspired it.

II
FATHER OF THE COMMUNITY

Monnet's role in the birth and rise of the European Community was an even more complex phenomenon, if only because of the Community's greater scope in time and space. Europe has been, and had to be, a broad, collective achievement. To speak only of the early founding years and of the main political leaders: Schuman and Adenauer, the German anvil on which plans were beaten into shape; Beyen, who launched the Common Market, and Spaak, who manoeuvred through the fog of Messina; and Mollet who, as Prime Minister, overrode French doubts in the two short years of the only window of opportunity for the Treaties of Rome; all, at different times, played crucial parts. That makes, with Monnet, at least six characters in search of Europe. They relied in turn on teams of committed politicians and civil servants, often of very high quality, who constituted, collectively, a powerful driving force. De Gaulle too deserves some of the credit for the Common Market. He said he would never have proposed it. But he made it credible by providing the authority for the French monetary reform of January 1959. He forced through its one initial common policy on any scale, that for agriculture, in the early 1960s. Europe was never a one-man show.

Inherent relativity is compounded by a factor peculiar to Monnet. From today's vantage point, the guts of the Community, indeed of the whole European Union, is the Common Market. Everything else pales in comparison. It is the paradox of Monnet's career that, though he launched the European revival of 1955, he played no direct part in the birth of the Common Market. Given half a chance, he would have postponed it in favour of Euratom. Whatever else Monnet may have been, he was not the father of the Common Market.

Indeed, the sectoral approach Monnet pioneered suffered swingeing blows a little later, around 1958–59. The European Coal and Steel Community, under weak leadership after the departure of René Mayer, was unable to face the coal crisis of those years. This was settled—or not settled—by deals between the governments which humiliated the High Authority. It is not certain that stronger leadership would have made much difference. The ECSC never really recovered and was overshadowed thenceforth by the EEC. As for Euratom, as soon as de Gaulle returned to power, it was living on borrowed time. So while the Common Market took off in the early 1960s, the Monnet formula of sectoral communities gradually fell out of the running. Moreover, in retrospect, it may never have had a strong chance of success. Both the steel and nuclear industries were opposed to the Communities that concerned them. The ECSC and Euratom also worked in industries where the states played a major regulatory role and were not inclined to share it with others.

These facts raise a basic question about Monnet's responsibility for the European Community as we know it today. Its solid and still expanding achievements have been secured almost exclusively through the Common Market. The Common Market is overwhelmingly a commercial and economic phenomenon. Though the Community has always made political claims for itself, all the efforts in the specifically political areas of union which have punctuated its history have produced marginal results verging on failure. The economic ones alone have been successful. Should one therefore conclude that the forces behind the European Community are really economic? May not the Common Market have been simply due to the awakening awareness of the governments in the "economic miracle" years—including an unlikely de Gaulle—that continuing growth demanded wider markets? If that has been, and is, the real world, and its fulcrum in Europe has been the Common Market, then the founding fathers of the Community, the Monnets and Schumans, are not "the fathers of Europe" at all. The fathers are the industrial-bureaucratic complex of Germany in 1956, and a persuasive few of like mind in other Community countries, such as Marjolin in France, who promoted the Common Market primarily for economic reasons.

There is no doubt that without the sudden discovery in the mid-1950s that Western Europe was launching into rapid growth and throwing off postwar mental depression—the "age of anxiety" of the nascent Cold War—there would probably have been no Treaties of Rome. The very phrase *economic miracle* conveyed surprise, relief and a budding self-confidence that was lacking before. The high tide gave even protectionists the courage to risk opening commercial frontiers. It defies belief that they would have prevailed in an era of low growth or recession. Nevertheless, it does not follow that because economic factors strongly favoured a common market, they sufficed to produce it on their own, still less that they predetermined it and that there were no plausible alternatives with other political aims.

Only six of the sixteen members of the OEEC in 1955–57 founded the Common Market. Ten did not. Of these ten, some grew and increased their trade with the Common Market countries, especially West Germany, the largest market, faster than some of the six themselves, others did not. There was no clear pattern in the years from 1952 to 1957, the years most relevant for defining attitudes to a still hypothetical Common Market. In all the cases, except perhaps those of Great Britain and Iberia, rates of growth were very respectable. The penalties for not joining the Common Market were, in the purely economic area, neither systematic nor self-evident.

Even among the six founding states, alternatives to the Common Market were considered at times. After France's rejection of the European Army treaty in late August 1954, powerful forces in all its Community partners leaned towards arrangements with Britain and the other states of the wider and looser West European OEEC. Free Trade Areas, though none had been proposed at the time, were theoretically well-known and written into the GATT. There were powerful forces, especially in Germany and the Netherlands, lined up, behind Erhard and the port of Rotterdam, under the banner of worldwide free trade. For them, a common market with France was a capitulation to protectionists. Similar but less decided schools of thought existed in parts of government in both Italy and Belgium. Had the British proposed a Free Trade Area there and then, they might conceivably have generated an unstoppable impetus. But, having no such ambitions, they did not and Spaak dammed up the tendencies to intergovernmentalism that surfaced most openly perhaps in Belgium.

It is true that the Netherlands, France and Italy were all interested in farm trade and that this argued for a common market. But both the major farm importers of Western Europe, Britain and the Federal Republic, preferred low price farm imports from the world. In reality, West Germany, which regarded farm imports as bargaining counters for its manufactured exports, did not want to be tied to a Western European agricultural preference system at all. Something like six years passed after the ratification of the Treaties of Rome before it became reasonably clear that the Common Market would include agriculture in fact as well as in fiction. The Common Agricultural Policy was treated as an extraordinary achievement when it emerged through successive "crises" and threats of walk-outs by de Gaulle. There is no sign the Germans would have given way if the "reconciliation with France" had not been a central plank of their policy. Though France, once it made up its mind on the EEC, gave high priority to its farmers politically and to agriculture in the Rome treaty, it had originally envisaged only bulk-buying contracts with Germany for wheat and sugar. In short, though agriculture was very important in the perceived balance of advantages of the EEC, it was ultimately dependent on the same factor that determined the Community strategy in the first place: the crucial relationship between France and Germany.

France did not want a common market at all until very late in the day. Marjolin has testified that the powerful French civil service, almost to a man, was as leery of the Common Market as Mendès-France, who led the parliamentary opposition. Christian Pineau, the Foreign Minister in the Mollet government, himself in favour of the Common Market, told more than one interlocutor early in 1956 that "a great deal of education" would be necessary before it could be accepted by the French Parliament. In short, it is hard to see the Common Market, which divided the OEEC countries, winning through on economic grounds alone. It does not follow that because integration has chalked up its major successes in the economic field, economic forces on their own would have produced them.

In fact, all the choices made by the various states for or against joining the Common Market seem to have been tipped one way or the other by political factors. The British stayed out because they still saw themselves as a world power, and not, Bevin once objected, as "just another European country." Equally political were the motives of other abstainers. Most of them were neutrals of various hues, and the Nordics shared with Britain a certain disdain for continental Europe.

Among the Six themselves, the Common Market proposal would not have emerged without political priorities. For Adenauer (who overrode Erhard) as for Spaak, finding a solid collective framework for Franco-German reconciliation was the heart of the strategy. The French failed to reject the Benelux Memorandum at Messina which contained the Common Market, because they felt it impossible to set their faces against "Europe" a second time after the EDC.

There was a potential majority in France itself for further integration, parts of it with a slow-burning anger at the rejection of the European Army Treaty. Mollet was to be decisive in the final French acceptance of the Treaties of Rome. For Mollet, the Prime Minister at the crucial juncture, fear of a German national army (provided by the Paris Agreements of October 1954) was probably the central motive for more European integration. One reason why he was nominated Prime Minister in January 1956 was because the President of the Republic, René Coty (who chose prime ministerial candidates to run the gauntlet of Parliament), considered that Mollet was a "European" and that Mendès-France, the alternative, was not. The reason Mollet then renegued on his promise to Mendès-France to choose him as Foreign Minister if he himself became Prime Minister was again because Mendès-France was felt not to be "European". The primacy of the federal or quasi-federal imperative in shaping relations between the new Germany and her neighbours, not only France, was never called in question. The new European drive after the conference of Messina was imbued with this specifically political energy.

The only model of a political structure to satisfy such a need was the European Coal and Steel Community. The natural approach was therefore to adapt it to new purposes. It is significant that whatever estimates of the ECSC may be today, it was widely accepted in 1955 to be a sufficient success as a pathfinder. It had functioned in a professional manner among the governments; and there was a strong cross-frontier party of "Europeans" who regarded it as the prototype of the only way to proceed. Economic motives came in the wake of this, not in its stead. Given that Franco-German reconciliation was at the heart of any scheme, France enjoyed a veto. Given French and to a lesser extent Italian protectionism, straight free trade was impossible. In any case, the Germans and Beyen themselves considered a sustainable Common Market had to have a regulatory system. This again pointed to solutions based on the Community model. The result—despite the veto after the EDC on anything smacking of a European "government" or High Authority—was a close family relationship between the institutions of the prototype ECSC and its two successors, the EEC and Euratom.[1]

1. All the Communities share decisions between the so-called Executive (High Authority or Commission) and the Council of Ministers. Formally, in the ECSC, the High Authority (claiming to be a government) took decisions after securing a concurring majority in the Council. In the later Communities, the Council decides by a majority vote on a proposal of the Commission (which is not accepted as a government). The practical effects are more alike

In reality, the Common Market was a particular case of a fact so basic it is easy to overlook. There was no functional reason why the members of the ECSC, the European Army, the European Political Community, Euratom and the EEC should always be the same six countries. For many, France was the last country with which to seek a privileged trade relationship. In the case of Euratom, there were good reasons for Britain, Norway and Switzerland to be members. Armand was fond of what he called Europe "à la carte", that is, technical schemes varying in national composition according to what made sense in terms of the matter in hand. This functionalism was anathema to Monnet. It would undermine the Community institutions and the Franco-German deal built into them. That this was not just a personal whim was evident from the fact that all three surviving Communities have had the same membership. The Common Market was adopted because the France of Monnet, Schuman and Mollet had a German policy acceptable to all the founder states of the Community, including Germany itself, while Britain, the fulcrum of any alternative solution, in effect had none.

There was a basic political continuity between the Schuman and two Rome treaties, symbolised by the partial fusion of all three Communities in a single structure in 1967. The political priorities which governed the Schuman Plan, *mutatis mutandis,* governed the later Communities as well. It would be wrong to argue that the Common Market obeyed economic forces in some sense free of the political motives of 1950. Economically, the Common Market did break with the sectoral concept. Politically, it flowed from the same preoccupations.

This brings one back to the Schuman Plan as the source of the European policy. Here too, as with the Common Market, there were powerful "objective" forces at work. The main one was the emergence of the Federal Republic of Germany. It was the writing on the wall for the kind of Allied controls over the Ruhr and German armaments which buttressed France's shaky sense of security in 1949. However, this is not the same as saying there was overwhelming force behind only one solution. It was Monnet who launched the Schuman Plan, not the French Foreign Ministry; and if the French steel industry opposed it violently for months in the name of a producer cartel, there were clearly other ideas of how to proceed.

Or even of how not to proceed. France went through three major crises over German policy in the postwar decade. In the summer of 1948, it was forced to accept the unification of the Western occupation zones as a preliminary in effect to the creation of the Federal Republic. Bidault lost the French Foreign Ministry as a result, the diplomats of the Quai d'Orsay wriggled on

---

than the doctrines. The one major difference was that, in the later Communities and before the Single Act, the Council could choose more often than in the ECSC not to decide at all. This bedevilled the period of Eurosclerosis (the 1970s and early 1980s).

the hook, trying to bargain the French zone in Germany against concessions and time, but France step by step gave way. Then in the spring and summer of 1950, the French were faced with the prospect of the Federal Republic escaping from all industrial constraints. The symptoms were remarkably similar to those of 1948. As Schuman wrote to Mayer on February 2, 1951,

> the Americans and British are ready to jettison the International Ruhr Authority in order to ease the way for German membership of the Allied defence system. We have . . . very specific indications of this.

In 1950, however, the responses were the Schuman Plan and then the EDC. Finally, in the summer of 1954, the French vetoed the EDC. During the ensuing winter, despite a first rejection of the Paris agreements by the Parliament, they found they had to swallow the very German national army inside NATO, which the EDC had been invented to avoid. In each case, the hands of the French were forced by the Americans backed by the British. In one case, France drew new political energy out of its predicament, the European strategy. In the other two, it was overborne. It could have been overborne a third time as well. The difference was that on this occasion there was a positive political response instead of a semi-hypnotised attempt to deny the nightmare.

The credit for this creative act belongs jointly to Schuman and Monnet. Schuman took what might have been the great risk to himself of launching it. He was also crucial to Monnet's later ability to establish the European Community. However, it is no slur on Schuman to recognise that without Monnet, the Schuman Plan would never have reached the agenda, let alone remained there. In particular, Monnet seems to have been decisive over some basic choices when Schuman wavered. The most obvious case was the twin pair of issues of supranationality and Britain. Monnet was determined not to let Britain into the Schuman treaty talks without a prior commitment to an authority with independent powers. Schuman was less clear about Britain because he was less clear about the powers. This difference may have had unseen roots. At first, Schuman was inclined to view his plan as a device to surmount immediate conflicts between France and Germany, not like Monnet, who saw it as the key to a European strategy. Schuman thought there might be more ways than one to union. Monnet by this time was convinced that without supranationality there was none.

Monnet's initial notion of the High Authority for coal and steel as a kind of European Monnet Plan office with sweeping powers but no federal government or Congress to provide a context, and so in political terms an object floating in orbit, was unsustainably crude. The Dutch introduction of a Council of Ministers gave the Monnet construct a realistic framework it lacked. This reinforced the basic principle, that a body with powers to act was the condition of there being any Europe worth speaking of.

The contributions of Schuman and the Dutch do not change the fact that Monnet was the driving force behind the Schuman Plan, the European Coal and Steel Community, and the basic strategy underlying them. The appreciation of the results depends on the point of view adopted. If one expected federal European domination of the coal and steel industries, the ECSC was a failure. If one expected a set of common institutions inserted into the round of government decision-making, then under Monnet and his first successor, Mayer, it succeeded. It also put a stamp on the coal and steel markets which was different from the sum of the earlier national arrangements. Above all, it proved to the satisfaction of those who wanted "Europe" for political reasons that here was a machine able to drive the strategy forward.

The existence of a working model of European government was vital after the wreck of the European Army treaty. It is doubtful whether the second Europe could have emerged without the ECSC's certificate of roadworthiness. The echoes of the crash of the EDC had hardly faded before Monnet and Spaak in the winter of 1954–55, providing very much the equivalent to Monnet and Schuman in 1950, prepared a new campaign of European integration. They started with Euratom, proposed by Monnet, before Beyen came up with the Common Market. At this juncture, Euratom, whatever its later fate, was the one Community proposal to which the French were willing to give some encouragement. As late as the Mollet government and 1956, the advance toward the Common Market took place warily through Euratom. The ECSC and Euratom provided the base for the Common Market a year later. The latter could not have been conjured out of the blue and included France. Sectoral integration made it possible.

Monnet was, then, until the late spring of 1955, the prime creator of virtually everything identified with an European union, the groundwork with the Schuman Plan, the failure with the European Army and the new hope with Euratom, not a man alone but the one man always in the van, whoever else might join him there from time to time. As Miriam Camps, who worked on Europe at the State Department until 1953, has put it, "Monnet was . . . the driving force . . . the philosopher and generally accepted leader of the movement for creating unity in Europe". There was also a direct line of descent from the Schuman Plan to the Common Market, as indeed there is to the Single Market of 1993. Monnet was not the father of the Common Market. He may have been its grandfather, but in essence he was something else. Surprisingly perhaps, that something else was not economic but political. He was the father of the Community.

III
MR. EUROPE

Becoming the father of the Community involved more than inventing it. If Monnet is the tutelary genius of the European Commission today, this is because he shaped the idea of Europe as no one else even tried to do and became its spiritual father as well.

There was plenty of talk about integration before the Schuman Plan. But ideas of it ran into one other in a kind of fog. For example, on February 13, 1948, Bidault told the French National Assembly that "it is high time France's desire to create a [political] Europe should at last find clear and precise expression. . . . [The] solution—there is no other—is to integrate a peace-loving Germany into a united Europe". It sounded like the banns for the Community Europe which later emerged. In fact, Bidault's career soon showed that he was opposed to virtually everything this comment would convey to a reader today, and in particular to supranationality. The Schuman Plan put an end to the confusion of categories. It took a little time. The Pentagon, in 1950–51, spoke in the same breath of the European Defence Force, by which a German national army was to be built into NATO, and the European Defence Community, which was designed initially to replace a German army by a supranational one of the Six. Still, once the Schuman Plan got into its stride, the mist began to lift.

Monnet was the main clarifying force. He narrowed the starting point of integration to the sectors of coal and steel. This side-stepped the French and other protectionists while tackling the political issue of the Ruhr as the industrial face of predatory nationalism. The corollary was that progress to unity would begin in the economic field and by a dialectic of partial unions. Monnet also insisted on supranationality, which led through the controversy with the British to the necessary separation of the sheep from the goats in a two-speed Europe, the condition of any serious effort to unite. He placed the emphasis on the linked features of "equality", institutions and the promotion of "peace". No one insisted in such specific detail as he did on the new constitutional system of the Community, not even Schuman or Monnet's immediate successor in Luxembourg, René Mayer. From the beginning, he worked on a close relationship with the Americans which embodied a concept of the politics of interdependence. In all these lasting strategic choices, settled virtually from the start, Monnet gave the intellectual, practical and political lead.

Once Monnet left the High Authority in 1955, his initiatives did not have the same impact. Not that his later campaigns, over Euratom, say, or the OECD or the European Council, were insignificant. Euratom was a tour de force for a politician out of office. But in the end, none fulfilled the hopes vested in them with anything like the effect of his plans earlier on. His main achievement in his later years was probably to establish the political language of the Community. It would have suffered greatly from the lack of one had the only policy ideas been (as in the political classes in general they tended to be) a dream of power for some and tactical pragmatism for others. Monnet had a matured conviction which held the policy together at a deeper level than the rhetoric of European revival which served most politicians.

This was, of course, the obligation, already described, to civilianise international relations. They should obey rules of law as close as possible to those of democracies at home. Countries could no longer refuse responsibility for the impact of their actions on others. Equality before the law embodied in common institutions was the only way to anchor international life in shared responsibility—the core of legitimate government and popular consent in civil society. Institutions alone could cement the social contract between countries. Monnet was addicted to a couple of aphorisms he ascribed to the nineteenth-century Genevese diarist Henri Frédéric Amiel and to which he contributed a good deal himself: "Each man begins the world afresh. Only institutions grow wiser; they store up the collective experience; and, from this experience and wisdom, men subject to the same laws will gradually find, not that their natures change but that their behaviour does". And: "Institutions govern relationships between people. They are the real pillars of civilisation".[2]

In the same spirit, Monnet told André Visson, "We should not create a nation Europe instead of a nation France". The means might have to differ outside Europe, but in a world increasingly intertwined, civilianising relations must mean moving to joint management of shared problems.

This approach was inherently inclusive and unifying. The Monnet Plan finessed the dilemma (conventional at the time) of socialism or the market by concentrating on the need to modernise. The Schuman Plan broke through the roadblock of Franco-German rivalry by setting a common destination, European Union. Monnet argued that European Union, far from being opposed to German reunification, was necessary to it. The "partnership of equals" turned its back on the iron choice for Europe of satellite status or chauvinist defiance of the United States. This "forward flight", as the French graphically call it, often worked and sometimes not. It is harder to imagine and set a common goal which did not previously exist than to analyse an

2. The one relevant entry in Amiel's *Journal* (October 4, 1873) reads: "Each man begins the world afresh, and not one fault of the first man has been avoided by his remotest ancestor. The collective experience of the race accumulates, but individual experience dies with the individual, and the result is that institutions become wiser and knowledge as such increases; but the young man, although more cultivated, is just as presumptuous, and not less fallible today than he ever was" (Mrs. Humphry Ward's translation, first edition, 1885). The extract is on p. 294 of Robert Bridges' anthology *The Spirit of Man*, Monnet's favourite bedside reading.

obvious "contradiction" built all too evidently into the current situation. But it worked often enough to suggest an uncommon capacity to point the way to new objectives.

This was reinforced by Monnet's attitudes close to the action. Professional politicians recognised in him someone as practical and adept and at least as energetic as they and knew that his contacts were often better than their own. On top of which, he was uniquely identified with European union. For all the other leaders, Europe was possibly a high point, but still only a phase, in variegated careers. They could not deal on Europe without people wondering about conflicting interests. Monnet, in contrast could bring together politicians and trade unionists of almost all stripes, some of whom could not normally afford to be seen together, and focus them on the one issue he personified. No one less uniquely identified with the European idea would have had the moral authority to take the lead.

Monnet, in short, alone linked up the whole European chain of being, from the conceptual background to the tiniest tactical detail. As a result, he coloured the European idea to an exceptional degree with his personality and concepts. "In the years after the war", wrote Spaak, "he played a preponderant role in the building of Europe. We all looked up to him as a mentor. We all sought his opinion and followed his advice".

This explains Monnet's exceptional ability to mobilise powerful and disparate coalitions of support for his major enterprises. It was clear enough with the Monnet and Schuman plans. More remarkable perhaps was the Action Committee. In it, a growing majority of political parties and trade unions from the Community countries held together over twenty years, during which European integration seemed unendingly on the defensive, most obviously but not only against de Gaulle. Whatever the Action Committee's practical uses, its main function was to keep the flag flying on the long march. With de Gaulle one minute patronising the Federal Republic as a privileged follower and the next treating it as a second-class citizen, there was a natural fear the Germans might succumb to the lure of national reunification at the expense of European Union. By maintaining the broadest possible consensus behind European orthodoxy, the Action Committee helped them not to.

Further, Monnet's semi-detached position conferred advantages. In France at the time of the Monnet Plan, he was a keeper of the crossroads, in touch with everyone in government (and the Americans) but not tied down to placating an irresponsible National Assembly. Later on again, on European issues, he was a keeper of the crossroads between the Community governments and between them and the United States. In many ways, he became the natural leader of a shadow party of internationalists on both sides of the Atlantic. Hallstein and the Common Market Commission in Brussels were one centre. Monnet and a core of leaders on the Action Committee were another. A third and very important one was in Washington, in the State Department and the White House.

Though not typical of any of their national milieus, these small elites—bureaucrats and politicians—were able to make the running for a decade and a half because they benefitted from American concentration on the Cold War in Europe and knew what they wanted. They also satisfied the interests of Germany and all its Community partners (bar de Gaulle's France), who wanted to run their Atlantic and European integration policies in tandem. It does not follow, however, that their policies were simply a mask for "the superpower hegemony rationalised in universal values". The instinctive attitude of many American policy-makers was to conduct bilateral relations as along spokes between themselves at the hub and individual Allies on the rim of the wheel, on the NATO model, not to encourage Europeans to build up a single separate weight as in the so-called dumbbell concept. European governments themselves normally preferred direct individual dealings with Washington.

In fact, partnership was an internationalists' policy. It is misleading to read the integrative policies of the early postwar period as those of states, such as America, France or Germany. They could not have worked had they violated the interests of those states. But other policies would have found champions in every capital. To an important extent, the ones actually chosen reflected the special convictions of tiny, temporarily dominant groups, imbued with the internationalism that flourishes after wars, and working together across frontiers, often against latent opposition at home. Monnet, in negotiating the Schuman Plan, worked as cheerfully with American as with French colleagues. As Ball has written:

> Tommy [Tomlinson] and I conspired with Monnet in full mutual confidence, sensitive to the problems he was encountering. Monnet, in turn, recognized Tommy's problems in dealing with Washington. Such a complete sharing of information and insights could only arise among individuals totally dedicated to a central idea; we all believed fervently in Monnet's goal of a united Europe, which, we thought, was quite as important to Americans as to Europeans.

An invisible "party" stretched hands across the Atlantic. In Tuthill's words, "The devil in *my* life, in international relations, is excessive [national] sovereignty".

Monnet proved the most creative of this small band. In fact, he was probably the one thoroughgoing internationalist so far who has made a marked impact on history. He was the long-sighted strategist and arguably major statesman of a Fourth Republic whose conventional politics did not produce one. His supreme achievement was to bring a new European political system into being. As a French diplomat, François Valéry, the son of the poet Paul Valéry, has put it, "Few men, in the final analysis, have enjoyed so little power and yet exerted so much influence, and one that was so lasting". In his *Memoirs,* Monnet wrote that "a great statesman is one who can work for long-term goals which eventually suit situations as yet unforeseen". He was ostensibly referring to Roosevelt, whom he regarded as a political genius. He might be forgiven for having also had himself in mind. Deficient in political theatre Monnet may have been. Judged by works, he is one of the few who have changed the modern world.

IV
WHAT IS NEW?

This judgement, of course, depends in part on whether European Union is as significant as has been claimed. Unexpected as any union may be against a thousand years of European wars, is it really such an act of innovation? May it not owe as much to underlying forces as to its architects? The Community was launched ostensibly to ensure peace in Europe. But France and Germany were no longer the arbiters of peace or war. The Cold War, the superpowers' control over Europe, the nuclear balance of terror, could have been necessary and sufficient to peace without benefit of European Union. In retrospect, it now appears that Hitler's suicide in the bunker buried the German lust for power as Waterloo once did that of the French. The spread of mass affluence in industrial societies bred, for a while at any rate, a civil outlook far from any military ethos. As for common markets, may they not be a European sub-species of an economy becoming more and more global? What has European integration added that is unique?

European Union would no doubt have been as utopian as for centuries without the surrounding change in conditions after the war. So long as Europe was the metropolis of world power, the unilateralism, the ambitions, of nation states left no room for a marriage of reason. At the same time, now that one has taken place, it is easy to take too much for granted. Nothing is more destructive of democracy or stability than rancorous nationalism. The Saar has disappeared as an issue, swallowed up in the European Community. But before the Schuman Plan, it showed every sign of reviving the old rehearsed responses between France and Germany. Had the issue been left unresolved, it is anyone's guess what effect the Algerian War, which almost produced an army coup, might have had on French politics. As for the Germans, their leaders were torn after the war between the desire to be rehabilitated in the West and the belief that it might be fatal to ignore the national feeling of their people. The issue bitterly divided Adenauer and the Socialist leader Kurt Schumacher until the latter's death in 1952. Had Adenauer's policy of European integration failed in the eyes of the electorate, the pull of a hankering after reunification, with all that meant in terms of unstable relations between East and West, could have been much stronger. That in turn would have woken the sleeping hound of French suspicions. Reciprocal hostility could easily have been aroused. Exactly how that would have affected either country, both of which were subject to substantial strains, and how the United States would have controlled such an unstable situation, are necessarily open questions.

We do know what happened instead. Because the Community states, for political reasons, were willing to envisage having common governing bodies with autonomous powers for some purposes and a form of majority voting, they were able to pass contracts among themselves that were beyond the scope of intergovernmental organisations. The new system gave guarantees of results and of mutual obligations that were not previously available. In the 1950s, supranational institutions in the EEC brought about the customs union the OEEC could not achieve. Later, in the 1960s, they made possible the hotly disputed Common Agricultural Policy and in the 1980s the Single Market, each of which was made up of a vast array of more specific policy decisions. The area of activity of the Communities has, by the standards of history, expanded rapidly even if at times, as in the 1970s, the system seemed becalmed.

The Community's effect has perhaps been even larger in political psychology than specifics. By introducing a rule of law into relations between Western European countries, it has cut off a whole dimension of destructive expectations in the minds of policy-makers. The need to think in terms of insurance policies against hostile intent among neighbours (and so, very often, to encourage the very behaviour feared) has been minimised and replaced by aspirations that come nearer to the "rights" and responsibilities which reign in domestic politics. With all its imperfections, the Community domesticates the balance of power into something which, if not as "democratic" as domestic norms, has made the international system in Europe take a huge step in their direction.

The Community is, in fact, a species of security policy. The French invented the Community as insurance against renascent German power. The United States was not enough in that regard. How long would the United States remain in Europe? And what would the French situation be if the United States and a strong Germany struck up a special relationship? France's sense of vulnerability was not unique. It was a cliché after the war that all the founding states of the Community, unlike Britain, had been defeated and shaken to their moral and material foundations. For West Germany, a postwar pariah, the Community provided an accommodating context for revival and an insurance against a decline in the United States' security guarantee. At least two chancellors voiced anxiety that Germany needed America more than America needed Germany. For the Benelux trio, initially very wary of supranational bodies, the Community increasingly represented protection against both conflict and a dominating alliance between France and Germany. Small countries have gained a say in the formation of policies they almost wholly lacked in the old balance of power, of which they always felt potential victims. Many able individuals of whom one would not have heard in the past because they came from minor countries have found a voice through the Community. It is no accident that the smaller countries look to the common rules and the Commission as bulwarks against a relapse into the old condition. The large countries even claim nowadays, with some justice, that the small ones are over-represented. For all member states, large and small, integration has meant insurance vis-à-vis superpowers and the globalisation of the world economy. Rightly or wrongly, it promises a stability in relations between members no alliance can offer. It has even given outsiders in Europe hope of a place "at the top table" if they can join. Its clubbable aspect makes the Community a very powerful magnet in Europe. Here is a formidable list of reasons for states to feel committed.

It is reasonable, then, despite the inherent impossibility of proof, to assume that European integration has produced a specific value-added which could not have been obtained in any other way. This seems palpable and active in the sense of solidarity which obtains between the Community's member states. In this sense, the European Community has already produced a political revolution. After the war, no government in Europe behaved as if Union were a realistic option. By the 1990s, it has become the common climate in which they operate. The huge effort of regulation to create a Continental market base for business makes it a political and administrative as much as economic achievement. Politically, the old nationalist norms have been modified by a civilian frame of rules which has gradually become habitual. For all their limitations, these laws mark the end of foreign policy and the advent of civil politics over much of a continent. One could hardly imagine a more radical change in international relations than to turn them, even partially, into domestic ones.

A new stratum has been deposited on the old and complex political geology of Europe. The new alluvium partially buries the nationalism dominant since the French Revolution. It reverts to the multinational systems of the old Habsburg and other empires but with what they lacked, the modern politics of consent. Nationalism was a crucial phase in the freeing of civil society, because power devolved to the citizen body. The vice of this process, however, was a shameless egocentricity in the name of the group to which few would dare to admit as individuals. As more and more peoples discovered nationhood, political fragmentation led Europe from eighteen states before the Congress of Berlin in 1878 to nearer fifty today. Yet, in contrast, material progress intensified interdependence. These contrary forces warred for two centuries before "Europe" at last began to moderate the anarchy by uniting the nations along democratic lines and so imposing the norms of civil society across frontiers.

At the same time, the end of the Cold War and the ever-increasing globalisation of the world economy could well test the fabric of European Union to the limit. When the EEC came into operation it was widely assumed that it would lead rapidly to economic union and that this in turn would create the conditions for political union. In fact, it has taken over thirty years for the EEC to erect most of the pillars of economic union it was supposed to raise in a decade. This is the meaning of the nearly three hundred regulations passed between 1988 and 1993 to produce the Single Market. But political union, in any real sense, has still escaped its would-be authors. The Maastricht treaty of European Union solves few of the problems. It raises all the issues—money, defence, foreign policy, law and order—but in practice is overwhelmingly intergovernmental on them all. The 1990s have fulfilled the European programme of the 1950s, but found that their political vision remains as elusive as ever.

This is not new. It has been a recurring pattern of European integration. The disappointments of Maastricht echo the failures or shortcomings of the EDC / ePC in 1954, the Werner Plan for monetary union in 1970, the European Council in 1974, and several lesser schemes. There remains, as a former French Foreign Minister, Jean Sauvagnargues, has pointed out, a qualitative gap between the enunciation of the Monnetist "general view", with which the European Commission and its predecessors have been endowed, and the exercise of sovereign power. Monnet spent his last fifteen years trying and failing to bridge this gap. In short, the founding fathers would have liked to work towards a federal union, but were unable to do so. Now, Maastricht has proved again that the states are more open to politically advanced forms of economic integration than to political union as such.

The European Union has grown up virtually in the opposite way to any of its supposed models. Past federations began with the commanding political heights, largely because the material and welfare aspects of government were far less developed than those of authority and power. Even under the Articles of Confederation, the United States Congress waged the War of Independence, issued money, contracted the alliance with France, concluded peace, and ordered the settlement of the new territories. In contrast, the European Communities were steps to a federation that might have to operate indefinitely in intermediate zones. It was federal minimalism confined to certain economic areas. New instruments and ideas had to be devised for dealing with such a partial condition of life. The creators of the Community were surprisingly ignorant of, and indifferent to, historical precedent. The system corresponds closely to no previous constitutional norm.

Critics have sometimes deplored the economic limits of the Community. Yet, as with the Monnet Plan, modesty may be its strength. The history of attempts at political federation is almost uniformly dismal, from ancient Greece to the German Bund in the nineteenth century. The three successes that were spontaneous and not imposed—Switzerland, the Netherlands and the United States—first came together in war against an overlord. Even with them, one needs in two cases out of three to take a telescope to history. The United Provinces (the pre–French Revolutionary incarnation of the Netherlands) hung back 250 years before being unified by Napoleon and the Treaty of Vienna. The Swiss, never to be hurried, achieved a federal constitution only after five civil wars and nearly six hundred years. It is hard to cite a single example of rapid union by consent between long-settled peoples, still less between former great powers without a common language.

Had the European Union not been forced to work through the dispersed economic medium, it might never have been the catchment area it has proved. Moreover, the Community has been the beneficiary of the decline of military influences between major powers and the corresponding rise of economic ones. When the use of force is constrained by nuclear deterrence, even its indirect employment to exert advantage is reduced. The Cold War was progressively stripped of its ancestral military rhetoric to reveal a form of political competition in which economic and cultural factors in the end proved decisive. (Even exhausting the Soviet Union by an arms race was an economic not a military strategy.) Can anyone seriously claim the British and French nuclear arsenals have delivered political dividends to compare with the yen or the Dentschemark? The more deterrence works, the more it shifts the ability to act to civilian factors, of which economics is the most integrated into government—persistent, flexible and pervading. As a result, the Community, as a huge and relatively coherent economic entity, despite obvious weaknesses, has acquired some of the political magnetism associated with "great" powers.

Nevertheless, the inability to carry European integration from the economic to political arena, from collective to unitary bodies, has left cracks potentially vulnerable to new pressures. Internally, Europe as it touches on more and more aspects of public life risks falling foul of grassroots democracy. This is partly because some national governments (such as the British and French) are trying to hinder the European Parliament from acting as the real one the Union needs. The charges of technocracy levelled against the Union are partly fraudulent because the governments are the main culprits, but that hardly disposes of the problem. Transnationally, the ever strengthening links of a global economy and its institutions will both complement and compete with the Union. The new World Trade Organisation could exert a centrifugal pull on a body based on many of the same economic elements. Finally, the end of the Cold War changes the context. A reunified

Germany will not need the European Union, one argument runs, as much as the old divided one. The endless procession of countries clamouring to join it could sink the Union under the weight of their diversity. On this reading, the future lies with loose compacts of the kind so dear to the British.

However, Union is associated in the core continental European countries with a political stability which has been a godsend to all of them, the Germans included. Now that the clear commitments of the Cold War are over, Europe could prove less, not more, secure. Instability in Russia and eastern Europe, American distractions elsewhere, competition from or frictions with very different cultures such as East Asia and Islam, at home the perceived imbalance between Germany and others, macroeconomics, the environment, could all reinforce the felt need for a structured Union. Already, the material interests vested in it are enormous. To handle their innumerable mutual obligations, the Community states will be under constant pressure to be effective. For that, actions, however fragmentary, will have to be federal in cumulative impact. "European options" will not disappear because the pace has become the slow march of history instead of an initial rush.

Still, the supposedly hybrid nature of the European Union, even with closer commitments than today, could prove durable. In an age of increasingly intense global interactions, Europe may never quite replicate the classic features of a federation—that is, of a variety of nation state—familiar from the eighteenth and nineteenth centuries. It could for a long time be unclear whether the European Union is moving to the clear-cut federal destination its founding fathers assumed or to some different terminus, perhaps a kind of collective geared to the global bargaining of contentious interdependence, a ganglion in a ganglionic international system. European Union is *inter alia* a way of exploring a new world.

This was essentially Monnet's own outlook. He kept in his office a model of the Kontiki raft on which Thor Heyerdahl and his companions crossed the South Pacific as a symbol of Europe's own voyage of discovery. Though he saw Europe in the relatively familiar terms of a political union he also saw it as a ferment of change. He stressed the virtues of rules and institutions in unifying peoples and not as new forms of the old game of coalitions of states. He favoured the "common management of common problems" beyond Europe. While circumstances have changed since Monnet's day, these insights are not time-bound. On an ever more technological, crowded planet the fragmented political authority inherited from the past is increasingly dangerous. The collapse of the Cold War has revealed a world torn between a growing multiplicity of nations and increasing functional interdependence in almost every field. The potential costs of failing to achieve political contracts between the many different societies are steadily piling up. The hegemony of a few leading powers will not suffice for long—first because the rising number of significant powers stacks the odds against cohesion, second because approaches not based on accepted and enforceable collective contracts will be neither efficient nor legitimate. European Union, raised in special circumstances—they always are—is not in any simple way a model for such a world, but it is the boldest instance yet of a civil answer to the threat of chaos. If Monnet had not launched it when he did, there is every sign no one else would have done so. He seized a brief opportunity to achieve one of the rarest feats in history, the deliberate introduction of a new theme.

Notes

Publications
First three letters of the surname, or more as far as necessary to be clear.[1]

Interviews by the author
(a) Taped interviews as above, plus an asterisk (*).
(b) Correspondence and other communications, as above, plus "-DF" (no asterisk).
N.B. Dates are recorded throughout the References in the order day-month-year.

Interviews from Archives
As for interviews *(a)* above, preceded by the code for the archive (see below).

A = United States archives
United States National Archives, Washington, D.C., are filed by numbered "record groups", as follows:
  A 59 = State Department (especially 840.50R Marshall aid + 850.33 Schuman Plan + European Coal and Steel Community + 851.51 Finance [e.g., A59 840.50R])
  A107 = War Department
  A165 = War Department, Civil Affairs Division
  A169 = Foreign Economic Administration (FEA) successor to Lend-Lease Administration (OLLA)
  A179 = War Production Board (WPB)

  1. Two or more authors of a single work are indicated by the first three letters of the surname of each (e.g., "BulPel" = Bullen and Pelly). When more than two books by an author are cited in the notes, the date of publication is added to the key (e.g., "Mon55" is a Monnet publication of 1955).

A218 = Chiefs of Staff

A466 = High Commission, Germany

A469 = Economic Cooperation Administration (ECA)

AE- = Eisenhower Library, Abilene, Kansas

AE-AH = papers Henry Aurand (dy = diary) + NL = papers Laurie Norstad

AE-Pre-Presidential + White House Central + Whitman papers

AE-Du1E* = interview Eleanor Dulles, 14.12.62

AP- = Princeton University (Seeley Mudd Library)

AP-DJF = papers John Foster Dulles

AP-Sha* = interviews George Sharp by Philip A Crowl, 8.7.64 and 10.7.64

AR- = Roosevelt Library, Hyde Park, New York

AR-CO = papers Oscar Cox (dy = diary) + HH = papers Harry Hopkins
+ MH = Henry Morgenthau "diary" (transcripts of conversations and
major office papers)

AR-OF = Official + PSF = President's Secretary's File

AT- = Truman Library, Independence, Missouri

AT-AD = papers Dean Acheson + SH = papers Henry Stimson + SJ =
papers John Snyder + VF = papers Fred Vinson

AT-Ach* = Princeton seminars, interviewing Dean Acheson October 1953 to
March 1954

AT-Ham* = interview Dag Hammarskjöld by Harry B. Price, 28.11.52

A- = private papers of American citizens

A-BD dy = diary David Bruce, Virginia Historical Society

A-CM = papers Miriam Camps

A-FF = papers Felix Frankfurter, Library of Congress

A-LJ = papers John Leddy

A-McC = papers and diary John J. McCloy, Amherst College, Massachusetts

A-SR = Robert Schaetzel, notes Rockefeller Fellowship year in Europe
1959–60

A-TJ = papers of John W. Tuthill

B- = Belgian Archives, essentially MAE (Foreign Ministry), Van der Meulen
papers, code 5216, Schuman Plan negotiations and ECSC (= B-MAE 5216)

C- = Canada, C-HBC Hudson's Bay Company archives

DF (or EU-DF) = author's papers or statements made to the author

EU- = European Community Archives (and assimilated)

EU- CEAB 2 = High Authority, Secretariat-General

EU- CEAB 3 = High Authority, Central Archives

EU- CEAB 4 = High Authority, Legal Service

EU- CM = Council of Ministers

EU- KM = archives of Max Kohnstamm

F- = French National Archives, including

F- 80 AJ = Monnet Plan + 81 AJ = Schuman Plan and ECSC

F-AP = private papers deposited in Archives Nationales: AP 363 = René Mayer + 457 AP = Georges Bidault + 496 AP = Edouard Daladier

F-AssNat = Archives of the National Assembly

F-B = Ministry of Finance

F- C = Cognac archives

F- F1a = Ministry of Interior + F12 = Public Works + F14 = Industry + F60 = Prime Minister's office + F60ter = Secretariat-General, Prime Minister's Office

F-LH = Légion d'Honneur, Grande Chancellerie, archives

F-MAE AP = private papers deposited in Ministry of Foreign Affairs AP 328 = Monnet papers (1939–40)

F-MAE-GU39 = Ministry of Foreign Affairs, Second World War + DECE Post-war Economic Cooperation

F-SHAT = Historical Archives of the Army

GB- = British archives, mainly Public Record Office, notably

GB-Avia = Ministry of Supply + Cab = Cabinet Office + FO = Foreign Office (371 Political 372 Treaty) + Premier = Prime Minister + T = Treasury

GB-O = Oxford, Bodleian Library, papers of Robert Henry, later Lord, Brand.

GB-RIIA = Royal Institute of International Affairs, London notably GB- Jac88 = Sir Ian Jacob, text on Monnet, 1988

L- = Luxembourg National Archives: AET, Ministry of Foreign Affairs.

M- = Jean Monnet archives at the Fondation Jean Monnet pour l'Europe, Ferme de Dorigny, Lausanne, Switzerland

M- C = 1919–33 + D = 1933–40 + E = World War II + F = Monnet Plan + G = Schuman Plan + H = European Coal and Steel Community + I = European Defence Community + J = European Political Community + K = Action Committee for the U.S. of Europe + Mon dy = office diary of Jean Monnet

M- FS = papers of Robert Schuman

M- PD = papers of Lord Perth (David Drummond) before transfer to Lausanne and classification

M-Alp* = interview of Hervé Alphand by Roger Massip 17.6.81

M-BeuM* = interview of Hubert Beuve-Méry by Antoine Marès 18.1.83

M-Bou* = interview of Libert Bou by Antoine Marès 9.11.83

M-Cle* = interview of Stanley Cleveland by Leonard Tennyson 12.6.81

M-Cou* = interview of Maurice Couve de Murville by Antoine Marès 16.1.84

M- Fre* = interview of Henri Frenay by Antoine Marès 2.12.83

M-Hir* = interview of Etienne Hirsch by Antoine Marès 2.7.80

M- Jav* = interview of Fernand Javel by François Fontaine and Jacques-René Rabier 22.3.79

M-Kap* = interview of Léon Kaplan by Antoine Marès 28.4.83

M-McC* = interview of John McCloy by Leonard Tennyson 15.6.81

M-MenF* = interview of Pierre Mendès-France by Roger Massip 29.1.81

M-Owe* = interview of Henry Owen by Leonard Tennyson 30.6.81

M-Ple* = interviews of René Pleven by (i) Massip and Marès 27.3.80 + (ii) Massip, Marès and F. Fontaine 8.5.80

M-Ram* = interviews of Aline Ramsay (née Monnet) by Leonard Tennyson 6.9.91 and 21.9.91

M-Reu* = interview of Paul Reuter by Antoine Marès 7.8.80

REFERENCES

Introduction: Why Jean Monnet?

21 neither a civil servant [Rot* 93] 22 persuasive power [Marj 175] this power [Zij* 10–11] deal of impatience [Pall* 5] slip cuttings [Whi 332–33] 23 domestic detail [MayR 5] hard taskmaster [Clap85, 21; McC] deal of scope [M-Ple* 4; Rab* 6–8] more dangerous than victory [Koh*; DF] crises are opportunities [DF] too clear to be true [Foc* 5] differently from those on my side [Koh*] sickening spectacle [M-Mon dy 2.1.60] 24 embarrassed when you thank him [Lin72, 51–52] utopian strain [Mon72, 5] commendation generous [Mon 595] picked the flowers [M-Reu*]

1   A Talent at Large

27   quasi-peasant [Alp 140] cow [M-BeuM*; Foc* 5]refined peasant [Gis 14] 28 Peasant met peasant [MayR 7] never come easily [Mon 42] 15 falling into the river [Mon 36] cellarman [Mon 37] wooden clogs [FonF 19] Vineyard Proprietors [C-HBC, AFG5/627, fo 86–87, Mon-Burbridge 15.9.11] Prince Charming [Dav 122] 29 corner of the world [M-Ple* 6] Cognac not nationalist [Mon 42] Barrès and Péguy [Hart171, 13] equal terms with the British [Mon 44] mutual trust [Mon 39] affection [Mon 71, 4] 30 very strict [Mon 71-1, 6–7;F-C] restless [FonF 17] left at 16 [Mon 39] Hercule Poirot [Anthony Sampson, *The New Europeans,* London 1971, 30] La Bordelaise [FonF89, 220] 31 expansion was assured [Mon 45–46] Two forms of patience [Mon 47] active heads [C-HBC, RG2/7/735 Sir John (Jean) Monnet, 31.10.31] since 1896 [C-HBC, A5/66, fo. 65] thorough trip [C-HBC, AFG5/627, fo 86–87, Mon-Burbridge 15.9.11] Titanic [M-Ram* 1] longstanding and cordial [C-HBC, RG2/7/735 idem] Kindersley [M-Ple* 4; Cos 138] 32 general mobilisation [Mon 48] precocious [AP-Sha* 10] long war [Mon 48–49; Gilli 4] strain of a large-scale conflict [LidH72, 38] Loucheur [Mon 57] big-headed [Mon 50] 33 Millerand [Mon 52] Mauclère [Mon 53; Mon 71-1, 14; F-LH to DF 26.1.94] Trafalgar House [Mon 53] early as August 1914 [C-HBC, A.1/265, 211-14 minutes meetings Governor & Committee #453,28.3.22] first contract signed October 9 [C-HBC, AFG2, contract #1, 9.10.14] initiative and efforts [C-HBC, A.1/265, 211–14 as above] friendly relations [Mon 54] called up [C-HBC, AFG 4/ 1 Sale-Weyers 5.11.17] 34 still in Bordeaux [C-HBC, AFG5/627, Mon-Ingrams ex-Bordeaux 20.11.14; Mon 53] little fleets [C-HBC Morton A, *Newsletter of the Maritime History Group* Vol II/1 Mar 88, 13–15] British concern [C-HBC, AFG4/1

Sale-Weyers 5.11.17] your exertions [C-HBC, AFG4/1 Kindersley-Mon 25.7.16]
neglected his own interests [C-HBC, A.1/265 as above] 35 Mikkelborg [C-HBC,
A.102/1504 Mikkelborg-Reynolds, 5.4.49] London 1917 [MortA-DF 18.8.93]
Clémentel [M-Ple* 6] tighter agreements [Mon 54] Clémentel [M-Ple* 6]
36 planned international economy [Clém 74–77; Dur 28; Tra 3–6] Wheat Executive [Clém 109; Sal67, 26] debt to Salter [Mon71-1, 16; NicH 212–13] 37 non-
combatant countries [Sal21, 91–92] 1917 losses [NicH 209] most advanced experiment [NicH 208] came to the fore [GB-0 # 50 Brand-Desborough 18.6.20] direct
line [Mon 55] head of French mission [GB-FO 372/1294/74905 Lord Robert Cecil,
British Mission to Supreme Economic Council, Paris-Lord Russell FO 14.5.1919]
on Allied Maritime Transport Executive [Nic 211; Sal21, 178; Dur 21–23] 38 confirmed in post [Mon 71] close to Clemenceau [Mill I 3.12.18, 26] officially thanked
[Dur 27] competitive panic [NicH 215] French member [Sal21, 178] 39 personal
confidence [Sal21, 179–180] not to penalise . . . war-time domination [Clém 337–
48; Mon 75; Tra vii–x, 1–27] 40 persist into the peace [Clém 302] not ready to
perpetuate [GB-Cab 23-5-312-6, 3.1.18] turned down flat [Mon 74–75] Keynes
and Dulleses [Mill I 379, 492–5; AE-DE* 14.12.62, 72] period of reconstruction
[Dur28–29; F-F12 7796, 2.11.18] begin all over again [Mon 75] 41 supranational
terms [Mon 71-1, 28; Mon 80] popular publicity [Mill IX, Monnet 27.5.19, 447–
453] sullen to belligerent [Wam 232–57] full fifteen years [Mon 85–89; Wam
267–70] 42 external intervention [Sal61, 176–77] first time an international body
[Mon 92–95] Monnet's hand [Sal61, 180–185] Saar and Schuman plan [Bal82,
82–83] means of pressure [Mon 98] little solutions [Mon55, 2.6.54, 106–07] 42–
43 telephone exchange [DF] 43 national veto a flaw [Mon71-1, 32] happiest
period of work [Sal61, 173] end of 1922 [Cos 146; *Le Temps* 21.12.22—Mon 99
mistakenly states 1921] great names of the day [Jox 97] clever diplomat [Bonn 56]
Drummond [Per* 1] great friends [Mon71-1, 27] old brandy [Mon 101] small
losses [Cos 138] near collapse [Cous 132–34; *Encyclopædia Britannica* 14th edn 1939
vol 4, 35–37] debts [C-HBC Mon-Sale 10.3.23] 44 younger spirits [Mon 101–02]
transition [FonF 9–10] Marie-Louise [Mon 99 says autumn 1923; Tav 519]
£40,000 [C-HBC, A.1/265, 211–14 Meeting Governor & Committee 28.3.22]
resigned from League [*Le Temps* 22.12.22 p. 2 col. 6] waive promised guarantees
[C-HBC, A92/97/1 Mon-Sale 2.3.23 and 23.5.23] rising prices [Cous 132–36]
profit in 1925–26 [Cos 147; DelAnd 720] Gaston Monnet [M-Ram* 6–7] Robert
Monnet [Mon 102; MonM*; M-Ram* 6–7] charming house [Mon101] repaid in
1930 [C-HBC, A unclass. Mon-HBC 17.9.30] kept his shares [MonM*] Blair
[Conn-DF 2.1.91; M-Ple* 4] 45 Wall Street [Dav 123] August 1926 [Mon 102–
03] floated in the US [Clar 20] mini Marshall Plan [M-McC* 4] 36 governments
and utilities [Swa 506] Monnet negotiated loans [Mon 102–07; More 213; Cos 150]
Salter's view [Sal61, 182] Finance Committee [More 214] Stetson [A59, 8600.51/
618, 620, 625, 636 &c. May to June 1927] 46 railways and utilities [Mon 111]
imperialist [Mon 104] bulwarks against Germany [Clar 29; More 504–05] lead in
operations [More 29.3.27, 268] Poland's borders [More, Jan + Feb 1927, 192,
214, 255] central figure [AP-Sha* 14] friend of Strong [More 24.7.26, 43] his aims
political [More 269] Strong takes a lead [More 29.3.27, 268 + 4.5.27, 301] credit
[More 28.2.27, 255] 47 conduit [More 58] $72 millions [AP-Sha* 14] fall of April
1928 [Swa 505] one match fewer [Mon 106] tyro [Mon 103] Pleven more gener-

ously [M-Ple* 5] Morrow [NicH 286; More 298–301] 48 Walker [Swa 500 fn 4 quoting Giannini] stratosphere [Swa 504 fn 1] honest Californians [M-C 1-1-35] 49 over $5 million [M-C 1-1-15, 30.1.32] SEC accused Giannini [M-C 1-1-39 + 40] good at making [money] [Mon 101] $25,000 [Dav 123] 50 cleared the debts [MonM* 21.11.92] Dulles steered [AP-Sha* 24–25] Paris flat [A. Churchill, *The Incredible Ivar Kreuger,* London, 1957, 9, 257] most widely distributed security [Gre 85] Galbraith called Kreuger [K. Galbraith, *The Great Crash,* Pelican 1961, 116, 208] financial intelligence [Gre 83] Polish and Rumanian loans [Gre 82; A59, 858.659 Matches 16.9.32, 145] half-mast [Gre 82–86] forgeries by Kreuger [Gre 86] Swedish opposition [AP-Sha* 22–5] 51 July 11, 1933 [A59, 858.659 Matches 21.7.33, 186] April 1935 [LisLip 131] T.V. Soong [M-D 1-1-1 Soong-Kung 10.11.32] champion of China [End 37] Rajchman [Mon 100] sole purchasing agent [End 35] could not fly over China [Per* 18–19] assets [GB-O #198 R H Brand memo of conversation with Monnet 24.2.43 + memo on JM assets by JM 23.2.43] 52 first meeting [M-D 1-1-4 Monnet-Soong 29.4.33] natural financier [LeiR 203] uncanny rapidity [End 34; Sal67 113] Consultative Committee [M-D 0-3-4; Bor 63–67] Lazards [End 35] English and American banks [Cob 127] lion's share [For33 III 521–524; For34 III 374; GB-FO 371/18078, 11.4.34] Taketomi [For33 III 25.7.33, 502–505] 53 stayed eight months [For34 III 403] foreign investment Shanghai [GB-FO 371/18078 Remer 18–22] Cognac with Chinese [Mon 114] Mazot [Per* 2 + 10] nobody knew [Per* 26] raise a single loan [MayR 45] wealthiest banks Chinese [MayR 46] genuine partnership [GB-FO371/18078 Ingram-Monnet talk 26.2.34; End 41] solid guarantees [M-D 0-3-1 Salter report 56–57] Railways [M-D 0-3-1 Salter report 89; GB-FO 371/18054, 60–61 of 12.3.34; + 70–73] Chinese bank [For33 III 523] and never would [End 131] no attention [Per* 32] 54 Japanese again frustrated [Bor 63] fight our battles [End 43] were won over [GB-FO371/18078 Sir A. Cadogan-FO-2.7.34] first railway bond [For34 III 421; End 42] south-east Chinese network [MayR 47; GB-FO 371/20225 HallPatch-FO 30.6.36, 263–272] Shanghai subscribe half [For34 III 421–423] one expert agreed [GB-FO 371/18079, 8.12.34] Export-Import Bank [For34 III 422] born in August 1907 [Cos 154; Conn-DF 18.3.91] elegant [M-McC* 5] forgot the other participants [Mon 109] April 6, 1929 [Conn-DF 18.3.91] employee of Monnet [M-McC* 5] fn 4 Programme Committees of AMTC [GB-FO 372/1294 Russell-Cecil 16.5.19] fn 4 secretariat of the League [GB-FO 371/9344/doct W3923, 22.5.23] 55 annulment [MayR 41] courtship by cable [Sal67, 26] legitimacy of a big country [FonF 45] Soviet government [Mon71-1, 34] a fortune [FonF 45] ambassadors in Moscow [For37 IV 30.5.37, 599; Sal67, 26] took refuge [MonM*] June 18, 1939 [Cos 154] fall of France [Dav 125] 56 Francesco Giannini died [MonM*] Lourdes [Mon 109–10] devout [M-Ple* 6] extreme unction [FonF 45] radical socialist [M-Ple* 6] weathered two millennia [DF] Adenauer; Marianne [Schä 134; MonM* 8.7.92] religious values [M-Owe* 8, 10–11] bored to death [Dav 124] hours writing [Jox 99] disinterested mind [Mon 71–1, 2] sequestered life [MonM*] 57 walking wounded [AR-MH #541, 19.6.42, 95] intimate friend [LisLip 111] $100,000 [AP-DF 14 Dulles-Monnet 30.1.35 + Dulles-MonMur 2.2.35 + Dulles-Green 2.2.35] Prince Edward [AR-MH #541, 19.6.42, 97] statue in Prague [Per* 43, 79] penned the armistice [AP-Sha* 9] advisory nature [AP-DF #14 Dulles-Monnet 2.2.35] 13 March 1935 memo [M-PD, Monnet-Drummond/Denis, 15.3.35] opportunities limitless [For34 III Mackay 12.10.34, 421–23] best understands China [M-PD, Monnet-Drummond/Denis 13.3.35] 56 per cent [GB-FO371/18708 Remer, Foreign Investments China 24.1.34, 4] 58 own ambassador [GB-FO 371/20216 Pratt 30.3.36] Monnet's arguments [End 132] appease Japan [Bor 129; End 108; For35 III 597 fn 9] adventurer [GB-FO 371/19243, 26.7.35] sabotage Monnet [GB-FO 371/19252, 10.12.35, 440, Waley to Browett] I only wish [GB-FO 371/19252 Leith-Ross 21.11.35, 437–440] left China [Mon 115] Turkish quota [MonM*] 58–59 China's debts mostly cleared [LeiR 225; M-PD, 16.10.36] 59 Lunghai railway [GB-FO 371/18053 Railway Gazette 9.3.34, 168, 395] there was nothing [Per* 45] crisis in relations [M-D 6-1-60→96+6−2−9, 12.7.38→May 1940] arrears of fees [M-PD 19.7.39] status unclear [M-D 10-5-11 + 12 Murnane-Roseborough 16.2.40] struggle to live [Per* 14] fn 7 [M-D 1-1 various + 12-4-60 & 62 &c + 13-3 various; Dav 123] papers burned [M-E 2-1-400] 60 Kelvinator [LisLip 113] four times [AR-MH #541, 19.6.42, 91-99] fortune for the Petscheks [Per* 49–53] Stuttgart [M-D 11-5-9] inimical to German Bosch [AR-MH #525, 7.5.42, 288–289] true [M-D 10-5-26 Murnane-Monnet 14.3.40] bored [Mon 115] 61 well understand [GB-O #198 R.H. Brand memo conversation with Monnet 23.1.44] petty financier [Pai 251] never groomed himself [Mon 46–47] 62 from private to public [Mon 41] conjuror [Mon 330] too soft [Mon 112–13] creative men of our time [Sal67, 25–26] 63 Swatland [M-McC* 2–4] Stimson and Harriman [Mon 154]

2 Arsenal of Democracy

64 little apartment [Lin76, 420–421; AR-MH #541, 95] husband and children [Lin76, 420–21, 426–27] air rearmament for France [Lin76, 420–21] in secret to Roosevelt [Mon 117–18; Hai 13] 65 desperate efforts [Ple 21–22] Bullitt persuaded Monnet [Mon 117] best of Frenchmen [F-496 AP 33-3c Daladier notes] Monnet the man [Mon 117] as a brother [AR-PSF #3 France, Bullitt-FDR 28.9.38] never admired more [Ple 21–22] Fear was everywhere [Mon 115–16] go to war [Mon 116] hoped for a settlement [AR-MH #525 Morgenthau-FDR 7.5.42, 289] profoundly anti-Hitler [M-Ple* 5] out of reach of enemy [Mon 117] 66 serious shortage [Mon 117] aluminium structures [Hai 4–5] avoid war [Hai 16] Douhet [Pea 201–04] knock-out attack [Pos 56; A. J. P. Taylor, *English History 1914–1945,* London 1965, 437–38] sheet of flame [Gilli 65; Sauvy 48, 53] mastery in the air [Sherw 239] no Munich [Mon 117–18; Hai 17–18, 22] Four days after Munich [Hai 13; For38 I 711–12] hundred fighters [Hai 8–13] 67 Hitler must be stopped [Div 19–23] study removal arms embargo [Hai 27] convenient locations [Mon 119] Arthur Murray [Hai 30–31] 600 warplanes a month [Hai 119–20] President could trust [Sherw 162] 68 a thousand in prison [Mon 120] Canadian assembly plants [Hai 39–43] French experts doubted [Hai 73] in Reynaud's presence [Mon 121] too optimistic [F-496 AP 39#163 Jaquin 12.9.40] 69 exposed by the military [Blu 64–78] Guam [Hai 204; Mon 135] went through hell [AR-MH #174, 23.3.39, 170–72; Hai 102] firm orders [Hai 69] quadrupled American capacity [F-496 AP 41 #327 Vuillemin; Hai 101] 70 repeal of the Neutrality Act [F-496 AP 33–3b Monnet-Reynaud 28.7.39] agents for the French government [M-E 7-1-29, 2.8.39] elderly Monnet died [Dav 122; *L'Indicateur* de Cognac

3.9.39] more affected [FonF 77; Koh* 130] as true today [F-AP 496 30–1, 26.7.39] no general coordination [GB-Cab 21 #746, Hopkinson 26.8.39 + 27.9.39; Daladier-Chamberlain 20.9.39] fourth mission to the States [Hai 136–37; For39 II Bullitt-SD 28.8.39, 518] prompt doubling or tripling [M-E 2-1-1 & 7-2-3, 3.9.39; F-SHAT, GN 346 #4 mission Monnet] conversations I had with Mr Roosevelt [Mon 125; GB-Cab 21 #748 Monnet-Wilson 7.11.39] 71 friend of Roosevelt [Dur86, 77–78] main fountainhead [HanGow 185] 72 retain the last word [GB-Cab 21 #746, 21.9.39] Cadogan [GB-Cab 21 #747 Cadogan-Bridges 29.9.39] God and the king [MayR 55] could do least harm [GB-Cab 21 #749 Bridges, British interdepartmental meeting 24.11.39; Lud 33 fn 149] deal of trouble [GB-Cab 21 #746 Waley-FPhilips 25.9.39] not prepared to take responsibility [GB-Cab 21 #748 Wilson-Simon 14.11.39] Purvis, a Scot [GB-Cab 21 #749] as well as with any other Frenchman [For 39 II 566–7] 73 organiser of Allied action [GB-Cab 21 #1270 "Coordination of the Economic War efforts of the UK and France" 4.4.40] inventory of . . . resources [HanGow 187] considerable standing [M-E 4-1-4, 29.4.40] conviction of need [HanGow 187] price of tallow [HanGow 194] destroyed his background [F-MAE AP 328 Monnet #1, 24.5.40; HanGow 195] 74 refusing on principle to share data [F-MAE AP 328 Monnet #6 Monnet, Note du Comité des programmes et des Achats Alliés 9.2.40] narrowly averted [F-MAE AP 328 Monnet #6 various texts 21.1.40–9.3.40; HanGow 189–90] shortfall in French imports [HanGow 191] drastically reduced [F-496 AP 20 Daladier 3DA5 dossier 2 Directives de la Politique Economique Française 24.2.40, §13; GB-Cab 21 #1270, British Memorandum in reply n.d. §9] concerned with almost every problem [GB-Cab 21 #1271 Hopkinson 9.5.40] special pleading [GB-Cab 21 #748 Note on arrangements for Anglo-French coordination 13.11.39] lack of Anglo-French cooperation [Hai 142–43 + 151] France's gold reserves [F-496 AP 33–3c Reynaud-Daladier Feb 1940; F-496 AP 39 #163 Jaquin 12.9.40] for lack of money [FDR press conference 16.12.40; MayR 96] 75 limit its prerogatives [M-E 7-2-12, 6.10.39] more forthcoming [M-E 7-6 & 7-7] Germans outnumbered [M-E 7-6-20, 30.1.40] dig deep in pockets [Mon 133–35] No such sum [HanGow 194] all-embracing balance sheet [F-MAE AP 328 Monnet #3, 8.4.40] goes considerably beyond [GB-Cab 21 #1270 Hopkinson-Bridges 4.4.40] relate London and Paris [GB-Cab 21 #1270 Coordination of the Economic War efforts of the UK and France 4.4.40; GB-Cab 21 #1271, 9.5.40] valuable with Washington [GB-Cab 21 #1271 Bridges-Churchill 6.6.40] coordination enabled discussion [Mon71–1, 41] 76 virtually lost [Gaul54, 52] non-Nazi German government [Lud 32] do not learn easily [Lud 25, 32] continue after the war [F-496 AP 30-1 Monnet-Daladier 18.12.39; M-E 8-3-1, 16.6.61] to every nation in Europe [Lud 35–36] answer to the Rhine claim [Lud 41 Halifax to Chamberlain 13.2.40] a single unit [Lud 41] go slow [GB-FO 800 #398 Halifax-Lothian 30.4.40] 77 deeper action [Mon 19] France a satellite [Hit ch XIII; Ple 50] Marjolin to Dunkirk [Marj 97–100] saw Churchill for the first time [Mon 20; GB-Cab 21 #1271 Bridges-Seal 6.6.40; M-E 4-9-6 Monnet-Churchill 6.6.40] did not receive me well [Mon71–1, 41] you are quite right [Chu 189] the control of events [Mon 21] matter of a group [M-Ple* 9] Monnet claims [M-E 8-3-1, 16.6.61] dramatic call for unity [M-E 8-1-2ff 14.6.40] talk about the future [Mon 22] 78 Vansittart [Mon 22–23] 79 de Gaulle–Reynaud [Dur86, 230; Spe54, 291] Monnet horrified [Mon 27] 79 tepid liquid

[Spe54, 323] June 18 [Gaul 54, 329–30; MayR 87] Monnet (and others) [Gillo 48] Concarneau [M-E 8-2-11, 17.6.40] embark for North Africa [Mon 30-31] to British ports [Chu 190–91] 80 *Claire* [Dav 214] cat's pyjamas [Harv 396] impracticable [Lud 44] no federalist overtones [Mon 34] 81 Constable [Chu 189] I think not [Mon 137] insight of genius [M-Ple* 12] never share power [M-Ple* 11; Gillo 49] war had to be won [Mon71–1, 43] great mistake [M-E 9-1-2; Mon 145] 82 clouds of aircraft [Mon 135; Hai 255] immense industrial [Ker 151, 170, 211] Noguès [Dur86, 237] asked Noguès to join [Mon 144] through Halifax [Spe66, 134–35] committee of individuals [NicN 98–99; Dilk 306] 83 honour of France [Mon 24] courage to take the decisive step [Moni 67] diverted to the UK [F-MAE-AP 328 Monnet #1 Purco(out) tg 149, 17.6.40] Bloch-Lainé [Hal 146–55] chaired by Salter [MayR 88] Monnet asked Churchill [Mon 147] passport signed by Churchill [GB-Avia 12 #33, 21.9.40 &c.] 84 fn 2 British pensioner [AR-MH #540 Morgenthau re talk Halifax + Lyttelton 17.6.42, 15; GB–O #198 R. H. Brand-Kindersley 16.6.43] stopover in Bermuda [Mon 150] blimp talk [GB-Cab 102 #95 Chance-Hancock 20.6.44] fully utilised [M-E 16-8-23, 15.1.41; GB-Avia 12 #33 Purvis-Brown 26.3.41] control his movements [Sal67, 27] complained to Purvis [AR-MH #727, 150--55; #733, 140–44] suspicious of Monnet [Jac* 2] 85 look askance [A-FF #38 Halifax-Frankfurter 8.2.46, 434] teacher to our defense [A-FF #51 Frankfurter-Halifax 14.11.41, 493–94] decisive share [A-FF #38 Frankfurter-Halifax 6.2.46, 433] I was a spy [DF] vetters as idiots [A107 #12/ASW 095 Jean Monnet 1.7.42] sacked from the BSC [AR-MH #540, 15–17] he was all right [AR-MH #542, 4–5] criminal tax evasion [AR-MH #542, 5 + #550, 99–101] Monnet, Murnane and Company Ltd., Hong Kong [AR-MH #527, 19–22] pay $45,000 [GB-O #198 R. H. Brand memo conversation with Monnet 23.1.44] 86 living expenses [GB-O #198 Kindersley-R H Brand 20.5.43] did not come through London [GB-O 198 Tyser-R. H. Brand 9.12.43] complete confidence [GB-O #198 R. H. Brand-Monnet 1.6.43] not a scratch [AR-MH #525, 279–93] fn 3 prevent Robert Brand [AR-MH #519, 22.4.42, 54–58; #520, 24.4.42, 164; #540, 17.6.42, 15–17] devotion to Roosevelt [Mon 119] 87 just the kind of service [GB-Cab 105 #417 Brand-Turner 13.8.40] overwhelm the enemy [GB-Cab 102 #95] Knudsen [GB-Cab 102 #95 RGD Allen 22.8.45] military self-sufficiency [Pos 54, 121, 128, 228, 231–34] 88 same language [Mon 156, 172–73] 2415 Foxhall [A-FF #51 Monnet-Frankfurter 20.12.42, 559] deep friendship [Mon 153] one tank too few [Sherw 288] artful [StiBun 369] replace potential lost [Hal 158] 89 before American rearmament [M-E 4-9-1, 22.5.40] Layton [Mon 156] state it in big terms [M-E 11-5-17, 15.11.40] stir the United States [Pos 237] restrictions on civilian manufacturing [Hal 255] credited with the phrase [McC81; Ros 260–261; Sherw 226; Mon 160] 90 without regard to cost [Mon 157–58; Hal 255, 268] Min Supply refused [Hal 264; Mon 162] Lend-Lease bill [Hal 306] comparable lines to the British [Hal 266] adequate outline of military requirements [Hal 307] Stacy May in London [e.g., GB-Cab 115 #7 mtg 28.8.41] British cabinet memo [GB-Cab 115 #7, August? 1941] 91 in proportion to his original irritation [Sherw 232; Mon 166–67] know you a bit better [Mon 167] buddies [Mon71–2 ex-McCloy 6] trick never failed [Fur 53 fn 101] with McCloy and Stacy May [M-E 13-9, 13-10, & 14-2] in a muffled way [GB-Avia 38 #1046 ff; GB-Cab 92 #28] communicated to Moscow [GB-Avia 38 #1048 BSC 34 minutes, item 6, 6.8.41] main adviser to Beaverbrook [M-E 13-2 + 13-12 + 14-2; Hal 328–35] give leverage [GB-Cab 102 #95 HanGow 1st draft 210] 92 without any doubt whatever [*ibid* 202] The OPM statisticians [Mon 172] fifty per cent increase [Hal 342] a fifth and a quarter [Natha 83; AR-HH #314 Bk 5 Beaverbrook-Hopkins "Raising the Sights" 30.12.41] 93 through Hopkins [GB-Cab 102 #95] raising the sights [A179 #971 Beaverbrook-Stimson 29.12.41; Nel 185–88; Hal 341–42] shortened the war [Moni 67–68] satisfaction of having contributed [Mon 174] strategic triumvirate [Jac* 8–9 + 14] joint Anglo-American board [GB-Avia 38 #1049, 55thBSC mtg 17.12.41 §4] 94 gently complain [Mon 175] ignore Allied claims [Jac* 5–6] Combined Production and Resources Board [GB-Avia 38 #1049, 55thBSC mtg 17.12.41, 3; GB-Cab 102 #95 Chance-Hancock 20.6.44; Hal 378] military resistance [A179-Policy #650 *(a)* 0831 CPRB Fesler-Planning Cte Sep 42, 14 pp; *(b)* 083.1C Knowlson-Nelson 13.11.42] hoarded by the US Pacific fleet [Jac* 6] 95 look to the USA [Fre 566–568; Mon 168] 96 how to play Washington [Jac* 2, 15] duplicate for its effect [A-FF #49 McCloy-Frankfurter 1.11.41, 297] four times a day [A-McC dy3 Dec 41] Aurand takes no offence [AE-AH dy ##6–7, 1941 17 & 21 Oct, 7 & 21 Nov, 23 & 30 Dec; 1942 12 & 18 June] the stoutest heart [AR-CO ##23 + 142–152] 97 all that was Monnet [GB-Cab 102 #95 Chance-Hancock 20.6.44] Consolidated Statement [GB-Cab 102 #95 RGD Allen-Hancock 22.8.45] Unsung Hero of World War II [Natha 67–85] shift War Department thinking [GB-Cab 102 #95 RGD Allen-Hancock 22.8.45] one of the real architects [A-FF #38 Halifax-Frankfurter 8.2.46, 434]

3 Algiers

98 JM Washington [AR-CO dy 27.10.43] 99 quagmire [For43 II 33] third person [Mon 207] 100 believe in democracy [Cha 342] Communist dictatorship [Bet 200] 100,000 troops [LidH70, 346] others should obey [Mcm84, 122] oath [AE-PP #132 Cables Off 18.6.43] 101 seizing power [Cha 158] new Wallonia [Ede 372–73; Ker 267–68] honest citizens [For43 Tehran 485, 514] Disdain for 1940 [Gaul56, 102–03] French deserts [F-MAE GU 39 #689, 110–15; Kim 222–27] not again become a first-class power [A218 Geographic 42–45 #580 file CCS 370 Fr (10-6-43) Sec 1, JCS mtg 15.11.43] rifles [Ede 372–73; Ker 267–68] lacked support [MorganT 717–18; AR-MH 8.1.44] 102 UN trusteeship [For43 Tehran 310, 509, 872; Ker 240, 321] local authorities [Agl 234–5] bases [Dur86, 631–32] New Caledonia [Vio 65–67, 84–87] right horse [Cha 228] loathing Darlan [For43 II 32] temporary expedient [Vio 124–25] nest of traitors [Vio 130] 103 shotgun wedding [Ker 236–241] breaking with de Gaulle [Ker 291–93, 307–09] Germans & N Africa [M-E 26-1; Mur 94, 114] Monnet & North Africa [M-E 26-1] 104 Lincoln's birthday [Ros 378] note 5 Feb 43 [M-E 26-1] third man [For43 III 610] FDR on Monnet [Gir 118] skirts clear [For43 III 809–10; Sherw 678–79] Béthouart [Bet 187] 105 Monnet to Algiers [M-E 26-4] London's reply [M-E 26-3] FDR-Eisenhower [AR-HH #330–7] a dud [Roo 91, 99] self-effacement [Mur 224] mission [M-E 26-4] 106 Christmas Eve 1942 [M-E 26-1; AR-HH #330-7] admirable statement [Sherw 680; Kas 31] Resistance de Gaulle [MayD

82] JM sceptical [Jox 99] **107** only French army [Gaul56, 412–14; Cha 124; Vio 123] with Alphand 10.1.43 [Alp 140] **108** Coordinating Council [M-E 26-1] Frankfurter [Las 185] Murphy on JM [Mur 224] **108** *perroquet* [Sherf* 12] Vichy Cabal [GB-Premier 3/442/6, 12.2.43] McCloy-Monnet in Washington [Mon 179] McCloy-Peyrouton [A-McC dy 1–8, 52a–f] credit for reform [AE-PP #75 McCloy(3); For43 II 68] **109** anti-Semite [Gir 119] Linarès [Sherf* 2] **132** break with Vichy [Bea 179–184] not valid [Kas 93–94] **110** note 8 Mar 43 [AR-HH #330-7] eight decrees [AR-HH #330-7] sweep Vichy out [F-SHAT 5 P 1] Nuremberg [AE-PP #75 McCloy(3)] Giraud a liberal [Sherf* 2–3] bombarded him [Mon 187] **111** New Deal [Mcm67, 299; GB-Premier 3/442/6, 24.3.43] liberalisation [Kas 154–58; 181] portraits Pétain [AR-HH #330-7] political prisoners [F-F1a 3805 Barel-Philip 18.6.43] Moslem majority [Gir 122] Gaullists' basic terms [Ker 268] **112** arms for French [AR-HH #330-7] publicity Allied supplies [MayR 174] assembly lines [Jox 99] six-room flat [Jav 294; Jox 97] **113** local *rosé* wine [Alp 162] Monnet-Macmillan, May [Mcm84, 83–86] Monnet-Philip [Kas 196] neighbours on the landing [Jox 98–99] **114** undressing for a swim [Man 343–44] kidnap and murder [Kas 131–32] putsch [MayR 174] weaving sharply [M-Jav* 19–21] Monnet's chauffeurs [M-Fre*] attempted assassination [AE-PP #166] **115** boasts of murder [AE-PP #132] shattered his jaw [Cat 391] de Gaulle depression [Cha 80, 87, 94] sectarian *émigrés* [Cat 343] worth a speech [Gir 124] **116** don't believe a word [Ord 560] fusion [GB-Premier 3/442/6 Macmillan-Churchill 12.2.43] note 8 Mar 43 [AR-HH #330-7] stay in London [Cha 104–107] **117** time on Giraud's side [Cha 100–119] paper dated April 1 [Ker 272] insurrectionary government [Gir 134–137] *loi Tréveneuc* [Las 164–65] men of Vichy [Gir 137–140] committee of five or seven [For43 II 94–95] **118** unconstitutional [Gir 140–152] attacked Giraud personally [Gir 359–365] Hitler [AR-HH #330-7; For43 II 108–10] Algiers nowhere else [Gir 152–157] **119** many remain that must go [AR-HH #330-7] not to be allowed to write it [Mcm67, 317] *éminence grise* [Mcm84, 82–86] Monnet's own priorities [Mcm67, 297–98] **120** Resistance National Council [Gaul56, 121–22] note 17 May 43 [Cha 148] end Vichy press laws [MayR 196] Monnet on de Gaulle's left [Gaul56, 126] demagogue or mad [Mcm84, 97] Macmillan told off Monnet [Mcm84, 98] Colomb-Bechar [Cha 210–215] nothing rash [MayR 205] **121** break with de Gaulle [For43 II 155–57 17.6.43] Eisenhower June 19 [For43 II 155–57] recognition [Ker 297] **122** prewar governments [For43 II 123–24] Committee decisions [M-E 31-1] imprisoned [For43 II 141; AE-PP #166 Eisenhower-CCS 10.6.43] only name the French would know [Hir 77] **123** talented team [M-Ple* 2] peace-maker [Alp 168] public menace [Ord 618] Massigli [F-F14, 13649 Mon-Mayer 20.12.43] olympian contempt [Pai 251] mouthpiece [Gaul-LNC V 25, 31] declared independence [Mur 227] **124** principles and programmes [GB-FO 371/36123 Makins–Strang 3.4.43] undiminished influence [Mur 227–228] Murphy criticism [For43 II 152–53] friendly chat [F-B 33000, 18.11.43] Eisenhower [Eis, Eisenhower-Marshall 18.6.43, 1193–94 + 22.6.43, 1205–06] Stimson [AE-PP #132 Off Cables 17.6.43; Las 260] Giraud lacked ability [For43 Tehran 484] volunteers for unity [Jox 95] **125** the inspirer [Jou II, de Gaulle 12.11.53, 197–98; Delou 141]

4   Liberation of France

126 last winter of war [Mon87, 272–285; Gaul56, 179] a new Lotharingia [Hir 78–79] **127** Alphand economic union [Mon 222] note of 5 August 1943 [Mon87, 272–285] single economic entity [Mon87, 287–291] France would take the lead [Alp 168–169] **128** great political influence [Hir 76] new Economic Committee [F-F60 #913 Queuille-Gaulle 9.2.44; #914 Joxe-Gaulle 4.4.44; #1722 JO 29.4.44; #896 Note Economic Committee 7.10.44; F-B33001, 17.9..44] **129** bored [Mcm84, 23.8.43, 191] constant chivvying [Hir 76] dropped arms [M-E 5-1-1, note Monnet 20.9.43] Provisional Government [Ker 322; Vio 195] modus vivendi [A59, 851R.24 #5075 NAEB 19.8.43, 155 + #5076, 25.9.43, 163] **130** fn 3, alcohol [F-F12 9972 Borocco-Queuille 29.5.44] postponed till August [F-MAE-GU39 Alger #689 Monnet-Giraud 8.7.43] fn 4 Director-General of UNRRA [LeiR 301–2] Monnet ill in bed [Alp 140] outside UNRRA [F-F60 #921 Note R Mayer 23.11.44 for CFLN summarising JM tgs] **131** strong impression [F-B 33000, 18.11.43] *de facto* recognition [F-363 AP 3 manuscript Monnet-Mayer 4 pp, 4.1.44] McCloy checked with Massigli [A107 ASW 095 Monnet-McCloy 28.12.43 + McCloy-Dunn 3.1.44 + encl. Massigli-Murphy 15.10.43] without reference to the CFLN [F-363 AP 3 note 13.1.44 Mayer based on Monnet tgs #47–50] **132** suspicion of his motives in Whitehall [F-MAE-GU39 Alger #697] CFLN administer all but the combat zones [A107 #25 ASW 370.8 France 1943–44] wanted a prompt settlement [F-363 AP 3 Alphand, conversations reconnaissance CFLN 21.3.44] Monnet amazes me [Alp 173] **133** democratic institutions in liberated France [F-F 14-13672, Alger-Wash'n tg Diplo #322 12.2.44] game which could go on for ever [F-363 AP 3 Alphand 21.3.44] wail of anguish [AR-HH #334 Bk 9 Civil Affairs France, Monnet-Hopkins 10.3.44] **134** Eisenhower to decide [F-F14 13672 tg Monnet, Diplo 591, 18.3.44] there would still be a price to pay [F-F14 13672, Monnet tgs Diplo 784, 787, 8.4.44] McCloy was almost dismissed [Schwart 35; Schwart-DF 4.6.93] too subject to the blandishments [A107 #25 ASW 370.8 France, McCloy-Stimson 17.1.44] outside the combat zones [F-F14 13672 Monnet #137, 30.3.44] give the Germans clues [A218 CCAC 400 France #121 3-14-44 sec 1 JSC 4.4.44; A165 CAD #16 Exec Office Adm 014 3-8-43(1) memo 10.4.44] adequate supplies not being obtained [AR-CO dy 21.4.44] now possible to establish plans [F-F60 920 tg Monnet–de Gaulle, Massigli &c 28.4.44] occupation as in Italy [For44 III 705–706] **135** on the wane [MorganT 717–18; AR-MH 8.1.44] we are subordinates [F-363 AP 3 Note 13.1.44 based on Monnet tgs #47-50, 9/10/1/44] Liberté, Egalité, Fraternité [F-F14 13672 tg #53 Monnet-Mayer 15.1.44] French reps not pleased [AR-OF #203 bk 2 France, Morgenthau-FDR 22.5.44; For44 III Stettinius-Chapin Algiers 10.6.44, 705] Pierre Mendès-France [F-B 37683] Prima donnas [For44 III FDR-Churchill 707–708] De Gaulle reproached Mendès-France [MayD 320–322] **136** kicked out of Washington [MorganT 721] supplementary francs [For44 III 709–710, 717, 722; MorganT, 721] independent British recognition [For44 III 716–724; Ker 373–74] Mayer in sessions of CFLN [F-F14 13672 tg Mon #53 15.1.44] **137** the issue had been settled [Alp 175] signs of irritation with Monnet [MayD 324–25] Monnet was also dropped from the Economic Committee [F-F60-903 Order of 23.11.44] balance-sheet—again! [F-F60-896 Comité Economique Interministériel (hereafter CEI) 23.8.44] negotiation with the Americans [F-F60-918, 10th CEI 20.11.44] **138** Mayer in Washington January 1945 [MayD 369–72] you want to nail down everything [AR-MH #729, 8.5.44] difficult to keep anything from him [AR-MH #814, 30/31.1.45] scorched earth [F-F14-13672 Monnet tg 259, 17.6.44] **138– 39** pump-priming then reconstruction [M-E 33-1-6 Monnet 22.9.43; F-B 33001 JM-Comité Reconstruction 8.10.43 + Note JM 15.10.43; F-F60 121 CAR-CFLN 16.10.43; F-MAE GU39-45 Alger #1502, 16.10.43] relief slipped in ahead [F-F60-896 CEI PV séance 20.11.43; F-F60 921 séance CEI 23.11.43 note by R Mayer on JM negotiations dated 22.11.43] occupation of major ports [F-F14-13663 (+ F60-918) 26.10.44] win their spurs [M-MenF*] 2nd Armoured Division [Gaul56, Ch 4] 4 per cent of prewar [AR-HH #336 folder 3 Monnet-Stettinius, 18.4.45] locomotives [MayR 225] **140** almost forgotten diseases [AR-OF 203 #2 Maury Maverick, France 2.4.45, 23–24] SHAEF bureaucracy [F-F60 918 Monnet 26.10.44] eight-month plan [AR-HH #334 Four Party Committee mtg 20.11.44 Attachment A, Monnet-Stettinius 2.1.45, 1; AR-OF 203 #2 Maury Maverick, France 2.4.45] **141** hoard of gold [F-B 33682, 1.2.44] Allies broke [AR-MH #729, 8.5.44, 33] greater part of their industrial equipment [F-F14-13672 tg Monnet 150, 11.4.44] long-term credit on easy terms [F-F14-13672, tg Monnet 184, 26.4.44] three years after Lend-Lease [F-F14-13663, Monnet, Alger 3.7.44] so Alphand claimed [F-MAE-GU39 #1465 tg Alger-Wash'n 27.7.44] denied [AR-MH #814, 30.1.45, incl. Glasser-Morgenthau] a new text [For44 III 20.7.44, 757–58] cut by three-quarters [F-F60-896 CEI 19.2.45] **142** industrial items [For44 Quebec Hull-Roosevelt 11.9.44, 419–20] long-term credits should be negotiated [For44 III 851.24, 11.9.44, 760–61] indefinitely postponed [For44 III 757–763; For44, 2nd Quebec Conference 419–23] seeds of the greatest difficulties [A218 CCAC 400 France (3-14-44) sec 1 #121 SHAEF mission to France, French Civil imports programs 26.11.44] master-agreement should be signed [AR-CO dy #151 Memo for Hopkins, Fr Lend-Lease 8.1.45] January 19 [AR-MH #814, 31.1.44] stay a few days [F-B 33682 Monnet tg 33, 26.1.45] **143** failure of mission [AR-CO #142 *NY Herald Tribune* 31.1.45 + *Washington Post* 1.2.45] Lend-Lease [F-F60-920 Monnet–de Gaulle 11.2.45] after some hesitation [MayD 24.1.45] unhoped for [F-F60-896 CEI 19.2.45] Truman [Dou 198–9, 201–04] **144** goods not formally ordered by September 2 [A169, entry 514 #3193 History Lend-Lease Administration XII France 363–64] $550 million loan [A59, 851.51 Acheson-USParis 10.9.45] commercial contacts [F-F60-918, 27th Cté Approv'ts Min Economie nationale 24.10.45] George Ball [F-B 33678, dossier A.9.a Réorganisation du Conseil Français des Approvisionnements en Amérique, memo Monnet 23.9.45; Mon 226–228; Bal82, 69 + 71 + 75–77] **145** long talk [*NY Times* 24.8.45, p 5:6] must modernise [Mon 228] liberals or *dirigistes* [Kui 221–222; F-80 AJ7 Beigel 388, ex A. Armengaud, *Cahiers Français d'Information,* Paris 19.5.46, 13] long-term [*NY Times* 22.9.45] longer range problems [A59 851.51 France-Finance 1945–48: (i) Acheson-Caffery 10.9.45 (ii) Caffery-SS 13.9.45 (iii) Monnet-Clayton 24.9.45 (iv) Byrnes-Caffery 8.10.45 (v) Byrnes-Caffery 19.10.45; A59, 851.50 Byrnes-Caffery 16.10.45; Mio87, 81–82].

5 Rebirth of France: The Monnet Plan

147 grandfather clock [Uppdraget (Sweden) 1993/3, 14–17] Wall Street [M-Kab*]
Jouhaux [FonF89, 220] 148 preparing the future [Mon 230–31] heated Bristol
[Mon 345; Hir-DF 31.10.91] host of people [Hir 89] commitment to a Plan
[Delou* 4; Lyn 81, 227–28 argues for Alphand on the basis of F-F60-918 meeting
at ministry of Economy 24.10.45] 149 not like plans [M-MenF* 29.1.81] point of
dying [Kui 201] eight-year sequel [F-F60-659 Plan d'Équipement 23.11.44] triptych [Lyn81,271] austerity [Kui 201] 150 barely functioning [Ass 108] disputed
it [Mio87, 78] covering letter [F-F60 900 doct 205 Monnet–de Gaulle 6.12.45]
short-circuit [F-F60 897 dossier 27 doct 66 9.10.44] 151 minor ministry [F-F12
10142 TanguyPrigent-MendèsFrance, n.d., end October 1944] killed [MenF 163]
sterile disputes [M-F 1-3-1 draft Monnet-Gouin 7.2.46] truly directed [Rou 29]
elementary facts [F-80 AJ7 Beigel 394 quoting Economist 29.12.45, 930] verbal
broadside [80 AJ26 Monnet-Philip 23.1.47] on a plate [M-Bou*] side-stepped [F-
F60 900 CEI 14.12.45 docts 205-208; Mio87, 114–117] all the vital forces [F-F60
900-1 CEI 14.12.45 doct 205, 6.12.45] 152 Billoux [F-F60 900 CEI 14.12.45
doct 208] data [M-F 1-3-1 of 7.2.46 + 4 of 12.2.46] incapacity of ministries [F-
F60 902 CEI doct 22, 18.2.46] counterweight [Pale 211; Mio87, 89] working
discipline [F-F60 896 Note pour M. Alphand 7.10.44; F-F60 897 dossier 27 annexe
9.10.44] Boris [BloBou 121] 196 creative team [Rab* 14] school certificate
[Delou* 11] Cézanne [Hir 93] trestle [Hir 91–92] intellectual void [Delou* 9] hot
air [M-Bou*] 154 team [Rab* 6–7] disinterested [M-Bou*] direct access [Uri* 73]
Lacoste [Bun 112 + 121 & Rou 30] Pflimlin [F-F60 904 CEI 18.6.48 doct 66; M-
Bou*] Moch [M-Bou*] tensions with Schuman [Bid 181] intractable [Delou* 13]
mutual seduction [BloBou 167–68] 155 close [BlochL 94–95] a friend [Rab*, 24]
swathe [F-80 AJ 11, 1er rapport Com'n Modernisation Sidérurgie, Nov 46, 11]
main credit [CGP, Rapport Général 1er Plan Nov46/Jan47, 101] half my time [EU-
DF, Monnet-Shone 27.4.62] 156 Monnet chose [M-F 9-5-5, 27.10.47 35^{B}Com'n
Modernisation Sidérurgie] Lynch [Lyn81, 275] French war aim [Mio87, 250 Men-
dèsFrance "Réformes de structure" Mar 45, 64–65] Alphand [Poi 248, 454] anti-
capitalist [Ass 109] 157 privileged classes [Ass 109] excuse [Kui 199 citing F-307
AP 123 Dautry, Note sur la Reconstruction 11.12.45] silk shirts [Kui 199 citing
F-307 AP 123 G Boris, La Politique du Plan: choix nécessaire 29.9.45] incompatible [F-80 AJ1, CGP, Council of Plan 16 + 19.3.46, DocF-NE 291, 27.4.46, 3]
crystallising [Mio87, 115] method [F-80 AJ266 13.2.47; M-F 1-3-4, 12.2.46]
specific target [Delou 143–44] solid start [F-80 AJ1, CGP, Council of Plan
16 + 19.3.46, DocF-NE 291, 27.4.46, 4] 158 30 per cent [M-F 4-1-15 Feb 46]
France would matter [A59, 851.51, Monnet-Clayton 24.9.45, 8.10.45, 19.10.45]
$3 billion [A59, 851.51 White-Collardo 23.1.46] Keynes [Block 65; Bonin 123]
against British loan [Block 72] 159 free trade [For45 IV 8.11.45, 768–771] key
concession [A59, 851.51,24.9 + 19.10 + 8.11 1945; Dob 216] pluriannual deficit
[AT-VF, NAC-US Top Committee 4.4.46] ignored the hint [Block 73] impressed
[AT-VF, NAC-US Top Cte 25.3.46 H. Dexter White 1; Moni 58] no endorsement
[For47 II Douglas-Lovett 1048] more for consumption [A59, 851.51 Byrnes-Caf-
fery 10.4.46; Wal 94] inflationary [Wal 97] exhausted [AT-SJ #18 Foreign Funds
Control (General), Snyder-Schuman Sep 46, table 13, Use of Foreign Credits 2] nine

weeks [Mon 250] too inflationary [Mio90, 34] 160 impetus [Mon 254; Delou 147]
fn 2 first year crucial [F-80 AJ266, 20.8.47] carried on [Alp*27] all the elements
[M-F 5-2-36, 6.6.46] basic activities [Delou* 6–7] geared to action [Hel 110–11]
161 40 percent of total [AT-VF, NAC 6.5.46; F-80 AJ1, 16.3.46] capital markets
[CGP, Cinq ans du Plan 1952, 323–4] battle of production [Ass 109] forty-eight-
hour week [AT-VF, NAC 6.5.46 Technical Committee final report 7] lunch [M-
Jav*] 162 international trade [CGP, Rapport Général Nov46/Jan47 (hereafter 1er
Rapport), 13, 15] big modern states [ibid., 25] Vichy plans [Lyn81, 251] Lubell
[Lub 102] potent means [Mio87, 151; M-F 5-2-10, 5.11.46] spectrum [Wal 102;
Shea 170, 257–83] machine tools [Mio87, 231–246] generation gap [Mio86 citing
Malcor 132] 163 Monnet in particular [Mio90, 39] security [CGP 1er Rapport 17–
18] pressed for cuts [F-80 AJ1, DocF-NE 291, 27.4.46 Conseil du Plan 16-
19.3.46; M-F 1-6-2, 21.1.46 + 1-6-8b, 3.2.46; A469 HQ European Programs,
Mediterranean, Country files 1948-9, France: Transport Money Public Finance #4,
French Budgetary Developments, C Dupont 22.12.47, 4] handicapped [M-FS 4-1-
2 Monnet-Schuman 1.5.50] 164 milk [F-81 AJ138 Bureau-Monnet 16.1.51; F-81
AJ 149, R5/Ib, n.d.] meet all needs [F-457 AP 20 Bidault, 9.7.47] German markets [AT-VF, NAC minutes 2nd mtg US-French financial negotiations 26.3.46, 7]
165 overseas markets [F-80 AJ11, 1er Rapport Com'n Sidérurgie, Nov 46, 43–44;
A469, SRE, Iron & Steel, France #6 Investment, Caffery-SD, 18.11.48; OEEC,
Industrial Statistics 1900–1959, table 55, 94] CGP priority [Hir-DF 31.10.91]
166 resign [F-F60 902 CEI 18.2.46; M-F 1-5-1bis draft 12.12.46] balance-sheet
[CGP Rapport 2nd half 1947 Mar48 preface] French capital [CGP 1er Rapport 94]
zero [F-80 AJ7 Beigel 384] eyes shut [BlochL 106] in every field [Hel* 4]
167 quarter of taxes [A469 Dupont 22.12.47, 9 see 163 above] society and fiscal
system [A469 #85 France I.7 #4, 29.7.48] Prices of food [Milw84 15 citing J.
Lehoulier, "l'évolution des salaires", Revue d'économie politique, nov-déc 1948, n° spé-
cial, La France économique et financière en 1947, 191; Ass 116] Frachon [F-80 AJ266]
Communists had been constructive [M-F 12-2, 26.9.47] French officials [M-F 12-2
ff; Bér 324–325] wooed [Auri 5.9.47, 438] lassitude and fear [Auri, 20.1.48, 44]
168 five-man group [F-457 AP 20 Monnet-Bidault 18.7.47] blur responsibilities
[Auri 4.8.47, 382] 168–69 heavily influenced [Ba182, 80] 169 uneasy compromise [A59 #5751, 840.50R Caffery-SS 11.3.48] intergovernmental [Beu 132–
133; Bal82, 80] Monnet refused [M-F 22-1-5 Monnet-Schuman 18.4.48] not much
on its own [OEEC, Annex of Convention, Paris 16.4.48] stronger institutions [M-
F 14-5-17bis, NY Herald Tribune 8.7.48] maximised [Milw84 180–181; Beu 139–
152] last flicker [Mon 271–72] major asset [Hir 100] 170 Pflimlin [Pfl 385–87]
railroad [Uri* 57] seeds of doubt [Wal 95–96] Nathan [Mio87, 136–138; M-F 5-
3 various] covering letter [Ann46, 276] on the road [F-80 AJ266 Monnet-Schuman
4.2.47] defence cuts [A469 Dupont, 22.12.47, 4 see 163 above; F-80 AJ266,
14.3.47] exempted [A59 #5754, 840.50R, 31.3.48; M-F 11-2-3a Monnet-Schuman 12.5.47, 27] fend off [Mon 275] stop inflation [F-363 AP 7 Monnet-Mayer
21.11.47] 171 Bernstein [Uri* 58] flair [BlochL 108] pioneer [BlochL 112; Gru
66–68] levy [F-363 AP 7 Monnet-Mayer 21.11.47; M-F 11-4-1a draft 6.12.47]
turning point [F-F60ter #378 Schweitzer papers: (i) 28.11.48 mtg Queuille Petsche
Bruce Tomlinson (ii) 3.12.48 letter Bruce-Queuille + conversation Tomlinson-
Schweitzer] financed by inflation [Lub 76] not been before [M-F 22-1-5, Monnet-

Schuman 18.4.48] largest [F-457 AP 20 Bidault 18.7.47] American net aid [AT MSA Statistics and Reports 30.11.52, Statement No 18.1, 28] 172 possible model [For47 III Marshall-USParis 12.6.47, 249–51] flood the region [Wal 94–95, 100–101] not orthodox [Wal 94–95; A59, 851.51 White-Marshall 8.4.47] pushed by Monnet [F-B18220, MAE-Fr embassy US 2.4.48; M-F 11-4-5, 19.2.48 + 7a draft 9.3.48 + 10 Monnet-Mayer 5.4.48] dawned [A469 ECA SRE France #78 Report France 1948, 105–106] interim aid [F-B18220 Bidault-Caffery 2.1.48 + 2.4.48, Caffery-Bidault 2.4.48] confirmed [A469 ECA SRE France #18 Report on Interim Aid July 1948; Wal 100] terribly powerful [Ver* 12] 173 insist [Hartm* 4–5] state funding [M-F 17-8-4a, 22.10.49, 4] four-year period [F-80 AJ10, 20.2.47] have a grip [EU-DF, Monnet-Shone 27.4.62] under CGP control [M-F 1-5-2, 12.12.46; M-F 11-2-1, 20.12.46] 174 guarantee investment [M-F 11-2-2 Monnet-Schuman 25] home and dry [M-F 11-4-3, 13.1.48 + 10, 5.4.48, both Monnet-Mayer] baronies [M-F 11-4-8 & 9, signature illegible, n.d. (March 1948?) to Monnet] resign [M-F 11-4-13 Monnet-Mayer 22.6.4] favourable enough [Guy*, 4, 6; Hir*, 36, 42–43] autonomous fund [M-F 11-1-6, Queuille + Petsche-Monnet 20.10.48] personalities [A469 SRE Confidential #1, 14.3.49] ministries failed [M-F 17-6-1 Monnet-Bidault 29.11.49] laurels [M-F 17-6-3 meeting Petsche's office 30.11.49] cut of a third [A469 Director Administration &c., Geographic 1948–1953, #85 France Investment #4] balance of payments [F-80 AJ 13 note Uri 18.10.48] wheat [Milw84 199–200] 176 shaved [F-B 42268 meeting 6.11.50 incl. Petsche Buron E Faure Monnet] Pinay [Yri* 1] Alphand protesting [F-B 33507 + M-F 22-2-1 Alphand-Schuman 29.11.48] half a dozen times [F-B 42268, meeting 11.12.48; M-F 11-7-15, *idem*] Prime Minister [F-B 42268, 15.12.48] charade [BloBou 167] capital markets [CGP, Cinq Ans du plan 1952 table 132, 323] halt operations [F-B 33507, Commission Investissements 1.10.48, 9; F-B 33508 Monnet-Petsche 17.11.50] 177 above Belgium [Bau 41] late 1920s [BloBou 155] consistent goals [Bau 346] German model [Mes 82] security [Sto 44] 178 continuous creation [CGP 1er Rapport 10; MonSch 25 + M-F 11-2-3a Monnet-Schuman 12.5.47] services rendered [BloBou 139] 179 punching bag [Bal82, 73 + 77–78] Cripps [Mon 237; Hir 89]

6 Europe's Breakthrough

182 postprandial [Spa 38] 183 terms of equality [Mon87, 272–285] eccentric map [Hir 78–79] backed by France [Mcm69, 188] true yielding of sovereignty [Dav 216] erase German industry [MorganT 734–36] hell-bent [AT-SH dy 6/7.9.44] 184 manufacturing core [AT-VF, NAC US/Fr financial negotiations 26.3.46, 7; For47 II Bonnet-Marshall 1000–03; A59, 862.60, 21.7.47 + Caffery-Marshall 19.8.47, 1039–41 + Douglas-Lovett 22.8.47, 1047–49; Lub 178–79; Milw 129] not consonant [F-80 AJ11, 1st report Com'n Mod'n Sidérurgie, Nov 46] nationalise French steel [Kui 193–194] Clayton no sympathy [For47 II 840.50R 30.7.47, 1011–12] make war [M-F 14-1-4, 22.7.47; Auri47, 375, 695–99] often in Paris [Dob 216] 185 international board [For47 II 30.7.47 ff, 1011–37; Milw 74–75, 141 ff] initial sketch [Ann49, 69–72] too weak for free trade [Dob 216] 186 festivities [Hel-DF 3.12.91; Hel* 116–17] Murphy [Mel80, 154–55] Bevin [Milw 235–36, 245–46] Monnet in London [MayR 246–47] Anglo-French foundation

[Auri 11.3.48, 144–46] **187** Federation of the West [M-F 22-1-5 Monnet-Schuman 18.4.48] so-called Atlantic [M-G 1-1-4 Réflexions 1/2.5.50] pet scheme [GB-T232/148 HallPatch-FO 13.12.49; GriLyn 31] **188** payments union [GriLyn 84/117 passim; A469 SRE Central D-F Fritalux #2 1949–50 various; A469 SRE Investment-Finance-Agriculture #11, various; F-MAE-DECE #56 Feb 1950 various; F-F 60bis #469 Le Groupement Régional 14.11.49; GB-T232/149 HallPatch-FO 30.1.50 + Cripps talk Petsche 2.2.50] exorcising the demons [Bal82, 83] find themselves disputing [GB-FO371/77933, Plowden-Makins 10.3.49 Note of four conversations 3 + 7.3.49] came to nothing [Hir 102; GB-FO 371/77933 Shuckburgh-Makins 2.4.49] **189** again and again [GB-T232/149 Discussion with M Monnet, Feb. 1, 1950] without Britain impossible [A59, 840.50R, 7th mtg SD Policy Planning Staff, 24.1.50; For50 III 840.00R, 24.1.50, 617–18; For50 III 896–98] Bruce summed it up [For50 III 25.4.50, 64] rash of Atlantic schemes [For50 III 75, 91–92] High Council for Peace [Ann50, 92–93] **190** Schuman on notice [For49 III 610; Clap85, 22] off the hook [For49 III 623] good intentions [Mis 31–33] **197** policies of Richelieu [*NY Times* 3.3.50; MayR 269] from de Gaulle [Ann50, 60–63; Wil 78–79] history repeating itself [Bal82, 82–83; M-G 28-0-8 Monnet-Schuman 1.2.52] timidity of the Saar settlement in 1922 [Mon 92] **198** back in the rut [M-FS 4-1-2 Monnet-Schuman 1.5.50; Bey 152–160] Pleven-Shinwell [Poi 250; BulPel86, 13.5.50, 38] already at war [M-FS 4-1-2 Monnet-Schuman 1.5.50; M-G 1-1-4, 1/2.5.50; M-I 4-1-1, 3.5.50] going to drop it [Reu 18] **199** system of domination [Mis 37] pondered deeply [Mon 292] tradition of mistrust [Mis 51] harassed men at the helm [Hel-DF 31.3.93] tart telegram [F-F14 13672 Mendès-France-Monnet tg #59, 22.2.44] suggested Schuman [Poi 145] through Clappier [Clap85, 23; Clap86, 55] not committed [Clap*] gift to caricaturists [BulPel89, 245] **200** convinced most people [Reu 24; For50 III 435] men of goodwill [BulPel86, 183] not a French trick [Bri* 11] believe what you say [Delou 149–51] plays fair [BulPel86, 959] focus for action [Mon 289] international lawyer [Reu 18; Elg 445] April 17 [Reu 20; F-81 AJ 152, dossier AI/a; Elg 445] April 20 [Elg 445] **201** secret envoy [Mis 63] jumping the gun [Mis 61–62] shock tactics [BulPel86, Harvey-Bevin 19.5.50, 74] stranglers [Foc* 25] Acheson [Ach 382] tears in his eyes [Hir 105] behind Britain's back [Ach 385] fury comprehensible [For50 III Bevin-Acheson 11.2.50, 627–29; F-MAE DECE Finebel #363 Schuman-Petsche 3.3.50] **202** without domination [M-FS 4-1-2, 1.5.50, 4] Shrewd old Adenauer [Mis 62] entry ticket [M-G 1-2-9, 6.5.50] old dream [Die 21] Ten in France alone [Poi 251–3] Arnold [Die 35] **203** steel, coal, electricity and transport [Wil 81] Thyssen works [Gros 204] Gascuel [Poi 252] McCloy [Schwart 74] Council of Europe [Mon 281–82] Moscow in 1947 [For50 III 695–96] Edwin Martin [A59, 840.50R 7.11.49] stake the ore of Lorraine [BulPel86, Franks-Makins 14.7.50, 259; BulPel86, Harvey-Younger 16.6.50, 183–85] impossible to swallow [BulPel86, Harvey-Younger 16.6.50, 183] **204** Pleven amazed Hirsch [Hir 107–8] economic annexation [F-373 AP 17 Mayer 12.5.53; A-BD dy 24.3.53] without full UK participation [A59 840.00R Acheson-Murphy 25.2.50] Rhineland in 1936 [Hir 106; Mon71-1, 62] with Germany alone [GB-T273/253, 16.5.50] could never succeed [Hir* 10] more we were impressed [Ach 384] **205** flesh and blood [Bri* 10] other than Schuman [BulPel86, Harvey-Younger 24.6.50, 220–21] rush ministers [BulPel86, 166–67 fn 2] **206** joint control over steel [F-MAE, Z-Europe,

Allemagne 40, Z-18-1, 210−213] *entente cordiale* [Clap*] patriotism cast in doubt [Mis 38] fought in German uniform [Guy* 12] victory of the minister [Bér 312-13] paid to fight [Guy* 12] Seydoux [EU−DF] produce results [Clap*] **207** Allies' absence [For50 III 23.5.50, 705−709] full equality [Mon 309] Hallstein [Bér 11.6.50, 323; Hir 106−07; M-G 2, LeroyBeaulieu-Monnet 2 notes 16.6.50] friends for life [Mon 311] **208** pig in a poke [BulPel86, Bevin 155] blank cheque [BulPel86, Harvey 160] in the dark [BulPel86, Makins 70] later repudiated [A59, 850.33, 26.5.50; BulPel86, Harvey-Younger 3.6.50, 159−163, 171−75, 182−86; Dum 502−03] virtually certain [A59, 850.33, 26.5.50] would be lost [BulPel86, Harvey-Younger 16.6.50, 184; Elg 449] not compatible [Bal68, 75; Stanley, T. W., *Nato in Transition,* New York, 1965, 42] organizing capacity [Milw 248] more general framework [BulPel86, 10.5.50, 9−11] **209** a single delegate [Bér 326; M-G 2 LeroyBeaulieu-Monnet 16.6.50] covertly uncommitted [GB-T229/749 Guillaume-Hayter 16.6.50] *youngest* candidate [For50 III 729] revived Lotharingia [Reu 19] so vague [A59 #4944, 850.33, 22.5.50; For50 III 724] plan to have a plan [MayR 304] several times a week [Bér 22.6.50, 331] technical details [For50 III 716−17] the difficult point [M-G 2-3-11; Mon 311, 450−51] dismissal of all material issues [A59 #4946, 850.33 Bonn-SD 19.10.50] amazed Bérard [Bér 325] left to them [BulPel86, Harvey-Younger 22.6.50, 214] **210** our problems and their solutions [B-MAE 5216 Note 3 Echanges de vues Monnet-Chefs des missions 23.6.50, 3; Gri 38] took ten [F-81 AJ131 doct F5 note (JM) pour Comité Interministériel 12.6.50; Schä 140] working document [F-81 AJ 152, dossier AII/a; For50 III 24.6.50, 727−738] not for a moment [GB-T232/393 HallPatch re Monnet 22.6.50] reserved the right [For50 III 728] European Monnet Plan [BulPel86, 47 fn 2 HallPatch-Makins 11.5.50] camouflaged cartels [B-MAE 5216 Note 3 Echanges de vues Monnet-Chefs des missions 23.6.50, 7−8] Upper Silesia [BulPel86, Monnet-Plowden 25.5.50, 94] suggestion of Philip [Hir 107] AGM [For50 III 728−38] **211** supervisory board [F-MAE, DECE 45-60 #500 Anglo-American Press, Paris 7.6.50] Zeus [For50 III 18.7.50, 740−41; Bri* 11−13; HarryKer 285−304] agreed, so long as [Hel* 124, 138] turning-point [F-81 AJ 131/H1/20.7.50; A59 Bruce-SS tg 187 850.33, 11.7.50] institutional pattern [For50 III Bruce-SS 31.7.50, 742−44] 80 per cent of national income [B-MAE 5216 Note 3 Monnet-Chefs des missions 23.6.50, 3] Sherman Act [Bern 53] cartel movement [For49 IV 444] **212** opposite of a cartel [Ach 383; F-81 AJ131 note Cartels 9.5.50; For50 III 12.5.50, 697, 701] public authority [BulPel86, 47 fn 2 HallPatch-Makins 11.5.50] competition and cartels [A59, #4945, 850.33 Paris-SD 3.7.50] Biblical abundance [A59, 850.33 1950, Deptels 1169 + 1177 Sep 7; 1209−10 Sep 8; 1447−48 Sep 21; 1687 Oct 2, 1717 Oct 3, 2205 Oct 26, 2729 Nov 17, 2743 Nov 18, 2941 Nov 28, 3072 Dec 4, &c.] fn3 Tomlinson [Bow* 43−4] and so he was [Ver* 19−22] **213** regional associations [F-81 AJ 132 L1/2 Textes de référence 28.9.50, 91 pp] shared by Monnet [For50 III 2.10.50, 753−59] diatribe against cartels [F-81 AJ 132 Observations sur le memorandum du 28.9.50; B-MAE 5216, 5.10.50] tone quite unlike [B-MAE 5216 Suetens-MAE 9.10.50] October 10 [Hel* 122, 127; B-MAE 5216 Suetens-MAE 16.10.50] Bowie [Bow-DF 31.3.93; Hel* 118; Hel-DF 24.4.92] draft of November 9 [Gri 39] Mr Tomlinson [B-MAE 5216 Suetens-MAE 9.1.51] **214** strong support to French [M-G 9-3-15; A59 #4946, 850.33, SD-Paris 17.11.50] full member of single market [A59 #4946, 850.33

USParis-SS 26.11.50] closer to the final outcome [BulPel86, 16.6.50, 60–61] concessions to the Germans [A59 #4947, 850.33 Bonsal - SD 28.1.51] 215 almost revolutionary [A-CM Schuman Plan & ECSC 68] Hallstein telephoned Monnet [Hel* 135] Germans formally reserved acceptance [For51 IV 87; A59 #4946, 850.33 Bruce-SS 25.11.50] 216 Adenauer was worried [M-G 6-6-3; MonSch 60–61; F-81 AJ 137 Monnet-Schuman 28.9.50] take away with one hand [M-G 6-6-3, 28.9.50] ceilings on German steel [Hel* 1.5.92] Monnet, Hallstein and the Americans [A59 #4946, 850.33, 21.12.50; F-81 AJ 148, 21.11.50] signature of the treaty [A59 #4946, 850.33, 11 & 17.12.50] 217 excessive powers [A59 #4946, 850.33 Bruce-SD 25.11.50] Wenzel [F-81 AJ 139 Pt 3/I Bureau-Monnet 7.4.51; BulPel86, Wilson-Pitblado 27.2.51, 414–6] Wenzel claimed [F-81 AJ 139 Bureau-Monnet 7.4.51] anti-cartel provisions [A59 #4946, 850.33 Bruce-SD 18.12.50] treaty clause by clause [A59 #4946, 850.33 Bruce-SD 30.12.50] steelmasters crowding round him [F-81 AJ 157 Bureau-Monnet 5.7.50] prewar cartel as a model [F-81 AJ 138 Pt 1/IV A. FrançoisPoncet 31.10.50; A59 #4946, 850.33 Bohlen-SS tg 2093, 18.10.50] declaration of war [A59 #4946, 850.33 Paris-SD 18.10.50] Franco-American front [F-363 AP 17 Monnet-Schuman 22.1.51] Formally [M-G 6-6-3 Monnet-Schuman 28.9.50] out of the hands of the Allies [F-81 AJ 137, 9.11.50; A59 #4946, 850.33 mtg Monnet Hallstein Bowie Tomlinson &c 21.11.50] handle the Ruhr itself [F-81 AJ 137 Pt 1 I + II Adenauer-High Commissions; A59 #4946, 850.33 Bruce-SS 21.11.50] reluctance of their own coal representatives [F-363 AP 17 Monnet-Picard 14.11.50] American determination [M-G 26-3-13 Monnet-Schuman 22.12.50] 218 dead duck [Schwart 186, 362 n 3] coal sales agency dissolved [F-81 AJ 137 Cleveland-Tomlinson 16.1.51] ready for a compromise [F-81 AJ 137 Pt 1 III LeroyBeaulieu-Monnet 18.1.51; A59 850.33 tg 6233 McCloy-SS 27.1.51] Erhard had been blocked [F81 AJ 137 mtg McCloy-Bowie-LeroyBeaulieu 22.2.51; 81 AJ 157 LeroyBeaulieu-Monnet 31.1.51] artificially preferred position [For51 IV 92–93] stood firm [F-81 AJ 137 McCloy-Monnet 19.2.51] who held the power? [F-81 AJ 137 LeroyBeaulieu 22.2.51] certain of failure [F-81 AJ 138 François Poncet 24.2.51] February 22 and 23 [F-81 AJ 138, 24.4.50; For51 IV 93] accepting terms [F-363 AP 17, 14.3.51; For51 IV McCloy-SS 15.3.51, 102–103; F-81 AJ 137, 16.1.51, Cleveland + Tomlinson re Bowie + Willner 15.1.51; F-81 AJ 157 François Poncet-Schuman 22.3.51] all seven steel plants [Die 362] without the firm assistance [A-BD dy 19.4.51] 219 parried or absorbed [F-81 AJ 136 dossiers N1–3] electricity in the air [M-G 10-3-13, 6.12.50; MonSch 89] refuse even to sign [A59, 850.33 McCloy-SS 7.4.51] agreed at once [A59 #4947, 850.33 McCloy 7.4.51] cordiality unequalled [A59, 850.33 Hague 28.3.51] conversation [B-MAE 5216 Suetens 18.9.50] How can I negotiate? [Koh* 279–80] lived in the House [A-CM 19.3.51] 220 trying to create something [Bow* 28-30] ballad [For51 IV 20.3.51, 106; Hel* 200–01] *Schritt!* [Bla* 7; Hel* 200–01; For51 IV 106] never seriously in doubt [Die 83] dispute over scrap [BulPel86, 439–740] 221 misused twice in the past [A59 #4946, 850.33 McCloy 21.12.50] output quotas [F-81 AJ135 M1a doc 1 Chambre Syndicale de la Sidérurgie Française 31.1.51] hardly budged since 1918 [Hel* 126] July 17, 1950 [A59 #4945, 850.33 McCloy-SD 17.7.50] sarcastic letters [F-81 AJ 135 passim] second Ruhr [F-363 AP 17 Monnet to For'n Affairs Commission Fr. National Assembly 26.11.51] easier than expected [Hir* 17] minority backed the Schuman Plan [F-81 AJ 155, 13.12.51] claw back concessions [BulPel86, 720–723] McCloy amazed [For51 IV 130–35; F-81 AJ 142] **222** agreement with Westrick [A59, 850.33, 24.6–8.7.52] European District [F-81 AJ 158 Monnet 30.5.52] fn 4 precarious [For52/4 VI:1 Dunn-SS 25.7.52, 136–39] **223** fn 4 Bech [A59, 850.33 Perle Mesta USMin Lux'g-SS 3.7.50] poor Europe [Hel* 64; A59, 850.33 USParis-SD 25.7.52] resign three times [BulPel86, 29.7.52, 922] a policy from a need [Fau 167–68] leap in the dark [Mon 305; Poi 263] quasi-monopoly of coke [F-363 AP 17 Monnet, For'n Affairs Commission Fr Assembly 26.11.51, 20pp] more the occasion than the cause [Hel* 118] **224** triple alliance [Hel 101] top of my form [FonF89, 221] **225** expert and determined generalship [GriLyn; MilwGri] clear-cut and determined [BulPel86, Harvey 981]

7 The First Europe

226 Pearl Harbor [Schwart 124] panic in Europe [Bal68, 49; Bal82, 90–91] **227** by August 5 [For50 III 138–41] European Minister of Defence [Roy 321–31] German force [*Washington Post* 9.9.50; *NY Times* 10.9.50; Schwart 135 + fn 40, 349] sixty divisions [Mon 342] Mme Moch [For50 III Acheson-Bruce 3.11.50, 426–31; Schwart 143] manufacture weapons [M-I 4-2, 1.8.50] Petsche [MayR 315–17] Schuman complained [For50 III Bruce-SS 7.9.50, 220–24, 269–70] urgent efforts [For50 III Spofford-SS 24.8.92, 246–48] transparent scheme [Wal 106] **228** our task [M-I 4-3-4 Monnet-Pleven 23.8.50; Mon 339–40] letter September 3 [MayR 320] bereft [M-I 4-4-1, 9.9.50; Mon 341] more nationalist [M-I 4-4-2, 14.9.50; M-I 4-6-1, 14.10.50] little choice [M-I 4-4-3 & 4, 16 + 18.9.50] Atlantic Council [AT-Ach* 931; M-I 4-5-1 Schuman 18.9.50; M-Alp* 17.6.81, 4] **229** European plan for defence [Hel* 24.4.92] only diplomat [BulPel89, Harvey 3.11.50, 243–45] do not apologise [Mon 344–45] convince Pleven [Hel* 68] Pleven's own impression [Elg 236; M-I 4-7-3, 21.10.50 + 4-4-7, 23.10.50, &c.] short shrift [Delou* 20] at best premature [A-SR 7.2 (i) Bruce (ii) Cleveland; Bow* 35; Delou* 20–21; Hartm* 27] flimsy European coating [Schwart 211; Schwarz86, 831] **230** postpones a solution [For50 III 17.10.50, 377–80, 385] labelled inferiors [*idem* 27.10.50, 411–12] hopeless situation [*idem* Acheson-Bonnet 25.10.50, 403–4] sincere [*idem* McCloy-Acheson 3.8.50, 180–82; Bow* 32; Cles 277 fn 49; A-BD dy 27.10.50; BulPel89, Kirkpatrick-Bevin 28.10.50, 228–30] Monnet opted for Alphand [Hel* 95] **231** special German-American relationship [Schwart 228–9, 232–3] second-class citizenship [Fur 107, 115, 122; Schwart 211] Monnet and Eisenhower [Bow* 32; A-SR 7.2 Cleveland 30.9.59] lean to the European Army [Schwart 221] putts [Bow-DF 5.2.92] June 21 [M-Mon dy] Franco-German tangle [Mon 358–60] political sense overrode [Mon 359] Eisenhower's conversion [SRA 3.3 Bruce-Schaetzel 20.10.59] English-Speaking Union [AE-PP #197, 3.7.51] **232** dominating element [For52/4 VI 9.7.52, 102] groupings [Hel* 75; Cles 44–5] team is not good [Hel 9.7.92] forcing the pace [For52/4 V 19.1.52, 587–89] in favour of a board [Hel-DF 31.3.93] committee for Armaments [Hir 111–12; Fur 113–14; For51 III 895–97] **233** covert steps [Gol 143–4] All but two [Hel* 76] immense drain [Auri 10.3.52, 196; For52/4 V 33 + 144–45; Yri* 1–2] withdraw from Indochina [A59 Lot 53 D 444 #6 Monnet-Sturm 21.3.52] force the issue [MonSch 129–31; M-G 28-0-8, 1.2.52] attacked Monnet bitterly

[A-SR 7.2 Cleveland 16.10.59] six months allotted [Hir 114] less than federal [Ann52, 522–56] no immediate attempt to ratify [For52/4 V 655, 663] Monnet's influence [Auri 18.2.52, 130 + 8.4.52, 192] **234** nominated to the presidency [Conr 37–38; B-MAE 5216 Muûls 22.2.52] civilian control [Hel* 9.7.92] Bruce recorded Monnet [A-BD dy 19.4.51] common political roof [A-BD dy 29.7.51 + 23.10.51] political Community in reserve [A59 Lot 53 D 444 #6, 21.9.51] cartel of generals [For52/4 VI 14.12.52, 249–55] **235** Europe's first government [e.g., EU-CEAB 2 #718 HA visit to FRG 1.12.53] real authority [A496 Director European Operations, Point IV 1948–53 Schuman Plan #19 Cleveland-SD (draft) 4.8.52] **236** constant consultation [EU-CEAB 2#713, 10.8.52] association with Britain [EU-CEAB 2#713, 1HA 10.8.52; Mon 346–50] not the nations [A59, 850.33, 11.8.52] Now that you are a fact [Mon 377] **237** Schuman encouraged [BulPel86, 855–56, 870–71, 886–87 &c.] only a limited function [BulPel86, Schuman-Eden 15.9.52, 962] Monnet's loss of influence [BulPel86, 999 fn 2 Hood 6.11.52] most dangerous suggestion [A59 Lot 53 D444 #6, 6.5.52] leading power in Europe [BulPel86, 812–18] prove stubborn [Mon 380–81; For52/4 VI 13.8.52, 153; EU-CEAB 2 #713, 5HA 29.8.52; BulPel86, 926] **238** under the floodlights [Koh* 20.7.92] appeal to the Court [BulPel86, Nutting-FO 23.9.52, 968] backpedal [BulPel86, WakefieldHarrey-FO 17.9.52, 965] direct access [Ezr* 14; Bul-Pel86, Marjoribanks 8.9.52, 954–55] nurtured [Gaud* 4, 16] **239** successive generations [Mon55, 11.9.52, 13–14] very powerful [Zij* 9] he *was* the High Authority [Wel* 50–51] Coppé agreed [EU-CEAB 2 #722 Coppé 9.11.54, 114] Ricard [GB-FO 371/116100 Christofas 31.1.55; Cop 126] deep change [Lil 19.4.52, 307] **240** friendship [Mon 373; Beh* 18–19 + 32–34; Gaud* 10–11; Wel* 48] Monnet complained [Conr 40] trinity [SpiPoi 69; Koh-DF 4.5.92] temporary contract [Conr 70–73; Gilli 315; MayR 351] working groups [SpiPoi 94–95; Conr 57–61] wide variety of subjects [GB-FO 371/116102 Weir-FO 10.6.55] **241** Parliamentary supervision [A59 #4953, 850.33, 1.12.54] institutions are working [Gaud 237; Gaud* 4] its prerogative [A59, 850.33 Tomlinson 4.12.52; SpiPoi 175–79] Van Zeeland [SpiPoi 254–55] **242** Suetens [SpiPoi 260–62] export prices [Die 242, 246] cost of transport [Die 171] one day to the next [SpiPoi 103] coal prices [SpiPoi 104, 111] **243** Erhard walked out [A59, 850.33 Tomlinson-SS 14.2.53] immense tax advantage [Mon 388] persuaded Adenauer [SpiPoi 111] irrelevant [Beh* 31] **244** Blair House [A59, 850.33 Bruce 19.5.53] ignorance [SpiPoi 181–82] not in search of dollar grants [EU-CEAB 2 #716, 101HA 14.6.53] wanted loans [F-MAE, DECE #542 Monnet, Common Assembly 19.6.53, 151–52] psychology of Marshall aid [For52/4 VI talks Dulles Humphrey Stassen Monnet &c. 13/15.12.53, 337–42] priorities for the year [EU-CEAB 2 #716] indirect assurances [For52/4 VI 346] **245** interest in Whitehall [Ann53 28.12.53, 461; GB-FO 371/111275, 30.9.54] tomfoolery [A59 #4953, 850.33, 20.12.54] Harriman [A59, 850.33 #4945 McCloy-SS re Blankenhorn conversation 28.6.50] sympathetic interest [For51 IV Mar51 107–08; EU-CEAB 2 #713, 5HA 29.8.52] psychology of Marshall aid [For52/4 VI talks Dulles Humphrey Stassen Monnet &c. 13/15.12.53, 337–42] any funds at all [SpiPoi 184–85] exceptional political act [For52/4 VI Dulles Humphrey Monnet etc., 8.4.54, 380–84; SpiPoi 192–93; Wel* 29.7.92, 3] for all it was worth [For52/4 VI Monnet-Tomlinson 26.1.54, 356–58] 4 per cent [Die 320–33] New York market [SpiPoi 428]

246 holy trinity [A469 SRE Industrial Resources, Coal, Multinational Orgs 1949–63 EPC-CSC #2 CSC General 19.3.51] lose face [EU-CEAB 2 #717, extraordHA 15.9.53, 78–81] energetic action [e.g. Gilli 330; M-H 23-10-1, 13.2.53; A59, 850.33, 21.4.53; EU-CEAB 2 #717, 117HA 18.9.53; EU-CEAB 2 #720, 163HA 18.3.54; EU-CM 1/1954, 12CM 3.3.54; For52/4 VI 13.5.54, 392–293 &c] German trustees [F-81 AJ 142 McCloy-Adenauer 27.8.51] 247 duly applied [EU-CEAB 4 #284 Hamburger 23.9.53, 196] must be liquidated [M-H 22-2-5 Monnet-HA 11.1.54] negotiations opened [SpiPoi 123–31] changing his job [SpiPoi 128] under René Mayer [Die 390–93; SpiPoi 353–59] ATIC [SpiPoi 127] easier to supply coking ovens {OEEC *Industrial Statistics 1900–1959*} enthusiastic report [F-457 AP 31 Achat de la mine Harpener 26.6.53; EU-CEAB 9 #104 Tezenas 2.2.55, 80–85; Gilli 358] 248 export price cartel [EU-CEAB4 #72 HA Legal Service 2.1.54] fines [A59 850.33 Baldwin (Düsseldorf)-SD 20.10.53] world exports [EU-CEAB2 #716, 127HA mtg 5.11.53; AE-US Council Foreign Economic Policy Papers #4 CFEP 520 ECSC pt I, Dec 1955, 19] act promptly [A59, 850.33 Bruce-SD reporting Hamburger HA Cartel Director 22.4.53] Webb-Pomarene Act [AE-US Council Foreign Economic Policy Papers #4 CFEP 520 ECSC pt I, Dec 1955, 19] depended on proof [EU-CEAB 4 #72 HA Legal Service 2.1.54] Wehrer [EU-CEAB3 #475, Albert Wehrer, "Le Plan Schuman et les Cartels" speech to Benelux section of International Law Association, Luxembourg 24.9.54] erode cartel [A59 #4952, 850.33, 9.4.54; SpiPoi 188] carving up the market [SpiPoi 136] vary prices up to 2.5 per cent [SpiPoi 146–47] Court [Die 258–60] 249 over a hundred cases [Die 357] deconcentrations maintained [SpiPoi 223] only yardstick [SpiPoi 235–36] gradually reconcentrate [Sim 35–36; SRA Cleveland 23.9.59] no Vereinigte Stahlwerke again [Wel* 44–45] fn 1 40 per cent German steel [Die 361; Lis 152] under 10 per cent [Die 356+362; Lis 152] 250 Marjoribanks [SpiPoi 277; GB-FO 371/105956 Marjoribanks-Christofas 11.9.53] power struggle [Zij* 12] turned largely to Monnet [AT-AD #67a Acheson-McCloy 23.12.53] premature [SpiPoi 119] talked out [Conr 41 ex-Wellenstein] voluntary cooperation [A59, 850.33 Goldenberg 13.2.53] fears of the labour unions [EU-CEAB 2 #720, 160HA 10.3.54, 62] unanimity achieved [EU-CEAB 2 #720, 165HA 18.3.54, 99] some form of organisation [EU-CEAB 2 #717, 117HA 17.9.53; SpiPoi 118] scrap [SpiPoi 150–72; Die 287–313] Free-market critics [Burn 422–30] rose more slowly [Mon 392; Burn 446–47; SpiPoi 370; Die 263–64] *liberalisers* in Britain [Ran 115, 117] restructuring [EU-CEAB 3 #468 Goudima n.d.] trade in steel doubled [OEEC *Industrial Statistics 1900–1959* Paris 1960 Table 55, p. 94] 252 rail charges [SpiPoi 219] increased rather than reduced [Lis 407–08] less independent [SpiPoi 179] ruling of the Court [Mon 384; Gaud 237] levy for steel [Gilli 353] Kreyssig [EU-CEAB 4 #63, 27.6.56, 33] 253 tangling up the threads [Hel* 92–94] salute to adventurers [F-MAE-DECE #542 + F-457 AP 34, Bidault speech to ad hoc Assembly 9.3.53] openly against the EDC [Hel* 181; F-457 AP 40 Seydoux 14 + 16 + 28.4.53] 254 democratic control [M-J 9-4-1 Commin, Council of the Republic 27.10.53] would-be simplification [Hel 47] too much on his plate [Mon 396] stateless hotch-potch [Cles 87; Jou I 255; Jou II 174] 255 stroke [MonM*; Hel89, 587] incapacitated [M-I 26-2-8 Monnet draft, early August 1954; Mel 54] renegotiation within the year [Ann54, 420–27] not concealed [M-MenF*] 256 come out in favour of the EDC [M-I 26-

2-13 + 14 + 15 + 16 Monnet-MendèsFrance 12 + 16 + 24 + 26.8.54,] should never break off [Koh* 20.7.92] *Marseillaise* [MayR 409] not normal [Den89, 169] 257 avoid any misunderstanding [Zij* 9]

8 The Most Hazardous Straits

258 [Schwarz91, 142. was the observer.] concussion [Rot* 12] automata [Hel* 3] early death [Hel* 4; Hel89, 588] bad business [Delou* 21] light-headed [Cam 20] balance in Europe [B-MAE 5216 Poswick–MAE 8.11.54] Drees [HarryKer 144– 45] 259 buried all this [Ann54, 433] single setback [Beu 307] if the EDC failed [BulPel86, 996–98] recapture the initiative [Küs89, 214] November 11 [Ann54, 478] nationalism in the air [A-FF #49 McCloy-Frankfurter 13.12.54, 350] all possible pressure [A59 #4956, 850.33 Düsseldorf-SD 4.5.55] 260 stay on [Ann54, 483] So did Adenauer [F-MAE-DECE #526 CECA FrançoisPoncet 16.11.54] Council of Ministers [A59 #4953, 850.33, 24.11.54] hour of need [Koh* 9] European federation [A59 #4953, 850.33 N°40, 31.10.54] High Authority-UK committee [BulPel86, Makins note on conversations with Monnet 22.8.52 doct 482, 926–928; Ran 114] met on November 17 [SpiPoi 274] 261 single U.K.-ECSC market in steel [Ran 117; SpiPoi 276] common rules [Rot* 12; GB-FO 371/106072 Weir-Pierson Dixon 7.12.53; GB-FO 371/105957/168 Monnet-Weir 24.12.53; SpiPoi 277] doldrums [DocD54, 546–547] root and branch [*The Times*, Coal-Steel Pact 20.12.54; GB-Cab 128/7-CC 54/27(3); GB-FO 371/111275, 30.9.54; A59 #4953, 850.33, 5.10.54] a non-state [DocD54, 674–675 + 750-752; A59 #4953, 850.33 N°39, Tomlinson-SS 31.10.54; Gaud* 13] the higher the level [Ran 114; For52/4 VI 23.7.54, 406] encroaching on trade policy [SpiPoi 278–295] 262 other fields [GB-FO 371/116100, 7.2.55 + 116101, 25.5.55 + 116035A, 21.11.55] 263 we must try [Stae* 5–6] September 12 [M-Mon dy] written . . . by Monnet [M-H 62-1-7; M-H 63-3-1 to 21 + 71-1-1; M-K 5-1-16 + 5-1 note 21.02.55] endorse it publicly [M-K 5, 4.1.55] fake integration [Harry 7–8] 264 supranational wedge [Hel* 21.2.91] insurmountable technical problems [Uri* 1] civil nuclear power [M-H 63-3 various] Isenbergh [A-SR 3.5 Isenbergh 2.3.60] 265 no point metering [Ise*] new industrial revolution [Ann55, 718; Hel* 50] commercial nuclear-power programme [Gol 282–83] self-denying ordinance [Gol 145; For55/7 IV 24.4.56, 443] temporary [Schwarz 91, 157–58, 299] inferiority complex [Hel* 31] Boussac [Pina* 3] radio talk Mendès-France [M-H 71-1-2, 5.1.55] 266 Holy Ghost [Hel* 131] Pleven [Hel-DF 21.2.91] woo Spaak [F-MAE DECE #526 memo mtg Faure-Spaak 7.2.55, 204–08] curious little incident [Mon 402; Koh* 10; Hel* 11] blocking Ramadier [Koh* 10] 267 lamentable surrender [Jou I 255] message twice over [Koh* 103] never denied [*Spiegel* 41, 9.10.54, 36– 39] December 17, 1954 [For55/7 IV 367–68] very bad, very dangerous [Hel* 28] 268 identified with Monnet [A59 #4953, 17.11.54] many enemies [GB-FO 371/ 116102 Weir-Macmillan 10.6.55] personal animus [B-MAE 5216 Guillaume-MAE 20.12.54] dislikes M. Monnet [GB-FO 371/116101 Allchin-FO 8.4.55] spearhead [GB-FO 371/116101 Meiklereid-FO 18.4.55] We must act [Rot* 12; Hel* 6] new proposals [GB-FO 371/116101 Boothby-FO 31.3.55] bursting with new ideas [GB-FO 371/116101 Allchin-FO 2.4.55] 269 eyrie in Luxembourg [F-MAE Europe Généralités 1949–55 #64, 108–11; Spa 62–63] first proposals [M-K 5–6]

rather depressed [Uri* 1–3] fn 2 Ophüls in Paris [Hel* 115–16; MayR 416, 419] **270** didn't dare [Hel 32] Monnet thinks it is not [Koh* 16] too complicated [Hel* 21.2.91] another rebuff [Spa 62] Free Trade Area [Harry 11; B-MAE 5216 Arrangements économiques franco-allemands, appendice, 4.12.54, 13] Van Houtte [Harry 20] Larock [Harry 19–20] **271** two confederations [Küs82, 67–68] not new [F-81 AJ 155 FrançoisPoncet 10.11.51] Beyen unimpressed [B-MAE 5216 Arrangements économiques franco-allemands 4.12.54, 8] sweeten a deal [B-MAE 5216 Hupperts re Bech 17.771/4, 29.10.54] nightmares [Rot* 61, 73] preferred collusion [Rot* 18, 62; GB-FO 371/109609, 9.11.54] integrate Germany [For55/7 IV 367–71] we must now act [F-MAE Europe Généralités #64, 108–11] against maintaining him [Spa 63–64] Faure does not like Monnet [Sno* 11a; GB-FO371/116102, 4.5.55; A59 #4956, 850.33, 17.5.55] most popular Premier [A59 #4956, 850.33, 12.5.55] **272** unsung heroes [Rot* 98–100; Rut*; Koh* 48, 291] further supranational [Harry 4] rejected the general opinion [Harry 27 + 38–39] tutelary power [Koh* 4] quays in Rotterdam [Rut* 21] **273** fn 5 if he were M. Bech [GB-FO 371/116049 Allchin-FO 14.9.55] like Spaak and Monnet [Harry 31 + 38–39] Tinbergen [Koh* 3, 281] Beyen sent to Spaak [Spa 64–65] at loggerheads [GB-FO371/116038, 18.4.55] in the style of Spaak [DocD55-1, 4.6.55, 731–32; GB-FO371/116057, 15.12.55] **274** free hand [Rut* 19–23] scared me [Spa 64–65] I wonder if [Harry 35] Rothschild remembers [Rot* 13–14] fall-back position [Rut* 5] **275** Adenauer sceptical [Küs82, 98; Koh* 11–12, 33, 48; Hel* 8–9; Hel 57; Schwarz86, 877; Schwarz91, 287, 299, 324–25] inclined to Britain [Koh* 4.2.55, 22] Saar conflict [Küs82, 98] tête-à-tête with Pinay [F-MAE, Z-Europe Allemagne 3.4.55 Pinay-Strauss 23–25] attached to Monnet [F-MAE, Z-Europe Allemagne, 19.4.55, FrançoisPoncet-Pinay 75–76] without supranational commitments [Ann55, 375–76] few German supporters [Küs82, 79–80, 113] **276** disintegration [Küs82, early draft (Fr.) 25, citing Hallstein-Erhard, 30.3.55] French hegemony [Koh* 23.11.54, 21–22; A59 #4953, 850.33, 23.8.54, West German attitudes, J W Tuthill 22 pp] criticisms of the Scientific Council [Groe* 5] vaguer on institutions [Küs82, 115–19; Ann55, 716–17] wily Adenauer [Koh* 16, 97] **277** Kiderlen-Wächter &c [Clém 68; Fis 6–12; Hartl92, 274] France and Turkey [Cal 18] Dresden [Clém 68] incomprehensible [Küs89, 232] technical departments [A59 #4956, 850.33 Rome-SD 27, 28, 31.5.55; For55/7 IV 29 + 31.5.55, 289–91] **278** hint of things to come [Ann55, 717–18] grouping of fifteen nations [B-MAE 5216, 17.771/4 Guillaume-Larock 19.4.55; Ann55, 34] outside control [Gol 143–44] Franco's Spain [Küs82, 104–05] under pressure [Mas 505] **279** all reference [A-SR 7.3 Hartmann 12.5.55] May 24 [GB-FO 371/116102 HA Press Release] obliged to accept [GB-FO 371/116100 Weir-FO 21.4.55] decline to chair [GB-FO371/115992 Marjoribanks-FO 2.5.55] sufficient justification [GB-FO371/116102 Allchin-FO 25.5.55] hang on [A59 #4956, 850.33 Lux'g-SD 23 + 28.5.55] mistake in leaving [MonM* 8.7.92] **280** several months ago [F-MAE, DECE 526 Valéry-MendèsFrance 23.11.54] four days before [source Bech A59 #4956 850.33, 17-25.5.55 Buchanan-SD; GB-FO371/116102 + 116038] withhold concessions [GB-FO371/116102 Marjoribanks-FO (citing Kohnstamm) 27.5.55] embarrassing for Spaak [Hel* 120–21; MayR 420] letter May 31 [MayR 425] under a double French veto [GB-FO371/116040 Jebb-Macmillan 15.6.55] very much mistaken [Koh* 13] **281** changeover would benefit the ECSC [A59

#4956, 850.33 Paris-SD 12.5.55; Lux-SD, 10.6.55; F-MAE, Europe Généralités #64 Garnier-MAE 4.6.55] licence for obstruction [L-AET 7689 PV Messine 25-29] German delegation to switch [A-SR 7.3 Hartman 30.6.55] veto a second time [Uri* 65–66] none to pool information [For55/7 IV 293–95] Behr [Koh* 14] 282 Sole Mio [Stae* 9–15; Rot* 28] take the sting out [GB-FO371/116040 Jebb-Macmillan 15.6.55, 43–48] Spaak deceived Pinay [Rot* 21] proposed Spaak [GB-FO371/116039 Brussels-FO 10.6.55; DocD55 I 13.6.55, 768 fn; A59 #4956, 850.33, 9.6.55, source Rothschild 8.6.55] No record was kept [Rot* 21; Stae* 11–13] warmest regard for Spaak [Pina* 2–3]

9 The Second Europe

284 returned [M-Mon dy; Koh*] I have me doots [A-FF #49 Frankfurter-McCloy 7.12.54, 348 + reply 13.12.54, 350] 285 Freitag [Mon 407; M-Mon dy] European-minded [A59 #4956, 850.33, 4.5.55] join as delegates [Mon 407] would give him a line [Hel* 24–25] fifty drafts [mainly M-H 63-3 + M-K 5-1] January 4 [M-Mon dy] Spinelli [M-K 5-1-1, 4.1.55] Action Committee [Koh* 23; M-K 5-1-8, 21.2.55] there was one in Algiers [MayD 310; M-E 31-1-57, 4.10.43] broad masses [EU-DF Monnet-Shone 4.62] 286 wooed them [Koh* 37–41] studies for the extension of the ECSC [Birkelbach Monde 15–16.5.55; Ann55, 414] Wehner [Ann55, 435–436] three years' experience of the Common Assembly [M-Mon dy] Ollenhauer sent a note [Mon 412] 287 party congress in March 1955 [Noë* 1] renunciation of weapons [Pine* 2] concessions to WEU [Ann54, 344 + 441–42; Noë* 5–6] accepted Monnet's thesis [Noë 5–6] immediate appointment [Hel* 34–35] Mollet's mentor [Noë* 5] asked Mendès-France [Hel* 23] weak link [Koh* 32, 43–44] 288 Mere cooperation [Rec 11–12] five-sixths of the Gaullists [Ann56, 22] Political passions [FauM* 15] 289 truly the relaunching [Hel 62] suggested by Monnet to Spaak [Spa 72; Groe* 9; Uri* 69–70; M-Mon dy] 290 Uri dictated [Uri* 73–76] Hupperts [Rot* 46–47] Council of Europe [Ann53, 394–95] Adenauer–Mendès-France [Ann54, 457–58 + 465–68] impressed Bonn [Cars* 8–9] Without a Saar settlement [Rot* 60] great deal of education [For55/7 IV 7.2.56, 407–408] electrified the parliamentarians [Koh* 148] barely brought to contemplate [Marj 282–94] 291 Socialist seminar [Noë* 30] shot to the top [Milward-DF; OEEC trade statistics] Marjolin persuaded Mollet [Noë* 24, 30–31] farmers' leaders [FauM* 9–10; Noë* 25–27] Monnet was first moved [Koh* 11, 32] farmers are in favour [Hel* 32] 292 ignoring many advisers [Küs82, 327] nomenklatura [Foc* 10; Mer* 21–22] fifty meetings [Mon dy] April 22 1955 [M-K 13 HA Division Relations Extérieures 5.4.55] 293 promoting a strong European industry [Tei 253–55] laggard Europeans [Arm55; Hel* 50–51; Hel 65] greater hurry than Armand [Hel-DF 26.11.91] 395 promptly dropped [A-SR 3.5 Isenbergh 2.3.60] patterned on the McMahon Act [Hel* 153] could not find fault [Hel* 45, 48–49, 51] AEC for six countries [A-SR 3.5 Isenbergh 2.3.60] ownership and monopoly [B-MAE 5216, 17.771/12 Spaak-Brentano/Hallstein, Bonn 14.11.55, 8ff; Hel 65] 294 atomic independence [For55/7 IV 397] reached most rapidly [Rec 17–22] meaning Britain [Rec 18–19; FonP 44 & 66–67; Ann56, 248] investiture speech [Ann56, 31.1.56, 257] impossible nationally [Ann56, 257 + 463–64] Cahiers Républicains [Sche 137–38] against the industries [Hel 108] major nuclear exporter

[For55/7 IV 346–48, 435–41] **295** mutilating our national defence [FraP 25–26] Were it not for Algeria [B-MAE 5216 17.771/6 Guillaume-MAE 2.5.56] chances almost zero [For55/7, 3.2.56, 401–02] Pinay [Spa 89] on budgetary grounds [Ins 33–35, 44–45, 82] Pflimlin [Sche 118–19] prototype nuclear weapon [Sche 122–25] clearing the road [L-AET 7691 PV CMEA Brussels 11-12.2.56; Schwarz91, 154] **296** moratorium [B-MAE 5216, 17.771/10 Spaak-MFaure 18.2.56 + MFaure-Calmès 20.3.56] Dulles [For55/7 IV 406–07] nor changed his own stance [Hel 62; Hel* 47–53] not renounce its right [Ann56 70; Wil 261] national nuclear lobby [B-MAE 5216, 17.771/6 Guillaume-Larock 3.5.56; For55/7 IV SD-AEC 7.8.55, 458] Guillaumat [Noë* 20–21] discrimination [For55/7 IV 9.2.56, 412–14] **296–97** SPD's anger [Koh* 11–12.9.56, 62] **297** socialism [For55/7 IV 435, 441, 473] Strauss in Germany and the CEA [Koh* 90–99] making Euratom impossible [Koh* 69] leak-proof controls [Rec 26] Mollet and Ollenhauer [Koh* 13.11.56, 109; Hel-DF 14.2.91 says Monnet did not intervene directly] told Adenauer [Groe* 5–7; Koh* 62–63; Schwarz91, 290] end of the year [Rec 30] Kohnstamm and Behr [Koh* 59, 70, 75, 88, 94] Cabinet in Bonn [Koh* 30.9.56, 74] attacked the Bonn government [Koh* 90 + 41, 77, 83] **298** haven of free enterprise [For55/7 IV 480–81] constant involvement [Koh* 96] first Community Summit [Hel* 64] negotiate foreign agreements [Hel* 14.2.92] first Five-Year Research Programme [Tei 263; Hel 65; Ren 148; Gué* 24] taxing powers [Hel 69] **299** declined to retract [Mer* 50–51; FauM* 14.9.88] reflected views of CEA [FauM* 20; Noë* 20] not very exciting [EU-KM Kohnstamm-Schaetzel 26.11.57] Is this all it is? [Foc* 18; Mer* 86] ample scope [Gué* 10] West's supplies of oil [Hel* 21.2.92] miracle of timing [Rec 29; Koh* 18, 24] godsend [Koh* 65] **300** emerged in a single day [M-Mon dy; Koh* 18, 24] nuclear power targets [M-K 13, 15.6.56 + 27.7.56 &c] some hesitation [Noë89, 376] Secord gave him a paper [M-K 13, 21.5.55] no respect [Koh* 146–49] Timbuctoo [Koh* 142 & 20.7.92] **301** forced Armand [Hel* 25.11.91 § 7] waiting in ambush [Koh* 146–49] exploratory stage [EU-KM Euratom Commission 1038/57e Summary Record of the Meetings of Three Wise Men Paris Brussels and Bonn 21–26.1.57, 5, 11] economic calamity [ArmEtzGio 18] third as large [ArmEtzGio 20–22] massive support [For55/7 IV 308] fissionable materials [For55/7 IV 367–68; Ann55, 543–44] not attach to the Common Market [For55/7 IV 399–400, 26.1.56] **302** twenty tons of uranium-235 [Ann56, 22.2.56, 262] Monnet wrote to members Action Committee [FonP 73] bilateral nuclear agreements [For55/7 IV 475–76] persuading Adenauer to squash [For55/7 IV 477–81] Shippingport [Tei 244–47; Gué* 4; Koh* 142] Atoms for Peace policy [Mel75, 77–88; Sche 176–79; Tei 254] antiproliferation [Mel75, 200–15] lowered in November 1956 [Sche 177] nothing like importance [Bow* 54] **303** administration was resigned [Tei 259–62] bilateral licensing agreements [e.g. For55/7 IV 347–48] partners and competitors [Tei 262–71] efficient help [For55/7 IV 279–569 passim] dire security risks [For55/7 IV 387, 390–99] **304** presented by Monnet [For55/7 IV 397] flying debris [For55/7 IV 403] inverted *Junktim* [Koh* 108–109; Mon 411–12, 419] the Action Committee will disintegrate [Koh* 41, 82–83] ambitions of the French CEA [Gol 149] European gas diffusion plant [Tei 252] from the ground up [Zij* 21] in a small room [Hel* 55] core of political will [Pine* 3; Hel* 21, 38, 55] **306** within a week of signature [Hel 69] clerk of the French National Assembly [M-Mon dy] Blamont

[Hel* 18–20, 39] Now only one did [Ann57, 71] uncommon [FauM* 14; Pine* 14] before the summer holidays [Rec 39–41] **307** diluted [Rec 35, 40; FonP 77–78] reunification plan [Ann57, 368, 580] without real difficulty [Mon 424; Koh* 163–69]

10   Europe in the World

310 committee wound up [Hel 79] tested the waters again [EU-KM 4.5.60] leaving for a year [A-SR 7.6, 20.5.60] Committee unique [EU-KM 4.5.60; Rec 11.10.68, 194–95] European statute [Rec 47] needs a focus [EU-KM Monnet-Buset 8.3.58] **311** location [EU-KM 25.7.57] Compiègne [Koh* 187, 216; Hel* 4.3.92] French takeover [Koh* 177] Strasbourg and Kehl [Koh* 201] Luxembourg [Koh* 201, 219] new Communities for Brussels [EU-KM Calmès-Kohnstamm 17.12.58] Larock [EU-KM Note sur la conférence des 6 ministres des affaires étrangères 7.3.58] change of Belgian government [Rot* 111–13] one Commission for three Communities [Rec 81–82] attacked by Buset [*Libre Belgique* 9.1.58] Buset and Lefèvre [FonP 82–83] conflict Brussels and District [EU-KM Monnet-Buset 8.3.58] highly committed [Tin 525] **312** article in Rome treaties [Hel-DF 31.3.93] easy to produce political union [EU-KM Monnet-Romme 22.11.58] Triffin [A-SR 13.1 Hinton 2.3.60] political in five years [Koh* 223] $655 million [Led* 2] **313** Monnet back seat [Koh* 191] propelled him [Koh* 223] suffered a breakdown [Koh* 122, 140, 212; EU-KM 20.1.58] October 13, 1957 [Koh* 190] informal group must prepare it [Koh* 190–92] preliminary work [Koh* 210] Monnet obliged [Koh* 213–14; EU-KM Farley-Kohnstamm 23.12.57 + Kohnstamm-Monnet 20.1.58] **314** take the initiative but not appear to do so [EU-KM Kohnstamm-Schaetzel 17.1.58 + Schaetzel-Kohnstamm 28.1.58] **314** Formal talks [EU-KM Kohnstamm-Armand 29.1.58] memorandum of understanding [EU-KM History Joint US-Euratom Programme EUR/C/849/59e, 23.4.59] What if Comecon [*NY Times* 13.4.58 + 8.6.58; Koh* 234] why subsidise Euratom [EU-KM Ball-Kohnstamm 18.7.58] echoed the objection [EU-KM Schaetzel-Kohnstamm 19.11.57] Buy American [Koh* 257; EU-KM Schaetzel-Kohnstamm 20.11.58] revolutionary change [EU-KM 20.1.57] more equal [Koh* 235, 237] the President early in August [EU-KM Kohnstamm-Monnet 1.7.58 + Monnet-Dulles 13.7.58; Koh* 239–40] Reuther [Koh* 240] trust oral reports [Hel* 64–67, 86; Hel 106] **315** first association of equals [EU-KM Monnet-CA drafts 17.6.58] when M. Monnet gave orders [Hir 171] **316** in favour constitution [Mon 429–30] Algeria referendum [Mon 484] vet appointments in the army [Delou* 3] too divided between countries [Ezr* 12] white paper [EU-KM Monnet-Daum 23.5.59] set up a joint group [Rec 64–65] The rest was silence [FonP 90] **317** break the High Authority [Koh* 219] up in heaven [Koh* 220] pathfinder [EU-KM les Institutions européennes en mai 1959] Bad Kreuznach [Hel 78] warning of last leaders [Koh* 166, 233—it was Maurice Faure at the Council of Foreign Ministers of the Six on May 20, 1958] Armand about to resign [Koh* 242] Monnet succeeding him [Koh* 254] post for Hirsch [Hir 147] close links [Gué* 23–24] **318** before de Gaulle Euratom [Hel* 21] arbiter between camps [Gaul 59, 178–80; Hart171, 207] Italo-French communiqué [Alb 220] quarterly meetings [Ann59, 550–51] obsolete [Mon 433–34] not what de Gaulle said [DF] progress and defence [Hel 83; Jou II 240–41] both surprised [Spa 357] Supreme Council [Mon 437] August 10 [Mon 433] **319** beyond states a delusion [Jou II 242–43; Hart171, 219] Franco-German agreement [Mon 435–36] resolution July 10–11 [Rec 104] Europe of States [Gaul-LNC 1958–60, 398–99] de Quay [Koh* 347] **320** scornful press conference [Jou II 264–68] Western orthodoxy [Hart171, 218–21] withdraw from NATO [Mac-millan-HeathcoteAmory 24.6.58] **321** everyone wants it [Koh* 209] natural nor wise [*The Times* 6.6.56; Cam 94] welcomed a Free Trade Area [Rec 35] leave FTA behind [M-K 89, 10.1.59; EU-KM 22.1.59] **322** Washington abruptly awoke [Mon 463; FonP 127] including Japan [Cam 282] primacy of the Six [Beu 332] Round Table [Rec 66–67] triangular relationship [A-TJ Tuthill memo of talk with Monnet 9.6.59] **323** Bar Harbour [Led* 9; M-K 89] Action Council [M-K 89] discredited OEEC [M-K 89-3-5, 23.7.59; FonP 126] jointly by de Gaulle and Ade-nauer [M-K 89] Tuthill paper October 1959 [Tut* 5–6] Monnet plans [Rec 79–81] Pinay and Etzel [A-SR 8, Kohnstamm 22.9.59] newfound dollar deficit [Mon 463; FonP 127] **324** EEC, the US, UK [Rec 79–82] establish the OECD [M-K 89, 13 + 19.12.59] annoyed with Hallstein [A-SR 5.1, 16.1.60 Kohnstamm-Duchêne; DF] inspirer of the OECD [Tut*; Clap*] **325** not reached a consensus [Cam 282] United Kingdom still hopes [AE-Whitman #10 Herter-Eisenhower, European Trade Problems, 28.2.60] acceleration [*NY Times* 16.3.60; Beu 348–49] Selwyn Lloyd [AE-WHC #80 Macmillan visit 26.3.50; Cam 282–85; Ann60, 397] Ball effect on Kennedy [Cam89, 133; Bal82, 213–17] **326** no exceptions for them in the rules [FonP 17.5.61, 120] You've heard many people say [Mon71-1, 66] future of the Atlantic alliance [AE-NL #98 Bowie-Herter, North Atlantic Nations, Tasks for the 1960s 143–59] genuine partnership of equals [AE-NL #98 August 1960, 144–46] Bowie saw Monnet [Bow* 7.9.92] real dialogue [Rec 87–93] Ball consulted Monnet [Win93, 6] July 4, 1962 [FonP 132] **327** Action Com-mittee voiced them too [Rec 26.6.62, 111–17] In Bowie's eyes [Bow* 60] outwards from such nuclei [For49 III Webb-Bruce 24.9.49, 666] association of equals [Hel* 113] nowhere near the interest in the Community [Bow* 54] impressed by the Community [Bal* 28; Schle 729] **328** we would have to cooperate [Bow* 50] I do not see why not [Hel 132] **329** He can't stop it [EU-DF, Monnet-Kleiman 24.5.61] negotiations must be pressed quickly [Mon 455; Monnet-AFP 1.8.61; MayR 480–86; EU-KM 31.10.61] without delay [Hel-DF 4.3.92] Hallstein denied [Hel* 213] Metz [*Monde* 4.7.91, 6; Kle 66] warned Macmillan [EU-KM, Duchêne-Kohnstamm 15.5.62; Hel 97] such a rage [M-Couv* 8] **330** fast and loose [EU-DF] in no uncertain terms [Hel 99; Koh* 12; M-Couv* 8] tarnished [MayR 495] like maidens and roses [Wil 317] author of the preamble [Lac86, 308; M-Couv*; Couv 55; Deb 425] not claim so much [Mon 468] Six no longer exist [MayR 499] **331** Bundestag resolution [M-K 117, 26.2.63] did not find it [Bal82, 272; AT-AD Post-Adm'n #86, 19.2.63] Free Democrats [M-K 117 Birrenbach-Monnet 16.3.63; Wil 315] ich bin ein Berliner [Win 367] endorsement MLF [Rec 131–49] boycotts [Wil 342–45; Hel 118] voted against its view [Mon 483–85; Hel 122; Jou I 239–40] **332** French rejection [MayR 507–08] Lecanuet [Hel-DF 9.7.92] Mitterrand [Hel 122; Ger 327] short of the plebiscites [Wil 347] national vetoes [Ger 319–29; Wil 349–53] **333** price rose steadily [EU-KM 27.7.59] out of date [Hir 171] five power reactors [Hel 104] forbid Euratom inspectors [Hir 169] campaign seeped [Hel* 191; Bommelle-Van Helmont 24.2.92] no longer invoke majority votes [Mer* 85–86; Gué* 38; Hel* 191] few reactor orders [Hel 104; Foc* 39–41] **334** up from the rotunda [FonP 186] defeat to defeat [Koh* 217] directorate of two [Hel 129] **335** Pompidou [Ger 349–50] European Reserve Fund [Hel 138] central bank insulated [Hel 138; Hel* 217] his plan, drafted by Van Helmont [Mon 503–04; Hel 152; Hel* 219] **336** diplomatic consultation [Hel 138, 153] Monnet suggested [Hel 155] Giscard and Sauvagnargues [Gis 26; Sauva* 20] European Council [Gis 12, 26] **337** British prevented majority voting [Sauva* 17–20] goal must be limited [FonP 197–98] buckshot [Rec passim] **338** circle of friends [Win93, 9–10; MKA Koh-Mon 20.2.75] IAEA and Euratom [Hel 108] semi-overtures from Pompidou [Hel 138] Europe in the world [Mon 494] not as sharp [MonM* 8.7.92] pneumonia [MonM* 8.7.92] thought of Brandt [Hel-DF 4.3.92] **339** memoirs of the future [Dur89, 194] egocentric + Bruce praised [FonF* 46] needed the money [Dur89, 191] twice his income [Zin-DF 30.12.92] directorships [Hel* 236] sold the family's controlling interest [Koh* 327–29; Cochet-DF26.6.91] old creditors [MonM* 8.7.92; Zin-DF 30.12.92] **340** sell Houjarray [Hel* 235] $150,000 [MonM* 8.7.92; Zin-DF 30.12.92] Honorary Citizen [FonP 169–170] isolation of retirement [MonM* 8.7.92] one never sees [Hel 158] added to growth [Hel 157] enough for any man [Tut* 15] grandchildren [Per-DF] more than one could have hoped [Koh-DF] Battle Hymn [Bal82, 99] felt left out [Gis 14] **341** face the sun [FonF 75; Hel89 (entry of 24.4.66) 590]

11   A Citizen among States

345 agricultural and other pools [Ger 145–49; MilGri passim] fn 1 Coudenhove-Kalergi [Vau 26–28] fn 1 Streit [AP-JFD Papers, correspondence, #19, 1940, Streit-Dulles 24.10.40 with enclosures & Dulles-Streit, 14.11.40] **346** endless fight [Mon 129, 231, 286–87] phrase repels [Mon 230] temptation to disperse [Mon 229] never taken a job [DF] self-evident [Den 172] **347** more realistic than what is possible [Mon 173–74] good at waiting [Mon 42] When ideas are lacking [Mon 231] do not know what to do [DF] **348** Rock Creek Park [Mon 50; Mon71-1, 1] fifteen kilometres [Lor 334] had no proposals [Mon 51] rest of the day [Koh* 7] *monsieur le Président* [DF] fn 2 real difficulties in writing French [Man 340] **350** formulated idea [M-Clev* 8–11] aphoristic summation [Bal82, 73] simplify not problems but solutions [Uri* 88] why it fitted [Bow* 8–9] What an expositor [A-FF #48 Frankfurter-McCloy 29.5.53, 328] flexible institutional setting [Ehr 285] Mendershausen [Ehr 285 + Review Economics and Statistics xxxv, 1953, 271] **351** so long as central theme [Led* 4] power of simple ideas [Mon 331] idea if concretized [Lil69, 241] thousand times [DF] Monotonous Mary [Mon 126, 259] that simple [Ten* 10] **352** having enemies [M-Ple* 2] same arguments with everyone [M-Couv* 6] said what he did [Mon 407] clear and precise [Noë* 8] actions coincide with words [Mon71-1, 37] moral authority [Bow89, 82–83; Des 177; Val 571] simplistic [Clap* 26] superficial side [Tei 238–39] **353** blot out complications [Marj 175] point of departure [Heinz Guderian, *Panzer Leader,* NY 1957, 14] no idea [Hel*'214] can't write read speak [Mon71-1, 21 source Salter] Stories used to circulate [Guy* 8–9] von Simson [Sim 33–34] hypnosis [Guy* 8] believed in ideas [Marj 175] new clarity of thought [Wel* 53] mania for secrecy [Bér 317, 327] **354** maze of telephoning [Jac88, 2] thin line [Beu 245–47 + 232–34] **355** three times a day [A-SR 13.1 Ball 2.4.60] get the credit [Mon 84] other peoples' jobs [Rot* 92] two kinds of people [Mon 519; NicH 286] 356 very junior man [Stad* 31–33] Palliser [Pall* 1–5; Rot* 91–92] what interests him [Owe-DF 31.3.93] 357 lucrative practice [Mon 153–54] alert sympathy [Ehr 411] laying down his hammer [Marj 176] peremptory [Bér 12.6.50, 325; Bu1Pe186, 953; Cam*] he listened [Jox 98] not all of the time [M-Kap* 10] Where is the snag [Uri* 21] 358 look together [Bri* 21] good idea [Hir 107] Tour d'Argent [Hir 91; BloL 164] 359 achieve results [M-Hir-MM* 31; Pale 211] the final effort [Mon 70] exceptional mobility [Stad* 3; Hel-DF 13.5.91] I during all my life [A-FF #51] Monnet-Frankfurter 13.2.48, 514] staying up late [Mon 323–24] not matters of detail [Mon 103] luggage in the boot [Nathu*] invincible obstinacy [Bu1Pe186, Kirkpatrick-Eden 7.9.52, 951] obsessional psychosis [Guy* 9] man possessed [Rot* 93] blinders [Frank 184–85; A-FF #48 Frankfurter-McCloy 29.5.53, 328] 360 even the obstacles [Mon 399] Justice Holmes [Ach 707] serviceable hypothesis [Bal82, 98] 361 never been alone [FonF 74] damn thing [DF] political base [Bow* 9] no progress without disorder [Mon 46] dislodge an admiral [Man 345] 362 creating not administering [Koh* 18.10.56, 84; NY Times 18.1.48, 25 col 2] 363 Couve de Murville [Mon 437, 482; Hel 122] coalitions of states [Mon55, 112] recurrence of wars [Hel 76] 364 domination intolerable [FonF89, 218] applying its own rules [Mon55 Société d'Économie Politique de Belgique 30.6.53, 20] today the law [FonF 23] widespread influence [Mon 85] politics of Versailles [Mon 71-1, 26–27] 365 imperfect understanding [Mil IX doct 996 memo Monnet 27.5.19, 447] how little alliance really means [Mon 18; Mon55, 33–35] Gibbon [Edward Gibbon *Decline and Fall of the Roman Empire* Everyman I 286] take a common view [Mon 20 and 76] same side of the table [EU-DF; Owe* 7] 366 milestones [Mon 127] restructuring power networks [Mon 129] general view [Mon 66] used the phrase increasingly [Mon55, 33–35] equality essential [Mon71-1, 30] 367 Hirsch introduced federalism [Hir* 11] too diverse [Bér 320] as if it were real [Hel89, 592]

12 Changing the Context

369 cross the dividing line [Mon 35] 370 Mendès-France [B-MAE 5216 PMF-Rasquin reported by Poswick-MAE 8.11.54] more urgent than a dollar loan [F-F60 902 CEI 18.2.46, 8] 371 haunted by German nationalism [BulPel86 Monnet-Harvey 7.9.51, 711 fn 1] anti-Poincaré [M-Alp* 5] Equality absolutely essential [Mon 97, 284] 373 Erfurt [Hel-DF 31.3.93] unity in a united Europe [Mon55, 110–12] 374 change the context [Mon 291] 376 chain reaction [Mon 463] now I have modernised [DF] continuous creation [MonSch 25; M-F 11-2-3a, 12.5.47] changed by what they do [W. H. Auden *Look Stranger!* 1936 xvii] not to lose momentum [Bal82, 82] frozen progression [Ball-DF 20.6.88] *solidarité de fait* [M-G 1-2-9, 6.5.50] 378 purely Franco-German [EU-DF] 379 closed Community [Mon55, 54] contracts with Poland [Koh* 188 + 84, 184] later the Scandinavians [Koh* 18.10.56, 84] 380 faith in ourselves [Mon55, 60–61] American nuclear policies [Smi* 12] genuine peace [*Le Monde* 13.6.61] lasting peaceful settlement [Rec 117] 381 best understood China [M-PD, Monnet-Drummond 13.3.35] support in the City [Mon 43–44] Britain the only dynamic force [GB-FO 371/77933 Monnet-Plowden 3/7.3.49] 382 a hundred years ago [Lil 13–14] as early as the

First World War [Mon 57] recognised official channels [BulPel86, 109] naughty—always has been [Lil 16.6.50, 20] undesirable effects [M-F 22-1-5, 18.4.48; MonSch 37] potential equals [FonP 87–93, 113–17] **383** more personal access [Bal* 13–14] as if there had never been a problem [Den 171–72] a great American [Hel-DF 9.12.91] always of a mind [Ser 385] **386** first time in history [Mon55, 2nd Assembly ECSC 19.6.53, 56] Dulles brushed aside [Beu 319] fragmented Europe [Mon 465] inferiority complex [Mon55, 22] **388** cannot exercise sovereignty on their own [Koh 70; Koh* 199–200] unlimited [Mel 76] by stealth [Kis 138–139]

13   Transforming Leader

390 MacGregor Burns [Burns 422–61] continuous reform [Mon 463] one reorganisation or another [GB-FO371/18078, 59–63 Drummond-Lindlay, Tokyo 27.4.34] **391** exert cumulative force [O1s] **392** farmcart stuck in the mud [Herbert Lüthy, *The State of France*, London 1955, 297] **394** Marjolin [Marj 282–83] **397** fn 1 not to decide at all [Wel-DF 29.7.92] Britain, Norway and Switzerland [Uri* 60] **398** jettison the International Ruhr Authority [F-363 AP 17 Schuman-Mayer 2.2.51] without supranationality none [Clap85, 26] **399** philosopher and generally accepted leader [Cam 12] **400** February 13, 1948 [Buf 79; Assemblée Nationale, *Annales* 13.2.48, 736–47] **401** their behaviour does [Mon55, 36] pillars of civilisation [Mon55, 37] not create a nation Europe [Koh* 18.10.56, 84] **402** followed his advice [Spa39] **403** rationalised in universal values [Cerny P G, *The Politics of Grandeur*, Cambridge 1980, 270] we all believed fervently [Bal82, 90] the devil in *my* life [Tut* 12] **407** qualitative gap [Sauva* 13–14] Articles of Confederation [MorganE 101–112]

Sources

1. ARCHIVES AND LIBRARIES

BELGIUM   Archives du Royaume, Fonds Snoy, &c.,
Brussels
Institut Royal des Relations Internationales,
Brussels
Ministère des Relations Extérieures, Brussels

BRITAIN   Bodleian Library, Oxford
British Library, London
Camps, Miriam, papers, Cambridge
Lord Perth, papers, London
Public Record Office, London
Royal Institute of International Affairs, London
University of Sussex Library, Brighton

CANADA   Hudson's Bay Company papers, Provincial
Archives of Manitoba, Winnipeg

EUROPEAN COMMUNITY   European University Institute, Florence
Kohnstamm Max, Diaries & Archives, Brussels

FRANCE (Paris)   Archives Nationales
Assemblée Nationale
Bibliothèque Nationale
Centre Pompidou
Cognac, Archives
Conseil Economique et Social
Documentation Française
Légion d'Honneur, Grande Chancellerie
Ministère des Affaires Etrangères
Ministère de l'Economie et des Finances

	Office Universitaire de Recherche Socialiste (OURS)
	Service Historique de l'Armée de Terre (SHAT)
LUXEMBOURG	Archives Nationales, Luxembourg City
SWITZERLAND	Bibliothèque des Nations Unies, Geneva
	Bibliothèque universitaire et cantonale, Lausanne
	Fondation Jean Monnet pour l'Europe, Lausanne
UNITED STATES	Amherst College (McCloy), Amherst, Massachusetts
	Dwight D. Eisenhower Library, Abilene, Kansas
	Library of Congress, Washington, D.C.
	National Archives, Washington, D.C.
	Princeton University, Seeley Mudd Library (Dulles)
	Public Library, New York City
	Franklin D. Roosevelt Library, Hyde Park, New York
	Schaetzel, J. Robert, papers, Washington, D.C.
	Harry S. Truman Library, Independence, Missouri
	Tuthill, John W., papers, Washington, D.C.
	Virginia Historical Society, Richmond, Virginia (Bruce)

2. INTERVIEWS BY THE AUTHOR

ALPHAND, Hervé	20 April 1988; 26 November 1990
BALINSKA, Martha	correspondence
BALL, George W.	10 August 1987 + correspondence
BEHR, Winrich	29 April & 22 June 1987
BLAISSE, Pieter	18 May 1989
BOWIE, Robert R.	12 May 1987; 28 September 1988 + correspondence
BRINK, van den, J. R. M.	17 May 1989
CAMPS, Miriam	31 August 1988 & 22 November 1989
CARROLL, Alison	22 June 1990
CARSTENS, Karl	27 April 1987
CHAUSSEBOURG, Fernand	11 April 1988
CLAPPIER, Bernard	18 April 1988
CONNELLY, Albert	16 October 1990 + correspondence
COPPE, Albert	4 April 1989
DELOUVRIER, Paul	5 May 1988
DILLON, Douglas	21 September 1988
Lord EZRA, Derek	20 January & 22 April 1989
FAURE, Maurice	4 March 1987

FOCH, René	28 April 1988
FONTAINE, François	29 April 1988
GAUDET, Michel	15 April 1988
GOLDSCHMIDT, Bertrand	19 April 1988
GROEBEN, von der, Hans	27 April 1987
GUERON, Jules	23 & 25 September 1987
GUYOT, Jean	21 April 1988
Lady HAMPDEN, Leila	21 February 1989
HARTMAN, Arthur	17 & 23 March 1990
HILLENBRAND, Martin	6 October 1988
HIRSCH, Etienne	22 & 24 September 1987 + correspondence
ISENBERGH, Max	13 May 1987
JACOB, Ian (Lt. Gen. Sir)	16 February 1989
KATZ, Milton	Correspondence
KOHNSTAMM, Max	18–19 January & 3–7 July 1986; 12 November 1988; 30 March–1 April 1989
LALOY, Jean	4 March 1987
LECOURT, Robert	6 March 1987
LEDDY, John	18 August 1987
MERCEREAU, Félix-Paul	12 April 1988
MONNET, Marianne	8 July 1992
MYERSON, Joseph	9 July 1987
NATHAN, Robert	15 May 1987
NATHUSIUS, Martin	n.d.
NOEL, Émile	19 October 1988
PALLISER, Michael (Sir)	16 September 1987
Lord PERTH (David Drummond)	23 January, 21 April, 21 May, & 4 July 1989
PINAY, Antoine	16 May 1986
PINEAU, Christian	25 September 1987
RABIER, Jacques	16 November 1988 + correspondence
RIPHAGEN, W.	19 May 1989
Baron ROTHSCHILD, Robert	13 & 20 February, 30 April, & 11 December 1986
RUTTEN, Charles	26 June 1987
SAUVAGNARGUES, Jean	5 March 1987; 25 April 1988 + correspondence
SCHAETZEL, Robert J.	18 May 1987
Lord SHERFIELD (Roger Makins)	18 January 1989
SMITH, Gerard C.	13 August 1987
Comte SNOY ET D'OPPUERS, Jean-Charles	25 June 1987
SOHL, Hans-Günter	22 June 1987
STADEN, von, Berndt	30 April 1987
DE STAERCKE, André	22 August 1986
TEISSIER DU CROS, Henri	3 May 1988
TENNYSON, Leonard	2 June 1987; 28 September 1988

TUTHILL, John W.   20 May 1987
URI, Pierre   9 April 1986; 22 April & 3 May 1988
VAN HELMONT, Jacques   12 April & 14 May 1986; 3 March 1987; 28
                           April & 2 May 1988; 6 August 1989; 19
                           August 1990 + correspondence
VERNON, Raymond   11 October 1988
WELLENSTEIN, Edmond   16 May 1989
YRISSOU, Henri   26 September 1986
ZIJLSTRA, Jelle   17 May 1989
ZINGG, Dory   30 December 1992

Publications Cited
in the Text

ACHESON, Dean	*Present at the Creation*	New York, 1969
ADAMS, William, & STOFFAES, Christian (eds.)	*French Industrial Policy*	Brookings, 1986
AGLION, Raoul	*De Gaulle et Roosevelt: la France Libre aux Etats-Unis*	Paris, 1984
ALBONETTI, Achille	*Préhistoire des Etats-Unis d'Europe*	Paris, 1963
ALPHAND, Hervé	*L'Etonnement d'Etre*	Paris, 1978
ANNEE POLITIQUE	1946 to 1961	Paris (annual)
ARMAND, Louis	*Quelques aspects du problème européen de l'énergie*	OEEC, Paris, 1955
ARMAND, Louis, ETZEL, Franz, & GIORDANI, Francesco	*A Target for Euratom*	Brussels, 1957
ASSELAIN, Jean-Charles	*Histoire Economique de la France,* Vol. 2: *de 1919 à la fin des années 1970*	Paris, 1984
AURIOL, Vincent, ed. NORA, Pierre	*Journal du Septennat,* 1947–54, 7 vols.	Colin, Paris 1970 ff.
BALL, George W.	*The Discipline of Power*	London, 1968
BALL, George W.	*The Past Has Another Pattern*	New York, 1982
BAUM, Warren	*The French Economy and the State*	Rand, 1958
BEAUFRE, André	*La Revanche de 1945*	Paris, 1966
BERARD, Armand	*Un Ambassadeur se souvient*	Paris, 1978
BERNIERE, Robert	"Un Citoyen du XXIe siècle", in RIEBEN (q.v.), 49–55	Lausanne, 1989
BETHOUART, M.-E.	*Cinq années d'espérance 1939–45*	Paris, 1968
BEUGEL, van der, Ernst H.	*From Marshall Aid to Atlantic Partnership*	Amsterdam, 1966

BEYER, Henri	*Robert Schuman: l'Europe par la réconciliation franco-allemande*	Lausanne, 1986
BIDAULT, Georges	*D'une Résistance à l'autre*	Paris, 1965
BLOCH-LAINE, François	*Profession: Fonctionnaire, Entretiens avec Françoise Carrère*	Paris, 1976
BLOCH-LAINE, F., & BOUVIER, J.	*La France Restaurée*	Paris, 1986
BLOCK, Fred L.	*The Origins of International Economic Disorder*	Berkeley, 1977
BLUM, John Morton	*The Morgenthau Diaries: Years of Urgency, 1938–1941*	Boston, 1965
BONIN, Hubert	*Histoire Economique de la IVe République*	Paris, 1987
BONNET, Georges	*Vingt ans de vie politique 1918–1938 De Clémenceau à Daladier*	Paris, 1969
BORG, Dorothy	*The United States and the Far Eastern Crisis, 1933–38*	Harvard, 1964
BOWIE, Robert R.	"Réflexions sur Jean Monnet", in RIEBEN (q.v.), 79–88	Lausanne, 1989
BRINKLEY, Douglas, & HACKETT, Clifford	*Jean Monnet: The Path to European Unity*	New York, 1991
BUFFET, Cyril	*La France et l'Allemagne 1945–1949*	Paris, 1991
BULLEN, R., & PELLY, M. E.	*Documents on British Policy Overseas,* Series II, Vol. I: *Schuman Plan*	London, 1986
BULLEN, R., & PELLY, M. E.	*Documents on British Policy Overseas,* Series II, Vol. III: *German Rearmament 1950*	London, 1989
BULLITT, Orville H. (ed.)	*For the President: Personal and Secret Correspondence between FDR and William C. Bullitt*	Boston, 1972
BUNGENER, Martine	"L'électricité et les trois premiers plans", in ROUSSO (q.v.)	Paris, 1986
BURN, Duncan	*The Steel Industry 1939–1959*	Cambridge, 1961
BURNS, James MacGregor	*Leadership*	New York, 1978
CALVOCORESSI, Peter	*Resilient Europe*	London, 1991
CAMPS, Miriam	*Britain and the European Community*	London, 1964
CAMPS, Miriam	"Jean Monnet and the United Kingdom", in MAJONE, NOEL, & VAN DEN BOSSCHE (q.v.)	Baden-Baden, 1989
CATROUX, Georges	*Dans la Bataille de Mediterranée*	Paris, 1949
CAZES, B., & MIOCHE, P.	*Modernisation ou Décadence*	U. Provence, 1990
CENTRE D'ETUDES DIPLOMATIQUES ET CONSULAIRES	*Le Marché Commun et l'Euratom: cycle de conférences faites au Ministère des Affaires Etrangères, 2–7 décembre*	Paris, 1957

(French Foreign Office)	1957	
CGP (COMMISSARIAT GENERAL AU PLAN)	Divers Rapports sur le Plan de Modernisation et d'Equipement	Paris, various
CHANDLER, Alfred D., Jr., & AMBROSE, Stephen E.	*The Papers of Dwight D. Eisenhower*	Baltimore, 1970
CHARBONNIERES, Guy de Girard de	*Le Duel Giraud–de Gaulle*	Paris, 1984
CHURCHILL, W. S.	*History of the Second World War,* Vol. II: *Their Finest Hour*	London, 1949
CLAPPIER, Bernard	"Bernard Clappier Témoigne", in RIEBEN H. (ed.), *L'Europe une longue marche*	Lausanne, 1985
CLAPPIER, Bernard	"L'Aventure du 9 mai 1950", in RIEBEN, H. (ed.), *Une Mémoire Vivante*	Lausanne, 1986
CLARKE, Stephen V. O.	*Central Bank Cooperation 1924–1931*	Federal Reserve, New York, 1967
CLEMENTEL, Etienne	*La France et la Politique économique Interalliée*	Paris, 1931
CLESSE, Armand	*Le Projet de CED du Plan Pleven au "crime" du 30 août*	Baden-Baden, 1986
COBLE, Parks M., Jr.	*The Shanghai Capitalists and the Nationalist Government 1927–1937*	Harvard, 1986
CONRAD, Yves	*Les débuts de la Fonction Publique Européenne: La Haute Autorité de la CECA 1952–1953*	Louvain, 1989
COPPE, Albert	"Des 'Executives' de 1914–1918 aux Etats Unis d'Europe de 1950", in RIEBEN (q.v.), 121–27	Lausanne, 1989
COSTON, Henri	*La Haute Banque et les Trusts*	Paris, n.d.
COUSSIE, Jean Vincent	*Le cognac et les aléas de l'histoire*	Jonzac, 1990
COUVE de MURVILLE, Maurice	*Le Monde en Face*	Paris, 1989
DALLEK, Robert	*Franklin D. Roosevelt and American Foreign Policy*	Oxford, 1979
DAVENPORT, John	"M. Jean Monnet of Cognac", in *Fortune,* August 1944, 121–25, 214, 216	New York, 1944
DEBRE, Michel	*Mémoires: Trois Républiques pour une France, III*	Paris, 1988

DELORME, Robert, & ANDRE, Christine	*L'Etat et l'Economie*	Paris, 1983
DELOUVRIER, Paul	"Quelques souvenirs sur Jean Monnet", in RIEBEN (q.v.), 135–63	Lausanne, 1989
DENIAU, Jean-François	"La méthode Monnet", in RIEBEN (q.v.), 165–72	Lausanne, 1989
DESCAMPS, Eugène	in RIEBEN (q.v.), 173–78	Lausanne, 1989
DIEBOLD, William, Jr.	*The Schuman Plan*	New York, 1959
DILKS, David	*The Diaries of Sir Alexander Cadogan 1938–45*	London, 1971
DIVINE, Robert A.	*Roosevelt and World War II*	Baltimore, 1969
DOBNEY, J. F.	*Selected Papers of Will Clayton*	Baltimore, 1971
DOCUMENTATION FRANÇAISE— NOTES ET ETUDES	Series, irregular dates	Paris
DOCUMENTS DIPLOMATIQUES FRANÇAIS	1954–1956	Paris, 1987–88
DOUGHERTY, James J.	*The Politics of Wartime Aid*	Westport, 1973
DUCHENE, François, & SHEPHERD, Geoffrey (eds.)	*Managing Industrial Change in Western Europe*	London, 1987
DUMAINE, Jacques	*Quai d'Orsay (1945–1951)*	Paris, 1955
DUROSELLE, Jean-Baptiste	*L'Abîme*	Paris, 1986
DUROSELLE, Jean-Baptiste	in RIEBEN (q.v.), 189–96	Lausanne, 1989
DUROSELLE, Jean-Baptiste	"Le rôle de Jean Monnet à Londres" (unpublished manuscript)	n.d.
EDEN, Anthony	*The Reckoning*	London, 1965
EHRMANN, Henry W.	*Organized Business in France*	Princeton, 1957
ELGEY, G.	*La République des Illusions*	Paris, 1965
ENDICOTT, Stephen L.	*Diplomacy and Enterprise: British China Policy 1933–37*	Vancouver, 1975
FAUVET, Jacques	*La IVe République*	Paris, 1959
FISCHER, Fritz	*War of Illusions: German Policies from 1911 to 1914*	London, 1975
FONTAINE, François	*Plus Loin avec Jean Monnet*	Lausanne, 1983
FONTAINE, François	"Jean Monnet nous disait", in RIEBEN (q.v.), 215–221	Lausanne, 1989
FONTAINE, Pascal	*Le Comité d'Action pour les Etats-Unis d'Europe de Jean Monnet*	Lausanne, 1974

FOREIGN RELATIONS OF THE UNITED STATES	State Department Documents	Washington, D.C. (annual)
FRANÇOIS-PONCET, Jean	"Historique des négociations de Bruxelles", in CENTRE D'ETUDES (q.v.), 17–34	Paris, 1957
FRANKFURTER, Felix	*Felix Frankfurter Reminisces* (ed. Harlan B. Philips)	London, 1960
FREEDMAN, Max (ed.)	*Roosevelt and Frankfurter: Their Correspondence 1928–1945*	Boston, 1967
FURSDON, Edward	*The European Defence Community*	London, 1980
GAUDET, Michel	"Un regard de Jean Monnet", in RIEBEN (q.v.), 233–39	Lausanne, 1989
GAULLE, Charles de	*Mémoires I—L'Appel, 1940–1942*	Paris, 1954
GAULLE, Charles de	*Mémoires II—L'Unité, 1942–1944*	Paris, 1956
GAULLE, Charles de	*Mémoires III—Le Salut, 1944–1946*	Paris, 1959
GAULLE, Charles de	*Discours et Messages, Vol. III*	Paris, 1970
GAULLE, Charles de	*Lettres, Notes et Carnets 1919–1966*	Paris, 1980 ff.
GERBET, Pierre	*La Construction de l'Europe*	Paris, 1983
GILLINGHAM, John	*Coal Steel and the Rebirth of Europe 1945–1955*	Cambridge, 1991
GILLOIS, André	*Histoire Secrète des Français à Londres de 1940 à 1944*	Paris, 1973
GIMBEL, John	*Origins of the Marshall Plan*	Stanford, 1976
GIRAUD, Henri	*Un seul But: la Victoire, Alger 1942–44*	Paris, 1949
GISCARD d'ESTAING, Valéry	*Jean Monnet*	Lausanne, 1989
GOLDSCHMIDT, Bertrand	*Le Complexe Atomique*	Paris, 1980
GREENBAUM, E. S.	*A Lawyer's Job*	New York, 1967
GRIFFITHS, R.	"The Schuman Plan Negotiations: The Economic Clauses", in SCHWABE (q.v.)	Brussels, 1988
GRIFFITHS, R., & LYNCH, F.	*The Fritalux/Finebel Negotiations 1949–1950*	European University Institute, 1984
GRIFFITHS, R., & MILWARD, A.	*The Beyen Plan and the European Political Community*	European University Institute, 1986
GROSSER, Alfred	*La IVe et sa Politique Etrangère*	Paris, 1961
GRUSON, C.	*Origine et espoirs de la planification française*	Paris, 1968
HAIGHT, John McV.	*American Aid to France 1938–40*	New York, 1970
HALL, H. Duncan	*Official History of the Second World War—North American Supply*	London, 1955

HANCOCK, W. K., & GOWING, M. M.	*The British War Economy: UK History of the Second World War*	London, 1975
HARRYVAN, Anjo G.	*The Netherlands, Benelux and the Origins of the Beyen-Spaak Initiative*	European University Institute, 1985
HARRYVAN, A. G., & KERSTEN, A. E.	"The Netherlands, Benelux and the relance européenne", in SERRA (q.v.)	Brussels, 1989
HARTLEY, Anthony	*Gaullism*	New York, 1971
HARTLEY, Anthony	*L'Europe hier et demain: de Rathenau à Briand et de Schuman à Rathenau in Commentaire N° 58 été 1992, 273–82*	Paris, 1992
HARVEY, J.	*Diplomatic Diaries of Oliver Harvey 1937–1940*	London, 1970
HELMONT, Jacques van	See VAN HELMONT, Jacques	
HIRSCH, Etienne	*Ainsi va la vie*	Lausanne, 1988
HITLER, Adolf	*Mein Kampf* (translation), Chap. XIII: "German Postwar Policy of Alliances"	London, n.d.
HOGAN, Michael J.	*The Marshall Plan: America, Britain and the Reconstruction of Western Europe 1947–1952*	Cambridge, 1987
INSTITUT CHARLES DE GAULLE	*L'Aventure de la Bombe: De Gaulle et la Dissuasion Nucléaire 1958–969*	Paris, 1985
JAVEL, Fernand	"Monnet à Alger", in RIEBEN (q.v.), 289–307	Lausanne, 1989
JOUVE, Edmond	*Le Général de Gaulle et la Construction Européenne*, 2 vols.	Paris, 1967
JOXE, Louis	*Victoires sur la Nuit: mémoires 1940–1966*	Paris, 1981
KASPI, André	*La Mission de Jean Monnet à Alger mars–octobre 1943*	Paris, 1971
KERSAUDY, François	*Churchill and de Gaulle*	London, 1981
KETTENACKER, Lothar	*Das andere Deutschland im zweiten Weltkrieg*	Stuttgart, 1977
KIMBALL, Warren F. (ed.)	*Churchill and Roosevelt: The Complete Correspondence*, II: *Alliance Forged November 1942–February 1944*	Princeton, 1984
KISSINGER, Henry	*Years of Upheaval*	New York, 1982
KLEIMAN, Robert	*Atlantic Crisis*	New York, 1964
KOHNSTAMM, Max	"Jean Monnet face à l'Union européenne", in MAJONE, NOEL, & VAN DEN BOSSCHE (q.v.)	Baden-Baden, 1989

KOHNSTAMM, Max	"Jean Monnet, technocrate, homme d'action, philosophe?", in RIEBEN (q.v.), 319–23	Lausanne, 1989
KRAFT, Joseph	*The Grand Design*	New York, 1962
KUESTERS, Hanns Jürgen	*Die Gründung der Europäischen Wirtschaftsgemeinschaft*	Baden-Baden, 1982
KUESTERS, Hanns Jürgen	"The Origins of the EEC Treaty", in SERRA (q.v.), 211–38	Baden-Baden, 1989
KUISEL, Richard F.	*Capitalism and the State in Modern France*	Cambridge, 1981
LACOUTURE, Jean	*De Gaulle:*	Paris
	1: Le Rebelle 1890–1944	1984
	2: Le Politique 1944–1959	1985
	3: Le Souverain 1959–1970	1986
LASH, Joseph P.	*From the Diaries of Felix Frankfurter*	New York, 1975
LEITH-ROSS, Frederick	*Money Talks: Fifty Years of International Finance*	London, 1968
LEMAIGRE-DUBREUIL, Jacques	*Les relations franco-américaines et la politique des généraux*	Paris, 1949
LIDDELL HART, Basil	*History of the Second World War*	London, 1970
LIDDELL HART, Basil	*History of the First World War*	London, 1972
LILIENTHAL, David E.	*Journals of,* Vol. III: *Venturesome Years, 1950–55*	Boston, 1966
	Vol. IV: *Road to Change, 1955–59*	Boston, 1969
LINDBERGH, Anne Morrow, Diaries 1922–44	*Bring Me a Unicorn (1922–28)* *The Nettle and the Flower (1936–38)*	London, 1972 Boston, 1976
LISAGOR, N., & LIPSIUS, F.	*A Law unto Itself: The Untold Story of the Law Firm Sullivan & Cromwell*	New York, 1988
LISTER, Louis	*Europe's Coal and Steel Community*	New York, 1960
LORIN, Paul	in RIEBEN (q.v.), 331–34	Lausanne, 1989
LUBELL, Harold	"The French Investment Program: A Defense of the Monnet Plan" (mimeo)	Littauer School, Harvard, 1951
LUDLOW, Peter	"The Unwinding of Appeasement", in KETTENACKER (q.v.)	Stuttgart, 1977
LYNCH, Frances	"The Political and Economic Reconstruction of France 1944–1947, in the International Context" (thesis, mimeo)	Manchester, 1981
LYNCH, Frances	*French Reconstruction in a European Context*	European University Institute, 1984
MACARTNEY, Maxwell H. H.	*Five Years of European Chaos*	London, 1923

MACMILLAN, Harold	*The Blast of War (1939–1945)*	London, 1967
MACMILLAN, Harold	*Tides of Fortune (1945–1955)*	London, 1969
MACMILLAN, Harold	*War Diaries*	London, 1984
MAJONE, G., NOEL, E., & VAN DEN BOSSCHE, P.	*Jean Monnet et l'Europe d'aujourd'hui*	Baden-Baden, 1989
MANDEREAU, Jean-Louis	in RIEBEN (q.v.), 337–47	Lausanne, 1989
MARGAIRAZ, Michel	"La mise en oeuvre du Plan Monnet (1947–1952)", in CAZES & MIOCHE (q.v.)	U. Provence, 1990
MARJOLIN, Robert	*Le Travail d'une Vie*	Paris, 1986
MASSIGLI, René	*Une Comédie des Erreurs*	Paris, 1978
MAYER, Denise	*René Mayer: études, Témoignages Documents*	Paris, 1983
MAYNE, Richard	"Father of Europe: Life and Times of Jean Monnet" (unpublished manuscript)	1972
McCLOY, John J.	*Congressional Record,* Senate 14634, 7.12.81	Washington, D.C., 1981
McDOUGALL, Walter A.	*France's Rhineland Diplomacy 1914–1924*	Princeton, 1979
MELANDRI, Pierre	*Les Etats Unis et le "Défi" Européen 1955–58*	Paris, 1975
MELANDRI, Pierre	*Les Etats-Unis face à l'Unification de l'Europe 1945–1954*	Paris, 1980
MELCHIONNI, M. G.	*Altiero Spinelli et Jean Monnet*	Lausanne, 1993
MENDES-FRANCE, Pierre	*Pour une République moderne*	Paris, 1963
MESSERLIN, Patrick	"France: The Ambitious State", in DUCHENE & SHEPHERD (q.v.)	London, 1987
MILLER, David Hunter	*My Diary at the Conference of Paris*	New York, 1924
MILWARD, Alan S.	*The Reconstruction of Western Europe 1945–1951*	London, 1984
MILWARD, Alan S.	"La Planification française et la reconstruction européenne", in CAZES & MIOCHE (q.v.)	U. Provence, 1990
MILWARD, Alan S.	*The European Rescue of the Nation State*	London, 1992
MILWARD, A., & GRIFFITHS, R.	*The European Agricultural Community 1948–1954*	European University Institute, 1986
MIOCHE, Philippe	"Les plans et la sidérurgie: du soutien mitigé à l'effacement possible", in ROUSSO (q.v.)	Paris, 1986
MIOCHE, Philippe	*Le Plan Monnet, genèse et élaboration 1941–1947*	Paris, 1987

MIOCHE, Philippe	"L'Invention du Plan Monnet", in CAZES & MIOCHE (q.v.)	U. Provence, 1990
MIOCHE, P., & RIOUX, J.	*Henri Malcor: un héritier des Maîtres des Forges*	Paris, 1988
MISCHLICH, Robert	*Une Mission Secrète à Bonn*	Lausanne, 1986
MONICK, Emanuel	*Pour Mémoire*	Paris, 1970
MONNET, Jean	*Les Etats-Unis d'Europe ont Commencé*	Paris, 1955
MONNET, Jean ("71-1")	Complete transcript of Alan Watson interview of Jean Monnet for BBC-2 (mimeo)	December 1971
MONNET, Jean ("71-2")	BBC-2 TV Money Programme, "The Father of Europe", presented by Alan Watson (mimeo)	December 31, 1971
MONNET, Jean	*L'Europe unie: de l'utopie à la réalité*	Lausanne, 1972
MONNET, Jean (translated by MAYNE, Richard)	*Memoirs*	London, 1978
MONNET, Jean	"Note de Réflexion de Jean Monnet, Alger 5 août 1943", in RIEBEN (q.v.)	Lausanne, 1987
MONNET, Jean & SCHUMAN, Robert	*Correspondance 1947–1953*	Lausanne, 1986
MOREAU, Emile	*Souvenirs d'un Gouverneur de la Banque de France: Histoire de la Stabilisation du franc 1926–1928*	Paris, 1954
MORGAN, Edmund S.	*The Birth of the Republic 1763–89*	Chicago, 1956
MORGAN, Ted	*FDR*	London, 1985
MURPHY, Robert	*A Diplomat among the Warriors*	London, 1964
NATHAN, Robert R.	"An Unsung Hero of World War II", in BRINKLEY & HACKETT (q.v.)	New York, 1991
NELSON, Donals	*Arsenal of Democracy—The Story of American War Production*	New York, 1946
NICOLSON, Harold	*Dwight Morrow*	New York, 1935
NICOLSON, Nigel	*Harold Nicolson: Diaries and Letters 1939–1945*	London, 1967
NOEL, Emile	"Jean Monnet et la négociation d'Euratom", in RIEBEN (q.v.), 371–76	Lausanne, 1989
OEEC (ORGANISATION FOR EUROPEAN ECONOMIC COOPERATION)	Various reports and statistical bulletins	Paris
OLSON, Mancur	*The Rise and Decline of Nations*	Yale, 1982
ORDIONI, Pierre	*Tout commence à Alger, 1940–1945*	Paris, 1985

PAILLAT, Claude	*L'Echiquier d'Alger,* 2 vols.	Paris, 1966
PALEWSKI, Gaston	*Mémoires d'Action*	Paris, 1988
PEARTON, Maurice	*Diplomacy, War and Technology since 1830*	Kansas, 1984
PFLIMLIN, Pierre	"Jean Monnet que j'ai connu", in RIEBEN (q.v.), 385–87	Lausanne, 1989
PLEVEN, René	*L'Union Européenne*	Lausanne, 1984
POIDEVIN, Raymond (ed.), ("86-1")	*Histoire des débuts de la Construction européenne mars 1948 à mai 950*	Bruxelles, 1986
POIDEVIN, Raymond ("86-2")	*Robert Schuman, homme d'Etat 1886– 1963*	Paris, 1986
POMPIDOU, Georges	*Pour rétablir une vérité*	Paris, 1982
POSTAN, M. M.	*British War Production*	London, 1952
RANIERI, Ruggero	"British Steel and ECSC 1950– 1954", in STIRK & WILLIS (q.v.)	London, 1991
RECUEIL	*Déclarations et Communiqués du Comité d'Action pour les Etats Unis d'Europe, 1955–65*	Lausanne, 1965
RENOU, Jean	"L'Euratom", in CENTRE D'ETUDES (q.v.), 147–60	Paris, 1957
REUTER, Paul	*La Naissance de l'Europe Communautaire*	Lausanne, 1980
RIEBEN, Henri (ed.)	*Des Guerres Européennes à l'Union de l'Europe*	Lausanne, 1987
RIEBEN, Henri (ed.)	*Témoignages*	Lausanne, 1989
ROOSEVELT, Elliott	*As He Saw It*	New York, 1946
ROSECRANCE, Richard	*The Rise of the Trading State*	New York, 1986
ROSENMAN, Samuel I.	*Working with Roosevelt*	New York, 1952
ROUSSO, Henri (ed.)	*De Monnet à Massé*	Paris, 1986
ROUSSO, Henri	"Le ministère de l'Industrie dans le processus de planification: une adaptation difficile", in ROUSSO (q.v.)	Paris, 1986
ROYAL INSTITUTE OF INTERNATIONAL AFFAIRS	*Yearbook 1950*	London, 1950
SALTER, Arthur	*Allied Shipping Control*	Oxford, 1921
SALTER, Arthur	*Memoirs of a Public Servant*	London, 1961
SALTER, Arthur	*Slave of the Lamp*	London, 1967
SAUVY, Alfred	*La Vie économique des Français 1939– 1945*	Paris, 1978
SCHAEFFERS, Hans	"Tagebuchaufzeichnung (Auszug) in Konrad Adenauer und der Schuman Plan: ein	Baden-Baden, 1988

Quellenzeugnis", in SCHWABE
(q.v.), 132–40

SCHEINMAN,
Lawrence
*Atomic Energy Policy in France under
the Fourth Republic*
Princeton, 1965

SCHLESINGER,
A. M., Jr.
*A Thousand Days: Kennedy in the
White House*
London, 1965

SCHWABE, Klaus
(ed.)
The Beginnings of the Schuman Plan
Baden-Baden,
1988

SCHWARTZ, Thomas
*America's Germany: John J. McCloy
and the Federal Republic of Germany*
Harvard, 1991

SCHWARZ, H.-P.
Adenauer: der Aufstieg 1876–1952
Stuttgart, 1986

SCHWARZ, H.-P.
Adenauer: der Staatsmann 1952–67
Stuttgart, 1991

SERRA, Enrico (ed.)
*Il rilancio dell'Europa e i tratatti di
Roma*
Brussels/Milan,
1989

SHEAHAN, John
*Promotion and Control of Industry in
Postwar France*
Harvard, 1963

SHERWOOD,
Robert E.
*The White House Papers of Harry L.
Hopkins: An Intimate History*
New York, 1948

SIMSON, Werner von
"Reflections on Monnet's Skillful
Handling &c", in MAJONE,
NOEL, & VAN DEN BOSSCHE
(q.v.)
Baden-Baden,
1989

SPAAK, Paul-Henri
Combats Inachevés, II
Paris, 1969

SPEARS, Edward
Assignment to Catastrophe, 2 vols.
London, 1954

SPEARS, Edward
*Two Men Who Saved France: Pétain
and de Gaulle*
London, 1966

SPIERENBURG, Dirk
in RIEBEN (q.v.), 509–11
Lausanne, 1989

SPIERENBURG, D. &
POIDEVIN, R.
*Histoire de la Haute Autorité de la
Communauté Européenne du Charbon
et de l'Acier: une Expérience
Supranationale*
Brussels, 1993

STIMSON, H. &
BUNDY, McG.
On Active Service in Peace and War
New York, 1947

STIRK, P. & WILLIS,
D. (eds)
*Shaping Postwar Europe: European
Unity and Disunity 1945–957*
London, 1991

STOFFAES, Christian
"Industrial Policy in the High
Technology Industries", in
ADAMS & STOFFAES (q.v.)
Brookings, 1986

SWAINE, Robert T.
The Cravath Firm since 1906
New York, 1948

TAVIANI, Paolo
Emilio
"L'adhésion de l'Italie à la
proposition de Schuman et de
Monnet", in RIEBEN (q.v.), 515–
19
Lausanne, 1989

TEISSIER DU CROS,
Henri
*Louis Armand: Visionnaire de la
Modernité*
Paris, 1987

TINDEMANS, Léo
"Monnet le Sage", in RIEBEN (q.v.),
521–27
Lausanne, 1989

TRACHTENBERG, Marc	*Reparation in World Politics: France and European Economic Diplomacy 1916–1923*	New York, 1980
VALERY, François	in RIEBEN (q.v.), 567–75	Lausanne, 1989
VAN HELMONT, Jacques	*Options Européennes 1945–1985*	Bruxelles, 1986
VAN HELMONT, Jacques	"Instants d'un quart de siècle", in RIEBEN (q.v.), 577–92	Lausanne, 1989
VAUGHAN, Richard	*Twentieth Century Europe: Paths to Unity*	London, 1979
VIORST, Milton	*Hostile Allies: FDR and de Gaulle*	New York, 1965
WALL, Irwin	"Jean Monnet, the United States and the French Economic Plan", in BRINKLEY & HACKETT (q.v.)	New York, 1991
WAMBAUGH, Sarah	*Plebiscites since the World War*	London, 1933
WEILEMANN, Peter	*Die Anfänge der Europäischen Atomgemeinschaft*	Baden-Baden, 1983
WELLENSTEIN, Edmond	"L'Affaire des Taxes", in RIEBEN (q.v.), 593–98	Lausanne, 1989
WHITE, Theodore	*In Search of History*	New York, 1978
WILLIS, F. Roy	*France, Germany and the New Europe 1945–67*	Stanford, 1968
WINAND, Pascaline	*Presidents' Advisers and the Uniting of Europe*	Brussels, 1990
WINAND, Pascaline	*Eisenhower, Kennedy and the United States of Europe*	New York, 1993
WINAND, Pascaline	*Lobbying Democracy, the Action Committee for the United States of Europe and Its Successor: A Case Study*	Brussels, 1993
WOODWARD, E. L., & BUTLER, R.	*Documents of British Foreign Policy 1919–1939*, 1st series	London, 1947 ff.

Index